Inspirational Travel

Vietnam ⚘ Cambodia ⚘ Laos ⚘ Thailand

Locally Based Specialists in Privately Guided, Fully Customised Holidays

email: info@buffalotours.com - **website:** www.buffalotours.com

Footprint story

It was 1921

Ireland had just been partitioned, the British miners were striking for more pay and the federation of British industry had an idea. Exports were booming in South America – how about a handbook for businessmen trading in that far away continent? The Anglo-South American Handbook was born that year, written by W Koebel, the most prolific writer on Latin America of his day.

1924

Two editions later the book was 'privatized' and in 1924, in the hands of Royal Mail, the steamship company for South America, it became The South American Handbook, subtitled 'South America in a nutshell'. This annual publication became the 'bible' for generations of travellers to South America and remains so to this day. In the early days travel was by sea and the Handbook gave all the details needed for the long voyage from Europe. What to wear for dinner; how to arrange a cricket match with the Cable & Wireless staff on the Cape Verde Islands and a full account of the journey from Liverpool up the Amazon to Manaus: 5898 miles without changing cabin!

1939

As the continent opened up, the South American Handbook reported the new Pan Am flying boat services, and the fortnightly airship service from Rio to Europe on the Graf Zeppelin. For reasons still unclear but with extraordinary determination, the annual editions continued through the Second World War.

1970s

Many more people discovered South America and the backpacking trail started to develop. All the while the Handbook was gathering fans, including literary vagabonds such as Paul Theroux and Graham Greene (who once sent some updates addressed to "The publishers of the best travel guide in the world, Bath, England").

1990s

During the 1990s the company set about developing a new travel guide series using this legendary title as the flagship. By 1997 there were over a dozen guides in the series and the Footprint imprint was launched.

2000s

The series grew quickly and there were soon Footprint travel guides covering more than 150 countries. In 2004, Footprint launched its first thematic guide: *Surfing Europe*, packed with colour photographs, maps and charts. This was followed by further thematic guides such as *Diving the World*, *Snowboarding the World*, *Body and Soul escapes*, *Travel with Kids* and *European City Breaks*.

2010

Today we continue the traditions of the last 89 years that have served legions of travellers so well. We believe that these help to make Footprint guides different. Our policy is to use authors who are genuine experts who write for independent travellers; people possessing a spirit of adventure, looking to get off the beaten track.

Vietnam, Cambodia & Laos

Andrew Spooner

Vietnam, Cambodia and Laos offer unrivalled attractions in the form of ruins, colonial remnants, stunning scenery, ethnic diversity and exotic food. Their shared history as part of Indochine is still evident in the fading French architecture, the cuisine and the ubiquitous reminders of bloody wars, but it is their distinct differences that render the area such a fantastic travel experience.

In Vietnam, vivid rice paddies climb up mountainsides or sit alongside beautiful coastal scenery; feverish Ho Chi Minh City plays noisier, more moneyed brother to the enchanting, romantic capital, Hanoi.

Cambodia is home to the magnificent Angkor Wat, the zenith of Southeast Asia architecture, and a multitude of other awe-inspiring monuments. Phnom Penh, the fascinating modern day capital, offers the glistening Royal Palace, eclectic markets and poignant relics of a turbulent past.

Laid-back Laos, rousing after years of isolation, provides a beautiful, postcard-like backdrop. From the picturesque gilded temples of the former royal capital, Luang Prabang, to the chilled-out Mekong islands of Siphandon, it's hard not to be inspired by this exquisite country and its charming people.

This page Woman working in fields, Northern Vietnam.
Previous page A young woman of the Dao tribe at the Khau Vai market in Northern Vietnam.

Vietnam, Laos & Cambodia

See colour maps in centre of book

1 Ha Giang province, a truly undiscovered border region of ethnic markets, towering terraced rice paddies and phallic limestone peaks. ▶▶ page 94.

2 An engaging capital city, Hanoi has a fascinating cultural legacy from the colonial to communist eras. ▶▶ page 68.

3 Limestone towers rise out of the waters of Halong Bay, a World Heritage Site. ▶▶ page 82.

4 Visit Hué, an imperial capital with imperial tombs in an imperial setting on the Perfume River. ▶▶ page 105.

5 Enjoy the silk emporiums, glorious food and Chinese temples of Hoi An. ▶▶ page 121.

6 Ho Chi Minh City is a manic, capitalistic hothouse clogged with traffic and bursting with energy, top

7 Luang Prabang is charming cafés and two rivers. ▶▶ page

8 Discover the tier archaeological site riverside Champas

9 The Four Thousa own laid-back trop

10 Marvel at Angko monument in the w

11 Use Kratie as a b Irrawaddy dolphins

12 The Royal Palace Penh's concoction

Clockwise from top
Imperial Tombs, Hué, Vietnam.
Ha Giang, Vietnam.
Ho Chi Minh Mausoleum, Hanoi, Vietnam.
Hoi An, Vietnam.

Opposite page top Halong Bay, Vietnam.
Opposite page bottom Ho Chi Minh City, Vietnam.

Clockwise from top

Four Thousand Islands, Laos.

Wat Mai, Luang Prabang, Laos.

Champasak, Laos.

Kratie, Cambodia.

Royal Palace, Phnom Penh, Cambodia.

Opposite page Angkor Wat, Cambodia.

The Mekong

The Mekong River is the heart and soul of mainland Southeast Asia, a sinuous thread that binds Vietnam, Cambodia and Laos geographically, historically, culturally and economically. Indeed, the Mekong – or the Mae Nam Khong (the Mother of Waters) – is the most important geographical feature of mainland Southeast Asia.

The Mekong's origins in eastern Tibet have only been pin-pointed in the last 15 years. From here the giant river plies 4500 km through six countries, cutting through almost the entire length of Laos, dissecting Cambodia, and plunging into Vietnam's Mekong Delta before emptying into the South China Sea. The river is the 12th longest river in the world and is the world's 10th largest by volume of water dispersed into the ocean – 475 cu km.

French explorer Francis Garnier once commented: "without doubt, no other river, over such a length, has a more singular or remarkable character". The Mekong has indeed woven itself into the cultural fabric, shaping the region's history. The river is the one constant from the ancient Funan settlement in the Mekong Delta, through to the Khmer Empire who established its capital at Angkor, relying on the river for transport and agricultural production. After several European expeditions, the French took an interest in the river and the region in the mid 19th century, developing grandiose plans to transform the Mekong into a river highway from China (the plans were thwarted upon discovering that the Mekong could not be traversed).

The river later played an integral role in shaping history during the Vietnam War when it became an important conduit for the running of Viet Cong supplies and was the scene of heavy fighting.

The river has been a major purveyor of culture, ushering in various religions, arts, customs and folklore. The enormous, colourful, boat racing festivals of Vietnam, Cambodia and Laos are staged on the water (pictured above). Similarly, the annual water festivals in Cambodia and Laos come from deep-rooted traditions stemming from the Mekong and its importance to agricultural production. Nor is the river free from superstition or strange phenomena. In Laos thousands of people gather each year to witness *naga* fireballs rising from the river's surface. Major arts have also developed from these waters including Vietnam's water puppetry (pictured at top of page). It also provided inspiration in the *Apocalypse Now* mission down the fictional Nung River, said to represent the Mekong.

Today, the Mekong is instrumental in the region's survival, with more than 60 million people in Southeast Asia dependent on the river and its tributaries for their survival.

Contents

Contents

Footprint features

Essentials

Planning your trip

Where to go

If time is limited, by far the best option is to get an open-jaw flight where you fly into one city and out of another or fly into Bangkok, which is the best major connected city to the region and the rest of the world. **Vietnam Airlines** has an excellent domestic network, too. Distances are huge in this region and in Cambodia and Laos, especially, roads are not always sealed, making overland journey times lengthy and sometimes tortuous, especially in the wet season. Note that there are strict regulations concerning visas that need to be noted before planning your trip, see Visas and immigration, page 63.

One week

A one-week trip will require careful planning and prioritizing. Either take internal flights, if you want to cover a lot of ground, or limit yourself to just one area. In Vietnam, fly from energetic and historic **Ho Chi Minh City** to the imperial city of **Hué**, followed by a trip to enchanting **Hoi An** and its beach. Then fly on to cultured **Hanoi**. If the countryside is of more interest, the **Mekong Delta** can be visited in a day trip from Ho Chi Minh City; magical **Halong Bay** can be done in a day/night trip from Hanoi but in order to visit **Sapa**, known for its stunning scenery and hilltribes, you'll have to spend two nights on a train. In Cambodia, up to four days could be spent around the exceptional ruins of **Angkor**, with one day in **Phnom Penh** and one in either the laid-back beaches of **Sihanoukville** or in colonial-inspired **Kampot**. For Laos, fly from Bangkok to **Vientiane** before heading north to wonderfully preserved **Luang Prabang** via **Vang Vieng**. Or fly from Vientiane to **Luang Namtha** to access the interesting trekking region in the north before overlanding it back to Luang Prabang. Alternatively, after visiting Luang Prabang, fly to Pakse for a trip to the tranquil, laid-back **Siphandon** (4000 islands) in the south.

Two weeks

Building on the one-week options, you have the chance to cross a border or two. If you fly into **Ho Chi Minh City** you could see the war relic of the **Cu Chi tunnels** and the fantastical **Cao Dai Temple** before making your way through the **Mekong Delta** (visiting the floating markets at **Can Tho**) to **Phnom Penh**, **Choeung Ek** and onto **Siem Reap** (**Angkor**) by boat, where you will have more time to visit some of the outlying ruins such as **Koh Ker** and **Beng Melea** and, at a push, the brilliant, clifftop temple of **Preah Vihear**. You could then fly from Siem Reap to **Pakse** for **Wat Phou**, the sublime **Tad Lo** and **Tad Fan falls** and **Siphandon**, or to **Vientiane** to access northern Laos. Alternatively, you could fly to Cambodia first and then fly from either **Phnom Penh** to **Vientiane** or **Ho Chi Minh City** or from **Siem Reap** to **Ho Chi Minh City**. If you fly into **Hanoi** you could visit both **Sapa** (by train) and **Halong Bay** and then fly to **Vientiane** in Laos continuing to **Siem Reap** or **Phnom Penh** by plane.

One month

With one month you can take things a little more slowly. Having explored **Sapa**, **Dien Bien Phu** and the area around **Mai Chau** in northwest Vietnam you could take an overnight train from **Hanoi** to **Hué**. You could either travel west into **central Laos** here or take the

Packing for Vietnam, Cambodia and Laos

Make sure your passport is valid for at least six months and take photocopies of essential documents, passport ID and visa pages, insurance policy details and student ID card. Spare passport photos are useful when applying for permits or in case of loss or theft.

You may also require a small first-aid kit, torch, penknife, insect repellent, padlock for locking bags in hotel rooms and while travelling, and a money belt. For clothing, pack long-sleeved cotton shirts, long light trousers and socks to prevent mosquitoes from biting in the evening. Warm clothing is necessary for certain areas and you may also want a jumper on buses and trains where the air conditioning can also be very cold.

Those intending to stay in budget accommodation should take a cotton sheet sleeping bag, padlock, earplugs, universal bath plug and student card.

You may want to pack antacid tablets for indigestion, antibiotics for diarrhoea (discuss with your doctor), antiseptic ointment, iodine drops, anti-malarials, mosquito repellent, travel sickness tablets, painkillers, condoms and contraceptives, tampons/sanitary towels, high-factor sun screen and sun hat, and a blow-up pillow.

For longer trips in more remote areas, consider a clean needle pack, clean dental pack and water filtration devices. However, be wary of carrying needles; customs officials may be suspicious.

splendid **train journey from Hué to Danang**. Close by is **Hoi An**. From there, travel to coastal **Nha Trang** for its islands or to the quieter, lovely resort of **Mui Ne**. From Nha Trang you could go to **Dalat**, the hub of the Central Highlands and the towns of **Buon Ma Thuot**, **Play Ku** and **Kontum**, then continue by air or overland to **Ho Chi Minh City**, from where a side trip to the golden-sand beaches of **Phu Quoc** is possible. To reach Cambodia, fly on to **Phnom Penh** or **Siem Reap** or go by bus and boat through the **Mekong Delta**. Visit **Angkor** and then, from Phnom Penh, go south to **Sihanoukville** and explore the beaches and outlying islands. A day or two can also be spent visiting **Kampot** and the seaside town of **Kep**, as well as exploring the eerie **Bokor Mountain National Park**. With one month it is better to start at the extreme north or the south of Laos to cover as much territory as possible. From Phnom Penh you could travel overland to **Siphandon** in southern Laos via Stung Treng. Before heading north take a side trip to the interesting **Bolaven Plateau** with its stunning coffee plantations and ubiquitous falls. Overland it to **Thakhek** and do the motorcycle loop around the limestone scenery of central Laos, visiting the **Kong Lor** River Cave en route. Or fly direct to **Vientiane** in order to catch a flight to **Phonsavanh** and explore the mysterious **Plain of Jars**, then overland it to **Xam Neua** to see the Pathet Lao caves at **Vieng Xai**. A long but interesting overland route will take you west from here via increasingly popular **Nong Khiaw** to **Luang Prabang**, from where you can head north to the trekking areas of **Luang Namtha**, **Muang Sing** and **Phongsali**, or catch a boat up the Mekong towards the Thai border.

When to go

Climatically the best time to visit the region is between November and April when it should be dry and not too hot. In the southern part of the region it is warm but not too hot with lovely cool evenings. However, in Cambodia wind-blown dust invades everything at this time of year. In the north of Vietnam and Laos the highlands will be a bit chilly but they should be dry with clear blue skies. However, temperatures in upland areas like the Plain of Jars, the Bolaven Plateau and some towns in the north of Laos can be extraordinarily cold.

From late-March to April the region heats up and temperatures can exceed 40°C. In northern Laos, the months from March through to the first rains in May or June can be very hazy as smoke from burning off the secondary forest hangs in the air. On the worst days this can cause itchiness of the eyes. It also means that views are restricted and sometimes flights are cancelled. Travel on the region's mud and laterite roads is difficult and sometimes impossible by June and July; transport will be slower and may cease altogether in some parts. It is also impossible to do any outdoor activities in June and July because of the rain. However, the area is at its most beautiful then. Travel in the south and Mekong Delta can be difficult at the height of the monsoon (particularly during September, October and November). The central regions and north of Vietnam sometimes suffer tropical storms from May to November. Hué is at its wettest wet from September to January.

Tet, the Vietnamese New Year, is not really a good time to visit. This movable feast usually falls between late January and March and lasts for about a fortnight. It is the only holiday most Vietnamese get in the year so popular destinations are packed, roads are jammed and, for a couple of days, restaurants are shut and all hotel prices increase and car hire prices rise by 50% or more. Problems also occur during **Khmer New Year** in Cambodia and **Pi Mai** in Laos, when public transport is full of and hotels booked out in popular places.

What to do

Vietnam and Laos are well known for their wonderful trekking opportunities amid stunning mountainous landscape, which is home to a variety of ethnic minorities. Other activities, such as rafting, kayaking, rock climbing and cycling, are slowly emerging and are not as developed as they are in a place like Thailand. Safety is always an issue when participating in adventurous sports: make sure you are fully covered by your travel insurance; check the credentials of operators offering adventure activities; and make sure that vehicles and safety equipment are in a good condition. Note that medical care in Cambodia and Laos is very limited, see page 52.

Caving
Laos has some of the most extensive and largest caves in the region. Some of the best can be found around Vang Vieng, where caving tourism has been developed. Contact **Green Discovery** ⓘ www.greendiscoverylaos.com. Another highlight is the amazing Kong Lor River Cave in the centre of the country. There are hundreds of caves around Vieng Xai (www.visit-viengxay.com) but only a few open to tourists, for those interested in history these caves should be a first stop.

Cycling and mountain biking
Large parts of Vietnam are flat, so cycling is a popular activity, although the traffic on the roads can be hazardous. It's therefore recommended that any tour is planned off-road or on minor roads. In Cambodia and Laos, cycling is offered by several tour agencies; Luang Namtha is a popular place to start, and **Green Discovery** ⓘ www.greendiscoverylaos.com,

runs excellent cycling tours. New cycling opportunities have opened up in Udomxai and in Xieng Khouang Province, the latter with the expertise of German NGO DED. Other operators include **Discover Adventure** ⓘ www.discoveradventure.com, **Symbiosis** ⓘ www.symbiosis-travel.com, **Spice Roads** ⓘ www.spiceroads.com, **Tien Bicycles** ⓘ www.tienbicycles.com. Many cyclists prefer to bring their own all-terrain or racing bikes but it's also possible to rent them from tour organizers. Other good cycling destinations include Hué, Dalat and the Mekong Delta.

Diving and snorkelling

Underwater adventures are limited in the seas around Vietnam, since much of the coast is a muddy deltaic swamp and, elsewhere, the water is turbid from high levels of soil erosion. In those places where snorkelling and diving is good (Nha Trang, Phu Quoc and Whale Island it is possible almost year round and is not necessarily dictated by the dry (October-November and April-May) and wet seasons. In Nha Trang, contact **Rainbow Divers** ⓘ www.divevietnam.com. The dive industry in Cambodia is in its infant years, but the coast boasts lots of pristine coral reefs and unexplored areas. There are several dive operators in Sihanoukville, including the nation's first PADI five-star dive centre **Scuba Nation Diving Centre** ⓘ T012-604680, www.divecambodia.com. Koh Kong town is now also emerging as a possible dive destination.

Kayaking

Kayaking in Vietnam is centred around Halong Bay. This World Heritage Site, crammed with islands and grottoes, is a fantastic place to explore by kayak. Head to the Nam Song River at Vang Vieng for kayaking, rafting and tubing in Laos. There is also excellent kayaking around the Bolaven Plateau.

Operators in Vietnam include **Buffalo Tours** ⓘ www.buffalotours.com, and **Exotissimo** ⓘ www.exotissimo.com. In Laos: **Green Discovery** ⓘ www.greendiscoverylaos.com, and **Riverside tours** ⓘ www.riversidetourlaos.com.

Kitesurfing and windsurfing

Kitesurfing and windsurfing are found largely in Mui Ne, Vietnam, which offers just about perfect conditions throughout the year. The wind is normally brisk over many days and the combination of powerful wind and waves enables good kitesurfers to get airborne for several seconds at a time. Equipment can be rented at many places, including **Jibe's Beach Club** ⓘ www.windsurf-vietnam.com. Windsurfing is popular in Nha Trang where dive schools offer this and other water sports.

Motorbiking tours

Touring northern Ha Giang province in Vietnam on a motorbike is one of the most exciting things you can do in the country. A permit and a great sense of adventure is required. Other cross-country and cross-border tours are possible (www.voyagevietnam.net). Tours are now offered across Indochina by multiple operators.

Rock climbing

Laos has stunning karst rock formations, caves and cliffs. Vang Vieng is the hot spot for this activity; contact **Green Discovery** ⓘ www.greendiscoverylaos.com. Climbing is a new activity in Vietnam and concentrated in Halong Bay. Contact **Asia Outdoors/Slo Pony Adventures** ⓘ Cat Ba town, T91-376 0025, www.slopony.com.

Visiting ethnic minorities: house rules

Scores of different ethnic minority groups inhabit northern Vietnam, the Central Highlands of Vietnam and northern Laos, in particular, and their distinctive styles of dress and age-old rituals may be of special interest to Western travellers. If you choose to visit or stay in a minority village, please remember that it is not a human zoo. Etiquette and customs vary between the minorities, but the following are general rules of good behaviour that should be adhered to whenever possible.

→ Organize your visit through a local villager or a travel agency that supports the village.
→ Inform yourself of local trekking rules and guidance.

→ Dress modestly and avoid undressing/changing in public.
→ Ask permission before entering a house.
→ Ask permission before photographing anyone (old people and pregnant women often object to having their photograph taken). Be aware that villagers are unlikely to pose out of the kindness of their hearts so don't begrudge them the money; for many, tourism is their livelihood.
→ Buy handicrafts that support local industry.
→ Avoid sitting or stepping on door sills.
→ Avoid excessive displays of wealth and do not hand out gifts.
→ Avoid introducing Western medicines.
→ Do not touch or photograph village shrines.

Spas

The only devoted spa resorts in Vietnam are the Ana Mandara in Nha Trang and the Evason Hideaway in Ninh Van Bay, www.sixsenses.com. There are other good hotels such as the Life Wellness Resorts and the Victoria Hotels that offer spa facilities. Hotels offering massage, treatments and therapies exist across the region and are good value for money.

There are also some wonderful spas in Luang Prabang; for extreme indulgence try the **Spa** at La Residence Phou Vao or for a cheaper luxury alternative the **Spa Garden**, see page 398.

Trekking

The main focus for trekking in Vietnam is Sapa but some trekking is also organized around Dalat and other opportunities are opening up around Ha Giang and in the Mai Chau area. Some treks are straightforward and can be done without guides or support, whereas others need accommodation and there may be a legal requirement to take a licensed guide. If staying with ethnic minorities in homestays this must be organized through a tour operator. In Laos, Luang Namtha, Muang Sing, around Savannakhet, Nong Khiaw, Muang Ngoi Neua and Phongsali all offer trekking in areas inhabited by a diverse range of ethnicities. There are also treks from Luang Prabang and Vang Vieng. For a different perspective on the landscape, elephant trekking is possible in Yok Don National Park, Vietnam. See also box, above.

Getting there

Gateway cities

Travelling to Southeast Asia by air offers up some of the cheapest and best-connected routes on the planet. Due to high tourist and business demand most major airlines from every major region in the world fly into the region. Yet not every country in the region is serviced by long-haul international flights, which means that flying into the hubs of Singapore, Bangkok and Kuala Lumpur is often the best option. From these different points on the map a spider's web of budget and short-haul carriers can then link the traveller to almost anywhere of note in the region. Direct flight times into each of these hubs are roughly 12 hours from Europe, 16 hours from the west coast of the US and eight to 12 hours from Australia and New Zealand (see box, page 25, for list of major carriers into the region). Be aware that in this highly competitive and cut-throat economic climate airlines and routes, particularly those of the budget players, are appearing and disappearing very fast – we've attempted to include what appear to be the safest and most stable regional and international airlines and their routes into the region.

Bangkok

Air **Suvarnabhumi International Airport** (pronounced su-wan-na-poom) opened in September 2006 and is around 25 km southeast of the city. Currently, the airport is only accessible by road but by the time this book hits the shelves the 29-km Suvarnabhumi Airport Rail Link should be running, offering travellers a 15-minute express ride into the Makassan City Air Terminal and a slower 27-minute commuter route with eight stops along the way. Travellers will be able to check in luggage at Makassan. The link will connect with the BTS Sukumvit Line and the MRT Blue Line at Phaya Thai. All facilities at the airport are 24 hours, so you'll have no problem exchanging money, getting something to eat or taking a taxi or other transport into the city at any time.

From the airport to the city centre It can take well over an hour to get to central Bangkok from the airport by road, depending on the time of day and the state of the traffic. Taking the expressway cuts the journey time significantly and outside of rush-hour the transit time should be 35-45 minutes. The Airport Rail Link, when open, will cut this time dramatically. The airport website, www.suvarnabhumiairport.com, offers excellent up-to-date information on transport services.

An **air-conditioned airport bus service** operates every 15 minutes (0500-2400), ฿150 to Silom Road (service AE1), Khaosan Road (service AE2), Wireless/Sukhumvit Road (service AE3) and Hualamphong train station (service AE4). Each service stops at between 12 and 20 popular tourist destinations and hotels. The airport offers full details at the stop located outside the Arrivals area on the pavement. Some of the more popular stops on each line are: **Silom service (AE1)**: Pratunam, Central World Plaza, Lumpini Park, Sala Daeng, Patpong, Sofitel Silom. **Khaosan service (AE2)**: Pratuman, Amari Watergate Hotel, Asia Hotel, Royal Princess Hotel, Democracy Monument, Phra Artit, Khaosan Road. **Wireless Road service (AE3)**: BTS (Skytrain) On Nuts, BTS Thonglor, Rex Hotel, Emporium Shopping Centre Sukhumvit 24, Novotel Sukhumvit, Westin Hotel, Amari Boulevard, Majestic Grande, Central Silom and Nana. **Hualamphong service (AE4)**:

Victory Monument, BTS On Nut, Asia Hotel Ratchathewi, Siam Centre, MBK/National Stadium, Hualamphong train station. Many visitors will see the ฿150 as money well spent (although note that for three or four passengers in a taxi it is as cheap or cheaper). However, there will still be a hardened few who will opt for the regular bus service. This is just as slow as it ever was, 1½ to three hours (depending on time of day), prices for air-conditioned buses linking the airport to the city are now a flat rate of ฿35.

The official taxi booking service is in the arrivals hall. Official airport limousines have green plates, public taxis have yellow plates; a white plate means the vehicle is not registered as a taxi. There are three sets of taxi/limousine services. First, **airport limos** (before exiting from the restricted area), next **airport taxis** (before exiting from the terminal building), and finally, a **public taxi** counter (outside, on the slipway). The latter are the cheapest. Note that airport flunkies sometimes try to direct passengers to the more expensive 'limousine' service: walk through the barriers to the public taxi desk. If taking a metered taxi, the coupon from the booking desk will quote no fare so ensure that the meter is turned on and keep hold of your coupon – some taxi drivers try to pocket it – as it details the obligations of taxi drivers. A public taxi to downtown should cost roughly ฿300. Note that tolls on the expressways are paid on top of the fare on the meter and should be no more than ฿55 per toll. There is a ฿50 airport surcharge on top of the meter cost. Don't be surprised if your driver decides to feign that he does not know where to go: it's all part of being new in town. Some regular airport visitors recommend going up to the departures floor and flagging down a taxi that has just dropped passengers off. Doing it this way will save you the ฿50 surcharge and possibly a long wait in a taxi queue.

Getting around Bangkok has the unenviable reputation of having some of the worst traffic in the world. The **Skytrain** – an elevated railway – along with the newer **Metro** have made things a lot easier for those areas of the city they cover. Plentiful **buses** travel to all city sights and offer the cheapest way to get around – visit the Bangkok Mass Transit Authority's website for full listings and a route planner, www.bmta.co.th/en. A **taxi** or **tuk-tuk** ride within the centre should cost ฿50-100. All taxis now have meters. Tuk-tuk numbers are dwindling and the negotiated fares often work out more expensive than a taxi. Walking can be tough in the heat and fumes, although there are some parts of the city where this can be the best way to get around. For an alternative to the smog of Bangkok's streets, hop onboard one of the express **river taxis**, which ply the Chao Phraya River and the network of *khlongs* (canals).

Orientation Begin in the bejewelled beauty of the **Old City**. The charming **Golden Mount** is a short hop to the east, while to the south are the bewildering alleyways and gaudy temples of Bangkok's frenetic **Chinatown**. Head west over the Chao Phraya River to the magnificent spire of **Wat Arun** and the **khlongs of Thonburi**. To the north are the broad, leafy avenues of **Dusit**, the home of the Thai parliament and the King's residence. Carry on east and south and you'll reach modern Bangkok. A multitude of mini-boutiques forms **Siam Square** and the Thai centre of youth fashion; **Silom** and **Sukhumvit roads** are vibrant runs of shopping centres, restaurants and hotels, while the **Chatuchak Weekend Market** (known to locals as JJ), in the northern suburbs, is one of Asia's best known markets.

Routes into the major hubs

Singapore

AirAsia	Kota Kinabalu, Kuala Lumpur, Kuching, Penang
Air China	Beijing-Capital
Air France	Paris-Charles de Gaulle
All Nippon Airways (ANA)	Tokyo-Narita
Asiana	Seoul-Incheon
British Airways	London-Heathrow, Sydney
Cathay Pacific	Bangkok, Colombo, Hong Kong
Cebu Pacific	Cebu, Clark, Manila
China Eastern	Shanghai-Pudong
Delta	Tokyo-Narita
Emirates Airline	Brisbane, Colombo, Dubai, Melbourne
Etihad	Abu Dhabi, Brisbane
Garuda	Jakarta-Soekarno Hatta, Denpasar
Japan Airlines	Osaka-Kansai, Tokyo-Narita
Jet Star	Auckland (from early 2011), Cairns, Darwin, Hong Kong, Melbourne, Perth, Osaka-Kansai, Taipei, Yangon
KLM	Amsterdam, Denpasar
Lufthansa	Frankfurt, Jakarta-Soekarno Hatta, Munich
Qantas Airways	Adelaide, Brisbane, Frankfurt, London-Heathrow, Melbourne, Mumbai, Perth, Sydney
Qatar Airways	Doha, Denpasar
SilkAir	Chiang Mai, Cochin, Kathmandu, Kunming, Trivandrum
Singapore Airlines	Adelaide, Amsterdam, Athens, Auckland, Cairo, Cape Town, Christchurch, Copenhagen, Frankfurt, Houston-Intercontinental, Johannesburg, Kolkata, London-Heathrow, Los Angeles, Malé, Manchester, Manila, Melbourne, Milan-Malpensa, New York-JFK, Newark, Paris-Charles de Gaulle, Rome-Fiumicino, San Francisco, Shanghai-Pudong, Sydney, Zürich
Tiger Airways	Bangalore, Guangzhou, Hong Kong, Perth, Shenzhen
United Airlines	Chicago-O'Hare, Tokyo-Narita, Washington-Dulles

Bangkok

Aeroflot	Moscow
AirAsia	Denpasar, Jakarta-Soekarno Hatta, Macau, Penang, Taipei
Air Berlin	Berlin-Tegel, Dusseldorf, Munich
Air China	Beijing-Capital, Chengdu, Chongqing
Air France	Paris-Charles de Gaulle
All Nippon Airways	Tokyo-Narita
Asiana	Seoul-Incheon
Austrian Airlines	Vienna
Bangkok Airways	Guilin, Yangon, Xi'an
British Airways	London-Heathrow, Sydney
Cathay Pacific	Colombo, Delhi, Hong Kong, Mumbai

Cebu Pacific	Clark, Manila
China Eastern	Kunming, Shanghai-Pudong
Emirates	Christchurch, Dubai, Hong Kong, Sydney
Etihad	Abu Dhabi
EVA Air	Amsterdam, London-Heathrow, Taipei, Vienna
Finnair	Helsinki
Jetstar	Melbourne
KLM	Amsterdam, Taipei
Lufthansa	Frankfurt, Ho Chi Minh City, Kuala Lumpur
Nepal Airlines	Kathmandu
Philippine Airlines	Manila
Qantas	London-Heathrow, Sydney
Qatar Airways	Doha
Royal Brunei Airlines	Bandar Seri Begawan
SAS	Copenhagen
Thai Airways International	Athens, Auckland, Chennai, Copenhagen, Delhi, Denpasar/Bali, Hanoi, Ho Chi Minh City, Jakarta, Kathmandu, London-Heathrow, Los Angeles, Madrid, Melbourne, Milan-Malpensa, Mumbai, Munich, Osaka-Kansai, Paris-Charles de Gaulle, Rome-Fiumicino, Shanghai-Pudong, Stockholm-Arlanda, Sydney, Xiamen, Zürich
Turkish Airlines	Istanbul-Atatürk
United Airlines	Tokyo-Narita
Kuala Lumpur	
AirAsia	Bandar Seri Begawan, Bangalore, Chengdu, Cochin, Colombo, Denpasar, Gold Coast. Guangzhou, Guilin, Hangzhou, Jakarta Soekarno Hatta, Kolkata, London Stansted, Taipei, Hong Kong, Macau, Makassar, Medan, Melbourne, Mumbai, New Delhi, Perth, Tianjin, Yogyakarta
Air China	Beijing-Capital
Cathay Pacific	Hong Kong
Emirates	Dubai, Melbourne
Etihad	Abu Dhabi
Japan Airlines	Osaka-Kansai, Tokyo-Narita
KLM	Amsterdam, Jakarta Soekarno Hatta
Lufthansa	Frankfurt
Malaysia Airlines	Adelaide, Amsterdam, Auckland, Bandar Seri Begawan, Beirut, Brisbane, Buenos Aires- Ezeiza, Cape Town, Delhi, Jakarta, Johannesburg, London-Heathrow, Los Angeles, Manila, Melbourne, Mumbai , Paris-Charles de Gaulle, Perth, Rome-Fiumicino, Shanghai-Pudong, Stockholm-Arlanda, Sydney, Tokyo-Narita, Xiamen
Nepal Airlines	Kathmandu
Qatar Airways	Doha

Tourist information **Tourism Authority of Thailand (TAT)** ① *main office at 1600 New Phetburi Rd, Makkasan, Ratchathewi, T02-250 5500, www.tourismthailand.org; also at 4 Rachdamnern Nok Av (intersection with Chakrapatdipong Rd), daily 0830-1630; 2 counters at Suvarnabhumi Airport, in the arrivals halls of Domestic and International Terminal, T02-134 0040, T02-134 0041, daily 0800-2400.* The two main offices are very helpful and provide a great deal of information for independent travellers – certainly worth a visit. For information, phone T1672 between 0800 and 2000 for the English-speaking TAT Call Centre. A number of good, informative, English-language magazines provide listings of what to do and where to go in Bangkok: *BK Magazine*, www.bk.asia-city. com, is a free weekly publication with good listings for clubs, restaurants and live acts. See also www.khaosanroad.com.

🛏 Sleeping

AL Metropolitan, 27 South Sathorn Rd, T02-625 3333, www.metropolitan.bangkok. como.bz.

A-B Atlanta, 78 Sukhumvit Soi 2, T02-252 1650, www.theatlantahotelbangkok.com.

A-D Charlie's House, Soi Saphan Khu, T02-679 8330, www.charliehousethailand.com.

A-D Phranakorn Nornlen Hotel, 46 Thewet soi 1, T02-628 8188, phranakorn-nornlen.com.

C-E Tavee, 83 Sri Ayutthaya Rd, Soi 14, T02-282 5983.

E Orchid House, Rambutri St, T02-280 2619.

🍴 Eating

Some of the best street food can be found on the roads between Silom and Surawong Rd, Soi Suanphlu off South Sathorn Rd. Also try the famous Chok Chai Si nightmarket on Lad Phrao Rd (take MRT to Lad Phrao and then a taxi). The street food in Chinatown is some of the best in Thailand. The Thai food sold along Khaosan Rd is some of the worst and least authentic in town.

¶¶¶ Nahm, Metropolitan Hotel, 27 South Sathorn Rd, T02-625 3333, www. metropolitan.bangkok.como.bz. Run by Michelin star winner David Thompson, **Nahm** is a superlative ining experience in sleek and warm contemporary surroundings. Offering fare from all over the country and showcasing market-fresh produce, this is Thai cuisine of the highest order. This is a restaurant at the cutting edge of Bangkok eating, miles ahead of the competition.

¶¶¶ Taling Pling, 60 Pan Rd, T02-236 4830. Daily 1100-2200. A favourite of locals, attracting a good mix of foreigners. Set in a comfortable converted house, serving up simple yet authentic dishes, decent desserts and offering a reasonable wine list.

¶ The Canton House, 530 Yaowarat Rd, 02-221 3335. This hugely popular dim sum canteen is set on the main drag. The prices – ฿15 – for a plate of dim sum are legendary. This has to be one of the best-value places to eat in town: the food is OK but nothing exceptional. The frenetic, friendly atmosphere is, however, 100% authentic Chinatown. Recommended.

Kuala Lumpur

Kuala Lumpur (KL) is well linked to the rest of Malaysia and to the wider world. **Kuala Lumpur International Airport (KLIA)** ① *Sepang, 72 km south, T03-8776 2000, www.klia.com.my*, provides a slick point of entry. Glitzy and high-tech, it has all the usual facilities including restaurants, shops and banks. The Tourism Malaysia desk has pamphlets and a useful map.

The Low **Cost Carrier Terminal (LCCT)** ① *20 km south of KLIA, lcct-klia.com*, is used by most budget airlines. Shuttle buses connect KLIA and the LCCT (20 minutes) for RM1.50. Always check your ticket to confirm which terminal you're flying from.

The LCCT terminal is dominated by the hugely successful **Air Asia** ① *T03-8775 4000, www.airasia.com*, which is the region's main low-cost carrier, with flights as far afield as China, Australia and the UK. Internet bookings provide the best deals. Tickets booked well in advance are the cheapest.

Transport from the airport From KLIA, **Airport Coach** ① *T03-8787 3894, www.airportcoach. com.my*, provides an efficient service into the city to KL Sentral. From the KLIA arrivals hall, go one floor down to where the coaches depart; follow the clearly marked signs. Coaches run every 30 minutes, 0630-0030 (KLIA – KL Sentral) 0500-2300 (KL Sentral–KLIA) one hour, RM10 one way.

The **KLIA Ekspres** ① *T03-2267 8000, www.kliaekspres.com*, runs an air-rail service every 15-20 minutes, 0500-0100 between the airport and **KL Sentral train station**. From here you can take a taxi to your hotel. The journey takes 28 minutes and costs RM35 one way. Travellers using the KLIA Ekspres can check their luggage in at KL Central for outgoing flights. Alternatively, the **KLIA Transit** ① *www.kliaekspres.com*, takes 35 minutes to make the same journey, and costs RM35. The train stops at three stations and runs 0550-0100. If your plane arrives outside these hours, take a taxi into KL or hire a car. Major car rental companies have desks in arrivals, open 24 hours.

For a taxi expect to pay RM80-100. Taxis operate on a coupon system; collect one from the taxi counter at the exit in arrivals (near Door 3). Touts charge more than double the official rate; bargain hard. Many hotels provide a pick-up service, but make sure they are aware of your arrival details; there is a hotel pick-up office just outside the terminal exit.

From the LCCT terminal the **Skybus** ① *www.skybus.com.my*, runs to KL Sentral Station. The journey takes 1¼ hours and costs RM9. It departs regularly 0700-0315. If arriving on **AirAsia** at the LCCT, the official taxi charge to KL city centre is RM75. Buy a coupon from the arrivals hall to avoid arguments.

The KLIA Transit now runs a service to the LCCT. Passengers ride the KLIA Transit rail link to Salak Tinggi and then transfer to a shuttle bus for the remainder of the journey to the LCCT RM12.50. Trains run from 0533 until 0033 from KL Sentral and minibuses leave from the LCCT from 0725 until 0035. This train and bus combination journey takes a little over an hour.

Getting around Kuala Lumpur is not the easiest city to navigate, with its sights spread thinly over a wide area. Pedestrians have not been high on the list of priorities for Malaysian urban planners, with many roads, especially outside the city centre, built without pavements, making walking both hazardous and difficult. The heavy pollution and the hot, humid climate add to the problem and, with the exception of the area around Central Market, Chinatown and Dayabumi, distances between sights are too great to cover comfortably on foot. Kuala Lumpur's bus system is labyrinthine and congested streets mean that travelling by taxi can make for a tedious wait in a traffic jam. Try to insist that taxi drivers use their meters, although don't be surprised if they refuse. The two **Light Rail Transit** (**LRT**), the **Monorail** and the **KMT Komuter** rail lines, are undoubtedly the least hassle and provide a great elevated and air-conditioned view of the city. The **Malaysian Tourism Centre**, see below, gives free, detailed pocket-sized maps of KL, with bus stops, monorail and LRT systems. See also www.kiat.net/malaysia/KL/transit.html.

Worth considering if short of time is the KL **Hop-on Hop-off City Tour** ① *T03-2691 1382, www.myhoponhopoff.com, daily 0830-2030, RM38*, a hi-tech variant on the London tour bus theme. Tickets are for 24 hours and can be bought at hotels, travel agents and on the bus itself, which stops at 22 clearly marked points around town. A recorded commentary is available in eight languages as the bus trundles around a circuit that includes KLCC, the Golden Triangle, Petaling Street (Chinatown), KL Central Station, the National Mosque and the Palace of Culture.

Orientation The **colonial core** is around the Padang and down Jalan Raja and Jalan Tun Perak. East of the Padang (the cricket pitch in front of the old Selangor Club, next to Merdeka Square), straight over the bridge on Lebuh Pasar Besar, is the main commercial area, occupied by banks and finance companies. To the southeast of Merdeka Square is KL's vibrant **Chinatown**. If you get disorientated in the winding streets around Little India and Chinatown a good point of reference is the angular Maybank Building situated in Jalan Pudu, very close to both Puduraya Bus Terminal and Jalan Sultan. The streets to the north of the Padang are central shopping streets with modern department stores and shops.

To find a distinctively Malay area, it is necessary to venture further out, along **Jalan Raja Muda Musa to Kampong Baru**, to the northeast. To the south of Kampong Baru, on the opposite side of the Klang River, is **Jalan Ampang**, once KL's millionaires row, where tin magnates, or *towkays*, and sultans first built their homes. The road is now mainly occupied by embassies and high commissions. To the southeast of Jalan Ampang is KL's so-called **Golden Triangle**, to which the modern central business district has migrated.

Tourist information **Malaysian Tourism Centre (MTC)** ① *109 Jln Ampang, T03-2163 3664, www.tourism.gov.my, daily 0700-2400*, is housed in an opulent mansion formerly belonging to a Malaysian planter and tin miner. It provides information on all 13 states, as well as money-changing facilities, an express bus ticket counter, tour reservations, a Malay restaurant, cultural shows on Tuesdays, Thursdays, Saturdays and Sundays at 1500 (RM5), demonstrations of handicrafts and a souvenir shop. There is a visitor centre on Level 3 of the airport's main terminal building.

Other useful contacts are: **Tourism Malaysia** ① *Level 2, Putra World Trade Centre, 45 Jln Tun Ismail, T03-2615 8188, tourist info T1300 88 5050, www.tourismmalaysia. gov.my, Mon-Fri 0900-1800*; **KL Tourist Police** ① *T03-2149 6593*, and the **Wildlife and National Parks Department** ① *Km 10, Jln Cheras, T03-9075 2872, www.wildlife.gov.my*.

Many companies offer half-day city tours, which include visits to Chinatown, the National Museum, railway station, Masjid Negara (National Mosque), the Padang area and Masjid Jamek; most cost about RM30. City night tours take in Chinatown, the Sri Mahmariamman Temple and a cultural show (RM60). Other tours visit sights close to the city such as Batu Caves, a batik factory and the Selangor Pewter Complex (RM30).

⊙ Sleeping

AL Swiss Garden, 117 Jln Pudu, T03-2141 3333, www.swissgarden.com.
A Nikko, 165 Jln Ampang, T03-2611 1111, www.hotelnikko.com.my.
B Bintang Warisan, 68 Jln Bukit Bintang, T03-2148 8111, www.bintangwarisan.com.

C Serai Inn, Jln Hang Lekiu, T03-2070 4728, www.seraiinn.com.
C-D Pondok Lodge, 20 Jln Cangkat Bukit Bintang, T03-2142 8449, www.pondok lodge.com.
C-E Grocer's Inn, 78 Jln Sultan, T03-2078 7906, www.grocersinn.com.my.

❶ Eating

In Chinatown head to Central Market for a good local breakfast of Ipoh coffee, kaya toast and half boiled eggs. Little India has some excellent pure veg restaurants and good international fare (particularly Middle Eastern) can be found around Bukit Bintang.

Seri Melayu, 1 Jln Conlay, T03-2145 1833. Open 1100-1500 and 1900-2300. One of the best Malay restaurants in town in traditional Minangkabau-style building, beautifully designed interior in style of Negeri Sembilan palace. Don't be put off by cultural shows or the big groups – the food is superb and amazing in its variety, including regional specialities; it's very popular with locals too. Individual dishes are expensive, the buffet is the best bet (choice of more than 50 dishes). Recommended.

Old China Café, 11 Jln Balai Polis, T03-2072 5915, www.oldchina.com.my. Good, interesting Nyonya and Malay favourites, including asam prawns, *mee siam* and plenty of seafood dishes. Lots of olde worlde ambience. Fine choice for a romantic evening out.

Nam Heong, 54 Jln Sultan. Open 1000-1500. Clean and non-fussy place specializing in delightful plates of delicious Hainanese chicken rice, but also featuring some wonderful Chinese delights including pork with yam (truly outstanding), asam fish and fresh tofu.

Sangeetha Veg Restaurant, 65 Jln Lebuh Ampang, T03-2032 3333. Open 1100-2230. With branches all over India, this tidy restaurant is a great place to sample some true Indian veg fare (including Jain) in a/c comfort. The thalis (most served 1100-1500) are truly gargantuan, and the *papad* are deliciously peppery.

Singapore

Changi Airport ① *on the eastern tip of the island, 20 km from downtown, www. changiairport.com*, is Southeast Asia's busiest airport and most long-haul airlines fly here. It is also a hub for budget Asian airlines. Changi is regularly voted the world's leading airport: it takes only 20 minutes from touchdown to baggage claim. Facilities include free Wi-Fi, boutique shops and a rooftop swimming pool. There is an arrivals lounge in Terminal 3 for those who arrive too early to check into a hotel. The lounge offers showers and peace. Car hire desks, open 0700-2300, are in the arrivals halls of the three terminals.

Changi also has a budget airline terminal – **Budget Terminal** ① *www.btsingapore.com*. It lacks the debonair ambience of Changi but has all necessary mod cons. Other than taxi, the best way to get to the budget terminal is to jump on the free five-minute shuttle bus service linking it with Terminal 2, where there are comprehensive transportation options. The service runs 24 hours a day every 10 minutes except between 0200 and 0500 when it runs every 30 minutes.

From Southeast Asia Useful airlines using Changi include: **AirAsia** ① *www.airasia.com*, with daily connections with Bangkok, Denpasar, Jakarta Kuala Lumpur and Penang. **Jetstar Asia** ① *www.jetstar.com*, has extensive connections with cities in Southeast Asia, China, India and Australia. Many of the cheapest fares are available exclusively on the internet. If you want to work out connections with specific cities, the Changi website has a useful flight planning facility.

Tiger Airways ① *www.tigerairways.com*, flies from the budget terminal and has some great deals around Southeast Asia, India and China.

From the airport to the city centre Most hotels offer an airport pickup service. Bus No 36 loops along Orchard Road passing many of the major hotels including the YMCA (0600-2400, S$2, have exact change ready). There are bus stops beneath Terminal 1, 2 and 3. Follow the signs. An airport shuttle runs every 15 minutes 0600-2400 and every 30 minutes outside these hours, S$9 (booking counter in arrivals) to destinations within Singapore other than Changi Village and Sentosa. If you are in a group of three or more and your hotel is not covered by the door-to-door service, it is probably cheaper to take a taxi. The airport is connected to the MRT underground line. The MRT station can be found beneath Terminal 2 and 3. Trains to the centre of Singapore run every 12 minutes 0530-2318, S$1.80, plus S$1 refundable deposit, journey time 30 minutes. Taxis queue up outside the arrival halls; they are metered but there is an airport surcharge of S$3 (S$5 on Friday, Saturday and Sunday and after 1700). A trip to the centre of town should cost about S$20-30 including the surcharge. Between midnight and 0559 fares increase by 50%.

Getting around Singapore's public transport system is cheap and easy to use. There is a comprehensive bus network, with convenient and regular services (make sure you have the correct money as bus drivers don't give change from notes). The **Mass Rapid Transit** (MRT) underground railway is quick and efficient. An **Ez-link card** ⓘ www.ezlink.com. sg, S$15 (S$3 travel deposit, S$7 travel value, S$5 non-refundable card deposit), is available from MRT stations and TransitLink ticket offices, www.transitlink.com.sg. It can be used on buses and the MRT and is worth buying if you plan to use public transport extensively. Alternatively, the Singapore Tourist Pass, www.thesingaporetouristpass.com, offers unlimited daily travel on the MRT and buses for S$8 (plus S$10 refundable deposit). Check the site for a list of places where the pass may be purchased. Visitors wishing to purchase this pass must produce their passport and white disembarkation card at point of sale.

Taxis are relatively cheap and the fastest and easiest way to get around the island in comfort (all taxis are metered and air conditioned). They are plentiful but should only be hailed at specified points; there are stands outside main shopping centres and hotels. Trishaws have all but left the Singapore street scene. A few genuine articles can be found in the depths of Geylang or Chinatown, but most cater only for tourists and charge accordingly. Agree a price before climbing in; expect to pay about S$30 for a 45-minute ride. Ferries to the southern islands such as Kusu and St John's, leave from Marina South Pier. Bumboats (motorized sampans) for the northern islands go from Changi Point. Ferries to the Indonesian islands of Batam and Bintan leave from HarbourFront.

Tourist infomation The best source of information is the **Singapore Visitor Centre** ⓘ Tourism Court, 1 Orchard Spring Lane, junction of Orchard and Cairnhill roads, T1800-736 2000 (24-hr and toll-free in Singapore), www.yoursingapore.com, daily 0930-2230, nearest MRT: Orchard. There are other offices at Liang Court Shopping Centre, Changi Airport, **The Galleria** (Suntec City Mall) and. The free Visitor's Guide to Singapore has good maps and listings information.

Sleeping

AL Naumi Hotel, 41 Seah St, T6403 6000, www.naumihotel.com.
AL Perak, 12 Perak Rd, T6299 7733, www.peraklodge.net.

AL-A Albert Court, 180 Albert St, T6339 3939, www.albertcourt.com.sg.
AL-B Hangout@Mt Emily, 10A Upper Wilkie Rd, T6438 5588, www.hangouthotels.com.

Train to Vietnam

If you've around three weeks to spare, you can travel from Europe to Vietnam overland by the Trans-Siberian Railway. It's safe, comfortable and relatively inexpensive, but good organisational skills are called for ...

Paris/London to Moscow takes roughly 48 hours. Travel by Eurostar and high-speed train to Cologne then take a direct Russian sleeping car from Cologne to Moscow.

Moscow to Beijing takes six nights on one of two weekly Trans-Siberian trains. Take train No 4 every Tuesday via Mongolia and the Gobi Desert, or train No 20 every Friday via Manchuria.

Beijing to Hanoi in Vietnam takes two nights on a twice-weekly train leaving every Sunday and Thursday.

Find more details on these routes at www.seat61.com/Trans-Siberian.htm.

A-B G4 Station, 11 Mackenzie Rd, T6334 5644, www.g4station.com.
A-C Sleepy Sam's, 55 Bussorah St, T9277 4988, www.sleepysams.com.

Eating

Head to any food court or hawker centre to sample the city's best selection of food and the cheapest beer in town. Places worth checking out include Maxwell Food Centre, Newton Circus and Lau Pa Sat. Little India has a huge selection of subcontinental delights and Chinatown is the place to sample delicious *hokkien mee*, chicken rice and Peranakan favourites. Good international fare comes at a price and can be found in Raffles Hotel, Dempsey Hill, Chijmes and Clarke Quay.

Jumbo Seafood, East Coast Seafood Centre, East Coast Park Service Rd, T6345 1211. Chilli crab, drunken prawns and views of the busy sea lanes.

True Blue Peranakan Cuisine, 47/49 Armenian St, T6440 0449. Located in a beautifully restored shophouse near the Peranakan Museum, this restaurant offers sensual, colourful Peranakan style in abundance, award-winning chefs and the city's most authentic Nyonya dining. Highly recommended.

Muthu's Curry, 138 Race Course Rd, T6392 1722. North Indian food, one of the finest authentic Indian restaurants in town, catering for Indians looking for contemporary flavours, good presentation and lively ambience. Muthu's fish-heads are famous. Highly recommended. Another branch in Suntec City.

Song Fa Bak Kut Teh, 111 New Bridge Rd, T6533 6128. Small and busy eatery with traditional Chinese decor, alfresco seating and bowls of delicious *bak kut teh* (a Hokkien pork rib herbal soup) and range of Chinese teas.

Air

The easiest – and cheapest – way to access the region is via **Bangkok**, **Kuala Lumpur** or **Singapore**. Most major airlines have direct flights from Europe, North America and Australasia to these hubs. International airports in Vietnam are at Tan Son Nhat Airport (SGN) in **Ho Chi Minh City** and Noi Bai Airport (HAN) in **Hanoi** and **Danang** (DAD). **Cambodia** and **Laos** are only accessible from within Asia. The most important entry point for Cambodia remains **Phnom Penh** though there are now more flights to **Siem Reap** (REP). Both are connected to Bangkok, Singapore, Kuala Lumpur and Ho Chi Minh

Overland travel

Overland travel between Vietnam, Cambodia and Laos is not only cheap, it's an essential part of the experience. Here's our guide to getting around the region without setting foot on a plane.

Vietnam to/from Laos

Buses leave Hanoi daily for the arduous but scenic 24-hour journey to Vientiane. In the other direction, buses leave Vientiane daily. There are also buses from Hué and Danang to the Laos border at Lao Bao, from where onward buses will take you to Vientiane.

Vietnam to/from Cambodia

Frequent buses leave Saigon for Phnom Penh and vice versa. You change buses at the border.

Many travellers opt for a tour from Ho Chi Minh City over three to four days that takes them through the Mekong Delta, onto a boat at Chau Doc, crossing into Cambodia on the Mekong River and ending in Phnom Penh. There are daily boats to Phnom Penh from Chau Doc and vice versa.

Cambodia to/from Thailand

Take a morning bus from Phnom Penh to Battambang. Buses run regularly between 0630 and 1245, journey time 5½ hours, fare around US$3-4. From there take a taxi, bus or pickup truck to Poiphet on the Thai frontier. After passing through customs, take a bus (฿10) or tuk-tuk (฿40-60) the few kilometres from Poiphet to the railway station at Aranyaprathet.

You might prefer to go via the Angkor Wat temples at Siem Reap. Regular buses link Phnom Penh with Siem Reap (six hours, US$10), or there's a daily boat along the river departing Phnom Penh at 0700 arriving Siem Reap 1330, US$25. Then take a share taxi from Siem Reap to

City. For Laos, there are direct flights to **Vientiane** from Phnom Penh, Siem Reap, Kuala Lumpur, Bangkok, Chiang Mai, Kunming, Nanning, Hanoi and Ho Chi Minh City. There are also international flights to Luang Prabang Pakse and Savannakhet. Flights operate from Bangkok, Udon Thani and Chiang Mai to **Luang Prabang**. A cheaper option for getting to Laos from Bangkok is to fly to **Udon Thani**, Thailand, about 50 km south of the border and travel overland via the Friendship Bridge or fly from Udon Thani to Luang Prabang. For full details on the land crossing, see box, page 381. An alternative route is to fly from Bangkok to **Chiang Rai,** Thailand, before overlanding it to **Chiang Khong** and crossing into northern Laos at **Houei Xai**. From Houei Xai there are flights to Vientiane and boats to Luang Prabang via Pak Beng.

Alternatively, take budget flights from Bangkok to Ubon Ratchathani in northeast Thailand and cross the border into southern Laos at Chongmek. Or take a flight to Sakhon Nakhon, also in northeast Thailand, and cross the border at Nakhon Phanom to Thakhek in central Laos. See regional flights, page 34. ⋙ *See also Ins and outs sections throughout the guide.*

International departure taxes in Vietnam are included in the price of the air ticket and not payable at the airport. In Cambodia the international departure tax is US$25, domestic tax is US$6. The international airport departure tax in Laos is now included in the cost of the ticket and so is not payable at the airport.

the Thai frontier at Poiphet. Journey time around three hours, cost about US$25 for the whole car or US$9 for the front seat.

Two reliable trains a day run from Aranyaprathet to Bangkok. You should be able to make the 1355 departure from Aranyaprathet, arriving Bangkok at 1955. If not, the other train leaves at 0640, arriving Bangkok at 1205. Both trains are third class only, but they are clean and it's a very pleasant ride. The fare is only ฿58.

In the other direction, take the daily 0555 train from Bangkok's main Hualamphong station to Aranyaprathet and onwards to the Cambodian border (open 0700-2000, visas available, bring photos and US$). Then just reverse the westbound journey.

Laos to/from Thailand
An overnight train links Bangkok with the new rail terminal at Thanaleng, 13 km outside Vientiane. In the other direction, it leaves Thanaleng in the afternoon. A change of train is required at Nong Khai. First- and second-class air-conditioned sleepers are available. Use local designated tuk-tuks or taxis between Thanaleng and central Vientiane.

To reach southern Laos take any one of seven daily trains from Bangkok to Ubon Ratchathani. The most recommended of these is the nightly sleeper leaving Bangkok at 2030 and arriving at 0730 the next morning. In the reverse direction, the sleeper leaves Ubon at 1830 and arrives into Bangkok at 0600; first-class sleeper fares are ฿1180, second-class sleeper ฿471 to ฿761. To and from Ubon/Pakse there are four buses a day that make the two hour journey for ฿200. You can buy your Laos visa at the Laos border but the bus won't wait if you're stuck in a queue – best to have it before travel.

Flights from Europe
There are direct flights to Vietnam from Paris and Frankfurt with **Vietnam Airlines**. Air France no longer calls in at Hanoi and now only offers direct flights to Ho Chi Minh. These code-shared flights last 12 hours. **Vietnam Airlines** has an office in the UK or flights can be booked online (www.vietnamairlines.com). There are also direct **Vietnam Airlines** flights from Moscow. Flights from London and other European hubs go via Bangkok, Singapore, Kuala Lumpur, Hong Kong and the Gulf states. From London to Vietnam takes around 16-18 hours, depending on the length of stopover. Airlines include **Air France**, **Cathay Pacific**, **Emirates**, **Lufthansa**, **Thai**, **Singapore Airlines**, **Malaysia Airlines** and **Qatar**. It is also possible to fly into Hanoi and depart from Ho Chi Minh City although this does seem to rack up the return fare. Check details with flight agents and tour operators (page 61). The best deals usually involve flying to Bangkok and then on from there to your destination. There are countless airlines flying to Bangkok from Europe and lots of good deals, so shop around.

Flights from the US and Canada
There are flights to Vietnam from several major US hubs. **Vietnam Airlines** flies from Los Angeles and San Francisco to both Hanoi and Ho Chin Minh via Taipei. The approximate flight time from Los Angeles to **Ho Chi Minh** is 21 hours. **United** fly to Ho Chi Minh via Hong Kong. It is often cheaper to fly via **Bangkok**, **Taipei**, **Tokyo** or **Hong Kong** and from there to Vietnam, Cambodia or Laos. **Thai**, **Delta**, and **United** fly to Bangkok from a number of US and Canadian cities.

Flights from Australia and New Zealand

Vietnam Airlines flies direct from Melbourne to both Ho Chi Minh and Hanoi. There are also direct flights to **Bangkok** from all major Australian and New Zealand cities with **Cathay Pacific, Korean Airlines, Qantas, Malaysia Airlines, Singapore Airlines** and **Thai**, among others. There is also the option of flying into Hanoi and out of Ho Chi Minh City, or vice versa.

Regional flights

If you have two weeks or less to spend in the region, it's important to factor in some flights if you want to cover a lot of ground. **Vietnam Airlines** (www.vietnamairlines.com) and **Lao Airlines** (www.laoairlines.com) and Cambodia **Angkor Air** also offer regional flights.

Within Vietnam, **Vietnam Airlines** flies all over the country. It also flies internationally to Phnom Penh, Siem Reap, Vientiane, Luang Prabang, Singapore, Kuala Lumpur and Bangkok. **Jet Star Pacific** (www.jetstar.com) is based in Ho Chi Minh with a secondary hub in Hanoi and flies to Danang, Haiphong, Hué, Nha Trang and Vinh. **AirAsia** have a significant stake in new start-up **Viet Jet**, which is to be based in Hanoi and will fly to Ho Chi Minh and Danang.

At the moment the only domestic route within Cambodia that operates safely and with any frequency is between Phnom Penh and Siem Reap with **Cambodia Angkor Air**. International connections with Cambodia are still poor – but improving – and most travellers will need to route themselves through Kuala Lumpur, Singapore or Bangkok, all of which have good onward connections to both Phnom Penh and Siem Reap.

To/from Phnom Penh these airlines currently operate international services to Phnom Penh's International Airport: **AirAsia** (Kuala Lumpur, Bangkok); **Bangkok Airways** (Bangkok); **China Airlines** (Taipei); **Silk Air** (Singapore); **Dragon Air** (Hong Kong); **Thai Airways** (Bangkok); **Malaysia Airlines** (Kuala Lumpur); **Vietnam Airlines** (Vientiane, Ho Chi Minh); **Shanghai Air** (Shanghai, Pudong); **China Southern Airlines** (Guangzhou); **Eva Air** (Taipei); **Jet Star** (Singapore); **Korean Air** and **Asiana Airlines** (Incheon). **Cambodia Angkor Air** flies to and from Ho Chi Minh.

To/from Siem Reap there are connections with **Bangkok Airways** (Bangkok); **AirAsia** (Kuala Lumpur); **Malaysia** (Kuala Lumpur); **Vietnam** (Hanoi and Ho Chi Minh); **Jet Star** (Singapore); **Silk Air** (Singapore); **Asiania Airlines** and **Korean Air** (Incheon); **Lao Airlines** (Luang Prabang).

Lao Airlines flies internationally to Hanoi , Bangkok, Siem Reap, Kunming, Chiang Mai, Phnom Penh and Udon Thani. It also flies domestically from Vientiane to Phonsavanh (Xieng Khouang), Luang Prabang, Pakse, Houei Xai, Oudomxai, Luang Namtha and Savannakhet. There are also flights from Luang Prabang to Pakse and from Phonsavanh to Luang Prabang. **Lao Airlines** now flies modern ATRs and MA-6s. **Phongsavanh Airlines** (T021-513 0000) has taken over the Lao Capricorn Air Company and operates flights to Xam Neua, Phongsali and Sayaboury province.

Thai (www.thaiair.com) flies to Ho Chi Minh City, Phnom Penh and Vientiane from Bangkok. **Bangkok Airways** flies daily between Bangkok and Luang Prabang. **AirAsia** (www.airasia.com) and **Nok Air** (www.nokair.com) fly to Udon Thani in northern Thailand for overland connections to Vientiane, see box, page 37. **AirAsia** also flies from Bangkok to Chiang Rai, Hanoi and Phnom Penh. **Thai** also flies to Chiang Rai. These budget airlines also fly to Ubon Ratchathani in northeast Thailand for crossing the border into southern Laos at Chongmek and to Sakhon Nakhon for crossing into Laos at Thakhek.

Getting around

For details of air travel within the region, see Regional flights opposite.

Vietnam

Open Tour Buses, see below, are very useful and cheap for bridging important towns. Train travel is exciting and overnight journeys are a good way of covering long distances. The Vietnamese rail network extends from Hanoi to Ho Chi Minh City and up to Sapa. Many travellers opt to take a tour to reach remote areas because of the lack of self-drive car hire and the dangers and slow speed of public transport.

Rail

Vietnam Railways (www.vr.com.vn) runs the 2600-km rail network. With overnight stays at hotels along the way to see the sights, a rail sightseeing tour from Hanoi to Ho Chi Minh City should take a minimum of 10 days but you would need to buy tickets for each separate journey. The difference in price between first and second class is small and it is worth paying the extra. There are three seating classes and four sleeping classes. The kitchen on the Hanoi-Ho Chi Minh City service serves soups and simple, but adequate, rice dishes (it is a good idea to take additional food and drink on long journeys, though). First-class long-distance tickets include the price of meals. Six trains leave Hanoi for Ho Chi Minh City daily and vice versa. The express trains (**Reunification Express**) take between 29½ to 34 hours. Most ticket offices have some staff who speak English. Queues can be long and sometimes confusing and some offices keep unusual hours. If you are short of time and short on patience it may well pay to get a tour operator to book your ticket for a small fee. All sleepers should be booked three days in advance.

River

There are services from Chau Doc to Phnom Penh, see border box, page 178 and from Rach Gia and Ha Tien to Phu Quoc, see page 179, and from Haiphong and Halong City to Cat Ba Island and Halong Bay, see page 81.

Road

Bus Since Highway 1 is so dangerous and public transport buses are poor and slow, most travellers opt for the cheap and regular Open Tour Bus (private minibus or coach) that covers the length of the country. Almost every Vietnamese tour operator/travellers' café listed in this guide will run a minibus service or act as an agent. The ticket is a flexible, one-way ticket from Ho Chi Minh City to Hanoi and vice versa. The buses run daily from their own offices and include the following stops: Ho Chi Minh City, Mui Ne, Nha Trang, Dalat, Hoi An, Hué, Ninh Binh and Hanoi. They will also stop off at tourist destinations along the way such as Lang Co, Hai Van Pass, Marble Mountains and Po Klong Garai. You may join at any leg of the journey, paying for one trip or several as you go. The Hanoi to Hué and vice versa is an overnight trip but although you might save on a night's accommodation you are unlikely to get much sleep.

Car hire Self-drive car hire is not available in Vietnam. It is, however, possible to hire cars with drivers and this is a good way of getting to more remote areas with a group of people. Cars with drivers can be hired for around US$60-110 per day. Longer trips would see a reduced overall cost. All cars are modern and air-conditioned. Car hire prices increase by 50% or more during Tet.

Motorbike and bicycle hire Most towns are small enough for bicycles to be an attractive option but if taking in a sweep of the surrounding countryside (touring around the Central Highlands, for example) then a motorbike will mean you can see more. Motorbikes can be rented easily and are an excellent way of getting off the beaten track. You do not need a driver's licence or proof of motorbike training to hire a motorbike in Vietnam. It became compulsory on 1 December 2007 for every rider in every location to wear a helmet. Take time to familiarize yourself with road conditions and ride slowly.

Bicycles can be rented by the day in the cities and are useful for getting out into the countryside. Hotels often have bicycles for hire and there is usually someone willing to lend their machine for a small charge (US$1-2 per day). Many travellers' cafés rent out bicycles and motorbikes too, the latter for around US$6 a day. Motorbikes are hired out with helmets and bicycles with locks. Always park your bicycle or motorbike in a guarded parking place (*gui xe*). Ask for a ticket. The small cost is worth every dong, even if you are just popping in to the post office to post a letter.

Motorbike taxi and cyclo Motorcycle taxis, known as *honda ôm* or *xe ôm* are ubiquitous and cheap. You will find them on most street corners, outside hotels or in the street. With their uniform baseball caps and dangling cigarette, *xe ôm* drivers are readily recognizable. If they see you before you see them, they will shout 'moto' to get your attention. In the north and upland areas the Honda is replaced with the Minsk. The shortest hop would be at least 10000d. Always bargain though.

Cyclos are bicycle trishaws. Cyclo drivers charge double or more than that of a xe ôm. A number of streets in the centres of Ho Chi Minh City and Hanoi are one-way or out of bounds to cyclos, necessitating lengthy detours which add to the time and cost. Do not take a cyclo after dark unless the driver is well known to you or you know the route. It is a wonderful way to get around the Old Quarter of Hanoi, though, and for those with plenty of time on their hands it is not so hazardous in smaller towns.

Taxi Taxis ply the streets of Hanoi and Ho Chi Minh City and other large towns and cities. They are cheap, around 12,000d per kilometre, and the drivers are better English speakers than cyclo drivers. See box, page 71 for an explanation of Vietnamese addresses. Always keep a small selection of small denomination notes with you so that when the taxi stops you can round up the fare to the nearest small denomination. At night use the better known taxi companies rather than the unlicensed cars that often gather around popular nightspots.

Cambodia

Rail

There are two lines out of Phnom Penh: one to Poipet on the Thai border which goes via Pursat, Battambang and Sisophon; and the second, which runs south to Sihanoukville on the coast via Takeo, Kep and Kampot. At time of publication in mid-2010 neither was operating.

Main border crossings

Visas can be obtained at land crossings into Laos except where mentioned; no Vietnam visas are available at land crossings.

Vietnam/Cambodia
Moc Bai–Bavet, page 178
Kaam Samnor–Chau Doc
(Vinh Xuong boat crossing), page 178
Ha Tien–Kep, page 262

Vietnam/Laos
Tay Trang–Sop Hun, page 94
Nam Xoi–Na Maew (Lao visa required in advance), page 421
Nam Khan–Nong Het
Lao Bao–Dansavanh, pages 116 and 433

Bo Y–Yalakhuntum, page 441
Laos/Cambodia
Voen Kham–Stung Treng
(Don Kralor crossing), page 280

Laos/Thailand
Houei Xai–Chiang Kong
Tha Na Leng–Nong Khai
(Friendship Bridge), page 381
Nakhon Phanom–Thakhek
Savannakhet–Mukdahan
Chongmek-Vang Tao
(near Pakse), page 435

Cambodia/Thailand
Koh Kong (Cham Yem crossing)–
Hat Lek, page 278

River

The route between Siem Reap and Phnom Penh is very popular while the route between Siem Reap and Battambang is one of the most scenic. With the new road opening, boats are no longer used as a main form of transport along the Mekong and in the northeast.

Road

Over the last few years the road system in Cambodia has dramatically improved. A trunk route of international standards, apart from a few gnarled stretches, now links Stung Treng to Koh Kong. New bridges are being built and other short cuts are being created. Much of the rest of the network is pretty basic and journeys can sometimes be long and laborious. Also, to some parts, such as Ratanakiri, the road is a graded, laterite track, untarmacked and potholed. In the rainy season expect to be slowed down on many roads to a slithering muddy crawl. The Khmer-American Friendship Highway (Route 4), which runs from Phnom Penh to Sihanoukville, is entirely tarmacked, as is the NH6 between Siem Reap and Phnom Penh. The infamous National Highway 6 between Poipet and Phnom Penh via Siem Reap has also had extensive work, as has National Highway 1. The Japanese in particular have put considerable resources into road and bridge building.

Bus and shared taxi There are buses and shared taxis to most parts of the country. Shared taxis (generally Toyota Camrys) or pickups are usually the quickest and most reliable public transport option. The taxi operators charge a premium for better seats and you can buy yourself more space. It is not uncommon for a taxi to fit 10 people in it, including two sitting on the driver's seat. Fares for riding in the back of the truck are half that for riding in the cab. The Sihanoukville run has an excellent and cheap air-conditioned bus service.

Car hire and taxi A few travel agents and hotels may be able to organize self-drive car hire and most hotels have cars for hire with a driver (US$30-50 per day). There is a limited taxi service in Phnom Penh.

Moto The most popular and sensible option is the motorbike taxi, known as 'moto'. This costs around the same as renting your own machine and with luck you will get a driver who speaks a bit of English and who knows where he's going. Once you have found a good driver stick with him: handing out the odd drink, a packet of cigarettes or an extra dollar or two is a good investment. Outside Phnom Penh and Siem Reap, do not expect much English from your moto driver.

Motorbike and bicycle hire Motorbikes can be rented from between US$5 and US$8 per day and around US$1 per day for a bicycle. If riding either a motorbike or bicycle be aware that the accident rate is very high. This is partly because of the poor condition of many of the cars, trucks and other vehicles on the road; partly because of poor roads; and partly because of horrendously poor driving. If you do rent a motorbike ensure it has a working horn (imperative) and buy some rear-view mirrors so you can keep an eye on the traffic. Wear a helmet (even if using a motodop); it may not be cool but neither is a fractured skull. More experienced motorcyclists can also rent more higher-powered dirt bikes of 250cc and over from about US$25 per day.

Laos

Roads have greatly improved. Many have been repaired or upgraded in recent years, making journeys infinitely more comfortable, as well as faster. Quite a few bus, truck, tuk-tuk, *songthaew* (see below) and taxi drivers understand the rudimentaries of English, French or Thai, although some of them (especially tuk-tuk drivers) aren't above forgetting the lowest price you thought you'd successfully negotiated before hopping aboard! It is best to take this sort of thing in good humour. Even so, in order to travel to a particular destination, it is a great advantage to have the name written out in Lao. Many people will not know road names, even if it's the road right outside their front door. However, they will know where all the sights of interest are – for example wats, markets, monuments, waterfalls, etc. In city centres make sure you have the correct money for your tuk-tuk as they are often conveniently short of change. Also opt to flag down a moving tuk-tuk rather than selecting one of the more expensive ones that sit out the front of tourist destinations.

Air
Lao Airlines runs domestic flights from Vientiane to Luang Prabang, daily, to Pakse and Xieng Khouang and three times a week to Houei Xai, Oudomxai, Luang Namtha and Savannakhet. There are also flights three times a week from Luang Prabang to Pakse and from Pakse to Savannakhet three times a week. **Lao Airlines** now flies modern ATRs and MA-6s. **Phongsavanh Airlines** (T021-513 0000) has taken over the Lao Capricorn Air Company and operates flights to Xam Neua, Phongsali and Sayaboury province.

River
It is possible to take river boats up and down the Mekong and its main tributaries. Boats stop at Luang Prabang, Pak Beng, Houei Xai, in the northwest and around Don Deth

and Don Khong in the south as well as other smaller towns and villages, such as Nong Khiaw and north to Phongsali on the Nam Ou River in the north. Luxury services operate between Houei Xai and Luang Prabang and between Pakse and Wat Phou, Champasak. Apart from the main route, Houei Xai to Luang Prabang, there are often no scheduled services and departures may be limited during the dry season. Take food and drink and expect somewhat crowded conditions aboard on the Houei Xai–Luang Prabang route. The most common riverboats are the *hua houa leim*, with no decks, the hold being enclosed by side panels and a flat roof (note that metal boats get very hot). Speedboats also chart some routes, but are very dangerous and never enjoyable.

Road

Bus/truck/minivan It is now possible to travel to most areas of the country by bus, truck or *songthaew* (converted pickup truck) in the dry season, although road travel in the rainy season can be tricky if not impossible in some areas. VIP buses are very comfortable night buses, usually allowing a good sleep during the trip – but watch out for karaoke on board. In the south of Laos there is a night bus that plies the route from Pakse to Vientiane; make sure you book a double bed, otherwise you could end up sleeping next to a stranger. Robberies have been reported on the night buses so keep your valuables secure.

On certain long routes, such as Vientiane/Luang Prabang to Xam Neua, big *Langjian* (Chinese) trucks are sometimes used. These trucks have been colourfully converted into buses with a wooden structure on the back, divided wooden seats and glassless windows. In more remote places (Xam Neua to Vieng Xai, for instance), ancient jeeps are common.

In the south of the country, Japanese-donated buses are used although you may see the occasional shiny Volvo bus. Few of the roads are now unsealed, and breakdowns, though not frequent, aren't uncommon either. For some connections you may need to wait a day. During the rainy season (June to December) expect journey times to be longer than those quoted; indeed some roads may be closed altogether.

A decent and reliable network of minivans now transport foreigners from one main tourist destination to another; for example, Luang Prabang to Vang Vieng. Costs are higher than public buses but journey times are shorter and pickups from guesthouses are usually part of the service.

Car hire This costs anything from US$60-100 per day, depending on the vehicle, with petrol and kilometre usage included. The price includes a driver. If you drive the car yourself, for insurance purposes you will probably need an international driver's permit. Insurance is generally included with car hire but it's best to check the fine print. A general rule of thumb: if you are involved in a car crash, you, the foreigner, will be liable for costs as you have more money.

Motorbike and bicycle hire There are an increasing number of motorcycles available from guesthouses and other shops in major towns. 110cc bikes go for around US$5-10 a day. Bicycles are available in many towns and are a cheap way to see the sights. Many guesthouses have bikes for rent for US$1-2 per day. Mountain bikes can be rented from more specialist outlets.

Tuk-tuk The majority of motorized three-wheelers known as 'jumbos' or tuk-tuks are large motorbike taxis with two bench seats in the back. You'll find them in most cities and metropolitan areas; expect to pay around 10,000-20,000 kip for a short ride. They can also be hired by the hour or the day to reach destinations out of town.

Sleeping

Vietnam

Accommodation ranges from luxury suites in international five-star hotels and spa resorts to small, family hotels (mini hotels) and homestays with local people in the Mekong Delta and with the ethnic minorities in the Central Highlands and northern Vietnam. During peak seasons – especially December to March and particularly during busy holidays such as Tet, Christmas, New Year's Eve and around Easter – booking is essential. Expect staff to speak English in all top hotels. Do not expect it in cheaper hotels or in more remote places, although most places employ someone with a smattering of a foreign language.

Private, mini hotels are worth seeking out as, being family-run, guests can expect quite good service. Mid-range and tourist hotels may provide a decent breakfast which is often included in the price. Many luxury and first-class hotels charge extra for breakfast and, on top of this, also charge VAT and service charge. There are some world-class beach resorts in Phu Quoc, Nha Trang, Mui Ne, Hoi An and Danang. In the northern uplands, in places like Sapa, Ha Giang province and Mai Chau, it is possible to stay in an ethnic minority house. Bathrooms are basic and will consist of a cold or warm shower and an alfresco or Western toilet. To stay in a homestay, you must book through a tour operator or through the local tourist office; you cannot just turn up. Homestays are also possible on farms and in orchards in the Mekong Delta. Here, guests sleep on camp beds and share a Western bathroom with hot and cold water. National parks offer everything from air-conditioned bungalows to shared dormitory rooms to campsites where, sometimes, it is possible to hire tents. Visitors may spend a romantic night on a boat in Halong Bay or on the Mekong Delta. Boats range from the fairly luxurious to the basic. Most people book through tour operators.

You will have to leave your passport at hotel reception desks for the duration of your stay. It will be released to you temporarily for bank purposes or buying an air ticket. Credit cards are widely accepted but there is often a 2-4% fee for paying in this manner. Tipping is not expected in hotels in Vietnam. See box opposite for details of what to expect within each price category.

Cambodia

Accommodation standards in Cambodia have greatly improved over the last couple of years. Phnom Penh now has a good network of genuine boutique hotels – arguably they are overpriced and sometimes management can be a bit Fawlty Towers but the bar has certainly been raised. Siem Reap, without doubt, has now become a destination for the upmarket international traveller. The range, depth and quality of accommodation here is of an excellent standard and is on a par with anywhere else in Asia. Even if you travel to some of the smaller, less visited towns, family-run hotels should now provide hot water, air conditioning and cable TV even if they can't provide first-class service. These places are often the best bargains in the country as many of the cheap backpacker places, while very cheap, are often hovels.

Sleeping price codes

LL Over US$200 Luxury: mostly found in Bangkok with some in Ho Chi Minh City, Hanoi, Luang Prabang, Phnom Penh and Siem Reap. Some beach and mountain resorts also fall into this category.

L-AL US$101-200 First class plus: there are a number of hotels in this category found in all the major cities and some smaller ones plus resorts across the region. A full range of facilities will be included.

A US$66-100 First class: these hotels are increasingly found in towns across Vietnam but less so in Cambodia and Laos. Hotels in this category should offer reasonable business services, a range of recreational facilities, restaurants and bars, although these services will be more limited in Cambodia and Laos.

B US$46-65 Tourist class: all rooms will have air conditioning and an attached bathroom with hot water. Other services should include one or more restaurants, a bar and room service. In Bangkok and Vietnamese beach resorts a pool may be available.

C US$31-45 Economy: rooms should be air conditioned in Vietnam and Laos but not necessarily in Cambodia and will have attached bathrooms with hot water and Western toilets. A restaurant and room service will probably be available. In Vietnam and Laos a pool may be available.

D-E US$12-30 Medium budget: air-conditioned en suite rooms in Vietnam and Laos although not necessarily in Cambodia.

F US$7-11 Budget/guesthouse: usually fan-cooled rooms and often shared bathrooms with basic facilities. Bed linen should be provided, towels may not be. Rooms are small and facilities few. In Vietnam, at the higher end, air conditioning will be available.

G US$6 and under Dormitory/guesthouse-type accommodation, with shared bathroom facilities, squat or Western toilets, fan-cooled and probably but not necessarily cold-water showers. Cleanliness will vary.

Laos

Rooms in Laos are rarely luxurious and standards vary enormously. You can end up paying double what you would pay in Bangkok for similar facilities and service. However, the hotel industry is expanding rapidly. There is a reasonable choice of hotels of different standards and prices in Vientiane, Luang Prabang and Pakse and an expanding number of budget options in many towns on the fast-developing tourist trail. First-class and boutique hotels exist in Vientiane and Luang Prabang. Vientiane, however, still lacks sufficient good budget choices. The majority of guesthouses and hotels have fans and attached bathrooms, although more and more are providing air conditioning where there is a stable electricity supply, while others are installing their own generators to cater for the needs of the growing tourist trade. Smaller provincial towns, having previously had only a handful of hotels and guesthouses – some of them quaint French colonial villas – are now home to a growing number of rival concerns as tourism takes off. In rural villages, people's homes are enthusiastically transformed into bed and breakfasts on demand. While Vientiane may still have little budget accommodation, many towns in the north, such as Vang Vieng, Muang Ngoi Neua, Muang Sing and Luang Namtha, have a large choice of very cheap, and in some cases very good accommodation, including dorm beds. In the southern provinces, upmarket and boutique accommodation has popped up in Champasak province. There are several excellent eco-lodges in the country, most notably the Boat Landing at Luang Namtha and the Kingfisher Ecolodge at Ban Kiet Ngong in the south. Many tour companies offer homestay in ethnic minority villages and camping as part of a package tour. At higher end hotels, rates are subject to 10% government tax and 10% service charge.

Eating

Vietnam

Vietnam offers outstanding Vietnamese, French and international cuisine in restaurants that range from first class to humble foodstalls. At either the quality will be, in the main, exceptional. The accent is on local, seasonal and fresh produce and the rich pickings from the sea, along Vietnam's 2000-km coastline will always make it far inland too. You will find more hearty stews in the more remote north and more salad dishes along the coast. All restaurants offer a variety of cuisine from the regions and some specialize in certain types of food – Hué cuisine, Cha Ca Hanoi etc. *Pho* (pronounced *fer*), noodle soup, is Vietnam's best known dish and is utterly delicious.

All Vietnamese food is dipped, whether in fish sauce, soya sauce, chilli sauce, peanut sauce or pungent prawn sauce (*mam tom*) before eating. As each course is served so a new set of dips will accompany. Follow the guidance of your waiter or Vietnamese friends to get the right dip with the right dish.

Locally produced fresh beer is called *bia hoi*. Bar customers have a choice of Tiger, Heineken, Carlsberg, San Miguel, 333, Saigon Beer or Huda. Many major cities in Vietnam produce their own beer, most of which are light, refreshing and far better than better known Thai and Indonesian beers. Rice and fruit wines are produced and consumed in large quantities in upland areas, particularly in the north of Vietnam. The Chinese believe that snake wines increase their virility and as such are normally found in areas of high Chinese concentration. Soft drinks and bottled still and sparkling mineral water are widely available. Tea and coffee is widely available. Coffee is drunk with condensed milk.

Cambodia

For a country that has suffered and starved in the way Cambodia has, eating for fun as opposed to eating for survival, has yet to catch on as a pastime. There are some good restaurants and things are improving but don't expect Cambodia to be a smaller version of Thailand, or its cuisine even to live up to the standards of Laos. Cambodian food shows clear links with the cuisines of neighbouring countries: Thailand, Vietnam, and to a lesser extent, Laos. The influence of the French colonial period is also in evidence, most clearly in the availability of good French bread. Chinese food is also available owing to strong business ties between Cambodia and China. True Khmer food is difficult to find and much that the Khmers would like to claim as indigenous food is actually of Thai, French or Vietnamese origin. Curries, soups, rice and noodle-based dishes, salads, fried vegetables and sliced meats all feature in Khmer cooking.

Eating price codes

🍴🍴🍴 over US$12   🍴🍴 US$6-12   🍴 under US$6

Prices refer to the cost of a meal for one, without a drink.

Phnom Penh and Siem Reap have the best restaurants with French, Japanese, Italian and Indian food being available. But those who want to sample a range of dishes and get a feel for Khmer cuisine should head for the nearest market where dishes will be cooked on order in a wok – known locally as a *chhnang khteak*.

International soft drink brands are widely available in Cambodia. Tea is drunk without sugar or milk. Coffee is also served black, or 'crème' with sweetened condensed milk. Bottled water is easy to find, as is local mineral water. Fruit smoothies – known locally as *tikalok* – are ubiquitous. Local and imported beers are also available everywhere.

Laos

Lao food is similar to that of Thailand, although the Chinese influence is slightly less noticeable. Lao dishes are distinguished by the use of aromatic herbs and spices such as lemon grass, chillies, ginger and tamarind. The best place to try Lao food is often from roadside stalls or in the markets. The staple Lao foods are *kao niao* (glutinous rice), which is eaten with your hands and fermented fish or *pa dek* (distinguishable by its distinctive smell), often laced with liberal spoons of *nam pa*, fish sauce. Being a landlocked country, most of the fish is fresh from the Mekong. One of the delicacies that shouldn't be missed is *Mok Pa* steamed fish in banana leaf. Most of the dishes are variations on two themes: fish and bird. *Laap*, also meaning 'luck' in Lao, is a traditional ceremonial dish made from (traditionally) raw fish or meat crushed into a paste, marinated in lemon juice and mixed with chopped mint. It is called *laap sin* if it has a meat base and *laap paa* if it's fish based. Beware of *laap* in cheap street restaurants. It is sometimes concocted from raw offal and served cold and should be consumed with great caution. Overall though *laap* is cooked well for the *falang* palate.

Restaurant food is, on the whole, hygienically prepared, and as long as street stall snacks have been well cooked, they are usually fine and a good place to sample local specialities. Really classy restaurants are only to be found in Vientiane and Luang Prabang. Good French cuisine is available in both cities. Salads, steaks, pizzas and more are all on offer. A better bet in terms of value for money are the Lao restaurants.

Far more prevalent are lower-end Lao restaurants which can be found in every town. Right at the bottom end – in terms of price if not necessarily in terms of quality – are stalls that charge a US$1-2 for filled baguettes or simple single-dish meals.

Soft drinks are expensive as they are imported from Thailand. Bottled water is widely available and produced locally, so it is cheap (about 2000 kip a litre). *Nam saa*, weak Chinese tea, is free. Imported beer can be found in hotels, restaurants and bars but is not particularly cheap. *Beer Lao* is a light lager (although the alcohol content is 5%). The local brew is rice wine (*lao-lao*), which is drunk from a clay jug with long straws.

Festivals and events

Colourful and serious ceremonies take place throughout the lunar calender in Vietnam. To help you work out on which day these events fall, check out the following website, which covers the Gregorian calendar to the lunar calendar: www.hko.gov.hk/gts/time/conversion1_text.htm; consult also www.vietnamtourism.com. There are some 30 public holidays celebrated each year in Cambodia. Most are celebrated with public parades and special events to commemorate the particular holiday. The largest holidays also see many Khmers – although less than used to be the case – firing their guns, to the extent that red tracer fills the sky. Being of festive inclination, the Lao celebrate New Year four times a year: the international New Year in January, Chinese New Year in January/February, Lao New Year (Pi Mai) in April and Hmong New Year in December. The Lao Buddhist year follows the lunar calendar, so many of the festivals are movable.

Thailand

Apr (movable, public holiday). **Songkran** marks the beginning of the Buddhist New Year. It is a 3- to 5-day celebration, with parades, dancing and folk entertainment.

Vietnam

Late Jan-Mar (movable, 1st-7th day of the new lunar year): **Tet** is the traditional new year. The big celebration of the year, the word Tet is the shortened version of *tet nguyen dan* ('first morning of the new period'). Tet is the time to forgive and forget and to pay off debts. It is also everyone's birthday – everyone adds one year to their age at Tet. Enormous quantities of food are consumed and new clothes are bought. It is believed that before Tet the spirit of the hearth, Ong Tao, leaves on a journey to visit the palace of the Jade Emperor where he must report on family affairs. To ensure that Ong Tao sets off in good cheer, a ceremony is held before Tet, Le Tao Quan, and during his absence a shrine is constructed (Cay Neu) to keep evil spirits at bay until his return. On the afternoon before Tet, Tat Nien, a sacrifice is offered at the family altar to dead relatives who are invited back to join in the festivities.

Great attention is paid to preparations for Tet, because it is believed that the first week of the new year dictates the fortunes for the rest of the year. The first visitor to the house on New Year's morning should be an influential, lucky and happy person, so families take care to arrange a suitable caller.

Apr (movable, 5th or 6th of the 3rd lunar month): **Thanh Minh** (New Year of the Dead or Feast of the Pure Light). The Vietnamese walk outdoors to evoke the spirit of the dead and family shrines and tombs are cleaned and decorated.

Aug (movable, 15th day of the 7th lunar month): **Trung Nguyen** (Wandering Souls Day). During this time, prayers can absolve the sins of the dead who leave hell and return, hungry and naked, to their relatives. The Wandering Souls are those with no homes to go to. There are celebrations in Buddhist temples and homes, food is placed out on tables and money is burnt.

Sep (movable, 15th day of the 8th lunar month): **Tet Trung Thi** (Mid-Autumn Festival). This festival is particularly celebrated by children. It is based on legend. In the evening families prepare food including sticky rice, fruit and chicken to be placed on the ancestral altars. Moon cakes (egg, green bean and lotus seed) are baked, lanterns are made and painted, and children parade through town with music.

Cambodia

Apr (13-15): **Bonn Chaul Chhnam** (**Cambodian New Year**). A 3-day celebration to mark the turn of the year when predictions are made for the forthcoming year. The celebration is to show gratitude to the departing demi-god, filled with offerings of food and drink. Homes are spring cleaned. Householders visit temples and traditional games like *angkunh* and *chhoal chhoung* are played and festivities are performed.

Apr/May Visak Bauchea (dates vary with the full moon), the most important Buddhist festival; a triple anniversary commemorating Buddha's birth, enlightenment and his *Paranirvana* (state of final bliss).

Oct/Nov (movable) **Bon Om Tuk** (**Water Festival** or **Festival of the Reversing Current**). Celebrates the movement of the waters out of the Tonlé Sap with boat races in Phnom Penh. Boat races extend over 3 days with more than 200 competitors but the highlight is the evening gala in Phnom Penh when a fleet of boats, studded with lights, row out under the full moon. Under the Cambodian monarchy, the king would command the waters to retreat.

Laos

Jan/Feb (movable): **Chinese New Year**. Celebrated by Chinese and Vietnamese communities. Many businesses shut down for 3 days.

Apr (13-15): **Pi Mai** (**Lao New Year**). The first month of the Lao new Year is actually Dec but it is celebrated in Apr when days are longer than nights. One of the most important annual festivals,

particularly in Luang Prabang. Statues of Buddha (in the 'calling for rain' posture) are ceremonially doused in water, which is poured along an intricately decorated trench (**hang song nam pha**). The small stupas of sand, decorated with streamers, in wat compounds are symbolic requests for health and happiness over the next year. It is celebrated with traditional Lao folksinging (*mor lam*) and the circle dance (*ramwong*). There is usually a 3-day holiday. 'Sok Dee Pi Mai' (good luck for the New Year) is usually said to one another during this period.

May (movable): **Boun Bang Fai**. The rocket festival is a Buddhist rain-making festival. Large bamboo rockets are built and decorated by monks and carried in procession before being blasted skywards. The higher a rocket goes, the bigger its builder's ego gets. Designers of failed rockets are thrown in the mud. The festival lasts 2 days.

Sep/Oct (movable): **Boun Ok Phansa**. The end of the Buddhist Lent when the faithful take offerings to the temple. It is the '9th month' in Luang Prabang and the '11th month' in Vientiane, and marks the end of the rainy season. Boat races take place on the Mekong River with crews of 50 or more men and women. On the night before the race small decorated rafts are set afloat on the river.

Oct: **Lai Heua Fai** (**Fireboat Festival**). See Luang Prabang, page 356.

Nov (movable): **Boun That Luang**. Celebrated in all Laos' *thats*, most enthusiastically and colourfully in Vientiane (see page 402).

Shopping

Vietnam

Vietnam is increasingly a good destination for shopping. A wide range of designer clothing, silk goods, high-quality handicrafts, ceramics and lacquerware are available at excellent value. The main shopping centres are Hanoi, Ho Chi Minh City and Hoi An. Hoi

An is the best place to get clothes made. Do not buy any marine turtle products. The majority of shops and markets in Vietnam are open from early in the morning to late at night every day of the week and do not close for lunch. Shops and markets will accept US dollars and Vietnamese dong and most shops also accept credit cards. Export of wood or antiques is banned and anything antique or antique-looking will be seized at customs. In order to avoid this happening you will need to get an export licence from the **Customs Department** ① *162 Nguyen Van Cu St, Hanoi, T04-3826 5260.*

Cambodia

Phnom Penh's markets are highly diverting. Cambodian craftsmanship is excellent and whether you are in search of silverware, *kramas* – checked cotton scarves – hand-loomed sarongs or bronze buddhas you will find them all in abundance. A great favourite for its range and quality of antiques, jewellery and fabrics is the **Russian Market** (Psar Tuol Tom Pong). Silverware, gold and gems are available in the **Central Market** (Psar Thmei). *Matmii* – ikat – is also commonly found in Cambodia. It may have been an ancient import from Java and is made by tie-dyeing the threads before weaving. It can be bought throughout the country. Other local textile products to look out for are silk scarves bags and traditional wall-hangings. Colourful *kramas* can be found in local markets across the country and fine woven sarongs in cotton and silk are available in Phnom Penh and Siem Reap. Silk and other textiles products can be bought throughout the country. There has been a strong revival of pottery and ceramics in Cambodia in the last 30 years. Other crafts include bamboo work, wooden panels with carvings of the *Ramayana* and temple rubbings.

Laos

Popular souvenirs from Laos include handicrafts and textiles, which are sold pretty much everywhere. The market is usually a good starting point as are some of the minority villagers. Boutique shops are now available predominantly in Luang Prabang with a handful in Vientiane. The smaller, less touristy towns will sell silk at the cheapest price (at about 40,000 kip a length). The best place to buy naturally dyed silk in Laos is in Xam Neua. This high-quality silk often makes its way to Luang Prabang and Vientiane but usually at much greater cost. Most markets offer a wide selection of patterns and embroidery though amongst the best places to go are **Talaat Sao** (Vientiane Morning Market) or, behind it, the cheaper **Talaat Kudin**, which has a textile section in the covered area. If you wish to have something made, most tailors can whip up a simple *sinh* (Lao sarong) in a day but you might want to allow longer for adjustments or other items. **Ock Pop Tok** in Luang Prabang also has a fantastic reputation for producing top-shelf, naturally dyed silk. Vientiane and Luang Prabang offer the most sophisticated line in boutiques, where you can get all sorts of clothes from the utterly exquisite to the frankly bizarre. Those on a more frugal budget will find some tailors who can churn out a decent pair of trousers on Sisavangvong in Luang Prabang and around Nam Phou in Vientiane. If you get the right tailor, they can be much better than those found in Thailand both in terms of price and quality but you do need to be patient and allow time for multiple fittings. It is also a good idea to bring a pattern/picture of what you want.

Most **silverware** is in the form of jewellery and small pots (though they may not be made of silver), and is traditional in Laos. The finest silversmiths work out of Vientiane

How big is your footprint?

The point of a holiday is, of course, to have a good time, but if it's relatively guilt-free as well, that's even better. Perfect ecotourism would ensure a good living for local inhabitants, while not detracting from their traditional lifestyles, encroaching on their customs or spoiling their environment. Perfect ecotourism probably doesn't exist, but everyone can play their part. Here are a few points worth bearing in mind:

- Think about where your money goes and be fair and realistic about how cheaply you travel. Try to put money into local people's hands; drink local beer or fruit juice rather than imported brands and stay in locally owned accommodation wherever possible.
- Haggle with humour and appropriately. Remember that you want a fair price, not the lowest one.
- Think about what happens to your rubbish. Take biodegradable products and a water filter to avoid using lots of plastic bottles. Be sensitive to limited resources such as water, fuel and electricity.
- Help preserve local wildlife and habitats by respecting rules and regulations, such as sticking to footpaths, not standing on coral and not buying products made from endangered plants or animals.
- Don't treat people as part of the landscape; they may not want their picture taken. Ask first and respect their wishes.
- Learn the local language and be mindful of local customs and norms. It can enhance your travel experience and you'll earn respect and be more readily welcomed by local people.
- And finally, use your guidebook as a starting point, not the only source of information. Talk to local people, then discover your own adventure.

and Luang Prabang. Chunky antique ethnic-minority jewellery, bangles, pendants, belts and earrings are often sold in markets in the main towns, or antique shops in Vientiane, particularly congregating around Nam Phou. Xam Neua market also offers a good range of ethnicminority-style silver jewellery. Look for traditional necklaces that consist of wide silver bands, held together by a spirit lock (a padlock to lock in your scores of souls). Gold jewellery is the preference of the Lao Loum (lowland Laos) and its bright yellow colour is associated with Buddhist luck (often it is further dyed to enhance its orange goldness), this is best bought in Vientiane. Craftsmen in Laos are still producing **wood carvings** for temples and coffins. Designs are usually traditional, with a religious theme.

Responsible travel

Since the early 1990s there has been a phenomenal growth in 'ecotourism', which promotes and supports the conservation of natural environments and is also fair and equitable to local communities. While the authenticity of some ecotourism operators needs to be interpreted with care, there is clearly both a huge demand for this type of activity and also significant opportunities to support worthwhile conservation and social development initiatives by this means.

The **International Eco-Tourism Society** (www.ecotourism.org), **Tourism Concern** (www.tourismconcern.org.uk), and **Planeta** (www.planeta.com) develop and promote ecotourism projects in destinations all over the world and their websites provide details for initiatives throughout Southeast Asia.

For opportunities to participate in an environmentally responsible and ethical manner, consult www.responsibletravel.com. See also box, page 47.

Essentials A-Z

Accident and emergency

Contact the relevant emergency service and your embassy. Make sure you obtain police/medical records in order to file insurance claims. If you need to report a crime visit your local police station and take a local with you who speaks English.

Vietnam Ambulance T115, Fire T114, Police T113.

Cambodia Ambulance T119 /724891, Fire T118, Police T117/112/012-999999.

Laos Ambulance T195, Fire T190, Police T191.

Children

The region is not particularly geared up for visiting children but there are activities that will appeal to both adults and children alike.

Some attractions in **Vietnam** offer a child's concession. The railways allow children under 5 to travel free and charge 50% of the adult fare for those aged 5-10. The Open Tour Bus tickets and tours are likewise free for children under 2 but those aged 2-5 pay 75% of the adult price. Baby products are found in major supermarkets in the main cities. In the remoter regions, such as the north and the Central Highlands and smaller towns, take everything with you.

In **Cambodia** be aware that expensive hotels as well as market stalls may have squalid cooking conditions and try to ensure that children do not drink any water (especially important when bathing). For babies, powdered milk is available in

provincial centres, although most brands have added sugar. Breast feeding is strongly recommended if possible. Baby food can also be bought in some towns – the quality may not be the same as equivalent foods bought in the West, but it is perfectly adequate for short periods. Disposable nappies can be bought in Phnom Penh, but are often expensive.

In **Laos**, disposable nappies can be bought in Vientiane and other larger provincial capitals, but again are often expensive.

Public transport may be a problem; long bus journeys are restrictive and uncomfortable. Chartering a car is the most convenient way to travel overland but rear seatbelts are scarce and child seats even rarer. Lao people love children and it is not uncommon for waiters and waitresses to spend the whole evening looking after your child.

Customs and duty free

Vietnam

Duty-free allowance is 400 cigarettes, 50 cigars or 100 g of tobacco, 1.5 litres of spirits, plus items for personal use. You can't import pornography, anti-government literature, photographs or movies, nor culturally unsuitable children's toys.

Cambodia

A reasonable amount of tobacco products and spirits can be taken in without incurring customs duty – roughly 200 cigarettes or the equivalent quantity of tobacco, 1 bottle of liquor and perfume for personal use. Taking any Angkorian-era images out of the country is strictly forbidden.

Laos
Duty-free allowance is 500 cigarettes, 2 bottles of wine and a bottle of liquor. Laos has a strictly enforced ban on the export of antiquities and all Buddha images.

Disabled travellers

Considering the proportion of the region's population that are seriously disabled, foreigners might expect better facilities for the immobile. However, some of the more upmarket hotels do have a few designated rooms for the physically disabled. For those with walking difficulties many of the better hotels have lifts. Wheelchair access is improving with more shopping centres, hotels and restaurants providing ramps for easy access. People sensitive to noise will find **Vietnam**, for example, at times, almost intolerable. The general situation in **Cambodia** is no better. The Angkor Complex can be a real struggle for disabled or frail persons. The stairs are 90 degrees steep and semi-restoration of areas means that visitors will sometimes need to climb over piles of bricks. Hiring an aide to help you climb stairs and generally get around is a very good idea and costs around US$5-10 a day. In **Laos** pavements are often uneven, there are potholes and missing drain covers galore, pedestrian crossings are ignored, ramps are unheard of, lifts are few and far between and escalators are seen only in magazines and high-end hotels and a sprinkling of shopping complexes.
RADAR, 12 City Forum, 250 City Rd, London, EC1V 8AF, T0207-250 3222, www.radar.org.uk.
SATH, 347 Fifth Avenue, Suite 605, New York City, NY 10016, T0212-447 7284, www.sath.org.

Drugs

Vietnam
Drugs are common and cheap and the use of hard drugs by Vietnamese is a rapidly growing problem. Attitudes towards users are incredibly lax and the worst that will happen is that certain bars and nightclubs may be closed for a few weeks. In such an atmosphere of easy availability and tolerance, many visitors may be tempted to indulge, and to excess, but beware that the end result can be disastrous. Attitudes to traffickers on the other hand are harsh, although the death penalty (now by lethal injection and not firing squad) is usually reserved for Vietnamese and other Asians whose governments are less likely to kick up a fuss.

Cambodia
Drug use is illegal in Cambodia but drugs are a big problem. Many places use marijuana in their cooking and the police seem to be quite ambivalent to dope smokers (unless they need to supplement their income with bribe money, in which case – watch out). The backpacker areas near the lake in Phnom Penh and Sihanoukville are particularly notorious for heavy drug usage by Westerners. It is important to note that cocaine and ecstasy do not really exist in Cambodia, despite what you may be told. Avoid *yaa baa*, a particularly insidious amphetamine. It has serious side effects and can be lethal.

Laos
Drug use is illegal and there are harsh penalties ranging from fines through to imprisonment or worse. Police have been known to levy heavy fines on people in Vang Vieng for eating so-called 'happy' foods, see page 417, or for being caught in possession of drugs. Note that 'happy' food can make some people extremely sick. Though opium has in theory been

eradicated it is still for sale in northern areas and people have died from overdosing. *Yaa baa* is also available here and should be avoided at all costs.

Electricity

Vietnam Voltage 110-240. Sockets are round 2-pin. Sometimes they are 2 flat pin. A number of top hotels now use UK 3 square-pin sockets.
Cambodia Voltage 220. Sockets are usually round 2-pin.
Laos Voltage 220, 50 cycles in the main towns. 110 volts in the country; 2-pin sockets. Blackouts are common outside Vientiane and many smaller towns are not connected to the national grid and only have power during the evening.

Embassies and consulates

Vietnamese
Australia, 6 Timbarra Cres, O'Malley Canberra, ACT 2606, T+61-2 6286 6059, www.vietnamembassy.org.au.
Cambodia, 436 Monivong, Phnom Penh, T+855 23-726274, www.vietnamembassy-cambodia.org.
Canada, 470 Wilbrod St, Ottawa, Ontario, K1N 6M8, T+1 613-2360772, www.vietnamembassy-canada.ca.
China, 32 Guanghua R, Jiangou menwai, PO Box 00600, Beijing, T+86-10 6532 1155; 5/F, Great Smart Tower, 230 Van Chai Rd, Wan Chai, Hong Kong, T852-2591 4517, http://www.vnemba.org.cn/en.
France, 62 R Boileau-75016, Paris, T+33 144-146400, www.vietnam embassy-france.org/en.
Laos, 85 23 Singha Rd, Vientiane, T+856 21-413409, www.mofa.gov.vn/vnemb.la.
South Africa, 87 Brooks St, Brooklyn, Pretoria, T+27 12-3628119, www. vietnamembassy-southafrica.org/en/.
Thailand, 83/1 Wireless Rd, Lumpini, Pathumwan, Bangkok 10330, T+66 2-251 5837, www.vietnamembassy-thailand.org/en.

UK, 12-14 Victoria Rd, London W8 5RD, T+44 (0)20-7937 1912, www.vietnamembassy.org. uk/consular.html.
USA, 1233, 20th St, NW Suite 400 Washington DC, 20036, T+1 202-861 0737, www.vietnamembassy-usa.org/.

Cambodian
For a full list of Cambodian embassies and consulates see www.cambodia.gov.kh.
Australia & NZ 5 Canterbury Cres, Deakin, Canberra, ACT 2600, T+61-2-6273 1259, www.embassyofcambodia.org.nz/au.htm.
France 4 rue Adolphe Yvon, 75116 Paris, T+33-1-4503 4720, ambcambodgeparis@ mangoosta.fr.
Germany Benjamin-Vogelsdorf Strasse, 213187, Berlin, T+49-30-4863 7901, www.kambodscha-botschaft.de.
Japan 8-6-9, Akasaka, Minato-Ku, Tokyo 1070052, T+81-3-5412 8522, www.cambodianembassy.jp.
Laos Thadeua Rd, KM2 Vientiane, BP34, T+856-2-131 4950, F1314951, recamlao@laotel.com.
Thailand 185 Rajdamri Rd, Lumpini Patumwan, Bangkok 10330, T+66-2-254 6630, recbkk@cscoms.com.
UK and **Scandinavia** 64 Brondesbury Park, Willesden Green, London, NW6 7AT, T020-8451 7850, www.cambodianembassy. org.uk.
USA 4500, 16th St, NW Washington, DC20011, T+1-202-726 8042, www.embassy.org/cambodia.
Vietnam 71 Tran Hung Dao St, Hanoi, T844-942 4789, arch@fpt.vn; 41 Phung Khac Khoan, Ho Chi Minh City, T848-829 2751, cambocg@hcm.vmn.vn.

Lao
Australia, 1 Dalman Cres, O' Malley, Canberra, ACT 2606, T02-62864595, www. laosembassy.net.
Cambodia, 15-17 Mao Tse Toung Blvd, Phnom Penh, T023-982632.
France, 74 Ave Raymonde-Poincaré 75116 Paris, T01-4553 0298, www.laoparis.com.

Thailand, 502/1-3 Soi Sahakarnpramoon 39, Thanon Pracha Uthit, Wangthonglang, Bangkok 10310, T02-539 6667, www.bkklaoembassy.com.
Vietnam, 22 Tran Binh Trong, Hanoi, T04-4285 4576; 181 Hai Ba Trung, Ho Chi Minh City, T08-3829 7667.

Gay and lesbian

Vietnam
The Vietnamese are tolerant of homosexuality. There are no legal restraints for 2 people of the same sex cohabiting in the same room be they Vietnamese or non-Vietnamese. There are several bars in central HCMC popular with gays. Cruising in dark streets is not advised. An Asian online resource for gays and lesbians which includes a list of scams and warnings in Vietnam as well as gay-friendly bars in Hanoi and HCMC is www.utopia-asia.com.

Cambodia
Gay and lesbian travellers will have no problems in Cambodia. Men often hold other men's hands as do women, so this kind of affection is nothing short of commonplace. Any kind of passionate kissing or sexually orientated affection in public is taboo – both for straight and gay people. The gay scene is just starting to develop in Cambodia but there is definitely a scene in the making. **Linga Bar** (www.lingabar.com) in Siem Reap and the **Salt Lounge** in Phnom Penh are both gay bars and are excellent choices for a night out.

Laos
Gay and lesbian travellers should have no problems in Laos. It does not have a hot gay scene per se and the Lao government is intent on avoiding the mushrooming of the gay and straight sex industry. Officially it is illegal for any foreigner to have a hetero or homosexual relationship with a Lao person they aren't married to. Openly gay behaviour is contrary to local culture and custom and

visitors, whether straight or gay, should not flaunt their sexuality. Any overt display of passion or even affection in public is taboo. In Vientiane there aren't any gay bars, although there are some bars and clubs where gays congregate. Luang Prabang has a few more options and is fast becoming one of Southeast Asia's most gay-friendly destinations.

Health

See your GP or travel clinic at least 6 weeks before departure for general advice on travel risks and vaccinations. Try phoning a specialist travel clinic if your own doctor is unfamiliar with health conditions in the region. Make sure you have sufficient medical travel insurance, get a dental check, know your own blood group and if you suffer a long-term condition such as diabetes or epilepsy, obtain a **Medic Alert** bracelet/necklace (www.medicalert.co.uk). If you wear glasses, take a copy of your prescription.

Vaccinations
It is advisable to vaccinate against polio, tetanus, typhoid, hepatitis A, and rabies if going to more remote areas. Japanese Encephalitis may be advised for some areas, depending on the duration of the trip and proximity to rice-growing and pig-farming areas. Yellow fever does not exist in Vietnam, Cambodia or Laos. However, the authorities may wish to see a certificate if you have recently arrived from an endemic area in Africa or South America.

Health risks
The most common cause of travellers' **diarrhoea** is from eating contaminated food. Drinking water is rarely the culprit in the region, although it's best to be cautious (see below). Swimming in sea or river water that has been contaminated by sewage can also be a cause; ask locally if it is safe. **Diarrhoea** may be also caused by viruses, bacteria (such as E-coli), protozoal (such

as giardia), salmonella and cholera. It may be accompanied by vomiting or by severe abdominal pain. Any kind of diarrhoea responds well to the replacement of water and salts. Sachets of rehydration salts can be bought in most chemists and can be dissolved in boiled water. If the symptoms persist, consult a doctor. Tap water in the major cities is in theory safe to drink but it may be advisable to err on the side of caution and drink only bottled or boiled water. Avoid having ice in drinks unless you trust that it is from a reliable source.

Travelling in high altitudes can bring on **altitude sickness**. On reaching heights above 3000 m, the heart may start pounding and the traveller may experience shortness of breath. Smokers and those with underlying heart or lung disease are often hardest hit. Take it easy for the first few days, rest and drink plenty of water, you will feel better soon. It's essential to get acclimatized before undertaking long treks or arduous activities.

Mosquitoes are more of a nuisance than a serious hazard but some, of course, are carriers of serious diseases such as **malaria**. This exists in rural areas in **Vietnam**. However, there is no risk in the Red River Delta and the coastal plains north of Nha Trang. Neither is there a risk in Hanoi, Ho Chi Minh City, Danang and Nha Trang. Malaria exists in most of **Cambodia**, except the capital Phnom Penh. Malaria is prevalent in **Laos** and remains a serious disease; about a third of the population contracts malaria at some stage in their lives. The choice of malaria prophylaxis will need to be something other than chloroquine for most people, since there is such a high level of resistance to it. Always check with your doctor or travel clinic for the most up-to-date advice. In addition to taking prophylaxis, try and avoid being bitten as much as possible by sleeping off the ground and using a mosquito net and some kind of insecticide. Mosquito coils

release insecticide as they burn and are available in many shops, as are tablets of insecticide, which are placed on a heated mat plugged into a wall socket.

Each year there is the possibility that **avian flu** or **swine flu** might rear their ugly heads. Check the news reports. If there is a problem in an area you are due to visit you may be advised to have an ordinary flu shot or to seek expert advice.

There are high rates of **HIV** in the region, especially among sex workers. Rabies and **schistosomiasis** (bilharzia, a water-borne parasite) may be a problem in Laos.

If you get sick

Contact your embassy or consulate for a list of doctors and dentists who speak your language, or at least some English. Doctors and health facilities in major cities are also listed in the Directory sections of this book. Make sure you have adequate insurance (see below).

Vietnam

Western hospitals exist in Hanoi and Ho Chi Minh City in Vietnam.
Columbia Asia (Saigon International Clinic), 8 Alexander de Rhodes St, HCMC, T8-3823 8455, www.columbiaasia.com. International doctors offering a full range of services.
International SOS, Central Building, 31 Hai Ba Trung St, Hanoi, T4-393 4066, www.internationalsos.com/countries/ Vietnam. Open 24 hrs for emergencies, routine and medical evacuation. It provides dental service too.

Cambodia

Hospitals are not recommended anywhere in Cambodia (even at some of the clinics that profess to be 'international'). If you fall ill or are injured the best bet is to get yourself quickly to either Bumrungrad Hospital or Bangkok Nursing Home, both in Bangkok. Both hospitals are of an exceptional standard, even in international terms.

Laos

Hospitals are few and far between and medical facilities are poor in Laos. Emergency treatment is available at the **Mahosot Hospital** and **Clinique Setthathirath** in Vientiane. The Australian embassy also has a clinic for Commonwealth citizens with minor ailments (see page 425). Better facilities are available in Thailand; emergency evacuation to Nong Khai or Udon Thani (Thailand) can be arranged at short notice. In cases of emergency where a medical evacuation is required, contact **Lao West Coast Helicopter**, Hangar 703, Wattay International Airport, T021-512023, www.laowestcoast.com. A charter to Udon Thani costs from US$1550, subject to availability and government approval.

Thailand

Aek Udon Hospital, Udon Thani, Thailand T+66-42-342555, www.aekudon.com. A 2½-hr trip from Vientiane.
Bumrungrad Hospital, 33 Sukhumvit 3, Bangkok, T+66-2-667 1000, www.bumrungrad.com. The best option: a world-class hospital with brilliant medical facilities.
Wattana Hospital Group, www.wattanahospital.net, is at Udon Thani, T+66 42-325999, and Nong Khai, T+66 42-465201; the latter in particular is a better alternative to the hospitals in Vientiane and only a 40-min trip from the capital.

Useful websites

www.btha.org British Travel Health Association.
www.cdc.gov US government site that gives excellent advice on travel health and details of disease outbreaks.
www.fco.gov.uk British Foreign and Commonwealth Office travel site has useful information on each country, people, climate and a list of UK embassies/consulates.
www.fitfortravel.scot.nhs.uk A-Z of vaccine/health advice for each country.
www.numberonehealth.co.uk Travel screening services, vaccine and travel health advice, email/SMS text vaccine reminders and screens returned travellers for tropical diseases.

Insurance

Always take out travel insurance before you set off and read the small print carefully. Check that the policy covers the activities you intend or may end up doing. Also check exactly what your medical cover includes, eg ambulance, helicopter rescue or emergency flights back home. Also check the payment protocol. You may have to cough up first before the insurance company reimburses you. It is always best to dig out all the receipts for expensive personal effects like jewellery or cameras. Take photos of these items and note down all serial numbers. You are advised to shop around. **STA Travel** and other reputable student travel organisations offer good-value policies. Young travellers from North America can try the **International Student Insurance Service** (ISIS), which is available through **STA Travel**, T01-800-777 0112, www.sta-travel.com. Other recommended travel insurance companies in North America include: **Access America**, www.accessamerica.com; **Travel Assistance International**, www.travelassistance.com; **Travel Guard**, www.noelgroup.com and **Travel Insurance Services**, www.travel insure.com. Older travellers should note that some companies will not cover people over 65 years old, or may charge higher premiums. The best policies for older travellers (UK) are offered by **Age UK**, www.ageuk.org.uk. Please also note your nation's ongoing travel warnings – if you travel to areas or places that are not recommended for travel your insurance may be invalid.

Internet

Vietnam

Although emailing is now usually easy and Wi-Fi is widespread, access to the internet is restricted as the authorities battle vainly to firewall Vietnam-related topics. Facebook is also restricted. Not all internet cafés have printing access.

Cambodia
Cambodia is surprisingly well-connected and most medium-sized to large towns have internet access. Not surprisingly, internet is a lot more expensive in smaller towns, up to a whopping US$5 per hr. In Phnom Penh internet rates are US$1-2 per hr and in Siem Reap should be US$1 per hr or under. Most guesthouses and hotels and many cafés and restaurants now have free Wi-Fi access. In the more developed areas you'll now also find an excellent 3G network, often operating at higher speeds than fixed line internet. See Telephone, page 60, for more details.

Laos
Internet cafés have been popping up all over Laos over the last few years. The connections are surprisingly good in major centres. Fast, cheap internet is available in Vientiane, Luang Prabang, Vang Vieng and Savannakhet for around 100-200 kip per minute. Less reliable and more expensive internet (due to long-distance calls) can be found in Phonsavanh, Don Khone, Don Deth, Luang Namtha, Thakhek, Savannakhet and Udomxai. Many internet cafés also offer international phone services. Wi-Fi is on the increase and can be found in a few places in major tourist centres.

Language

Vietnam
You are likely to find good to a smattering of English wherever there are tourist services but outside tourist centres, communication can be a problem for those who have no knowledge of Vietnamese. Furthermore, the Vietnamese language is not easy to learn. For example, pronunciation presents enormous difficulties as it is tonal. On the plus side,

Vietnamese is written in a Roman alphabet making life much easier: place and street names are instantly recognizable. French is still spoken and often very well by the more elderly and educated.

Cambodia
In Cambodia the national language is Khmer (pronounced Khmei). It is not tonal and the script is derived from the southern Indian alphabet. French is spoken by the older generation who survived the Khmer Rouge era. English is the language of the younger generations. Away from Phnom Penh, Siem Reap and Sihanoukville it can be difficult to communicate with the local population.

Laos
Lao is the national language but there are many local dialects, not to mention the ubiquitous languages of the minority groups. Lao is closely related to Thai and, in a sense, is becoming more so as the years pass. Though there are important differences between the languages, they are mutually intelligible – just about. French is spoken, though only by government officials, hotel staff and many educated people over 40. However, most government officials and many shopkeepers have some command of English.

Media

Vietnam
Unlike western newspapers, Vietnamese papers are less interested in what has happened (that is to say, news), preferring instead to report on what will happen or what should happen, featuring stories such as 'Party vows to advance ethical lifestyles' and 'Output of fertilizer to grow 200%'. The English language daily *Viet Nam News* is widely available. Inside the back page is an excellent 'What's on' section. *The Word* (www.wordhcmc.com and www.wordhanoi. com) is a tourism and culture magazine, which is available throughout the country and is the most useful. *The Guide*, a monthly

magazine on leisure and tourism produced by the *Vietnam Economic Times*, can be found in tourist centres. Good hotels will have cable TV with a full range of options.

On the internet, check out the new Hanoian (www.newhanoian.xemzi.com) and Grapevine (www.hanoigrapevine.com) for news, views and events. Vietnam's official news agency is www.vietnamnews.vnagency.com.vn.

Cambodia

Cambodia has a vigorous English-language press which fights bravely for editorial independence and freedom to criticize politicians. The principal English-language newspapers are the fortnightly *Phnom Penh Post*, (www.phnompenhpost.com) which many regard as the best and the *Cambodia Daily*, published 5 times a week. There are also several tourist magazine guides. The **BBC World Service** provides probably the best news and views on Asia (available on 100 FM).

Laos

The *Vientiane Times*, www.vientianetimes.org.la, is published 5 times a week and provides some interesting cultural and tourist-based features, as well as quirky stories translated from the local press and wire service. Television is becoming increasingly popular as more towns and villages get electricity. The national TV station broadcasts in Lao. In Vientiane, **CNN**, **BBC**, **ABC** and a range of other channels are broadcast. Thailand's **Channel 5** subtitles the news in English. The **Lao National Radio** broadcasts news in English. The **BBC World Service** can be picked up on shortwave.

Money

Vietnam

The unit of currency is the **dong**. The exchange rate at the time of going to press was US$1 = 19,060d;

£1 = 29,000d, €1 = 24,000d. Under law, shops should only accept dong but in practice this is not enforced and dollars are accepted almost everywhere. If possible, however, try to pay for everything in dong as prices are usually lower and in more remote areas people may be unaware of the latest exchange rate. Also, to ordinary Vietnamese, 18,000d is a lot of money, while US$1 means nothing. ATMs are plentiful in HCMC and Hanoi and are pretty ubiquitous in other major tourist centres, but it is a good idea to travel with US$ cash as a back-up. Banks in the main centres will change other major currencies including UK pound sterling, Hong Kong dollar, Thai baht, Swiss franc, Euros, Australian dollars, Singapore dollars and Canadian dollars. Credit cards are increasingly accepted, particularly Visa, MasterCard, Amex and JCB. Large hotels, expensive restaurants and medical centres invariably take them but beware a surcharge of between 2.5 and 4.5%. Most hotels will not add a surcharge onto your bill if paying by credit card. Traveller's cheques are best denominated in US$ and can only be cashed in banks in the major towns. Commission of 2-4% is payable if cashing into dollars but not if you are converting them direct to dong.

Cambodia

The **riel** is the official currency though US dollars are widely accepted and easily exchanged. US$1 = 4260 riel, £1= 6478 riel, €1 = 5366 riel.

In Phnom Penh and other towns most goods and services are priced in dollars and there is little need to buy riel. In remote rural areas prices are quoted in riel (except accommodation). Money can be exchanged in banks and hotels. US$ traveller's cheques are easiest to exchange – commission ranges from 1 to 3%. Cash advances on credit cards are available. Credit card facilities are limited but some banks, hotels and restaurants do accept them, mostly in the tourist centres.

ANZ Royal Bank has a number of ATMs throughout Phnom Penh and Siem Reap. Machines are also now appearing in other towns and a full ATM network should be established in the next couple of years.

Laos

The kip is the official currency. At the time of going to press the exchange rate was US$1 = 8255 kip, £1 = 12,553 kip, €1 = 10,400 kip. The lowest commonly used note is the 500 kip and the highest is the 50,000 kip which tends to shadow the Thai baht but with a rather quaint one-week delay. It is getting much easier to change currency and traveller's cheques. Banks are generally reluctant to give anything but kip in exchange for hard currency.

US dollars and sometimes Thai baht can be used as cash in most shops, restaurants and hotels and the Chinese Renminbi (Yuan) is starting to be more widely accepted in northern parts of Laos (closer to the Chinese border). A certain amount of cash (in US dollars or Thai baht) can also be useful in an emergency. Banks include the **Lao Development Bank** and **Le Banque pour Commerce Exterieur Lao (BCEL)**, which change most major international currencies (cash) and traveller's cheques denominated in US dollars and pounds sterling. Many of the BCEL branches offer cash advances on Visa/MasterCard and thankfully they have rolled out Visa and MasterCard ATMs in all tourist centres. ATMs will only dispense 700,000 kip at one time but apparently you can withdraw this amount 7 times in one day. Note that some banks charge a hefty commission of US$2 per TC. While banks will change traveller's cheques and cash denominated in most major currencies into kip, some will only change US dollars into Thai baht, or into US dollars cash.

Payment by credit card is becoming easier – although beyond the larger hotels and restaurants in Vientiane and Luang Prabang do not expect to be able to get by on plastic. American Express, Visa,

MasterCard/Access cards are accepted in a limited number of more upmarket establishments. Note that commission is charged on credit card transactions.

Cost of travelling

Vietnam is better overall value than Cambodia and Laos as it has a better established tourism infrastructure and more competitive services. On a budget expect to pay around US$6-15 per night for accommodation and about the same each day for food. A good mid-range hotel will cost US$12-30. There are comfort and cost levels anywhere from here up to more than US$200 per night. For travelling many use the Open Tour Buses as they are inexpensive and, by Vietnamese standards, 'safe'. Slightly more expensive are trains followed by planes.

The budget traveller will find that a little goes a long way in **Cambodia**. Numerous guesthouses offer accommodation at around US$3-7 a night. Food-wise, the seriously strapped can easily manage to survive healthily on US$4-5 per day, so an overall daily budget (not allowing for excursions) of US$7-9 should be enough or the really cost-conscious. For the less frugally minded, a daily allowance of US$30 should see you relatively well-housed and fed, while at the upper end of the scale, there are, in Phnom Penh and Siem Reap, plenty of restaurants and hotels for those looking for Cambodian levels of luxury. A mid-range hotel (attached bathroom, hot water and a/c) will normally cost around US$25 per night and a good meal at a restaurant around US$5-10.

The variety of available domestic flights means that the bruised bottoms, dust-soaked clothes and stiff limbs that go hand-in-hand with some of the longer bus/boat rides can be avoided by those with thicker wallets in **Laos**. As the roads improve and journey times diminish, buses have emerged as the preferred (not to mention most reasonably priced) transportation option. Budget accommodation costs US$3-10, with a mid-range hotel costing from US$20-30. Local food is very cheap and it is possible to eat well for under US$2. Most Western restaurants will charge between US$2-5 although it's possible to splurge in Luang Prabang and Vientiane.

Opening hours

Vietnam
Shops Daily 0800-2000. Some stay open for another hour or two, especially in tourist centres.
Banks Mon-Fri 0800-1600. Many close 1100-1300 or 1130-1330.
Offices Mon-Fri 0730-1130, 1330-1630.
Restaurants, **cafés**, **bars** Daily from 0700 or 0800 although some open earlier. Bars are meant to close at 2400 by law.

Cambodia
Shops Daily from 0800-2000. Some, however, stay open for a further hour or two, especially in tourist centres. Most markets open daily between 0530/0600-1700.
Banks Mon-Fri 0800-1600. Some close 1100-1300. Some major branches are open until 1100 on Sat.
Offices Mon-Fri 0730-1130, 1330-1630.
Restaurants, **cafés** and **bars** Daily from 0700-0800 although some open earlier. Bars are meant to close at 2400 by law.

Laos
Shops Shops keep regular business hours but those whose clients are tourists stay open longer into the night.
Banks Mon-Fri 0830-1600 (some close at 1500).
Offices Mon-Fri 0900-1700; those that deal with tourists stay open a bit later and are also usually open over the weekends. Government offices close at 1600.
Bars and **nightclubs** Usually close around 2200-2300 depending on how strictly the curfew is being inforced. In smaller towns, most restaurants and bars will be closed by 2200.

Police and the law

Vietnam
If you are robbed in Vietnam, report the incident to the police (for your insurance claim). Otherwise, the police are of no use whatsoever. They will do little or nothing (apart from log the crime on an incident sheet which you will need for your insurance claim). Vietnam is not the best place to come into conflict with the law. Avoid getting arrested. If you are arrested, however, ask for consular assistance immediately and English-speaking staff.

Involvement in politics, possession of political material, business activities that have not been licensed by appropriate authorities, or non-sanctioned religious activities (including proselytizing) can result in detention. Sponsors of small, informal religious gatherings such as bible-study groups in hotel rooms, as well as distributors of religious materials, have been detained, fined and expelled. (Source: US State Department.) The army are extremely sensitive about all their military buildings and become exceptionally irate if you take a photo. There are signs to this effect outside all military installations, of which there are hundreds.

Cambodia
A vast array of offences are punishable in Cambodia, from minor traffic violations through to possession of drugs. If you are arrested or are having difficulty with the police contact your embassy immediately. As the police only earn approximately US$20 a month, corruption is a problem and contact should be avoided, unless absolutely necessary. Most services, including the provision of police reports, will require paying bribes. Law enforcement is very haphazard, at times completely subjective and justice can be hard to find. Some smaller crimes receiving large penalties while perpetrators of greater crimes often get off scot-free.

Laos

If you are robbed insurers will require that you obtain a police report. The police may try to solicit a bribe for this service. Although not ideal, you will probably have to pay this fee to obtain your report. Laws aren't strictly enforced but when the authorities do prosecute people the penalties can be harsh, ranging from deportation through to prison sentences. If you are arrested seek embassy and consular support. People are routinely fined for drugs possession, having sexual relations with locals (when unmarried) and proselytizing. If you are arrested or encounter police, try to remain calm and friendly. Although drugs are available throughout the country, the police levy hefty fines and punishments if caught.

Post

Vietnam

Postal services are pretty good. Post offices open daily 0700-2100; smaller ones close for lunch.

Cambodia

International service is unpredictable but it is reasonably priced and fairly reliable (at least from Phnom Penh). Only send mail from the GPO in any given town rather than sub POs or mail boxes. **Fedex** and **DHL** also offer services.

Laos

The postal service is inexpensive and reliable but delays are common. As the National Tourism Authority assures: in Laos the stamps will stay on the envelope. Contents of outgoing parcels must be examined by an official before being sealed. Incoming mail should use the official title, **Lao PDR**. There is no mail to home addresses or guesthouses, so mail must be addresses to a PO Box. The post office in Vientiane has a *poste restante* service. EMS (Express Mail Service) is available from main post offices in larger towns. In general, post offices open 0800-1200, 1300-1600. In provincial areas, **Lao Telecom**

is usually attached to the post office. DHL, **Fedex** and **TNT** have offices in Vientiane.

Public holidays

Vietnam

1 Jan New Year's Day.
3 Feb Founding anniversary of the Communist Party of Vietnam.
30 Apr Liberation Day of South Vietnam and HCMC.
1 May International Labour Day.
19 May Anniversary of the Birth of Ho Chi Minh (this is a government holiday). The majority of state institutions will be shut but businesses in the private sector carry on regardless.
2 Sep National Day.
3 Sep President Ho Chi Minh's Anniversary.

Cambodia

1 Jan National Day and Victory over Pol Pot.
7 Jan Celebration of the fall of the Khmer Rouge in 1979.
8 Mar Women's Day. Processions, floats and banners in main towns.
17 Apr Independence Day.
1 May Labour Day.
9 May Genocide Day.
1 Jun International Children's Day.
18 Jun Her Majesty Preah Akkaek Mohesey Norodom Monineath Sihanouk's Birthday.
Sep (movable) End of Buddhist 'lent'.
24 Sep Constitution Day.
23 Oct Paris Peace Accord.
30 Oct-1 Nov King's Birthday.
9 Nov Independence Day (1953).
10 Dec Human Rights Day.

Laos

1 Jan New Year's Day.
6 Jan Pathet Lao Day.
20 Jan Army Day.
8 Mar Women's Day.
22 Mar People's Party Day.
1 May Labour Day.
1 Jun Children's Day.
2 Dec Independence Day.

Safety

Travel advisories

The US State Department's travel advisories: **Travel Warnings & Consular Information Sheets**, www.travel.state.gov/travel_warnings.html.

The **UK Foreign and Commonwealth Office**'s travel warning section, www.fco.gov.uk/travel/.

Vietnam

Do not take any valuables on to the streets of HCMC as bag and jewellery snatching is a common and serious problem. Thieves work in teams, often with beggar women carrying babies as a decoy. Beware of people who obstruct your path (pushing a bicycle across the pavement is a common ruse); your pockets are being emptied from behind. Young men on fast motorbikes also cruise the central streets of HCMC waiting to pounce on unwary victims. The situation in other cities is not as bad but take care in Nha Trang and Hanoi. Never go by cyclo in a strange part of town after dark.

Lone women travellers have fewer problems than in many other Asian countries. The most common form of harassment usually consists of comic and harmless displays of macho behaviour.

Unexploded ordnance is still a threat in some areas. It is best not to stray too far from the beaten track and don't unearth bits of suspicious metal.

Single Western men will be targeted by prostitutes on street corners, in tourist bars and those cruising on motorbikes.

Cambodia

Cambodia is not as dangerous as some would have us believe. The country has really moved forward in protecting tourists and violent crime towards visitors is comparatively low. Since large penalties have been introduced for those who kill or maim tourists, random acts of violence aren't as common these days. Safety on the night-time streets of Phnom Penh is a problem. Robberies and hold-ups are common. Many robbers are armed, so do not resist. As Phnom Penh has a limited taxi service, travel after dark poses a problem. Stick to moto drivers you know. Women are, obviously, particularly targeted by bag snatchers. Khmer New Year is known locally as the 'robbery season'. Theft is endemic at this time of year so be on red alert. A common trick around New Year is for robbers to mess around with tourists (usually throwing water and talcum powder in the eyes) and rob them blind. Leave your valuables in the hotel safe or hidden in your room. Sexual harassment is not uncommon. Many motos/tour guides will try their luck with women but generally it is more macho posturing than anything serious.

Outside Phnom Penh safety is not as much of a problem. Visitors should be very cautious when walking in the countryside, however, as landmines and other unexploded ordnance is a ubiquitous hazard. Stick to well-worn paths, especially around Siem Reap and when visiting remote temples. Motorbike accidents have serious fatality rates as they do in Vietnam. Keep an eye on the ongoing situation with Thailand as the 2 nations have come close to conflict in the last 2 years – if this flares up again, borders may be closed.

Laos

Crime rates are very low but it is advisable to take the usual precautions. Most areas of the country are now safe – a very different state of affairs from only a few years ago when foreign embassies advised tourists not to travel along certain roads and in certain areas (in particular Route 13 between Vientiane and Luang Prabang, and Route 7 between Phonsavanh and Route 13). Today these risks have effectively disappeared. However, the government will sometimes make areas provisionally off-limits if they think there is a security risk – take heed!

There has been a reported increase in motorcycle drive-by thefts in Vientiane, but these and other similar crimes are still at a low level compared with most countries. If riding on a motorbike or bicycle, don't carry your bag strap over your shoulder – as you could get pulled off the bike if someone goes to snatch your bag. In the Siphandon and Vang Vieng areas, theft seems more common. Use a hotel security box if available.

Road accidents are on the increase. The hiring of motorbikes is becoming more popular and consequently there are more tourist injuries. Wear a helmet.

Be careful around waterways, as drowning is one of the primary causes of tourist deaths. Be particularly careful during the rainy season (May-Sep) as rivers have a tendency to flood and can have extremely strong currents. Make sure if you are kayaking, tubing, canoeing, travelling by fast-boat, etc, that proper safety gear, such as life jackets, is provided. 'Fast-boat' river travel can be dangerous due to excessive speed and the risk of hitting something in the river and capsizing. Low Mekong River levels in the dry season in 2010 – the lowest for over 50 years – have also caused damage and capsizing to boats. Seek advice before setting out.

Xieng Khouang Province, the Bolaven Plateau, Xam Neua and areas along the Ho Chi Minh Trail are littered with bombies (small anti-personnel mines and bomblets from cluster bomb units). There are also numerous, large, unexploded bombs; in many villages they have been left lying around. They are very unstable so DO NOT TOUCH. Only walk on clearly marked or newly trodden paths. Consult the **Mines Advisory Group** (www.maginternational. org), which works in Laos.

Student travellers

There are discounts available on the train in **Vietnam**. Discount travel is provided to those under 22 and over 60. There are no specific student discounts in **Cambodia** or **Laos**. Anyone in full-time education

is entitled to an **International Student Identity Card** (www.isic.org). These are issued by student travel offices and travel agencies and offer special rates on all forms of transport and other concessions and services. They sometimes permit free admission to museums and sights, at other times a discount on the admission.

Telephone

Vietnam
To make a domestic call dial 0 + area code + phone number. Note that all numbers in this guide include the 0 and the area code. Most shops or cafés will let you call a local number for 2000d: look for the blue sign '**dien thoai cong cong**' (meaning public telephone). All post offices provide international telephone services. The cost of calls has greatly reduced but some post offices and hotels still insist on charging for a minimum of 3 mins. You start paying for an overseas call from the moment you ring even if the call is not answered. By dialling 171 or 178 followed by 0 or 00 to make an international call, it is approximately 30% cheaper. Vietnam's country code is +84; IDD is 0084; directory enquires 1080; operator-assisted domestic long-distance calls 103; international directory enquiries 143; Yellow pages 1081. Numbers beginning with 091 or 090 are mobile numbers. Pay-as-you-go sim cards are available and calls are cheap.

Cambodia
It is now relatively easy for foreigners to buy mobile phone sim cards in Cambodia. If you have an unlocked handset that allows you to use any sim card this is by far the easiest and cheapest choice for travellers in Cambodia for both local and international calls. Mobile network company **M-Fone** offer a good nationwide coverage and pay-as-you-go service–it is easy to buy top-up for their services via scratch cards of various denominations. They also offer high speed mobile internet services via their 3G

network for an extra charge – this can often be cheaper, quicker and more reliable than using an internet café.

Landline linkages are so poor in Cambodia that many people and businesses prefer to use mobile phones instead. In 2009 Cambodia liberalized and deregulated their mobile networks and there are now several to choose from depending on your needs. It's not uncommon for some Khmers to have 3 or 4 sim cards/numbers. For landlines the 3-digit prefix included in a 9-digit landline telephone number is the area (province) code. If dialling within a province, dial only the 6-digit number. International calls can be made from most guesthouses, hotels and phone booths. Don't anticipate being able to make international calls outside Phnom Penh, Siem Reap and Sihanoukville. Use public MPTC or Camintel card phone boxes dotted around Phnom Penh to make international calls (cards are usually sold at shops near the booth). International calls are expensive, starting at US$4 per minute in Phnom Penh, and more in the provinces. To make an overseas call from Cambodia, dial 007 or 001 + IDD country code + area code minus first 0 + subscriber number. The country code for Cambodia is +855.

Laos

Public phones are available in Vientiane and other major cities. You can also go to **Lao Telecom** offices to call overseas. Call 178 in Vientiane for town codes. Most towns in Laos have at least one telephone box with IDD facility. The one drawback is that you must buy a phonecard. Because these are denominated in such small units, even the highest-value card will only get you a handful of minutes talk time with Europe. Most call are charged between US$0.80 and US$2 per min. All post offices, telecoms offices and many shops sell phone cards.

Mobile telephone coverage is now good across the country. Pay-as-you-go sim cards are available for 30,000 kip to 50,000 kip and calls and SMS are very cheap.

In summer 2010, the National Authority of Post and Telecommunications added an extra digit to all 7-digit mobile phone numbers. Depending on mobile phone providers, a 5, 9, 7 or 2 will need to be added to the front of phone numbers. Footprint has added these extra digits in this guide.

Many internet cafés have set up call facilities that charge US$0.20 per min and under to make a call. In Vientiane, Pakse, Luang Prabang and Vang Vieng most internet cafés are equipped with Skype, including headphones and webcam, which costs a fraction of the price for international calls (as long as you have an account already established).

International operator: 170. Operator: 16. The IDD for Laos is 00856.

Time

Vietnam, Cambodia and Laos are 7 hrs ahead of Greenwich Mean Time.

Tipping

Vietnamese do not normally tip if eating in small family restaurants but may tip extravagantly in expensive bars. Foreigners normally leave the small change. Big hotels and some restaurants add 5-10% service charge and the government tax of 10% to the bill. Taxis are rounded up to the nearest 5000d, hotel porters 20,000d. Tipping is rare but appreciated in Cambodia. Neither is it common practice in Laos, even in hotels. However, it is a kind gesture to tip guides and some more expensive restaurants. If someone offers you a lift, it is a courtesy to give them some money for fuel.

Tour operators

Numerous operators offer organized trips to this region, ranging from a whistle-stop tour of the highlights to specialist trips that focus on a specific destination or activity. The advantage of travelling with a reputable operator is that your transport, accommodation and activities are all arranged for you in advance, which is particularly valuable if you only have limited time. By travelling independently, however, you can be more flexible and spontaneous about where you go and what you do. You will be able to explore less-visited areas and you will save money, if you budget carefully. On arrival in Vietnam, many travellers hire operators to take them on day and week-long trips. These tours cater for all budgets and you will benefit from an English-speaking guide and safe vehicles. Some of the most popular trips include week-long tours around the northwest or into the Mekong Delta.

For regional tour operators, such as **Asian Trails** (www.asiantrails.com), refer to the Activities and tours listings throughout this guide.

In the UK

Adventure Company, Cross & Pillory House, Cross & Pillory Lane, Alton, Hampshire GU34 1HL, T0845-450 5316, www.adventurecompany.co.uk.
Audley Travel, New Mill, New Mill Lane, Witney, Oxfordshire OX29 9SX, T01993-838000, www.audleytravel.com.
Buffalo Tours UK, The Old Church, 89B Quicks Road, Wimbledon, London, SW19 1EX, T020-8545 2830, www.buffalotours.com.
Exodus, Grange Mills, Weir Road, London, SW12 0NE, T020-8772 3936, www.exodus.co.uk.
Explore, Nelson House, 55 Victoria Road, Farnborough, Hampshire, GU14 7PA, T0845-013 1537, www.explore.co.uk.
Guerba Adventure & Discovery Holidays, Wessex House, 40 Station Rd, Westbury, Wiltshire BA13 3JN, T01373-826611, www.guerba.co.uk.
KE Adventure Travel, 32 Lake Rd, Keswick, Cumbria, CA12 5DQ, T01768-773966, www.keadventure.com.
Silk Steps, Odyssey Lodge, Holywell Rd,

Edington, Bridgwater, Somerset TA7 9JH, T01278-722460, www.silksteps.co.uk.
Steppes Travel, 51 Castle St, Cirencester, Glos, GL7 1QD, T01285-880980, www.steppestravel.co.uk.
Symbiosis Expedition Planning, 1 Frenchies View, Denmead, Waterlooville, Hampshire, T0845-1232844, www.symbiosis-travel.com.
Trans Indus, 75 St Mary's Road and the Old Fire Station, Ealing, London, W5 5RH, T020-8566 3729, www.transindus.co.uk.
Travel Indochina Ltd, 2nd floor, Chester House, George St, Oxford OX1 2AY, T01865-268940, www.travelindochina.co.uk.
Travelmood, 214 Edgware Rd, London W2 1DH; 1 Brunswick Court, Leeds LS2 7QU; 16 Reform St, Dundee DD1 1RG, T0800-298 9815, www.travelmoodadventures.com.
Tucan Travel, 316 Uxbridge Rd, London, W3 9QP, T020-8896 1600, www.tucantravel.com.
Visit Asia 30-32 Fulham High St, London SW6 3LQ, T020-7736 4347, www.visitasia.co.uk.

In North America

Adventure Center, 1311 63rd St, Suite 200, Emeryville, CA, T+1-800 227 8747, www.adventurecenter.com.
Global Spectrum, 3907 Laro Court, Fairfax, VA 22031, T+1-800 419 4446, www.globalspectrumtravel.com.
Hidden Treasure Tours, 509 Lincoln Blvd, Long Beach, NY 11561, T877-761 7276 (USA toll free), www.hiddentreasuretours.com.
Journeys, 107 April Drive, Suite 3, Ann Arbor, MI 48103-1903, T734-665 4407, www.journeys./travel.
Myths & Mountains, 976 Tree Court, Incline Village, Nevada 89451, T+1-800 670-MYTH, www.mythsandmountains.com.

In Australia and New Zealand

Buffalo Tours, L9/69 Reservoir St, Surry Hills, Sydney, Australia 2010, T61-2-8218 2198, www.buffalotours.com.
Intrepid Travel, 360 Bourke St, Melbourne,

Victoria 3000, T+61-03-8602 0500,
www.intrepidtravel.com.au
Travel Indochina, Level 10, HCF House,
403 George St, Sydney, NSW 2000,
T1300-138755 (toll free),
www.travelindochina.com.au.

Tourist information

Contact details for tourist offices and other
information resources are given in the
relevant Ins and Outs sections throughout
the book.

Vietnam
The national tourist office is **Vietnam
National Administration of Tourism**
(www.vietnamtourism.com), whose role is
to promote Vietnam as a tourist destination
rather than to provide tourist information.
Visitors to their offices can get some
information and maps but are more likely to
be offered tours. There are exceptions, such
as **Saigontourist** (www.saigon-tourist.com).
Good tourist information is available from
tour operators in the main tourist centres.

Cambodia
Government tourism services are minimal at
best. The **Ministry of Tourism**, 3 Monivong
Blvd, T023-426876, is not able to provide any
useful information or services. The tourism
office in Siem Reap is marginally better but
will only provide services, such as guides,
maps, etc, for a nominal fee. In all cases in
Cambodia you are better off going through
a private operator for information and price.

Laos
The **Laos National Tourism Authority**, Lane
Xang, Vientiane, T021-212248, provides
maps and brochures. Some provincial
tourist offices are excellent and staffed
with helpful, knowledgeable and willing
people. Others are woeful. The German
NGO DED are doing an excellent job in
many provinces to assist with providing
tourist information and providing

information about and creating new
activities. Be patient in the less good ones
and eventually they may come through
with the information you need. There
are particularly good tourism offices in
Thakhek, Vieng Xai, Xam Neua, Udomxai
and Phongsali. Unfortunately the front
desk operation in Vientiane is pretty
useless. You might be lucky enough to get
a bus timetable, though, if they can be
raised from their slumber. The authority
has teamed up with local tour operators
to provide a number of ecotourism
opportunities, such as trekking and village
homestays, www.ecotourismlaos.com.
Many provincial tourist offices now have an
Eco Guide Unit attached or operating from
a separate office. The best in the country is
the one in Savannakhet.

Visas and immigration

30-day tourist visas are granted on arrival
in Bangkok.

Vietnam
Valid passports with visas issued by a
Vietnamese embassy are required by all
visitors. Visas are normally valid only for
arrival by air at Hanoi and HCMC. Those
wishing to enter or leave Vietnam by land
must specify the border crossing when
applying. It is possible to alter the point
of departure at immigration offices in
Hanoi and HCMC. Visas on arrival at land
crossings are not available.

The standard tourist visa is valid for 1
month for 1 entry only. Tourist visas cost
US$67 and generally take 5 days to process.
Express visas cost more and take 2 days.
2-month tourist visas are now available
for US$129. If you are planning on staying
for a while or making a side trip to Laos or
Cambodia with the intention of coming
back to Vietnam then a 1-month multiple
entry visa will make life much simpler.
Visa regulations are ever changing: usually
it is possible to extend visas within Vietnam.

Travel agencies and hotels will probably add their own mark-up but for many people it is worth paying to avoid the difficulty of making 1 or 2 journeys to an embassy. Visas can be extended for 1 month. Depending on where you are it will take between 1 day and a week. A visa valid for 1 month can only be extended for 1 month. Visas on arrival at land crossings are not available and visas on arrival at airports are not exactly as they appear; they must be arranged in advance with licensed companies, paperwork signed before arriving and handed at desks at airports to get the visa. This may or may not work out cheaper than the embassy approach.

Cambodia

In 2009 Cambodia began an e-visa system which will allow tourists to negotiate arrivals much quicker. The charge is US$20 plus a US$5 admin charge. These visas are valid for 3 months from date of issue for a single entry of 30 days. They can ONLY be used at the following points of entry: Siem Reap Airport, Phnom Penh Airport, Poipet, Koh Kong and Bavet. The usual tourist visas for a 30-day stay are still available on arrival at these and several other entry points. Fill in a form and hand over 1 photograph (4 cm x 6 cm). Tourist visas cost US$20 and your passport must be valid for at least 6 months from the date of entry. More details of the e-visa plus an up-to-date list of border crossings and requirements can be found at www.evisa.mfaic.gov.kh/e-visa.

Cambodia also has missions overseas from which visas can be obtained (see Embassies and consulates, page 50).

Travellers leaving by land must ensure that their Vietnam visa specifies Moc Bai or Chau Doc as points of entry otherwise they could be turned back. You can apply for a Cambodian visa in Ho Chi Minh City and collect in Hanoi and vice versa.

Extensions can be obtained at the Department for Foreigners on the road to the airport, T023-581558 (passport photo required). Most travel agents arrange visa extensions for around US$40 for 30 days. Those overstaying their visas are fined US$5 per day, although officials at land crossings often try to squeeze out more.

Laos

A 30-day tourist visa can be obtained at most (but not all) borders. See box, page 37.

Visa prices are based on reciprocity with countries and cost US$30-42. 'Overtime fees' are often charged if you enter after 1600 or at a weekend. To get a visa you need to provide a passport photograph. Where visas are not available on arrival they must be obtained at Laos embassies.

The Lao government also issues business visas that are available for 30 days with the possibility of extending for months beyond. This is a more complicated process and usually requires a note from an employer or hefty fees from a visa broker. These visas are best organized from your home country and can take a long time to process.

Tourist visa extensions can be obtained from the Lao Immigration Office in the Ministry of the Interior opposite the Morning Market on Phai Nam Rd, in Vientiane, T021-212529. They can be extended for up to a month at the cost of US$2 per day (although if you want to extend for a month it works out cheaper to cross the border); you will need 1 passport photo. It takes a day to process the extension and if you drop the paperwork off early in the morning it will often be ready by the afternoon. Travel agencies in Vientiane and other major centres can also handle this service for you for a fee (eg an additional US$1-2 per day). Visitors who overstay their visas are charged US$10 for each day beyond the date of expiration; they will be asked to pay this on departure from Laos.

Contents

Footprint features

Border crossings

Vietnam

At a glance

⊖ **Getting around** Open Tour Bus, rail, plane and boat.

⊙ **Time required** 2-6 weeks.

☼ **Weather** Dec-March is best.

⊗ **When not to go** Monsoon season in the Mekong is Sep-Nov. Central region can suffer tropical storms May-Nov. Around Tet transport and hotels are booked up.

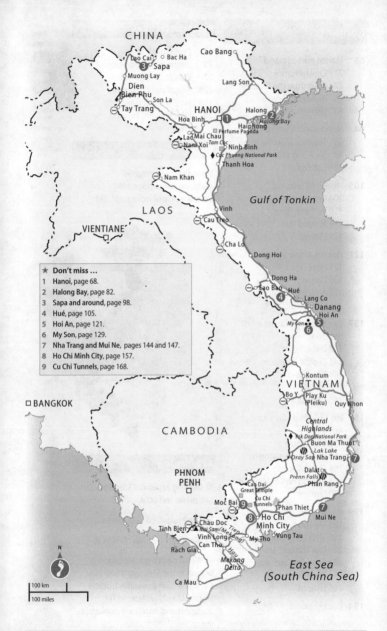

CHINA

Lao Cai
Bac Ha
Cao Bang
Sapa
Muong Lay
Lang Son
Dien
Bien Phu
Son La
Tay Trang
HANOI
Halong
Hoa Binh
Haiphong
Halong Bay
Lac Mai Chau
Perfume Pagoda
Nam Xoi
Tam Coc
Ninh Binh
Cuc Phuong National Park
Thanh Hoa
Nam Khan

LAOS

Gulf of Tonkin

VIENTIANE

Vinh
Cau Treo
Cha Lo
Dong Hoi

Dong Ha
Lao Bao
Hué
Lang Co
Danang
Hoi An
My Son

Kontum

VIETNAM

Bo Y
Play Ku
(Pleiku)
Quy Nhon

BANGKOK

CAMBODIA

Central
Highlands
Yok Don National Park
Buon Ma Thuot
Lak Lake
Dray Sap
Nha Trang

PHNOM
PENH

Dalat
Prenn Falls
Phan Rang

Cao Dai
Great Temple
Moc Bai
Cu Chi
Tunnels
Phan Thiet
Chau Doc
Tien
Nui Sam (Mekong)
Ho Chi
Minh City
Mui Ne
Tinh Bien
Vinh Long
My Tho
Vung Tau
Can Tho
Rach Gia
Mekong
Delta
Ca Mau

East Sea
(South China Sea)

N

100 km
100 miles

Introduction

In modern-day Vietnam one thing in particular stands out. It is, quite simply, the remarkable speed at which the country is developing and the extraordinary ambitions its leaders are planning to achieve. Vietnam now hovers in an enigmatic and paradoxical time zone, somewhere between the late Industrial Revolution and the post-industrial age. High school children in Ho Chi Minh City vie for the trendiest motorbikes, mobile phones and trainers, while children in the Northern Highlands are happy with a pair of sandals. Youngsters in the Mekong Delta have email accounts yet 10 years ago they didn't have a telephone. And while staff in call centres gossip about the latest fashions, their parents harvest rice by hand. Vietnam has experienced war and bloody revolution in the past 100 years, but the revolution it is now undergoing is peaceful and prosperous. Vast strides in economic development are apace with the government hoping to be crowned a middle income country by 2020. It is, in part, these changes that make Vietnam the absorbing and gripping place that it is.

War? Yes, Vietnam has survived several, in fact, over the last century. The Vietnamese people have seen much water flow under the bridge since the war ended but the government will not let it drop. Even now, more than 30 years on, new war memorials are being erected. It is as if legitimacy of the government somehow depends on having won the war, resulting in an odd mixture of war legacy in modern Vietnam. Heroic communist monuments and war memorabilia abound in museums but the Vietnamese people have set their sights firmly on the future. There is no looking back, no nostalgia for the past. And this explains the lack of fuss every time an old building is flattened. Forget yesterday, look to tomorrow.

Hanoi and around

→ *Colour map 2, B4.*

Hanoi is a small city of broad tree-lined boulevards, lakes, parks, weathered colonial buildings, elegant squares and some of the newest office blocks and hotels in Southeast Asia. It lies nearly 100 km from the sea on a bend in the Red River and from this geographical feature the city derives its name – Hanoi – meaning 'within a river bend'.

Hanoi is the capital of the world's 14th most populous country, but, in an age of urban sprawl, the city remains small and compact, historic and charming. Much of its charm lies not so much in the official 'sights' but in the unofficial and informal: the traffic zooming around the broad streets or the cyclos taking a mellow pedal through the Old Quarter, small shops packed with traders' goods or stacks of silk for visitors, skewered poultry on pavement stalls, mobile flower stalls piled on the backs of bikes, the bustle of pedestrians, the ubiquitous tinkle of the ice cream man's bicycle, and the political posters, now raised to an art form, dotted around the city.

At the heart of the city is Hoan Kiem Lake and the famous Sunbeam Bridge. The Old Quarter (36 Streets and Guilds) area, north of the lake, is bustling with commerce, its ancient buildings crumbling from the weight of history and activity. The French Quarter, which still largely consists of French buildings, is south of the lake.

Accessible on a tour from the city, the primates at Cuc Phuong National Park and the waters of Halong Bay make this area one of the most visited in Vietnam. ▶▶ *For listings, see pages 83-94.*

Ins and outs

Getting there
Air **Noi Bai Airport** (HAN) is 35 km from Hanoi, a 45-minute to one-hour drive, and is the hub for international and domestic flights.

The official **Noi Bai Taxi**, T04-3873 3333, charges a fixed price of US$12-15 to the city centre. The airport minibus service (every 30 minutes, daily 0900-2000, US$2), terminates opposite the **Vietnam Airlines** office, Quang Trung Street, T04-3825 0872. Return buses leave the Vietnam Airlines office at regular intervals from 0500-1800, 50 minutes.

Bus Open Tour Buses leave and depart from tour operator offices in the city for destinations in the south, including Hué, Hoi An, Dalat, Nha Trang, Mui Ne and Ho Chi Minh City.

Train The train station is a short taxi ride from the Old Quarter. There are trains to Ho Chi Minh City, and all points on the route south, as well as to Lao Cai (for Sapa) in the north. ▶▶ *See Transport, page 92.*

Getting around
At the heart of the city is Hoan Kiem Lake. The majority of visitors make straight for the Old Quarter (36 Streets and Guilds) area north of the lake, which is densely packed and bustling with commerce. In the French Quarter, south of the lake, you'll find the Opera House and the grandest hotels, shops and offices. A large block of the city west of Hoan Kiem Lake (Ba Dinh District) represents the heart of the government and the civil and military administration of Vietnam. To the north of the city is the West Lake, Tay Ho District, fringed with the suburban homes of the new middle class and a new emerging expat quarter with bars and restaurants.

Hanoi is getting more frenetic by the minute but, thanks to the city's elegant, tree-lined boulevards, walking and cycling can still be delightful. If you like the idea of being pedalled around town, then a cyclo is the answer but be prepared for some concentrated haggling. There are also motorbike taxis (*xe ôm*), and self-drive motorbikes for hire as well as a fleet of metered taxis. Local buses have also improved.

Best time to visit

For much of the year Hanoi's weather is decidedly non-tropical. It benefits from glorious Europe-like springs and autumns, when temperatures are warm but not too hot and not too cold. From May until early November Hanoi is fearfully hot and steamy. You cannot take a step without breaking into a sweat. The winter months from November to February can be chilly and Hanoians wrap themselves up well in warm coats, woolly hats, gloves and scarves. Most museums are closed on Mondays.

Tourist information

The privately run **Tourist Information Center** ① *7 Dinh Tien Hoang St, T04-3926 3366, www.ticvietnam.com, daily 0800-2200*, at the northern end of the lake, is proving useful. It provides information and maps and will book hotels and transport tickets at no extra cost; also currency exchange and ATM. Also see www.hanoitourism.gov.vn. Useful information is also available from the multitude of tour operators in the city. ▶ *See Activities and tours, page 90.*

Background

The origins of Hanoi as a great city lie with a temple orphan, Ly Cong Uan. Ly rose through the ranks of the palace guards to become their commander and in 1010, four years after the death of the previous King Le Hoan, was enthroned, marking the beginning of the 200-year Ly Dynasty. On becoming king, Ly Cong Uan moved his capital from Hoa Lu to Dai La, which he renamed Thang Long (Soaring Dragon). Thang Long is present-day Hanoi. Hanoi celebrated its 1000th anniversary with a series of special events in October 2010.

During the period of French expansion into Indochina, the Red River was proposed as an alternative trade route to that of the Mekong. The French attacked and captured the citadel of Hanoi under the dubious pretext that the Vietnamese were about to attack. Recognizing that if a small expeditionary force could be so successful, then there would be little chance against a full-strength army, Emperor Tu Duc acceded to French demands. At the time that the French took control of Annam, Hanoi could still be characterized more as a collection of villages than a city. From 1882 onwards, Hanoi, along with the port city of Haiphong, became the focus of French activity in the north. Hanoi was made the capital of the new colony of Annam and the French laid out a 2 sq km residential and business district, constructing mansions, villas and public buildings incorporating both French and Asian architectural styles. At the end of the Second World War, with the French battling to keep Ho Chi Minh and his forces at bay, Hanoi became little more than a service centre. After the French withdrew in 1954, Ho Chi Minh concentrated on building up Vietnam and in particular Hanoi's industrial base.

Although Ho Chi Minh City has attracted the lion's share of Vietnam's foreign inward investment, Hanoi, as the capital, also receives a large amount. But whereas Ho Chi Minh City's investment tends to be in industry, Hanoi has received a great deal of attention from property developers, notably in the hotel and office sectors.

Vietnamese addresses

Odd numbers usually run consecutively on one side of the street, evens on the other; bis after a number, as in 16 bis Hai Ba Trung Street, means there are two houses with the same number and ter after the number means there are three houses with the same number. Large buildings with a single street number are usually subdivided 21A, 21B, etc; some buildings may be further subdivided 21C1, 21C2, and so on. An oblique (/ sec or tren in Vietnamese) in a number, as

in 23/16 Dinh Tien Hoang Street, means the address is to be found in a small side street (hem) – in this case running off Dinh Tien Hoang by the side of no 23: the house in question will probably be signed 23/16 rather than just 16. Usually, but by no means always, a hem will be quieter than the main street. Q stands for quân (district); this points you in the right general direction and is important in locating your destination as a long street may run through several quan.

Central Hanoi

Hoan Kiem Lake

Hoan Kiem Lake, or Ho Guom (Lake of the Restored Sword) as it is more commonly referred to in Hanoi, is named after an incident that occurred during the 15th century. Emperor Le Thai To (1428-1433), following a momentous victory against an army of invading Ming Chinese, was sailing on the Lake when a golden turtle appeared from the depths to take back the charmed sword which had secured the victory and restore it to the Lake from whence it came. Like the sword in the stone of British Arthurian legend, Le Thai To's sword assures the Vietnamese of divine intervention in time of national crisis and the story is graphically portrayed in water puppet theatres across the country. There is a modest and rather dilapidated tower (the **Tortoise Tower**) commemorating the event on an islet in the southern part of the lake. In fact, the lake does contain large turtles, believed to be a variety of Asian soft-shell tortoise; one captured in 1968 was reputed to have weighed 250 kg.

Located on a small island on the lake, the **Ngoc Son Temple** ① *daily 0730-1800, 3000d*, was constructed in the early 19th century on the foundations of the old Khanh Thuy Palace, which had been built in 1739. The temple is dedicated to Van Xuong, the God of Literature, although the 13th-century hero Tran Hung Dao, the martial arts genius Quan Vu and the physician La To are also worshipped here. The island is linked to the shore by a red, arched wooden bridge, **The Huc (Sunbeam) Bridge**, constructed in 1875.

The park that surrounds the shore is used by the residents of the city every morning for jogging and t'ai chi (Chinese shadow boxing) and is regarded by locals as one of the city's beauty spots.

Old Quarter and 36 Streets

Stretching north from the lake is the Old Quarter (36 Streets and Guilds or 36 Pho Phuong), the most beautiful area of the city. The narrow streets are each named after the products that are (or were) sold there (**Basket Street**, **Paper Street**, **Silk Street**, etc) and create an intricate web of activity and colour. By the 15th century there were 36 short lanes here, each specializing in a particular trade and representing one of the 36 guilds. Among them were the **Phuong Hang Dao** (Dyers' Guild Street), and the **Phuong Hang Bac** (Silversmiths' Street). Some of the area's past is still in evidence: at the south end of **Hang Dau Street**,

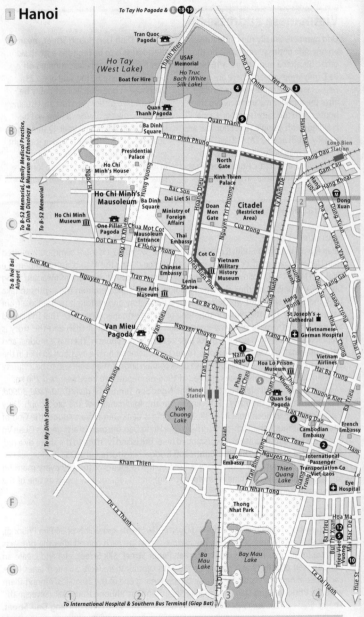

1 Hanoi

To Tay Ho Pagoda & 8 18 19

A

Tran Quoc
Pagoda

Ho Tay
(West Lake)

USAF
Memorial

Ho Truc
Bach (White
Silk Lake)

Boat for Hire

Thanh Nien

Pho Duc Chinh

Yen Phu

4

3

Quan
Thanh Pagoda

Quan Thanh

9

B

Ba Dinh
Square

Phan Dinh Phung

Hang Than

Long Bien
Station

Presidential
Palace

Hang Dau Station

Gam Cau

Ho Chi
Minh's House

Hung Vuong

North
Gate

Kinh Thien
Palace

Hang Khoai

Dong Xuan

M

Luong Van Can

Bac Son

Dai Liet Si

Citadel
(Restricted
Area)

Ly Nam De

Cha Ca

Ba Dinh
Square

Doan
Mon Gate

Ministry of
Foreign
Affairs

Ho Chi Minh
Mausoleum

To B-52 Memorial, Family Medical Practice,
Ba Dinh District & Museum of Ethnology

Ngoc Ha

Ong Ich Khiem

To B-52 Memorial

C

Ho Chi Minh
Museum

One Pillar
Pagoda

Chua Mot Cot
Mausoleum
Entrance

Doi Can

Le Hong Phong

Thai
Embassy

Cua Dong

Nguyen Tri Phuong

Cot Co

Vietnam Military
History Museum

Hang Gai

Hang Bong

Duong Thanh

Ly Quoc Su

Chinese
Embassy

Lenin
Statue

Dien Bien Phu

D

To & Noi Bai
Airport

Kim Ma

Nguyen Thai Hoc

Tran Phu

Fine Arts
Museum

Cao Ba Quat

Cat Linh

Van Mieu
Pagoda

11

Nguyen Khuyen

Van Mieu

St Joseph's
Cathedral

Vietnamese-
German Hospital

Tran Thi

Nha Chung

Ly Thai To

Dinh Tien

Quoc Tu Giam

Ton Duc Thang

13

Nam
Ngu

Hoa Lo Prison
Museum

Vietnam
Airlines

E

To My Dinh Station

Le Duan

Tran Quy Cap

Phan Boi Chau

5

Quan Su

Khol Thien

Quan Su
Pagoda

6

Hai Ba Trung

Ly Thuong Kiet

Hanoi
Station

Van
Chuong
Lake

Tran Hung Dao

Cambodian
Embassy

2

French
Embassy

Ham

Tran Quoc Toan

Le Duan

Nguyen Du

Lao
Embassy

International
Passenger
Transportation Co
Viet-Laos

Le

Kham Thien

Tran Binh Trong

Thien
Quang
Lake

Quang Trung

Eye
Hospital

De La Thanh

Tran Nhan Tong

F

Thong
Nhat Park

Hoa Ma

Ba Trieu

Bui Thi Xuan

Trieu Viet Vuong

Mai Hac De

12

10

Hue St

G

Ba
Mau
Lake

Bay Mau
Lake

Le Dai Hanh

1   2   3   4

To International Hospital & Southern Bus Terminal (Giap Bat)

72 · Vietnam Hanoi & around

→ **Hanoi maps**
1 Hanoi, page 72
2 Hoan Kiem, page 74

N

| 400 metres |
| 400 yards |

Sleeping 🛏
De Syloia & Cay
 Cau Restaurant **2** *F5*
Hoa Linh **7** *E5*
InterContinental Hanoi
 Westlake **8** *A2*
Movenpick **5** *E3*

Eating 🍴
Café 129 **10** *D3*
Chim Sáo **12** *F4*
Cong Café **5** *F4*
Duy Tri **3** *B4*
Hanoi Cooking Centre **4** *B3*
Kitchen **19** *A3*
KOTO **11** *D2*
La Badiane **1** *D3*
Le Cooperative **18** *A3*
Pho Yen **9** *B3*
Quan An Ngon **13** *D3*
Song Thu **6** *E4*
Verticale **2** *E4*

Bars & clubs 🍸
Tadiato **23** *F5*

for example, is a mass of stalls selling nothing but shoes, while Tin Street is still home to a community of pot and pan menders (and sellers). Generally, however, the crafts and trades have given way to new activities – karaoke bars and tourist shops – but it is remarkable the extent to which the streets still specialize in the production and sale of just one type of merchandise.

The dwellings in this area are known as *nha ong* (**tube houses**); they have narrow shop fronts, sometimes only 3 m wide, but can stretch back from the road for up to 50 m. In the countryside the dimensions of houses were calculated on the basis of the owner's own physical dimensions; in urban areas the tube houses evolved so that each house

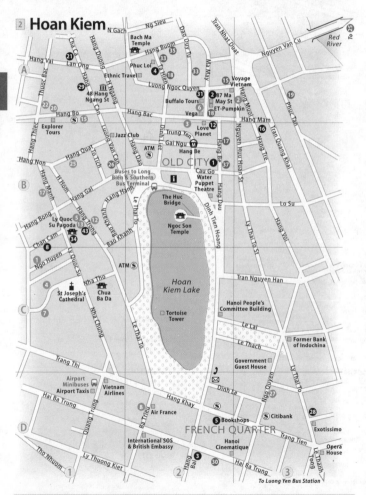

2 Hoan Kiem

could have an, albeit very small, area of shop frontage facing onto the main street, its width determined by the social class of the owner. The houses tend to be interspersed by courtyards or 'wells' to permit light into the house and allow some space for outside activities like washing and gardening. The structures were built of bricks 'cemented' together with sugar-cane juice. The older houses tend to be lower; commoners were not permitted to build higher than the Emperor's own residence. Other regulations prohibited attic windows looking down on the street; this was to prevent assassination and to stop people from looking down on a passing king. As far as colour and decoration were concerned, purple and gold were strictly for royal use only, as was the decorative use of the dragon.

By the early 20th century, traditional tube houses were being replaced with buildings inspired by French architecture. Many fine buildings from this era remain and are best appreciated by standing back and looking upwards. Shutters, cornices, columns and wrought-iron balconies and balustrades are common decorative features. An ornate façade sometimes conceals a pitched roof behind. There are some good examples on **Nguyen Sieu Street**. On Ma May Street, the shophouse at **No 87** ① *daily 0800-1200, 1300-1700, 5000d, guide included*, is a wonderfully preserved example of an original Hanoi building.

N

200 metres
200 yards

Sleeping 🛏
Cinnamon **4** *C1*
Freedom **12** *B1*
Gold Spring **2** *A3*
Golden Lotus **5** *B1*
Hang Trong **13** *B1*
Hanoi Backpackers'
  Hostel **1** *C1*
Hoa Linh **15** *A1*
Hong Ngoc **17** *B1*
Hong Ngoc 2 **6** *A2*
Hong Ngoc 3 **3** *B2*
Joseph's **7** *C1*
My Lan **20** *A1*
Ngoc Diep **22** *A1*
Real Darling Café **25** *B1*
Sofitel Legend Metropole
  Hanoi & Le Beaulieu
  Restaurant **27** *D3*
Zephyr **8** *D2*

Eating 🍴
69 **2** *A2*
Al Fresco's **3** *D2*
Café Puku **43** *B1*
Cha Ca La Vong **21** *A1*

Chica **4** *A2*
Green Tangerine **1** *B2*
Hanoi Press Club **28** *D3*
Highway 4 **16** *B3*
Kem Trang Tien **5** *D2*
Lá **34** *B1*
Madame Hiem **8** *B1*
My Burger My **12** *B2*
Restaurant 22 **29** *A1*
Tamarind & Handspan
  Adventure Travel **31** *A2*

Bars & clubs 🍷
Cheeky Quarter Tet **33** *A2*
Dragonfly **35** *A2*
Funky Buddha **37** *B2*
Jo Jo's **30** *D2*
Half Man/Half Noodle **15** *A2*
Le Pub **17** *B2*
Mao's Red Lounge **18** *A2*
Phuc Tan **19** *A3*
Roots **18** *A2*
Solace **25** *A3*
Rock Billy **26** *B1*

Further north is the large and varied **Dong Xuan Market**, on Dong Xuan Street. This covered market was destroyed in a fire in 1994. It has since been rebuilt and now specializes in clothes and household goods.

To the west, along Phung Hung Street is another live market selling fish, dog, birds, vegetables and betel nut. It makes for a wonderful wander.

St Joseph's Cathedral

To the west of Hoan Kiem Lake, in a little square stands the twin-towered neo-Gothic **Saint Joseph's Cathedral** ① *Open 0500-1130*. Built in 1886, the cathedral is important as one of the very first colonial-era buildings in Hanoi finished, as it was, soon after the Treaty of Tientsin, which gave France control over Vietnam. Some fine stained-glass windows remain.

Opera House

① *Not open to the public except during public performances. See the billboards outside or visit the box office for details.*

To the south and east of Hoan Kiem Lake is the proud-looking French-era Opera House. It was built between 1901 and 1911 by François Lagisquet and is one of the finest French colonial buildings in Hanoi. Some 35,000 bamboo piles were sunk into the mud of the Red River to provide foundations for the lofty edifice. The exterior is a mass of shutters, wrought-iron work, little balconies and a tiled frieze. The top balustrade is capped with griffins. Inside, there are dozens of little boxes and fine decoration evocative of the French era. Having suffered years of neglect, the Opera House was eventually lavishly restored, opening in time for the Francophone Summit held in 1997. The restoration cost US$14 million, a colossal sum to spend on the reappointment of a colonial edifice.

Other interesting French Quarter buildings include the **Sofitel Metropole** and **Government Guesthouse** on Ngo Quyen Street. **Hanoi University** is at 19 Le Thanh Tong Street.

Museum of Vietnamese History
① *1 Trang Tien St, Tue-Sun 0800-1130, 1330-1630, 15,000d.*

The history museum (**Bao Tang Lich Su**) is housed in a splendid building, completed in 1931. It was built as the home of the École Française d'Extrême-Orient, a distinguished archaeological, historical and ethnological research institute, by Ernest Hébrard. The collection spans Vietnamese history from the Neolithic period to the 20th century of Ho Chi Minh and is arranged in chronological order.

Galleries on the first floor lead from the Neolithic (Bac Son) represented by stone tools and jewellery to the Bronze Age (Dong Son) with some finely engraved ceremonial bronze drums, symbolizing wealth and power. Wooden stakes that were used to impale invading Chinese forces in 1288 were found in 1976 at the cross of the Chanh River and Bach Dang River – a photo of some remaining in the river bed is interesting and a giant oil painting depicting the famous battle is hypnotically fascinating. The giant turtle, a symbol of longevity, supports a vast stela which praises the achievements of Le Loi (reigned 1428-1433), founder of the Le Dynasty who harnessed nationalist sentiment and repelled the war-hungry Chinese. A replica of the oldest Buddha Amitabha statue dominates the far end of the first floor. Amitabha is the Buddha of Infinite Light and the original dates from 1057 and was from Phat Tich Pagoda in Bac Ninh Province. Opposite the statue the oldest minted coins in Vietnam are displayed. They date from AD 968 and were minted by the Dinh Dynasty. A collection of outsized paper currency from the French colonial days is also interesting. These date from 1875 when the French established the Bank of Indochina. The second floor begins with the 15th century to the present day. Champa is represented by some well-preserved stone carvings of apsaras, mythical dancing girls and a head of Garuda, found at Quang Nam. There are relics such as 18th-century, unusually shaped, bronze pagoda gongs and urns of successive royal dynasties from Le to Nguyen. Unfortunately, some of the pieces are reproductions, including a number of the stelae.

Hoa Lo Prison
① *1 Hoa Lo, Tue-Sun 0800-1130, 1330-1630, 10,000d.*

Hoa Lo Prison (Maison Centrale), better known as the **Hanoi Hilton**, is the prison where US POWs were incarcerated during the Vietnamese War. Up until 1969, prisoners were also tortured here. Two US Air Force officers, Charles Tanner and Ross Terry, rather than face torture, concocted a story about two other members of their squadron who had been court-martialled for refusing to fly missions against the north. Thrilled with this piece of propaganda, visiting Japanese Communists were told the story and it filtered back to the US. Unfortunately for Tanner and Terry, they had called their imaginary pilots Clark Kent and Ben

Casey (both TV heroes). When the Vietnamese realized they had been made fools of, the two prisoners were again tortured. The final prisoners of war were not released until 1973, some having been held in the north since 1964. At the end of 1992, a US mission was shown around the prison where 2000 inmates had been housed in squalid conditions.

Despite pleas from war veterans and party members, the site was sold to a Singapore-Vietnamese joint venture and is now a hotel and shopping complex, **Hanoi Towers**. As part of the deal the developers had to leave a portion of the prison for use as a museum. There are recreations of conditions under colonial rule when the French incarcerated patriotic Vietnamese from 1896: by 1953 they were holding 2000 prisoners in a space designed for 500. Less prominence is given to the role of the prison for holding American pilots, but Douglas 'Pete' Peterson, the first post-war American Ambassador to Vietnam (1997-2001), who was one such occupant (imprisoned 1966-1973), has his mug-shot on the wall, as does John McCain (imprisoned 1967-1973), a US presidential candidate in the 2008 elections.

West from the Citadel

Vietnam Military History Museum
ⓘ *28 Dien Bien Phu St, T04-3733 6453, Tue-Thu, Sat and Sun 0800-1130, 1300-1630, 20000d, camera use, 5000d. ATM and Highlands Coffee Café on site.*
Tanks, planes and artillery fill the courtyard of the Army Museum (Bao Tang Quan Doi). Symbolically, an untouched Mig-21 stands at the museum entrance while wreckage of B-52s, F1-11s and Q2Cs is piled up at the back. The museum illustrates battles and episodes in Vietnam's fight for independence, from the struggles with China through to the resistance to the French and the Battle of Dien Bien Phu (illustrated by a good model). Inevitably, of course, there are lots of photographs and exhibits of the American war and, although much is self-evident, a lot of the explanations are in Vietnamese only.

In the precincts of the museum is the **Cot Co**, a flag tower, raised up on three platforms. Built in 1812, it is the only substantial part of the original **citadel** still standing. There are good views over Hanoi from the top. The walls of the citadel were destroyed by the French between 1894 and 1897, presumably as they symbolized the power of the Vietnamese emperors. The French were highly conscious of the projection of might, power and authority through large structures, which helps explain their own remarkable architectural legacy. Other remaining parts of the citadel are in the hands of the Vietnamese army and out of bounds to visitors. Across the road from the museum's front entrance is a **statue of Lenin**.

Ho Chi Minh's Mausoleum and Ba Dinh Square
ⓘ *Summer Tue-Thu, Sat and Sun 0730-1100, Winter Tue-Thu, Sat and Sun 0800-1100, closed 6 weeks from Sep. Before entering the mausoleum, visitors must leave possessions at the office (Ban To Chuc) on Huong Vuong, just south of and a few minutes' walk from the Mausoleum. Visitors must be respectful: dress neatly, walk solemnly, do not talk and do not take anything in that could be construed as a weapon, for example a penknife. Ba Dinh Square is a public space with no opening hour restrictions.*
The Vietnamese have made the mausoleum housing Ho Chi Minh's body a holy place of pilgrimage and visitors march in file to see Ho's embalmed corpse inside the mausoleum (Lang Chu Tich Ho Chi Minh). The embalming and eternal display of Ho Chi Minh's body was contrary to Ho's own wishes: he wanted to be cremated and his ashes placed in

three urns to be positioned atop three unmarked hills in the north, centre and south of the country. He once wrote that "cremation is not only good from the point of view of hygiene, but it also saves farmland". The embalming of Ho's body was undertaken by the chief Soviet embalmer, Dr Sergei Debrov, who also pickled such Communist luminaries as Klenient Gottwald (President of Czechoslovakia), Georgi Dimitrov (Prime Minister of Bulgaria) and Forbes Burnham (President of Guyana). Debrov was flown to Hanoi from Moscow as Ho lay dying, bringing with him two transport planes packed with air conditioners (to keep the corpse cool) and other equipment. To escape US bombing, the team moved Ho to a cave, taking a full year to complete the embalming process. Russian scientists still check-up on their handiwork, servicing Ho's body regularly. Their embalming methods and the fluids they use are still a closely guarded secret. In an interview, Debrov noted with pleasure the poor state of China's Chairman Mao's body, which was embalmed without Soviet help.

The mausoleum, built between 1973 and 1975, is a massive, square and forbidding structure and must be among the best constructed, maintained and air-conditioned buildings in Vietnam. Opened in 1975, it is modelled closely on Lenin's Mausoleum in Moscow. Ho lies with a guard at each corner of his bier and visitors march past in file to see his body.

In front of Ho Chi Minh's Mausoleum is Ba Dinh Square where Ho read out the Vietnamese Declaration of Independence on 2 September 1945. Following Ho's declaration, 2 September became Vietnam's National Day. Coincidentally, 2 September was also the date on which Ho died in 1969, although his death was not officially announced until 3 September in order not to mar people's enjoyment of National Day in the beleaguered north of the country.

Ho Chi Minh's house and the Presidential Palace

ⓘ *1 Bach Thao St, T04-3804 4529, summer Tue-Thu, Sat and Sun 0730-1100, 1400-1600, Fri 0730-1100, winter Tue-Thu, Sat and Sun 0800-1100, 1330-1600, Fri 0800-1100, 15000d. The Presidential Palace is not open to the public.*

From the mausoleum, visitors are directed across Ba Dinh Square to **Ho Chi Minh's house** built in the compound of the former **Presidential Palace**. The palace, now a party guesthouse, was the residence of the Governors-General of French Indochina and was built between 1900 and 1908. In 1954, when North Vietnam's struggle for independence was finally achieved, Ho Chi Minh declined to live in the palace, saying that it belonged to the people. Instead, he stayed in what is said to have been an electrician's house in the same compound. He lived here from 1954 to 1958, before moving to a new stilt house built on the other side of the small lake (Ho Chi Minh's 'Fish Farm', swarming with massive and well-fed carp). The house was designed by Ho and an architect, Nguyen Van Ninh. This modest house made of rare hardwoods is airy and personal and immaculately kept. Ho conducted meetings under the house, which is raised up on wooden pillars, and slept and worked above from May 1958 to August 1969. Behind the house is Ho's bomb shelter and, behind that, the hut where he died in 1969.

One Pillar Pagoda and Ho Chi Minh Museum

Close by is the **Chua Mot Cot** (One Pillar Pagoda), one of the few structures remaining from the original foundation of the city. It was built in 1049 by Emperor Ly Thai Tong, although the shrine has since been rebuilt on several occasions, most recently in 1955 after the French destroyed it, before withdrawing from the country. The emperor built the pagoda in a fit of religious passion after he dreamt that he saw the goddess Quan Am (Vietnam's equivalent of the Chinese goddess Kuan-yin), sitting on a lotus and holding a young boy, whom she handed to the Emperor. On the advice of counsellors who interpreted the dream, the Emperor built a little lotus-shaped temple in the centre of a water-lily pond and shortly afterwards his queen gave birth to a son. As the name suggests, it is supported on a single (concrete) pillar with a brick and stone staircase running up one side. The pagoda symbolizes the 'pure' lotus sprouting from the sea of sorrow. Original in design, with dragons running along the apex of the elegantly- curved tiled roof, the temple is one of the most revered monuments in Vietnam.

Overshadowing the One Pillar Pagoda is the **Ho Chi Minh Museum** ① *19 Ngoc Ha St, T04-3846 3752, Tue-Thu and Sat 0800-1130, 1400-1600, Fri 0800-1130, 10,000d, 40,000d for guide,* opened in 1990 in celebration of the centenary of Ho's birth. Contained in a large and impressive modern building, it is the best arranged and most innovative museum in Vietnam. The displays trace Ho's life and work from his early wanderings around the world to his death and final victory over the south.

Temple of Literature
① *Entrance on Quoc Tu Giam St, T04-3845 2917, open daily summer 0730-1730, winter daily 0730-1700, 5000d, 45-min tour in French or English 50,000d, 3000d for brochure. ATM inside.*

The temple of literature (Van Mieu Pagoda) is the largest and, probably, the most important, temple complex in Hanoi. It was founded in 1070 by Emperor Ly Thanh Tong, dedicated to Confucius who had a substantial following in Vietnam, and modelled, so it is said, on a temple in Shantung, China, the birthplace of the sage. Some researchers while acknowledging the date of the foundation, challenge the view that it was built as a Confucian institution pointing to the ascendancy of Buddhism during the Ly Dynasty. Confucian principles and teaching rapidly replaced Buddhism, however and Van Mieu subsequently became the intellectual and spiritual centre of the kingdom as a cult of literature and education spread amongst the court, the mandarins and then among the common people. At one time there were said to be 20,000 schools teaching the Confucian classics in northern Vietnam alone.

The temple and its compound are arranged north-south; visitors enter at the southern end from Quoc Tu Giam Street. On the pavement two pavilions house stelae bearing the inscription *ha ma* (climb down from your horse), a nice reminder that even the most elevated dignitaries had to proceed on foot. The main **Cong Van Mieu Mon** (Van Mieu Gate) is adorned with 15th-century dragons. Traditionally, the large central gate was opened only on ceremonial occasions. The path leads through the Cong Dai Trung to a second courtyard and the **Van Khue Gac Pavilion**, which was built in 1805 and dedicated to the Constellation of Literature. The roof is tiled according to the yin-yang principle.

Beyond lies the **Courtyard of the Stelae** at the centre of which is the rectangular pond or Cieng Thien Quang (**Well of Heavenly Clarity**). More important are the stelae themselves, on which are recorded the names of 1306 successful examination scholars (*tien si*). Of the 82 stelae that survive (30 are missing), the oldest dates back to 1442 and the most recent to 1779. Each stela is carried on the back of a tortoise, symbol of strength and longevity. The stelae are arranged in no order but three chronological categories can be identified. Fourteen date from the 15th and 16th centuries; they are the smallest and embellished with floral motifs and yin-yang symbols but not dragons (a royal emblem). Twenty-five stelae are from the 17th century and ornamented with dragons (by now permitted), pairs of phoenix and other creatures mythical or real. The remaining 43 stelae are of 18th-century origin; they are the largest and decorated with two stylized dragons, some merging with flame clouds.

Passing the examination was not easy: in 1733, out of some 3000 entrants only eight passed the doctoral examination (*Thai Hoc Sinh*) and became Mandarins, a task that took 35 days. This tradition was begun in 1484, on the instruction of Emperor Le Thanh Tong, and continued through to 1878, during which time 116 examinations were held. The Temple of Literature was not used only for examinations, however: food was also distributed from here to the poor and infirm, 500 g of rice at a time. In 1880, the French Consul Monsieur de Kergaradec recorded that 22,000 impoverished people came to receive this meagre handout.

Continuing north, the **Dai Thanh Mon** (Great Success Gate) leads on to a courtyard flanked by two buildings which date from 1954, the originals having been destroyed in 1947. These buildings were reserved for 72 disciples of Confucius. Facing is the **Dai Bai Duong** (Great House of Ceremonies) which was built in the 19th century but in the earlier style of the Le Dynasty. The carved wooden friezes with their dragons, phoenix, lotus flowers, fruits, clouds and yin-yang discs are all symbolically charged, depicting the order of the universe and by implication reflecting the god-given hierarchical nature of human society, each in his place. It is not surprising that the Communist government has hitherto had reservations about preserving a temple extolling such heretical doctrine. Inside is an altar on which sit statues of Confucius and his closest disciples. Adjoining is the **Dai Thanh Sanctuary** (Great Success Sanctuary), which also contains a statue of Confucius.

Vietnam Museum of Ethnology
ⓘ *Nguyen Van Huyen Rd, some distance west of the city centre in Cau Giay District, T04-3756 2193, www.vme.org.vn, Tue-Sun 0830-1730, 25,000d, photography 50,000d, tour guide 50,000d. Take a taxi or catch the No 14 minibus from Dinh Tien Hoang St, north of Hoan Kiem Lake, to the Nghia Tan stop, turn right and walk down Hoang Quoc Viet St for 1 block, before turning right at the Petrolimex station down Nguyen Van Huyen, the museum is on the left.*

The collection here of some 25,000 artefacts, 15,000 photographs and documentaries of practices and rituals is excellent and, more to the point, is attractively and informatively presented with labels in Vietnamese, English and French. It displays the material culture (textiles, musical instruments, jewellery, tools, baskets and the like) of the majority Kinh people as well as Vietnam's 53 other designated minority peoples. While much is historical, the museum is also attempting to build up its contemporary collection. There is a shop attached to the museum and ethnic minorities' homes have been recreated in the grounds.

Ho Truc Bach and Ho Tay
North of the Old City is **Ho Truc Bach** (White Silk Lake). Truc Bach Lake was created in the 17th century by building a causeway across the southeast corner of Ho Tay. Ho Tay (West Lake) which is much larger **Ho Tay** (West Lake) was originally a meander in the Red River. Around these lakes are a growing number of restaurants, bars and hotels.

There are a number of worthwhile day and overnight trips from Hanoi: the Perfume Pagoda lies to the southwest; Tam Coc and Cuc Phuong National Park are some three hours south, while Halong Bay, best visited on an overnight trip, is three hours to the east.

Perfume Pagoda→ *Colour map 2, B4.*
ⓘ *30,000d entrance plus 210,000d for the boat (maximum 4 people). Taking a tour is the best way to get here.*

The Perfume Pagoda (Chua Huong or Chua Huong Tich) is 60 km southwest of Hanoi. A sampan takes visitors along the Yen River, a diverting 4-km ride through a flooded landscape to the Mountain of the Perfume Traces. From here it is a 3-km hike up the mountain to the cool, dark cave where the Perfume Pagoda is located. The stone statue of Quan Am in the principal pagoda was carved in 1793 after Tay Son rebels had stolen and melted down its bronze predecessor to make cannon balls. Dedicated to Quan Am, it is one of a number of shrines and towers built amongst limestone caves and is regarded as one of the most beautiful spots in Vietnam. Emperor Le Thanh Tong (1460-1497) described it as *"Nam Thien de nhat dong"* or "foremost cave under the Vietnamese sky". It is a popular pilgrimage spot, particularly during the festival months of March and April.

Tam Coc → *Colour map 2, B4.*
ⓘ *The turning to Tam Coc is 4 km south of Ninh Binh on Highway 1. 60,000 (one to two people) for the boat, 30,000d for the grottoes. It can easily be reached from Hanoi on a day trip, either as part of an organized tour or by hiring a car and driver. Take plenty of sun cream and a hat.*

An area of enchanting natural beauty, Tam Coc means literally 'three caves'. Those who have seen the film *Indochine*, some of which was shot here, will be familiar with the nature of the beehive-type scenery created by limestone towers, similar to those of Halong Bay. The highlight of this excursion is an enchanting boat ride up the little Ngo Dong River through the eponymous three caves. The exact form varies from wet to dry season; when flooded, the channel disappears and one or two of the caves may be drowned; in the dry season, the shallow river meanders between fields of golden rice. Women punt pitch-and-resin tubs that look like elongated coracles through the tunnels. It is a leisurely experience and a chance to observe at close quarters the extraordinary method of rowing with the feet. The villagers have a rota to decide whose turn it is to row and, to supplement their fee, will try and sell visitors embroidered tablecloths. Enterprising photographers snap you setting off from the bank and will surprise you 1 km upstream with copies of your cheesy grin already printed. On a busy day the scene from above is like a two-way, nose-to-tail procession of water boatmen, so to enjoy Tam Coc at its best, visit in the morning.

Cuc Phuong National Park → *Colour map 2, B4.*
ⓘ *Nho Quan district, 120 km south of Hanoi and 45 km west of Ninh Binh, T030-384 8006, www. cucphuongtourism.com, 40,000d. Can be visited as a day trip from Hanoi, either on an organized tour (a sensible option for lone travellers or pairs) or by hiring a car with a driver or a motorbike.*

Located in an area of deeply cut limestone and reaching elevations of up to 800 m, this park is covered by 22,000 ha of humid tropical montagne forest. It is home to an estimated 2000 species of flora, including the giant parashorea, cinamomum and sandoricum trees. Wildlife, however, has been much depleted by hunting, so that only 117 mammal, 307 bird species and 110 species of reptile and amphibian are thought to remain. April and May sees fat grubs and pupae metamorphosing into swarms of beautiful butterflies that mantle the forest in fantastic shades of greens and yellows. The government has resettled a number of the park's 30,000 Muong minority people but Muong villages do still exist and can be visited. The **Endangered Primate Rescue Centre** ① *www.primatecenter.org, daily 0900-1100, 1330-1600, limited entrance every 30 mins, 10,000d*, is a big draw in the park, with more than 30 cages, four houses and two semi-wild enclosures for the 130 animals in breeding programmes.

Halong Bay → *Colour map 2, B5.*

① *Most boats depart from Halong City, 110 km east of Hanoi. Quang Ninh Tourism opposite the Halong 1 Hotel and near the Novotel, T033-362 8862, www.halongtourism.com.vn, is super helpful. 30,000d admission for each cave and attraction. You need 4-5 hrs to see the bay properly but an overnight stay aboard a boat is enjoyable. The majority of people visit on an all-inclusive tour with tourist cafés or tour operators from Hanoi (see page 90). It can be stormy in Jun-Aug; Jul and Aug are also the wettest months, winter is cool and dry, rain is possible at all times of year.*

Halong means 'descending dragon'. An enormous beast is said to have careered into the sea at this point, cutting the fantastic bay from the rocks as it thrashed its way into the depths. Vietnamese poets, including the 'Poet King' Le Thanh Tong, have traditionally extolled the beauty of this romantic area, with its rugged islands that protrude from a sea dotted with sailing junks. Artists, too, have drawn inspiration from the crooked islands, seeing the forms of monks and gods in the rock faces, and dragon's lairs and fairy lakes in the depths of the caves. Another myth says that the islands are dragons sent by the gods to impede the progress of an invasion flotilla. The area was the location of two famous sea battles in the 10th and 13th centuries and is now a UNESCO World Heritage Site.

Geologically, the tower-karst scenery of Halong Bay is the product of millions of years of chemical action and river erosion working on the limestone to produce a pitted landscape. At the end of the last ice age, when the glaciers melted, the sea level rose and inundated the area turning hills into islands. The islands of the bay are divided by a broad channel: to the east are the smaller outcrops of Bai Tu Long, while to the west are the larger islands with caves and secluded beaches. Rocks can be treacherously slippery, so sensible footwear is advised. Many of the caves are a disappointment, with harrying vendors, mounds of litter and disfiguring graffiti. Among the more spectacular, however, are **Hang Hanh**, which extends for 2 km. Tour guides will point out fantastic stalagmites and stalactites which, with imagination, become heroes, demons and animals. **Hang Luon** is another flooded cave, which leads to the hollow core of a doughnut-shaped island. It can be swum or navigated by coracle. **Hang Dau Go** is the cave in which Tran Hung Dao stored his wooden stakes prior to studding them in the bed of the Bach Dang River in 1288 to destroy the boats of invading Mongol hordes. **Hang Thien Cung** is a hanging cave, a short 50-m haul above sea level, with dripping stalactites, stumpy stalagmites and solid rock pillars.

Cat Ba → *Colour map 2, B5.*

Cat Ba is the largest island in a coastal archipelago that includes more than 350 limestone outcrops. It is adjacent to and geologically similar to the islands and peaks of Halong Bay but separated by a broad channel. The islands around Cat Ba are larger than the outcrops of Halong Bay and generally more dramatic. Cat Ba is the ideal place from which to explore the whole coastal area. Outside Cat Ba town there are only a few small villages. Perhaps the greatest pleasure is to hire a motorbike and explore, a simple enough process given the island's limited road network. Half of the island forms part of a national park and the interior scenery is stunning; there are also some beautiful beaches near Cat Ba Town.

Hotel and guesthouse prices

LL over US$200	**L** US$151-200	**AL** US$101-150
A US$66-100	**B** US$46-65	**C** US$31-45
D US$21-30	**E** US$12-20	**F** US$7-11
G US$6 and under		

Restaurant prices

🍴🍴🍴 over US$12   🍴🍴 US$6-12   🍴 under US$6

⊜ Sleeping

Central Hanoi *p71, maps p72 and p74*

LL InterContinental Hanoi Westlake, 1A Nghi Tam, Tay Ho District, T04-3829 3939, www.intercontinental.com. One of the newer 5-star hotels in the city, the **InterContinental** sits on West Lake, almost beside the **Sheraton**. Rooms are large and decorated using traditional Vietnamese elements. The bar and pool areas facing the lake are lovely, especially in early evening when *den choi* (fire-powered paper balloons) drift across the sky above the water. Cocktails are good but prices are international standard.

LL-L Sofitel Legend Metropole Hanoi, 15 Ngo Quyen St, T04-3826 6919, www.accorhotels-asia.com. The French-colonial-style cream building with green shutters is beautifully and lusciously furnished and exudes style. The historic **Metropole** wing contains the original rooms while the new wing is named the **Opera**. It boasts a diversity of bars and restaurants. **Le Beaulieu** is one of the finest restaurants in Hanoi. A small pool is boosted by the attractive poolside **Bamboo Bar**. The new **Le Spa du Metropole** is seriously chic.

LL-AL Movenpick, 83A Ly Thuong Kiet St, T4-38222800, www.moevenpick-hotels.com. Formerly the **Guoman**, this Swiss-run hotel chain is housed in an attractive building on Ly Thuong Kiet street, in the middle of Hanoi's business district. Rooms are smart and stylish.

L-AL De Syloia, 17A Tran Hung Dao St, T04-3824 5346, www.desyloia.com. An attractive and friendly small boutique, business hotel south of the lake. 33 rooms and suites, a business centre and gym in good central location. The popular **Cay Cau** restaurant specializes in Vietnamese dishes and the daily set lunch is excellent value.

AL Zephyr, 4 Ba Trieu St, T04-3934 1256, www.zephyrhotel.com.vn. Popular among business travellers, **Zephyr** is under a minute's walk to the lake and sits at the end of Ba Trieu street, which heads south to the city's interesting Hai Ba Trung district, home to Hanoi's only international standard cinema. There is a café and restaurant downstairs. Special deals are offered in the low season.

B Gold Spring Hotel, 22 Nguyen Huu Huan St, T04-3926 3057, www.goldspring hotel. com.vn. On the edge of the Old Quarter. 22 fine rooms that are attractively decorated. Breakfast and free internet included.

B Hong Ngoc, 30-34 Hang Manh St, T04-3828 5053, www.hongngochotel.com. A real find. A small, family-run hotel, with comfy rooms and huge bathrooms with baths. Spotlessly clean and run by cheerful and helpful staff. Breakfast included. There are 2 others in the Old Quarter: **Hong Ngoc 2**, 99 Ma May St, T04-3828 3631, www.hongngoc hotel.com, and **Hong Ngoc 3** (see below).

B Joseph's Hotel, 5 Au Trieu St, T04-3938 1048, www.josephshotel.com. Right near St Joseph's Cathedral, on Au Trieu street – a cosy street filled with good cafés, salons and souvenir shops – **Joseph's Hotel** is small, with just 10 rooms. However, small can equal cosy, and it certainly does here. This mid-range hotel has Wi-Fi in all rooms, as well as standards such as a/c, cable TV and minibar. Breakfast is included.

C-D Hong Ngoc 3, 39 Hang Bac St, T04-3926 0322, www.hongngochotel.com. Some staff are exceptionally helpful, others are not. Rooms are clean and comfy with TVs, a/c and baths. It's in a great central location and quiet. You may want to pass on breakfast.

D Freedom, 57 Hang Trong St, T04-3826 7119, freedomhotel@hn.vnn.vn. Not far from Hoan Kiem lake and cathedral. 11 spacious rooms with desks. Some have baths. Friendly. Breakfast is not included on the cheaper rate.

D Hang Trong, 56 Hang Trong St, T04-3825 1346, thiencotravelvn@yahoo.com. A/c and hot water, a few unusual and decent rooms set back from the road, either on a corridor or in a courtyard. The ones that don't overlook the courtyard are dark and airless. Convenient for every part of town. Internet and booking office for Sinh Café tours.

D-E Hoa Linh, 35 Hang Bo St, T04-3824 3887, hoalinhhotel@hn.vnn.vn. Right in the centre of the Old Quarter, this hotel has lovely bedrooms decked out in the dark wood of Hué imperial style. The larger, more expensive rooms have a double and a single bed and a balcony. It is worth paying extra for a view of the decoration on the crumbling buildings opposite. Bathrooms are basic with plastic showers and no curtains. Breakfast included.

D-F Hanoi Backpackers' Hostel, 48 Ngo Huyen St, T04-3828 5372, www.hanoiback packershostel.com. Dorm rooms and double suites in a house that belonged to the Brazilian ambassador. A friendly and busy place with plenty of opportunities to meet other travellers and gather advice. Breakfast, internet, tea and coffee, and luggage store is included. Don't miss the barbecues on the roof terrace and the sessions on Sun.

D-F Real Darling Café, 33 Hang Quat St, T04-3826 9386, darling_cafe@hotmail.com. Travellers' café that has 16 rooms, though only 10 have a/c. Food is available, excellent English is spoken and visas for both overseas and extensions for within Vietnam can be organized. Wi-Fi.

E-F My Lan, 70 Hang Bo St, T04-3824 5510, hotelmylan@yahoo.com. Go through the dentist's surgery where an elderly French-speaking doctor has 10 rooms to rent, a/c or fans. Rather tightly packed but light

and breezy; also 1 nice rooftop apartment with kitchen and terrace, US$400 a month. Recommended.

F Ngoc Diep, 83 Thuoc Bac St, through the Chinese pharmacy, T04-3825 0020, thugiangguesthouse@yahoo.com. Cheaper rooms all have fan; more expensive rooms a/c. All rooms have hot water and TV, and free internet; breakfast can be included. Bus station and railway station pick up. Popular and friendly, long-stay discounts available.

Cat Ba Town *p82*

L-A Catba Island Resort & Spa, Cat Co 1, T031-368 8686, www.catbaislandresort-spa.com. There are 109 pleasant rooms decorated with white rattan furniture across 3 buildings facing the bay with a lovely out look and fronting right on to the beach. The obtrusive water slides cannot be seen from the 2nd and 3rd building. 3 restaurants provide Western and Asian food and there are 2 pools, water slides, jacuzzi, massage, billiards and a tennis court. Trekking and Halong Bay tours are offered.

D Family (Quang Duc), just west of pier, T031-388 8231. The original 'Family' Hotel, a/c, hot water, 7 spotlessly clean rooms, views from most, a very well-run little hotel, owners are knowledgeable on local matters and helpful, newly renovated and now offers a range of water sports.

D-E Cat Tien Tourism Complex, Cat Co 1 and 2, T031-388 7988, giathanh@flamingovietnam.com. Cat Co 2 is more beautiful but Cat Co 1 is more easily accessible from town. There are 7 fan-cooled small bungalows and 2 large ones on Cat Co 2; camping (**F**) with your own tents is possible.

E Noble House, T031-388 8363. Overlooking the pier with 5 comfortable and well-appointed rooms. A/c and fridge, good views, more expensive rooms include breakfast. Popular bar and restaurant serving reasonably priced Vietnamese and Western dishes (avoid the tasteless pepperoni pizza). Tours are offered.

🍴 Eating

Hanoi has Western-style coffee bars, restaurants and watering holes that stand up well to comparison with their equivalents in Europe. It also has a good number of excellent Vietnamese restaurants.

Note Dog (*thit chó* or *thit cay*) is an esteemed delicacy in the north but is mostly served in shacks on the edge of town – so you are unlikely to order it inadvertently.

Central Hanoi *p71, maps p72 and p74*

††† Hanoi Press Club, 59A Ly Thai To St, T4-3934 0888, www.hanoi-pressclub.com. This is an odd building with some style inside directly behind the Sofitel Metropole Hotel; The Restaurant has remained consistently one of the most popular dining experiences in Hanoi. The dining room is luxuriously furnished with polished, dark wood floors and print-lined walls. The food is imaginative and superb and there's a fine wine list. Service has definitely slipped, though. **The Terrace**, a large outdoor space, hosts live music events and at the time of writing was still holding big parties popular with every hard networking local and expat in town the first Fri of each month. The **Library Bar** stocks a good range of cigars and whiskies.

††† Lá, 25 Ly Quoc Su St, T04-3928 8933. This attractive green and cream building houses a restaurant serving up marvellous Vietnamese and international food. Behind the modest exterior is one of the best-loved restaurants in the city. Chef Wayne Sjothun's menu offers traditional Vietnamese as well as a range of unpretentious fusion meals and daily specials. The bistro atmosphere is comfortable and the wine list excellent. The small bar is surprisingly well stocked.

††† Le Beaulieu, in the Metropole Hanoi, T04-3826 6919. A good French and international restaurant open for breakfast, lunch and dinner. Its Sun brunch buffet is regarded as one of the best in Asia. The buffet is good enough that even *Forbes* magazine waxed ecstatic over it. A great selection of French seafood, oysters, prawns, cold and roast meats and cheese.

†††-†† La Badiane, 10 Nam Ngu St, T04-3942 4509. A relative newcomer to Hanoi, from a couple of Hanoi old hands, La Badiane's French aesthetic stops at the food. Fusion, and of more than Vietnamese and French, is what this restaurant is about and while its intricately decorated plates of seasonal meals won't appeal to everyone there are many who swear this is the best restaurant in town. Service is good, if over attentive at times. Portions have increased but order a starter too if you're hungry. The converted colonial villa is delightful. The set lunch menu is a bargain at US$10.

†††-†† Verticale, 19 Ngo Van So St, T04-3944 6317, verticale@didiercorlou.com. Open 0900-1400 and 1700-2400. Didier Corlou, former chef at the Sofitel Metropole, opened this new restaurant in a small street in the French quarter. The tall, multi-storey building includes a spice shop, restaurant, private rooms and a terrace bar. The food and presentation are an adventurous culinary journey of gustatory delight; this is certainly one of the best dining experiences in the city.

†††-† Green Tangerine, 48 Hang Be St, T04-3825 1286, greentangerine@vnn. vn. This is a gorgeous French restaurant with a lovely spiral staircase, wafting fans, tasselled curtain cords and abundant glassware. It's a Hanoi stalwart in a lovely 1928 house serving fusion and Vietnamese food. Recommended dining areas are the courtyard and downstairs; upstairs can lack atmosphere. Many have decried the drop in quality but it remains popular with the tourist crowd. However, the set lunch is still excellent and extraordinarily good value. The cheese cake (not cheesecake) platter is intriguing and delicious.

†† Al Fresco's, 23L Hai Ba Trung St, T04-3826 7782. This is a popular Australian-run grill bar serving ribs, steak, pasta, pizza and fantastic salads. Portions are large and it's a very child-friendly place, with paper tablecloths and crayons on every table.

Luna d'Autonno, 78 Tho Nhuom St, T04-3823 7338. Regarded as one of the city's best Italian restaurants, Luna has a large menu of pizza, pasta and mains. Though it has recently moved to a far less prepossessing setting, the food, if not ambience, remains good.

Song Thu, 28A Ha Hoi St (off Tran Hung Dao St), T04-3942 4448, www.hoasuaschool. com. Daily 0700-2200. French training restaurant for disadvantaged youngsters, where visitors eat excellently prepared French and Vietnamese cuisine in an attractive and secluded courtyard setting. Reasonably cheap and popular. Cooking classes now available.

69 Restaurant Bar, 69 Ma May St, T04-3926 1720. Daily 0700-2300. The restaurant is up a steep flight of wooden stairs in a restored 19th-century house in the Old Quarter, with 2 tables on the tiny shuttered balcony. Plenty of Vietnamese and seafood dishes, including Hong Kong duck (chargrilled and stuffed with 5 spices, ginger, onion and garlic) and sunburnt beef: beef strips deep fried in 5 spice butter. Special mulled wine is offered on cold nights.

Chim Sáo, 65 Ngo Hué St, T04-3976 0633, www.chimsao.com. Set in an atmospheric old colonial villa, Chim Sao is famous for its speciality Northern Vietnamese food, cooked by a French chef. Seating is on the floor upstairs.

Highway 4, 3 Hang Tre St, T04-3926 4200. Open 0900-0200. There are other branches too. The original restaurant has moved next door. It specializes in ethnic minority dishes from North Vietnam (Highway 4 is the most northerly road in Vietnam running along the Chinese border and favoured by owners of Minsk motorbikes) but now includes a full menu of dishes from other provinces. The fruit and rice wines – available in many flavours – are the highlight of this place. There's plenty to eat and it's a great fun and memorable experience.

Café 129, 129 Mai Hac De St. Does excellent breakfast fry-ups and cheap but filling Mexican meals in what is still one of Hanoi's most basic settings. Despite serving a mostly western menu, Café 129 has never moved past its pho shop vibe of low tables and plastic stools. And its long-standing fan club wouldn't have it any other way.

Cha Ca La Vong, 14 Cha Ca St, T04-3825 3929. Open 1100-2100. Serves 1 dish only, the eponymous *cha ca Hanoi*, fried fish fillets in mild spice and herbs served with noodles. It's utterly delicious and popular with visitors and locals, although expensive at 1300,000d for the meal and the service is now complacent, slapdash and verging on the rude. They've definitely had too much of a good thing and treat the customers now with disdain rather than a warm welcome.

My Burger My, 5 Hang Bac St, T04-7309 0777. Though portions are small, American My Burger My serves US-style burgers with many toppings, on grilled buns in a small but comfortable shop in the Old Quarter. Those preferring gut-busters are advised to look elsewhere but for a snack it's worth the stop.

Quan An Ngon, 18 Phan Boi Chau St, T04-3942 8162, ngonhanoi@vnn.vn. Daily 0700-2130. This place is insanely popular at lunch and dinner time. In a massive open-air courtyard setting with enormous umbrellas shading wooden tables you can wander around looking at all the street stalls with signage in Vietnamese. The menu is in English and you order from a waitress. All the food is delicious and you'll be keen to return again to sample the huge array on display.

Tamarind, 80 Ma May St, T04-3926 0580, tamarind_café@yahoo.com. A vegetarian restaurant that goes beyond traditional 'veggie' fare. There is a comfortable café at the front and a smart restaurant behind in the **Handspan Adventure Travel** office. There's a lengthy vegetarian selection, delicious juices and the recommended Thai glass noodle salad.

West from the Citadel *p77, map p72*

⍦ KOTO, 59 Van Mieu St, T04-3747 0337, www.koto.com.au. Mon 0730-1800, Tue-Sun 0730-2230. A training restaurant for under-privileged young people. Next to the Temple of Literature, pop in for lunch after a morning's sightseeing. The food is international, filling and delicious. Upstairs is the **Temple Bar** with Wi-Fi. Recommended.

North of the Old City *p80, maps p72 and p74*

⍦⍦⍦-⍦⍦ Bobby Chinn, 77 Xuan Dieu, T04-3719 2640, www.bobbychinn.com. Bobby has been in Vietnam for many years having ventured out on his culinary career in HCMC. The restaurant is arguably one of Hanoi's most famous restaurants thanks to its TV star chef. Though now moved from its central Hoan Kiem Lake location, the food and decor remain the same: rich reds, comfortable tables and the same intricate fusion that made Bobby famous.

⍦⍦-⍦ Le Cooperative, 46 An Duong St, T04-3716 6401. A French-run restaurant and bar from the same people behind famous Vietnamese restaurant **Chim Sáo**. Le Cooperative has a compact but good French menu of classics and the best-value steak in the city. The cold cuts are recommended. The Vietnamese menu is large but receives mixed reviews. Upstairs is done up like an ethnic minority stilt house and there's also a selection of rice wines; some are even drinkable.

⍦⍦ Hanoi Cooking Centre, 44 Chau Long St, T04-3715 0088, http://hanoicookingcentre. com. A restaurant, café and cooking centre housed in a restored colonial villa near Truc Bach Lake, this place has quickly become popular with expats and tourists. Past the excellent cooking classes, which provide a useful overview of street food dishes and others, the cooking centre serves things rarely seen in Hanoi, such as a seasonal Sunday roast.

⍦⍦ Pho Yen, 66 Cua Bac St, T04-3715 0269. This down-at-heel tables and chair joint

does very very tasty *pho cuon*. It's very popular with locals.

⍦ Kitchen, Lane 40, 7A Xuan Dieu, T04-3719 2679. Open 0700-2130. Down an alley with a small courtyard, a cheap and cheerful very popular hang-out serving great Mexican, sandwiches and salads and healthy juices. Greg's chicken shawarma pitta is hugely filling.

Cafés

Café Puku, 16/18 Tong Duy Tan St, T04-3928 5244. An old favourite recently relocated to a new location in a large colonial villa. Puku has kept everything that made it good and still managed improvements, such as cheaper beer and an astonishing 24-hr license. Set on the famous Food Street now, it still even smells the same: like a university café, all friendly garlic and fresh brewed coffee.

Cong Café, 152D Trieu Viet Vuong St. A communist parody in a city which, in the main, doesn't view such a sense of humour favourably. Music here is generally excellent and coffee a cut above the rest. Trieu Viet Vuong St is the café quarter of Hanoi.

Duy Tri, 43A Yen Phu St, T04-3829 1386. Considered the best coffee in Hanoi. This tiny tube café is full on atmosphere and the smell of beans. The coffee with yoghurt (*ca phe sua chua*) is the signature drink.

Kem Trang Tien, 35 Trang Tien St. This is probably the most popular ice cream parlour in the city and it's a drive-in and park your moto affair. It's also a flirt joint for Hanoian young things. Flavours are cheap and change as to what's available.

Cat Ba Town *p82*

⍦ Green Mango, T031-388 7151. This is an outstanding addition to Cat Ba cuisine. The sesame-encrusted ahi tuna on a bed of cellophane noodles is worth the ferry trip to Cat Ba alone. Other culinary delights include home-smoked duck with vindaloo rice, green mustard and pomegranate jus and warm chocolate pudding, raspberry purée and cream. Indoor and outdoor seating is available. Highly recommended.

🍸 Bars and clubs

Hanoi *p71, maps p72 and p74*
Hanoi's main bar street is Ta Hien, heading towards Hang Buom after it has cut across the famous Bia Hoi Corner (at Luong Ngoc Quyen). Though officially all bars are supposed to close at midnight, it's a rule sporadically enforced and one that often leads to a convivial, speakeasy atmosphere – as long as you know which closed roller door to knock on.
Funky Buddha, 2 Ta Hien St, T04-3926 7615. A lounge/club bar that is something of an anomaly in Hanoi: equally popular with foreigners and Vietnam's rapidly growing middle class. Though it looks plenty glitzy, spirit prices are only a shade above anything else on the street and staff are extremely competent. Bottle service is on offer.
Le Pub, 25 Hang Be St, T04-3926 2104, www.lepub.org. One of Hanoi's best pubs, now with a second location on the shores of West Lake. Popular with tourists and expats, prices remain reasonable, beer is some of the coldest in the city and nightly drinks' specials keep the wallet intact. Food is reasonably priced and competent but, excepting the breakfasts and Vietnamese, largely uninspiring.
Mao's Red Lounge, 7 Ta Hien St, T04-3926 3104. A hugely popular hole-in-the-wall bar mostly frequented by young English teachers. Music is good though dependent on whomever of the publican's friends has control of the iPod. Some of the cheapest beers in town with famously honest staff.
Phuc Tan Bar, 51 Phuc Tan St. An out-and-out dive bar, and proud of it. Come the weekend there are precious few places open late at night where you can both drink and dance. Though basic, and with nightmare toilets, Phuc Tan Bar has a gorgeous view over the Red River, large outdoor seating area and often stays open late. Be very wary of catching any cabs from outside the bar on your way home. Ask staff to phone for one instead.
R & R Tavern, 10 Tho Nhuom St, T04-6295 8215. One of Hanoi's oldest bars, this new location outside the Old Quarter has everything its predecessor had, right down to the crowd. A mostly American bar, with reasonably priced Tex-Mex meals and one of Vietnam's best beers: the hard-to-find Huda.
Tadioto, 113 Trieu Viet Vuong St, T04-2218 7200, www.tadioto.com. **Tadioto** has no precedent in the city or other neighbours in the area. An art gallery-cum-bar, it's one of the few places to host poetry readings or play Tom Waites albums. Far from the centre of town it might be, but it's always worth the trip.
Tet bar, 2A Ta Hien St, T04-3926 3050. One of the city's late-night mainstays and formerly known as **Le Marquis**, **Tet** closes when the last customers go home, pretty much. For some reason better known to fate, the toasted sandwiches here – a Croque Monsieur – are considered the best after-hours snack in the city.

Cat Ba Town *p82*
Flightless Bird, on the seafront, T031-388 8517. Run by Graeme Moore, a New Zealander, the only real pub in town. Also a book exchange. See also **Noble House**, Sleeping, above.

🎭 Entertainment

Hanoi *p71, maps p72 and p74*
Dance and theatre
Opera House, T04-3933 0113, nthavinh@ hn.vn.vn. Box office daily 0800-1700. Housed in an impressive French-era building at the east end of Trang Tien St (see page 75). A variety of Vietnamese and Western concerts, operas and plays are staged. See the schedule in *Vietnam News* or from the box office.

Water puppet theatre

Water Puppetry House, 57 Dinh Tien Hoang St, T04-3936 4335, www.thanglongwaterpuppet.org. Fabulous shows with exciting live music and beautiful comedy: the technical virtuosity of the puppeteers is astonishing. Performances 1530, 1700, 1830 and 2000 and 2130, additional matinee Sun 0930. Admission 60,000d (1st class), 40,000d (2nd class); children half price on Sun. This is not to be missed.

❀ Festivals and events

Around Hanoi *p81*

Perfume Pagoda Festival From 6th day of the 1st lunar month to end of 3rd lunar month (15th-20th day of 2nd lunar month is the main period). This festival focuses on the worship of the Goddess of Mercy (Quan Am). Thousands flock to this famous pilgrimage site. Worshippers take part in dragon dances and a royal barge sails on the river.

O Shopping

Hanoi *p71, maps p72 and p74*

The city is a shopper's paradise with cheap silk and expert tailors, handicrafts and antiques and some good designer shops. Hang Gai St is well geared to the souvenir hunter and stocks an excellent range of clothes, fabrics and lacquerware.

Art and antiques

Apricot Gallery, 40B Hang Bong St, T04-3828 8965, www.apricot-artvietnam.com. High prices but spectacular exhibits.
Art Vietnam Gallery, 7 Nguyen Khac Nhu St, T04-3927 2349, www.artvietnamgallery.com. Mon-Sat 1000-1800. Art director Suzanne Lecht has created a cool interior in a chic space to display delectable works of art by Vietnamese and Vietnam-based artists. This is Hanoi's premier art space. Highly recommended.

Dien Dam Gallery, 4B Dinh Liet St, T04-3825 9881, www.dien dam-gallery.com. Beautiful photographs.
Hanoi Gallery 17 Nha Chung St, T04-3928 7943, propaganda_175@yahoo.com. This is a great find: hundreds of propaganda posters for sale. Original posters cost US$200 upwards; US$8 for a rice paper copy. Some of the reproductions aren't faithful to the colours of the originals; choose carefully.

Clothes, fashions, silk and accessories

The greatest concentration is in the Hoan Kiem Lake area particularly on Nha Tho, Nha Chung, Hang Trong and Hang Gai.
Bo Sua, beside skate shop Boo on Ta Hien St. Owned by the same people as Boo, Bo Sua is revolutionary for a Hanoian label. Plastic bags have been banned, T-shirts carry environmental awareness cartoons, and designs are mainly done by young Hanoians. If you want a sartorial souvenir that goes beyond the standard Captain Vietnam shirt – the Vietnamese flag shirt – shop here. Day-to-day objects, such as coal briquettes, plastic sandals or foamy glasses of bia hoi have been turned into stylish T-shirt icons.
Co, 18 Nha Tho St, T04-3928 9925, conhatho@yahoo.com. Daily 0830-1900. Clothes shop with a very narrow entrance. Some unusual prints, the craftsmanship is recommended.
Ipa Nima, 34 Han Thuyen St, T04-3933 4000, www.ipa-nima.com. Shiny shoes, bags, clothes and jewellery boxes. Hong Kong designer Christina Yu is the creative force behind the label.
Song, 27 Nha Tho St, T04-3928 8733, www.asiasongdesign.com. Daily 0900-2000. The Song shop is run by friendly staff and has beautiful designer clothes, accessories and homeware but its floor space is much smaller than the HCMC store (see page 176).
Things of Substance, 5 Nha Tho St, T04-3828 6965, contrabanddesign@hn.vnn.vn. Open 0900-2000. Selling swimwear, silk jewellery bags and attractive jewellery, this small shop, with excellent service in the

shadow of the cathedral, offers something a bit different. An Australian designer is in charge and everything is made with the motto 'Western sizes at Asian prices' in mind. Popular enough that you're likely to run into someone else sporting your outfit, at some stage.

Tina Sparkle, 17 Nha Tho St, T04-3928 7616. Daily 0900-2000. Funky boutique that sells bags in an array of designs, from tropical prints to big sequinned flowers. Also stocks items by Spanish design team Chula. A good option if you want an IpaNima bag without a taxi ride to the next district.

Handicrafts

Chi Vang, 63 Hang Gai St, T04-3936 0601. Exquisite hand-embroidered cloths, babies' bed linen and clothing, cushion covers, tablecloths and unusual-shaped cushions.
Mosaique, 22 Nha Tho St, T04-3928 6181. Daily 0830-2000. Embroidered table runners, lamps and stands, silk flowers, silk curtains, metal ball lamps, and lotus flower-shaped lamps.

◐ Activities and tours

Hanoi *p71, maps p72 and p74*
Halong Bay trips
Many Hanoi tour operators run tours to **Halong Bay** (see page 82). Some also offer kayaking trips. Other dedicated Halong Bay operators include:

Cruise Halong Co, Suite 328, 33B Pham Ngu Lao St, Hanoi, T04-3933 5561, www. cruisehalong.com. Operates the *Halong Ginger* luxury junks.
Emeraude Classic Cruises, 46 Le Thai To St, T04-3935 1888, www.emeraude-cruises. com. Has one of the best ways to see Halong Bay in style on a reconstructed French paddle steamer, the *Emeraude*.
Huong Hai Junk Halong Company, www. halong discovery.com. Also operates in the bay.
Life Heritage Resort Halong Bay, www. life-resorts.com. 22 private de luxe boats with a living area, sun deck, DVD player and TV and their own captain and staff. Therapy treatments will be available on board.

Tour operators
The most popular option for travellers are the budget cafés, which offer reasonably priced tours but make sure you know exactly what you are getting for your fee especially where food and drink is concerned. Operators match their rivals' prices and itineraries closely and many operate a clearing system to consolidate passenger numbers to more profitable levels.
Asia Pacific Travel, 66 Hang Than St, Ba Dinh, T04-3836 4212, www. asia-pacifictravel.com. Arranges tours throughout Vietnam.

Blue Star Hotel, 21 Bat Dan St, T04-3923 1585, www.bluestar-hotels.com. Recommended for its budget Halong Bay excursions, which are good value.

Buffalo Tours Vietnam, 94 Ma May St, T04-3828 0702, www.buffalotours.com. Well-regarded. Has its own boat for Halong Bay trips and offers tours around the north as well as day trips around Hanoi.

Discovery Indochina, 63A Cua Bac St, T04-3716 4132, www.discoveryindochina.com. Organizes private and customized tours throughout Vietnam, Cambodia and Laos.

Ethnic Travel, 35 Hang Giay St, T04-3926 1951, www.ethnictravel.com.vn. Owner, Mr Khanh, runs original individual tours to Bai Tu Long Bay (next to Halong Bay) and to Ninh Binh. Offers homestays and always tries to show travellers the 'real' Vietnam.

ET-Pumpkin, 89 Ma May St, T04-3926 0739, www.et-pumpkin.com. Very professional in attitude, offering a good selection of travel services, particularly for visitors to the northwest. Now offering motorbike tours of the north. Also has its own very comfortable train carriage which goes to Sapa. Footprint received reports that it is not as helpful as it used to be.

Exotissimo, 26 Tran Nhat Duat St, T04-3828 2150, www.exotissimo.com. Specializes in more upmarket tours, good nationwide service.

Footprint Vietnam, 6 Le Thanh Tong, T04-3933 2844, www.footprint.vn. Customized tour packages.

Halong Discovery Indochina, 63A Cua Bac St, T04-3716 4132, www.discoveryindochina.com. Private and customized tours throughout Vietnam, Cambodia and Laos.

Halong Travel, 10 Hang Be St, T04-3926 3606, www.halongtravel.com. A countrywide operator with friendly staff.

Handspan Adventure Travel, 80 Ma May St, T04-3926 2828, www.handspan.com. Reputable business specializing in adventure tours, trekking in the north, mountain biking and kayaking in Halong Bay. Has its own junk.

Hanoi Toserco, 8 To Hien Thang St, T04-3976 0066, www.tosercohanoi.com. It runs an efficient Open Tour service.

Love Planet, 25 Hang Bac St, T04-3828 4864, www.loveplanettravel.com. Individual and small group tours; organizes visas. Helpful.

Luxury Travel Co, 5 Nguyen Truong To St, T04-3927 4120, www.luxurytravelvietnam.com. A newer tour operator offering countrywide tours and alternative excursions across the region.

Real Darling Café, 33 Hang Quat St, T04-3826 9386, darling_café@hotmail.com. Long-established and efficient. Concentrates on tours of the north and has a visa service.

Voyage Vietnam Co, Mototours Asia, 1-2 Luong Ngoc Quyen St and 20 Nguyen Huu Huan, T04-3926 2373, www.voyagevietnam.net. Well-organized, reliable, great fun and knowledgeable off-road 4WD motorbiking, trekking and kayaking tours, especially of the north. The super-friendly and knowledgeable Tuan will take professional

bikers to China, Laos, and the Golden Triangle. Trips are well-organised with all protective gear and nights are spent in homestays and hotels. 4WD car hire also available. This is the only company permitted to import your bike into Vietnam and to organize trips from Vietnam through to China and Tibet.

Cat Ba town *p82*
Tour operators
Cat Hai District People's Committee Tourism Information Centre, along the seafront, T031-368 8215. Daily 0700-2200. Runs guided tours to the national park and Halong Bay; organizes *xe ôm* to park HQ; 1-hr boat trip to Lan Ha Bay; boat charter; car hire; motorbike hire; bicycle hire.
Slo Pony Adventures/Asia Outdoors, 222 1/4 St, Group 19, Ward 4, T031-368 8450, www.slopony.com. Rock climbing, kayaking, trekking, environmentally conscious boat cruises and other adventures. **Slo Pony** works directly with the local community on Cat Ba Island, employs domestic and international staff and assists the national park with efforts to protect the endangered langur as well as with the park's conservation efforts.

⊖ Transport

Hanoi *p71, maps p72 and p74*
Air
Airline offices AirAsia, 30 Le Thai To St, www.airasia.com. **Air France**, 1 Ba Trieu St, T04-3825 3484, www.airfrance.com. **Cathay Pacific**, 49 Hai Ba Trung St, T04-3826 7298, www.cathaypacific.com/vn. **Jetstar**, 204 Tran Quang Khai St, Hoan Kiem District, www.jetstar.com/vn. **Lao Airlines**, 46 Tho Nhuom St, Hoan Kiem District, T04-3822 9951, www.laoairlines.com. **Malaysian Airlines**, 49 Hai Ba Trung St, T04-3826 8820, www.malaysiaairlines.com. **Singapore Airlines**, 17 Ngo Quyen St, T04-3826 8888, www.singaporeair.com. **Thai**, 44B Ly Thuong Kiet St, T04-3826 7921, www.thaiair.com. **Vietnam Airlines**, 1 Quang Trung St, T04-3832 0320, www.vietnamairlines.com.

Bicycle
An excellent way to get around. Bikes can be hired from the shops at 29-33 Ta Hien St and from most tourist cafés and hotels for about US$2 per day.

Bus
Tour operators run Open Tour Buses from offices in the Old Quarter to major tourist destinations in the south. See page 68.

Cyclo
Cyclos are ubiquitous especially in the Old Quarter. A trip from the railway station to Hoan Kiem Lake should cost no more than 30,000d. The trip on a *xe ôm* would be 15,000d.

Motorbike
A good way of getting to some of the more remote places. Tourist cafés and hotels rent

This guidebook gives you the country's facts.

We show you the local insights and offer you a true value in travel.

Footprint® Vietnam Travel

Call us: +844 3933 2844 - Visit us: www.Footprint.Vn

machines for US$5-40 per day. Note that hire shops insist on keeping the renter's passport, so it can be hard to rent other than at your hotel. See **Voyage Vietnam**, above.

Taxi and private car

There are plenty of metered taxis in Hanoi, the following companies are recommended: **Airport Taxi**, T04-3873 3333; **Mai Linh Taxi**, T04-3822 2666. Private cars with drivers can be chartered from most hotels and from tour operators, see page 90.

Train

The central station (*Ga Hanoi*) is at 120 Le Duan St (a 10-min taxi ride from the centre of town) T04-3942 2770. For trains to **HCMC** and the south, enter the station from Le Duan St. For trains to **Lao Cai** (for Sapa) enter the station from Tran Quy Cap St. There are regular daily connections with **HCMC**; advance booking required.

Overnight trains from Hanoi to **Lao Cai**, 8½-10 hrs, from where a fleet of minibuses ferries passengers on to **Sapa**. The train carriages are run by different companies and prices vary depending on the company and the berth type.

ET-Pumpkin, www.et-pumpkin.com and **Ratraco**, www.ratraco.com.vn, run standard comfortable a/c 4-berth cabins in its carriages with complimentary water, bedside lights and space for luggage. For luxury, the **Victoria Hotel** carriages (http://www.victoriahotels-asia.com/eng/hotels-in-vietnam/sapa-resort-spa/victoria-express-train) run Sun-Fri at 2150 to **Sapa** arriving 0630. The dining carriage is only available Mon, Wed and Fri. Places are only available to **Victoria Sapa** hotel guests.

Cat Ba Town *p82*
Boat

To get to **Cat Ba** jump on a tourist boat for a 1-way (4 hr) ride for 200,000d from the Bai Chay Tourist Wharf (Halong Rd, Halong City, T033-3846592) open 0730-1700 daily; get there early as last group departures (ie cheaper leave around 1230) and get off at the port of Gia Luan, which is in the north of Cat Ba. A bus runs from Gia Luan to Cat Ba Town, 10,000d. Ferries also run from Tuan Chau 'Island' to Gia Luan in the summer at 0730, 0930, 1100, 1330, 1600, and in winter at 0800 and 1400, 30,000d. Or get to Haiphong: **Transtour Co** runs the Cat Ba-**Haiphong** ferry, T031-388 8314, office on the seafront. **Hoang Long Co**, T031-388 7244 (Cat Ba), with an office on the seafront, runs a bus from Hanoi's Luong Yen bus station to Haiphong and then 30 mins by bus to the Dinh Vu ferry (1½ hrs) and then from Phu Long on Cat Ba to Cat Ba Town. Several buses a day.

⊙ Directory

Hanoi *p71, maps p72 and p74*
Banks Commission is charged on cashing TCs into US$ but not into dong. It is better to withdraw dong from the bank and pay for everything in dong. Most hotels will change dollars, often at quite fair rates. There are now ATMs in a lot of places. **ANZ Bank**, 14 Le Thai To St, T04-3825 8190, Mon-Fri 0830-1600. 24-hr ATMs. **Citibank**, 17 Ngo Quyen St, T04-3825 1950, cashes TCs into dong. **Embassies and consulates** Australia, 8 Dao Tan St, T04-3831 7755. Cambodia, 71 Tran Hung Dao St, T04-3942 7646. **Canada**, 31 Hung Vuong St, T04-3734 5000. **France**, 57 Tran Hung Dao St, T4-3944 5700. **Laos**, 22 Tran Binh Trong St, T04-3942 4576. **Malaysia**, 43-45 Dien Bien Phu St, T4-3734 3836. **Singapore**, 41-43 Tran Phu St, T4-3944 5700. **Thailand**, 63-65 Hoang Dieu St, T04-3823 5092. **UK**, Central Building, 31 Hai Ba Trung St, T04-3936 0500. **USA**, 7 Lang Ha St, T04-3772 1500; Consulate: 1st Floor, Rose Garden Tower, 170 Ngoc Khanh St, T4-3850 5000. **Immigration** Immigration Dept, 40A Hang Bai St, T04-3826 6200. **Internet** Internet access and emailing is cheap and easy in Hanoi. Many hotels now have free internet use. Failing that, all the travel cafés have internet services. Wi-Fi is everywhere and even outer suburban cafés with no

sit-down toilet will have Wi-Fi. **Medical services** Family Medical Practice Hanoi, Building A1, Van Phuc Compound, 298 I Kim Ma Rd, Ba Dinh, T04-3843 0748, 24-hr emergency services, dental care. **Hospital Bach Mai**, Giai Phong St, T04-3869 3731. English-speaking doctors. **International SOS**, Central Building, 31 Hai Ba Trung St, T04-3934 0555, www.internationalsos.com/countries/ Vietnam/. 24-hr, emergencies and medical evacuation. **Post office** GPO, 75 Dinh Tien Hoang St. International telephone service also available at the PO at 66-68 Trang Tien St; 66 Luong Van Can St and at the PO on Le Duan next to the train station. DHL, at the GPO.

Cat Ba Town *p82*
Banks Agribank, T031-388 8227, on the back road will change dollars. ATM on seafront. Internet available.

Northwest Vietnam

The north is a mountainous region punctuated by limestone peaks and luscious valleys of terraced paddy fields, tea plantations, stilt houses and water hyacinth-quilted rivers. Large cones and towers, some with vertical walls and overhangs, rise dramatically from the flat alluvial plains. This landscape, dotted with bamboo thickets, is one of the most evocative in Vietnam; its hazy images seem to linger deep in the collective Vietnamese psyche and perhaps symbolize a sort of primaeval Garden of Eden.

Sapa, in the far northwest, is a former French hill station, home of the Hmong and set in a stunning valley, carpeted with Alpinese flowers. It is a popular centre for trekking. Scattered around are market towns and villages populated by Vietnam's ethnic minorities such as the Black Hmong, Red Dao, Flower Hmong, Phu La, Dao Tuyen, La Chi and Tay – the latter being Vietnam's largest ethnic minority.

Nor is the region without wider significance; the course of world history was altered at Dien Bien Phu in May 1954 when the Vietnamese defeated the French. In 2004 a vast bronze statue commemorating the victory was erected; it towers over the town. Closer to Hanoi is Hoa Binh where villages of the Muong and Dao can be seen and the beautiful Mai Chau Valley, home to the Black and White Thai whose attractive houses nestle amid the verdant paddies of the hills.
▶▶ For listings, see pages 101-104.

Ins and outs

Getting there and around
There are three points of entry for the northwest circuit: the south around Hoa Binh (reached by road); to the north around Lao Cai/Sapa (reached by road or preferably by train) and, bang in the middle, Dien Bien Phu reached by road or by plane. Which option you pick will depend upon how much time you have available and how much flexibility you require. Most people arrive by train or by luxury bus, the cheapest option, to Sapa.

Expect overland journeys to be slow and sometimes arduous in this mountainous region but the discomfort is more than compensated for by the majesty of the landscapes. The road south of Dien Bien Phu has been significantly upgraded over recent years but the route north to Sapa is still poor and a 4WD is recommended. Jeeps with driver can be hired from some tour operators in Hanoi (see page 90) for the five- or six-day round trip. A good and slightly cheaper option is to leave the jeep in Sapa and catch the overnight train back to Hanoi from Lao Cai. For those willing to pay more, Japanese land cruisers offer higher levels of comfort.

Another option is to do the whole thing by motorbike. The rugged terrain and relatively quiet roads make this a popular choice for many people. It has the particular advantage of allowing countless side trips and providing access to really remote and untouched areas. It is not advised to attempt the whole circuit using public transport as this would involve fairly intolerable levels of discomfort and a frustrating lack of flexibility.
▸▸ *See Transport, page 104.*

Best time to visit
The region is wet from May to September. This makes travel quite unpleasant. Owing to the altitude of much of the area winter can be quite cool, especially around Sapa, so make sure you go well prepared.

Towards Dien Bien Phu → *For listings, see pages 101-104. Colour map 2, B4.*

The road from Hanoi to Dien Bien Phu winds its way for 420 km into the Annamite Mountains that mark the frontier with Laos. The round trip from Hanoi and back via Dien Bien Phu and Sapa is about 1200 km and offers some of the most spectacular scenery anywhere in Vietnam. Opportunities to experience the lives, customs and costumes of some of Vietnam's ethnic minorities abound. The loop can be taken in a clockwise or anti-clockwise direction; the advantage of following the clock is the opportunity to recover from the rigours of the journey in the tranquil setting of Sapa.

Highway 6, which has been thoroughly rebuilt along almost the entire route from Hanoi to Son La, leads southwest out of Hanoi to Hoa Binh. Setting off in the early morning (this is a journey of dawn starts and early nights), the important arterial function of this road to Hanoi can be clearly seen: ducks, chickens, pigs, bamboo and charcoal all pour in – the energy and building materials of the capital – much of it transported by bicycle. Beyond the city limits, the fields are highly productive, with market gardens and intensive rice production.

Hoa Binh → *Colour map 2, B4.*
Hoa Binh, on the banks of the Da (Black) River, marks the southern limit of the interior highlands and is 75 km from Hanoi, a journey of about 2½ hours. Major excavation sites of the Hoabinhian prehistoric civilization (10,000 BC) were found in the province, which is its main claim to international fame.

Bao Tang Tinh Hoa Binh (Hoa Binh Province Museum) ① *daily 0800-1030, 1400-1700, 10,000d*, contains items of archaeological, historical and ethnographical importance. Relics of the First Indochina War, including a French amphibious landing craft, remain from the bitterly fought campaign of 1951-1952, which saw Viet Minh forces dislodge the French.

Muong and **Dao minority villages** are accessible from Hoa Binh. **Xom Mo** is 8 km from Hoa Binh and is a village of the Muong minority. There are around 10 stilt houses, where overnight stays are possible; contact **Hoa Binh Tourism** ① *T218-385 4374, www. hoabinhtourism.com.* There are also nearby caves to visit. **Duong** and **Phu** are villages of the Dao Tien (Money Dao), located 25 km up river. Boat hire is available from **Hoa Binh Tourism**. A permit is required for an overnight stay.

Mai Chau and Lac → *Colour map 2, B4.*
After leaving Hoa Binh, Highway 6 heads in a south-southwest direction as far as the Chu River. Thereafter it climbs through spectacular mountain scenery before descending into the beautiful Mai Chau Valley. During the first half of this journey, the turtle-

Tay Trang–Sop Hun

The border linking Dien Bien Phu in Vietnam with Laos in this part of the country is now open. The border at Sop Hun, Laos, is open 0800-1700 daily, and is 34 km from Dien Bien Phu. A Lao visa is obtainable on arrival. Vietnamese visas are not available on arrival.

Transport There is little transport on the Laos side to Muang Khua and the road is still maybe under construction so expect delays. There is a direct bus from Muang Khua to Dien Bien Phu, 50,000 kip, which lets you off for border formalities at Sop Hun and Tay Trang. It leaves from the opposite side of the river bank to Muang Khua at 0600. There's a bus leaving Dien Bien Phu to the border crossing at Tay Trang and onto Muang Khua (Laos) every other day leaving at 0500.

shaped roofs of the Muong houses predominate but, after passing Man Duc, the road enters the territory of the Thai, northwest Vietnam's most prolific ethnic minority, heralding a subtle change in the style of stilted-house architecture. This region is dominated by Black Thai communities (a sub-ethnic group of the Thai) but White Thai also live in the area.

The growing number of foreign and domestic tourists visiting the area in recent years has had a significant impact on the economy of Mai Chau and the lifestyles of its inhabitants. Some foreign visitors complain that the valley offers a manicured hill-tribe village experience to the less adventurous tourist who wants to sample the quaint lifestyle of the ethnic people without too much discomfort. There may be some truth in this allegation, yet there is another side to the coin. Since the region first opened its doors to foreign tourists in 1993, the **Mai Chau People's Committee** has attempted to control the effect of tourism on the valley. **Lac** (White Thai village) is the official tourist village to which tour groups are led and, although it is possible to visit and even stay in the others, the committee hopes that by 'sacrificing' one village to tourism, the impact on other communities will be limited. Income generated from tourism by the villagers of Lac has brought about a significant enhancement to the lifestyles of people throughout the entire valley, enabling many villagers to tile their roofs and purchase consumer products such as television sets, refrigerators and motorbikes.

Lac is easily accessible from the main road from the direction of Hoa Binh. Take the track to the right, immediately before the red-roofed **People's Committee Guesthouse**. This leads directly into the village. You can borrow or rent a bicycle from your hosts and wobble across narrow bunds to the neighbouring hamlets, enjoying the ducks, buffalos, children and lush rice fields as you go – a delightful experience.

About 5 km south of Mai Chau on Route 15A is the Naon River on which, in the dry season, a boat can be taken to visit a number of large and impressive grottoes. Others can be reached on foot. If you wish to visit them, ask your hosts or at the **People's Committee Guesthouse** for details.

Moc Chau and Chieng Yen

North of Mai Chau on the road to Son La is Chieng Yen. Home to 14 villages of Thai, Dao, Muong and Kinh, there are new homestay options with trekking and biking opportunities as well as tea farm visits at Moc Chau. A highlight is the weekly Tuesday market, see Sleeping, page 101.

People of the north

Ethnic groups belonging to the Sino-Tibetan language family such as the Hmong and Dao, or the Ha Nhi and Phula of the Tibeto-Burman language group are relatively recent arrivals. Migrating south from China only within the past 250-300 years, these people have lived almost exclusively on the upper mountain slopes, practising slash-and-burn agriculture and posing little threat to their more numerous lowland-dwelling neighbours, notably the Thai.

Thus was established the pattern of human and political settlement that would persist in North Vietnam for more than 1000 years right down to the colonial period – a centralized Viet state based in the Red River Delta area, with powerful Thai vassal lordships dominating the Northwest. Occupying lands located in some cases almost equidistant from Hanoi, Luang Prabang and Kunming, the Thai, Lao, Lu and Tay lords were obliged during the pre-colonial period to pay tribute to the royal courts of Nam Viet, Lang Xang (Laos) and China, though in times of upheaval they could – and frequently did – play one power off against the other for their own political gain. Considerable effort was thus required by successive Viet kings in Thang Long (Hanoi) and later in Hué to ensure that their writ and their writ alone ruled in the far north. To this end there was ultimately no substitute for the occasional display of military force, but the enormous cost of mounting a campaign into the northern mountains obliged most Viet kings simply to endorse the prevailing balance of power there by investing the most powerful local lords as their local government mandarins, resorting to arms only when separatist tendencies became too strong. Such was the political situation inherited by the French colonial government following its conquest of Indochina in the latter half of the 19th century. Its subsequent policy towards the ethnic minority chieftains of North Vietnam was to mirror that of the Vietnamese monarchy whose authority it assumed; throughout the colonial period responsibility for colonial administration at both local and provincial level was placed in the hands of seigneurial families of the dominant local ethnicity, a policy which culminated during the 1940s in the establishment of a series of ethnic minority 'autonomous zones' ruled over by the most powerful seigneurial families.

Dien Bien Phu → Colour map 1, B2.
ⓘ *The airport is 2 km north of town. The battlefield sites, most of which lie to the west of the Nam Yum River, are a bit spread out and best visited by car or by motorbike.*

Dien Bien Phu lies in the Muong Thanh valley, a region where, even today, ethnic Vietnamese still represent less than one-third of the total population. For such a remote and apparently insignificant little town to have earned itself such an important place in the history books is a considerable achievement. And yet, the Battle of Dien Bien Phu in 1954 was a turning point in colonial history. It was the last disastrous battle between the French and the forces of Ho Chi Minh's Viet Minh and was waged from March to May 1954. The French, who under Vichy rule had accepted the authority of the Japanese during the Second World War, attempted to regain control after the Japanese had surrendered. Ho, following his Declaration of Independence on 2 September 1945, thought otherwise, heralding nearly a decade of war before the French finally gave up the fight after their catastrophic defeat here. It marked the end of French involvement in Indochina and heralded the collapse of its colonial empire. Had the Americans, who shunned French appeals for help, taken more careful note of what happened at Dien Bien Phu they might have avoided their own calamitous involvement in Vietnamese affairs just a decade later.

General de Castries' bunker ① *daily 0700-1100, 1330-1700, 5000d*, has been rebuilt on the sight of the battlefield and eight of the 10 French tanks are scattered over the valley, along with US-made artillery pieces. East of the river, **Hill A1** ① *daily 0700-1800*, known as Eliane 2 to the French, was the scene of the fiercest fighting. Remains of the conflict include a bunker, the bison (tank) known as Gazelle, a war memorial dedicated to the Vietnamese who died on the hill and, around at the back, the entrance to a tunnel dug by coal miners from Hon Gai. Their tunnel ran for several hundred metres to beneath French positions and was filled with 1000 kg of high explosives. It was detonated at 2300 on 6 May 1954 as a signal for the final assault. The huge crater is still there. Opposite the hill, the renovated **Nha Trung Bay Thang Lich Su Dien Bien Phu** (Historic Victory Exhibition Museum) ① *daily 0700-1100, 1330-1800, 5000d*, has a good collection of assorted Chinese, American and French weapons and artillery in its grounds. Inside are photographs and other memorabilia, together with a large illuminated model of the valley illustrating the course of the campaign and an accompanying video. While every last piece of Vietnamese junk is carefully catalogued, displayed and described, French relics are heaped into tangled piles. **The Revolutionary Heroes' Cemetery** ① *opposite the Exhibition Museum next to Hill A1, daily 0700-1100, 1330-1800*, contains the graves of 15,000 Vietnamese soldiers killed during the course of the Dien Bien Phu campaign. At the north end of town, the **Tuong Dai Chien Dien Bien Phu** (Victory monument) ① *entrance next to the TV station on 6 Pho Muong Thanh, look for the tower and large pond*, erected on D1 at a cost of US$2.27 million, is the largest monument in Vietnam. The 120-tonne bronze sculpture depicts three Vietnamese soldiers standing on top of de Castries' bunker. It was commissioned to mark the 50th anniversary of the Vietnamese victory over the French.

Sapa and around → *For listings, see pages 101-104. Colour map 2, A2.*

Despite the thousands of tourists who have poured in every year for the past decade, Sapa retains great charm. Its beauty derives from two things: the impressive natural setting high on a valley side, with Fan Si Pan, Vietnam's tallest mountain either clearly visible or brooding in the mist; and the clamour and colour of the ethnic minorities selling jewellery and clothes. Distinctly oriental but un-Vietnamese in manner and appearance are the Hmong, Dao and other groups who come to Sapa to trade. Interestingly, the Hmong (normally so reticent) have been the first to seize the commercial opportunities presented by tourism. Saturday night is always a big occasion for Black Hmong and Red Dao teenagers in the Sapa area, as youngsters from miles around come to the so-called 'Love Market' to find a partner. The market proved so popular with tourists that the teenagers now arrange their trysts in private. Sapa's regular market is at its busiest and best on Sunday mornings, when most tourists scoot off to Bac Ha (see page 101).

Ins and outs
Getting there and around Travel to Sapa is either by road on the northwest circuit or by overnight train from Hanoi, via Lao Cai. A fleet of minibuses ferries passengers from Lao Cai railway station to Sapa. Sapa is small enough to walk around easily. From Sapa there are a great many walks and treks to outlying villages. **Sapa Tourist Information Center** ① *2 Phan Si Pang Street, T20-387 1975, www.sapa-tourism.com.* ▸▸ *See Transport, page 104.*

Best time to visit At 1650 m Sapa enjoys warm days and cool evenings in the summer but gets very cold in winter. Snow falls, on average, every couple of years and settles on the surrounding peaks of the Hoang Lien Son Mountains. Rain and cloud can occur at any time of year but the wettest months are May to September with nearly 1000 mm of rain in July and August alone, the busiest months for Vietnamese tourists. December and January can be pretty miserable with mist, low cloud and low temperatures. Spring blossom is lovely but even in March and April a fire or heater may be necessary in the evening.

Background

Originally a Black Hmong settlement, Sapa was first discovered by Europeans when a Jesuit missionary visited the area in 1918. By 1932 news of the quasi-European climate and beautiful scenery of the Tonkinese Alps had spread throughout French Indochina. By the 1940s an estimated 300 French buildings, including a sizeable prison and the summer residence of the Governor of French Indochina, had sprung up. Until 1947 there were more French than Vietnamese in the town, which became renowned for its many parks and flower gardens. However, as the security situation began to worsen during the latter days of French rule, the expatriate community steadily dwindled, and by 1953

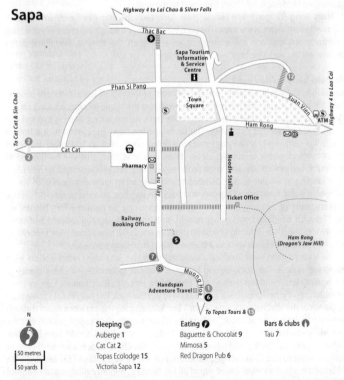

Sapa

Highway 4 to Lai Chau & Silver Falls
Thac Bac 9
Sapa Tourism Information & Service Centre
Highway 4 to Lao Cai
Phan Si Pang
Xuan Vien
To Cat Cat & Sin Chai
Town Square
ATM
Ham Rong
Cat Cat 2
Pharmacy
Cau May
Noodle Stalls
Ticket Office
Railway Booking Office
Ham Rong (Dragon's Jaw Hill)
5
7
Muong Hoa
Handspan Adventure Travel
6
To Topas Tours & 15

N
50 metres
50 yards

Sleeping
Auberge 1
Cat Cat 2
Topas Ecolodge 15
Victoria Sapa 12

Eating
Baguette & Chocolat 9
Mimosa 5
Red Dragon Pub 6

Bars & clubs
Tau 7

virtually all had gone. Following the French defeat at Dien Bien Phu in 1954, victorious Vietnamese forces razed a large number of Sapa's French buildings to the ground.

Sights

Sapa is a pleasant place to relax in and unwind. Being comparatively new it has no important sights but several French buildings in and around are worth visiting. The huge scale of the Fan Si Pan range gives Sapa an Alpine feel and this impression is reinforced by *haut savoie* vernacular architecture, with steep pitched roofs, window shutters and chimneys. Each house has its own neat little garden of temperate flora – foxgloves, roses, apricot and plum trees – carefully nurtured by generations of gardeners. But in an alluring blend of European and Vietnamese vegetation, the gardens are cultivated alongside thickets of bamboo and delicate orchids, just yards above the paddy fields.

The small **church** in the centre of Sapa was built in 1930. In the churchyard are the tombs of two former priests, including that of Father Thinh, who was brutally murdered. In the autumn of 1952, Father Thinh confronted a monk named Giao Linh who had been discovered having an affair with a nun at the Ta Phin seminary. Giao Linh obviously took great exception to the priest's interference, for shortly after this, when Father Thinh's congregation arrived at Sapa church for mass one foggy November morning, they discovered his decapitated body lying next to the altar.

Ham Rong (Dragon's Jaw Hill) ① *daily 0600-1800, 30,000d, free for children under 5*, offers excellent views of the town. The path winds its way through a number of interesting limestone outcrops and miniature grottoes as it nears the summit. Traditional dance performances take place here. ▸▸ *See Entertainment, page 104.*

Around Sapa → *Colour map 2, A2.*

Trekking to the villages around Sapa is a highlight of this region. It is a chance to observe rural life led in reasonable prosperity. Wet rice forms the staple income, weaving for the tourist market puts a bit of meat on the table. Here, nature is kind: there is rich soil and no shortage of water. It's clear how the landscape has been engineered to suit human needs: the terracing is on an awesome scale (in places more than 100 steps), the result of centuries of labour to convert steep slopes into level fields that can be flooded to grow rice. Technologically, and in no sense pejoratively, the villages might be described as belonging to a bamboo age: bamboo trunks carry water huge distances from spring to village; water flows across barriers and tracks in bamboo aqueducts; mechanical rice huskers made of bamboo are driven by water requiring no human effort; houses are held up with bamboo; bottoms are parked on bamboo chairs; and tobacco and other substances are inhaled through bamboo pipes. In late 2004, regulations were brought in, which mean that trekking without a licensed guide is no longer possible.

The track heading west from Sapa through the market area offers either a short 5-km round-trip walk to the Black Hmong village of **Cat Cat** (accessible without a guide) or a longer 10-km round-trip walk to **Sin Chai** (Black Hmong). Both options take in some beautiful scenery; foreigners must pay 15,000d to use the track. The path to Cat Cat leads off to the left of the Sin Chai track after about 1 km, following the line of pylons down through the rice paddies to Cat Cat village; beyond the village over the river bridge you can visit the **cascade waterfall** (from which the village takes its name) and an old French hydro-electric power station that still produces electricity. Sin Chai village is 4 km northwest of here. Walking to **Lau Chai village** (Black Hmong) and **Ta Van village** (Zay or Giay) with a licensed guide is a longer round trip of 20 km taking in minority villages and beautiful scenery. **Mount Fan Si Pan**, at a height of 3143 m, is Vietnam's highest mountain and is a three-day trek from Sapa. It lies on a bearing of 240° from Sapa; 9 km as the crow flies but 14 km by track. The route involves dropping to 1200 m and crossing a rickety bamboo bridge before ascending.

North of Sapa is an **abandoned French seminary**, where the names of the bishop who consecrated it and the presiding Governor of Indochina can be seen engraved on stones at the west end. Built in 1942 and under the ecclesiastical jurisdiction of the Parish of Sapa, the building was destroyed 10 years later by militant Vietnamese hostile to the intentions of the order. Beyond the seminary, the path descends into a valley of beautifully sculpted rice terraces and past Black Hmong settlementsge.

Bac Ha, located to the northeast of Sapa, is really only notable for one thing and that is its Sunday morning market. Hundreds of local minority people flock in from the surrounding districts to shop and socialize, while tourists from all corners of the earth pour in to watch them do it. The market draws in the Flower Hmong, Phu La, Dao Tuyen, La Chi and Tay, and is a riot of colour and fun. While the women trade and gossip, the men consume vast quantities of rice wine; by late morning they can no longer walk so are heaved onto donkeys by their wives and led home. If you have your own transport arrive early; if you haven't, nearly all the hotels and all the tour operators in Sapa organize trips.
➤ *See Activities and tours, page 104.*

◉ Northwest Vietnam listings

For Sleeping and Eating price codes and other relevant information, see pages 40 -43.

◉ Sleeping

Hoa Binh *p95*
C-D Hoa Binh 1, 54 Phuong Lam, T0218-385 2051. On Highway 6 towards Mai Chau. Clean rooms with a/c and TV; some rooms built in ethnic minority style. There's also an ethnic minority dining experience complete with rice drunk through bamboo straws. Gift shop stocks local produce.

Mai Chau and Lac *p95*
AL-A Mai Chau Lodge, a short walking distance southwest of Lac village, T018-386 8959, www.maichaulodge.com. Owned and operated by **Buffalo Tours** and staffed by locals, there are 16 warmly furnished rooms with modern facilities. The attractive lodge has 2 restaurants, a bar, pool, sauna and jacuzzi. Bicycling, kayaking and trekking tours are offered. Room prices include round-trip transfer from Hanoi.

E Ethnic Houses, Lac Village. Trips to homestays must be booked by tour operators, usually in Hanoi. In Mai Chau, visitors can spend the night in a White Thai ethnic house on stilts. Mat, pillow, duvet, mosquito net, communal washing facilities and sometimes fan provided. Particularly recommended, as the hospitality and easy manner of the people is a highlight of many visitors' stay in Vietnam. Food and local rice wine provided. Avoid the large houses in the centre if possible. **Guesthouse No 6**, T218-3867168, is popular, with plentiful food and rice wine. The owner fought the French at Dien Bien Phu. Minimal English is spoken.

Moc Chau and Chieng Yen *p96*
G Homestays, with meals are possible. Contact Son La Province, T022-385 5714, or tour operator **Handspan** in Hanoi. Breakfasts are 12000-15000d; lunch and dinner 40,000-50,000d each.

Dien Bien Phu *p97*
D Muong Thanh Hotel, 25 Him Lam-TP, T230-381 0043. Breakfast included with the

more expensive rooms. 62 standard rooms with TV, a/c, minibar and fan. Internet service, swimming pool (10,000d for non-guests), karaoke, Thai massage and free airport transfer. Souvenir shop and bikes for rent.
F Airport, Tran Dang Ninh, near the bus station, T230-382 5052. Fairly basic, 20 rooms, a/c, hot water.

Sapa and around *p98, map p99*

A host of guesthouses has sprung up to cater for Sapa's rejuvenation and the appeal of the town has, perhaps, been a little compromised by the new structures. Prices tend to rise Jun-Oct to coincide with northern hemisphere university holidays and at weekends. Hoteliers are accustomed to bargaining; healthy competition ensures fair rates.
AL Victoria Sapa, T020-387 1522, www.victoriahotels-asia.com. With 77 rooms, this hotel is the best in town. Comfy, with well-appointed rooms, it is a lovely place in which to relax. In winter there are open fires in the bar and dining rooms. The food is very good and the set buffets are excellent value. The Health Centre offers everything from the traditional massage to reflexology. The centre, pool, tennis courts and sauna are open to non-guests. Packages available.
A Topas Ecolodge, 18 km southeast from Sapa, www.topasecolodge.com (Sapa office: 24 Muong Hoa St, T020-387 1331). 25 bungalows with balconies built from white granite are built around a hill over-looking Ban Ho village in the stunning valley. Bungalows are simply furnished and powered by solar energy. The food is good and abundant. Butterflies, flowers and fire flies abound. Treks organized from the lodge can take you to less touristy Red Dao areas. Unfortunately, a hydroelectric power station is being built in the valley, near Seo Trung Ho, spoiling some views. For nature, views, peace and an eco-philosophy, the lodge is unique in Vietnam. Highly recommended.
B-C Sapa Rooms, 18 Phan Xi Pang St, T020-387 2130, www.saparooms.com. New and popular hotel in town with smart rooms and heaps of facilities including TV, DVD library and Wi-Fi. Good atmosphere and recommended restaurant, see Eating below. Supports the local ethnic-minority community.
B-D Cat Cat, 46 Phan Xi Pang St, on the Cat Cat side of town through the market. T020-3871946, www.catcathotel.com. The guesthouse has expanded up the hillside, with new terraces and bungalows with balconies all with views down the valley. Friendly and popular, its 40 rooms represent good value for money. Some enjoy the best views in Sapa. The hotel has a good restaurant and, like most others, arranges tours and provides useful information.
D-E Auberge, Muong Hoa St, T020-387 1243. Mr Dang Trung, the French-speaking owner, shows guests his wonderful informal garden with pride: sweet peas, honeysuckle, snap dragons, foxgloves, roses and irises – all familiar to visitors from temperate climes – grow alongside sub-Alpine flora and orchids. The rooms are simply furnished but clean and boast baths and log fires in winter. There's a restaurant on the lovely terrace.

Around Sapa *p100*

It is possible to spend the night in one of the ethnic houses in the Sapa district. However, homestays must be organized through reputable tour operators. The Black Hmong villages are probably the best bet, though facilities are considerably more basic than in the Muong and Thai stilted houses of Hoa Binh and Mai Chau and travellers need to bring their own bedding and mosquito net.

🍽 Eating

Hoa Binh *p95*

The **Hoa Binh 1** hotel (see Sleeping, above) is open for breakfast, lunch and dinner.

Mai Chau and Lac *p95*

Most people eat with their hosts. Mai Chau town has a couple of simple *com pho* places near the market. The rice wine is excellent, particularly when mixed with local honey. The **Mai Chau Lodge**, see Sleeping, has 2 restaurants.

Dien Bien Phu *p97*
❦ **Lien Tuoi**, 27 Muong Thanh 8 St, next to the Vietnamese cemetery and Hill A1, T230-382 4919. Daily 0700-2200. Delicious local fare in a family-run restaurant.
❦ **Muong Thanh Hotel Restaurant**, 25 Him Lam-TP, T230-381 0043. Daily 0600-2200. Breakfasts, plenty of Vietnamese dishes and a few pasta dishes. Also duck, boar, pork, frog, curry, seafood and some tofu dishes.

Sapa and around *p98, map p99*
There are rice and noodle stalls in the market and along the path by the church.
❦❦❦ **Ta Van**, in Victoria Sapa, see Sleeping, T020-387 1522. The food is very good, served in the large dining room with an open fire, and the set buffets are excellent value.
❦❦-❦ **Cha Pa Garden**, 23b Cau May St, T020-387 2907, www.chapagarden.com. A peaceful little oasis where you can hide from the street vendors during a romantic meal. Try to ignore the bizarre lounge area with flatscreen TV right off the main dining room while you watch the staff prepare roasted red peppers in a wood fire beside you for a tasty sandwich. The soft-spoken staff are kind, though might be confused by substitutions. Restaurant boasts an extensive wine selection.
❦❦-❦ **Sapa Rooms**, 18 Phan Xi Pang St, T020-3872130, www.saparooms.com. If you can't manage to snag a room at this boutique hotel, stop in for a meal at its delightful restaurant. An Aussie owner and an Hanoian artist have worked together to decorate this establishment with whimsical, hilltribe-inspired works, while the KOTO-trained chefs (see page 87) whip up delicious meals, though the portions are on the smaller side. Try the homemade cookie and ice-cream dessert. Across the street, check out **Sapa Rooms**' small gallery and cooking school.

❦ **Baguette & Chocolat**, Thac Bac St, T020- 387 1766, www.hoasuaschool.com. Daily 0700-2100. The ground floor of the guest-house comprises a stylish restaurant and café, with small boulangerie attached; lovely home-made cakes for exhausted trekkers. Picnic kits from 32,000d.
❦ **Mimosa**, up a small path off Cay Mau St, T020-387 1377. Daily 0700-2300. A small, slightly chaotic, family-run restaurant. Sit indoors or in the fresh air on a small terrace. A long menu of good Western and Asian dishes. Very popular – service is incredibly slow when busy. Pizzas, pastas and burgers as well as boar, deer, pork and vegetarian dishes.
❦ **Red Dragon Pub**, 21 Muong Hoa St, T020-387 2085, reddragonpub@hn.vnn.vn. Daily 0750-2300. Done out like an English tearoom with mock Tudor beams and red and white checked table cloths. Tea, cornflakes and shepherd's pie. Pub upstairs. Fantastic views.

🍸 Bars and clubs

Sapa and around *p98, map p99*
Red Dragon Pub, see above. The balcony is perfect for a sunset drink.
Tau Bar, 42 Cau May St, beneath **Tau Hotel**, T0912-927756. Daily 1500-late. It must have the longest bar made of a single tree trunk in the world and worth a beer just to see it. Minimalist, with white walls, stools, darts board and pool table.

🎭 Entertainment

Hoa Binh *p95*
Hoa Binh Ethnic Minority Culture Troupe, Hoa Binh 1 Hotel, see Sleeping. Shows featuring dance and music of the Muong, Thai, Hmong and Dao.

Mai Chau and Lac *p95*
Mai Chau Ethnic Minority Dance Troupe. Thai dancing culminating in the communal drinking of sweet, sticky rice wine through

straws from a large pot. This troupe performs most nights in Lac in one of the large stilt houses. Admission is included for people on tours; otherwise give a small contribution.

Sapa and around *p98, map p99*
Ethnic minority dancing at Dragon's Jaw Hill, daily at 0930 and 1500, 10,000d. Also at the **Bamboo Hotel**, 2030-2200; free as long as you buy drinks at **Victoria Sapa** Sat at 2030.

O Shopping

Mai Chau and Lac *p95*
Mai Chau is probably the best place for handicrafts in the northwest. Villagers sell woven goods and fabrics and are dependent on them for a living. There are also paintings and wicker baskets and pots.

Sapa and around *p98, map p99*
Sapa is good for ethnic clothes but it is not possible to buy walking shoes, rucksacks, coats, jackets or mountaineering equipment.

O Activities and tours

Hoa Binh *p95*
Hoa Binh Tourism, next to Hoa Binh 1, T218-385 4374, www.hoabinhtourism.com. Can arrange boat hire as well as visits to minority villages, trekking and transport.

Mai Chau and Lac *p95*
Hanoi tour operators run overnight tours to the area.

Sapa and around *p98, map p99*
Victoria Sapa, see Sleeping. Massage and other treatments are available in the hotel spa. There's a pool, gym and tennis court.

Tour operators
Handspan, 7 Cau May St, T20-387 1214, www.handspan.com. Diverse range of tours in the vicinity of Sapa, including a range of

treks, mountain-bike excursions, homestays and jeep expeditions.
Topas, 24 Muong Hoa St, T020-387 1331, http://topastravel.vn. A Danish and Vietnamese operator offering treks from fairly leisurely 1-day walks to an arduous 4-day assault on Mount Fan Si Pan. Also organizes cycling tours, horse riding and family tours. Well run, with an office in Hanoi.

O Transport

Dien Bien Phu *p97*
For overland transport, see page xxx.
Air The airport is 2 km north of town, off Highway 12. Flights to and from **Hanoi** with **Vietnam Airlines**, Nguyen Huu Tho Rd, T230-382 4948.

Sapa and around *p98, map p99*
Train For train details, see page 93. Passengers alighting at Lao Cai will either be met by their hotel or there is a desk selling minibus tickets to Sapa. Tour operators in Hanoi can also book your ticket for you for a small fee. It is often less hassle than organizing it yourself.

O Directory

Dien Bien Phu *p97*
Banks Vietcombank and Agribank.
Internet Muong Thanh Hotel, 25 Him Lam St.

Sapa and around *p98, map p99*
Banks Agribank, 1 Pho Cau May St, T020-387 1206. Changes many currencies, as will most hotels, but at poor rates. Also changes US$ and € TCs. BIDV, Ngu Chi Son St, T020-387 2569, opposite the lake, has a visa ATM and changes cash and TCs. **Internet** There are now a dozen internet cafés in town. **Post office** There are 2.

Hué and around

→ Colour map 3, B5.

Hué, a gracious imperial city that housed generations of the country's most powerful emperors, was built on the banks of the Huong Giang (Perfume River), 100 km south of the 17th parallel. The river is named after a scented shrub that is supposed to grow at its source.

In many respects, Hué epitomizes the best of Vietnam and, in a country that is rapidly disappearing under concrete, it represents a link to a past where people live in old buildings and don't lock their doors. Whether it is because of the royal heritage or the city's Buddhist tradition, the people of Hué are the gentlest in the country. They speak good English and drive their motorbikes more carefully than anyone else.

Just south of the city are the last resting places of many Vietnamese emperors. A number of war relics in the Demilitarized Zone (DMZ) can be easily visited from Hué. ►► For listings, see pages 115-120.

Ins and outs

Getting there Hué's Phu Bai airport is a 25-minute drive from the city. There are daily connections with Hanoi and Ho Chi Minh City. **Vietnam Airlines** runs a bus service in to town which costs 40,000d. The railway station is more central. The trains tend to fill up, so advance booking is recommended, especially for sleepers. ►► *See Transport, page 119.*

Getting around For the city itself, walking is an option, interspersed, perhaps, with the odd cyclo journey. However, most guesthouses hire out bicycles and this is a very pleasant and slightly more flexible way of exploring Hué and some of the surrounding countryside. A motorbike makes it possible to visit many more sights in a day. Cyclos are pleasant for visiting the more central attractions. *Xe ôm* are a speedier way to see the temples.

Getting to and around the **Imperial Tombs** is easiest by motorbike or car as they are spread over a large area. Most hotels and cafés organize tours either by minibus, bike or by boat. Sailing up the Perfume River is the most peaceful way to travel but only a few of the tombs can be reached by boat so *xe ôm* wait at the riverbank to take passengers on to the tombs. All the tombs are accessible by bicycle but you'll need to set out early. It is also possible to go on the back of a motorbike taxi. Further details are given for each tomb. ►► *See Activities and tours, page 118.*

Best time to visit Hué has a reputation for bad weather. Rainfall of 2770 mm has been recorded in a single month. The rainy season runs from September to January and rainfall is particularly heavy between September and November; the best time to visit is therefore between February and August. However, even in the 'dry' season an umbrella is handy. Temperatures in Hué can also be pretty cool in winter, compared with Danang, Nha Trang and other places to the south, as cold air tends to get bottled here, trapped by mountains to the south. For several months each year neither fans nor air conditioning are required.

Background

Hué was the capital of Vietnam during the Nguyen Dynasty, which ruled Vietnam between 1802 and 1945. For the first time in Vietnamese history a single court controlled the land from Yunnan (southern China) southwards to the Gulf of Siam. To link the north and south (more than 1500 km), the Nguyen emperors built and maintained the Mandarin Road (Quan Lo), interspersed with relay stations. Even in 1802, when it was not yet complete, it took couriers just 13 days to travel between Hué and Ho Chi Minh City, and five days between Hué and Hanoi. If they arrived more than two days late, couriers were punished with a flogging. There cannot have been a better road in Southeast Asia nor a more effective incentive system.

Although the Confucian bureaucracy and some of the dynasty's technical achievements may have been remarkable, there was continued discontent and uprisings. Court was packed with scheming mandarins, princesses, eunuchs and scholars.

In 1883 a French fleet assembled at the mouth of the Perfume River and opened fire. After taking heavy casualties, Emperor Hiep Hoa sued for peace and signed a treaty making Vietnam a protectorate of France. As French influence over Vietnam increased, the power and influence of the Nguyen waned. The undermining effect of the French presence was compounded by significant schisms in Vietnamese society. In particular, the spread of Christianity was undermining traditional hierarchies. Although the French and then the Japanese found it to their advantage to maintain the framework of Vietnamese imperial rule, the system became hollow and, eventually, irrelevant. The last Nguyen Emperor, Bao Dai, abdicated on 30 August 1945.

During the 1968 Tet offensive, Viet Cong soldiers holed up in Hué's Citadel for 25 days. The bombardment which ensued, as US troops attempted to root them out, caused extensive damage to the Thai Hoa Palace and other monuments. During their occupation of Hué, the NVA forces settled old scores, shooting, beheading and even burning alive 3000 people, including civil servants, police officers and anyone connected with, or suspected of being sympathetic to, the government in Ho Chi Minh City.

Central Hué → *For listings, see pages 115-120.*

Imperial City

ⓘ *Entrance through the Ngo Mon Gate, 23 Thang 8 St, 0700-1700, 55,000d. Guided tour 100,000d for 1½ hrs, guiding can last until 1900.*

The Imperial City at Hué is built on the same principles as the Forbidden Palace in Beijing. It is enclosed by thick outer walls (**Kinh Thanh**), 7-10 m thick, along with moats, canals and towers. Emperor Gia Long commenced construction in 1804 after geomancers had decreed a suitable location and orientation for the palace. The site enclosed the land of eight villages (for which the inhabitants received compensation) and covered 6 sq km, sufficient area to house the emperor and all his family, courtiers, bodyguards and servants. It took 20,000 men to construct the walls alone. Not only has the city been damaged by war and incessant conflict, but also by natural disasters such as floods which, in the mid-19th century, inundated the city to a depth of several metres.

Chinese custom decreed that the 'front' of the palace should face south (like the Emperor) and this is the direction from which visitors approach. Over the outer moat, a pair of gates pierce the outer walls: the **Hien Nhon** and **Chuong Duc** gates. Just inside are two groups of massive cannon; four through the Hien Nhon Gate and five through the Chuong Duc Gate. These are the Nine Holy Cannon (**Cuu Vi Than Cong**), cast in bronze in 1803 on the orders of Gia Long. The cannon are named after the four seasons and the five elements, and on each is carved its name, rank, firing instructions and how the bronze of which they are made was acquired. They are 5 m in length but have never been fired. Like the giant urns outside the Hien Lam Cac (see page 109), they are meant to symbolize the permanence

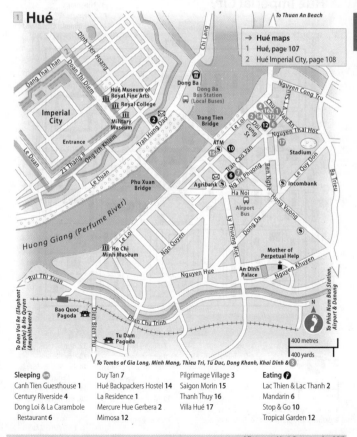

Hué

→ **Hué maps**
1 Hué, page 107
2 Hué Imperial City, page 108

of the empire. Between the two gates is a massive **flag tower**, from which the flag of the National Liberation Front flew for 24 days during the Tet Offensive in 1968.

Northwards from the cannon, and over one of three bridges which span a second moat, is the **Ngo Mon**, or Royal Gate (**1**), built in 1833 during the reign of Emperor Minh Mang. (The ticket office is just to the right.) The gate, remodelled on a number of occasions since its original construction, is surmounted by a pavilion from where the emperor would view palace ceremonies. Of the five entrances, the central Ngo Mon was only opened for the emperor to pass through. UNESCO has thrown itself into the restoration of Ngo Mon with vigour and the newly finished pavilion atop the gate now gleams and glints in the sun; those who consider it garish can console themselves with the thought that this is how it might have appeared in Minh Mang's time.

North from the Ngo Mon is the **Golden Water Bridge** (**2**) – again reserved solely for the emperor's use – between **two tanks** (**3**), lined with laterite blocks. This leads

2 Hué Imperial City

→ **Hué maps**
1 Hué, page 107
2 **Hué Imperial City, page 108**

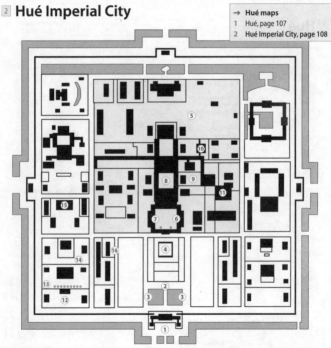

N

| 100 metres |
| 100 yards |

1 Ngo Mon (Royal Gate)
2 Golden Water Bridge

3 Tanks
4 Dai Trieu Nghi (Great Rites Courtyard) & Thai Hoa Palace (Palace of Supreme Harmony)
5 ☐ Tu Cam Thanh (Purple Forbidden City)
6 Ta Pavilion

7 Huu Vu Pavilion
8 Central Pavilion, private apartments of the Emperor
9 Quang Minh Palace
10 Royal Reading Pavilion
11 Royal (East) Theatre

12 Hien Lam Cac
13 9 Bronze urns
14 Thé Temple (Temple of Generations)
15 Hung Temple
16 Waiting Pavilion (Huu Ta Dai Lam Vien)

to the **Dai Trieu Nghi** (Great Rites Courtyard, **4**), on the north side of which is the **Thai Hoa Palace** (Palace of Supreme Harmony), constructed by Gia Long in 1805 and used for his coronation in 1806. From here, sitting on his throne raised up on a dais, the emperor would receive ministers, foreign emissaries, mandarins and military officers during formal ceremonial occasions. In front of the palace are 18 stone stelae, which stipulate the arrangement of the nine mandarinate ranks on the Great Rites Courtyard: the upper level was for ministers, mandarins and officers of the upper grade; the lower for those of lower grades. Civil servants would stand on the left and the military on the right. Only royal princes were allowed to stand in the palace itself, which is perhaps the best-preserved building in the complex. Its columns, tiled floor and ceiling have all been restored.

North of the Palace of Supreme Harmony is the **Tu Cam Thanh** (Purple Forbidden City **5**), reserved for the use of the emperor and his family, and surrounded by walls, 1 m thick, to form a city within a city. Tragically, the Forbidden City was virtually destroyed during the 1968 Tet offensive. The two **Mandarin Palaces** and the **Royal Reading Pavilion** (**10**) are all that survive. The Royal Reading Pavilion has been rebuilt but, needless to say, has no books.

At the far side of Thai Hoa Palace are two enormous **bronze urns** (Vac Dong) decorated with birds, plants and wild animals, and weighing about 1500 kg each. On either side are the **Ta** (**6**) and **Huu Vu** (**7**) pavilions, one converted into a souvenir art shop, the other a mock throne room in which tourists can pay US$5 to dress up and play the part of king. On the far side of the palace are the outer northern walls of the citadel and the north gate.

Most of the surviving buildings of interest are to be found on the west side of the palace, running between the outer walls and the walls of the Forbidden City. At the southwest corner is the well-preserved and beautiful **Hien Lam Cac** (**12**), a pavilion built in 1821, in front of which stand nine massive **bronze urns** (**13**) cast between 1835 and 1837 on the orders of Emperor Minh Mang. It is estimated that they weigh between 1500 kg and 2600 kg, and each has 17 decorative figures, animals, rivers, flowers and landscapes representing between them the wealth, beauty and unity of the country. The central, largest and most ornate urn is dedicated to the founder of the empire, Emperor Gia Long. Next to the urns walking northwards is **Thé Temple** (Temple of Generations, **14**). Built in 1821, it contains altars honouring 10 of the kings of the Nguyen Dynasty (Duc Duc and Hiep Hoa are missing) behind which are meant to be kept a selection of their personal belongings. It was only in 1954 that the stelae depicting the three Revolutionary emperors, Ham Nghi, Thanh Thai and Duy Tan, were brought into the temple. The French, perhaps fearing they would become a focus of discontent, prevented the Vietnamese from erecting altars in their memory. North of the Thé Temple is **Hung Temple** (**15**), built in 1804 for the worship of Gia Long's father, Nguyen Phuc Luan, the father of the founder of the Nguyen Dynasty.

Hué Museum of Royal Fine Arts
ⓘ *3 Le Truc St, Tue-Sun 0700-1700, until 1730 in summer (14 Apr-14 Oct), 35,000d. No cameras or video cameras, over shoes are provided, information in English. The collection still may be temporarily housed at An Dinh Palace, 97 Phan Dinh Phung St and also with an entrance at 150 Nguyen Hué St.*

Housed in the Long An Palace, the museum contains a reasonable collection of ceramics, furniture, screens and bronzeware and some stunning, embroidered imperial clothes. The building itself is worthy of note for its elegant construction. Built by Emperor Thieu Tri in 1845, it was dismantled and erected on the present site in 1909.

As the geographical and spiritual centre of the Nguyen Dynasty, Hué and the surrounding area is the site of numerous pagodas, seven imperial tombs and the tombs of numerous other royal personages, countless courtiers and successful mandarins. Many of these are located close to the Perfume River.

Each of the tombs follows the same stylistic formula, although they also reflect the individual tastes of the emperor in question. The tombs were built during the lifetime of each emperor, who took a great interest in their design and construction; they were, after all, meant to ensure his comfort in the next life. Each mausoleum, variously arranged, has five design elements: a courtyard with statues of elephants, horses and military and civil mandarins (usually approached through a park of rare trees); a stela pavilion (with an engraved eulogy composed by the king's son and heir); a Temple of the Soul's Tablets; a pleasure pavilion, and a grave. Geomancers decreed that they should also have a stream and a mountainous screen in front. The tombs faithfully copy Chinese prototypes, although most art historians claim that they fall short in terms of execution.

Thien Mu Pagoda → Colour map 3, B5.

ⓘ *Easy 4-km bicycle (or cyclo) ride from the city, following the north bank of the river upstream.*

Thien Mu Pagoda (the Elderly Goddess Pagoda), also known as the Thien Mau Tu Pagoda, and locally as the **Linh Mu Pagoda** (the name used on most local maps), is the finest in Hué and beautifully sited on the north bank of the Perfume River. It was built in 1601 by Nguyen Hoang, the governor of Hué, after an old woman appeared to him and said that the site had supernatural significance and should be marked by the construction of a pagoda. The monastery is the oldest in Hué, and the seven-storey **Phuoc Duyen** (Happiness and Grace Tower), built later by Emperor Thieu Tri in 1844, is 21 m high, with each storey containing an altar to a different Buddha. The summit of the tower is crowned with a water pitcher to catch the rain, water representing the source of happiness. Arranged around the tower are four smaller buildings one of which contains the **Great Bell**, cast in 1710 under the orders of the Nguyen Lord, Nguyen Phuc Chu, and weighing 2200 kg. Beneath another of the surrounding pavilions is a monstrous **marble turtle** on which is a stela, carved in 1715 and 2.6 m high, recounting the development of Buddhism in Hué. Beyond the tower, the entrance to the pagoda is through a triple gateway patrolled by six carved and vividly painted guardians, two on each gate. The roof of the sanctuary itself is decorated with *jataka* stories (birth stories of the Buddha). At the front of the sanctuary is a laughing Buddha in brass. Behind that are an assortment of gilded Buddhas and a crescent-shaped gong, cast in 1677 by Jean de la Croix. Thich Quang Duc, the first monk to commit suicide through self immolation, came from this pagoda (see page 162); the grey Austin in which he made the journey to his death in Ho Chi Minh City is still kept here in a garage in the temple garden.

Tomb of Emperor Gia Long → Colour map 3, B5.

ⓘ *South of town on a tributary of the Perfume River, daily 0630-1730, 55,000d for the upkeep of the tomb. Get there by bicycle or motorbike.*

The Tomb of Emperor Gia Long is the most distant from Hué and is rarely visited. Overgrown with venerable mango trees and devoid of tourists, touts and ticket sellers, it is the most atmospheric of all the tombs. And, given the historical changes that were to be wrought by the dynasty Gia Long founded, this is arguably the most significant tomb in Hué.

Nguyen Anh, or Gia Long as he was crowned in 1802, came to power with French support. His reign was despotic: when his European advisers suggested that encouragement of industry would lead to the betterment of his poorer subjects, Gia Long replied that he preferred them poor. In fact, the poor were virtual slaves during his reign: the price for one healthy young buffalo was one healthy young girl. It's not surprising, then, that a study by a Vietnamese scholar estimated that there were 105 peasant uprisings between 1802 and 1820 alone. The Vietnamese have never forgiven Gia Long for his despotism nor for the fact that he gave the French a foothold in Vietnam; they still say of him that "*cong ran can ga nha*" (he carried home the snake that killed the chicken).

To reach Gia Long's tomb, take Dien Bien Phu Street out of town. After a couple of kilometres turn right at the T-junction facing pine-shrouded Dan Nam Giao Temple and take the first left onto Minh Mang. Continue past the sign marking your departure from Hué and take the right-hand branch of the fork in the road. After a short distance the road joins the riverbank and heads for some 2 km towards the new Hué bypass (Highway 1) across the river. Follow the riverbank directly underneath this bridge and continue straight on as the road begins to deteriorate. A few metres beyond the Ben Do 1 km milestone is a red sign to 'Gia Long Tomb'. Down a steep path a sampan waits to ferry passengers across this tributary of the Perfume River (bargain but expect to pay US$2-3 return); on the far side, follow the track upstream for about 1 km. Turn right by a café with two billiard tables and then, almost immediately, turn left. Keep on this path. Ask for directions along the way.

Gia Long's geomancers did a great job finding this site: with the mountainous screen in front it is a textbook example of a final resting place. Interestingly, although they had first choice of all the possible sites, this is the furthest tomb from the palace: clearly they took their task seriously. Gia Long's mausoleum was built between 1814 and 1820 and, as the first of the dynasty, set the formula for the later tombs. There is a surrounding lotus pond and steps lead up to a courtyard, where the Minh Thanh ancestral temple stands resplendent in red and gold. To the right is a double burial chamber, walled and locked, where Gia Long and his wife are interred (the emperor's tomb is fractionally the taller). The chamber is perfectly lined up with the two huge obelisks on the far side of the lake. Beyond this is a courtyard with five, now headless, mandarins, horses and elephants on each side; steps lead up to the stela eulogizing the emperor's reign, composed, presumably, by his eldest son, Minh Mang, as was the custom. This grey monolith, engraved in Chinese characters, remained miraculously undisturbed during two turbulent centuries.

Tomb of Emperor Minh Mang → *Colour map 3, B5.*
ⓘ *12 km south of Hué, daily 0630-1730, 55,000đ. To get there by bicycle or motorbike follow the directions for Gia Long's tomb (opposite) but cross the Perfume River using the new road bridge; on the far side of the bridge turn left.*

The Tomb of Emperor Minh Mang is possibly the finest of all the imperial tombs. Built between 1841 and 1843, it is sited south of the city. In terms of architectural poise and balance, and richness of decoration, it has no peer in the area. The tomb's layout, along a single central and sacred axis (*Shendao*), is unusual in its symmetry; no other tomb, with the possible exception of Khai Dinh, achieves the same unity of constituent parts, nor draws the eye onwards so easily and pleasantly from one visual element to the next. The tomb was traditionally approached through the **Dai Hong Mon**; today, visitors pass through a side gate into the ceremonial courtyard, which contains an array of statuary. Next is the stela pavilion in which there is a carved eulogy to the emperor composed by his son, Thieu Tri. Continuing downwards through a series of courtyards visitors see, in turn, the **Sung An Temple** dedicated to Minh Mang and his empress; a small garden with flower beds that once formed the Chinese character for 'longevity', and two sets of stone bridges. The first consists of three spans, the central one of which (**Trung Dao Bridge**) was for the sole use of the emperor. The second, single bridge, leads to a short flight of stairs with naga balustrades at the end of which is a locked bronze door (no access). The door leads to the tomb itself which is surrounded by a circular wall.

Tomb of Tu Duc → Colour map 3, B5.
① *7 km south Hué, daily 0630-1730, 55,000d. If you're travelling by boat, a return* xe ôm *trip from the riverbank is 30,000d.*
The Tomb of Tu Duc was built between 1864 and 1867 in a pine wood. The complex is enclosed by a wall and encompasses a lake, with lotus and water hyacinth. An island on the Lake has a number of replicas of famous temples, built by the king, which are now rather difficult to discern. Tu Doc often came here to relax, and composed poetry and listened to music. The **Xung Khiem Pavilion**, built in 1865, has recently been restored with UNESCO's help and is the most attractive building here.

West of the lake, the tomb complex follows the formula described above: ceremonial square, mourning yard with pavilion and then the tomb itself. To the left of Tu Duc's tomb are the tombs of his Empress, Le Thien Anh, and adopted son, Kien Phuc. Many of the pavilions are crumbling and ramshackle, lending the complex a rather tragic air. This is appropriate since, though he had 104 wives, Tu Duc fathered no sons and was therefore forced to write his own eulogy, a fact which he took as a bad omen. The eulogy itself recounts the sadness in Tu Duc's life. It was shortly after Tu Duc's reign that France gained full control of Vietnam.

Tomb of Khai Dinh
① *10 km south of Hué, daily 0630-1730, 55,000d. To get there by motorbike or bicycle follow the directions for Gia Long's tomb but turn immediately left past small shops after the new river crossing (Highway 1) and head straight on, over a small crossroads, parallel to the main road. If you're travelling by boat, a return* xe ôm *trip from the riverbank is 30,000d.*
The Tomb of Khai Dinh was built between 1920 and 1932 and is the last mausoleum of the Nguyen Dynasty. By the time Khai Dinh was contemplating the afterlife, brick had given way in popularity to concrete, so the structure is now beginning to deteriorate. Nevertheless, it occupies a fine position on the Chau Mountain facing southwest towards a large white statue of Quan Am, also built by Khai Dinh. The valley, used for the cultivation of cassava and sugar cane, and the pine-covered mountains, make this one of the most beautifully sited and peaceful of the tombs. Indeed, before construction begin, Khai Dinh had to remove the tombs of Chinese nobles who had already selected the site for its beauty and auspicious orientation. A total of 127 steep steps lead up to the Honour Courtyard with statuary of mandarins, elephants and horses. An octagonal stela pavilion in the centre of the mourning yard contains a stone stela engraved with a eulogy to the emperor. At the top of some more stairs are the tomb and shrine of Khai Dinh, containing a bronze statue of the emperor sitting on his throne and holding a jade

sceptre. The body is interred 9 m below ground level. The interior is richly decorated with ornate and colourful murals (the artist incurred the wrath of the emperor and only just escaped execution), floor tiles, and decorations built up with fragments of porcelain. It is the most elaborate of all the tombs and took 11 years to build. Such was the cost of construction that Khai Dinh had to levy additional taxes to fund the project.

Amphitheatre and Elephant Temple
ⓘ *South bank of the river, about 3 km west of Hué railway station, free. To get there by bicycle or motorbike turn left up a paved track opposite 203 Bui Thi Xuan St, the track for the Elephant Temple runs in front of the amphitheatre (off to the right).*

The Ho Quyen (Amphitheatre) was built in 1830 by Emperor Minh Mang as a venue for the popular duels between elephants and tigers. This royal sport was in earlier centuries staged on an island in the Perfume River or on the riverbanks themselves but, by 1830, it was considered desirable for the royal party to be able to observe the duels without placing themselves at risk from escaping tigers. The amphitheatre is said to have been last used in 1904. The walls of the amphitheatre are 5 m high and the arena is 44 m in diameter. On the south side, beneath the royal box, is one large gateway (for the elephant) and, to the north, five smaller entrances for the tigers.

Den Voi Re, the Temple of the Elephant Trumpet, dedicated to the call of the fighting elephant, is a few hundred metres away. It is a modest little place and fairly run down, with a large pond in front and two small elephant statues. Presumably this is where elephants were blessed before battle or perhaps where the unsuccessful ones were mourned.

Thanh Toan Covered Bridge
ⓘ *8 km west of Hué.*

The bridge was built in the reign of King Le Hien Tong (1740-1786) by Tran Thi Dao, a childless woman, as an act of charity, hoping that God would bless her with a baby. The structure, with its shelter for the tired and homeless, attracted the interest of several kings who granted the village immunity from a number of taxes. Unfortunately, the original yin-yang tiles have been replaced with ugly green enamelled tube tiles but the bridge is still in good condition. The route to the bridge passes through beautiful countryside. Travel there by bicycle or motorbike in the glow of the late afternoon sun.

Around Hué

The Demilitarized Zone (DMZ) → *Colour map 3, B4.*

ⓘ *Most visitors see the sights of the DMZ, including Khe Sanh and the Ho Chi Minh Trail, on a tour. A 1-day tour of all the DMZ sights can be booked from any of Hué's tour operators from US$10, depart 0600, return 1800-2000.*▸▸ *See Activities and tours, page 118.*

The incongruously named Demilitarized Zone (DMZ), scene of some of the fiercest fighting of the Vietnam War, lies along the **Ben Hai River** and the better-known **17th Parallel**. The **Hien Luong Bridge** on the 17th parallel is included in most tours. The DMZ was the creation of the 1954 Geneva Peace Accord, which divided the country into two spheres of influence prior to elections that were never held. Like its counterpart in Germany, the boundary evolved into a national border, separating Communist from Capitalist but, unlike its European equivalent, it was the triumph of Communism that saw its demise.

At **Dong Ha**, to the north of Hué, Highway 9 branches off the main coastal Highway 1 and heads 80 km west to the border with Laos (see below). Along this route is **Khe Sanh** (now called Huong Hoa), the site of one of the most famous battles of the war. The battleground is 3 km from the village. There's also a small **museum** ⓘ *25,000d*, at the former Tacon military base, surrounded by military hardware.

A section of the **Ho Chi Minh Trail** runs close to Khe Sanh. This is another popular but inevitably disappointing sight, given that its whole purpose was to be as inconspicuous as possible and anything you see was designed to be invisible, from the air at least. However, it's worthy of a pilgrimage considering the sacrifice of millions of Vietnamese porters and the role it played in the American defeat (see box, page 165).

Tours to the DMZ usually also include the **tunnels of Vinh Moc** ⓘ *13 km off Highway 1 and 6 km north of Ben Hai River, 20,000d*, which served a similar function to the better-known Cu Chi tunnels in the south. They evolved as families in the heavily bombed village dug themselves shelters beneath their houses and then joined up with their neighbours. Later the tunnels developed a more offensive role when Viet Cong soldiers fought from them. Some regard these tunnels as more 'authentic' than the 'touristy' tunnels of Cu Chi.

The **Rock Pile** is a 230-m-high limestone outcrop just south of the DMZ. It served as a US observation post, with troops, ammunition, Budweiser and prostitutes all being helicoptered in. Although it was chosen as an apparently unassailable position, the sheer walls of the Rock Pile were eventually scaled by the Viet Cong.

Hai Van Pass and Lang Co → *Colour map 4, B5.*

Between Hué and Danang a finger of the Truong Son Mountains juts eastwards, extending all the way to the sea: almost as though God were somewhat roguishly trying to divide the country into two equal halves. The mountains act as an important climatic barrier, trapping the cooler, damper air masses to the north and bottling them up over Hué, which accounts for Hué's shocking weather. They also mark an abrupt linguistic divide: the Hué dialect (the language of the royal court) to the north is still the source of bemusement to many southerners. The physical barrier to north-south communication has resulted in some spectacular engineering solutions: the single track and narrow gauge **railway line** closely follows the coastline, sometimes almost hanging over the sea while Highway 1 winds its way equally precariously over the Lang Co lagoon and Hai Van Pass.

The road passes through many pretty, red-tiled villages, compact and surrounded by clumps of bamboo and fruit trees, which provide shade, shelter and sustenance. The idyllic fishing village of **Lang Co** is just off Highway 1, about 65 km south of Hué, and has a number of cheap and good seafood restaurants.

Shortly after crossing the Lang Co lagoon, dotted with coracles and fish traps, the road begins the long haul up to **Hai Van Pass** (Deo Hai Van or 'Pass of the Ocean Clouds'), known to the French as 'Col des Nuages'. The pass is 497 m above the waves and once marked the border between Vietnam and Champa. The pass is peppered with abandoned pillboxes and crowned with an old fort, originally built by the Nguyen Dynasty from Hué and used as a relay station for the pony express on the old Mandarin Road. Subsequently used by the French, it is a pretty shabby affair today, collecting wind-blown litter and sometimes used by the Army for a quiet brew-up and a smoke. Looking back to the north, stretching into the haze is the littoral and lagoon of Lang Co; to the south is Danang Bay and Monkey Mountain, and at your feet lies a patch of green paddies that belong to the leper colony, accessible only by boat.

◉ Hué and around listings

For Sleeping and Eating price codes and other relevant information, see pages 40-43.

◉ Sleeping

Hué *p105, map p107*
Most hotels lie to the south of the Perfume River, although there are a couple to the north in the old Vietnamese part of town. Hué suffers from a dearth of quality accommodation but this has improved in recent years.

LL Vedana Lagoon Resort & Spa, Zone 1, Phu Loc, T054-381 9397, www.vedanalagoon. com. Due to open in Dec 2010, this resort is set on a lagoon with villas, bungalows and houseboats. There's also a spa.

LL-AL La Residence Hotel & Spa, 5 Le Loi St, T054-383 7475, www.la-residence-hue. com. For lovers of art deco, this is an essential place to stay. Home of the French governor of Annam in the 1920s, it has been beautifully restored with 122 rooms, a restaurant, lobby bar, spa and swimming pool. The rooms in the original governor's residence are the most stylish, with 4-poster beds; other rooms are extremely comfortable too, with all mod cons. Filling breakfasts and free internet. Highly recommended.

LL-B Saigon Morin, 30 Le Loi St, T054-382 3526, www.morinhotel.com.vn. The best hotel in Hué, this is still recognizable as the fine hotel built by the Morin brothers in the 1880s. Arranged around a courtyard with a small pool, the rooms are large and comfortable. All have a/c, satellite TV and hot water. The courtyard is a delightful place to sit in the evening and enjoy a quiet drink.

L-A Century Riverside, 49 Le Loi St, T054-382 3390, www.centuryriversidehue. com. Fabulous river views and comfortable, nicely furnished rooms in this very imposing building. Note that not all rooms have been renovated, so enquire before booking. There's a pool, tennis courts and a massage service. Used by dozens of tour operators.

AL-L The Pilgrimage Village, 130 Minh Mang Rd, T054-388 5461, www. pilgrimagevillage.com. Tastefully designed rooms in a village setting ranging from honeymoon and pool suites to superior rooms. The rooms in small houses with private pools are gorgeous and recommended. There are 2 restaurants including **Junrei**, see page 117, a number of bars, a beautiful and atmospheric spa (the Vietnamese aromatherapy massage is outstanding), open to outside guests also, and 2 inviting pools. Cooking and t'ai chi classes are available. There's a complimentary shuttle service to and from town.

AL-B Mercure Hué Gerbera, 38 Le Loi St, T054-393 6688, www.mercure.com. This brings a new class of hotel to Hué with 110 rooms a pool and restaurant that serves an excellent buffet breakfast. The vast lobby is rather characterless but service is excellent. The hotel location is downtown and rooms are super comfortable.

A-B Villa Hué, 4 Tran Quang Khai St, T054-383 1628, www.villahue.com. Villa Hué, in an attractive building, is a 12-room hotel used by the Hué Tourism School to train up future hotel managers in conjunction with the Luxembourg Development Cooperation. All rooms are spacious and comfortable and have TV, a/c, and tea- and coffee-making facilities and come with attractive soft furnishings. Vietnamese and Western food is served at the restaurant. There's a lobby bar and an outdoor seating area in the courtyard. Cooking classes are offered. Recommended.

A-D Duy Tan, 12 Hung Vuong St, T054-382 5001, www.duytanhotel.com.vn. Large building in a bustling part of town, with comfortable superior rooms. The standard rooms are spartan but fully equipped.

E Dong Loi, 19 Pham Ngu Lao St, T054-382 2296, www.hoteldongloi.com. Well situated and surrounded by internet cafés, shops and restaurants, this is a bright, breezy, airy and comfortable hotel. All rooms have a/c and hot water and all except the cheapest have a bath. Family-run, friendly and helpful service. The excellent **La Carambole Restaurant** adjoins the hotel.

The little *hem* (alley) opposite the **Century Riverside** has some comfortable and cheerful guesthouses – easily the best-value accommodation in Hué. Recommended are:

E-F Canh Tien Guesthouse, 9/66 Le Loi St, T054-382 2772, http://canhtienhotel.chez-alice.fr. 12 rooms with fan or a/c. Cheaper rooms have fans; the most expensive have a balcony. Welcoming family.

E-G Hué Backpackers' Hostel, 10 Pham Ngu Lao St, T054-382 6567, www.vietnambackpackershostels.com. A fabulous new travellers' focus with a bar downstairs and ultra-clean rooms and dorms upstairs with a lovely balcony over the street for chilling. Tours offered too. Prices include breakfast. Happy hour 2000-2100.

E-G Thanh Thuy, 66/6 (6 Kiet 66) Le Loi St, T54-3824585, thanhthuy66@dng.vnn.vn. Another small, peaceful, clean and friendly family-run guesthouse, with 6 rooms, a/c and hot water. Can arrange car hire at good rates (around US$25 per day). Super helpful. Offers an excellent tour to the elephant springs, Lang Co, Hai Van Pass, Cham Museum and Marble Mountains for US$30. Rents motos and car with driver.

F Mimosa, 66/10 (10 Kiet 66) Le Loi St, T054-382 8068. French is spoken when the owner is here. 8 rooms, with a/c, hot water and bath that are quiet, simple and clean. Rooms with fan are cheaper.

🍴 Eating

Hué cuisine is excellent; delicately flavoured and painstakingly prepared. Hué dishes are robust, notably the famed *bun bo Hué* – round white noodles in soup, with slices of beef, laced with chilli oil of exquisite piquancy. Restaurants for locals tend to close early; get there before 2000. Traveller cafés and restaurants keep serving till about 2200.

Hué *p105, map p107*

¶¶-¶ **Junrei**, Pilgrimage Village, 130 Minh Mang Rd, T054-388 5461. Open 0600-2200. Lovely Hué-lite stylized restaurant building serving delicious Vietnamese Bun Bo Hué and passionfruit mousse among other delights. Western menu too. Attentive service.

¶¶ **La Carambole**,19 Pham Ngu Lao St, T054-381 0491, la_carambole @hotmail.com. Daily 0700-2300. One of the most popular restaurants in town and deservedly so. It is incredibly busy especially for dinner when the imperial-style dinner is recommended.

¶¶ **Saigon Morin**, see Sleeping. Excellent buffets in a garden setting with a range of specialty Hué cuisine. While you dine, be entertained by Royal Music performers.

¶¶-¶ **Mediterraneo D2 Hué**, 7 Ben Nghe St, T054-381 9849. The softest, doughiest pizza in Vietnam. Highly recommended. Ice cream served too in the double courtyard set-up.

¶¶-¶ **Tropical Garden Restaurant**, 27 Chu Van An St, T054-3847 1431. Dine alfresco in a small leafy garden just a short walk from the Perfume River. Beef soup with starfruit and mackerel baked in pineapple.

¶ **Jardin de Y Thao**, 3 Thach Han St, T054-352 3018, ythaogarden@gmail.com. Eating here is an extraordinary experience. The set menu of 8 courses is a culinary adventure with some amazing animals-from-food sculptures. The old house in a pretty garden is delightful. Recommended.

¶ **Lac Thanh**, 6A Dinh Tien Hoang St, T054-352 4674 and ¶ **Lac Thien**, 6 Dinh Tien Hoang St, T054-352 7348. Arguably Hué's most famous restaurants, run by schismatic branches of the same deaf-mute family in adjacent buildings. You go to one or the other: under no circumstances should clients patronize both establishments. **Lac Thien** serves excellent dishes from a diverse and inexpensive menu, and the family is riotous and entertaining, but service has been known to be slack.

¶ **Mandarin**, 24 Tran Cao Van St, T054-382 1281, www.mrcumandarin.com. Recently moved again to larger premises but stil with the trademark lovely photos adorning the walls. Serves a variety of cheap food. Travel services and bike rental. Mr Cu is one of the most helpful café owners in the whole of Vietnam and is helped by his staff. Highly recommended.

¶ **Stop and Go**, 3 Huong Vuong St, T54-3827051, stopandgocafe@yahoo.com. Travel café run by the relatives of the silver-haired Mr Do. His specialities include rice pancakes and the Hué version of spring rolls, which are excellent and cheap.

🍸 Bars and clubs

Hué *p105, map p107*

DMZ Bar, 60 Le Loi St, T054-382 3414, www.dmz-bar.com. Daily 0900-0200. Hué's first bar, with pool table, cold beer and spirits at affordable prices. Good place to meet people and pick up tourist information.

Why Not?, 21 Vo Thi Sau St. Slightly arty café bar, with a decent selection of food and drink.

🎭 Entertainment

Hué *p105, map p107*

Rent a **dragon boat** and sail up the Perfume River with private singers and musicians; tour offices and major hotels will arrange groups.

See a **Royal Court performance** in the Imperial City's theatre or listen to performers during the **Saigon Morin**'s evening buffet.

O Shopping

Hué p105, map p107

Shops around the **Century Riverside Hotel**, for example Le Loi and Pham Ngu Lao streets, sell ceramics, silk and clothes. The non bai tho or poem hats are also available. These are a unique Hué form of the standard conical hat (non lá), made from bamboo and palm leaves, with love poetry, songs, proverbs or simply a design stencilled on to them. The decoration is only visible if the hat is held up to the light and viewed from the inside.

No Vietnamese visitor would leave Hué without having stocked up on me xung, a sugary, peanut and toffee confection coated in sesame seeds.

Healing the Wounded Heart Shop, 23 Vo Thi Sau St, T054-383 3694, www.spiralfoundation.org. Recycled products such as water bottles and electricity wires are fashioned into bags and homeware by disabled people. Profits fund heart surgery for poor children and support the livelihoods of Hué's disabled craftsmen.

O Activities and tours

Hué p105, map p107

Bus and boat tours to the Imperial Tombsare organized by tour operators and hotels. Local tour operators charge round US$5-6 per person (but excluding tomb entrance fees) to visit Thien Mu Pagoda, Hon Chien Temple, Tu Duc, Minh Mang and Khai Dinh's Tombs, 0800-0830, returning 1530-1630.

There are also day tours to some of the sights of the Vietnam War, from US$8-75 for a day's programme depending on group size and mode of transport for sights including **Vinh Moc** tunnels and museum, the **Ho Chi Minh Trail** and **Khe Sanh**. Those wishing to travel overland to Laos can arrange to be dropped off in Khe Sanh and pay less.

SNV, a Dutch NGO, in conjunction with local tour operators, have developed new Hué region tours to promote tourism in disadvantaged communities. These include a handicrafts village tour; a trip to the ancient village of Phuoc Tic with its preserved old Hué-style houses; visiting a fishing village at Tam Giang Lagoon with a homestay option; a visit to the Katu ethnic minority area of Nam Dong with homestay option and visit to A Luoi district home of Ta Oi ethnic minorities, also with a homestay option. One operator includes **Asia Travel Land**, 42 Nguyen Tri Phuong St, T054-384 0888, www.asiatravelland.com.

Tour operators

Café on Thu Wheels, 3/34 Nguyen Tri Phuong St, T54-3832241, minhthuhue@yahoo.com. Run by Minh Toan Thu. Good-value US$10 motorbike tours. The formidable Thu allows you to tailor your own tour taking in the best pagodas and sites around Hué, with well-informed English-speaking guides. DMZ tours are US$13.

DMZ Café Open Tour, T09-8519 7538, dmzdodienat@gmail.com. Mr Do Dien was a translator for the US Army, making this a unique experience to speak to and be guided by someone who can speak English. Mr Dien is knowledgable and can take you to the principal spots but you will need patience as his English is now not clearly understood. However, a private tour with him beats a large minibus tour any day.

Mandarin Café, 24 Tran Cao Van St, T54-382 1281, www.mrcumandarin.com. This café offers a multitude of services and its staff are also extremely helpful. Open Tour Buses arranged. All day trip to the tombs, US$5; DMZ tour, US$14. Sunset boat trip US$10. Free internet available.

Sinh Tourist (formerly Sinh Café), 60 Nguyen Tri Phuong St,12 Hung Vuong St, T054-382 6867, www.thesinhtourist.vn. Offers a number of competitively priced tours and money-changing facilities.

Stop and Go Café, 3 Huong Vuong St, T054-382 7051, T090-512 6767 (mob),

Border essentials: Vietnam–Laos

The Vietnamese border post is 3 km beyond Lao Bao village at the western end of Highway 9; Lao immigration is 500m west at Dansavanh. Once in Laos, Route 9 heads west over the Annamite Mountains to Xepon (45 km) and on to Savannakhet (236 km from the border). We have received reports of long delays at this crossing, particularly entering Vietnam, as paperwork is scrutinized and bags are checked and doublechecked. Don't be surprised if formalities take an hour – and keep smiling! Expect to pay 'overtime fees' on the Lao side if you come through on a Saturday or Sunday or after 1600 on a weekday. Lao immigration can issue 30-day tourist visas for US$30-45. You can also get a Lao visa in advance, if need be, from the Lao consulate in Danang (12 Tran Qui Cap Street, T0511-3382 1208, ketkeomanivong@yahoo.com, open 0800-1130 and 1330-1630). The closest Vietnamese consulate is in Savannakhet; see page 434.

Transport There are buses from Hué direct to Savannakhet. There are also buses direct to the border from Le Duan St in Dong Ha, 1-1½ hours. *Xe ôm* from Lao Bao village to the border, US$1. **Sepon Travel**, 189 Le Duan Street, Dong Ha, T053-385 5289, www.sepontour.com, runs buses to Laos. There are daily departures for the Lao town of Savannakhet from Dansavanh inside Laos. Buses also depart from Xepon (45 km west of the border) to Savannakhet daily 0800, 30,000 kip. Those crossing into Vietnam from Laos may be able to get a ride with the DMZ tour bus from Khe Sanh back to Hué (see page 118) in the late afternoon. Otherwise, there are Vietnam-bound buses from Savannakhet (see page 433) and numerous *songthaews* to the border from the market in Xepon, 45 km, one hour, 20,000 kip, but you'll need to get there by 0700 to ensure a space.

Accommodation **Mountain**, Lao Bao village. A simple, clean and friendly guesthouse.

---

stopandgocafe@yahoo.com. Known for its tours of the DMZ (all-day tour, US$35 on a motorbike, US$75 in a car) which are led by ARVN veterans which brings the landscape to life and an insight you won't get on a much cheaper tour. Highly recommended. Run by the helpful Thien and his sister. City tours and public transport arranged.
Tien Bicycles, 12 Nguyen Thien Ke St, T054-382 3507, www.tienbicycles.com. Mr Tien runs recommended bicycling tours around the country, including one to the DMZ, including bike, support car, guide, accommodation and entrance fees.

⊖ Transport

Hué *p105, map p107*
Air
There are flights to **Hanoi** and **HCMC**. Phu Bai Airport is a 25-min drive south of Hué.
 Airline offices Vietnam Airlines, 23 Nguyen Van Cu St, T054-382 4709, 0715-1115, 1330-1630. Airport bus, 30 mins, 40,000d, from 20 Ha Noi St; leaves 1 hr 40 mins before the flight. Returns also after flights.

Bicycle and motorbike
Bicycles can be hired from most hotels, guesthouses and cafés; bicycles are about 20-25,000d a day. **Nam Thanh**, 48 Le Loi St, T054-382 8951, has a good solid selection. Bikes can be hired from most hotels and guesthouses for around US$6 per day with a driver or US$3 without.

Boat

Boats can be hired through tour agents and from any berth on the south bank of the river, east of Trang Tien Bridge. Good for either a gentle cruise, or an attractive way of getting to some of the temples and mausoleums, around US$5-10. If you travel by boat you may have to pay a moto driver to take you to the tomb as they are often 1 km or so from the riverbank.

Bus

The **Ben Xe Phia Nam** bus station, 97 An Duong Vuong St, T054-382 5070, serves destinations mostly south of Hué with services also to **Savannakhet** on Tue-Fri, Sun, 0830, 200,000d. Buses to **Vientiane** leave at 1930 Wed and Sun, 350,000d. To **Pakse** at 0830. Book with tour operators, see above. The **Hoang Long co**, departs for **Hanoi** from here, 9 a day, 210,000d.

The **Ben Xe Phia Bac** bus station, An Hoa Ward, T54-3580562, is up at the northwest corner of the citadel and serves destinations north of Hué. Also buses to **Lao Bao**, for **Laos** at 0630, 0700, 0730, 0800, 0830, 0900, 50,000d. Open Tour Buses can be booked to major destinations from hotels or from tour agencies. Tourist buses to **Savannakhet**, Laos, via Lao Bao, leave at 0600 on odd days

arriving 1600, US$16-19. Returns 0800 on even days, arriving 1730. **Sepon Travel** is recommended. There is a bus change at the border.

Taxi

Mai Linh Taxi, T054-389 8989.

Train

Hué Railway Station, 2 Bui Thi Xuan, west end of Le Loi St, T54-3822175, booking office open daily 0700-2200. It serves all stations south to **HCMC** and north to **Hanoi**. Advance booking, especially for sleepers, is essential. The 4-hr journey to **Danang** is recommended.

❶ Directory

Hué p105, maps p107

Banks Vietinbank, 2A Le Quy Don St, daily 0700-1130, 1330-1700. Vietcom Bank, 2A Hung Vuong St, 0800-1100, 1345-1600. A number of ATMs in town. **Internet** Most hotels and guesthouses offer internet services. **Medical services** Hué General Hospital, 16 Le Loi St, T054-382 2325. **Post office** 8 Hoang Hoa Tham St; 91 Tran Hung Dao, daily 0630-2130.

Hoi An, Danang and around

The ancient town of Hoi An (formerly Faifo) lies on the banks of the Thu Bon River. During its heyday 200 years ago, when trade with China and Japan flourished, it was a prosperous little port. Much of the merchants' wealth was spent on family chapels and Chinese clan houses that remain little altered today. The city of Hoi An is currently experiencing a revival: the river may be too shallow for shipping but it is perfect for tourist boats; the silk merchants may not export any produce but that's because everything they make leaves town on the backs of satisfied customers. The city of Danang has no real charm and no sense of permanence but few cities in the world have such spectacular beaches on their doorstep, let alone three UNESCO World Heritage Sites – Hué, Hoi An and My Son – within a short drive. ▶▶ *For listings, see pages 131-136.*

Hoi An → *For listings, see pages 131-136. Colour map 3, B6.*

Hoi An's tranquil riverside setting, its diminutive scale, friendly people and its shops and galleries have made it one of the most popular destinations in Vietnam for tourists. There is much of historical interest in the town, plus a nearby beach and plenty of superb, inexpensive restaurants. That said, Hoi An's historic character is being slowly submerged by the rising tide of tourism. Although physically intact, virtually every one of its fine historic buildings either markets some aspect of its own heritage or touts in some other way for the tourist dollar; increasingly it is coming to resemble the 'Vietnam' pavilion in a Disney theme park. Nevertheless, visitors to Hoi An are charmed by the gentleness of the people and the sedate pace of life. A promenade has been built around the water's edge.

Most of Hoi An's more attractive buildings and assembly halls (*hoi quan*) are found either on, or just off, Tran Phu Street, which stretches west to east from the Japanese Covered Bridge to the market, running parallel to the river.

Ins and outs

Getting there and around There are direct minibus connections with Ho Chi Minh City, Hanoi, Hué and Nha Trang. The quickest way of getting from Hanoi or Ho Chi Minh City is by flying to Danang airport (see page 126) and then getting a taxi direct to Hoi An (40 minutes, US$12-15). The town itself is compact, quite busy and best explored on foot, although guesthouses also hire out bicycles. ▶▶ *See Transport, page 136.*

Best time to visit On the 14th day of the lunar month the town converts itself into a Chinese lantern fest and locals dress in traditional costume. The old town is pedestrianized for the night and poetry and music are performed in the streets.

Tourist information Entrance to most historic buildings is by sightseeing ticket, 90,000d, on sale at **Hoi An Tourist Office** ① *see map for locations, T0510-386 327, www. hoianworldheritage.org.vn, open 0700-1730*, which has English-speaking staff and can arrange car and minibus hire as well as sightseeing guides (70,000d for two hours). The sightseeing ticket is segregated into five categories of different sights, allowing visitors admission to one of each. It is valid for three days. If you want to see additional sights and have used up your tokens, you must buy additional tickets. The tourist kiosks provide a good map colour-coding the categories for ease of use. At least a full day is needed to see the town properly.

Background

Hoi An is divided into five quarters, or 'bangs', each of which would traditionally have had its own pagoda and supported one Chinese clan group. The Chinese, along with some Japanese, settled here in the 16th century and controlled trade between the islands of Southeast Asia, East Asia (China and Japan) and India. Portuguese and Dutch vessels also docked at the port. Chinese vessels tended to visit Hoi An during the spring, returning to China in the summer. By the end of the 19th century the Thu Bon River had started to silt up and Hoi An was gradually eclipsed by Danang as the most important port of the area.

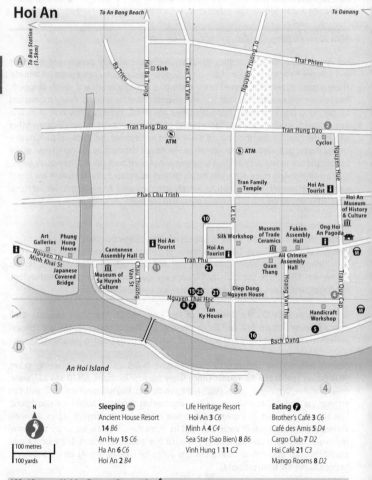

Sleeping	Life Heritage Resort	Eating
Ancient House Resort	Hoi An **3** C6	Brother's Café **3** C6
14 B6	Minh A **4** C4	Café des Amis **5** D4
An Huy **15** C6	Sea Star (Sao Bien) **8** B6	Cargo Club **7** D2
Ha An **6** C6	Vinh Hung 1 **11** C2	Hai Café **21** C3
Hoi An **2** B4		Mango Rooms **8** D2

Japanese Covered Bridge (Cau Nhat Ban)

ⓘ *Tran Phu St, 1 'other' token; keep your ticket to get back across the bridge.*

The Japanese Covered Bridge – also known as the Pagoda Bridge and the Faraway People's Bridge – is Hoi An's most famous landmark and was built in the 16th century. Its popular name reflects a long-standing belief that it was built by the Japanese, although no documentary evidence exists to support this. One of its other names, the Faraway People's Bridge, is said to have been coined because vessels from far away would moor close to the bridge. On its north side there is a pagoda, Japanese in style, for the protection of sailors, while at each end of the bridge are statues of two dogs (at the west end) and two monkeys (at the east end). It is said that the bridge was begun in the year of the monkey and finished in the year of the dog, although some scholars have pointed out that this would mean a two-year period of construction, an inordinately long time for such a small bridge. They maintain, instead, that the two animals represent points of the compass, WSW (monkey) and NW (dog). Father Benigne Vachet, a missionary who lived in Hoi An between 1673 and 1683, notes in his memoirs that the bridge was the haunt of beggars and fortune tellers hoping to benefit from the stream of people crossing over it.

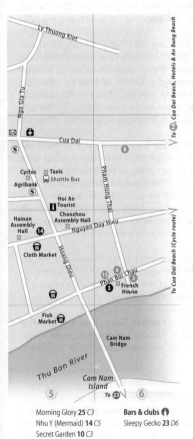

Bach Dang Street and the French quarter

Just south of the Covered Bridge is Bach Dang Street, which runs along the bank of the Thu Bon River, where there are boats, activity and often a cooling breeze, before looping round to the Hoi An Market. Further on, the small but interesting French quarter around Phan Boi Chau Street is worth taking time over; it's not on the regular 'tourist circuit' and requires no entry fee but the colonnaded fronts here are particularly attractive. As in all historical quarters of Vietnamese towns, visitors should raise their gaze above street level to appreciate the architectural detail of upper floors, which is more likely to have survived, and less likely to be covered up.

Morning Glory **25** *C3*
Nhu Y (Mermaid) **14** *C5*
Secret Garden **10** *C3*
Tam Tam Café **15** *C2*
Thanh **16** *D3*

Bars & clubs 🎵
Sleepy Gecko **23** *D6*

Assembly Halls (Hoi Quan)

Chinese traders in Hoi An (like elsewhere in Southeast Asia) established self-governing dialect associations or clan houses that owned their own schools, cemeteries, hospitals and temples. The clan houses (*hoi quan*) may be dedicated to a god or an individual and may contain a temple, although they are not themselves temples. There are five *hoi quan* in Hoi An, four for use by people of specific ethnicities – Fukien, Cantonese, Hainan, Chaozhou – and the fifth for use by any visiting Chinese sailors or merchants.

Strolling east from the Covered Bridge down Tran Phu Street all the assembly halls can be seen. Merchants from Guangdong would meet at the **Quang Dong Hoi Quan** (Cantonese Assembly Hall) ① *176 Tran Phu St, 1 'assembly hall' token*. This assembly hall is dedicated to Quan Cong, a Han Chinese general and dates from 1786. The hall, with its fine embroidered hangings, is in a cool, tree-filled compound and is a good place to rest.

Next is the **All Chinese Assembly Hall** (Ngu Bang Hoi Quan) ① *64 Tran Phu St, free*, sometimes referred to as **Chua Ba** (Goddess Temple). Unusually for an assembly hall, it was a mutual aid society open to any Chinese trader or seaman, regardless of dialect or region of origin. The assembly hall would help shipwrecked or ill sailors and also performed the burial rites of merchants with no relatives in Hoi An. Built in 1773 as a meeting place for all five groups (the four listed above plus Hakka) and also for those with no clan house of their own, today it accommodates a Chinese School, **Truong Le Nghia**, where children of the diaspora learn the language of their forebears.

The **Phuc Kien Hoi Quan** (Fukien Assembly Hall) ① *46 Tran Phu St, 1 'assembly hall' token*, was founded around 1690 and served Hoi An's largest Chinese ethnic group, those from Fukien. It is an intimate building within a large compound and is dedicated to Thien Hau, goddess of the sea and protector of sailors. She is the central figure on the main altar, clothed in gilded robes, who, together with her assistants, can hear the cries of distress of drowning sailors. Immediately on the right on entering the temple is a mural depicting Thien Hau rescuing a sinking vessel. Behind the main altar is a second sanctuary housing the image of Van Thien whose blessings pregnant women invoke on the lives of their unborn children.

Further east, the **Hai Nam Hoi Quan** (Hainan Assembly Hall) ① *10 Tran Phu St, free*, has a more colourful history. It was founded in 1883 in memory of more than 100 sailors and passengers who were killed when three ships were plundered by an admiral in Emperor Tu Duc's navy. In his defence the admiral claimed that the victims were pirates; some sources maintain he even had the ships painted black to strengthen his case.

Exquisite wood carving is the highlight of the **Chaozhou (Trieu Chau) Assembly Hall** ① *362 Nguyen Duy Hieu St, 1 'assembly hall' token*. The altar and its panels depict images from the sea and women from the Beijing court, which were presumably intended to console homesick traders.

Merchants' houses and temples

Tan Ky House ① *101 Nguyen Thai Hoc St, 1 'old house' token*, dates from the late 18th century. The Tan Ky family had originally arrived in Hoi An from China 200 years earlier and the house reflects not only the prosperity the family had acquired in the intervening years but also the architecture of their Japanese and Vietnamese neighbours, whose styles had presumably influenced the aesthetic taste and appreciation of the younger family members.

At the junction of Le Loi and Phan Chu Trinh streets, the **Tran Family Temple** ① *1 'old house' token*, has survived for 15 generations (although the current generation has no son, which means the lineage has been broken). The building exemplifies Hoi An's construction methods and the harmonious fusion of Chinese and Japanese styles. It is roofed with heavy yin and yang tiling, which requires strong roof beams; these are held up by a triple-beamed support in the Japanese style (also seen on the roof of the covered bridge). Some beams have Chinese-inspired ornately carved dragons. The outer doors are Japanese, the inner are Chinese. On a central altar rest small wooden boxes containing the photograph or likeness of the deceased together with biographical details. Beyond, at the back of the house, is a raised Chinese herb, spice and flower garden. As at all Hoi An's family houses, guests are received warmly and served lotus tea and dried coconut.

Diep Dong Nguyen House ⓘ *80 Nguyen Thai Hoc St*, with two Chinese lanterns hanging outside, was once a Chinese dispensary. The owner is friendly, hospitable and not commercially minded. He takes visitors into his house and shows them everything with pride and smiles.

Just west of the Japanese Bridge is **Phung Hung House** ⓘ *4 Nguyen Thi Minh Khai St, 1 'old house' token*. Built over 200 years ago it has been in the same family for eight generations. The house, which can be visited, is constructed of 80 columns of ironwood on marble pedestals. During the floods of 1964, Phung Hung House became home to 160 locals who camped upstairs for three days as the water rose to a height of 2.5 m.

Ong Hoi An Pagoda and around

At the east end of Tran Phu Street, at No 24, close to the intersection with Nguyen Hué Street, is the **Ong Hoi An Pagoda** ⓘ *1 'other' token*. This temple is in fact two interlinked pagodas built back-to-back: Chua Quan Cong, and behind that Chua Quan Am. Their date of construction is not known, although both certainly existed in 1653. In 1824 Emperor Minh Mang made a donation of 300 luong (1 luong being equivalent to1½ oz of silver) for the support of the pagodas. They are dedicated to Quan Cong and Quan Am respectively.

Virtually opposite the Ong Hoi An Pagoda is **Hoi An Market** (Cho Hoi An). The market extends down to the river and then along the river road (Bach Dang Street, see page 123). At the Tran Phu Street end it is a covered market selling mostly dry goods. Numerous cloth merchants and seamstresses will produce made-to-measure shirts in a few hours but not all to the same standard. On the riverside is the local **fish market**, which comes alive at 0500-0600 as boats arrive with the night's catch.

Cua Dai Beach

ⓘ *4 km east of Hoi An. You must leave your bicycle (5000d) or moto (10000d) just before Cua Dai beach in a car park. The first shop kiosk on the beach at the end of the road offer lockers for 20,000d.*

A white-sand beach with a few areas of shelter, Cua Dai Beach is a pleasant 20-minute bicycle ride or one-hour walk from Hoi An. Head east down Tran Hung Dao Street or, for a quieter route, set off down Nguyen Duy Hieu Street, which peters out into a walking and cycling path. This is a lovely route past paddy fields and ponds; nothing is signed but those with a good sense of direction will make their way back to the main road a kilometre or so before Cua Dai and those with a poor sense of direction can come to no harm. Behind the beach are a handful of hotels where food and refreshments can be bought. Four kilometres north of Hoi An, off the new dual carriageway, is **An Bang Beach** where a collection of popular beach bars has gathered.

Danang, Vietnam's third largest port and a trading centre of growing importance, is situated on a peninsula of land at the point where the Han River flows into the South China Sea. It was first known as Cua Han (Mouth of the Han River) and renamed Tourane (a rough transliteration of Cua Han) by the French. It later acquired the title Thai Phien, and finally Danang. An important port from French times, it gained world renown when two US Marine battalions landed here in March 1965 to secure the airfield. They were the first of many more US military personnel who would land on the beaches and airfields of South Vietnam.

Ins and outs

Getting there There are international and domestic flights to Danang airport on the edge of the city; a taxi into town costs US$3-5 and takes five to 10 minutes. Danang is on the north-south railway line linking Hanoi and Ho Chi Minh City. Regular bus and minibus connections link Danang with all major cities in the south as far as Ho Chi Minh City, and in the north as far as Hanoi. There are also daily buses from Danang to the Lao town of Savannakhet on the Mekong via the border at Lao Bao (see border box, page 126). ▸▸ See Transport, page 136.

Getting around Danang is a sizeable town, rather too large to explore on foot, but there is abundant public transport, including cyclos, taxis and *Honda ôm*. Bicycles and motorbikes are available for hire from most hotels and guesthouses.

Tourist information Sinh Tourist ⓘ *154 Bach Dang St, T511-384 3259, www.thesinhtourist. vn*, is helpful and can book buses as well as help with information, see page 118. The website www.indanang.com is worth consulting for news and events.

Museum of Cham Sculpture

ⓘ *Intersection of Trung Nu Vuong and Bach Dang streets, daily 0700-1730, 30,000d. Labels are in English. Guided tours are held 0800-1030 and 1400-1630, 5 people minimum, T511-357 2414.*

The museum contains the largest display of Cham art in the world and testifies to a creative and long-lasting civilization. Each room is dedicated to work from a different part of the Champa kingdom and, since different parts of Champa flowered artistically at different times from the fourth to the 14th centuries, the rooms reveal the evolution of the art and its outside influences, from Cambodia to Java.

Many pieces from **My Son** (see page 129) illustrate the Hindu trinity: Brahma the Creator, Vishnu the Preserver and Siva the Destroyer. An altar is inscribed with scenes from the wedding story of Sita and Rama, taken from the *Ramayana*, the Hindu epic. Ganesh, the elephant-headed son of Siva, was a much-loved god and is also well represented here.

At the end of the ninth century **Dong Duong** replaced My Son as the centre of Cham art. At this time Buddhism became the dominant religion of court, although it never fully replaced Hinduism. The Dong Duong room is illustrated with scenes from the life of Buddha. Faces from this period become less stylistic and more human and the bodies of the figures are more graceful and flowing.

The subsequent period of Cham art is known as the late **Tra Kieu** style. In this section there are *apsaras* (celestial dancing maidens), whose fluid and animated forms are exquisitely captured in stone. Thereafter Cham sculpture went into artistic decline.

The **Thap Mam** style (late 11th to early 14th century) sees a range of mythical beasts whose range and style is unknown elsewhere in Southeast Asia. Also in this room is a pedestal surrounded by 28 breast motifs. It is believed they represent Uroha, the mythical mother of the Indrapura nation (incorporating My Son, Tra Kieu, Dong Duong), but the meaning of the pedestal and others like it is unknown.

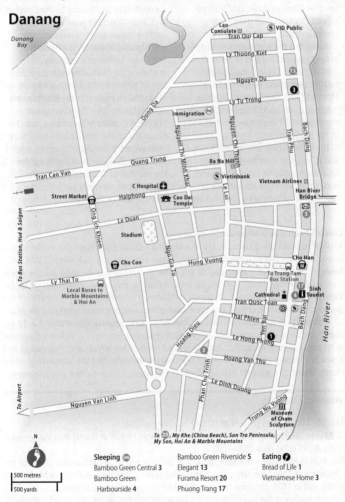

Danang

Sleeping	Bamboo Green Riverside 5	Eating
Bamboo Green Central 3	Elegant 13	Bread of Life 1
Bamboo Green	Furama Resort 20	Vietnamese Home 3
Harbourside 4	Phuong Trang 17	

Kingdom of Champa

The powerful kingdom of Champa was one of the most glorious in ancient Southeast Asia. Chinese texts suggest that in AD 192 a group of tribes, probably of Indonesian descent, formed a union known as Lin-Yi, later to become Champa. The first Champa capital, Tra Kieu (fourth to 10th centuries), was about 30 km from Danang, but the kingdom's territories extended far afield and other major sites included Dong Duong (eighth to 10th centuries), Po Nagar, Thap Mam and Cha Ban. Tra Kieu, My Son (see opposite) and Dong Duong were the three most important centres of the kingdom.

The polytheistic religion of Champa was a fusion of Buddhism, Sivaism, local elements and, later, Islam, and was expressed in an abundance of religious (and secular) sculptures and monuments. The kingdom reached its apogee in the 10th and 11th centuries but, unlike the Khmers, Champa never had the opportunity to create a capital city matching the magnificence of Angkor. For long periods the Cham were compelled to pay tribute to the Chinese and, after that, they were dominated in turn by the Javanese, Annamese (the Vietnamese) and then the Khmers. The Cham kingdom was finally eradicated in 1471, although there are still an estimated 90,000 Cham living in central Vietnam (mostly Brahmanists and Muslims). Given this turbulent history, it is perhaps surprising that the Cham found any opportunity for artistic endeavours. It should perhaps be added that since the demise of the kingdom, the number of Cham sculptures has increased enormously as forgers have carved more of these beautiful images.

China Beach (My Khe Beach) → *Colour map 3, B6.*

An R&R retreat during the war, My Khe became popular with American soldiers, who named it China Beach. It became a fabled resort celebrated in rock songs. Since 1975, however, it has been called T20 Beach, after the military code used by the North Vietnamese Army. Today the whole area, including the hotels, still belongs to the Vietnamese Army. It was a quiet area until relatively recently but now resonates to the sound of construction clatter. This once-abandoned, wild stretch of beach is now nearly all sectioned off for massive hotel development. Only several kilometres of a 30-km stretch between Danang and Hoi An remains untainted. For those who knew it just five years ago, it is quite incredible. It has miles and miles of fine white sand, clean water and a glorious setting: the hills of Monkey Mountain to the north and the Marble Mountains clearly visible to the south. At times, there is a dangerous cross-current and undertow.

Around Danang

Marble Mountains (Nui Non Nuoc) → *Colour map 3, B6.*
ⓘ *12 km from Danang, 20 km from Hoi An, many visitors stop off at Marble Mountain en route to Hoi An, 15,000d, daily 0600-1700.*

The Marble Mountains overlook the city of Danang and its airfield, about 12 km to the west of town. The name was given to these five peaks by the Nguyen Emperor Minh Mang on his visit in 1825, although they are in fact limestone crags with marble outcrops. They are also known as the mountains of the five elements (fire, water, soil, wood and metal).

An important religious spot for the Cham, the peaks became havens for Communist guerrillas during the war, owing to their commanding view over Danang airbase. From here, a force with sufficient firepower could control much of what went on below, and the guerrillas harried the Americans incessantly. The views from the mountain, overlooking Danang Bay, are impressive although they will be less impressive once every chain resort on the planet has made its stake on the beach. On the Marble Mountains are a number of important sites, often associated with caves and grottoes formed by chemical action on the limestone.

Of the mountains, the most visited is **Thuy Son**. There are several grottos and cave pagodas in the mountain, which are marked by steps cut into the rock. The **Tam Thai Pagoda**, reached by a staircase cut into the mountain, is on the site of a much older Cham place of worship. Constructed in 1825 by Minh Mang, and subsequently rebuilt, the central statue is of the Buddha Sakyamuni (the historic Buddha) flanked by the Bodhisattva Quan Am (a future Buddha and the Goddess of Mercy) and a statue of Van Thu (symbolizing wisdom). At the rear of the grotto is another cave, the **Huyen Khong Cave**. Originally a place of animist worship, it later became a site for Buddhist pilgrimage. The entrance is protected by four door guardians. The high ceiling of the cave is pierced by five holes through which the sun filters and, in the hour before midday, illuminates the central statue of the Buddha Sakyamuni. In the cave are various natural rock formations which, according to the cave guides look like storks, elephants, an arm, a fish and a face.

A few hundred metres to the south on the right is a track leading to **Chua Quan The Am**, which has its own grotto, complete with stalactites, stalagmites and pillars.

My Son → *Colour map 3, B5.*
ⓘ *60 km south of Danang via Tra Kieu or 45-km west of Hoi An via Nam Phuoc. From the ticket office (6 km beyond the village of Kiem Lam) it's a 2-km jeep ride (included in the ticket price) and a short walk to My Son, daily 0630-1630, 60,000d. Tour operators in Hoi An and Danang offer tours. It is not clear how thoroughly the area has been de-mined so do not stray too far from the road and path. Take a hat, sun cream and water.*

My Son, with its detailed carved masonry, was the spiritual centre of the Cham empire (see box, page 128). Declared a World Heritage Site by UNESCO in 1999, it is one of Vietnam's most ancient monuments. Weather, jungle and years of strife have wrought their worst on My Son. But, arguably, the jungle under which My Son remained hidden to the outside world provided it with its best protection, for more has been destroyed in the past 40 years than the previous 400. Today, far from anywhere, My Son is a tranquil archaeological treasure. Not many visitors have time to make an excursion to see it, which makes it all the more appealing to those that do. The thin red bricks of the towers and temples have been beautifully carved and the craftsmanship of many centuries still remains abundantly visible today. The trees and creepers have been pushed back but My Son remains cloaked in green; shoots and saplings sprout up everywhere and one senses that were its custodians to turn their backs for even a short time, My Son would be quickly reclaimed by nature.

My Son consists of more than 70 monuments spread over a large area. It was rediscovered and investigated by French archaeologists of the École Française d'Extrême-Orient in 1898. Their excavations revealed a site that had been settled from the early eighth to the 15th centuries, the longest uninterrupted period of development of any monument in Southeast Asia. Its maximum population is unknown but it seems to have had a holy or spiritual function rather than being the seat of power and was, very probably, a burial place of its god kings. Unfortunately, My Son was a Viet Cong field headquarters, located within one of the US 'free fire' zones during the Vietnam War. The finest sanctuary in the complex was demolished by US sappers and temple groups A, E and H were badly damaged. Groups B and C have largely retained their temples but many statues, altars and linga have been removed to the Museum of Champa Sculpture in Danang (see page 126). Currently Group C is being restored by UNESCO; the F building is covered in cobwebs and propped up by scaffolding.

It is important to see My Son in the broader context of Indian influence on Southeast Asia, not just in terms of architecture but also in terms of spiritual and political development around the region. Falling as it did so strongly under Chinese influence, it is all the more remarkable to find such compelling evidence of Indian culture and iconography in Vietnam. Indeed this was one of the criteria cited by UNESCO as justification for My Son's World Heritage listing.

Angkor in Cambodia, with which My Son is broadly contemporaneous, is the most famous example of a temple complex founded by a Hindu or Sivaist god king (deva-raja). The Hindu cult of deva-raja was developed by the kings of Angkor and later employed by Cham kings to bolster their authority but, because Cham kings were far less wealthy and powerful than the god kings of Angkor, the monuments are correspondingly smaller and more personal. One of the great joys of Cham sculpture and building is its unique feel, its graceful lines and unmistakable form.

The characteristic Cham architectural structure is the tower, built to reflect the divinity of the king: tall and rectangular, with four porticoes, each of which is 'blind' except for that on the west face. Originally built of wood (not surprisingly, none remains), they were later made of brick, of which the earliest (seventh century) are located at My Son. The bricks are exactly laid and held together with a form of vegetable cement, probably the resin of the day tree. Sandstone is sometimes used for plinths and lintels but, overwhelmingly, brick is the medium of construction. It is thought that on completion, each tower was surrounded by wood and fired over several days in what amounted to a vast outdoor kiln. The red bricks at My Son have worn amazingly well and are intricately carved with Hindu, Sivaist and Buddhist images and ornaments. Sivaist influence at My Son is unmissable, with Siva often represented, as in other Cham relics throughout Vietnam, by the linga or phallus.

For Sleeping and Eating price codes and other relevant information, see pages 40-43.

⊖ Sleeping

Hoi An *p121, map p122*

LL The Nam Hai, Hamlet 1, Dien Duong Village, 11 km north of Hoi An, 30 km south of Danang on Ha My Beach, T0510-394 0000, www.ghmhotels.com. The Nam Hai is a stunning creation of 100 beachside villas overlooking the East Sea. Raised platforms inside the villas create a special sleeping and living space enveloped with white silk drapes; egg-shell lacquered baths in a black marble surround are incorporated into the platform. There are 2 restaurants flanking the vast infinity pool. 3 pools, a gym, tennis, badminton and basketball courts. For relaxing there's a lovely library and spa.

LL-AL Hoi An Riverside Resort, 175 Cua Dai Rd, Cua Dai Beach, T0510-386 4800, www.hoianriverresort.com. A short, 5-min cycle ride from the beach and a 15-min pedal from town, this hotel faces the Thu Bon River. There is a pool set in landscaped gardens with hammocks. Standard rooms have balconies and all rooms have showers. **Song Do** restaurant is the best place to be at sunset.

LL-AL Life Heritage Resort Hoi An, 1 Pham Hong Thai St, T0510-391 4555, www.life-resorts.com. This small, quiet resort is in an excellent location right on the river next to the town and has had a recent makeover and is boosted by a new spa. The rooms are spacious and extremely comfortable. There's a restaurant, café and bar on site. The passion fruit mojito – an exciting twist on a cocktail classic – is drink of the year; it's absolutely unmissable.

LL-AL Victoria Hoi An Beach Resort & Spa, Cua Dai Beach, T0510-392 7040, www.victoriahotels-asia.com. A charming, recently upgraded resort right on the beach with 105 beautifully furnished rooms

facing the sea or the river. There is a large pool, the **L'Annam Restaurant** (which serves very tasty but expensive dishes), a couple of bars, a kids' club, barbecue beach parties, live music and dancing, a host of water sports and all with charming service. A free shuttle bus runs between the hotel and the town.

AL-A Ancient House Resort, 377 Cua Dai St, T0510-392 3377, www.ancienthouse resort.com. A beautiful, small hotel set around a garden. There is a pool, shop, billiards, free shuttle to town and beach, free bicycle service and a restaurant. Behind the hotel is a traditional Ancient House. Breakfast included.

AL-A Hoi An, 10 Tran Hung Dao St, T0510-386 1445, www.hoiantourist.com. An attractive colonial building set well back from the road in spacious grounds with attractively furnished, comfortable rooms with all mod cons and en suite bathrooms with baths. Has a pool and new zen spa and beauty salon. Discounts offered in Hoi An's summer low season. Staff are welcoming and there are a host of activities from Chinese lantern making to trips to local villages.

A Vinh Hung 1, 143 Tran Phu St, T0510-386 1621, www.vinhhunghotels.com.vn. An attractive old building with a splendid and ornate reception room decorated with dark wood in Chinese style. It halved its room capacity and upgraded the 6 remaining rooms to some very lovely stylish retreats; these are now some of the most appealing rooms in the old city. Recommended.

A-B Ha An Hotel, T0510-386 3126, 6-8 Phan Boi Chau St, http://haanhotel.com. This is a lovely hotel with a flourishing courtyard garden. Rooms are decorated with ethnic minority accents but are on the small side but the overall ambience is delightful and relaxing in the garden is a bonus in a city with no outdoor green space.

C-D An Huy Hotel, 30 Phan Boi Chau St, T0510-386 2116, www.anhuyhotel.com.

Opposite **Brother's Café**, with courtyards that create a breeze and shutters that keep the noise out. Spacious rooms are beautifully decorated in Japanese style and the staff are very friendly. Breakfast and free internet.

E-F Minh A, 2 Nguyen Thai Hoc St, T0510-386 1368. This is a very special little place. An old family house with just 5 guestrooms that are all different. Guests are made to feel part of the family. Communal bathrooms have hot water. Next to the market in a busy part of town. Very welcoming, and recommended.

E-F Sea Star (Sao Bien), 489 Cua Dai St, on the road to the beach, T0510-386 1589, saobien_hotel@yahoo.com. A privately run hotel with all rooms coming with a/c and hot water. Travel services, bicycle, motorbike and car hire on offer. Efficient and popular.

Danang *p58, map p127*

LL-AL Furama Resort, 68 Ho Xuan Huong St, Bac My An Beach, 8 km from Danang, T0511-384 7888, www.furamavietnam.com. 198 rooms and suites beautifully designed and furnished. It has 2 pools, 1 of which is an infinity pool overlooking the private beach. All its facilities are first class. Water sports, diving, mountain biking, tennis and a health centre offering a number of massages and treatments. Operates a free and very useful shuttle to and from the town, Marble Mountains and Hoi An. Surprisingly the price does not include breakfast

A-C Bamboo Green, there are 3 hotels in this chain: **Bamboo Green Central**, 158 Phan Chu Trinh St, T0511-382 2996, www.bamboogreenhotel.com.vn; **Bamboo Green Harbourside** (a somewhat tenuous claim), 177 Tran Phu St, T0511-382 2722; and **Bamboo Green Riverside**, 68 Bach Dang St, T0511-383 2591. All are well-run, well-equipped, comfortable, business-type hotels with efficient staff and in central locations offering excellent value for money. Riverside has a particularly attractive outlook opposite the cathedral and is currently being rebuilt in a more fashionable boutique style.

C Elegant Hotel, 22A Bach Dang St, T0511-389 2893, elegant@dng.vnn.vn. It's fairly elegant and in a good position overlooking the river. 32 standard rooms including breakfast and Wi-Fi.

E Phuong Trang (formerly Tan Minh), 142 Bach Dang St, T0511-389 9900. On the riverfront, a small, well-kept hotel with Wi-Fi; friendly staff speak good English.

❼ Eating

Hoi An *p121, map p122*

A Hoi An speciality is *cao lau*, a noodle soup with slices of pork and croutons, traditionally made with water from one particular well. The quality of food in Hoi An, especially the fish, is outstanding and the value for money is not matched by any other town in Vietnam. Bach Dang St is particularly pleasant in the evening, when tables and chairs are set up almost the whole way along the river.

♥♥♥-♥♥ Brother's Café, 27-29 Phan Boi Chau St, T0510-391 4150, www.brothercafehoian. com.vn. These little cloistered French houses have been renovated in exquisite taste. The house and garden leading down to the river are beautifully restored. The menu is strong on Vietnamese specialities, especially seafood, and the daily set menu offers good value in such charming surroundings.

♥♥♥-♥♥ Secret Garden, 132/2 Tran Phu St, off Le Loi St, T0510-391 1112, www.secretgardenhoian.com. An oasis amid the shopping malestrom of downtown Hoi An. Superior and attentive service in a delightful courtyard garden with delicious dishes. Try the sublime thin slices of beef with garlic and pepper, lemon juice, soya sauce, and black sesame oil or the star fruit soup. Live music is played nightly and there's a cooking school.

♥♥ Nhu Y (aka Mermaid), 2 Tran Phu St, T0510-386 1527, www.hoianhospitality.com. Miss Vy turns out all the local specialities as well as some of her own. The 5-course set dinner is particularly recommended.

Streets Restaurant Café, 17 Le Loi St, www.streetsinternational.org. A professional training restaurant for disadvantaged youngsters that serves up very tasty Vietnamese and Western cuisine in a lovely old property. Trainee chefs complete an 18-month programme here.

Tam Tam Café, 110 Nguyen Thai Hoc St, T0510-386 2212, www.tamtamcafe-hoian.com. A great little café in a renovated tea house. Cocktails, draft beer, music, book exchange. Attached restaurant serves French and Italian cuisine. A relaxing place for a drink or meal.

Thanh, 76 Bach Dang St, T0510-386 1366. A charming old house overlooking the river, recognizable by its Chinese style and flowering *hoa cat dang* creepers; the shrimp is excellent. Friendly service.

Café des Amis, 52 Bach Dang St, near the river, T0510-386 1616. The set menu of fish/seafood or vegetarian dishes changes daily and is widely acclaimed and excellent value. The owner, Mr Nguyen Manh Kim, spends several months a year cooking in Europe. Highly recommended.

Mango Rooms, 111 Nguyen Thai Hoc St, T0510-391 0839, www.mangorooms.com. A very welcome addition to Hoi An and the superior cooking makes a repeat visit a must. Enjoy slices of baguette layered with shrimp mousse served with a mango coconut curry or the delicious ginger and garlic-marinated shrimps wrapped in tender slices of beef and pan-fried with wild spicy butter and soy-garlic sauce; the seared tuna steak with mango salsa is outstanding. Complimentary tapas-style offerings such as tapioca crisps are a welcome touch. Highly recommended.

Cargo Club, 107-109 Nguyen Thai Hoc St, T0510-391 0489. This extremely popular venue with a new upstairs dining area serves up filling Vietnamese and Western fodder including club sandwiches, Vietnamese salads and overpriced fajitas. The service is quicker downstairs than up on the balcony overlooking the river. The patisserie, groaning with cakes and chocolate, is the best thing.

Hai Café, 111 Tran Phu St/98 Nguyen Thai Hoc St, T0510-386 3210, www.visithoian. com. The central area of this back-to-back café has a photographic exhibition of the WWF's invaluable work in the threatened environment around Hoi An. It offers good food in a relaxing courtyard or attractive café setting. Cookery courses can be arranged.

Morning Glory, 106 Nguyen Thai Hoc St, T0510-324 1555. In an attractive building with a balcony serving up Vietnamese street food such as crispy mackerel and mango salsa, caramel fish in clay pot and spicy prawn curry. The restaurant is run by Miss Vy of Mermaid fame.

Danang *p126, map p127*

Seafood is good here and Danang has its own beers, Da Nang 'Export' and Song Han. There are a number of cafés and restaurants along Bach Dang St, overlooking the river.

Bread of Life, 12 Le Hong Phong St, T0511-356 5185, www.breadoflifedanang.com.

Closed Sun. This is a restaurant that provides training and jobs to deaf people. It's a worthwhile cause to support and the pizzas are very tasty. Baked goods and other comfort food too. Motorbike rental also.

Vietnamese Home, 34 Bach Dang St, T0511-388 9575. A very popular place, both with Vietnamese and Westerners, in an interior courtyard setting with fountain and bamboo chairs. The menu is full of fish, frog, eel and pork as well as those catering to the Western palate.

Bars and clubs

Hoi An *p121, map p122*
Phattie's, An Bang Beach. A popular hangout for backpackers and expats with a genial atmosphere and pool table.
Sleepy Gecko, first major right (signposted) on Cam Nam Island, past **Randy's BookXchange**. A lovely little haven of jollity with beers, breakfasts and Saturday barbecues from 1600. Friendly and genuinely helpful with advice. Ask about **Steve's Byke** tours (T090-842 6349, sleepygecko@gmail.com). There are movies to view too.
Tam Tam Café, 110 Nguyen Thai Hoc St. Mainly a café/restaurant but also has a good bar and a pool table.

Entertainment

Hoi An *p121, map p122*
Hoi An Handicraft Workshop, 9 Nguyen Thai Hoc St, T0510-391 0216, www.hoian handicraft.com. Traditional music perform-ances Tue-Sun at 1015, 1515 and 1930 (part of the ticket programme), with the Vietnamese monochord and dancers. At the back there is a potter's wheel, straw mat making, embroiderers, conical hat makers, wood carvers and iron ornament makers.

Shopping

Hoi An *p121, map p122*
Hoi An is a shopper's paradise. **Tran Phu** and **Le Loi** are the main shopping streets. 2 items stand out – paintings and clothes.

Art
Vietnamese artists have been inspired by Hoi An's old buildings and a Hoi An school of art has developed. Countless galleries sell original works of art but the more serious galleries are to be found in a cluster on Nguyen Thi Minh Khai St, west of the Japanese Bridge.

Books
Randy's BookXchange, Cam Nam Island, T093-608 9483, randy@randysbookxchange. com. Randy's got a proper bookstore here with a range of genres including travel guides. It's a welcoming place to browse.

Handicrafts and jewellery
Hoi An is the place to buy handbags and purses and attractive Chinese silk lanterns, indeed anything that can be made from silk, including scarves and shoes. **41 Le Loi Street** is a silk workshop where the whole process from silkworm to woven fabric can be seen and fabrics purchased, daily 0745-2200. There is also chinaware available, mainly modern, some reproduction and a few antiques.
Memory, 96A Bach Dang St and 62 Le Loi St, T0510-391 1483. Wonderful, imaginative designs using a range of materials.
Reaching Out Handicrafts, 103 Nguyen Thai Hoc, T0510-391 0168, www. reachingoutvietnam.com. Fairtrade shop selling arts and crafts, cards and notebooks, textiles and silk sleeping bags all made by disabled artisans living in Hoi An. Profits support the disabled community.

Tailors
Hoi An is famed for its tailors – there are now reckoned to be more than 140 in town – who will knock up silk or cotton clothing

in 24 hrs. The quality of the stitching varies from shop to shop, so see some samples first, and the range of fabrics is limited, so many people bring their own. A man's suit can cost anywhere from US$55-395 and a woman's from US$55-395, depending on fabric and quality of workmanship. Thai silk costs more than Vietnamese silk and Hoi An silk is quite coarse.

Visitors talk of the rapid speed at which shops can produce the goods but bear in mind that, if every visitor to Hoi An wants something made in 12-24 hrs, this puts enormous strain on staff. Quite apart from the workers having to stay up all night, the quality of the finished garment could suffer. So, if you are in Hoi An for a few days, give yourself time to accommodate 2nd or 3rd fittings, which may be necessary. Tailors themselves recommend a minimum 36-hr period.

Lan Ha, 1A Hai Ba Trung St, T0510-391 0706, leco50@hotmail.com. Daily 0900-2200. This shop unit is recommended because of the speed of service, the quality of the goods, the excellent prices and the fact that, unlike many other tailors in town, 2nd, 3rd or even 4th fittings are usually not required.

Yaly, 47 Nguyen Thai Hoc St, T0510-391 0474, yalyshop@dng.vnn.vn. Daily 0700-2030. Professional staff, very good, quality results across a range of clothing, including shoes. Women's blouses are around US$20 and dresses US$30.

⚙ Activities and tours

Hoi An *p121, map p122*
Boat rides
Boat rides are available on the Thu Bon River. Local boatwomen charge US$1 or so per hr.

Cookery classes
Red Bridge Cooking School, run out of the Hai Café, 98 Nguyen Thai Hoc St, T0510-386 3210 and Thon 4, Cam Thanh, T0510-393 3222, www.visithoian.com. Operates all year, 0815-1330. Visit the market to be shown local produce, then take a 20-min boat ride to the cooking school where you're shown the herb garden. Next, you watch the chefs make a number of dishes such as warm squid salad served in half a pineapple and grilled aubergine stuffed with vegetables. Move inside and you get to make your own fresh spring rolls and learn Vietnamese food carving, which is a lot harder than it looks. From US$24.

Diving and snorkelling
Cham Island Diving Center, 88 Nguyen Thai Hoc St, T0510-391 0782, www.chamislanddiving.om. Its Cham Island excursion is recommended for snorkellers as it gives time to explore the village on Cham Island, US$40, led by Italians who lived on the island for a year.
Rainbow Divers, 39B Tran Hung Dao St, T0510-391 1914. A well-regarded Western-run national operation.

Motorbiking
Hoi An Motorbike Adventures, 54A Phan Chau Trinh St, T091-823 0653, www.motorbiketours-hoian.com. Runs good half-day to 5-day tours in the area.

Tour operators
Asia Pacific Travel, 79 Thang St, Hai Chau District, T0511-628 6088, www.asia-pacifictravel.com. Arranges tours throughout Vietnam.
Hoi An Travel, Hotel Hoi An, 10 Tran Hung Dao St, and at **Hoi An Beach Resort**, T510-3910911, www.hoiantravel.com. Offers a variety of tours including some unusual ones: a visit to a vegetable village, fishing at Thanh Ha pottery village, and visiting the Cham Islands. Can also arrange trips to Savannakhet and Pakse, Laos and from Bangkok to Hoi An, Danang and Hué and returning to Laos and Thailand.
Seventeen's, 17 Tran Hung Dao St, T0510-386 1947, www.seventeenstravel.com. Offers tours to My Son, from US$4; My Lai, US$55 in car; motorbike hire, US$5; snorkelling

at Cham Islands, US$25; river tour US$20; canoeing, US$25; diving US$65 and organizes transport to the Central Highlands. Taxi to Danang, US$10.

Sinh Tourist (formerly Sinh Café), 587 Hai Ba Trung St, T0510-386 3948, www. thesinhtourist.vn. Open 0630-2200. Branch of the ubiquitous chain offering tours and transport My Son tour, 96,000d; with return boat trip via Kim Bong carpentry village, 115,000d.

⊖ Transport

Hoi An *p121, map p122*
Bicycle and motorbike
Hotels have 2WD and 4WD vehicles for hire. Bicycle hire, 20,000d per day, motorbike US$4-6 per day.

Bus
The bus station is 1 km west of the centre of town on Ly Thuong Kiet St. There are regular connections from **Danang**'s bus station, from 0530 until 1800, 1 hr, 20,000d. Open Tour Buses go north to **Hanoi** and South to **HCMC**. Book through local tour operators (see above).

Danang *p126, map p127*
Air
The airport is 2.5 km southwest of the city. A taxi from Danang airport to Hoi An will cost about US$15 or less (bargain hard), 40 mins.

Vietnam Airlines and Jetstar sales agent, 10 Tran Hung Dao St, T510-3910912.

Taxi
Airport Taxi, T0511-327 2727.

Train
Danang Railway Station, 122 Haiphong St, 2 km west of town, T0511-375 0666. Express trains to and from **Hanoi**, **HCMC** and **Hué**.

❶ Directory

Hoi An *p121, map p122*
Banks Vietinbank, 4 Hoang Dieu St, T0510-386 1340. Accepts most major currencies, US dollar withdrawal from credit/debit card, no commission for cashing Amex TCs, ATM. **Internet** Widely available in cafés and hotels. **Medical services** 4 Tran Hung Dao St, T0510-386 4750, daily 0700-2200. **Post office** 4 Tran Hung Dao St, T0510-386 1480.

Danang *p126, map p127*
Banks Eximbank, 205 Phan Chu Trinh St. ATM. **Vietinbank**, 5 Tran Quoc Toan St. With ATM. **Lao Consulate**, 12 Tran Quy Cap St, T0511-3821208, ketkeomanivong@ yahoo.com, 0800-1130, 1330-1630. **Internet** There are numerous internet cafés all over town. **Medical services** Family Medical Practice, 50-52 Nguyen Van Linh St, Nam Duong ward, Hai Chau district, T0511-358 2699, www. vietnammedicalpractice.com. **Post office** 64 Bach Dang St, corner of Bach Dang and Le Duan streets.

Central Highlands and the coast

The Central Highlands consist of the Truong Son Mountain Range and its immediate environs. The mountain range is commonly referred to as the backbone of Vietnam and borders Laos and Cambodia to the west. The highlands provide flowers and vegetables to the southern lowlands and have several tea and coffee plantations that supply the whole world. Tourism is an additional source of revenue. Most highlanders belong to one of 26 indigenous groups and, beyond the main towns of Dalat, Buon Ma Thuot, Play Ku (Pleiku) and Kontum, their way of life remains unchanged.

East of the highlands, on the coast, Nha Trang is a seaside resort with diving, boat tours and spas to entice foreign visitors. Further south, Mui Ne has golden sands and the best kitesurfing in Vietnam. ➤➤ For listings, see pages 148-156.

Ins and outs

In terms of climate, the best time to visit this region is from December to April. However, as there are many different indigenous groups within its borders, there are festivals in the region all year round.

Background

The Central Highlands have long been associated with Vietnam's hilltribes. Under the French, the colonial administration deterred ethnic Vietnamese from settling here but missionaries were active among the minorities of the region, although with uneven success. Bishop Cuenot (see page 143) dispatched two missionaries to Buon Ma Thuot, where they received a hostile reception from the M'nong, however in Kontum, among the Ba-na, they found more receptive souls for their evangelizing. Today many of the ethnic minorities in the Central Highlands are Roman Catholic, although some (such as the Ede) are Protestant.

At the same time French businesses were hard at work establishing plantations to supply the home market. Rubber and coffee were the staple crops. The greatest difficulty they faced was recruiting sufficient labour. Men and women of the ethnic minorities were happy in their villages drinking rice wine and cultivating their own small plots. They were poor but content and saw no reason to accept the hard labour and slave wages of the plantation owners. Norman Lewis travelled in the Central Highlands and describes the situation well in his book, *A Dragon Apparent*.

Since 1984 there has been a bit of a free-for-all and a scramble for land in the highlands. Ethnic Vietnamese have encroached on minority land and planted it with coffee, pepper and fruit trees. As an indicator of progress, Vietnam is now the second largest producer of coffee in the world, although it produces cheaper robusta rather than arabica coffee. The way of life of the minorities is disappearing with the forests: there are no trees from which to build traditional stilt houses nor shady forests in which to live and hunt.

Dalat → For listings, see pages 148-156. Colour map 4, B2.

Dalat is situated on a plateau in the Central Highlands, at an altitude of almost 1500 m. The town itself, a former French hill station, is centred on a Lake – Xuan Huong – amidst rolling countryside. To the north are the five volcanic peaks of **Langbian Mountain**, rising to 2400 m. The ascent is recommended for stunning views and abundant birdlife. In the vicinity of Dalat are lakes, forests, waterfalls, and an abundance of orchids, roses and other temperate flora. Dalat is the honeymoon capital of southern Vietnam and there is a quaint belief that unless you go on honeymoon to Dalat you are not really married at all.

Ins and outs

Getting there and around There are daily direct flights to Dalat from Ho Chi Minh City and Hanoi and a new route to Danang. Open Tour Buses pass through Dalat heading to Nha Trang, Mui Ne and Ho Chi Minh City and innumerable local buses plough the inter-provincial routes between Dalat, Play Ku, Kontum, Ho Chi Minh City, Nha Trang, Buon Ma Thuot, Phan Thiet and Phan Rang. Alternatively it is possible to hire a car and driver. Taxis and *xe ôm* are available around town and the cool climate means that it is very pleasant to reach outlying attractions by bicycle. In fact a day spent travelling can be more enjoyable than the sights themselves. ▸▸ *See Transport, page 155.*

Tourist information **Dalat Travel Bureau** ⓘ *www.dalattourist.com.vn*, is the state-run travel company for Lam Dong Province. There are also a number of tour operators in town. ▸▸ *See Activities and tours, page 153.*

Dalat

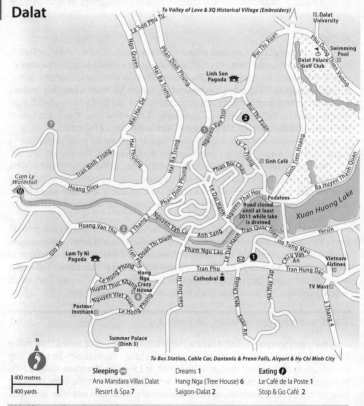

Sleeping 🛏
Ana Mandara Villas Dalat
Resort & Spa **7**
Dreams **1**
Hang Nga (Tree House) **6**
Saigon-Dalat **2**

Eating 🍴
Le Café de la Poste **1**
Stop & Go Café **2**

Background

Dr Alexandre Yersin, a protégé of Luis Pasteur, founded Dalat in 1893. He stumbled across Dalat as he was trying to find somewhere cool to escape from the sweltering summer heat of the coast and lowlands. The lush alpine scenery impressed the French and it soon became the second city in the south after Saigon. In the summer months the government and bureaucrats moved lock, stock and barrel to Dalat where it was cooler. There are still plenty of original French-style villas in town, many of which have been converted into hotels. The last Emperor of Vietnam Bao Dai also lived here.

Dalat soon took on the appearance of Paris in the mountains. A golf course was made and a luxurious hotel was built. In both the Second World War and the American War, high-ranking officials of the opposing armies would while away a pleasant couple of days playing golf against each other before having to return to the battlefields. Of all the highland cities, Dalat was the least affected by the American War. The main reason being that, at the time, the only way to Dalat was via the Prenn pass. There was a small heliport at Cam Ly and also a radio-listening station on Langbian Mountain but nothing else of note.

Xuan Huong Lake and the centre

Xuan Huong Lake was created as the Grand Lake in 1919, after a small dam was constructed on the Cam Ly River, and renamed in 1954. It is a popular exercise area for the local inhabitants, many of whom walk around the lake first thing in the morning, stopping every so often to perform t'ai chi exercises. The lake was drained in 2010 so as to remove accumulated silt and construct a new road across the centre. It should be refilled by the time you read this. At the northeast end of the Lake is the **Dalat Flower Garden** ① *0700-1800, 10000d*. Established in 1966, it supports a modest range of temperate and tropical plants including orchids (of which Dalat is renowned throughout Vietnam), roses, camellias, lilies and hydrangeas.

Dalat Cathedral ① *Mass is held twice a day Mon-Sat, and 5 times on Sun*, is a single-tiered cathedral, visible from the lake. It is referred to locally as the 'Chicken Cathedral' because of the chicken-shaped wind dial at the top of the turret. Construction began in 1931, although the building was not completed until the Japanese 'occupation' in the 1940s. The stained-glass windows, with their vivid colours and use of pure, clean lines, were crafted in France by Louis Balmet, the same man who made the windows in Nha Trang and Danang cathedrals, between 1934 and 1940. Sadly, most have not survived the ravages of time.

At the end of Nguyen Thi Minh Khai Street, **Dalat Market (Cho Dalat)** sells an array of exotic fruits and vegetables: plums, strawberries, carrots, potatoes, loganberries, cherries, apples, onions and avocados. The forbidding appearance of the market is masked by the riot of colourful flowers also on sale, including gladioli, irises, roses, chrysanthemums and marigolds.

Tran Hung Dao Street

Many of the large **colonial villas**, almost universally washed in pastel yellow, are 1930s and 1940s vintage. Some have curved walls, railings and are almost nautical in inspiration; others are reminiscent of houses in Provençe. Many of the larger villas can be found along **Tran Hung Dao Street**, although many have fallen into a very sorry state of repair. Perhaps the largest and most impressive house on Tran Hung Dao is the former residence of the Governor General at No12. It occupies a magnificent position set among mountain pines, overlooking the town. The villa, now the **Hotel Dinh 2**, is 1930s in style, with large airy rooms and uncomfortable furniture.

Summer Palace (Dinh 3)

① *Le Hong Phong St, about 2 km from the town centre, daily 0730-1100 and 1330-1600, 10000d, visitors have to wear covers on their shoes to protect the wooden floors.*

Vietnam's last emperor, Bao Dai, chose Dalat for his Summer Palace, built between 1933 and 1938 on a hill with views on every side, it is art deco in style, both inside and out, and rather modest for a palace. The stark interior contains little to indicate that this was the home of an emperor, especially since almost all of Bao Dai's personal belongings have been removed. The impressive dining room contains an etched-glass map of Vietnam, while the study has Bao Dai's desk, books, a few personal ornaments and, notably, photographs of the royal family, who were exiled permanently to France in 1954. One of the photos shows Bao Dai's son, the prince Bao Long, in full military dress uniform. He was a distinguished and gallant soldier who died during the war. Of all the members of the royal family, he is the only one that is regarded with respect by the government. He is considered to be a good, patriotic Vietnamese who fought for his country. The emperor's bedroom, balcony and bathroom are also open to the public, as is the family drawing room. The gardens are colourful and well maintained.

Lam Ty Ni Pagoda and around

Lam Ty Ni Pagoda, off Le Hong Phong St, is unremarkable save for the charming monk, Vien Thuc, who has lived here since 1968. He has created a garden, almost Japanese in inspiration, around the pagoda, known as the Divine Calmness Bamboo Garden. Vien Thuc is a scholar, poet, artist, philosopher, mystic, divine and entrepreneur but is best known for his paintings of which, by his own reckoning, there are more than 100,000. Wandering through the maze of rustic huts and shacks tacked on to the back of the temple you will see countless hanging sheets bearing his simple but distinctive calligraphy and philosophy: "Living in the present how beautiful this very moment is", "Zen painting destroys millennium sorrows", and so on. Vien Thuc's work is widely known and has been exhibited in Paris, New York and the Netherlands, as well as on the internet.

The slightly wacky theme is maintained at the **Hang Nga Guest House and Art Gallery** (Crazy House) ① *3 Huynh Thuc Khang, T063-382 2070, art gallery daily 0700-1800, 10,000d,* where Doctor Hang Viet Nga has, over many years, built up a hotel in organic fashion. Rooms resemble scenes from a fairy storybook; guests sleep inside mushrooms, trees and giraffes, and sip tea under giant cobwebs. It is not a particularly comfortable place to stay and visitors limit privacy but it is well worth visiting. ›› *See Sleeping, page 148.*

Bao Dai's hunting lodge (Dinh 1)

Emperor Bao Dai also had a hunting lodge that used to be a museum. East of the town centre, Dinh 1 sported 1930s furniture, antique telephone switchboards, and had a feel of authenticity. It has now closed and there is talk of it reopening as a casino.

Railway to Trai Mat Village

Dalat Railway Station, off Quang Trung Street to the east of the centre, was opened in 1938 and is the last station in Vietnam to retain its original French art deco architecture and coloured-glass windows. In 1991, a 7-km stretch of railway to the village of **Trai Mat** was reopened and every day a small **Russian-built diesel car** makes the journey ① *daily at 0800, 0930, 1100, 1400, 1530, US$5 return, 30 mins, minimum 6 people.* The journey to Trai Mat takes you near the **Lake of Sighs**, 5 km northeast of Dalat. The lake is said by some to be named after the sighs of the girls being courted by handsome young men from the military academy in Dalat. Another theory is that the name was coined after a young Vietnamese maiden, Mai Nuong, drowned herself in the lake in the 18th century, believing that her lover, Hoang Tung, had rejected her. Not long ago the lake was surrounded by thick forest but today it is a thin wood. The track also passes immaculately tended vegetable gardens; no space on the valley floors or sides is wasted and the high intensity agriculture is a marvellous sight. Trai Mat itself is a prosperous K'Ho village with a market selling piles of produce from the surrounding area. Walk 300 m up the road and take a narrow lane to the left to reach Chua Linh Phuoc, an attractive Buddhist temple, notable for its huge Buddha and mosaic-adorned pillars, made from broken rice bowls and fragments of beer bottle.

Waterfalls around Dalat

More cascades can be found south of town off Highway 20 towards Ho Chi Minh City. The first of these is **Datanla Falls** ① *5 km out of town, T063-383 1804, 0700-1700, 5000d.* A path leads steeply downwards into a forested ravine; it is an easy hike to get there, but tiring on the return journey. However, the **Alpine Coaster** ① *T063-383 1804, 35,000d return,* a toboggan on rails, makes the journey faster and easier. The falls are hardly spectacular but few people come here, except at weekends, so they are usually peaceful. Not far from the falls is the terminus of the **Dalat cable car** (**Càp Treo**) ① *daily 0730- 1700 but may be closed May-Nov if the wind is too strong, 35,000d 1 way, 50,000d return,* which starts from the top of Prenn Pass, about 100 m from the bus station. The journey from top to bottom takes about 15 minutes and gives a different perspective of the Dalat area.

 Prenn Falls, next to Highway 20, 12 km south of Dalat, were dedicated to Queen Sirikit of Thailand when she visited in 1959. The falls are not that good but there is a rope bridge that can be crossed and pleasant views of the surrounding area. Though it underwent renovations a few years ago, the falls began to suffer pollution and degredation in 2010 because dredged silt from Xuan Huong lake in Dalat was being dumped at the source of the falls. About 20 km north of Bao Loc on the Bao Loc Plateau are the **Dambri Falls** ① *Highway 20, 120 km from Dalat, Jul-Nov only; get an xe ôm from Bao Loc or take a tour.* These are considered the most impressive falls in southern Vietnam and are worth an excursion for those who have time.

Nam Cat Tien National Park

ⓘ *50,000d. Guides can be hired and accommodation is available. Take tough, long-sleeved and long-legged clothing, jungle boots and leech socks if possible and plenty of insect repellent.*

This newly created national park is about 150 km north of Ho Chi Minh City en route for Dalat. About 50 km south of Bao Loc (at the small town of Tan Phu) turn off Highway 20 to Nam Cat Tien, which is about 25 km down a rough road (not well signposted). The park is one of the last surviving areas of natural bamboo and dipterocarp forest in southern Vietnam. It is also one of the few places where populations of large mammals can be found in Vietnam – tiger, elephant, bear and the last few (possibly only four or five) remaining Javan rhino (see page 235). There are also 300 species of bird, smaller mammal, reptile and butterfly. The park is managed by 20 rangers who besides helping protect the flora and fauna also conduct research and show visitors around. They do not speak English. The **E Park Guesthouse and Bungalows**, T/F61-379 1228, offers basic accommodation with fan and or a/c, cold showers and semi-operational TV. There is a very basic restaurant on site and several small restaurants outside the entrance that provide reasonable food and snacks. Tour operators in Dalat and HCMC offer trips to Nam Cat Tien, see pages 153 and 176.

Central provinces → *For listings, see pages 148-156*

Ins and outs

Getting there and around There are direct flights from Ho Chi Minh City and Danang to Buon Ma Thuot and Play Ku. Local buses plough the inter-provincial routes between Dalat, Play Ku, Kontum, Ho Chi Minh City, Nha Trang, Buon Ma Thuot, Phan Thiet and Phan Rang. Alternatively, hire a car and driver. ⇥ *See Transport, page 155.*

Buon Ma Thuot → *Colour map 4, B2.*

Buon Ma Thuot, the provincial capital of Daklak Province, is located at the junction of Highway 14 and Highway 26. Until the 1950s big game hunting was Buon Ma Thuot's main claim to fame but now the town has surpassed its illustrious and renowned neighbour of Dalat to be the main centre for tea and coffee production and the area has become the second largest producer of coffee in the world. With the rise of the Trung Nguyen coffee empire, Buon Ma Thuot has changed from a sleepy backwater to a thriving modern city. The government also instigated a resettlement programme here, taking land from the ethnic minority groups to give to Vietnamese settlers. The Ede did not take kindly to having their land encroached upon by outsiders; tensions reached their peak in late 2001 and early 2002, when there was widespread rioting in Buon Ma Thuot. Today, the best Ede village to visit is **Buon Tur**, southwest of Buon Ma Thuot, off Highway 14. Apart from the odd TV aerial, life has changed little in this community of 20 stilt houses and, despite the efforts of the government to stop it, Ede is still taught in school. **Daklak Tourist Office** ⓘ *3 Phan Chu Trinh St (within the grounds of Thang Loi Hotel), T0500-385 2246, www.daklaktourist.com.vn,* provides useful information about the province and has knowledgeable, English-speaking staff.

Dray Sap waterfalls → *Colour map 4, B2.*

ⓘ *2 km off Highway 14 towards Ho Chi Minh City, 20 km from Buon Ma Thuot, daily 0700-1700, 6000-8000d.*

The waterfalls consist of several different cascades all next to each other. The 100-m-wide torrent is particularly stunning in the wet season when the spray justifies the name 'waterfall of smoke'. There are two paths to choose from: one down by the river and the other on the high ground. Note, though, that access may occasionally be limited in the wet season, if the paths are too treacherous to use.

Lak Lake → Colour map 4, B2.

The serene Lak Lake is about 50 km southeast of Buon Ma Thuot and can be explored by dugout. It is an attraction in its own right but is all the more compelling on account of the surrounding **Mnong villages**. Early morning mists hang above the calm waters and mingle with the columns of woodsmoke rising from the longhouses. The Mnong number about 50,000 and are matriarchal. They have been famed as elephant catchers for hundreds of years, although the elephants are now used for tourist rides rather than in their traditional role for dragging logs from the forest. In order to watch the elephants taking their evening wallow in the cool waters and to appreciate the tranquillity of sunrise over the lake, stay overnight at a Mnong village, **Buon Juin**. An evening supping with your hosts, sharing rice wine and sleeping in the simplicity of a Mnong longhouse is an ideal introduction to these genial people. ▸▸ *See Sleeping, page 148.*

Yok Don National Park → Colour map 4, B1.

ⓘ *40 km northwest of Buon Ma Thuot, T0500-378 3049, yokdonecotourism@vnn.vn. Tour guide Mr Hung T090-519 7501 (mob), daily 0700-2200. Tours range from elephant riding (US$40 for 2 hrs) to elephant trekking (US$190 for 2 for 3 days) to riverboat rides (US$20 for 1 hr) to trekking (US$15 for 3 hrs). There is an additional entry fee to the park, for under US$1. Accommodation is available.*

This 115,545-ha wildlife reserve is home to 250 species of bird and at least 63 species of mammal, 17 of which are on the worldwide endangered list. It is believed that rare white elephants survive here. The best chance of spotting wildlife is on an overnight guided hike or elephant safari. Within the park boundaries are also 17 different ethnic tribes.

Play Ku (Pleiku) and around → Colour map 4, A2.

Nearly 200 km north of Buon Ma Thuot, Play Ku is located in a valley at the bottom of a local mountain and is visible from 12 km away. It is a modern, thriving, bustling town, surrounded by rubber, pepper, coffee and tea plantations. There was fierce fighting here during the American War and, as a result, the town itself has little to offer the tourist but nearby are several Jarai villages that are worth a visit. Contact **Gia Lia Tourist** ⓘ *215 Hung Vuong St (in Hung Vuong Hotel), T059-387 4571, www.gialaitourist.com, daily 0730-1100, 1330-1630,* for information and, for the sake of preserving the traditional way of life, only visit those villages where foreigners are permitted to visit.

Plei Fun is about 16 km north of Play Ku and is the village **Gia Lai Tourist** will take you to if you book a tour through them. The local villagers have wised up to tourism and may try and charge you 30,000d to see their graveyard, in which tiled or wooden roofs shelter the worldly possessions of the deceased: bottles, bowls and even the odd bicycle. Traditional Jarai carved hardwood statues guard the graves. Push on to **Plei Mun**, another 5 km down the road and left 2 km down a dirt road, for some even finer examples. There is also a traditional wooden *rong* house here but it has a corrugated iron roof.

Kontum → Colour map 4, A2.

Kontum is a small, sleepy market town, 44 km north of Play Ku on Highway 14. There are a couple of notable sights that make a side trip to Kontum worthwhile, plus scores of Ba-na villages in the vicinity that can be reached by motorbike and on foot. Contact **Kontum Tourist Office** ⓘ *2 Phan Dinh Phung St (on the ground floor of the Dakbla Hotel 1), T060-386 1626, daily 0700-1100, 1300-1700,* for details about tours and further information.

The French Bishop and missionary Stephano Theodore Cuenot founded Kontum in the mid 1800s and succeeded in converting many of the local tribespeople to Christianity. He was arrested on Emperor Tu Duc's orders but died in Binh Dinh prison on 14 November 1861, a day before the beheading instructions arrived. He was beatified in 1909. Cuenot and other French priests and missionaries slain by Emperor Tu Duc are commemorated by a plaque set into the altar of **Tan Huong Church** ⓘ *92 Nguyen Hué St (if the church is shut ask in the office adjacent and they will gladly open it).* The whitewashed façade has an interesting depiction of St George and the dragon. It is not immediately evident that the church is built on stilts, but crouch down and look under one of the little arches that run along the side and the stilts, joists and floorboards are clear. Many of the windows are original but, unfortunately, the roof is a modern replacement, although the original style of fish-scale tiling can still be seen in the tower. The interior of the church is exquisite, with dark wooden columns and a fine vaulted ceiling made of wattle and daub.

Further east (1 km) on the same street is the superb **Wooden Church**. Built by the French with Ba-na labour in 1913, it remains largely unaltered, with the original wooden frame and wooden doors. Inside, the blue walls combine with the dark-brown polished wood to produce a very serene effect. Unfortunately the windows are modern tinted glass and rather crude. In the grounds to the right stands a *rong* house and a statue of Cuenot, the first Catholic bishop of East Cochin China diocese.

Nha Trang → *For listings, see pages 148-156. Colour map 4, B3.*

Nha Trang is Vietnam's only real seaside city, with a long, golden beach. The centuries-old fishing settlement nestles in the protective embrace of the surrounding hills and islands at the mouth of the Cai Estuary. The light here has a beautifully radiant quality and the air is clear: colours are vivid, particularly the blues of the sea, sky and fishing boats moored on the river. The name Nha Trang is thought to be derived from the Cham word *yakram*, meaning bamboo river. Certainly, the surrounding area was a focal point of the Cham Kingdom (see box, page 128), with some of the country's best-preserved Cham towers located nearby.

Nha Trang's clear waters and offshore islands won wide acclaim in the 1960s and its current prosperity is based firmly on tourism. Word has spread and Nha Trang's days as an undiscovered treasure are over. The town is now a well-established favourite of Vietnamese as well as foreign visitors. There is a permanent relaxed holiday atmosphere, the streets are not crowded and the motorbikes cruise at a leisurely pace. There are, in reality, two Nha Trangs: popular Nha Trang, which is a sleepy, sedate seaside town consisting of a long, palm and casuarina-fringed beach and one or two streets running parallel to it, and commercial Nha Trang to the north of Yersin Street, which is a bustling city with an attractive array of Chinese shophouses.

Ins and outs

Getting there The airport is 34 km from Nha Trang at Cam Ranh. There are daily flights to Hanoi and Ho Chi Minh City and regular flights to Danang. The town is on the main north-south railway line, with trains to Ho Chi Minh City, Hanoi and stops between. The main bus terminal is west of the town centre. Note that inter-provincial buses do not go into Nha Trang but drop off on Highway 1 which bypasses the town. *Xe ôms* take passengers into town. ►► *See Transport, page 156.*

Nha Trang

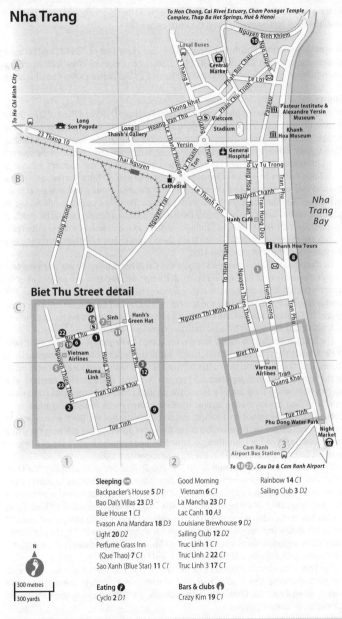

Sleeping 🛏

Backpacker's House **5** *D1*
Bao Dai's Villas **23** *D3*
Blue House **1** *C3*
Evason Ana Mandara **18** *D3*
Light **20** *D2*
Perfume Grass Inn
  (Que Thao) **7** *C1*
Sao Xanh (Blue Star) **11** *C1*

Eating 🍽

Cyclo **2** *D1*

Good Morning
  Vietnam **6** *C1*
La Mancha **23** *D1*
Lac Canh **10** *A3*
Louisiane Brewhouse **9** *D2*
Sailing Club **12** *D2*
Truc Linh **1** *C1*
Truc Linh 2 **22** *C1*
Truc Linh 3 **17** *C1*

Bars & clubs 🍸

Crazy Kim **19** *C1*

Rainbow **14** *C1*
Sailing Club **3** *D2*

Getting around Nha Trang is just about negotiable on foot but there are also bicycles and motorbikes for hire everywhere and the usual cyclos.

Tourist information **Khanh Hoa Tours** ① *1 Tran Hung Dao St, T058-352 6753, www. nhatrangtourist.com.vn, daily 0700-1130, 1330-1700,* is the official tour office and can arrange visa extensions, car and boat hire and tours of the area. It's also Vietnam Airlines booking office.

Sights

Known as Thap Ba, the temple complex of **Cham Ponagar** ① *follow 2 Thang 4 St north out of town, Cham Ponagar is just over Xom Bong bridge, daily 0600-1800, 15000d,* is on a hill just outside the city. Originally the complex consisted of eight towers, four of which remain. Their stylistic differences indicate they were built at different times between the seventh and 12th centuries. The largest (23 m high) was built in AD 817 and contains a statue of Lady Thien Y-ana, also known as Ponagar (the beautiful wife of Prince Bac Hai), as well as a fine and very large linga. She taught the people of the area weaving and new agricultural techniques, and they built the tower in her honour. The other towers are dedicated to gods: the central tower to Cri Cambhu (which has become a fertility temple for childless couples); the northwest tower to Sandhaka (wood cutter and foster-father to Lady Thien Y-ana); and the south tower to Ganeca (Lady Thien Y-ana's daughter). The best time to visit the towers is in the afternoon, after 1600.

En route to the towers, the road crosses the **Cai River estuary**, where you'll see Nha Trang's elegant fleet of blue fishing boats, decorated with red trim and painted eyes for spotting the fish. The boats have coracles (*cái thúng*) for getting to and from the shore and mechanical fish traps, which take the form of nets supported by long arms; the arms are hinged to a platform on stilts and are raised and lowered by wires connected to a capstan which is turned, sometimes by hand but more commonly by foot.

The best known pagoda in Nha Trang is the **Long Son Pagoda** ① *23 Thang 10 St,* built in 1963. Inside the sanctuary is an unusual image of the Buddha, backlit with natural light. Murals depicting the *jataka* stories (birth stories of the Buddha) decorate the upper walls. To the right of the sanctuary, stairs lead up to a 9-m-high white Buddha, perched on a hill top, from where there are fine views. The pagoda commemorates those monks and nuns who died demonstrating against the Diem government, in particular those who, through their self-immolation, brought the despotic nature of the Diem regime and its human rights abuses to the attention of the American public. Before reaching the white pagoda, take a left on the stairs. Through an arch behind the pagoda you'll see a 14-m long reclining Buddha. Commissioned in 2003, it is an impressive sight.

The **Alexandre Yersin Museum** ① *10 Tran Phu St, T058-382 9540, Mon-Fri 0700-1130, 1330-1700, 26,000d,* is contained within the colonnaded **Pasteur Institute** founded by the great scientist's protégé, Dr Alexandre Yersin. Swiss-born Yersin first arrived in Vietnam in 1891 and spent much of the rest of his life in Nha Trang. He was responsible for identifying the bacillus that causes the plague. The museum contains the lab equipment used by Yersin, his library and stereoscope through which visitors can see in 3-D the black-and-white slides, including shots taken by Yersin on his visits to the highlands. The museum's curator is helpful, friendly, and fluent in French and English.

The **Cho Dam** (central market) close to Nguyen Hong Son Street is a good place to wander and browse and is quite well-stocked with useful items. In the vicinity of the market, along **Phan Boi Chau Street** for example, are some bustling streets with old colonial-style shuttered houses.

Long Thanh is one of Vietnam's most distinguished photographers and has a **gallery** ① *126 Hoang Van Thu St, near the railway station, T058-382 4875, www.longthanhart.com. 0900-1900*, in his native Nha Trang. Long Thanh works only in black and white and has won a series of international awards and recognition for his depictions of Cham children and of wistful old men and women, who have witnessed generations of change in a single lifetime. Many of his famous pictures were taken in and around Nha Trang. Long Thanh speaks English and welcomes visitors to his gallery.

Islands around Nha Trang
① *The islands are reached on boat trips from Cau Da pier, departures 0900, around 100,000d including a seafood lunch and snorkelling equipment, cold beers cost extra. Boat charters also available.* The islands are sometimes known as the **Salangane** islands after the sea swallows that nest here. The sea swallow (*yen*) produces the bird's nest from which the famous soup is made.

There's an uninspiring aquarium on **Mieu Island** but no other sights. The islands (including **Hon Mun**, and **Hon Mot**) are usually a bit of an anti-climax for, as so often in Vietnam, to travel is better than to arrive; it's often a case of lovely boat trip, disappointing beach. The best part is anchoring offshore and jumping into the cool water while your skipper prepares a sumptuous feast and chills some beers. The best known boat trips to the islands are run by **Hanh's Green Hat** and **Mama Linh**. ▸▸ *See Activities and tours, page 153.*

Mui Ne → *For listings, see pages 148-156. Colour map 4, C2.*

Further down the coast and east of the small fishing town of **Phan Thiet** is Mui Ne, a 20-km sweep of golden sand where Vietnam's finest resorts can be found. Water sports are available as well as one of the country's most attractive golf courses. ▸▸ *See Activities and tours, page 153.*

Ins and outs
Getting there Open Tour Buses nearly all divert to Mui Ne and drop off/pick up from just about every hotel along the beach. It is also possible and quicker to hire a car; from Ho Chi Minh City it will cost about US$75. ▸▸ *See Transport, page 155.*

Best time to visit The weather is best in the dry season, December to April. Mui Ne is most popular with overseas visitors in the Christmas to Easter period when prices at the some of the better hotels rise by 20% or more. From December to March, Mui Ne loses part of its beach to the sea.

Sights
Mui Ne (Cape Ne) is the name of the famous sandy cape and the small fishing village that lies at its end. Mui Ne's two claims to fame are its *nuoc mam* (fish sauce) and its **beaches**, where it's possible to play a host of water sports, including kitesurfing, for which it is justly famous. The cape is dominated by some impressive **sand dunes**, which are quite red in parts due to the underlying geology.

Around the village, visitors may notice a strong smell of rotting fish. This is the unfortunate but inevitable by-product of fish sauce fermenting in wooden barrels. The process takes a year but to Vietnamese palates it is worth every day. The *nuoc mam* of Phan Thiet is made from anchovies and is highly regarded but not as reverentially as that from the southern island of Phu Quoc.

For Sleeping and Eating price codes and other relevant information, see pages 40-43.

⊜ Sleeping

Dalat *p137, map p138*
LL-AL Ana Mandara Villas Dalat Resort & Spa, Le Lai St, T063-355 5888, www.anamandararesortdalat.com. Restored

French villas are perched on a hillside, surrounded by fruit farms. Each villa has a couple of bedrooms, a sitting room and dining room. The heated pool, buried amid the secluded hillside villas, is lovely. There is also a central villa that houses a French bistro and wine bar. The spa experience has been created in one of the villas.

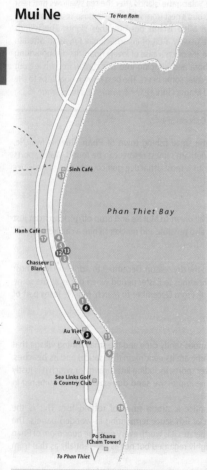

Mui Ne

To Hon Rom

Sinh Café

Phan Thiet Bay

Hanh Café

Chasseur Blanc

Au Viet
Au Phu

Sea Links Golf & Country Club

Po Shanu (Cham Tower)

To Phan Thiet

1 km
1 mile

N

Sleeping ⊜
Bamboo Village **1**
Beach Resort **9**
Coco Beach (Hai Duong) **3**
Full Moon Beach **4**
Hiep Hoa **5**
Mui Ne Resort **13**
Sailing Club & Airwaves **11**
Small Garden
(Vuon Nho) **14**
Thuy Thuy **17**
Victoria Phan Thiet
Beach Resort & Spa **18**

Eating ⊘
Forest **6**
Luna D'Autonno **3**

Bars & clubs ⊙
Sankara **12**
Wax **13**

AL-C Hang Nga (Tree House), 3 Huynh Thuc Khang St, T063-382 2070. If you fancy a fantasy night in a mushroom, a tree or a giraffe then this is the place for you. It is an architectural meander through curves, twists and bizarre rooms and ornamentation. The guesthouse was designed by Hang Nga, whose father, Truong Chinh, formed the triumvirate of power following the death of Ho Chi Minh. Prices have risen and the rooms tend to be visited by curious tourists. The furniture is sturdily made and not too comfortable.

A Saigon-Dalat Hotel, 2 Hoang Van Thu, T063-355 6789, www.saigondalathotel.com. The government-owned Saigon-Dalat is one of the largest in the city. The striking white exterior with bright orange, alpine-style roof is visible throughout western Dalat. The hotel has 2 restaurants and a bar, plus the **Moulin Rouge Restaurant** across the street.

C Empress Hotel, 5 Nguyen Thai Hoc St, T063-383 3888, empressdl@hcm.vnn.vn. This is a particularly attractive hotel in a lovely position overlooking the lake. All rooms are arranged around a small courtyard that traps the sun and is a great place for breakfast or to pen a postcard. The rooms are large with very comfortable beds and the more expensive ones have luxurious bathrooms so try to get a room upgrade. Attentive and courteous staff. A great value hotel with the best view of Xuan Huong Lake.

C Golf 3 Hotel, 4 Nguyen Thi Minh Khai St, T063-382 6042, www.vinagolf.vn. Smart, centrally located hotel with comfortable rooms; cheaper rooms have showers only. It has a good range of facilities, including bar, restaurant, massage, nightclub and karaoke. The location by Dalat market is excellent. One drawback though is that because it is so near to the market the rooms facing the street are noisy. Breakfast is included.

E Dreams Hotel, 5 Hai Thuong St, T063-383 3748. Though 10 years old, this immaculate hotel looks brand new. The top floor has a jacuzzi, sauna and stream room, and there is free Wi-Fi throughout.

F Hoa Binh 1 (Peace Hotel 1), 64 Truong Cong Dinh St, T063-382 2787, peace12@hcm.vnn.vn. One of the better low-cost places with 16 rooms in a good location, including 5 at the back around a small yard; quiet but not much view. Rooms at the front have a view but can be a bit noisy. The rooms have TV, fan and mosquito nets. A friendly place with an all-day café.

Buon Ma Thuot *p142*

C Damsan Hotel, 212-214 Nguyen Cong Tru St, T0500-385 1234, www.damsan hotel. com.vn. A good hotel with a pool and tennis court and large restaurant. Service is good and rooms are comfortable. There's a lovely balconied coffee shop and bar, Da Quy, opposite.

E Thang Loi Hotel, 1 Phan Chu Trinh St, T0500-385 7615, www.daklaktourist.com. vn. In a central location, opposite the victory monument. The rooms are large and come with en suite facilities. The staff speak good English. Food in the restaurant is fresh, well presented, good value and plentiful. ATM.

F Duy Hoang Hotel, 30 Ly Thuong Kiet St, T0500-385 8020. Spacious, well-furnished rooms with en suite facilities and a/c. Cheaper rooms have fan and shared bathrooms. Staff are efficient and friendly and have a reasonable grasp of English. Excellent value for money.

Lak Lake *p143*

It costs US$5 to stay in a Mnong long-house at Buon Jun; contact **Daklak Tourist** for arrangements.

Play Ku *p143*

E Ialy Hotel, 89 Hung Vuong St, T059-382 4843, ialyhotel@dng.vnn.vn. Excellent location opposite the main post office. Reasonable sized, good-value rooms with en suite facilities, a/c and satellite TV. Staff are friendly enough but no English is spoken. The restaurant on the 1st floor is only open for breakfast. ATM in the lobby.

Kontum *p143*

C-D Indochine (Dong Duong) Hotel, 30 Bach Dang St, T060-386 3335, indochinevn@kontumtourism.com. The views from this new hotel are fantastic. You can look right up the river to the mountains beyond. Decent-sized rooms with mod cons including hairdryer. A riverfront pool was due to open. The breakfasts could be better.

E Dakbla 1 Hotel, 2 Phan Dinh Phung St, T060-386 3333. Set amid attractive grounds, this hotel has a small restaurant and jetty on the riverbank. Staff are friendly and helpful and have a basic understanding of English and French. Rooms have minibars, satellite TV, a/c, hot water and en suite bathrooms. The restaurant provides good food at a reasonable price.

Nha Trang *p144, map p145*

LL Evason Ana Mandara, Tran Phu St, T058-352 2222, www.sixsenses.com. Nha Trang's finest beach resort (recently upgraded) and, despite the increasing competition, still the loveliest resort in Vietnam, where those who can afford it relax in unashamed and exquisite luxury. The resort has 74 rooms in sea view or garden villas that are all beautifully furnished with special touches and new outdoor bathtubs. Every conceivable facility is available in this enchanting retreat, including 2 pools, a tennis court, an enlarged gym, bicycles and restaurants. For those wanting further pampering there is the Six Senses Spa.

LL Evason Hideaway & Six Senses Spa at Ana Mandara, Ninh Vinh Bay; 30 km north of Nha Trang, T058-372 8222, www.sixsenses.com. Beach Villas, Rock Villas and Hilltop Villas are laid out in the full dramatic curve of Ninh Van Bay. Exceptional luxury; the Rock Villas are perched on rocks at the tip of the bay with bathrooms overlooking the sea and fronted by small infinity pools. The resort is large; from the Rock Villas to the main restaurant is an enormous hike. Beach Villas are more centrally located. While your

days away in the herb garden, Six Senses Spa, library or bar and be attended by your personal butler. It's highly romantic, very secluded and very expensive; the food is exceptional. The resort is 1 hr ahead of real time which is far too confusing.

A-B The Light Hotel, 86B Tran Phu St, T058-625 2333, www.thelighthotel.com.vn. This is in a great location opposite **Louisiane Restaurant**. Views are incredible and there's a small pool streetside. Music blares in the afternoon but all in all it's a good choice. Staff are very helpful.

A-D Bao Dai's Villas, Tran Phu St (just before Cau Da village), T058-359 0147, http://baodaivillas.khatoco.com. Several villas of former Emperor Bao Dai, with magnificent views over the harbour and outlying islands, sited on a small promontory, with large elegant a/c rooms. There are an additional 40 rooms in assorted buildings that lack the scale and elegance, not surprisingly, of the emperor's own quarters. Overrun with sightseers during holiday periods.

B-C Whale Island Resort, off Nha Trang, T058-384 0501, www.iledelabaleine.com. This is a great place in which to relax amid the aquamarine waters of the South China Sea. Bungalows right on this island beach, 2½ hrs north of Nha Trang. The price includes breakfasts. Activities include diving, windsurfing, canoeing and catamaran sailing and there's plenty of wildlife to observe. Return transfers to Nha Trang are arranged.

C-E Perfume Grass Inn (Que Thao), 4A Biet Thu St, T058-352 4286, www.perfume-grass.com. Well-run and friendly family hotel with 21 rooms. Restaurant and internet service. Good value for money. Book in advance.

D-E Sao Xanh (Blue Star), 1B Biet Thu St, T058-352 5447, quangc@dng.vnn.vn. Another popular, clean and friendly family-run hotel. 28 rooms, free coffee and bananas, more expensive rooms have breakfast included. Near the beach and in a popular area.

D-F Backpackers' House, 54G Nguyen Thien Thuat St, T058-352 4500, www.backpackershouse.net. A super clean and bright new place with dorms and private rooms with cable TV and DVD players set up in a courtyard along with the attached **Green Apple Restaurant** and hang out joint. Tours also arranged. A dollar from each booking is invested in the Anh Dao Orphanage (http://heartsofnamfoundation.com)

E-G Blue House, 12/8 Hung Vuong St, T58-3824505, ngovietthuy57@yahoo.com.vn. Down a little alley in a quiet setting. 16 a/c and cheaper fan rooms in a small, neat blue building. Friendly, warm welcome and excellent value for money.

Mui Ne p147, map p148

LL Victoria Phan Thiet Beach Resort & Spa, T062-381 3000, www.victoriahotels-asia.com. Part of the French-run Victoria Group, the resort has thatch-roof bungalows with outdoor rain showers and 3 villas, built in country-house style in an attractive landscaped setting. It is well equipped with restaurants, several bars, an attractive pool and a spa.

AL Bamboo Village, T062-384 7007, www.bamboovillageresortvn.com. Attractive, simple, hexagonal bamboo huts peppered around a lovely shady spot at the top of the beach. More expensive rooms have a/c and hot-water showers. An excellent restaurant and attractive swimming pool.

AL Coco Beach (Hai Duong), T062-3847 111, www.cocobeach.net. Coco Beach was the first resort on Mui Ne and remains among the best. Not luxurious but friendly and impeccably kept. Wooden bungalows and 2-bedroom 'villas' facing the beach in a beautiful setting with a lovely pool. Price includes a decent buffet breakfast. There are 2 restaurants: the French **Champa** (Tue-Sun 1500-2200 only) and **Paradise Beach Club** (open all day).

A Sailing Club, T062-384 7440, www.sailingclubvietnam.com. This is a stunning resort, designed in the most charming style with bungalows and rooms that are simple and cool and surrounded by dense vegetation. Its pool has been extended and the bathrooms for the superior rooms enlarged. It has an excellent restaurant and bar. A good buffet breakfast is included.

B The Beach Resort, T062-384 7626, www.thebeachresort.com.vn. A very attractive resort with 40 rooms set in luscious gardens with a lovely pool surrounded by tip-top shrubbery and thatched umbrellas on the beach. Good value.

B Full Moon Beach, T062-384 7008, www.windsurf-vietnam.com. Visitors are assured of a friendly reception by the French and Vietnamese couple who own and run the place. Some rooms are spacious, others a little cramped, some brick, some bamboo. The most attractive rooms have a sea view. There is a good restaurant.

B Thuy Thuy, T062-384 7357, T091-816 0637 (mob), thuythuyresort2000@yahoo.com. 7 pleasant a/c bungalows with TV run by the friendly Elaine. Newer bungalows are a bit more expensive but the originals are perfectly comfortable. Set on the 'wrong' side of the road (eg away from the beach) this is nevertheless a rather charming and nicely run little place, highly praised by guests. Attractive pool.

C Mui Ne Resort (Sinh Tourist), T062-384 7542, This recommended resort has cleverly packed the narrow site with 48 rooms and brick-built bungalows, rather like a crowded Sinh Tourist tour bus though the prices aren't as cheap as they once were. It has a nice pool. Bar and restaurant (with extensive menu and Fanny ice cream) for guests and for those waiting for their bus to come along.

D Small Garden (Vuon Nho), T062-387 4012, nguyengrimm@yahoo.com. Run by a Vietnamese family, it consists of simple and bamboo hut accommodation near the road and new, small, a/c concrete bungalows nearer the beach. Although lacking in amenities it is in a good part of the beach with plenty of cafés and restaurants nearby.

E Hiep Hoa, T062-384 7262, T091-8124149 (mob), hiephoatourism@yahoo.com.

Attractive and simple little place with 25 a/c rooms. It's quiet, clean and with its own stretch of beach. Popular and should be booked in advance. Rates are excellent value for Mui Ne; they go down in the low season.

🍴 Eating

Dalat *p137, map p138*

In the evening, street stalls line Nguyen Thi Minh Khai St, leading to Dalat market, which is itself the ideal place to buy picnic provisions. Lakeside cafés and restaurants may look attractive but they serve indifferent food.

¶¶-¶ Empress Restaurant, Empress hotel. Open all day and specializing in Chinese fare but with a good selection of Vietnamese and Western dishes. Ideal breakfast setting, al fresco around the fountain in the courtyard.

¶¶-¶ Le Café de la Poste, 12 Tran Phu St. Adjacent to the Sofitel and under the same management. International comfort food at near-Western prices in an airy and cool building. The 3-course lunch menu is great value. A pool table dominates the café. Upstairs is a Vietnamese restaurant.

¶ Hoa Binh 1, 67 Truong Cong Dinh St. An all-day eatery serving standard backpacker fare: fried noodles, vegetarian dishes and pancakes at low prices.

¶ Long Hoa, 63 Thang 2, T063-382 2934. In the best traditions of French family restaurants, this place has delicious food with fish, meat, venison and super breakfasts. Popular with Dalat's expats and visitors. The chicken soup and beefsteak are particularly recommended and sample Madame's home-made strawberry wine. Erratic service.

¶ Stop and Go Café, 2A Ly Tu Trong St, T063-382 8458. A café and art gallery run by the local poet, Mr Duy Viet. Sit inside or on the terrace as he bustles around rustling up breakfast, pulling out volumes of visitors' books and his own collected works. The garden is an overrun wilderness.

Nha Trang *p144, map p145*

A local speciality is *nem nuong*, grilled pork wrapped in rice paper with salad leaves and *bun*, fresh rice noodles. The French bread in Nha Trang is also excellent.

¶¶-¶ Good Morning Vietnam, 19B Biet Thu St, T058-3522071. Daily 1000-2300. Popular Italian restaurant, part of a small chain to be found in major tourist centres.

¶¶-¶ La Mancha, 78 Nguyen Thien Tuat St, T058-352 7978. Open 1100-2400. Great atmosphere, with Spanish and sangria decor, barbecued meat on the street. Garlic galore and great dishes but not served together (ie tapas style) and sadly the chorizo is not real. Nonetheless, highly recommended.

¶¶-¶ Louisiane Brewhouse, 29 Tran Phu St, opposite the turning for the old airport, T058-352 1948, www.louisianebrewhouse.com.vn. Open 0700-0100. This place has been transformed into a restaurant and brewery but has maintained its pool so is popular with families for lunch and has a great seating area. Serves a range of Western dishes and seafood; the fish menu is enormous. You can eat facing the beach, the pool or on converted beer barrels.

¶¶-¶ Sailing Club, 72-74 Tran Phu St, T058-352 4628, sailingnt@dng.vnn.vn. Daily 0700-2300. Although best known as a bar, this busy and attractive beachfront area also includes several restaurants: Japanese, Italian and global cuisine. None is cheap but all serve good food and represent decent value.

¶ Cyclo, 130 Nguyen Thien Thuat St, T058-352 4208, khuongthuy@hotmail.com. Daily 0700-2400. Outstanding little family-run restaurant. Italian and Vietnamese dishes. Real attention to detail in the cooking.

¶ Lac Canh, 44 Nguyen Binh Khiem St, T058-382 1391. Specializes in beef, squid and prawns, which you barbecue at your table. Also excellent fish and a special dish of eel mixed with vermicelli. Smoky atmosphere and can be hard to get a table. Highly recommended.

¶ Truc Linh, 11 Biet Thu St, T058-352 6742. Deservedly popular with sensible prices.

Good fruit shake and *op la* (fried eggs).
There's also **Truc Linh 2**, at 21 Biet Thu St,
T058-352 1089, and **Truc Linh 3**, at 80 Hung
Vuong St, T058-352 5259. Nos 2 and 3 are
recommended as the best.

Mui Ne *p147, map p148*
Of the hotel restaurants the **Sailing Club**,
Bamboo Village and **Coco Beach** stand out,
see Sleeping.
¶ Forest Restaurant, 7 Nguyen Dinh Chieu
St, T062-384 7589, www.forestrestaurant.
com. Local dishes and lots of seafood,
this atmospheric garden-jungle setting
puts on live music and dance shows
throughout the evening.
¶ Luna D'Autonno, T062-384 7591. One of
the best Italian restaurants in the country.
Inspired menu that goes way beyond the
standard pizzas and pasta with daily fish specials
and barbecues. Huge portions, good wine.

❶ Bars and clubs

Nha Trang *p144, map p145*
Crazy Kim, 19 Biet Thu St, T058-381 6072.
Open until late. A busy, lively bar in the
heart of a popular part of town. Pool, table
tennis, food.
The Rainbow, 90a Hung Vuong St, T058-352
4351. 0600-2400. This popular bar, run by
Rainbow Divers, is a current hotspot.
Sailing Club, 74-76 Tran Phu St, T058-352
4628. Open until late. Lively bar, especially
on Sat nights when locals and visitors enjoy
pool, cold beer, dancing and music.

Mui Ne *p147, map p148*
Sankara, 78 Nguyen Dinh Chieu St , T062-
374 1122, www.sankaravietnam.com. This
chic new beachside bar with pool has made
a lot of noise since its much-anticipated
opening in 2009. The place to see and be
seen on weekends and holidays.
Wax, 68 Nguyen Dinh Chieu St, T062-
384 7001. Located beside the beach at
Windchamp Resort, Wax is dance party
central, especially during holidays.

❍ Shopping

Dalat *p137, map p138*
Dalat has a well-deserved reputation
for producing not only beautiful flowers
but also some of the best handmade silk
paintings in Vietnam.

❍ Activities and tours

Dalat *p137, map p138*
Golf
Dalat Palace Golf Club, 1 Phu Dong
Thien Vuong St, T063-382 3507, www.
dalatpalacegolf.vn. Originally built for
Emperor Bao Dai in 1922, it was rebuilt in
1994 and is now an 18-hole championship
golf course. Rated by some as the finest in
Vietnam and one of the best in the region.
Green fees from US$55, include caddie fee.

Tour operators
Dalat Toserco, No7, 3 Thang 2 St, T063-
382 2125. Budget transport and a good
selection of tours. Slightly more expensive
than **Sinh Café**.
Dalat Travel Bureau, 1 Nguyen Thi Minh
Khai, T063-351 0104, www.dalattourist.
com.vn. The state-run travel company
for Lam Dong Province. Tours include:
city, trekking, canyoning, rock climbing,
exploring and biking; the majority of these
tours cost upwards of US$20 per person.
Highland Holiday Tour, 49 Truong Cong
Dinh St, T090-284 8967, haitours@gmail.
com. Recently recommended by CNN,
Highland Holiday's guides are highly
trained and graduated from a 4-year
university tourism program.
Phat Tire Adventures, 73 Truong
Cong Dinh St, T063-382 9422, www.
phattireventures.com. Canyoning from
US$29; rock climbing US$35; mountain
biking from US$38; trekking from US$22;
kayaking, US$30.
Sinh Tourist, 4a Bui Thi Xuan, T063-382
2663, www.theSinhtourist.vn. Part of the
nationwide **Sinh Café** chain. Primarily

provides cheap travel to HCMC and Nha Trang. Also arranges local tours.

Buon Ma Thuot *p142*
Tour operators
Vietnam Highland Travel, 24 Ly Thuong Kiet, T0500-385 5009, highlandco@dng.vnn.vn. Offers adventure packages, including elephant trekking and homestays. Recommended.

Nha Trang *p144, map p145*
Diving
Rainbow Divers, 90A Hung Vuong St, T058-352 4351, www.divevietnam.com. A full range of training and courses, including the National Geographic dive courses. Good reports regarding equipment and focus on safety. Qualified instructors speak a variety of European languages. Top professional operation. Rainbow also operates out of **Whale Island Resort**, see page 150.

The **Evason Hideaway** also offers diving packages.

Therapies
Six Senses Spa, Ana Mandara Resort, www.sixsenses.com. Japanese and Vichy showers, hot tubs and massages in beautiful surroundings. Programmes for vitality, stress-management and meditation that include tailored spa treatments. 5-day lifestyle packages are US$990 (no accommodation).

Súspa, 93AB Nguyen Thien Thuat St, T58-352 3242, www.suspa.vn. An upmarket new spa in zen-like surrounds.

Tour operators
The following tour operators can also arrange trips to **Buon Ma Thuot** and the **Central Highlands**.
Mama Hanh/Hanh's Green Hat, 2C Biet Thu St, T058-352 6494, www.biendaotour.com. Boat trips (US$5 including lunch and pick-up from hotel, excluding entrance fees and Con Se Tre village fees). Mama Hanh also offers less crowded half-day and 1-day

tours for US$14. Also other local tours, fishing tours, car, motorbike and bicycle hire.
Mama Linh, 144 Hung Vuong St, T58-3522844, mamalinhvn@yahoo.com. Organizes standard boat trips 100,000d and sells minibus tickets to Hoi An, Phan Thiet, HCMC and Dalat. Not as helpful as Mama Hanh.
Sinh Tourist, 2A Biet Thu St, T058-3521981, www.thesinhtouristvn. Offers tours and Open Tour Bus tickets. **Sinh Café** buses arrive and depart from here.

Water sports
The **Sailing Club** offers water sports.

Mui Ne *p147, map p148*
Golf
Ocean Dunes Golf Club, 1 Ton Duc Thang St, T062-382 3366, www.oceandunesgolf.vn. Phan Thiet's 18-hole golf course, designed by Nick Faldo, is highly regarded. Fully equipped club house with bar and restaurant. Green fees from US$55 including caddie fees.

Therapies
Lotus Day Spa, Sailing Club, T062-384 7440, www.sailingclubvietnam.com. Massage treatments are available in special cabins in the grounds.

Tour operators
Sinh Tourist, 144 Nguyen Dinh Chieu, T062-384 7542, muine@thesinhtourist.vn. Good for Open Tour tickets and local tours.

Water sports
Windsurfing, kitesurfing and other water sports are popular in Mui Ne, the water sports capital of Vietnam. The wind is normally brisk and the sight of the kitesurfers zooming around on the waves is great for those of us too cowardly to try. Equipment and training is offered by a couple of resorts. Make sure your operator is licensed.
Jibe's Beach Club, T062-384 7405, T091-316 2005 (mob) www.windsurf-vietnam.

com. Jibe's is the importer of sea kayaks, windsurfers, surfboards, sailboats, SUP (stand up paddle) and kitesurf equipment. Equipment is available for purchase or for hire by the hr, day or week. Hourly windsurf lessons US$45 and hourly kitesurf lessons are $50; US$7.50 surfboard hire, boogie board hire US$2.50, kayaking US$5 per hr per person.

Storm, T062-384 7442 www.storm kiteboarding.com. This place has a station at the beachfront of the **Sailing Club**

✈ Transport

Dalat *p137, map p138*
Air
See page 138. **Vietnam Airlines**, No 2 and No 40 Ho Tuong Mau St, T063-383 3499, daily 0730-1130, 1330-1630, closes 30 mins earlier at weekends.

Bus
Open Tour Buses operate daily trips to **HCMC**, 7 hrs, **Nha Trang**, 6 hrs, and **Mui Ne**, 6 hrs.

Car
It is possible to hire cars and taxis. Many tour operators have cars for hire and there are numerous taxis to choose from.

Central provinces *p142*
Air
Vietnam Airlines has offices at Buon Ma Thuot (T0500-395 4442) and Play Ku (T059-382 3058) and at 129 Ba Trieu St in Kontum, T060-386 2282.

Bus
Regular local buses link provincial centres throughout the region.

Car
Cars with drivers are available for hire; contact the provincial tourist offices or your hotel. Play Ku to **Buon Ma Thuot**, 3½ hrs, US$50.

Nha Trang *p144, map p145*
Air
See page 144. Some hotels offer free bus rides to town. The airport bus costs 80,000d from the airport and 40,000d from Nha Trang, 34 km. Taxis wait at the bus station to transport passengers to hotels. A taxi from the airport to town costs 260,000d. **Vietnam Airlines**, 91 Nguyen Thien Thuat St, T058-352 6768.

Bicycle and motorbike
Bicycles can be hired from almost every hotel and every café for around 20,000d per day for a bicycle. Motorbikes available too.

Bus
The long-distance bus station is out of town at 23 Thang 10 St and has connections with **HCMC, Phan Rang, Danang, Quy Nhon, Buon Ma Thuot, Dalat, Hué** and **Vinh**. Open Tour Buses arrive at and depart from their relevant operator's café (see Tour operators, above).

Taxi
Mai Linh, T058-391 0910.

Train
There are regular train connections with stops to and from **Hanoi** and **HCMC**. The station is at 17 Thai Nguyen St, T058-382 0666.

Mui Ne *p147, map p148*
Bus
A local bus plies the route from Phan Thiet COOP Supermarket to **Mui Ne**, as do taxis. **Sinh Tourist** and **Phuong Trang** (www. phuongtrangdalat.com) Open Tour Buses drop off and pick up from all resorts on **Mui Ne**.

❻ Directory

Dalat *p137, map p138*
Banks BIDV, 42 Hoa Binh Sq. Vietinbank, 46-48 Hoa Binh Sq, Mon-Fri 0700-1000, 1300-1600, Sat until 1100. It has a bureau de change, an ATM and also cashes TCs.

Internet Internet cafés galore along Nguyen Chi Thanh St, heading from Hoa Binh Sq to Xuan Huong Lake. **Medical services** 4 Pham Ngoc Thach St, T063-382 2154. Well-equipped hospital. Doctors speak English and French. **Post office and telephone** 14 Tran Phu St, opposite Novotel Hotel.

Nha Trang *p144, map p145*

Banks Vietcombank, 17 Quang Trung St. Will change most major currencies, cash, TCs (2% commission), and arrange cash advances on some credit cards. There's a Vietcombank exchange bureau at 8A Biet Thu St. **Internet** Internet cafés all over town, particularly in Biet Thu St and Hong Vuong St. **Medical services** General Hospital, 19 Yersin St,

T058-382 2168. **Post office** GPO, 1 Hung Vuong St.

Mui Ne *p147, map p148*

Banks No banks but a couple of ATMs; the Saigon Mui Ne Resort has one; there's one at Wind Champ Resort and there is one in front of the Ocean Star Resort that is next to the Sailing Club. **Internet** Coco Café is the best traditional internet café, located across from Full Moon Resort. Most Resorts and large restaurants or bars offer free Wi-Fi. **Medical services** Polyclinic, next to Swiss Resort, T091-821 0504 (mob), daily 1130-1330, 1730-2100. An-Phuoc Hospital, 235 Tran Phu St, Ward Phu Trinh, Phan Thiet, T062-383 1056, is the best hospital in the province.

Ho Chi Minh City and around

→ Colour map 5, A3 and A4.

Ho Chi Minh City is a manic, capitalistic hothouse, clogged with traffic, bustling with energy and enlivened by top restaurants, shops and bars. Its streets are evidence of a vibrant historical past with pagodas and temples and a bustling Chinatown. During the 1960s and early 1970s, Saigon, the Pearl of the Orient, boomed and flourished under the American occupation. In more recent times it was the seat of the South Vietnam government until the events that led to the country's reunification.

Today, Ho Chi Minh City is dedicated to commerce and hedonistic pleasures. Officially renamed in 1975, it remains to most the bi-syllabic, familiar 'Saigon'. It is the largest city in Vietnam and still growing at a prodigious rate. It is also the nation's foremost commercial and industrial centre, a place of remorseless, relentless activity and expanding urban sprawl. For the visitor, Ho Chi Minh City is a fantastic place to shop, eat and drink, while admiring its historical past and enjoying its energetic present.

The city is surrounded by fascinating historical sites to the north and by the liquid fingers of the river delta to its south. The Mekong region is a veritable Garden of Eden, stuffed full of bountiful fruit trees, decorated in pink bougainvillea and carpeted with brilliant green rice paddies. Waterways are as busy as highways, with fishing boats chugging their way along the brown river. Elsewhere in the south, historical, cultural, religious and pleasurable treasures abound: the Viet Cong tunnels at Cu Chi, the fantastical Cao Dai temple at Tay Ninh and dazzling white, remote beaches at Phu Quoc. ▶▶ *For listings, see pages 170-178.*

Ins and outs

Getting there **Tan Son Nhat airport** (SGN), is 30 minutes from the centre. By taxi the cost is about US$6-7. The official flat fare to downtown organized through a desk at the airport is US$8. Taxi drivers may try and demand a flat fee in US dollars but you should insist on using the meter, which is the law, and pay in dong. On the right of the international terminal is the domestic terminal.

Open Tour Buses generally depart and leave from offices in the Pham Ngu Lao district. There is also a daily bus service from Ho Chi Minh City to Phnom Penh (Cambodia). The railway station is northwest of the city centre. There are regular daily connections to/from Hanoi and all stops on the line north. ▶▶ *See Transport, page 177.*

Getting around Ho Chi Minh City has abundant transport. Metered taxis, motorcycle taxis and cyclos vie for business. Those who prefer some level of independence opt to hire (or even buy) a bicycle or motorbike. There are now so many motorbikes on the streets of Ho Chi Minh City that intersections seem lethally confused. Miraculously, the riders miss each other (most of the time), while pedestrians carefully make their way through waves of machines. Take an organized tour to reach sights outside the city.

Orientation Virtually all of Ho Chi Minh City lies to the west of the Saigon River. Most visitors to Ho Chi Minh City head straight for hotels in Districts 1 or 3. Many will arrive on buses in De Tham or Pham Ngu Lao streets, the backpacker area, in District 1, not far from the city centre. Many of the sights are also in District 1 (also still known as Saigon). Cholon or Chinatown (District 5) is a mile west of the centre. All the sights of Central Ho Chi Minh City can be reached on foot or cyclo in no more than 30 minutes from the major hotels on Nguyen Hué, Dong Khoi and Ton Duc Thang streets. The eastern side of the river, District 2, is for the most part marshy, poor and rather squalid, although a growing expat city has evolved.

Safety

It is not safe to carry handbags and purses on the streets of Ho Chi Minh City. Drive-by snatchings are on the increase.

Tourist information

A **Tourist Information Center** ① *92-96 Nguyen Hué St, T08-8322 6033, www.ticvietnam. com, daily 0800-2100,* provides free information, hotel reservations, an ATM and currency exchange and free internet.

Background

Before the 15th century, Ho Chi Minh City was a small village surrounded by a wilderness of forest and swamp. Through the years it was ostensibly incorporated into the Funan and then the Khmer empires but it's unlikely that these kingdoms had any lasting influence on the community. In fact, the Khmers, who called the region *Prei Nokor*, used it for hunting. By 1623 the town had become an important commercial centre and, in the mid-17th century, it became the residence of the so-called Vice-King of Cambodia. In 1698, the Viets managed to extend their control to the far south and Saigon was finally brought under Vietnamese control. By 1790, the city had a population of 50,000 and Emperor Gia Long made it his place of residence until Hué was selected as the capital of the Nguyen Dynasty.

In the middle of the 19th century, the French began to challenge Vietnamese authority in the south. Between 1859 and 1862, in response to Nguyen persecution of the Catholics in Vietnam, the French attacked and captured Saigon. The Treaty of Saigon in 1862 ratified the conquest and created the new French colony of Cochin China. Saigon was developed in French style, with wide, tree-lined boulevards, street-side cafés, elegant French architecture, boutiques and the smell of baking baguettes.

During the course of the Vietnam War, as refugees spilled in from a devastated countryside, the population of Saigon almost doubled from 2.4 million in 1965 to around 4.5 million by 1975. With reunification in 1976, the new Communist authorities pursued a policy of depopulation, believing that the city had become too large and parasitic, preying on the surrounding countryside.

The population of Ho Chi Minh City today is officially more than seven million and rising fast as the rural poor are lured by tales of streets paved with gold. Vietnam's economic reforms are most in evidence in Ho Chi Minh City, where average annual incomes, at US$2800, are more than double the national average. It is also here that the country's largest population (around 380,000) of Hoa (ethnic Chinese) is to be found. Once persecuted for their economic success, they still have the greatest economic influence and acumen. Under the current regime, best described as crony capitalism, the city is once more being rebuilt.

City centre

The centre of Ho Chi Minh City is, in many respects, the most interesting. A saunter down **Dong Khoi Street**, the old rue Catinat, can still give an impression of life in a more elegant and less frenzied era. Much remains on a small and personal scale and within a 100 yard radius of Dong Khoi or Thai Van Lung streets there are dozens of cafés, restaurants and boutiques.

However, the character of the street has altered with the opening of luxury chain names and will alter further with the completion of the Times Square mega hotel development.

Around Lam Son Square

Lam Son Square is the centre of Ho Chi Minh City. The **Rex Hotel**, a pre-Liberation favourite with US officers, stands at the intersection of Le Loi and Nguyen Hué boulevards. This was the scene of the daily 'Five O'clock Follies' where the military briefed an increasingly sceptical press corps during the Vietnam War. A short distance northeast of the Rex, is the once impressive, French-era **Opera House**, once home to the National Assembly. When it is open, it provides a varied programme of events.

At the north end of Nguyen Hué Boulevard is the yellow and white **City Hall**, now home to Ho Chi Minh City People's Committee, which overlooks a **statue of Bac Ho** (Uncle Ho) offering comfort, or perhaps advice, to a child. On weekend evenings literally thousands of young city men, women and families cruise up and down Nguyen Hué and Le Loi boulevards and Dong Khoi street on bicycles and motorbikes; this whirl of people and machines is known as *chay long rong*, 'cruising', or *song voi*, 'living fast'.

To the left of the Opera House is the **Continental Hotel**, built in 1880 and an integral part of the city's history. Graham Greene stayed here and the hotel features in the novel *The Quiet American*. The old journalists' haunt, the 'Continental Shelf', was described as "a famous veranda where correspondents, spies, speculators, traffickers, intellectuals and soldiers used to meet during the war to glean information and pick up secret reports, half false, half true or half disclosed. All of this is more than enough for it to be known as Radio Catinat".

Cong Xa Paris (Paris Square)

In the middle of Cong Xa Paris is the imposing and austere **Notre Dame Cathedral** ① *open to visitors Mon-Fri 0500-1100 and 1500-1730*, built between 1877 and 1880, allegedly on the site of an ancient pagoda. The red-brick, twin-spired cathedral overlooks a grassy square with a statue of the Virgin Mary holding an orb.

Facing onto Paris Square is the **General Post Office** ① *daily 0730-1930*, built in the 1880s, a particularly distinguished building despite the veneer of junk that has been slapped onto it. The front façade has attractive cornices with French and Khmer motifs and the names of distinguished French men of letters and science. Inside, the high, vaulted ceiling and fans create a deliciously cool atmosphere in which to scribble a postcard. Note the old wall map of Cochin-China, which has miraculously survived.

Reunification Hall

① *135 Nam Ky Khoi Nghia St, T08-3822 3652, daily 0730-1100, 1300-1600, 15,000d, brochure 10000d. There are tours every 10 mins, the guides are friendly but their English is not always very good. The hall is sometimes closed for state occasions.*

The residence of the French governor was built on this site in 1868 and later became Ngo Dinh Diem's **Presidential Palace**. In February 1962, a pair of planes took off to attack Viet Cong emplacements but turned back to bomb the Presidential Palace in a futile attempt to assassinate President Diem, who had been living there since 1954. The president escaped with his family to the cellar but the palace had to be demolished and replaced with a new building, now renamed Reunification Hall, or **Thong Nhat Conference Hall**. One of the two pilots, Nguyen Thanh Trung, is now a Vice President of Vietnam Airlines and still flies government officials around to keep his pilot's licence current.

One of the most memorable photographs taken during the war was of a North Vietnamese Army (NVA) tank crashing through the gates of the Palace on 30 April 1975, symbolizing the end of South Vietnam and its government. A similar tank is now displayed in the forecourt. The President of South Vietnam, General Duong Van Minh, along with his entire cabinet, was arrested in the palace shortly afterwards but the hall has been preserved as it was found in 1975. In the Vice President's Guest Room is a lacquered painting of the Temple of Literature in Hanoi, while the Presenting of Credentials Room contains a fine 40-piece lacquer work showing diplomats presenting their credentials during the Le Dynasty (15th century). In the basement, there are operations rooms, military maps, radios and other official paraphernalia.

1 Ho Chi Minh City

War Remnants Museum

① *28 Vo Van Tan St, District 3, T08-3930 6325, daily 0730-1200, 1330-1700, 15,000d.*

All the horrors of the Vietnam War from the Vietnamese perspective are piled up in a new museum building. The courtyard is stacked with tanks, bombs, planes and helicopters, while the new museum, arranged in five new sections, record man's inhumanity to man, with displays of deformed foetuses alongside photographs of atrocities and of military action. The exhibits cover the Son My (My Lai) massacre on 16 March 1968, the effects of napalm and phosphorous, and the after-effects of Agent Orange defoliation. Many of the pictures are horrific.

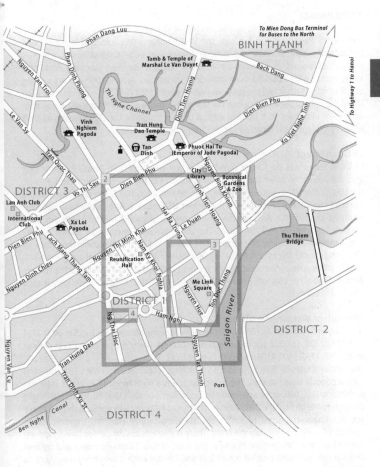

One of the most interesting rooms is dedicated to war photographers and their pictures. It is a requiem to those who died pursuing their craft and, unusually, depicts the military struggle from both sides. The war, as captured through the lens, is an Heironymous Bosch-like hell of mangled metal, suffocating mud and injured limbs. The wall-to-wall images include shots from Robert Capa's last roll of film (before the famous photographer stood on a land mine on 25 May 1954 and died); *Life* magazine's first colour coverage of the conflict, and quotes from those that perished, including a memorable one from Georgette Louise Meyer, aka Dickey Chapelle, who described the thrill of being on the "bayonet border" of the world. Understandably, there is no record of North Vietnamese atrocities carried out on US and South Vietnamese troops.

Xa Loi Pagoda

ⓘ *89 Ba Huyen Thanh Quan St, daily 0630-1100, 1430-1700.*

The Xa Loi Pagoda is not far from the War Remnants Museum and is surrounded by foodstalls. Built in 1956, the pagoda contains a multi-storeyed tower, which is particularly revered, as it houses a relic of the Buddha. The main sanctuary contains a large, bronze-gilded Buddha in an attitude of meditation. Around the walls are a series of silk paintings depicting the previous lives of the Buddha (with an explanation of each life to the right of the entrance into the sanctuary). The pagoda is historically, rather than artistically, important as it became a focus of dissent against the Diem regime in 1963 when several monks committed suicide through self-immolation.

Le Duan Street

Le Duan Street was the former corridor of power with Ngo Dinh Diem's Palace at one end, the zoo at the other and the former embassies of the three major powers, France, the US and the UK, in between. Nearest the Reunification Hall is the compound of the **French Consulate**. A block away is the **former US Embassy**. After diplomatic ties were resumed in 1995, the Americans lost little time in demolishing the 1960s embassy, which held so many bad memories. The US Consulate General now stands on this site. A **memorial** outside, on the corner of Mac Dinh Chi Street, records the attack by Viet Cong special forces during the Tet Offensive of 1968 and the final victory in 1975. On the other side of the road, a little further northeast at 25 Le Duan, is the **former British Embassy**, erected in the late 1950s, now the British Consulate General and British Council.

Museum of Vietnamese History

ⓘ *2 Nguyen Binh Khiem St, T08-3829 8146, www.baotanglichsuvn.com, Tue-Sun 0800-1130 and 1330-1700, 15,000d, photography permit 32,000d. Water puppet shows held daily at 0900, 1000, 1100, 1400, 1500 and 1600, 15 mins, US$2.*

The history museum (Bao Tang Lich Su Viet Nam) occupies an elegant 1928 building with a pagoda-based design. The collection spans a wide range of artefacts from the prehistoric (300,000 years ago) and the Dong Son periods (3500 BC to AD 100), right through to the birth of the Vietnamese Communist Party in 1930. Particularly impressive are the Cham sculptures, of which the standing bronze Buddha, showing Indian stylistic influence, is probably the finest. There is also a delicately carved Devi (goddess) dating from the 10th century, as well as the head of Siva (Hindu destroyer and creator) and Ganesh (elephant-headed son of Siva and Parvati) both dating from the eighth to the ninth century.

② Ho Chi Minh City centre

→ **Ho Chi Minh City maps**
1 Ho Chi Minh City, page 160
2 Ho Chi Minh City centre, page 163
3 Ho Chi Minh City centre detail, page 164
4 Pham Ngu Lao, page 166

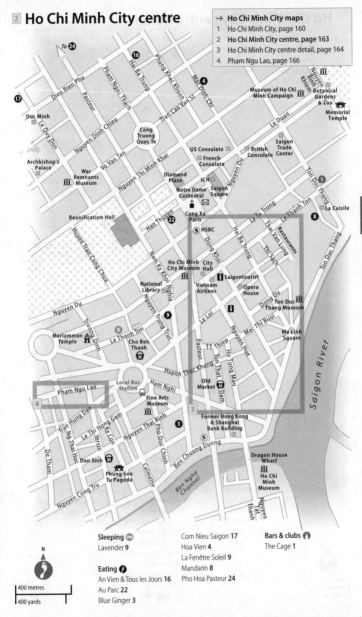

Sleeping 🛏
Lavender **9**

Eating 🍴
An Vien & Tous les Jours **16**
Au Parc **22**
Blue Ginger **3**

Com Nieu Saigon **17**
Hoa Vien **4**
La Fenêtre Soleil **9**
Mandarin **8**
Pho Hoa Pasteur **24**

Bars & clubs 🍸
The Cage **1**

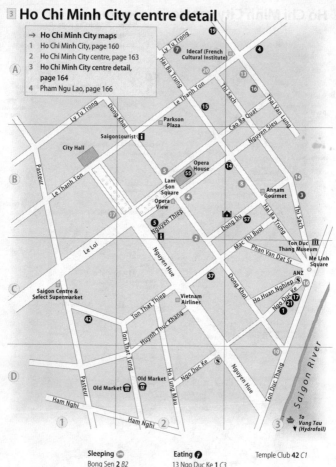

→ **Ho Chi Minh City maps**
1 Ho Chi Minh City, page 160
2 Ho Chi Minh City centre, page 163
3 **Ho Chi Minh City centre detail, page 164**
4 Pham Ngu Lao, page 166

N

100 metres
100 yards

Sleeping 🛏
Bong Sen **2** *B2*
Caravelle **4** *B2*
Continental **5** *B2*
Ho Sen **14** *B3*
Khach San 69 **8** *B3*
Majestic **10** *D3*
Orchid **13** *A3*
Renaissance
  Riverside **16** *C3*
Rex **17** *B1*
Spring **20** *A2*

Eating 🍴
13 Ngo Duc Ke **1** *C3*
Al Fresco's **57** *B3*
Ashoka **4** *A3*
Augustin **5** *B2*
Hoang Yen **17** *C3*
La Fourchette **21** *C3*
Le Jardin **19** *A2*
Pacharan **14** *B3*
Qucina & Q Bar **55** *B2*
Refinery, Hua Tuc
  & Vasco's **15** *A2*
Saigon Indian
  & Worda **37** *C2*

Temple Club **42** *C1*

Bars & clubs 🍸
Alibi **16** *A3*
Apocalypse Now **3** *B3*
Blue Gecko **7** *A2*

Ho Chi Minh Trail

The Ho Chi Minh Trail was used by the North Vietnamese Army to ferry equipment from the North to the South via Laos. The road, or more accurately roads (there were between eight and 10 routes to reduce 'choke points') were camouflaged in places, allowing the NVA to get supplies to their comrades in the South through the heaviest bombing by US planes. Even the USA's use of defoliants such as Agent Orange only marginally stemmed the flow. Neil Sheehan, in his book *A Bright Shining Lie*, estimates that at no time were more than one third of the supply trucks destroyed and, by marching through the most dangerous sections, the forces themselves suffered a loss rate of only 10-20%.

The Ho Chi Minh Trail was built and kept operational by 300,000 full-time workers and by another 200,000 part-time North Vietnamese peasants. Initially, supplies were carried along the trail on bicycles; later, as supplies of trucks from China and the Soviet Union became more plentiful, they were carried by motorized transport. By the end of the conflict the Trail comprised 15,360 km of all-weather and secondary roads. One Hero of the People's Army is said, during the course of the war, to have carried and pushed 55 tonnes of supplies a distance of 41,025 km – roughly the circumference of the world.

The Ho Chi Minh Trail represents perhaps the best example of how, through revolutionary fervour, ingenuity and weight of people (not of arms), the Viet Cong were able to vanquish the might of the US. But American pilots did exact a terrible toll through the years. Again, Sheehan writes: "Driving a truck year in, year out with 20-25% to perhaps 30% odds of mortality was not a military occupation conducive to retirement on pension."

The cemetery for those who died on the trail covers 16 ha and contains 10,306 named headstones; many more died unnamed and unrecovered.

Representative pieces from the Chen-la, Funan, Khmer, Oc-eo and Han Chinese periods are also on display, along with items from the various Vietnamese dynasties and some ethnic minority artefacts. Other highlights include the wooden stakes planted in the Bach Dang riverbed to repel the war ships of the Mongol Yuan in the 13th century; a beautiful Phoenix head from the Tran Dynasty (13th to 14th century); and a Hgor (big drum) of the Jorai people, made from the skin of two elephants.

Ben Thanh Market (Cho Ben Thanh)

A large, covered central market, Ben Thanh Market faces a statue of Tran Nguyen Han at a large and chaotic roundabout, known as the Ben Thanh gyratory system. Ben Thanh is well stocked with clothes, household goods, a good choice of souvenirs, lacquerware, embroidery and so on, as well as some terrific lines in food, including cold meats, fresh and dried fruits. It is not cheap (most local people window-shop here and purchase elsewhere) but the quality is high and the selection probably without equal. Outside the north gate (*cua Bac*) on Le Thanh Ton Street are some particularly tempting displays of fresh fruit (the oranges and apples are imported) and beautiful cut flowers. The **Ben Thanh Night Market** has flourished since 2003; starting at dusk and continuing until after midnight, it offers clothes and cheap jewellery and an abundance of foodstalls.

Phung Son Tu Pagoda and Dan Sinh market

On Nguyen Cong Tru Street is **Phung Son Tu Pagoda**, a small temple built just after the Second World War by Fukien Chinese; its most notable features are the wonderful painted entrance doors with their fearsome armed warriors. Incense spirals hang in the open well of the pagoda, which is dedicated to Ong Bon, the Guardian of Happiness and Virtue.

Close to the pagoda, on the same street, is the **War Surplus Market** (**Dan Sinh**). Merchandise on sale includes dog tags and military clothing and equipment (not all of it authentic). The market is popular with Western visitors looking for mementoes of their visit, so bargain particularly hard.

Pham Ngu Lao

Most backpackers arriving overland in Ho Chi Minh City are dropped off in this bustling district, a 10 to 15-minute walk from downtown. There are countless hotels, guesthouses and rooms to rent and the area is peppered with restaurants, cafés, bars, email services, tour agencies and money changers, all fiercely competitive.

Cholon (Chinatown)

Cholon (*Cho lon* or 'big market' or Chinatown), which encompasses District 5 to the southwest of the city centre, is inhabited predominantly by Vietnamese of Chinese origin. Since 1975, the authorities have alienated many Chinese, causing hundreds of thousands to leave the country. (Between 1977 and 1982, 709,570 refugees were recorded by the UNHCR as having fled Vietnam.) In making their escape many have died, either through drowning – as their perilously small and overladen craft foundered – or at the hands of pirates in the South China Sea. By the late 1980s, the flow of boat people was being driven by economic rather than by political forces: there was little chance of making good in a country as poor, and in an economy as moribund, as that of Vietnam.

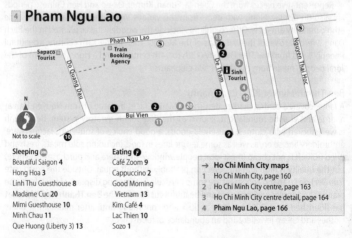

Sleeping
Beautiful Saigon **4**
Hong Hoa **3**
Linh Thu Guesthouse **8**
Madame Cuc **20**
Mimi Guesthouse **10**
Minh Chau **11**
Que Huong (Liberty 3) **13**

Eating
Café Zoom **9**
Cappuccino **2**
Good Morning Vietnam **13**
Kim Café **4**
Lac Thien **10**
Sozo **1**

→ **Ho Chi Minh City maps**
1 Ho Chi Minh City, page 160
2 Ho Chi Minh City centre, page 163
3 Ho Chi Minh City centre detail, page 164
4 Pham Ngu Lao, page 166

Even with this exodus of Chinese out of the country, there is still a large population of Chinese Vietnamese living in Cholon, an area which, to the casual visitor, appears to be the most populated, noisiest and, in general, the most vigorous part of Ho Chi Minh City, if not of Vietnam. It is here that entrepreneurial talent and private funds are concentrated; both resources that the government are keen to mobilize in their attempts to reinvigorate the economy.

Cholon is worth visiting not only for the bustle and activity, but also because the temples and assembly halls found here are the finest in Ho Chi Minh City. As with any town in Southeast Asia boasting a sizeable Chinese population, the early settlers established meeting rooms that offered social, cultural and spiritual support to members of a dialect group. These assembly halls (*hoi quan*) are most common in Hoi An and Cholon. Temples within the buildings attract Vietnamese as well as Chinese worshippers and, today, the halls serve little of their former purpose.

Assembly halls and temples

Nghia An Assembly Hall ⓘ *678 Nguyen Trai St,* has a magnificent, carved, gold-painted wooden boat hanging over the entrance. To the left, on entering the temple, is a larger than-life representation of Quan Cong's horse and groom. At the main altar are three figures in glass cases: the central red-faced figure with a green cloak is Quan Cong himself; to the left and right are his trusty companions, General Chau Xuong (very fierce) and the mandarin Quan Binh respectively. On leaving the temple, note the fine gold figures of guardians on the inside of the door panels.

Thien Hau Temple ⓘ *710 and 802 Nguyen Trai St,* is one of the largest in the city. Constructed in the early 19th century, it is Chinese in inspiration and is dedicated to the worship of both the Buddha and the Goddess Thien Hau (goddess of the sea and the protector of sailors). Thien Hau was born in China and, as a girl, saved her father from drowning but not her brother. Thien Hau's festival is marked here on the 23rd day of the third lunar month. Inside, the principal altar supports the gilded form of Thien Hau, with a boat to one side. Silk paintings depicting religious scenes decorate the walls. By far the most interesting part of the pagoda is the roof, which can be best seen from the small open courtyard. It is one of the finest and most richly ornamented in Vietnam, with a high-relief frieze depicting episodes from the Legends of the Three Kingdoms. In the post-1975 era, many would-be refugees prayed here for safe deliverance before casting themselves adrift on the South China Sea. A number of those who survived the perilous voyage sent offerings to the merciful goddess and the temple has been well maintained since. Look up on leaving to see, over the front door, a picture of a boiling sea peppered with sinking boats. A benign Thien An looks down mercifully from a cloud.

Dinh Minh Huong Gia Thanh (Ming Dynasty Assembly Hall) ⓘ *380 Tran Hung Dao St,* was built by the Cantonese community, which arrived in Ho Chi Minh City via Hoi An in the 18th century. The assembly hall was built in 1789 to the dedication and worship of the Ming Dynasty, although the building today dates largely from an extensive renovation carried out in 1960s. In the main hall there are three altars, which following imperial tradition: the central altar is dedicated to the royal family (Ming Dynasty in this case); the right-hand altar to two mandarin officers (military), and the left-hand altar to two mandarin officers (civil).

Quan Am Pagoda ⓘ *12 Lao Tu St, just off Luong Nhu Hoc St,* is thought to be one of the oldest in the city. Its roof supports four sets of impressive mosaic-encrusted figures, while inside, the main building is fronted with gold and lacquer panels of guardian spirits.

The altar supports a seated statue of A-Pho, the Holy Mother. In front of the main altar is a white ceramic statue of Quan Am, the Goddess of Purity and Motherhood (Goddess of Mercy).

Outer districts

The outlying areas of Ho Chi Minh City include a clutch of scattered pagodas in districts 3, 10, 11 and Binh Thanh. All are accessible by cyclo, moto or taxi.

Pagodas

Giac Vien Pagoda (Buddha's Complete Enlightenment) ⓘ *at the end of a narrow, rather seedy 400-m-long alley running off Lac Long Quan Street, District 11,* was built in 1771 and dedicated to the worship of the Emperor Gia Long. Although restored, Giac Vien remains one of the best preserved temples in Vietnam. It is lavishly decorated, with more than 100 carvings of various divinities and spirits, dominated by a large gilded image of the Buddha of the Past (Amitabha or *A Di Da Phat* in Vietnamese).

In District 10, the **Giac Lam Pagoda** (Forest of Enlightenment) ⓘ *118 Lac Long Quan St, T08-3865 3933, daily 0500-1200, 1400-2100, through an arch and down a short track about 300 m from the intersection with Le Dai Hanh St,* was built in 1744 and is the oldest pagoda in Ho Chi Minh City. There is a sacred Bodhi tree in the temple courtyard and the pagoda is set among fruit trees and vegetable plots. The interior of Giac Lam feels, initially, like a rather cluttered private house. In one section, there are rows of funerary tablets with pictures of the deceased. The main altar is particularly impressive, with layers of Buddhas, dominated by the gilded form of the Buddha of the Past. Note the 49-Buddha oil lamp with little scraps of paper tucked in to it. On these scraps are the names of the mourned. Behind the main temple in the section with the funerary tablets is a bust of Ho Chi Minh. At the very back of the pagoda is a hall with murals showing scenes of torture from hell. Each sin is punished in a very specific and appropriate way. An unusual feature is the use of blue and white porcelain plates to decorate the roof and some of the small towers in the garden facing the pagoda. These towers are the burial places of former head monks.

Phuoc Hai Tu (Emperor of Jade Pagoda) ⓘ *73 Mai Thi Luu St, off Dien Bien Phu St, daily 0700-1800,* can be found, nestling behind low pink walls, just before the Thi Nghe Channel. The Emperor of Jade is the supreme god of the Taoists, although this temple, built in 1900, contains a wide range of other deities. These include the archangel Michael of the Buddhists, a Sakyamuni (historic) Buddha, statues of the two generals who tamed the Green Dragon (representing the east) and the White Dragon (representing the west) to left and right of the first altar respectively and Quan Am. The Hall of Ten Hells in the left-hand sanctuary has reliefs depicting the 1000 tortures of hell.

Around Ho Chi Minh City

The Cu Chi Tunnels are the most popular day trip, followed closely by an excursion to the Mekong Delta, especially My Tho. ▶▶ *See Activities and tours, page 176.*

Cu Chi Tunnels → *Colour map 5, A3.*
ⓘ *About 40 km northwest of Ho Chi Minh City, daily 0700-16.30, 75,000d. Most visitors reach Cu Chi on a tour or charter a car and include a visit to Tay Ninh.*

Begun by the Viet Minh in 1948, these tunnels were later expanded by the Viet Cong and used for storage and refuge. Between 1960 and 1970, 200 km of tunnels were built, containing sleeping quarters, hospitals and schools. The original tunnels were only 80 cm high and the width of the tunnel entry at ground level was 22 cm by 30 cm. The tunnels are too narrow for most Westerners, but a short section of the 250 km of tunnels has been especially widened to allow tourists to share the experience.

Cu Chi was one of the most fervently Communist districts around Ho Chi Minh City and the tunnels were used as the base from which the VC mounted the operations of the Tet Offensive in 1968. When the Americans first discovered this underground network on their doorstep (Dong Du GI base was nearby) they would simply pump CS gas down the tunnel openings and then set explosives. They also pumped river water in and used German Shepherd dogs to smell out air holes, although the VC smothered the holes in garlic to deter the dogs. Around 40,000 VC were killed in the tunnels in 10 years but, later, realizing the tunnels might also yield valuable intelligence, the Americans sent volunteer 'tunnel rats' into the earth to capture prisoners.

Cu Chi district initially was a free-fire zone and was assaulted using the full battery of ecological warfare. Defoliants were sprayed and 20-tonne Rome Ploughs carved up the area in the search for tunnels. It was said that even a crow flying over Cu Chi district had to carry its own lunch. Later it was carpet bombed: 50,000 tonnes were dropped on the area in 10 years evidenced by the B-52 bomb craters.

At **Cu Chi 1** (Ben Dinh) ① *75,000d*, visitors are shown a somewhat antique but interesting film of the tunnels during the war before being taken into the tunnels themselves and seeing some of the rooms and the booby traps the GIs encountered. You will also be invited to a firing range to try your hand with ancient AK47s at a buck a bang. **Cu Chi 2** (Ben Duoc), has a temple, built in 1993, devoted to the memory of the dead and visited by those whose relatives are still 'missing'. The sculpture behind the temple is of a massive tear cradled in the hands of a mother.

Cao Dai Great Temple → Colour map 5, A2.

① *Tay Ninh, 64 km beyond Cu Chi town (96 km northwest of Ho Chi Minh City). It can be visited on a day trip from the city and can easily be combined with a visit to the Cu Chi tunnels. Ceremonies 1 hr long, daily 0600, 1200, 1800 and 2400; visitors should not wander in and out during services but can watch from the balcony. At other times keep to the side aisles and do not enter the central portion of the nave. Photography is allowed. Shoes must be removed.*

The Cao Dai religion was founded on Phu Quoc Island (page 184) in 1920, when civil servant Ngo Van Chieu communed with the spirit world and made contact with the Supreme Being. The idiosyncratic, twin-towered Cao Dai Great Temple, the 'cathedral' of the religion, was built from 1933 to 1955 and is European in inspiration but with distinct Oriental features. On the façade are figures of Cao Dai saints in high relief and, at the entrance to the cathedral, there is a painting depicting writer Victor Hugo flanked by the Vietnamese poet Nguyen Binh Khiem and the Chinese nationalist Sun Yat Sen.

The temple provokes strong reactions: Novelist Graham Greene in *The Quiet American* called it "The Walt Disney Fantasia of the East". Monsieur Ferry, an acquaintance of travel writer Norman Lewis, described the cathedral in even more outlandish terms, saying it "looked like a fantasy from the brain of Disney, and all the faiths of the Orient had been ransacked to create the pompous ritual ...". Lewis himself was clearly unimpressed with the structure and the religion, writing in *A Dragon Apparent* that this "cathedral must be the most outrageously vulgar building ever to have been erected with serious intent".

After removing shoes and hats, women enter the cathedral through a door to the left, men to the right, and they then proceed down their respective aisles towards the altar, usually accompanied by a Cao Dai priest dressed in white with a black turban. During services they don red, blue and yellow robes signifying Confucianism, Taoism and Buddhism respectively. Two rows of pink pillars entwined with green, horned dragons line the nave, leading up to the main altar which supports a large globe on which is painted a single staring eye: the divine, all-seeing eye. Above the altar is the Cao Dai pantheon: at the top in the centre is Sakyamuni Buddha; next to him, on the left, is Lao Tzu, master of Taoism; left of Lao Tzu is Quan Am, Goddess of Mercy, sitting on a lotus blossom; on the other side of the Buddha statue is Confucius; right of the sage is the red-faced Chinese God of War, Quan Cong; below Sakyamuni Buddha is the poet and leader of the Chinese saints, Li Ti Pei; below him is Jesus, and, below Christ, is Jiang Zhia, master of Geniism.

◉ Ho Chi Minh City and around listings

For Sleeping and Eating price codes and other relevant information, see pages 40-43.

● Sleeping

City centre *p158, maps p160, p163 and p164*

LL-L Majestic, 1 Dong Khoi St, T08-3829 5517, www.majesticsaigon.com. Built in 1925, this riverside hotel has character and charm and has been tastefully restored and recently expanded. More expensive and large rooms have superb views over the river; from the new bar on the top floor there are magnificent views of the riverfront, especially at night.

LL-L Renaissance Riverside, 8-15 Ton Duc Thang St, T08-3822 0033, www.marriott.com. Despite its 21 floors and 319 rooms and suites this is, in style and feel, almost a boutique hotel. Very well run, comfortable and popular with its customers. It also boasts Vietnam's highest atrium. It has several excellent restaurants, including **Kabin** Chinese restaurant, and an attractive pool.

LL-AL Caravelle, 19-23 Lam Son Sq, T08-3823 4999, www.caravellehotel.com. Central and one of HCMC's top hotels and recently renovated. Comfortable with well-trained and friendly staff. **Restaurant Nineteen** serves a fantastic buffet lunch and dinner with free flow of fine French wine included (see Eating), and **Saigon**, the rooftop bar, draws the crowds until the early hours of the morning (see Bars and clubs). Also has a suite of boutique shops and ATM.

L-AL Rex, 141 Nguyen Hué Blvd, T08-3829 2185, www.rexhotelvietnam.com. A historically important hotel in the heart of Saigon with unusual interior decor and a new fabulous side extension that has become the principal entrance. The original lobby is decorated entirely in wood, furnished with numerous wicker chairs, and dominated by the ceiling, a vast replica of a Dongson Drum, while the new wing is a vast cathedral of glass and marble. New wing premium rooms are very smart; cheaper 'Superior' rooms in the old wing have small bathtub and are interior facing.

L-A Lavender Hotel, 208-210 Le Thanh Ton St, T8-2222 8888, www.lavenderhotel.com.vn. In an excellent location. The standard rooms are small but nicely furnished so you may want to opt for a superior. Helpful staff. In-room internet access and breakfast included.

AL-A Bong Sen, 117-123 Dong Khoi St, T08-3829 1516, www.hotelbongsen.com. Well-run and in a perfect location in the heart of the shopping district. Good value for the location but standard rooms are very small. Larger superior rooms are only slightly more expensive and have baths. Few rooms have views. There is a restaurant and the **Green Leaf** café.

AL-A Continental, 132-134, Dong Khoi St, T08-3829 9201, www.continentalhotel. com.vn. Built in 1880 and renovated in 1989, the **Continental** has an air of faded colonial splendour and its large but still-dated rooms need upgrading. The exterior has had a lick of paint. (A US$10 million renovation has been approved.) The hotel has a couple of restaurants, a business centre, fitness room and a pool. Probably in an attempt to stamp out the theft of souvenirs, you can purchase every item in the room. Don't opt for the balconied rooms overlooking Lam Son Square if you value your sleep.

A-C Ho Sen, 4B-4C Thi Sach St, T08-3823 2281, www.hosenhotel.com.vn. This bland-looking hotel in a very central location is a good find. Surprisingly, rooms are very quiet, fairly spacious and comfortable with TV. Staff are friendly and helpful and will store luggage.

A-C Spring, 44-46 Le Thanh Ton St, T08-3829 7362, www.springhotelvietnam.com. Central, comfortable with charming and helpful staff. Book well in advance if you want to stay in this well-run family hotel that is excellent value; breakfast included. Recommended.

B-D Orchid, 29A Thai Van Lung St, T08-3823 1809, www.orchid-hotel.com. In a good, central spot, surrounded by restaurants and bars, worth taking a look at. Rooms have a/c and satellite TV.

D Khach San 69, 69 Hai Ba Trung St, T08-3829 1513, hotel69haibatrung@yahoo.com. vn. Central location with clean a/c rooms that back onto HCMC's Indian mosque. It's an ancient hotel but spotless and staff are super polite. Possibly the cheapest accommodation in the heart of downtown. Free Wi-Fi.

Pham Ngu Lao *p166, map p166*
Shared rooms can be had for as little as US$5 per night and dormitory rooms for less but facilities and comfort levels at the bottom end are very basic.

AL-A Que Huong (Liberty 4), 265 Pham Ngu Lao St, T08-3836 4556, www.libertyhotels. com.vn. A perfectly comfortable hotel. It has had to moderate its prices which means it is now possibly fair value but priced way too high for this area. Breakfast is included.

B-D Beautiful Saigon, 62 Bui Vien St, T08-3836 4852, www.beautifulsaigonhotel. com. A new addition to the backpacker zone replacing an old hotel, this is more for the flashpackers and welcome it is too. Very nice smart and tidy rooms all with mod cons, Wi-Fi and breakfast at fair prices and recommended by happy guests.

D-E Hong Hoa, 185/28 Pham Ngu Lao St, T08-3836 1915, www.honghoavn.com. A well-run family hotel with 9 rooms, all a/c, hot water and private bathroom. Downstairs has free email terminals and a supermarket.

E Mimi Guesthouse, 40/5 Bui Vien St, T08-3836 9645, mimihotel405@yahoo.fr. 10 rooms with private bathroom, a/c, TV and Wi-Fi in rooms and hot water. Motorbikes, bicycles and the internet.

E Minh Chau, 75 Bui Vien St, T08-3836 7588, minhchauhotel@hcm.vnn.vn. Some a/c, hot water and private bathrooms. Spotlessly clean and run by 2 sisters. It has been recommended by lone women travellers. Free internet but breakfast not included.

E-F Hotel Madam Cuc, 64 Bui Vien St, T08-3836 5073; 127 Cong Quynh St, T08-836 8761; and 184 Cong Quynh St, T08-3836 1679, www.madamcuchotels.com. The reception staff at No 64 could be a lot friendlier. Rooms are quite small but the US$20 room is the bargain of the place.

E-F Linh Thu Guesthouse, 72 Bui Vien St, T08-3836 8421, linhthu_72bv@yahoo.com. vn. Fan rooms with bathroom and some more expensive a/c rooms too.

❶ Eating

HCMC has a rich culinary tradition and, as home to people from most of the world's imagined corners, its cooking is diverse. Do not overlook street-side stalls, staples consist of *pho* (noodle soup), *bánh xeo* (savoury pancakes), *cha giò* (spring rolls) and *banh mi pate* (baguettes stuffed with pâté and salad) all usually fresh and very cheap.

City centre *p158, maps p160, p163 and p164*

¶¶¶ An Vien, 178A Hai Ba Trung St, T08-3824 3877. Daily 1200-2300. Excellent and intimate restaurant that serves the most fragrant rice in Vietnam. Attentive service and rich decor. The *banh xeo* and crispy fried squid are recommended.

¶¶¶ Hoa Tuc, 74 Hai Ba Trung St, T08-3825 1676. Open 1000-2230. A new addition to this popular courtyard dining space. Dine amid the art deco accents on soft shell crab or a salad of pink pomelo, squid and crab with herbs. The desserts are tantalising. Try the Earl Grey tea custard. Portions a tad on the small side. Cooking classes available.

¶¶¶ La Fourchette, 9 Ngo Duc Ke St, T08-3829 8143. Daily 1200-1430, 1830-2230. Truly excellent and authentic French bistro offering a warm welcome, well-prepared dishes and generous portions of tender local steak. Booking advised. Recommended.

¶¶¶ Mandarin, 11A Ngo Van Nam St, T08-3822 9783. Daily 1130-1400, 1730-2300. One of the finest restaurants in HCMC serving up a culinary mix of exquisite flavours from across the country amid elegant decor including stunning, richly coloured silk tablecloths. The food is delicious but it's not very Vietnamese and the service is a little over the top.

¶¶¶ Qucina, 7 Lam Son Sq, T08-3824 6325. Mon-Sat 1800-2300. Smart and stylish Italian restaurant in the basement of the Opera House. The sophisticated menu includes grilled tuna in black butter and rolled chocolate cake with vanilla cream – enough to satisfy any gourmet.

¶¶¶-¶¶ Pacharan, 97 Hai Ba Trung St, T08-3825 6024. Daily 1100-late. A hit from the beginning, this Spanish restaurant is nearly full every night with happy and satisfied customers. The open-air rooftop bar that overlooks the Park Hyatt Hotel is a winner when there's a cool breeze blowing through the terrace. Fans of Spanish fare will love the (expensive) Iberian cured ham from rare, semi-wild, acorn-fed black-footed pigs as well as staples such as anchovies, olives, mushrooms and prawns; all the tapas are beautifully presented.

¶¶¶-¶¶ Restaurant Nineteen, Caravelle Hotel, Lam Son Sq, T08-3823 4999, daily 1130-1430, 1745-2200. Japanese sushi, Chinese dim sum, seafood, cheeses and puddings galore. The food is stacked up so luxuriously and abundantly, it is like a gastro-cinematic experience. Weekends are especially extravagant with tender roast beef. The free wine makes it tremendous value for money.

¶¶¶-¶¶ Temple Club, 29 Ton That Thiep St, T08-3829 9244. Daily 1100-1400, 1830-2230. Beautifully furnished club and restaurant open to non-members. French-colonial style and tasty Vietnamese dishes. Excellent value. The restaurant is popular so it's wise to book.

¶¶ Augustin, 10 Nguyen Thiep St, T090-866 8081. Mon-Sat 1100-1400 and 1800-2230. Fairly priced and some of the best, unstuffy French cooking in HCMC; tables pretty closely packed, congenial atmosphere. Excellent onion soup, baked clams and rack of lamb.

¶¶ Blue Ginger (Saigon Times Club), 37 Nam Ky Khoi Nghia St, T08-3829 8676. Daily 0700-1430, 1700-2200. A gorgeous restaurant that offers a feast of Vietnamese food for diners with more than 100 dishes on the menu. Dine indoors in the cellar-like restaurant or outdoors in a small courtyard. Charming staff offer courteous and discrete service.

¶¶ Hoa Vien, 28 bis Mac Dinh Chi St, T08-3829 0585. Daily 0900-2400. A vast Czech bierkeller boasting Ho Chi Minh City's first micro-brewery. Freshly brewed dark and light beer available by the litre or in smaller measures. Grilled mackerel, pork and sausages are very useful for soaking up the alcohol.

¶¶ Le Jardin, 31 Thai Van Lung St, T08-3825 8465. Mon-Sat 1100-1400 and 1800-2100. Excellent French café, part of the **French Cultural Institute**. Eat inside or in the shady garden, good food, fairly priced.

¶¶ The Refinery, 74 Hai Ba Trung St, T08-3823 0509. Open 1100-2300. This former opium factory (through the arch and on the left) is a little understated in its reincarnation. The herb-encrusted steak and grilled barramundi are delicious but the seared tuna with lentil salad is outstanding. Braised rabbit and duck and apple tagine with raisin and butter couscous are other menu offerings.

¶¶ Saigon Indian, 1st floor, 73 Mac Thi Buoi St, T08-3824 5671. Daily 1115-1430, 1730-2230. Proving to be a very popular Indian restaurant with a wide range of dishes from the north and south, including tandoori dishes and plenty of veggie options. Delicious garlic naan bread.

¶¶-¶ Al Fresco's, 27 Dong Du St, T08-3822 7317. Daily 0830-1400, 1830-2300. A huge success from its first day. Australian run. Specializes in ribs, steak, pizzas, hamburgers and Mexican dishes which are all excellent and highly recommended. Book or be prepared to wait. Delivery available.

¶¶-¶ Ashoka, 17A/10 Le Thanh Ton St, T08-3823 1372. Daily 1100-1400, 1700-2230. Delicious food from an extensive menu. The set lunch lists 11 options with a further 19 curry dishes. Highlights are the mutton *shami* kebab, prawn vindaloo and *kadhai* fish – barbecued chunks of fresh fish cooked in *kadhai* (a traditional Indian-style wok with Peshwari ground spices and sautéed with onion and tomatoes). Those with a sweet tooth should try the bizarre Coke with ice cream for pudding.

¶¶-¶ Warda, 71/7 Mac Thi Buoi St, T08-3823 3822, www.wardavn.com. Mon-Sat 0900-2400, Sun 1500-2400. A Bedouin tent huddles over plump pumpkin-coloured cushions on sofas amid a few shisha pipes at the end of this buzzy alley. The menu options are tantalising and this is a wonderful way to break from Vietnamese menus. It's a meat lover's paradise but vegetarians are not ignored. The hot chocolate and fig pudding with cardamom is a must try.

¶ 13 Ngo Duc Ke, 15 Ngo Duc Ke St, T08-3823 9314. Daily 0600-2300. Fresh, well cooked, honest Vietnamese fare. Chicken in lemongrass (no skin, no bone) is a great favourite and *bo luc lac* melts in the mouth. Popular with locals, expats and travellers.

¶ Au Parc, 23 Han Thuyen St, T08-3829 2772. Mon-Sat 0730-2230, Sun 0800-1700. Facing on to the park in front of the old Presidential Palace, this attractive café serves snacks and light meals including sandwiches, salads, juices and drinks. Also does a good Sun brunch 1100-1530; a lovely spot for a leisurely breakfast.

¶ Com Nieu Saigon, 19 Tu Xuong St, Q3, T08-3932 2799. Best known for the theatrics that accompany the serving of the speciality baked rice: one waiter smashes the earthenware pot before tossing the contents across the room to his nimble-fingered colleague standing by your table. Deserves attention for its excellent food and selection of soups.

¶ Hoang Yen, 5-7 Ngo Duc Ke St, T08-3823 1101. Daily 1000-2200. Plain setting and decor but absolutely fabulous Vietnamese dishes, as the throngs of local lunchtime customers testify. Soups and chicken dishes are ravishing.

¶ Pho Hoa Pasteur, 260C Pasteur St. Daily 0600-2400. Probably the best known *pho* restaurant and packed with customers. The *pho*, which is good, and costs more than average, comes in 10 options. Chinese bread and wedding cake (*banh xu xe*) provide the only alternative in this specialist restaurant.

Cafés

La Fenêtre Soleil, 2nd floor, 135 Le Thanh Ton St (entrance at 125 Nam Ky Khoi Nghia), T08-3822 5209. Mon-Sat café 0900-1900, bar 1900-2400. Don't be put off by the slightly grimy side entrance; climb up into the boho-Indochine world of this gorgeous café/bar, artfully cluttered with antiques, lamps, comfy sofas and home-made cakes, muffins, smoothies and other delights. The high-energy drinks of mint, passion fruit, and ginger juice are lovely. Highly recommended.

Foodstalls
Just north of the centre on the south side of Tan Dinh market **Anh Thu**, 49 Dinh Cong Trang St (and numerous other stalls nearby) serve excellent *cha gio, banh xeo, bi cuon* and other Vietnamese street food. Also head north of the market to the foodstalls on Hia Ba Trung St. Everyone has their favourite but Nos 362-376 and No 381 (**Hong Phat**) are particularly good. All charge just over US$2 for steamed chicken and rice (*com gà hap*) with soup.

Pham Ngu Lao *p166, map p166*
Pham Ngu Lao, the backpacker area, is chock-a-block with low-cost restaurants many of which are just as good as the more expensive places elsewhere. All restaurants here are geared to the habits and tastes of Westerners.
❢ **Good Morning Vietnam**, 197 De Tham St, T08-3837 1894. Daily 0900-2400. Italian owned and serving authentic Italian flavours. Good but not cheap. The pizzas are delicious and salads are good.
❢ **Café Zoom**, 169A De Tham St, T01222-993585, www.vietnamvespaadventure.com. Laid-back vibe and venue serving top burgers and fries.
❢ **Cappuccino**, 258 De Tham St, T08-3837 4114, and 86 Bui Vien St, T08-3920 3134. A good range of well-prepared Italian food at sensible prices. Very good lasagne and zabaglione.
❢ **Kim Café**, 268 De Tham St, T08-3836 8122. Open all day. Wide range of food, popular with travellers and expats. The breakfast must rate among the best value in the country.
❢ **Lac Thien**, 207 Bui Vien St, T090-445 6103. Daily 0800-2300. Vietnamese food. Outpost of the well-known Lac Thien in Hué and

run by the same family. *Banh xeo* (savoury pancake) is a major feature on the menu.
❢ **Sozo**, 176 Bui Vien, T08-6271 9176, www.sozocentre.com. As well as coffees of every shade, this place serves up bagels, and excellent cookies with proceeds going to charity.

◑ Bars and clubs

Some of these bars sometimes succeed in staying open until 0200 or 0300 but at other times the police shut them down at 2400. Those in the Pham Ngu Lao area tend to be busy later at night and tend to stay open longer than those in the centre.

Ho Chi Minh City *p158, maps p160, p163 and p164*
In Pham Ngu Lao, the **Go2** and **Buffalo** cluster are the junction of De Tham and Bui Vien streets is always busy and for much later night jinks, move to the **T&R Tavern** on Do Quang Dau St.
Alibi, 11 Thai Van Lung St, T08-3822 3240. Goes on after hours and is a magnet for tourists and expats. There's a small terrace to escape the inner heat.
Apocalypse Now, 2BCD Thi Sach St, T08-3825 6124. Free admission for Westerners. Open 2100-0300. This legendary venue remains one of the most popular and successful bars and clubs in HCMC. Draws a very wide cross section of punters of all ages and nationalities. Quite a large outside area at the back where conversation is possible.
Blue Gecko, 31 Ly Tu Trong St, T08-3824 3483. This bar has been adopted by HCMC's Australian community so expect cold beer and Australian flags above the pool table.
The Cage, 3A Ton Duc Thang St. Fashionable new clubby hangout for the young and beautiful. Guest DJs spin the tunes for the city's clubbing denizens. Drinks are expensive.
Q Bar, 7 Lam Son Sq, T08-3823 3479. Daily 1800-late. Haunt of a wide cross-section of HCMC society: the sophisticated, intelligent, witty, rich, handsome, cute, curvaceous,

camp, glittering and famous are all to be found here. Striking decor and design, with Caravaggio-esque murals.

Rex Hotel Bar, see Sleeping, above. An open-air rooftop bar which has a kitsch revolving crown. There are good views, cooling breeze, snacks and meals – and a link with history (page 159).

Saigon Saigon, 10th floor, **Caravelle Hotel**, 19 Lam Son Sq, T08-3824 3999. Breezy and cool, with large comfortable chairs and superb views by day and night. Excellent cocktails but not cheap.

Vasco's, 74/7D Hai Ba Trung St, T08-3824 2888. Open 1600-2400. A hugely popular expat spot now in its new courtyard setting.

Evening cafés

Vietnamese tend to prefer non-alcoholic drinks. Young romantic couples sit in virtual darkness listening to Vietnamese love songs, all too often played at a deafening volume, while sipping coffee. These cafés are an agreeable way of relaxing after dinner in a more typically Vietnamese setting.

⊕ Entertainment

Ho Chi Minh City *p158, maps p160, p163 and p164*
Cinema
Diamond Plaza, 34 Le Duan St. The cinema on the 13th floor of this shopping centre screens English-language films.
French Cultural Institute (Idecaf), 31 Thai Van Lung, T08-3829 5451, www.idecaf.gov. vn. Shows French films.

○ Shopping

Ho Chi Minh City *p158, maps p160, p163 and p164*
Antiques
Most antique shops are on Dong Khoi, Mac Thi Buoi and Ngo Duc Ke streets but for less touristy stuff visitors are advised to browse the shops along Le Cong Trieu St. It runs between Nam Ky Khoi Nghia and Pho

Duc Chinh streets just south of Ben Thanh market. Among the bric-a-brac are some interesting items of furniture, statuary and ceramics. Bargaining is essential.
Lac Long, 143 Le Thanh Ton St, T08-3829 3373. Daily 0800-1900. Mr Long sometimes has some unusual items for sale even if there is nothing of interest on display.

Art, crafts and home accessories
Ancient/Apricot, 50-52 Mac Thi Buoi St, T08- 3822 7962, www.apricotgallery.com.vn. Specializes in famous artists; high prices.
Dogma, 175 De Tham St, www.dogma. vietnam.com. Sells propaganda posters, funky T-shirts and postcards and other Communist kitsch.
Gaya, 1 Nguyen Van Trang St, corner of Le Lai St, T08-3925 2495, www.gayavietnam. com. A 3-storey shop with heavy items: embroidered tablecloths, ceramics and screens. The 2nd floor has silk designer clothes by Romyda Keth.
Lotus Gallery, 47 Dong Khoi St, T08-3829 2695, www.lotusgallery.com. Another expensive gallery at the top end of the market. Many are members of the Vietnam Fine Arts Association and many have exhibited around the world.
Mosaique, 98 Mac Thi Buoi, T08-3823 4634. Daily 0900-2100. Like its sister store in Hanoi, this boutique is a home-accessories parlour.
Nga Shop, 49-57 Dong Du St, T08-3823 8356, www.huongngafinearts.vn. **Nga** has become one of the best-known lacquer stores as a result of her high-quality designs. Other top-quality rosewood and ceramic handicrafts suitable for souvenirs are available.
Nguyen Freres, 2 Dong Khoi St, T08-3823 9459, www.nguyenfreres.com. An absolute Aladdin's cave. Don't miss this – even if it's just to potter among the collectable items.

Clothing and silk
Many female visitors head straight for Dong Khoi St for Vietnamese silk and traditional dresses (*ao dai*). Also check out Ben Thanh market in Binh Thanh District.

Khai Silk, 107 Dong Khoi, T08-3829 1146. Part of Mr Khai's growing empire. Beautifully made, quality silks in a range of products.

Mai's, 132-134 Dong Khoi St, T08-3827 2733, www.mailam.com.vn. One of the most exciting designers working in Vietnam.

Song, 76D Le Thanh Ton, T08-3824 6986. Daily 0900-2000, www.valeriegregorimc kenzie.com. Beautiful clothes emporium. Lovely, flowing summer dresses from designer Valerie Gregori McKenzie plus other stylish and unique pieces and accessories.

Department stores

Diamond Department Store, Diamond Plaza 1st-4th floor, 34 Le Duan St, T08-3822 5500. Open 1000-1000. HCMC's central a/c department store set over a couple of floors.

⏾ Activities and tours

Ho Chi Minh City *p158, maps p160, p163 and p164*

Tour operators

Asia Pacific Travel, 127 Ban Co St, District 3, T08-3833 4083, www.asia-pacifictravel.com. Arranges tours throughout Vietnam.

Asian Trails, 5th floor, 21 Nguyen Trung Ngan St, District 1, T08-3910 2871, www. asiantrails.travel. Southeast Asia specialists.

Buffalo Tours, Satra House, Suite 601, 58 Dong Khoi St, T8-3827 9170, www. buffalotours.com. Organizes trips to the Mekong Delta, city tours, the Cu Chi tunnels and Cao Dai Temple and arranges a home concert in HCMC with a family who have mastered and perform traditional Vietnamese instruments; this latter trip is a delightful way to spend an evening. Staff are helpful. Good countrywide operator with longstanding reputation.

Cuu Long Tourist, 190 Cong Quynh St, T08-3920 0339, www.cuulongtourist.com. Branch of Vinh Long provincial tourist authority. Tours to the Mekong Delta.

Delta Adventure Tours, 267 De Tham St, T08-3920 2112, www.deltaadventuretours. com. Slow and express bus and boat tours through the Mekong Delta to Phnom Penh, Cambodia at very good prices.

Exotissimo, 64 Dong Du St, T08-3827 2911, www.exotissimo.com. An efficient agency that can handle all travel needs of visitors to Vietnam. Its local excursions are very well guided.

Handspan Adventure Travel, F7, Titan Building, 18A Nam Quoc Cang, T08-3925 7605, www.handspan.com. Reputable and well-organized. Specializes in adventure tours.

Kim Café, 270 De Tham St, District 1, T08-3920 5552, www.kimtravel.com. Organizes minibuses to Nha Trang, Dalat, etc, and tours of the Mekong. A good source of information.

SinhBalo, 283/20 Pham Ngu Lao, T08-3837 6765, www.sinhbalo.com. Mr Sinh, formerly of **Sinh Café**, is a recommended tour operator organizing a number of tours including cycling, adventure and cross-country tours.

Sinh Tourist (formerly Sinh Café), 246-248 De Tham St, T08-3838 9597, www. thesinhtourist.vn. **Sinh Tourist** now has branches and agents in all main towns in Vietnam. Its tours are generally good value and its open ticket is excellent value. For many people, especially budget travellers, Sinh is the first port of call. It is tempting to tour the entire country with them as it makes travelling easy. Like many other tour operators, trips to the Mekong Delta (from180,000d) and onwards to Cambodia are organized (from 580,000d). It also offers round trip bus and plane journeys to Phnom Penh and Siem Reap. The company also deals with visa extensions, flight, train and hotel bookings and car rentals. Children under 2 are free; 2-5 year-olds are charged 75% of the full price. Beware that there are numerous copycat **Sinh Cafés**; make sure you know which ones are the real deal as many of the fake Sinhs are to be avoided. This one is the HQ.

TM Brother's Café, 230 De Tham St, T08-3837 7764, tmbrothertours@yahoo.com. Reliable Open Tour Bus operator. Runs trips to the Mekong Delta and into Cambodia.

⊖ Transport

Ho Chi Minh City *p158, maps p160, p163 and p164*

Air
See page 157.

Airline offices AirAsia, 254 De Tham St, T08-3838 9810, www.airasia.com. Air France, 130 Dong Khoi St, T08-3829 0981, www.airfrance.com. Bangkok Airways, Unit 103, Saigon Trade Center, 37 Ton Duc Thang St, T08-3910 4490, www.bangkokair. com. Cathay Pacific, 72-74 Nguyen Thi Minh Khai St, T08-3822 3203, www.cathaypacific. com. Emirates Airlines, 170-172 Nam Ky Khoi Nghia, District 3, T08-3930 2939, www. emirates.com. Eva Air, 2A-4A, Ton Duc Thang St, T8-38445211, www.evaair.com. Gulf Air, 18 Dang Thi Nhu St, Q1, T08-3915 7614, www.gulfair.com. Jetstar, 112 Hong Ha, Q Tan Binh, T08-3845 0092, www.jetstar. com. Lao Airlines, www.laoairlines.com. Lufthansa, 19-25 Nguyen Hué Blvd, T08-3829 8529, www.luft hansa.com. Malaysia, Saigon Trade Center, 37 Ton Duc Thang St, T08-3829 2529, www.malaysiaairlines.com. Qantas, HT&T Vietnam, Level 2, Ben Thanh TSC Building,186-188 Le Thanh Ton St, T08-3910 5373, www.quantas.com.au. Qatar, Suite 8, Petro Vietnam Tower, 1-5 Le Duan St, T08-3827 3777, www.qatarairways.com. Thai Airways, 29 Le Duan St, T8-38223365, www. thaiairways.com.vn. Vietnam Airlines, 6th floor, Sun Wah Tower, 115 Nguyen Hué St, T08-3832 0320, www.vietnamairlines.com.

Bicycle and motorbike
Bikes and motorbikes can be hired from some of the cheaper hotels and cafés, especially in Pham Ngu Lao St. They should always be parked in the roped-off compounds (*gui xe*), found all over town; they will be looked after for a small fee (12,000d; always get a ticket).

Bus
All city buses start from or stop by the Ben Thanh bus station opposite Ben Thanh Market, District 1, T08-3821 4444. A free map of all bus routes can also be obtained here. The buses are green or yellow and run at intervals of 10-20 mins depending on the time of day; during rush hours they are jammed with passengers and can run late. There are bus stops every 500 m. Tickets cost 3000d per person.

Open Tour Buses leave from company offices in the centre, including **Sinh Café** in Pham Ngu Lao.

Cyclo
Cyclos are a peaceful way to get around the city. They can be hired for approximately 250,000d per hr or to reach a specific destination. Some drivers speak English. Some visitors complain that cyclo drivers in HCMC have an annoying habit of 'forgetting' the agreed price, however, the drivers will argue that cyclos are being banned from more and more streets in the centre of HCMC, which means that journeys are often longer and more expensive than expected.

Motorcycle taxi
Honda om or *xe ôm* are the quickest way to get around town and are cheaper than cyclos; just agree a price and hop on the back. *Xe ôm* drivers can be recognized by their baseball caps and their tendency to chain smoke; they hang around on most street corners. Short journeys should be around 10-15,000d but you may end up paying more.

Taxi
All taxis are metered. Mai Linh Taxi (green and white, but note that the de luxe version is more expensive), T08-3822 2666.Vinasun (white), T08-3827 2727. Vinataxi (yellow), T08-3811 1111.

Train

Thong Nhat Railway Station, 1 Nguyen Thong St, Ward 9, District 3, T08-3931 2795, is 2 km from the centre of the city. There is now also a **Train Booking Agency**, 275c Pham Ngu Lao St, T08-3836 7640, daily 0730-1830, which saves a journey out to the station. Daily connections with **Hanoi** and all points north. Express trains take between 29½ and 42½ hrs to reach Hanoi; hard and soft berths are available. Sleepers should be booked in advance.

❶ Directory

Ho Chi Minh City *p158, maps p160, p163 and p164*

Banks There are now dozens of ATMs. Remember to take your passport if cashing TCs and withdrawing money from a bank. **ANZ Bank**, 2 Ngo Duc Ke St, T08-3829 9319, www.anz.com/vietnam, a 2% commission is charged on cashing TCs into US$ or VND, ATM. **HSBC, Hong Kong and Shanghai Bank**, 235 Dong Khoi St, T08-829 2288, provides all financial services, 2% commission on TCs, ATM. **Sacombank**, 11-213 Pham Ngu Lao St, Q1, T08-3837 1526. **Embassies and consulates** Australia, Landmark Building, 5B Ton Duc Thang St, T08-3521 8100, www.hcmc.vietnam.embassy.gov. au. **Cambodia**, 41 Phung Khac Khoan St, T08-3829 2751. **Canada**, 235 Dong Khoi St, T08-3827 9899, www.canadainternational. gc.ca. **France**, 27 Nguyen Thi Minh Khai St, T08-3520 6800, www.consulfrance-hcm.

org. **Laos**, 9B Pasteur St, T08-3829 7667. **New Zealand**, Room 909, Metropole Building, 235 Dong Khoi St, T08-3822 6907. **Thailand**, 77 Tran Quoc Thao St, District 3, T08-3932 7637. **UK**, 25 Le Duan St, T08-3829 8433. **USA**, 4 Le Duan St, T08-3520 4200, http://hochiminh.usconsulate.gov. **Immigration** Immigration Office, 254 Nguyen Trai St, T08-3832 2300. For visa extensions and to change visas to specify overland travel to Cambodia via Moc Bai (see box, page 183) or for overland travel to Laos or China. **Internet** There are numerous internet cafés but most guesthouses and hotels offer services and Wi-Fi now. **Laundry** There are several places that will do your laundry around Pham Ngu Lao St. **Medical services** Columbia Asia (Saigon International Clinic), 8 Alexander de Rhodes St, T08-3823 8455, www. columbiaasia.com, international doctors. **Family Medical Practice HCMC**, Diamond Plaza, 34 Le Duan St, T08-3822 7848, www.vietnammedicalpractice.com, well-equipped practice, 24-hr emergency service and an evacuation service, Australian and European doctors. Also provides a useful major and minor disease outbreak service on its website. **French Vietnam Hospital**, 6 Nguyen Luong Bang St, Saigon South, Q7, T08-5411 3333, www.fvhospital.com. **Post office and telephone** The GPO is at 2 Cong Xa Paris (facing the cathedral). Daily 0630-2100. Telex, telegram and international telephone services available.

Far south

At its verdant best the Mekong Delta is a riot of greens: pale rice seedlings deepen in shade as they sprout ever taller; palm trees and orchards make up an unbroken horizon of foliage. But at its muddy worst the paddy fields ooze with slime and sticky clay; grey skies, hostile clouds and incessant rain make daily life a misery and the murky rising waters, the source of all the natural wealth of the delta, also cause hundreds of fatalities.

Boat trips along canals and down rivers are the highlights of this region, as is a visit to Phu Quoc – Vietnam's largest island. Lying off the southwest coast, Phu Quoc remains largely undeveloped with beautiful sandy beaches along much of its coastline and forested hills inland. *▶▶ For listings, see pages 186-193.*

Ins and outs

Getting there and around There are several highways throughout the Mekong Delta linking the major towns. Highway 1 from Ho Chi Minh City goes to My Tho, Vinh Long and Can Tho and Highway 91 links Can Tho, Long Xuyen and Chau Doc. Beyond these towns, however, roads are narrow and pot-holed and travel is generally slow. Ferry crossings make travel more laborious but two new bridges in recent years have speeded up travel. The easiest way to explore the region is to take a tour from Ho Chi Minh City to Can Tho, My Tho or Chau Doc; some operators organise through trips to Phnom Penh over three days or more, a great way to see the delta and enter Cambodia in one go. ▶▶ *See Transport, page 191; for transport to Phu Quoc Island, see page 192.*

Best time to visit December to May is when the Mekong Delta is at its best. During the monsoon, from June to November, the weather is poor, with constant background drizzle, interrupted by bursts of torrential rain. In October flooding may interrupt movement particularly in remote areas and around Chau Doc and Dong Thap Province.

Background

The Mekong River enters Vietnam in two branches known traditionally as the Mekong (to the north) and the Bassac but now called the Tien and the Hau respectively. Over the 200 km journey to the sea they divide to form nine mouths, the so-called 'Nine Dragons' or Cuu Long of the delta. In response to the rains of the southwest monsoon, river levels in the delta begin to rise in June, usually reaching a peak in October and falling to normal in December. This seasonal pattern is ideal for growing rice, around which the whole way of life of the delta has evolved. Even prior to the creation of French Cochin China in the 19th century, rice was being transported from here to Hué, the imperial capital.

The region has had a restless history. Conflict between Cambodians and Vietnamese for ownership of the wide plains resulted in ultimate Viet supremacy (although important Khmer relics remain). From 1705 onwards Vietnamese emperors began building canals to improve navigation in the delta. This task was taken up enthusiastically by the French in order to open up new areas to rice cultivation and export. By the 1930s the population of the delta had reached 4.5 million with 2.2 million ha of land under rice cultivation. The Mekong Delta, along with the Irrawaddy (Burma) and Chao Phraya (Thailand) became one of the great rice-exporting areas of Southeast Asia, shipping over 1.2 million tonnes annually. During the French and American wars, the Mekong Delta produced many of the most fervent fighters for independence.

Today, the Mekong Delta remains Vietnam's rice bowl. The delta covers 67,000 sq km, of which about half is cultivated. Rice yields are in fact generally lower than in the north but the huge area under cultivation and the larger size of farms means that both individual households and the region produce a surplus for export. In the Mekong Delta there is nearly three times as much rice land per person as there is in the north.

My Tho → *For listings, see pages 186-193. Colour map 5, B3.*

My Tho is an important riverside market town on the banks of the Tien River, a tributary of the Mekong. The town has had a turbulent history: it was Khmer until the 17th century, when the advancing Vietnamese took control of the surrounding area. In the 18th century Thai forces annexed the territory, before being driven out in 1784. Finally, the French gained control in 1862. This historical melting pot is reflected in **Vinh Trang Pagoda** ① *60 Nguyen Trung Truc St, daily 0900-1200, 1400-1700 (best to go by bicycle or Honda ôm)*, which was built in 1849 and displays a mixture of architectural styles – Chinese, Vietnamese and colonial. The façade is almost fairytale in inspiration and the entrance to the temple is through an ornate porcelain-encrusted gate.

Ins and outs
From Ho Chi Minh City to My Tho the main route is Highway 1. The majority of travellers join an inclusive tour or catch an Open Tour Bus, which allows greater flexibility. ›› *See Transport, page 191.*

Tien River islands
① *The best way of getting to the islands is to take a tour from the tourist dock on 30 Thang 4 St. Hiring a private boat is not recommended due to the lack of insurance, the communication difficulties and lack of explanations. Prices vary according to the number of people.* ›› *See Activities and tours, page 190.*

There are four islands in the Tien River between My Tho and Ben Tre: Dragon, Tortoise, Phoenix and Unicorn. Immediately opposite My Tho is **Tan Long** (Dragon Island), noted for its longan cultivation. Honey tea is made on the islands from the longan flower, with a splash of kumquat juice to balance the flavour. There are many other fruits to sample here, as well as rice whisky. It is also pleasant to wander along the island's narrow paths.

The Island of the Coconut Monk, also known as **Con Phung** (Phoenix Island), is about 3 km from My Tho. The 'Coconut Monk' established a retreat on this island shortly after the end of the Second World War where he developed a new 'religion', a fusion of Buddhism and Christianity. He is said to have meditated for three years on a stone slab, eating nothing but coconuts. Persecuted by both the South Vietnamese government and by the Communists, the monastery on the island has since fallen into disuse.

On **Con Qui** (Tortoise Island) there is an abundance of dragon fruit, banana and papaya. Here visitors are treated to singing accompanied by a guitar and Vietnamese monochord.

Vinh Long and around → *For listings, see pages 186-193. Colour map 5, B2.*

Vinh Long is a rather ramshackle riverside town on the banks of the Co Chien River. It was one of the focal points in the spread of Christianity in the Mekong Delta and there is a cathedral and Roman Catholic seminary in town as well as a Cao Dai church. The main reason for visiting Vinh Long is to spend a night at a homestay on the lovely and tranquil island of An Binh.

Ins and outs

Tourist information **Cuu Long Tourist** ⓘ *No 1, 1 Thang 5 St, T070-382 3616, http://cuu longtourist.com, daily 0700-1700*, is one of the friendlier and more helpful of the state-run companies and runs tours and homestays.

Around Vinh Long

The river trips taking in the islands and orchards around Vinh Long are as charming as any in the delta but can be expensive. See Tour operators, page 190. Local boatmen are prepared to risk a fine and take tourists for one-tenth of the amount. **Binh Hoa Phuoc Island** makes a pleasant side trip or you could spend a morning visiting the floating market at **Cai Be**, about 10 km from Vinh Long. It's not quite as spectacular as the floating markets around Can Tho (see page 182) but nevertheless makes for a diverting trip.

An Binh Island is just a 10-minute ferry ride from Phan Boi Chau Street and represents a great example of a delta landscape, stuffed with fruit-bearing trees and flowers. It is a large island that is further sliced into smaller islands by ribbons of small canals. Sights include the ancient **Tien Chau Pagoda** and a *nuoc mam* (fish sauce factory). Travel is by sampan or walking down the winding paths that link the communities. If you choose to stay on the island, you will be given tea and fruit at a traditional house, see rice cakes and popcorn being made, and visit a brick factory, where terracotta pots are made and then fired in pyramid-shaped kilns.

Sa Dec → For listings, see pages 186-193. Colour map 5, B2.

Sa Dec's biggest claim to fame is that it was the birthplace of French novelist Marguerite Duras, and the town's three main avenues – Nguyen Hué (on the riverfront), Tran Hung Dao and Hung Vuong garlanded with fragrant frangipani – together with some attractive colonial villas betray the French influence on this relatively young town. It is completely untouched by tourism and offers an untainted insight into life in one of the last attractive towns of the delta.

Many of the scenes from the film adaptation of Duras' novel *The Lover* were filmed in front of the shop terraces and merchants' houses on Nguyen Hué St. Huynh Thuy Le was Duras' lover and his house **Nha Co Huynh**, *Thuy Le, 255A Nguyen Hué St, Ward 2, T067-377 3937, huynhthuyle@dongthaptourist.com, 10,000d entrance, Mon-Sat 0730-1700, Sun 0830-1700*, a lovely Sino-influenced building on the main street is open to visitors. There are stunning gold-leaf carved animal figures framing arches and the centrepiece is a golden shrine to Chinese warrior Quan Cong. See Sleeping, page 186.

Can Tho and around → For listings, see pages 186-193. Colour map 5, B2.

Can Tho is a large and rapidly growing commercial town situated in the heart of the Mekong Delta. Lying chiefly on the west bank of the Can Tho River, it is the largest city in the delta and also the most welcoming and agreeable. It is the launch pad for trips to some of the region's floating markets. A small settlement was established at Can Tho at the end of the 18th century, although the town did not prosper until the French took control of the delta a century later and rice production for export began to take off. Despite the city's rapid growth there are still vestiges of French influence apparent in the broad boulevards, as well as many elegant buildings. Can Tho was also an important US base.

Ins and outs

Getting there and around Virtually all visitors arrive by road. With the My Thuan Bridge (near Vinh Long) and the new bridge linking Vinh Long and Can Tho, journey times have fallen. Most of Can Tho can be explored on foot but the floating markets are best visited by boat. ▸▸ *See Transport, page 191.*

Sights

Hai Ba Trung Street, alongside the river, is the heart of the town, where, at dusk, families stroll in the park in their Sunday best. There is also a bustling **market** here, along the bank of the river. Opposite the park, at number 34, is **Chua Ong Pagoda**, dating from 1894 and built by Chinese from Guangzhou. Unusually for a Chinese temple it is not free standing but part of a terrace of buildings. The right-hand side of the pagoda is dedicated to the Goddess of Fortune, while the left-hand side belongs to General Ma Tien, who, to judge from his unsmiling statue, is fierce and warlike and not to be trifled with.

Floating markets

ⓘ *Busiest at around 0600-0900. Sampans are available to rent in Hai Ba Trung St. Expect to pay about US$15 for 2 people for 3 hrs. Set off as early as possible to beat the tour boats.*
The river markets near Can Tho are colourful confusions of boats, goods, vendors, customers and tourists. From their boats the market traders attach samples of their wares to bamboo poles, which they hold out to attract customers. Up to seven vegetables can be seen dangling from the staffs – wintermelon, pumpkin, spring onions, giant parsnips, grapefruit, garlic, mango, onions and Vietnamese plums – and the boats are usually piled high with more produce. Housewives paddle their sampans from boat to boat to barter, haggle and gossip; small sampans are the best means of transport as they can negotiate the narrowest canals to take the shopper (or the visitor) into the heart of the area. Take at least a five-hour round trip in order to see the landscape at a leisurely pace.

Chau Doc and around → *For listings, see pages 186-193. Colour map 5, B1.*

Chau Doc was once an attractive, bustling riverside town on the west bank of the Hau or Bassac River, bordering Cambodia. It is still a bustling market town but no longer so appealing, since it has become an important trading and marketing centre for the surrounding agricultural communities. One of its biggest attractions, however, is the nearby **Nui Sam** (Sam Mountain), which is dotted with pagodas and tombs, and from whose summit superb views of the plains below can be enjoyed.

Ins and outs

Getting there Chau Doc is an increasingly important border crossing into Cambodia. There are connections by boat with Phnom Penh as well as by road from the crossing at Tinh Bien south of Chau Doc. There are tours to Chau Doc from Ho Chi Minh City.

Getting around Chau Doc itself is easily small enough to explore on foot and Nui Sam, the nearby sacred mountain, can be reached by motorbike. ▸▸ *See Transport, page 191.*

Best time to visit Nui Sam is one of the holiest sites in southern Vietnam and, as such, has vast numbers of pilgrims visiting it on auspicious days. From a climatic viewpoint, the best time to visit is between December and April.

Border essentials: Vietnam–Cambodia

Chau Doc, Tinh Bien, Xà Xía, Mekong Delta and Moc Bai, Tay Ninh province
The river crossing is on the Mekong Chau Doc and there are two further land crossings south of Chau Doc; the other land crossing is at Moc Bai, close to Tay Ninh in Vietnam.
Transport Daily morning boat departures to Phnom Penh from Chau Doc through the crossing at Vinh Xuong and can be arranged through tour operators in Chau Doc, five to 10 hours, US$10-25. **Mekong Tours**, see Tour operators, Chau Doc, runs a bus to Phnom Penh via Tinh Bien near Nha Ban (Phnom Den, Takeo, on the Cambodian side). Further south, outside of Ha Tien, it's possible to cross the border at Xà Xía. Either take a *Xe ôm* to the border or buy a bus ticket to Kep, Kampot, Sihanoukville or Phnom Penh with Ha Tien Tourism, see Tour operators, Ha Tien, page 191.
There is also an uncomfortable 10-hour public bus ride from Chau Doc to Phnom Penh via Moc Bai. Budget tour operators in Ho Chi Minh City such as **Sinh Tourist**, 248 De Tham Street, Ho Chi Minh City, T08-3838 9597, www.thesinhtourist.vn, run a two-day tour through the Mekong Delta from Ho Chi Minh City to Phnom Penh by land, from 180,000d. To travel direct from Ho Chi Minh City to Moc Bai takes about three hours, and from Moc Bai to Phnom Penh a further six hours, with one ferry crossing.
Note Cambodia entry visas can be obtained at the border. Vietnam visas are not available on arrival at the border.

Background

Until the mid-18th century Chau Doc was part of Cambodia: it was given to the Nguyen lord, Nguyen Phuc Khoat, after he had helped to put down an insurrection in the area. The area still supports a large Khmer population, as well as the largest Cham settlement in the delta. Cambodia's influence can be seen in the tendency for women to wear the *kramar*, Cambodia's characteristic chequered scarf, instead of the *non lá* conical hat, and in the people's darker skin, indicating Khmer blood.

Nui Sam (Sam Mountain) → *Colour map 5, B1.*

Nui Sam, 5 km southwest of Chau Doc, is one of the holiest sites in southern Vietnam. Rising from the flood plain, it is a favourite spot for Vietnamese tourists who throng here, especially at festival time. The mountain, really a barren, rock-strewn hill, can be seen at the end of the continuation of Nguyen Van Thoai Street. It is literally honeycombed with tombs, sanctuaries and temples. It is possible to walk or drive right up the hill for good views of the surrounding countryside and from the summit it is easy to appreciate that this is some of the most fertile land in Vietnam.

The **Tay An Pagoda**, at the foot of the hill, facing the road, represents an eclectic mixture of styles – Chinese, Islamic, perhaps even Italian – and contains a bewildering display of more than 200 statues. A short distance on from the pagoda, to the right, past shops and stalls, is the **Chua Xu**. It is rather a featureless building, though highly revered by the Vietnamese and honours the holy Lady Xu, whose statue is enshrined in the new multi-roofed pagoda. From the 23rd to the 25th of the fourth lunar month the holy lady is commemorated, during which time, hundreds of Vietnamese flock to see her being washed and reclothed. Lady Xu is a major pilgrimage for traders and business from Ho Chi Minh City and the south, all hoping that sales will soar and profits leap during this auspicious time.

On the other side of the road is the tomb of **Thoai Ngoc Hau** (1761-1829); an enormous head of the man graces the entranceway. Thoai is a local hero who played a role in the resistance against the French but is known more for his engineering feats in canal building and draining swamps.

Hang Pagoda is a 200-year-old temple situated halfway up Nui Sam. In the first level of the temple are some vivid cartoon drawings of the tortures of hell. The second level is built at the mouth of a cave, which, last century, was home to a woman named Thich Gieu Thien. Her likeness and tomb can be seen in the first pagoda. Fed up with her lazy and abusive husband she left her home in Cholon and came to live in this cave, as an ascetic supposedly waited on by two snakes.

Ha Tien → For listings, see pages 186-193.

Ha Tien used to be a quaint small town with a tranquil pace of life and an attractive US-built pontoon bridge that carried bikers and pedestrians across to the opposite bank of the river. It has quite rapidly become a sprawling urban mess with ugly hotels cluttering the riverbank and construction running rampant with no regard to aesthetics. The boom has no doubt been helped by the opening of the border with Cambodia at Xà Xía. Step back off the main thoroughfare and you will find vestiges of the quaint appeal that once made this city worth visiting.

Ha Tien can be reached from all over the delta. The border crossing to Cambodia is now in full operation. See box, page 183.

Phu Quoc Island → For listings, see pages 186-193. Colour map 6, C2.

Lying off the southwest coast of the country, Phu Quoc is Vietnam's largest island. Just a few years ago it remained largely undeveloped, with beautiful sandy beaches along much of its coastline and forested hills inland, but the arrival of numerous new resorts sees some of its virgin land disappearing under concrete. Most of the beaches benefit from crystal-clear waters, making them perfect for swimming. After the rigours of sightseeing, Phu Quoc is well worth a visit for a few days' relaxation in southern Vietnam.

Ins and outs

Getting there and around You can get to Phu Quoc by plane from Ho Chi Minh City and Rach Gia. Most hotels will provide a free pick-up service from the airport if accommodation is booked in advance. There is also a high-speed boat service to the island from Rach Gia and Ha Tien. Hiring a motorbike is cheap and convenient but makes for dusty and very hot travelling although as more roads are tarmacked conditions will improve; limited signposting can make some places pretty hard to find without local assistance. There are also plenty of motorbike taxis available, as well as cars with drivers at fairly reasonable prices; ask at hotels. ▶▶ *See Transport, page 191.*

Around the island

Vietnamese fish sauce (*nuoc mam*) is produced on Phu Quoc. You'll see dozens of fish laid out to dry on land and on trestle tables, destined for fish sauce factories at **Duong Dong**, the island's main town. The Khai Hoan factory can be visited.

The island is also a centre for South Sea pearls, with 10,000 collected offshore each year. At the **Phu Quoc Pearl Gallery** ① *10 km south of Duong Dong, daily 0800-1800,* a video demonstrates the farming operation, the tasting of pearl meat and pearl-making is illustrated in the gallery. South of the pearl farm, on the coast road, are two **whale dedication temples**. Whales have long been worshipped in Vietnam. Ever since the days of the Champa, the whale has been credited with saving the lives of drowning fishermen. The Cham believed that Cha-Aih-Va, a powerful god, could assume the form of a whale in order to rescue those in need. Emperor Gia Long is said to have been rescued by a whale when his boat sank. After he ascended to the throne, Gia Long awarded the whale the title 'Nam Hai Cu Toc Ngoc Lam Thuong Dang Than' – Superior God of the Southern Sea. Coastal inhabitants always help whales in difficulty. If a whale should die, a funeral is arranged.

Inland, the **Da Ban** and **Chanh** streams and waterfalls are not very dramatic in the dry season but still provide a relaxing place to swim and walk in the forests.

The stunning, dazzling white sands of **Sao Beach**, on the southeast coast, are worth visiting by motorbike but finding the beach can be difficult, as it is not well signposted, so you made need your resort or a tour operator to help you. One of the biggest draws are the boat trips around the **An Thoi islands**, which are scattered off the southern coast and offer opportunities for swimming, diving, snorkelling and fishing.

Phu Quoc Island

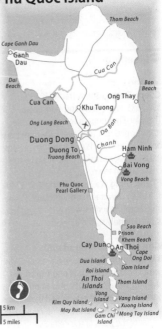

For Sleeping and Eating price codes and other relevant information, see pages 40-43.

⊟ Sleeping

My Tho *p180*

C Song Tien, 33 Trung Trac St, T0730-397 7883, www.tiengiangtourist.com. This place has undergone a remarkable transformation into a lovely 20-room hotel boasting large beds and bathtubs on legs. Price includes breakfast and it's now the best place in town.

F Rang Dong, No 25, 30 Thang 4 St, T730-3874400, www.rangdonghotel.net. Private mini hotel, near river with a/c, TV and hot water. Friendly staff are helpful.

Vinh Long and around *p180*

B Mekong Homestays, An Binh Island, Vinh Long. Organized by **Cuu Long Tourist**, or **Mekong Travel**, page 190. Accommodation is basic, with camp beds, shared bathrooms and mosquito nets, and a home-cooked dinner of the fruits of the delta. Evening entertainment consists of chatting with the owner. The price includes a boat trip around the island, transfers from Vinh Long, guide, 1 dinner and 1 breakfast.

C-D Cuu Long (B), No 1, 1 Thang 5 St (ie No 1 May St), T070-382 3616, www.cuulongtourist.com. Set back from the river, in the centre of action. 34 comfortable a/c rooms; price includes breakfast (over the road at the **Phuy Thuong Restaurant**). The **Hoa Vien Club** in the grounds next to the hotel is also good for a drink.

E-F Nam Phuong, 11 Le Loi St, T070-382 2226, khachsannamphuongvl@yahoo.com. These comfortable rooms have a/c and hot water. They're clean and cheap with very friendly service. There's a big co-op mart nearby. Bikes to rent too.

Sa Dec *p181*

D Nha Co Huynh Thuy Le, 255A Nguyen Hué St, Ward 2, T067-377 3937. Run by Dong Thap Tourist, this lovely home has 4 fan rooms with 2 single beds in each and would be the most enjoyable way to spend time in Sa Dec. The 2 front rooms are much more attractive than the plain 2 back rooms, with stained-glass windows and carved wooden doors. The shared bathroom is at the back with cold water. The price includes breakfast and dinner.

Can Tho *p181*

LL Victoria Can Tho Resort, Cai Khe Ward, T0710-381 0111, www.victoriahotels-asia.com. This is one of the most beautiful hotels in Vietnam. With its riverside garden location, combined with a harmonious interior, breezy reception area, emphasis on comfort and plenty of genuine period features, it inspires relaxation. The centre-piece is the gorgeous, flood-lit pool, flanked by the lobby bar and restaurant. Rooms are elegantly decorated. Other facilities include a tennis court and therapies in divine massage cabins. The hotel offers a complimentary shuttle bus and boat to the town centre.

L-AL Golf Hotel, 2 Hai Ba Trung St, T0710-381 2210, www.vinagolf.vn. No longer the tallest hotel in town with its 10 floors. The services and facilities are on a par with the better hotels in HCMC and Hanoi but it always seems empty. The staff are friendly, knowledgeable and multilingual. The rooms are well equipped with all mod cons and en suites. The restaurants on the 8th, 9th and 10th floors provide fine dining and the views from the **Windy Sky Bar** (8th floor) are superb. The swimming 'fool' is a draw. ATM on site.

A-C Kim Tho, 14 Ngo Gia Tu St, T0710-322 2228, www.kimtho.com. The closest thing to boutique hotel in the delta with low-slung beds and white linens. Don't bother paying extra for a room with a view. Choose a standard with a bathtub. The standout attraction is the rooftop café with fabulous views. Price includes breakfast.

E-F Tay Ho, 42 Hai Ba Trung St, T0710-382 3392, tay_ho@hotmail.com. This lovely place has a variety of rooms and a great public balcony that can be enjoyed by those paying for back rooms. All rooms now have private bathrooms. River view rooms, inevitably, cost more. The staff are friendly.

Chau Doc p182

LL-L Victoria Chau Doc, 32 Le Loi St, T076-386 5010, www.victoriahotels-asia.com. This old, cream building with its riverfront pool is the perfect location in which to relax. All rooms are attractively decorated. The hotel group runs a speedboat to Phnom Penh.

C-D Ben Da Sam Mountain Resort, Highway 91, T076-386 1745. This resort consists of 4 hotels, a restaurant and bar. The staff speak good English. The place to stay for a bit of luxury. Sam Mountain is 5 mins' walk away.

E Thuan Loi, 18 Tran Hung Dao St, T076-386 6134, hotelthuanloi@hcm.vnn.vn. A/c and good river views, clean and friendly. The expanded and attractively designed restaurant enjoys a great location right on the river and is recommended especially in the late afternoon for coffee. This is a highly popular place; reserve in advance if possible.

E-F Thanh Nam 2, 10 Quang Trung St, T076-321 2616, thanhnam2hotel@yahoo.com. Rooms are better at this one than the **Vinh**

Phuoc if you can stand the bright green floor tiles. There are 10 rooms; those with a/c are slightly more expensive.

Ha Tien p184

C-E Ha Tien Hotel, 36 Tran Hau St, T077-385 1563. In a convenient location close to the ferry station with a good alfresco restaurant. However, the 30 rooms are a little lacklustre despite it being a new hotel and are a tad overpriced; those with balconies cost more.

E Du Hung, 27A Tran Hau St, T077-395 1555, www.dongtamhotel.com. A hotel with spacious rooms and all facilities close to the ferry station. Recommended.

E-G Hai Van, 55 Lam Son St, T077-385 2872. This new hotel with attached restaurant offers comfortable rooms a few block backs from the hustle, bustle and building works on Tran Hau St. Recommended.

Phu Quoc Island p187, map p185

During peak periods, such as Christmas and Tet, it is advisable to book accommodation well in advance. Most of the resorts lie along the west coast to the south of Duong Dong and are within a few kilometres of the airport. Others are on On Lang Beach.

LL-AL La Veranda, Tran Hung Dao St, Long Beach, T077-398 2988, www.laverandaresort. com. A beautiful luxury resort with rooms and villas set in luscious gardens leading on to the main beach on the island. All rooms are beautifully furnished and come with TV, DVD player and wireless internet. De luxe rooms

and villas come with gorgeous 4-poster beds and drapes. There's a spa, pool and the delicious food of the **Peppertree Restaurant**. The welcome and service is exceptional.

L-AL Chenla Resort & Spa, Ong Lang Beach, T077-399 5895, www.chenla-resort. com. A very inviting resort with lovely villas set back from the white-sand beach with alfresco bathrooms. Smaller-roomed semi-detached bungalows face the sea. The golden sands are dotted with paprika-coloured umbrellas, and there's an infinity pool, spa, water sports and atmospheric restaurant.

AL-B Mango Bay Resort, Ong Lang Beach, T090-338 2207 (mob), www. mangobayphuquoc.com. A small and environmentally friendly resort located on the beach close to pepper farms. Bungalows are made from rammed earth and come with fans and coconut doorknobs and are kitted out with bamboo furniture and tiled floors. The 5 rooms share a wonderful, large communal veranda, some have outdoor bathrooms. There's information on birds and fish, and the restaurant provides a mixture of Vietnamese and Western food at very reasonable prices.

A-B Mai House Resort, Long Beach, T077-384 7003, maihouseresort@yahoo. com. This is really lovely resort run by Tuyet Mai and Gerard Bezardin set in large flourishing gardens in front of a delicious slice of beach dotted with palms. The 20 bungalows feature 4-poster beds, pretty tiled bathrooms and balconies with carved balustrades. Sea view rooms are bigger. The small restaurant (with Wi-Fi access) overlooks the beach. Raw black kingfish is recommended.

A-C Bo Resort, Ong Lang Beach, T077-986142/3, www.boresort.com. This feels like a great escape with 18 stilted bungalows set on a hillside amid flourishing gardens. Rooms come with large rustic bathrooms and alfresco showers. There's no road access to the wild stretch of beach where there are pines, hammocks, kayaks and a beach bar. There's Wi-Fi in the restaurant/bar and

candlelight at night. The owners are warm and friendly.

B-D Sao Bien, Tran Hung Dao St, Long Beach, T077-398 2161, www.seastarresort. com. Spacious but spartan rooms at this resort with 38 bungalows of mixed price and a long stretch of beach. Garden rooms at the rear of the property are cheaper than those nearer the beachfront. Cheapest are those in a hotel block. Wi-Fi at reception and restaurant only.

C-E Beach Club, Long Beach, T077-398 0998, www.beachclubvietnam.com. Luscious golden sands and thatched beach umbrellas at this small resort, the furthest from the town and thus not conveniently located. If you want to stay in the resort and kick back for a while this is perfect. If you want more activity, choose a resort closer to town. The ochre-coloured 6 rooms and 4 bungalows are all close to the sea. It's good value and so always booked up. Reserve well in advance.

D Freedomland, Ong Lang Beach, 10 mins' walk from beach, T077-399 4891, www. freedomlandphuquoc.com. Run by Peter, this laid-back resort creates a community vibe as all guests eat together at the large dinner table. Bungalows are scattered around the grounds; the cutest being a stilted room with a tiny balcony. Four of the rooms have private bathroom and 4 share. It's a 12-min walk to the beach. Boat and motos can be rented. Recommended.

🍴 Eating

My Tho *p180*
A speciality of the area is *hu tieu my tho* – a spicy soup of vermicelli, sliced pork, dried shrimps and fresh herbs. At night, noodle stalls spring up on the pavement on Le Loi St at the junction with Le Dai Han St.

🍴 **Banh Xeo 46**, 11 Trung Trac St. Serves *bánh xèo*, savoury pancakes filled with bean-sprouts, mushrooms and prawns; delicious.

🍴 **Hu Tien 44**, 44 Nam Ky Khoi Nghia St. Daily 0500-1200. Specializes in *hu tien* *my tho*. At 16000d for a good-sized bowl filled to top.

¶ Lac Hong, 63, 30 Thang 4 St. This is the latest place to be seen. Sip your coffee in the cool and watch the world go by.

Vinh Long and around *p180*

¶ Phuong Thuy Restaurant, No 1, 1 Thang 5 St, T070-382 4786. Daily 0600-2100. A 'stilt' restaurant on the river with Vietnamese and Western dishes and welcoming service. Cuttlefish and shrimp feature strongly.

Sa Dec *p181*

¶¶¶ Nha Co Huynh Thuy Le, 255A Nguyen Hué St, Ward 2, T067-377 3937. Run by Dong Thap Tourist, reserve a day in advance for the chance to dine in the home of Marguerite Duras' lover. Attended to by Xuan and Tuyen who are guides at the house, dine on spring rolls, fried fish, lotus salad, noodles, fried vegetables with pork and fruit. Lunch and dinner menus are US$6 each for 5 courses.

Can Tho *p181*

Hai Ba Trung St by the river has a range of excellent and well-priced little restaurants; the riverside setting is an attractive one.

¶¶-¶ Sao Hom, Nha Long Cho Co, T0710-381 5616, http://saohom.transmekong.com. This new and very busy restaurant on the riverfront serves plentiful food and provides very good service. Watching the river life and the floating pleasure palaces at night is a good way to spend an evening meal here. Shame about the illuminated billboards on the opposite bank. This place is hugely popular with very large tour groups that alter the character of the restaurant when they swarm in.

¶ Mekong, 38 Hai Ba Trung St. Perfectly good little place near the river in this popular restaurant strip. Serves decent Vietnamese fare at reasonable prices.

¶ Nam Bo, 50 Hai Ba Trung St, T0710-382 3908. Delightful French house on the corner of a street. Its balcony seating area overlooks the market clutter and riverside promenade. Tasty Vietnamese and French dishes. The set menu is 170,000d. Small café downstairs. Recommended.

¶ Phuong Nam, 48 Hai Ba Trung St, T0710-381 2077. Similar to the next door Nam Bo, good food, less stylish, a popular travellers' haunt and reasonable prices.

Chau Doc *p182*

¶¶¶-¶¶ La Bassac, in Victoria Chau Doc. The French and Vietnamese menus at this riverside restaurant include rack of lamb coated in Mekong herbs, sweet potato puree and pork wine reduction or spaghetti with flambéed shrimps in vodka paprika sauce.

¶ Bay Bong, 22 Thung Dang Le St, T076-386 7271. Specializes in hot pots and soups and also offers a good choice of fresh fish. The staff are friendly.

¶ Mekong, 41 Le Loi St, T076-386 7381, opposite Victoria Chau Doc. Open for lunch and dinner. It is located in a lovingly restored French villa. Good selection of food and the staff are friendly.

Ha Tien *p184*

¶¶-¶ Hai Van, 55 Lam Son St, T077-385 2872. This restaurant has moved from its popular riverside spot to be at the back end of a hotel of the same name and has smartened up its appearance. It serves up a reasonable selection of Chinese, Vietnamese and international cuisine.

¶ Ha Tien Floating Restaurant, T077-395 9939. Quite a nice surprise for Ha Tien with Australian beef on the menu. There's a huge menu of chicken, frog and eel as well as fish. Popular with local business people.

Phu Quoc Island *p189, map p185*

¶¶-¶ Ocean Bar & Grill & Winestore, 60 Tran Hung Dao St, T077-399 4268, winestore.pq@ gmail.com. The owner of this place gives the biggest welcome in Phu Quoc. Friendly ambience, tasty and varied Vietnamese and pan-Asian dishes and a great view of the sunset for an early dinner.

♦♦–♥ Pepper's, 89 Tran Hung Dao St, T077-384 8773. An Italian restaurant set away from the beach which is hugely popular. Service is a bit slack, though.
♥ Buddy's, 26 Nguyen Trai St, T077-399 4181. Western-style café with roadside view serving up delicious kiwi-made ice cream at 20,000d per scoop.

☉ Activities and tours

My Tho *p180*
You can hire boats to take you to visit the islands. Once there, walk or cycle.

Tour operators
Chuong Duong Tourist, next to the hotel, T0730-387 0875, cdhoteltravel@vnn. vn. Offers the same tour as **Tien Giang Tourist** for the same price but for 3 hrs. Recommended tour guides.
Tien Giang Tourist, Dockside location is at No 8, 30 Thang 4 St, T0730-387 3184, www. tiengiangtourist.com. Dinner with traditional music on the Mekong for US$28. Canoe hire is US$50 per hr for 2 people and a boat is US$12 for 1½ hrs.

Vinh Long and around *p180*
Cuu Long Tourist, No 1, 1 Thang 5 St, T070-382 3616, www.cuulongtourist.com. Trips to An Binh Island – a highlight of the area – include a visit to the small floating market of Cai Be. A tour of the area including homestay, dinner and breakfast can be arranged (see Sleeping above). A day trip to Cai Be passing the floating market is possible, as is the arrangement from HCMC.
Mekong Travel, No 8, 30 Thang 5 St, T070-383 6252, www.mekongtravel.com.vn. Breaking the monopoly of **Cuu Long Tourist** is this new company offering the same homestay and floating market options.

Can Tho *p181*
Boat trips
Trans Mekong, 97/10 Ngo Quyen, P An Cu, T0710-382 9540, www.transmekong.com.

Operates 3 *Bassac* boats, converted rice barges that sleep passengers in a/c cabins with private bathrooms.

Swimming
The **Victoria Can Tho Resort** has a pool open to the public for a fee.

Tour operators
Can Tho Tourist, 20 Hai Ba Trung St, T0710-382 1852, http://canthotourist.vn. It's quite expensive and organizes tours in small boats and powerful boats – the latter not the best way to see the delta. The staff are helpful and knowledgeable. Tours include trips to Cai Rang, Phong Dien and Phung Hiep floating markets, to Soc Trang, city tours (328,000d), canal tours, bicycle tours, trekking tours, stork sanctuary tour and homestays that involve working with farmers in the fields. General boat tours also arranged. It charges US$60 for a 1-night tour for two including floating market and bike tour.

Chau Doc *p182*
Mekong Tours, Vinh Phuoc Hotel, and at 14 Nguyen Huu Canh St, T076-386 8222, and at the **Thanh Nam 2 hotel** where they are particularly helpful, www.mekongtours. net. Local trips include the fish farms, floating markets and Cham village. Trips to Phu Quoc and boat trips to Phnom Penh (US$10, departs 0700, 8-10 hrs or express boat, US$25, departs 0800, 5 hrs; Cambodian visas can be bought at the border). A/c and public buses also booked; air ticketing; Open Tour Bus ticketing (to Can Tho hourly , US$5, 3 hrs; to Ha Tien, US$7, 3 hrs; to HCMC hourly, US$9, 6 hrs); and visa applications. Onward bus transport to Can Tho and HCMC can include tour stops on the way (from US$16-37). You need to ask exactly what your payment includes and whether any accommodation included is individual or shared. Private express boat transfer to My Tho, US$450; slow boat to Can Tho, 4½ hrs, US$180, 6 people maximum.

Ha Tien p184

Ha Tien Tourism Coop Ltd, 1 Phuong Thanh St, T077-395 9598, hatientourism@gmail.com. Organizes boat tickets to Phu Quoc for US$9 and US$10. Open buses to HCMC, US$10 at 0900, 1130, 2200. Also to Can Tho, Chau Doc, Vinh Long, My Tho. 3-day Mekong tours ending in HCMC offered from US$55. Organizes buses to Cambodia at 1200 and 1600: to Kep, US$12; to Kampot US$15; to Sihanoukville, US$20; to Phnom Penh at 1200 and 0600, US$18. Cambodian visa organized, US$25. These trips do not involve a change of bus. Vietnam visa extensions also organized. Very helpful.

Phu Quoc Island p191, map p185
Diving

Rainbow Divers, Tran Hung Dao St, close to the market, T091-723 9433 (mob), www.divevietnam.com. Long-standing operation with a very good reputation.

Tour operators

John's Tours, New Star Café, 143 Tran Hung Dao St, T091-910 7086, www.johnislandtours.com. Run by the super helpful and friendly John Tran out of the **New Star Café** (next to the alley to La Veranda) and various kiosks on the beach as well as hotel desks. Snorkelling, squid fishing, island tours and car hire can be arranged. Prices from US$15. Car hire with driver also arranged.

Tony Travel, 100 Tran Hung Dao St or based at the **Rainbow Divers** office on Tran Hung Dao St opposite the market, T0913-197334, tonytravelpq@yahoo.com.vn. Kiosks on the beach too. Tony knows Phu Quoc extremely well and speaks fluent English. He would be able to organize almost anything. In his stable are island tours, snorkelling to the south and north islands, deep-sea fishing excursions, car and motorbike rental and hotel and transport reservations. Prices from US$15. Snorkelling tours make sure you're fitted with a mask and snorkel properly and water and fruit are offered in abundance.

⊖ Transport

My Tho p180

As in all Mekong Delta towns, local travel to visit the orchards, islands and remoter places is often by boat. On land there are *xe ôms*. There are public bus connections to Ho Chi Minh City.

Vinh Long and around p180

The local bus station is on 3 Thang 2 St, between Hung Dao Vuong and Hung Vuong in the centre of town with services to Sa Dec and Can Tho. The long-distance bus station is at Dinh Tien Hoang St, Ward 8 for hourly connections with **HCMC**'s Mien Tay station.

Can Tho p181
Air

Vietnam Airlines, 66 Chau Van Liem St. The airport is situated about 7 km from the city centre. Flights to **Hanoi**. A taxi from the airport is 40,000-50,000d.

Boat

A bridge has been built to Can Tho but ferries will still operate for direct routing as the bridge is 10 km from Can Tho. There are no public boats leaving Can Tho.

Bus

The bus station is about 2 km northwest of town along Nguyen Trai St, at the intersection with Hung Vuong St. Xe-om is 10,000d into town. Hourly connections to **HCMC**'s Mien Tay terminal, 4-5 hrs, 80,000d (Phuong Trang bus company, T710-3769768 provides a good service), and other towns in the Mekong Delta.

Chau Doc p182
Boat

There are daily departures to **Phnom Penh**. A couple of tour operators in town organize boat tickets. See also box, page 183.

 Victoria Hotels & Resorts, www.victoriahotels-asia.com, runs boats from **Chau Doc** to Phnom Penh, 0700, 5 hrs, US$100 per person, min 2 people.

Bus

The new station is 3 km south from the town centre T076-386 7171. No English is spoken at the ticket office. There is an uncomfortable 10-hr bus ride from Chau Doc to **Phnom Penh** via **Moc Bai**. Mekong Tours, see Tour operators, runs a bus to Phnom Penh via Tinh Bien (see box, page 183) at 0815, 5 hrs, US$25 with no change of bus.

Ha Tien p184

The ferry wharf is opposite the **Ha Tien** hotel. Ferries to **Phu Quoc** leave at 0800-0830 (120,000d) and at 1000, 100,000d. Note that the 1000 service arrives at Nam Ninh where there are few public transport options. (There are also twice daily boats from Rach Gia to Phu Quoc).

Bus

The bus station is on the way to the Cambodia border on Highway 80 north of town. There are buses to **HCMC**, at 0700, 0800 and 0900, 10-12 hrs, 100,000d and regular connections with **Rach Gia**, 4 hrs, 38,000d, **Chau Doc**, 52,000d **Can Tho**, 83,000d as well as other Delta towns. Reliable **Mai Linh** runs to Rach Gia, 45,000d. Footprint has received news of scams involving illegally operated buses running out of Ha Tien and the Cambodia border. Make sure you buy a ticket at the real Ha Tien bus station. All real buses provide tickets in Vietnam. (*Phong Ve* means ticket office in Vietnamese). Ha Tien bus station is new and substantial in size with a ticket office. *Xe ôm*s wait outside. *Xe ôm* to the Cambodia border, 30,000d; into town, 10,000d.

Phu Quoc Island p192, map p185
Air

There are daily flights to **HCMC** and **Rach Gia**.
   Airline offices Vietnam Airlines, 122 Nguyen Trung Truc St, Duong Dong, T077-399667.

Boat

Ferries leave from Bai Vong port in the southeastern part of the island and Ham Ninh in the east. An Thoi port in the south is closed for renovation.

   Superdong, 1 Tran Hung Dao St, Duong Dong, T077-348 6180, to **Rach Gia** from Bai Vong at 1300 arriving 1535. Adults 200,000d.

   Duong Dong Express leaves for Rach Gia at 1245 arriving 1515, 270,000d; children 200,000d, www.duongdongexpress.com.vn.

   Savanna, 36 Tran Hung Dao St, T077-399 2999, at Bai Vong, T077-399 2555. Leaves at 1305 arriving Rach Gia at 1535, 270,000d.

   Vinashin, 21 Nguyen Trai St, T077-260 0155, leaves 0810.

   Cawaco from Ham Ninh to **Ha Tien** at 0830 arriving 1000, 160,000d. Also departs Bai Vong 1400 arriving 1520. Bus picks up from agents, at 1200, 20,000d, for the Bai Vong departure. No public transport to Ham Ninh; taxi 160,000d.

Car, motorbike and bicycle

Cars, motorbikes and bicycles can be rented from resorts.

● Directory

My Tho p180
Bank EXIM, Le Van Duyet St.
Internet The post office and Choung Dong hotel offer internet and there's Wi-Fi at the Lac Hong café. **Post office** No 59, 30 Thang 4 St.

Vinh Long and around p180
Banks Agribank, 47 1 Thang 5 St. With ATM. ATM next to the Cuu Long (B) hotel.
Internet Post office and Cuu Long (B) hotel. **Post office** 12c Hoang Thai Hieu St, 0600-2100.

Can Tho p181
Banks Agribank, 3 Phan Dinh Phung St. Vietcombank, 7 Hoa Binh Blvd, T0710-820445. **Internet** Pizza_CT, 9 Chau Van

Liem St. **Post office** 2 Hoa Binh Blvd, T0710-382 7280.

Chau Doc *p182*
Banks Vietinbank, 68-70 Nguyen Huu Canh St with ATM. **Internet** Post office, Victoria Chau Doc Hotel and 30 Nguyen Huu Canh St. **Medical services** Opposite the Victoria Chau Doc Hotel. **Post office** 73 Le Loi St, daily 0600-2100, internet access.

Ha Tien *p184*
Banks Agribank is located on 37 Lam Son St on the corner of Phung Thanh St with a currency exchange and ATM. **Hospitals** On the corner of Mac Cuu and Bach Dang streets, T077-385 2666 **Internet** In the main post office and at Ha Tien Tourism. **Post office** 3 To Chau St, T077-385 2182.

Phu Quoc Island *p193, map p185*
Banks Agribank, 2 Tran Hung Dao St, Duong Dong, also cashes TCs; ATM. **Internet** Available at resorts; some have Wi-Fi. Terminals at John's Tours, New Star Café, 143 Tran Hung Dao St. **Medical services** Hospital: Khu Pho, 1 Duong Dong, T077-384 8075. **Post office** Phu Quoc Post Office, Khu Pho 2, 2 Tran Hung Dao St, Duong Dong, daily 0645-2030, internet.

Background

Vietnam prehistory

The earliest record of humans in Vietnam is from an archaeological site on Do Mountain, in the northern Thanh Hoa Province. The remains discovered here have been dated to the Lower Palaeolithic (early Stone Age). So far, all early human remains have been unearthed in North Vietnam, invariably in association with limestone cliff dwellings. Unusually, tools are made of basalt rather than flint, the more common material found at similar sites in other parts of the world.

Archaeological excavations have shown that between 5000 and 3000 BC, two important Mesolithic cultures occupied North Vietnam: these are referred to as the **Hoa Binh** and **Bac Son** cultures after the principal excavation sites in Tonkin. Refined stone implements and distinctive hand axes with polished edges (known as Bacsonian axes) are characteristic of the two cultures. These early inhabitants of Vietnam were probably small, dark-skinned and of Melanesian or Austronesian stock.

There are 2000 years of recorded Vietnamese history and another 2000 years of legend. The Vietnamese people trace their origins back to 15 tribal groups known as the **Lac Viet** who settled in what is now North Vietnam at the beginning of the Bronze Age. Here they established an agrarian kingdom known as Van-lang that seems to have vanished during the third century BC.

A problem with early **French archaeological studies** in Vietnam was that most of the scholars were either Sinologists or Indologists. In consequence, they looked to Vietnam as a receptacle of Chinese or Indian cultural influences and spent little time uncovering those aspects of culture, art and life that were indigenous in origin and inspiration. The French archaeologist Bezacier for example, expressed the generally held view that 'Vietnamese' history only began in the seventh century AD. Such sites as Hoa Binh, Dong Son and Oc-Eo, which pre-date the seventh century, were regarded as essentially Chinese or Indonesian, their only 'Vietnamese-ness' being their location. This perspective was more often than not based on faulty and slapdash scholarship, and reflected the prevailing view that Southeast Asian art was basically derivative.

Pre-colonial history

The beginning of Vietnamese recorded history coincides with the start of **Chinese cultural hegemony** over the north, in the second century BC. The Chinese dominated Vietnam for more than 1000 years until the 10th century AD and the cultural legacy is still very much in evidence, making Vietnam distinctive in Southeast Asia. Even after the 10th century, and despite breaking away from Chinese political domination, Vietnam was still overshadowed and greatly influenced by its illustrious neighbour to the north. Nonetheless, the fact that Vietnam could shrug off 1000 years of Chinese subjugation and emerge with a distinct cultural heritage and language says a lot for Vietnam's strength of national identity.

Ly Dynasty

The Ly Dynasty (1009-1225) was the first independent Vietnamese dynasty. Its capital, Thang Long, was at the site of present-day Hanoi and the dynasty based its system of government and social relations closely upon the Chinese Confucianist model. The Vietnamese owe a considerable debt to the Chinese – mainly in the spheres of government, philosophy and the arts – but they have always been determined to maintain their independence. Vietnamese Confucianist scholars were unsparing in their criticism of Chinese imperialism. Continuous Chinese invasions, all ultimately futile, served to cement an enmity between the two countries, which is still in evidence today – despite their having normalized diplomatic relations in October 1991.

The first Ly emperor, and one of Vietnam's great kings, was Ly Cong Uan who was born in AD 974. He is usually known by his posthumous title, **Ly Thai To**, and reigned for 19 years from 1009-1028. Ly Cong Uan was raised and educated by monks and acceded to the throne when, as the commander of the palace guard in Hoa Lu (the capital of Vietnam before Thang Long or Hanoi) and with the support of his great patron, the monk Van Hanh, he managed to gain the support of the Buddhist establishment and many local lords. During his reign, he enjoyed a reputation not just as a great soldier, but also as a devout man who paid attention to the interests and well-being of his people. He also seemed, if the contemporary records are to be believed, to have been remarkably sensitive to those he ruled. He tried to re-establish the harmony between ruler and ruled which had suffered during the previous years and he even sent his son to live outside the walls of the palace so that he could gain a taste of ordinary life and an understanding of ordinary people. As he approached death he is said to have increasingly retired from everyday life, preparing himself for the everlasting.

Ly Cong Uan was succeeded by his son, Ly Phat Ma, who is better known as **Ly Thai Tong** (reigned 1028-1054). Ly Phat Ma had been prepared for kingship since birth and he proved to be an excellent ruler during his long reign. It is hard to generalize about this period in Vietnamese history because Ly Phat Ma adapted his pattern of rule no less than six times during his reign. Early on he challenged the establishment, contending for example that good governance was not merely a consequence of following best practice (which the logic of bureaucratic Confucianism would maintain) but depended upon the qualities of the man at the helm. Later he was more of an establishment figure, holding much greater store by the institutions of kingship. Perhaps his greatest military success was the mounting of a campaign to defeat the Cham in 1044 from which he returned with shiploads of plunder. His greatest artistic legacy was the construction of the One Pillar Pagoda or Chua Mot Cot in Hanoi (see page 78).

Ly Phat Ma was succeeded by his son, Ly NhatTon, posthumously known as **Ly Thanh Tong** (reigned 1054-1072). History is not as kind about Ly Thanh Tong as it is about his two forebears. Nonetheless he did challenge the might of the Chinese along Vietnam's northern borders – largely successfully – and like his father also mounted a campaign against Champa (see page 198) in 1069. Indeed his expedition against the Cham mirrored his father's in most respects and, like his father, he won. Records indicate that he spent a great deal of time trying to father a son. At last, a son was born to a concubine of common blood in 1066 and named Ly Can Duc.

Ly Can Duc was proclaimed emperor in 1072 when he was only six years old and, surprisingly, remained king until he died in 1127. During the early years of his reign the kingdom faced a succession of crises, largely due to the fact that his young age meant that there was no paramount leader. His death marks the end of the Ly Dynasty for he left no heir and the crown passed to the maternal clan of his nephew. There followed a period of instability and it was not until 1225 that a new dynasty – the **Tran Dynasty** – managed to subdue the various competing cliques and bring a semblance of order to the country.

Tran Dynasty

Scholars do not know a great deal about the four generations of kings of the Tran Dynasty. It seems that they established the habit of marrying within the clan, and each king took queens who were either their cousins or, in one case, a half-sister. Such a long period of intermarriage, one imagines, would have had some far-reaching genetic consequences, although ironically the collapse of the dynasty seems to have been brought about after one foolish king decided to marry outside the Tran clan. The great achievement of the Tran Dynasty was to resist the expansionist tendencies of the Mongol forces who conquered China in the 1250s and then set their sights on Vietnam. In 1284 a huge Mongol-Yuan force, consisting of no fewer than four armies, massed on the border to crush the Vietnamese. Fortunately the Tran were blessed with a group of brave and resourceful princes, the most notable of whom was Tran Quoc Tuan, better known – and now immortalized in street names in just about every Vietnamese town – as **Tran Hung Dao**. Although the invading forces captured Thang Long (Hanoi) they never managed to defeat the Vietnamese in a decisive battle and in the end the forces of the Tran Dynasty were victorious.

Le Dynasty and the emergence of Vietnam

Le Loi

During its struggle with the Cham, nascent Dai Viet had to contend with the weight of Ming Chinese oppression from the north, often in concert with their Cham allies. Despite 1000 years of Chinese domination and centuries of internal dynastic squabbles the Viet retained a strong sense of national identity and were quick to respond to charismatic leadership. As so often in Vietnam's history one man was able to harness nationalistic sentiment and mould the country's discontent into a powerful fighting force: in 1426 it was Le Loi. Together with the brilliant tactician **Nguyen Trai**, Le Loi led a campaign to remove the Chinese from Vietnamese soil. Combining surprise, guerrilla tactics and Nguyen Trai's innovative and famous propaganda, designed to convince defending Ming of the futility of their position, the Viet won a resounding victory which led to the enlightened and artistically distinguished Le period. Le Loi's legendary victory lives on in popular form and is celebrated in the tale of the restored sword in water puppet performances across the country. Following his victory against the Ming he claimed the throne in 1428 and reigned until his death five years later.

Le Thanh Ton

With Le Loi's death the Le Dynasty worked its way through a succession of young kings who seemed to hold the throne barely long enough to warm the cushions before they were murdered. It was not until 1460 that a king of substance was to accede: Le Thanh Ton (reigned 1460-1497). His reign was a period of great scholarship and artistic accomplishment. He established the system of rule that was to guide successive Vietnamese emperors for 500 years. He also mounted a series of military campaigns, some as far as Laos to the west.

Le expansion

The expansion of the Vietnamese state, under the Le, south from its heartland in the Tonkin Delta, followed the decline of the Cham Kingdom at the end of the 15th century. By the early 18th century the Cham were extinct as an identifiable political and military force and the Vietnamese advanced still further south into the Khmer-controlled territories of the Mekong Delta. This geographical over-extension and the sheer logistical impracticability of ruling from distant Hanoi, disseminating edicts and collecting taxes, led to the disintegration of the – ever tenuous – imperial rule. The old adage 'The edicts of the emperor stop at the village gate' was particularly apt more than 1000 km from the capital. Noble families, locally dominant, challenged the emperor's authority and the Le Dynasty gradually dissolved into internecine strife and regional fiefdoms, namely Trinh in the north and Nguyen in the south, a pattern that was to reassert itself 300 years later. But although on paper the Vietnamese – now consisting of two dynastic houses, Trinh and Nguyen – appeared powerful, the people were mired in poverty.

There were numerous peasant rebellions in this period, of which the most serious was the **Tay Son rebellion** of 1771. One of the three Tay Son brothers, Nguyen Hué, proclaimed himself **Emperor Quang Trung** in 1788, only to die four years later.

The death of Quang Trung paved the way for the establishment of the **Nguyen Dynasty** (the last Vietnamese dynasty) in 1802 when Emperor Gia Long ascended to the throne in Hué. Despite the fact that this period heralded the arrival of the French, it is regarded as a golden period in Vietnamese history. During the Nguyen Dynasty, Vietnam was unified as a single state and Hué emerged as the heart of the kingdom.

History of the non-Viet civilizations

Any history of Vietnam must include the non-Vietnamese peoples and civilizations. The central and southern parts of Vietnam have only relatively recently been dominated by the Viets. Before that, these lands were in the hands of people of Indian or Khmer origins.

Funan (AD 100-600)

According to Chinese sources, Funan was a Hindu kingdom founded in the first century AD with its capital, Vyadhapura, close to the Mekong River near the border with Cambodia. A local legend records that Kaundinya, a great Indian Brahmin, acting on a dream, sailed to the coast of Vietnam carrying with him a bow and arrow. When he arrived, Kaundinya shot the arrow and where it landed he established the capital of Funan. Following this act, Kaundinya married the princess Soma, daughter of the local King of the Nagas (giant water serpents). The legend symbolizes the union between Indian and local cultural traditions – the naga representing indigenous fertility rites and customs, and the arrow, the potency of the Hindu religion.

Oc-Eo

Funan built its wealth and power on its strategic location on the sea route between China and the islands to the south. Maritime technology at the time forced seafarers travelling between China and island Southeast Asia and India to stop and wait for the winds to change before they could continue on their way. This sometimes meant a stay of up to five months. The large port city of Oc-Eo offered a safe harbour for merchant vessels and the revenues generated enabled the kings of the empire to expand rice cultivation, dominate a host of surrounding vassal states as far away as the Malay coast and South Burma, and build a series of impressive temples, cities and irrigation works. Although the Chinese chronicler K'ang T'ai records that the Funanese were barbarians – "ugly, black, and frizzy-haired" – it is clear from Chinese court annals that they were artistically and technologically accomplished. It is recorded for example that one Chinese emperor was so impressed by the skill of some visiting musicians in AD 263 that he ordered the establishment of an institute of Funanese music.

Funan reached the peak of its powers in the fourth century and went into decline during the fifth century AD when improving maritime technology made Oc-Eo redundant as a haven for sailing vessels. No longer did merchants hug the coastline; ships were now large enough, and navigation skills sophisticated enough, to make the journey from South China to the Malacca Strait without landfall. By the mid-sixth century, Funan, having suffered from a drawn-out leadership crisis, was severely weakened. Neighbouring competing powers took advantage of this crisis, absorbing previously Funan-controlled lands. Irrigation works fell into disrepair as state control weakened and peasants left the fields to seek more productive lands elsewhere. The Cham ultimately conquered Funan, having lost both the economic wealth and the religious legitimacy on which its power had been based.

What is interesting about Funan is the degree to which it provided a model for future states in Southeast Asia. Funan's wealth was built on its links with the sea, and with its ability to exploit maritime trade. The later rulers of Champa, Langkasuka (Malaya), Srivijaya (Sumatra) and Malacca (Malaya) repeated this formula.

Champa (AD 200–1720)

In South Vietnam, where the dynastic lords achieved hegemony only in the 18th century, the kingdom of Champa – or Lin-yi as the Chinese called it – was the most significant power. The kingdom evolved in the second century AD and was focused on the narrow ribbon of lowland that runs north-south down the Annamite coast with its various capitals near the present-day city of Danang. Chinese sources record that in AD 192 a local official, Kiu-lien, rejected Chinese authority and established an independent kingdom. From then on, Champa's history was one of conflict with its neighbour; when Imperial China was powerful, Champa was subservient and sent ambassadors and tributes in homage to the Chinese court; when it was weak, the rulers of Champa extended their own influence and ignored the Chinese.

The difficulty for scholars is to decide whether Champa had a single identity or whether it consisted of numerous mini-powers with no dominant centre. The accepted wisdom at the moment is that Champa was more diffuse than previously thought and that only rarely during its history is it possible to talk of Champa in singular terms. The endless shifting of the capital of Champa is taken to reflect the shifting centres of power that characterized this kingdom.

Like Funan, Champa built its power on its position on the maritime trading route through Southeast Asia. During the fourth century, as Champa expanded into formerly Funan-controlled lands, they came under the influence of the Indian cultural traditions of the Funanese. These were enthusiastically embraced by Champa's rulers who tacked the suffix '-varman' onto their names (for example Bhadravarman) and adopted the Hindu-Buddhist cosmology. Though a powerful trading kingdom, Champa was geographically poorly endowed. The coastal strip between the Annamite highlands to the west, and the sea to the east, is narrow and the potential for extensive rice cultivation limited. This may explain why the Champa Empire was never more than a moderate power: it was unable to produce the agricultural surplus necessary to support an extensive court and army, and therefore could not compete with either the Khmers to the south nor with the Viets to the north. But the Cham were able to carve out a niche for themselves between the two, and to many art historians, their art and architecture represent the finest that Vietnam has ever produced (see page 126). Remains are to be found on the central Vietnamese coast from Quang Tri in the north, to Ham Tan 800 km to the south.

For over 1000 years the Cham resisted the Chinese and the Vietnamese. But by the time Marco Polo wrote of the Cham, their power and prestige were much reduced. After 1285, when invading Mongol hordes were repelled by the valiant Viets, Champa and Dai Viet enjoyed an uneasy peace maintained by the liberal flow of royal princesses south across the Col des Nuages (Hai Van Pass) in exchange for territory. During the peaceful reign of Che A-nan a Franciscan priest, Odoric of Pordenone, reported of Champa "'tis a very fine country, having a great store of victuals and of all good things". Of particular interest, he refers to the practice of suti, writing "When a man dies in this country, they burn his wife with him, for they say that she should live with him in the other world also". Clearly, some of the ancient Indian traditions continued.

Champa saw a late flowering under King Binasuos who led numerous successful campaigns against the Viet, culminating in the sack of Hanoi in 1371. Subsequently, the treachery of a low-ranking officer led to Binasuos' death in 1390 and the military eclipse of the Cham by the Vietnamese. The demographic and economic superiority of the Viet coupled with their gradual drift south contributed most to the waning of the Cham Kingdom, but finally, in 1471 the Cham suffered a terrible defeat at the hands of the Vietnamese. 60,000 of their soldiers were killed and another 36,000 captured and carried into captivity, including the King and 50 members of the royal family. The kingdom shrank to a small territory in the vicinity of Nha Trang. It survived until 1720 when members of the royal family and subjects fled to Cambodia to escape from the advancing Vietnamese.

Colonial period

One of the key motivating factors that encouraged the **French** to undermine the authority of the Vietnamese emperors was their treatment of Roman Catholics. Jesuits had been in the country from as early as the 17th century – one of them, Alexandre-de-Rhodes, converted the Vietnamese writing system from Chinese characters to Romanized script – but persecution of Roman Catholics began only in the 1830s. Emperor Minh Mang issued an imperial edict outlawing the dissemination of Christianity as a heterodox creed in 1825. The first European priest to be executed was François Isidore Gagelin who was strangled by six soldiers as he knelt on a scaffold in Hué in 1833. Three days later, having been told that Christians believe they will come to life again, Minh Mang had the body exhumed to confirm the man's death. In 1840 Minh Mang actually read the Old Testament in Chinese translation, declaring it to be 'absurd'.

Yet Christianity continued to spread as Buddhism declined and there was a continual stream of priests willing to risk their lives proselytizing. In addition, the economy was in disarray and natural disasters common. Poor Vietnamese saw Christianity as a way to break the shackles of their feudal existence. Fearing a peasants' revolt, the Emperor ordered the execution of 25 European priests, 300 Vietnamese priests, and 30,000 Vietnamese Catholics between 1848 and 1860. Provoked by these killings, the French attacked and took Saigon in 1859. In 1862 **Emperor Tu Duc** signed a treaty ceding the three southern provinces to the French, thereby creating the colony of **Cochin China**. This treaty of 1862 effectively paved the way for the eventual seizure by the French of the whole kingdom. The French, through weight of arms, also forced the Emperor to end the persecution of Christians in his kingdom. In retrospect, although many Christians did die cruelly, the degree of persecution was not on the scale of similar episodes elsewhere: Minh Mang's successors Thieu Tri (1841-1847) and Tu Duc (1847-1883), though both fervently anti-Christian, appreciated French military strength and the fact that they were searching for pretexts to intervene.

Ho Chi Minh: 'He who enlightens'

Ho Chi Minh, one of a number of pseudonyms Ho adopted during his life was born Nguyen Sinh Cung, or possibly Nguyen Van Thanh (Ho did not keep a diary during much of his life, so parts of his life are still a mystery), in Nghe An Province near Vinh on 19 May 1890, and came from a poor scholar-gentry family. In the village, the family was aristocratic; beyond it they were little more than peasants. His father, though not a revolutionary, was a dissenter and rather than go to Hué to serve the French, he chose to work as a village school teacher. Ho must have been influenced by his father's implacable animosity towards the French, although Ho's early years are obscure. He went to Quoc Hoc College in Hué and then worked for a while as a teacher in Phan Thiet, a fishing village in South Annam.

In 1911, under the name Nguyen Tat Thanh, he travelled to Saigon and left the country as a messboy on the French ship Amiral Latouche-Tréville. He is said to have used the name 'Ba' so that he would not shame his family by accepting such lowly work. This marked the beginning of three years of travel during which he visited France, England, America (where the skyscrapers of Manhattan both amazed and appalled him) and North Africa. Seeing the colonialists on their own turf and reading such revolutionary literature as the French Communist Party newspaper L'Humanité, he was converted to Communism. In Paris he mixed with leftists, wrote pamphlets and attended meetings of the French Socialist Party. He also took odd jobs: for a while he worked at the Carlton Hotel in London and became an assistant pastry chef under the legendary French chef Georges Escoffier.

An even more unlikely story emerges from Gavin Young's A Wavering Grace. In the book he recounts an interview he conducted with Mae West in 1968 shortly after he had returned from reporting the Tet offensive. On hearing of Vietnam, Mae West innocently said that she "used to know someone very, very important there ... His name was Ho ... Ho ... Ho something". At the time she was staying at the Carlton while starring in a London show, Sex. She confided to Young: "There was this waiter, cook, I don't know what he was. I know he had the slinkiest eyes though. We met in the corridor. We – well ..." Young writes that "Her voice trailed off in a husky sigh ..."

Gradually Ho became an even more committed Communist, contributing articles to radical newspapers and working his way into the web of Communist and leftist groups. At the same time he remained, curiously, a

The **French conquest of the north** was motivated by a desire to control trade and the route to what were presumed to be the vast riches of China. In 1883 and 1884, the French forced the Emperor to sign treaties making Vietnam a French protectorate. In August 1883 for example, just after Tu Duc's death, a French fleet appeared off Hué to force concessions. François Harmand, a native affairs official on board one of the ships, threatened the Vietnamese by stating: "Imagine all that is terrible and it will still be less than reality ... the word 'Vietnam' will be erased from history." The emperor called on China for assistance and demanded that provinces resist French rule; but the imperial bidding proved ineffective, and in 1885 the **Treaty of Tientsin** recognized the French protectorates of Tonkin (North Vietnam) and Annam (Central Vietnam), to add to that of Cochin China (South Vietnam).

French cultural chauvinist, complaining for example about the intrusion of English words like *le manager* and *le challenger* (referring to boxing contests) into the French language. He even urged the French prime minister to ban foreign words from the French press. In 1923 he left France for Moscow and was trained as a Communist activist – effectively a spy. From there, Ho travelled to Canton where he was instrumental in forming the Vietnamese Communist movement. This culminated in the creation of the Indochina Communist Party in 1930. His movements during these years are scantily documented: he became a Buddhist monk in Siam (Thailand), was arrested in Hong Kong for subversive activities and received a six-month sentence, travelled to China several times, and in 1940 even returned to Vietnam for a short period – his first visit for nearly 30 years. Despite his absence from the country, the French had already recognized the threat that he posed and sentenced him to death in absentia in 1930. He did not adopt the pseudonym by which he is now best known – Ho Chi Minh – until the early 1940s.

Ho was a consummate politician and, despite his revolutionary fervour, a great realist. He was also a charming man, and during his stay in France between June and October 1946 he made a great number of friends. Robert Shaplen in his book *The Lost Revolution* (1965) talks of his "wit, his oriental courtesy, his savoir-faire ... above all his seeming sincerity and simplicity". He talked with farmers and fishermen and debated with priests; he impressed people wherever he travelled. He died in Hanoi at his house in the former governor's residence in 1969 (see page 78).

Since the demise of Communism in the former Soviet Union, the Vietnamese leadership have been concerned that secrets about Ho's life might be gleaned from old comintern files in Moscow by nosy journalists. To thwart such an eventuality, they have, reportedly, sent a senior historian to scour the archives. To date, Ho's image remains largely untarnished – making him an exception amongst the tawdry league of former Communist leaders. But a Moscow-based reporter has unearthed evidence implying Ho was married, challenging the official hagiography that paints Ho as a celibate who committed his entire life to the revolution. It takes a brave Vietnamese to challenge established 'fact'. In 1991, when the popular Vietnamese Youth or *Tuoi Tre* newspaper dared to suggest that Ho had married Tang Tuyet Minh in China in 1926, the editor was summarily dismissed from her post.

Resistance to the French: the prelude to revolution

Like other European powers in Southeast Asia, the French managed to achieve military victory with ease, but they failed to stifle Vietnamese nationalism. After 1900, as Chinese translations of the works of Rousseau, Voltaire and social Darwinists such as Herbert Spence began to find their way into the hands of the Vietnamese intelligentsia, so resistance grew. Foremost among these early nationalists were Phan Boi Chau (1867-1940) and Phan Chau Trinh (1871-1926) who wrote tracts calling for the expulsion of the French. But these men and others such as Prince Cuong De (1882-1951) were traditional nationalists, their beliefs rooted in Confucianism rather than revolutionary Marxism. Their perspectives were essentially in the tradition of the nationalists who had resisted Chinese domination.

Quoc Dan Dang (VNQDD), founded at the end of 1927, was the first nationalist party, while the first significant Communist group was the **Indochina Communist Party (ICP)** established by **Ho Chi Minh** in 1930 (see box, page 201). Both the VNQDD and the ICP organized resistance to the French and there were numerous strikes and uprisings, particularly during the harsh years of the Great Depression. The Japanese 'occupation' from August 1940 (Vichy France permitted the Japanese full access to military facilities in exchange for allowing continued French administrative control) saw the creation of the **Viet Minh** to fight for the liberation of Vietnam from Japanese and French control.

Vietnam wars

First Indochina War (1945–1954)

The Vietnam War started in September 1945 in the south of the country and in 1946 in the north. These years marked the onset of fighting between the Viet Minh and the French and the period is usually referred to as the First Indochina War. The Communists, who had organized against the Japanese, proclaimed the creation of the **Democratic Republic of Vietnam (DRV)** on 2 September 1945 when Ho Chi Minh read out the Vietnamese **Declaration of Independence** in Hanoi's Ba Dinh Square. The US was favourably disposed towards the Viet Minh and Ho. Operatives of the OSS (the wartime precursor to the CIA) met Ho and supported his efforts during the war and afterwards Roosevelt's inclination was to prevent France claiming their colony back. Only Winston Churchill's persuasion changed his mind.

The French, although they had always insisted that Vietnam be returned to French rule, were in no position to force the issue. Instead, in the south, it was British troops (mainly Gurkhas) who helped the small force of French against the Viet Minh. Incredibly, the British also ordered the Japanese, who had only just capitulated, to help fight the Vietnamese. When 35,000 French reinforcements arrived, the issue in the south – at least superficially – was all but settled, with Ca Mau at the southern extremity of the country falling on 21 October. From that point, the war in the south became an underground battle of attrition, with the north providing support to their southern comrades.

In the north, the Viet Minh had to deal with 180,000 rampaging Nationalist Chinese troops, while preparing for the imminent arrival of a French force. Unable to confront both at the same time, and deciding that the French were probably the lesser of two evils, Ho Chi Minh decided to negotiate. To make the DRV government more acceptable to the French, Ho proceeded cautiously, only nationalizing a few strategic industries, bringing moderates into the government, and actually dissolving the Indochina Communist Party (at least on paper) in November 1945. But in the same month Ho also said: "The French colonialists should know that the Vietnamese people do not wish to spill blood, that it loves peace. But if it must sacrifice millions of combatants, lead a resistance for long years to defend the independence of the country, and preserve its children from slavery, it will do so. It is certain the resistance will win."

Chinese withdrawal

In February 1946, the French and Chinese signed a treaty leading to the withdrawal of Chinese forces and shortly afterwards Ho concluded a treaty with French President de Gaulle's special emissary to Vietnam, Jean Sainteny, in which Vietnam was acknowledged as a 'free' (the Vietnamese word *doc lap* being translated as free, but not yet independent) state that was within the French Union and the Indochinese Federation.

It is interesting to note that in negotiating with the French, Ho was going against most of his supporters who argued for confrontation. But Ho, ever a pragmatist, believed at this stage that the Viet Minh were ill-trained and poorly armed and he appreciated the need for time to consolidate their position. The episode that is usually highlighted as the flashpoint that led to the resumption of hostilities was the French government's decision to open a customs house in Haiphong at the end of 1946. The Viet Minh forces resisted and the rest, as they say, is history. It seems that during the course of 1946 Ho changed his view of the best path to independence. Initially he asked: "Why should we sacrifice 50 or 100,000 men when we can achieve independence within five years through negotiation?" although he later came to the conclusion that it was necessary to fight for independence. The customs house episode might, therefore, be viewed as merely an excuse. The French claimed that 5000 Vietnamese were killed in the ensuing bombardment, versus five Frenchmen; the Vietnamese put the toll at 20,000.

In a pattern that was to become characteristic of the entire 25-year conflict, while the French controlled the cities, the Viet Minh were dominant in the countryside. By the end of 1949, with the success of the Chinese Revolution and the establishment of the Democratic People's Republic of Korea (North Korea) in 1948, the US began to offer support to the French in an attempt to stem the 'Red Tide' that seemed to be sweeping across Asia. At this early stage, the odds appeared stacked against the Viet Minh, but Ho was confident that time was on their side. As he remarked to Sainteny "If we have to fight, we will fight. You can kill 10 of my men for every one I kill of yours but even at those odds, I will win and you will lose". It also became increasingly clear that the French were not committed to negotiating a route to independence. A secret French report prepared in 1948 was obtained and published by the Viet Minh in which the High Commissioner, Monsieur Bollaert, wrote: "It is my impression that we must make a concession to Vietnam of the term, independence; but I am convinced that this word need never be interpreted in any light other than that of a religious verbalism."

Dien Bien Phu (1954) and the Geneva Agreement
The decisive battle of the First Indochina War was at Dien Bien Phu in the hills of the northwest, close to the border with Laos. At the end of 1953 the French, with American support, parachuted 16,000 men into the area in an attempt to protect Laos from Viet Minh incursions and to tempt them into open battle. The French in fact found themselves trapped, surrounded by Viet Minh and overlooked by artillery. There was some suggestion that the US might become involved, and even use tactical nuclear weapons, but this was not to be. In May 1954 the French surrendered – the most humiliating of French colonial defeats – effectively marking the end of the French presence in Indochina. In July 1954, in Geneva, the French and Vietnamese agreed to divide the country along the 17th parallel, so creating two states – the Communists occupying the north and the non-Communists occupying the south. The border was kept open for 300 days and over that period about 900,000 – mostly Roman Catholic – Vietnamese travelled south. At the same time nearly 90,000 Viet Minh troops along with 43,000 civilians went north, although many Viet Minh remained in the south to continue the fight there.

Second Indochina War (1954-1975)
The Vietnam War, but particularly the American part of that war, is probably the most minutely studied, reported, analysed and recorded in history. Yet, as with all wars, there are still large grey areas and continuing disagreement over important episodes. Most crucially, there is the question of whether the US might have won had their forces

been given a free hand and were not forced, as some would have it, to fight with one hand tied behind their backs. This remains the view among many members of the US military.

Ngo Dinh Diem

At the time of the partition of Vietnam along the 17th parallel, the government in the south was chaotic and the Communists could be fairly confident that in a short time their sympathizers would be victorious. This situation was to change with the rise of Ngo Dinh Diem. Born in Hué in 1901 to a Roman Catholic Confucian family, Diem wished to become a priest. He graduated at the top of his class from the French School of Administration and at the age of 32 was appointed to the post of minister of the interior at the court of Emperor Bao Dai. Here, according to the political scientist William Turley, "he worked with uncommon industry and integrity" only to resign in exasperation at court intrigues and French interference. He withdrew from political activity during the First Indochina War and in 1946 Ho Chi Minh offered him a post in the DRV government – an offer he declined.

In July 1954 Diem returned from his self-imposed exile at the Maryknoll Seminary in New Jersey to become Premier of South Vietnam. It is usually alleged that the US administration was behind his rise to power, although this has yet to be proved. He held two rigged elections (in October 1955, 450,000 registered voters cast 605,025 votes) that gave some legitimacy to his administration in American eyes. He proceeded to suppress all opposition in the country. His brutal brother, Ngo Dinh Nhu, was appointed to head the security forces and terrorized much of Vietnamese society.

During the period of Diem's premiership, opposition to his rule, particularly in the countryside, increased. This was because the military's campaign against the Viet Minh targeted – both directly and indirectly – many innocent peasants. At the same time, the nepotism and corruption that was endemic within the administration also turned many people into Viet Minh sympathizers. That said, Diem's campaign was successful in under-mining the strength of the Communist Party in the south. While there were perhaps 50,000-60,000 party members in 1954, this figure had declined through widespread arrests and intimidation to only 5000 by 1959.

The erosion of the Party in the south gradually led, from 1959, to the north changing its strategy towards one of more overt military confrontation. The same year also saw the establishment of Group 559, which was charged with the task of setting up what was to become the Ho Chi Minh Trail, along which supplies and troops were moved from the north to the south (see box, page 165). But, even at this stage, the Party's forces in the south were kept from open confrontation and many of its leaders were hoping for victory without having to resort to open warfare. There was no call for a 'People's War' and armed resistance was left largely to guerrillas belonging to the Cao Dai and Hoa Hao (Buddhist millenarian) sects. The establishment of the National Liberation Front of Vietnam in 1960 was an important political and organizational development towards creating a credible alternative to Diem – although it did not hold its first congress until 1962.

Escalation of the armed conflict (1959-1963)

Viet Cong

The armed conflict began to intensify from the beginning of 1961 when all the armed forces under the Communists' control were unified under the banner of the **People's Liberation Armed Forces (PLAF)**. By this time the Americans were already using the term Viet Cong (or VC) to refer to Communist troops. They reasoned that the victory at Dien Bien Phu had conferred almost heroic status on the name Viet Minh. American psychological warfare specialists therefore invented the term Viet Cong, an abbreviation of *Viet-nam Cong-san* (or Vietnamese Communists) and persuaded the media in Saigon to begin substituting it for Viet Minh from 1956.

The election of **John F Kennedy** to the White House in January 1961 coincided with the Communists' decision to widen the war in the south. In the same year Kennedy dispatched 400 special forces troops and 100 special military advisers to Vietnam, in flagrant contravention of the Geneva Agreement. With the cold war getting colder, and Soviet Premier Nikita Khrushchev confirming his support for wars of 'national liberation', Kennedy could not back down and by the end of 1962 there were 11,000 US personnel in South Vietnam. At the same time the NLF had around 23,000 troops at its disposal. Kennedy was still saying that: "In the final analysis, it's their war and they're the ones who have to win or lose it". But just months after the Bay of Pigs debacle in Cuba, Washington set out on the path that was ultimately to lead to America's first large-scale military defeat.

The bungling and incompetence of the forces of the south, the interference that US advisers and troops had to face, the misreading of the situation by US military commanders, and the skill – both military and political – of the Communists, are most vividly recounted in Neil Sheehan's massive book, *A Bright Shining Lie*. The conflict quickly escalated from 1959. The north infiltrated about 44,000 men and women into the south between then and 1964, while the number recruited in the south was between 60,000 and 100,000. In August 1959, the first consignment of arms was carried down the **Ho Chi Minh Trail** into South Vietnam. Meanwhile, Kennedy began supporting, arming and training the Army of the Republic of Vietnam (ARVN). The US however, shied away from any large-scale, direct confrontation between its forces and the Viet Cong.

An important element in Diem's military strategy at this time was the establishment of **strategic hamlets**, better known simply as 'hamleting'. This strategy was modelled on British anti-guerrilla warfare during Malaya's Communist insurgency, and aimed to deny the Communists any bases of support in the countryside while at the same time making it more difficult for Communists to infiltrate the villages and 'propagandize' there. The villages which were ringed by barbed wire were labelled 'concentration camps' by the Communists, and the often brutal, forced relocation that peasants had to endure probably turned even more of them into Communist sympathizers. Of the 7000-8000 villages sealed in this way, only a fifth could ever have been considered watertight.

In January 1963 at **Ap Bac**, not far from the town of My Tho, the Communists scored their first significant victory in the south. Facing 2000 well-armed ARVN troops, a force of just 300-400 PLAF inflicted heavy casualties and downed five helicopters. After this defeat, many American advisers drew the conclusion that if the Communists were to be defeated, it could not be left to the ARVN alone – US troops would have to become directly involved.

In mid-1963 a Buddhist monk from Hué committed suicide by dousing his body with petrol and setting it alight. This was the first of a number of **self-immolations**, suggesting that even in the early days the Diem regime was not only losing the military war but also the 'hearts and minds' war. He responded with characteristic heavy handedness by ransacking suspect pagodas. On 2 December 1963, Diem and his brother Nhu were both assassinated during an army coup.

American war in Vietnam

The US decision to enter the war has been the subject of considerable disagreement. Until recently, the received wisdom was that the US administration had already taken the decision, and manufactured events to justify their later actions. However, the recent publication of numerous State Department, Presidential, CIA, Defence Department and National Security Council files – all dating from 1964 – has shed new light on events leading up to American intervention (these files are contained in the United States Government Printing Office's 1108 page-long *Vietnam 1964*).

In Roger Warner's *Back Fire* (1995), which deals largely with the CIA's secret war in Laos, he recounts a story of a war game commissioned by the Pentagon and played by the Rand Corporation in 1962. They were asked to play a week-long game simulating a 10-year conflict in Vietnam. At the end of the week, having committed 500,000 men, the US forces were bogged down, there was student unrest and the American population had lost confidence in their leaders and in the conduct of the war. When the game was played a year later but, on the insistence of the US Air Force, with much heavier aerial bombing, the conclusions were much the same. If only, if only …

By all accounts, **Lyndon Johnson** was a reluctant warrior. In the 1964 presidential campaign he repeatedly said: "We don't want our American boys to do the fighting for Asian boys". This was not just for public consumption. The files show that LBJ always doubted the wisdom of intervention. But he also believed that John F Kennedy had made a solemn pledge to help the South Vietnamese people, a pledge that he was morally obliged to keep. In most respects, LBJ was completely in agreement with Congress, together with sections of the American public, who were disquietened by events in South Vietnam. The Buddhist monk's self-immolation, broadcast on prime-time news, did not help matters.

It has usually been argued that the executive manufactured the **Gulf of Tonkin Incident** to force Congress and the public to approve an escalation of America's role in the conflict. It was reported that two American destroyers, the *USS Maddox* and *USS C Turner Joy*, were attacked without provocation in international waters on the 2 August 1964 by North Vietnamese patrol craft. The US responded by bombing shore installations while presenting the Gulf of Tonkin Resolution to an outraged Congress for approval. Only two Congressmen voted against the resolution and President Johnson's poll rating jumped from 42% to 72%. In reality, the *USS Maddox* had been involved in electronic intelligence-gathering while supporting clandestine raids by South Vietnamese mercenaries – well inside North Vietnamese territorial waters. This deception only became apparent in 1971 when the **Pentagon papers**, documenting the circumstances behind the incident, were leaked to the *New York Times* (the Pentagon papers were commissioned by Defense Secretary McNamara in June 1967 and written by 36 Indochina experts).

But these events are not sufficient to argue that the incident was manufactured to allow LBJ to start an undeclared war against North Vietnam. On 4 August, Secretary of State Dean Rusk told the American representative at the United Nations that: "In no sense is this destroyer a pretext to make a big thing out of a little thing". Even as late as the end of 1964, the President was unconvinced by arguments that the US should become more deeply involved. On 31 August, McGeorge Bundy wrote in a memorandum to Johnson: "A still more drastic possibility which no one is discussing is the use of substantial US armed forces in operation against the Viet Cong. I myself believe that before we let this country go we should have a hard look at this grim alternative, and I do not at all think that it is a repetition of Korea."

But events overtook President Johnson, and by 1965 the US was firmly embarked on the road to defeat. In March 1965, he ordered the beginning of the air war against the north perhaps acting on Air Force General Curtis Le May's observation that "we are swatting flies when we should be going after the manure pile". **Operation Rolling Thunder**, the most intense bombing campaign any country had yet experienced, began in March 1965 and ran through to October 1968. In 3½ years, twice the tonnage of bombs was dropped on Vietnam (and Laos) as during the entire Second World War. During its peak in 1967, 12,000 sorties were being flown each month – a total of 108,000 were flown throughout 1967. North Vietnam claimed that 4000 out of its 5788 villages were hit. Most terrifying were the B-52s that dropped their bombs from such an altitude (17,000 m) that the attack could not even be heard until the bombs hit their targets. Each aircraft carried 20 tonnes of bombs. By the end of the American war in 1973, 14 million tonnes of all types of munitions had been used in Indochina, an explosive force representing 700 times that of the atomic bomb dropped on Hiroshima. As General Curtis Le May explained on 25 November 1965 – "We should bomb them back into the Stone Age". In the same month that Rolling Thunder commenced, marines landed at Danang to defend its airbase, and by June 1965 there were 74,000 US troops in Vietnam. Despite President Johnson's reluctance to commit the US to the conflict, events forced his hand. He realized that the undisciplined South Vietnamese could not prevent a Communist victory. Adhering to the domino theory, and with his own and the US's reputation at stake, he had no choice. As Johnson is said to have remarked to his press secretary Bill Moyers: "I feel like a hitchhiker caught in a hail storm on a Texas highway. I can't win. I can't hide. And I can't make it stop."

Dispersal of the North's industry

In response to the bombing campaign, industry in the north was decentralized and dispersed to rural areas. Each province was envisaged as a self-sufficient production unit. In order to protect the population in the north, they too were relocated to the countryside. By the end of 1967 Hanoi's population was a mere 250,000 essential citizens – about a quarter of the pre-war figure. The same was true of other urban centres. What the primary US objective was in mounting the air war remains unclear. In part, it was designed to destroy the north's industrial base and its ability to wage war; to dampen the people's will to fight; to sow seeds of discontent; to force the leadership in the north to the negotiating table; and perhaps to punish those in the north for supporting their government. By October 1968 the US realized the bombing was having little effect and they called a halt. The legacy of Operation Rolling Thunder, though, would live on. Turley wrote: "... The bombing had destroyed virtually all industrial, transportation and communications facilities built since 1954, blotted out 10 to 15 years' potential economic growth, flattened three major cities and 12 of 29 province capitals, and triggered a decline in per capita agricultural output".

However, it was not just the bombing campaign that was undermining the north's industrial and agricultural base. Socialist policies in the countryside were labelling small land owners as 'landlords' – in effect, traitors to the revolutionary cause – thus alienating many farmers. In the cities, industrial policies were no less short-sighted. Though Ho's policies in the battlefield were driven by hard-headed pragmatism, in the field of economic development they were informed – tragically – by revolutionary fervour.

William Westmoreland, the general appointed to command the American effort, aimed to use the superior firepower and mobility of the US to 'search and destroy' PAVN forces. North Vietnamese bases in the south were to be identified using modern technology, jungle hideouts revealed by dumping chemical defoliants and then attacked with shells, bombs and by helicopter-borne troops. In 'free-fire zones' the army and air force were permitted to use whatever level of firepower they felt necessary to dislodge the enemy. 'Body counts' became the measure of success and collateral damage – or civilian casualties – was a cost that just had to be borne. As one field commander famously explained: 'We had to destroy the town to save it'. By 1968 the US had more than 500,000 troops in Vietnam, while **South Korean, Australian, New Zealand, Filipino** and **Thai** forces contributed another 90,000. The ARVN officially had 1.5 million men under arms (100,000 or more of these were 'flower' or phantom soldiers, the pay for whom was pocketed by officers in an increasingly corrupt ARVN). Ranged against this vastly superior force were perhaps 400,000 PAVN and National Liberation Front forces.

1964-1968: who was winning?

The leadership in the north tried to allay serious anxieties about their ability to defeat the American-backed south by emphasizing human over physical and material resources. **Desertions** from the ARVN were very high – there were 113,000 from the army in 1965 alone (200,000 in 1975) – and the PAVN did record a number of significant victories. The Communists also had to deal with large numbers of desertions – 28,000 men in 1969. By 1967 world opinion, and even American public opinion, appeared to be swinging against the war. Within the US, **anti-war demonstrations** and 'teach-ins' were spreading, officials were losing confidence in the ability of the US to win the war, and the president's approval rating was sinking fast.

But although the Communists may have been winning the psychological and public opinion wars, they were increasingly hard-pressed to maintain this advantage on the ground. Continual American strikes against their bases, and the social and economic dislocations in the countryside, were making it more difficult for the Communists to recruit supporters. At the same time, the fight against a vastly better equipped enemy was also taking its toll in sheer exhaustion. Despite what is now widely regarded as a generally misguided US military strategy in Vietnam, there were notable US successes (for example, the Phoenix Programme, see page 210). American GIs were always sceptical about the 'pacification' programmes that aimed to win the 'hearts and minds' war. GIs were fond of saying, "If you've got them by the balls, their hearts and minds will follow". At times, the US military and politicians appeared to view the average Vietnamese as inferior to the average American. This latent racism was reflected in General Westmoreland's remark that Vietnamese "don't think about death the way we do" and in the use by most US servicemen of the derogatory name "gook" to refer to Vietnamese.

At the same time as the Americans were trying to win 'hearts and minds', the Vietnamese were also busy indoctrinating their men and women, and the population in the 'occupied' south. In Bao Ninh's moving *The Sorrow of War* (1994), the main character, Kien, who fights with a scout unit describes the indoctrination that accompanied the soldiers from their barracks to the field: "Politics continuously. Politics in the morning, politics in the afternoon, politics again in the evening. 'We won, the enemy lost. The enemy will surely lose. The north had a good harvest, a bumper harvest. The people will rise up and welcome you. Those who don't just lack awareness. The world is divided into three camps.' More politics."

By 1967, the war had entered a period of military (though not political) stalemate. As Robert McNamara writes in his book *In Retrospect: the Tragedy and Lessons of Vietnam*, it was at this stage that he came to believe that Vietnam was "a problem with no solution". In retrospect, he argues that the US should have withdrawn in late 1963, and certainly by late

1967. Massive quantities of US arms and money were preventing the Communists from making much headway in urban areas, while American and ARVN forces were ineffective in the countryside – although incessant bombing and ground assaults wreaked massive destruction. A black market of epic proportions developed in Saigon, as millions of dollars of assistance went astray. American journalist Stanley Karnow once remarked to a US official that "we could probably buy off the Vietcong at US$500 a head". The official replied that they had already calculated the costs, but came to "US$2500 a head".

Tet Offensive, 1968: the beginning of the end

By mid-1967, the Communist leadership in the north felt it was time for a further escalation of the war in the south to regain the initiative. They began to lay the groundwork for what was to become known as the Tet (or New Year) Offensive – perhaps the single most important series of battles during the American War in Vietnam. During the early morning of 1 February 1968, shortly after noisy celebrations had welcomed in the New Year, 84,000 Communist troops simultaneously attacked targets in 105 urban centres. Utterly surprising the US and South Vietnamese, the Tet Offensive had begun.

Preparations for the offensive had been laid over many months. Arms, ammunition and guerrillas were smuggled and infiltrated into urban areas and detailed planning was undertaken. Central to the strategy was a 'sideshow' at **Khe Sanh**. By mounting an attack on the marine outpost at Khe Sanh, the Communists convinced the American and Vietnamese commanders that another Dien Bien Phu was underway. General Westmoreland moved 50,000 US troops away from the cities and suburbs to prevent any such humiliating repetition of the French defeat. But Khe Sanh was just a diversion, a feint designed to draw attention away from the cities. In this the Communists were successful; for days after the Tet offensive, Westmoreland and the South Vietnamese President Thieu thought Khe Sanh to be the real objective and the attacks in the cities the decoy.

The most interesting aspect of the Tet Offensive was that although it was a strategic victory for the Communists, it was also a considerable tactical defeat. They may have occupied the US embassy in Saigon for a few hours but, except in Hué, Communist forces were quickly repulsed by US and ARVN troops. The government in the south did not collapse nor did the ARVN. Cripplingly high casualties were inflicted on the Communists – cadres at all echelons were killed – morale was undermined and it became clear that the cities would not rise up spontaneously to support the Communists. Tet, in effect, put paid to the VC as an effective fighting force. The fight was now increasingly taken up by the North Vietnamese Army (NVA). This was to have profound effects on the government of South Vietnam after reunification in 1975; southern Communists and what remained of the political wing of the VC – the government in waiting – were entirely overlooked as northern Communists were given all the positions of political power, a process that continues. This caused intense bitterness at the time and also explains the continued mistrust of many southerners for Hanoi. Walt Rostow wrote in 1995 that "Tet was an utter military and political defeat for the Communists in Vietnam", but adding "yet a political disaster in the United States". But this was not to matter; Westmoreland's request for more troops was turned down and US public support for the war slumped still further as they heard reported that the US embassy itself had been 'over-run'. Those who for years had been claiming it was only a matter of time before the Communists were defeated seemed to be contradicted by the scale and intensity of the offensive. Even President Johnson was stunned by the VC's successes. As it turned out the VC incursion was by a 20-man unit from Sapper Battalion C-10 who were all killed in the action. Their mission was not to take the embassy but to 'make a psychological gesture'. In that regard at least, the mission must have exceeded the leadership's wildest expectations.

The **Phoenix Programme**, established in the wake of the Tet Offensive, aimed to destroy the Communists' political infrastructure in the Mekong Delta. Named after the Vietnamese mythical bird the Phung Hoang, which could fly anywhere, the programme sent CIA-recruited and trained Counter Terror Teams – in effect assassination units – into the countryside. The teams were ordered to try and capture Communist cadres; invariably they fired first and asked questions later. By 1971, it was estimated that the programme had led to the capture of 28,000 members of the VCI (Viet Cong Infrastructure), the death of 20,000 and the defection of a further 17,000. By the early 1970s the countryside in the Mekong Delta was more peaceful than it had been for years; towns that were previously strongholds of the Viet Cong had reverted to the control of the local authorities. Critics have questioned what proportion of those killed, captured and sometimes tortured were Communist cadres, but even Communist documents admit that it seriously undermined their support network in the area. In these terms, the Phoenix Programme was a great success.

The costs

The Tet Offensive concentrated American minds. The costs of the war by that time had been vast. The US budget deficit had risen to 3% of Gross National Product by 1968, inflation was accelerating, and thousands of young men had been killed for a cause that, to many, was becoming less clear by the month. Before the end of the year President Johnson had ended the bombing campaign. Negotiations began in Paris in 1969 to try and secure an honourable settlement for the US. Although the last American combat troops were not to leave until March 1973, the Tet Offensive marked the beginning of the end. It was from that date the Johnson administration began to search seriously for a way out of the conflict. The illegal bombing of Cambodia in 1969 and the resumption of the bombing of the north in 1972 (the most intensive of the entire conflict) were only flurries of action on the way to an inevitable US withdrawal.

Paris Agreement (1972)

US Secretary of State **Henry Kissinger** records the afternoon of 8 October 1972, a Sunday, as the moment when he realized that the Communists were willing to agree a peace treaty. There was a great deal to discuss, particularly whether the treaty would offer the prospect of peaceful reunification, or the continued existence of two states: a Communist north, and non-Communist south. Both sides tried to force the issue: the US mounted further attacks and at the same time strengthened and expanded the ARVN. They also tried to play the 'Madman Nixon' card, arguing that **President Richard Nixon** was such a vehement anti-Communist that he might well resort to the ultimate deterrent, the nuclear bomb. It is true that the PAVN was losing men through desertion and had failed to recover its losses in the Tet Offensive. Bao Ninh in his book *The Sorrow of War* about Kinh, a scout with the PAVN, wrote: "The life of the B3 Infantrymen after the Paris Agreement was a series of long suffering days, followed by months of retreating and months of counter-attacking, withdrawal, then counter-attack. Victory after victory, withdrawal after withdrawal. The path of war seemed endless, desperate, and leading nowhere."

But the Communist leadership knew well that the Americans were committed to withdrawal – the only question was when, so they felt that time was on their side. By 1972, US troops in the south had declined to 95,000, the bulk of whom were support troops. The north gambled on a massive attack to defeat the ARVN and moved 200,000 men towards the demilitarized zone that marked the border between north and south. On 30 March the PAVN crossed into the south and quickly overran large sections of Quang Tri province. Simultaneous attacks were mounted in the west highlands, at Tay Ninh and in the Mekong Delta. For a while it looked as if the south would fall altogether. The US responded by mounting a succession of intense bombing raids that eventually forced the PAVN to retreat. The spring offensive may have failed, but like Tet, it was strategically important, for it demonstrated that without US support the ARVN was unlikely to be able to withstand a Communist attack.

Both sides, by late 1972, were ready to compromise. Against the wishes of South Vietnam's President Nguyen Van Thieu, the US signed a treaty on 27 January 1973, the ceasefire going into effect on the same day. Before the signing, Nixon ordered the bombing of the north – the so-called Christmas Campaign. It lasted 11 days from 18 December (Christmas Day was a holiday) and was the most intensive of the war. With the ceasefire and President Thieu, however shaky, both in place, the US was finally able to back out of its nightmare and the last combat troops left in March 1973.

Final Phase (1973-1975)
The Paris Accord settled nothing; it simply provided a means by which the Americans could withdraw from Vietnam. It was never going to resolve the deep-seated differences between the two regimes and with only a brief lull, the war continued, this time without US troops. Thieu's government was probably in terminal decline even before the peace treaty was signed. Though ARVN forces were at their largest ever and, on paper, considerably stronger than the PAVN, many men were weakly committed to the cause of the south. Corruption was endemic, business was in recession, and political dissent was on the increase. The North's Central Committee formally decided to abandon the Paris Accord in October 1973; by the beginning of 1975 they were ready for the final offensive. It took only until April for the Communists to achieve total victory. ARVN troops deserted in their thousands, and the only serious resistance was offered at Xuan Loc, less than 100 km from Saigon. President Thieu resigned on 27 April. ARVN generals, along with their men, were attempting to flee as the PAVN advanced on Saigon. The end was quick: at 1045 on 30 April a T-54 tank (number 843) crashed its way through the gates of the Presidential Palace, symbolizing the end of the Second Indochina War. For the US, the aftermath of the war would lead to years of soul searching; for Vietnam, to stagnation and isolation. A senior State Department figure, George Ball, reflected afterwards that the war was "probably the greatest single error made by America in its history".

Legacy of the Vietnam War

The Vietnam War (or 'American War' to the Vietnamese) is such an enduring feature of the West's experience of the country that many visitors look out for legacies of the conflict. There is no shortage of physically deformed and crippled Vietnamese. Many men were badly injured during the war, but large numbers also received their injuries while serving in Cambodia (1979-1989). It is tempting to associate deformed children with the enduring effects of the herbicide **Agent Orange** (1.7 million tonnes had been used by 1973), although this has yet to be proven scientifically; American studies claim that there is no significant difference in congenital malformation. One thing is certain: Agent Orange is detectable today only in tiny isolated spots, often near former military bases.

Bomb damage

Bomb damage is most obvious from the air: well over five million tonnes of bombs were dropped on the country (north and south) and there are said to be 20 million bomb craters – the sort of statistic people like to recount, but no one can legitimately verify. Many craters have yet to be filled in and paddy fields are still pockmarked. Some farmers have used these holes in the ground to farm fish and to use as small reservoirs to irrigate vegetable plots. War scrap was one of the country's most valuable exports. The cities in the north are surprisingly devoid of obvious signs of the bombing campaigns; Hanoi remains remarkably intact. In Hué the Citadel and the Forbidden Palace were extensively damaged during the Tet offensive in 1968 although much has now been rebuilt.

Psychological effect of the war

The Vietnamese Communist Party leadership still seem to be preoccupied by the conflict and school children are routinely shown war museums and Ho Chi Minh memorials. But despite the continuing propaganda offensive, people harbour surprisingly little animosity towards America or the West. Indeed, of all Westerners, it is often Americans who are most warmly welcomed, particularly in the south.

But it must be remembered that about 60% of Vietnam's population has been born since the US left in 1973, so have no memory of the American occupation. Probably the least visible but most lasting of all the effects of the war is in the number of elderly widowed women and the number of middle aged women who never married.

The deeper source of antagonism is the continuing divide between the north and south. It was to be expected that the forces of the north would exact their revenge on their foes in the south and many were relieved that the predicted bloodbath didn't materialize. But few would have thought that this revenge would be so long lasting. The 250,000 southern dead are not mourned or honoured, or even acknowledged. Former soldiers are denied jobs and the government doesn't recognize the need for national reconciliation.

This is the multiple legacy of the War on Vietnam and the Vietnamese. The legacy on the US and Americans is more widely appreciated. The key question that still occupies the minds of many, though, is, was it worth it? Economic historian Walt Rostow, ex-Singaporean prime minister Lee Kuan Yew and others would probably answer 'yes'. If the US had not intervened, Communism would have spread farther in Southeast Asia; more dominoes, in their view, would have fallen. In 1973, when the US withdrawal was agreed, Lee Kuan Yew observed that the countries of Southeast Asia were much more resilient and resistant to Communism than they had been, say, at the time of the Tet offensive in 1968. The US presence in Vietnam allowed them to reach this state of affairs. Yet Robert McNamara in his book *In Retrospect: the Tragedy and Lessons of Vietnam*, wrote:

"Although we sought to do the right thing – and believed we were doing the right thing – in my judgment, hindsight proves us wrong. We both overestimated the effects of South Vietnam's loss on the security of the West and failed to adhere to the fundamental principle that, in the final analysis, if the South Vietnamese were to be saved, they had to win the war themselves."

After the war

The Socialist Republic of Vietnam (SRV) was born from the ashes of the Vietnam War on 2 July 1976 when former North and South Vietnam were reunified. Hanoi was proclaimed as the capital of the new country. But few Vietnamese would have guessed that their emergent country would be cast by the US in the mould of a pariah state for almost 18 years. First President George Bush I, and then his successor Bill Clinton, eased the US trade embargo bit by bit in a dance of appeasement and procrastination, as they tried to comfort American business clamouring for a slice of the Vietnamese pie, while also trying to stay on the right side of the vociferous lobby in the US demanding more action on the MIA issue. Appropriately, the embargo, which was first imposed on the former North in May 1964, and then nationwide in 1975, was finally lifted a few days before the celebrations of Tet, Vietnamese New Year, on 4 February 1994.

On the morning of 30 April 1975, just before 1100, a T-54 tank crashed through the gates of the Presidential Palace in Saigon, symbolically marking the end of the Vietnam War. Twenty years later, the same tank – number 843 – became a symbol of the past as parades and celebrations, and a good deal of soul searching, marked the anniversary of the end of the War. To many Vietnamese, in retrospect, 1975 was more a beginning than an end: it was the beginning of a collective struggle to come to terms with the war, to build a nation, to reinvigorate the economy and to excise the ghosts of the past. Two decades after the armies of the South laid down their arms and the last US servicemen and officials frantically fled by helicopter to carriers waiting in the South China Sea, the Vietnamese government is still trying, as they put it, to get people to recognize that 'Vietnam is a country, not a war'. A further 20 years from now, it may seem that only in 1995 did the war truly end.

Re-education camps

The newly formed Vietnam government ordered thousands of people to report for re-education camps in 1975. Those intended were ARVN members, ex-South Vietnam government members and those that had collaborated with the South regime including priests, artists, teachers and doctors. It was seen as a means of revenge and a way of indoctrinating the 'unbelievers' with Communist propaganda. It was reported in the *Indochina Newsletter* in 1982 that some 80 camps existed with an estimated 100,000 still languishing in them seven years after the war ended. Detainees were initially told that they would be detained for between three days and one month. Those that were sent to the camp were forced to undertake physical labour and survived on very little food and without basic medical facilities, all the while undergoing Communist indoctrination.

Boat people

Many Vietnamese also fled, first illegally and then legally through the Orderly Departure Programme. The peak period of the crisis spanned the years 1976-1979, with 270,882 leaving the country in 1979 alone. The flow of refugees slowed during 1980 and 1981 to about 50,000 and until 1988 averaged about 10,000 each year. But in the late 1980s the numbers picked up once again, with most sailing for Hong Kong and leaving from the north. It seems that whereas the majority of those sailing in the first phase (1976-1981) were political refugees, the second phase of the exodus was driven by economic pressures. With more than 40,000 refugees in camps in Hong Kong, the Hong Kong authorities began to forcibly repatriate those screened as economic migrants at the end of 1989. Such was the international outcry as critics highlighted fears of persecution that the programme was suspended. In May 1992, an agreement was reached between the British and the Vietnamese governments to repatriate the 55,700 boat people living in camps in Hong Kong and the orderly return programme was quietly restarted.

Ironically, the evidence is that those repatriated are doing very well – better than those who never left the shores of Vietnam. With the European Community and the UN offering assistance to returnees, they have set up businesses, enrolled on training courses and become embroiled in Vietnam's thrust for economic growth.

Invasion of Cambodia

In April 1975, the Khmer Rouge took power in Cambodia. Border clashes with Vietnam erupted just a month after the Phnom Penh regime change but matters came to a head in 1977 when the Khmer Rouge accused Vietnam of seeking to incorporate Kampuchea into an Indochinese Federation. Hanoi's determination to oust Pol Pot only really became apparent on Christmas Day 1978, when 120,000 Vietnamese troops invaded. By 7 January they had installed a puppet government that proclaimed the foundation of the **People's Republic of Kampuchea (PRK)**: Heng Samrin, a former member of the Khmer Rouge, was appointed president. The Vietnamese compared their invasion to the liberation of Uganda from Idi Amin – but for the rest of the world it was an unwelcome Christmas present. The new government was accorded scant recognition abroad, while the toppled government of Democratic Kampuchea retained the country's seat at the United Nations.

But the country's 'liberation' by Vietnam did not end the misery; in 1979 nearly half of Cambodia's population was in transit, either searching for their former homes or fleeing across the Thai border into refugee camps. The country reverted to a state of outright war again, for the Vietnamese were not greatly loved in Cambodia – especially by the Khmer Rouge. American political scientist Wayne Bert wrote: "The Vietnamese had long seen a special role for themselves in uniting and leading a greater Indochina Communist movement and the Cambodian Communists had seen with clarity that such a role for the Vietnamese could only be at the expense of their independence and prestige."

Under the Lon Nol and Khmer Rouge regimes, Vietnamese living in Cambodia were expelled or exterminated. Resentment had built up over the years Hanoi – exacerbated by the apparent ingratitude of the Khmer Rouge for Vietnamese assistance in fighting Lon Nol's US-supported Khmer Republic in the early 1970s. As relations between the Khmer Rouge and the Vietnamese deteriorated, the Communist superpowers, China and the Soviet Union, polarized too – the former siding with Khmer Rouge and the latter with Hanoi.

The Vietnamese invasion had the full backing of Moscow, while the Chinese and Americans began their support for the anti-Vietnamese rebels.

Following the Vietnamese invasion, three main anti-Hanoi factions were formed. In June 1982 they banded together in an unholy alliance of convenience to fight the PRK and called themselves the **Coalition Government of Democratic Kampuchea (CGDK)**, which was immediately recognised by the UN. The three factions of the CGDK were firstly: the Communist Khmer Rouge, whose field forces had recovered to at least 18,000 by the late 1980s. Supplied with weapons by China, they were concentrated in the Cardamom Mountains in the southwest and were also in control of some of the refugee camps along the Thai border. The second faction was the National United Front for an Independent Neutral Peaceful and Co-operative Cambodia (Funcinpec) – known by most people as the **Armée National Sihanoukiste (ANS)**. It was headed by Prince Sihanouk – although he spent most of his time exiled in Beijing; the group had fewer than 15,000 well-equipped troops – most of whom took orders from Khmer Rouge commanders. Thirdly was the anti-Communist **Khmer People's National Liberation Front (KPNLF)**, headed by Son Sann, a former prime minister under Sihanouk. Its 5000 troops were reportedly ill-disciplined in comparison with the Khmer Rouge and the ANS.

The three CGDK factions were ranged against the 70,000 troops loyal to the government of President Heng Samrin and Prime Minister Hun Sen (previously a Khmer Rouge cadre) they were backed by Vietnamese forces until September 1989.

In the late 1980s the Association of Southeast Asian Nations (ASEAN) – for which the Cambodian conflict had almost become its raison d'être – began steps to bring the warring factions together over the negotiating table. ASEAN countries were united in wanting the Vietnamese out of Cambodia. After Mikhail Gorbachev had come to power in the Soviet Union, Moscow's support for the Vietnamese presence in Cambodia gradually evaporated. Gorbachev began leaning on Vietnam as early as 1987, to withdraw its troops. Despite saying their presence in Cambodia was 'irreversible', Vietnam completed its withdrawal in September 1989, ending nearly 11 years of Hanoi's direct military involvement. The withdrawal led to an immediate upsurge in political and military activity, as forces of the exiled CGDK put increased pressure on the now weakened Phnom Penh regime to begin a round of power-sharing negotiations.

Border incursions with China
In February 1979 the Chinese marched into the far north of Vietnam justifying the invasion because of Vietnam's invasion of Cambodia, its treatment of Chinese in Vietnam, the ownership of the Paracel and Spratley Islands in the East Sea (South China Sea) also claimed by China and a stand against Soviet expansion into Asia (Hanoi was strongly allied with the then USSR). They withdrew a month later following heavy casualties although both sides have claimed to be victorious. Vietnamese military hardware was far superior to the Chinese and their casualties were estimated to be between 20,000 and 60,000; Vietnamese casualties were around 15,000. In 1987 fighting again erupted on the Sino-Vietnamese border resulting in high casualties.

Modern Vietnam

Politics
The **Vietnamese Communist Party (VCP)** was established in Hong Kong in 1930 by Ho Chi Minh and arguably has been more successful than any other such party in Asia in mobilizing and maintaining support. While others have fallen, the VCP has managed to stay firmly in control. To enable them to get their message to a wider audience, the Communist Party of Vietnam have launched their own website, www.cpv.org.vn.

Vietnam is a one-party state. In addition to the Communist Party the posts of president and prime minister were created when the constitution was revised in 1992. The president is head of state and the prime minister is head of the cabinet of ministries (including three deputies and 26 ministries), all nominated by the National Assembly. The current president is Nguyen Minh Triet and the current prime minister is Nguyen Tan Dung. Although the National Assembly is the highest instrument of state it can still be directed by the Communist Party. The vast majority of National Assembly members are also party members. Elections for the National Assembly are held every five years. The Communist Party is run by a politburo of 15 members. The head is the general secretary, currently Nong Duch Manh. The politburo, last elected in 2006 at the Tenth Party Congress, meets every five years and sets policy directions of the Party and the government. The Eleventh Party Congress is scheduled for 2011 In addition, there is a Central Committee made up of 161 members, who are also elected at the Party Congress.

In 1986, at the Sixth Party Congress, the VCP launched its economic reform programme known as *doi moi*, which was a momentous step in ideological terms. However, although the programme has done much to free up the economy, the party has ensured that it retains ultimate political power. Marxism-Leninism and Ho Chi Minh thought are still taught to Vietnamese school children and even so-called 'reformers' in the leadership are not permitted to diverge from the party line. In this sense, while economic reforms have made considerable progress – particularly in the south – there is a very definite sense that the limits of political reform have been reached, at least for the time being.

From the late 1990s to the first years of the new millennium there have been a number of arrests and trials of dissidents charged with what might appear to be fairly innocuous crimes (see The future of Communism in Vietnam, page 219) and, although the economic reforms enacted since the mid-1980s are still in place, the party resolutely rejects any moves towards greater political pluralism.

Looking at the process of political succession in Vietnam and the impression is not one of a country led by young men and women with innovative ideas. Each year commentators consider the possibility of an infusion of new blood and reformist ideas but the Party Congress normally delivers more of the same: dyed-in-the-wool party followers who are more likely to maintain the status quo than challenge it along with just one or two reformers. The Asian economic crisis did, if anything, further slow down the pace of change. To conservative party members, the Asian crisis – and the political instability that it caused – were taken as warnings of what can happen if you reform too far and too fast. The latest change of faces in leadership occurred during the Ninth Party Congress in April 2001.

For many Westerners there is something strange about a leadership calling for economic reform and liberalization while, at the same time, refusing any degree of political pluralism. How long the VCP can maintain this charade, along with China, while other Communist governments have long since fallen, is a key question. Despite the reforms, the leadership is still divided over the road ahead. But the fact that debate is continuing, sometimes openly, suggests that there is disagreement over the necessity for political reform and the degree of economic reform that should be encouraged. One small chink in the armour is the proposed bill to allow referenda. The draft report indicates that referenda would be held on the principles of universality, equality, directness and secret ballot but that the subject of referenda would be decided by the party.

In the country as a whole there is virtually no political debate at all, certainly not in the open. There are two reasons for this apparently curious state of affairs. First there is a genuine fear of discussing something that is absolutely taboo. The police have a wide network of informers who report back on a regular basis and no one wants to accumulate black marks that make it difficult to get the local police reference required for a university place, passport or even a job. Second, and more importantly, is the booming economy. Since the 1990s, economic growth in Vietnam has been unprecedented. As every politician knows, the one thing that keeps people happy is rising income. Hence with not much to complain about most Vietnamese people are content with their political status quo.

Nevertheless it would be foolish to think that everyone was happy. That political tensions are bubbling somewhere beneath the surface of Vietnamese society became clear in 1997 with serious disturbances in the poor coastal northern province of Thai Binh, 80 km southeast of Hanoi. In May, 3000 local farmers began to stage protests in the provincial capital, complaining of corruption and excessive taxation. There were reports of rioting and some deaths – strenuously denied, at least at first, by officials. However, a lengthy report appeared in the army newspaper *Quan Doi Nhan Dan* in September detailing moral decline and corruption in the Party in the province. For people in Thai Binh, and many others living in rural areas, the reforms of the 1980s and 1990s have brought little benefit. People living in Ho Chi Minh City may tout mobile phones and drive cars and motorbikes, but in much of the rest of the country average monthly incomes are around US$50-80. The Party's greatest fear is that ordinary people might lose confidence in the leadership and in the system. The fact that many of those who demonstrated in Thai Binh were, apparently, war veterans didn't help either. Nor can the leadership have failed to remember that Thai Binh was at the centre of peasant disturbances against the French. A few months later riots broke out in prosperous and staunchly Roman Catholic Dong Nai, just north of Ho Chi Minh City. The catalyst to these disturbances was the seizure of church land by a corrupt Chairman of the People's Committee. The mob razed the Chairman's house and stoned the fire brigade. Clearly, pent up frustrations were seething beneath the surface, for Highway 1 had to be closed for several days while the unrest continued. While the Dong Nai troubles went wholly unreported in Vietnam, a *Voice of Vietnam* broadcast admitted to them and went on to catalogue a list of previous civil disturbances, none of which was known to the outside world; it appears the purpose was to advise Western journalists that this was just another little local difficulty and not the beginning of the end of Communist rule. But reports of disturbances continue to filter out of Vietnam. At the beginning of 2001 thousands of ethnic minorities rioted in the Central Highland provinces of Gia Lai and Dac Lac and the army had to be called in to re-impose order. All foreigners were banned from the Central Highlands.

Again in April 2004 violence between ethnic minorities and the government flared in the Central Highlands, resulting in 'unknown numbers of dead and injured and reports of people missing' according to Amnesty International. Once more the cause was religious freedom and land rights although the government persists in its implausible conspiracy theory about 'outside forces' and extremists in the US wanting to destabilize it; a pretext, some fear, for the use of the jackboot and the imprisonment of trouble makers. To its shame (not that they are aware of such a concept) the Cambodian government simply hands refugees – many of who are asylum seekers in the strictest meaning – straight back to the Vietnamese forces. Much of the border area is a no-go zone in both countries, neither country allowing representatives of UNHCR anywhere near.

HRW reports than more than 350 ethnic minority people from the Central Highlands have been jailed, charged under Vietnam's Penal Code.

In more recent years, others have been prepared to voice their views. In 2006 Bloc 8406, a pro-democracy group named after its founding date of 8 April 2006, was set up. Catholic priest Father Nguyen Van Ly, editor of the underground online magazine *Free Speech* and a founding member of Bloc 8406, was sentenced to eight years in jail for anti-government activity. Four others were also sentenced with him. His trial can be seen on You Tube, including images of him having his mouth covered up and being bundled out of the courtroom. In March 2007 Nguyen Van Dai and Le Thi Cong Nhan, two human rights lawyers, were arrested on the grounds of distributing material "dangerous to the State" and were sentenced to four and five years in prison respectively.

As well as Bloc 8406, other pro-democracy movements include the US-based Viet Tan Party, www.viettan.org, with offices also in Australia, France, Japan, and the People's Democratic Party, among others.

International relations

In terms of international relations, Vietnam's relationship with the countries of the Association of Southeast Asian Nations (ASEAN) have warmed markedly since the dark days of the early and mid-1980s and in mid-1995 Vietnam became the association's seventh – and first Communist – member. The delicious irony of Vietnam joining ASEAN was that it was becoming part of an organization established to counteract the threat of Communist Vietnam itself – although everyone was too polite to point this out. No longer is there a deep schism between the capitalist and Communist countries of the region, either in terms of ideology or management. The main potential flashpoint concerns China. The enmity and suspicion which underlies the relationship between the world's last two real Communist powers stretches back over 2000 years. Indeed, one of the great attractions to Vietnam of joining ASEAN was the bulwark that it created against a potentially aggressive and actually economically ascendant China.

China and Vietnam, along with Malaysia, Taiwan, Brunei and the Philippines, all claim part (or all) of the South China Sea's Spratly Islands. These tiny islands, many no more than coral atolls, would have caused scarcely an international relations ripple were it not for the fact that they are thought to sit above huge oil reserves. Whoever can prove rights to the islands lays claim to this undersea wealth. Although the parties are committed to settling the dispute without resort to force, most experts see the Spratly Islands as the key potential flashpoint in Southeast Asia – and one in which Vietnam is seen to be a central player. The Paracel Islands further north are similarly disputed by Vietnam and China.

Rapprochement with the US   One of the keys to a lasting economic recovery was a normalization of relations with the US. From 1975 until early 1994 the US made it largely illegal for any American or American company to have business relations with Vietnam. The US, with the support of Japan and other Western nations, also blackballed attempts by Vietnam to gain membership to the IMF, World Bank and Asian Development Bank, thus cutting off access to the largest source of cheap credit. In the past, it has been the former Soviet Union and the countries of the Eastern Bloc that have filled the gap, providing billions of dollars of aid (US$6 billion 1986-1990), training and technical expertise. But in 1990 the Soviet Union halved its assistance to Vietnam, making it imperative that the government improve relations with the West and particularly the US.

In April 1991 the US opened an official office in Hanoi to assist in the search for Missing in Action (MIAs), the first such move since the end of the war, and in December 1992 allowed US companies to sign contracts to be implemented after the US trade embargo had been lifted. In 1992, both Australia and Japan lifted their embargoes on aid to Vietnam and the US also eased restrictions on humanitarian assistance. Support for a full normalization of relations was provided by French President Mitterand during his visit in February 1993, the first by a Western leader since the end of the war. He said that the US veto on IMF and World Bank assistance had "no reason for being there", and applauded Vietnam's economic reforms. He also pointed out to his hosts that respect for human rights was now a universal obligation, which did not go down quite so well. Nonetheless he saw his visit as marking the end of one chapter and the beginning of another.

This inexorable process towards normalization continued with the full lifting of the trade embargo on 4 February 1994 when President Bill Clinton announced the normalization of trade relations. Finally, on 11 July 1995 Bill Clinton declared the full normalization of relations between the two countries and a month later Secretary of State Warren Christopher opened the new American embassy in Hanoi.

Even though the embargo is now a thing of the past, there are still the families of over 2000 American servicemen listed as Missing in Action who continue to hope that the remains of their loved ones might, some day, make their way back to the US. (The fact there are still an estimated 300,000 Vietnamese MIAs is, of course, of scant interest to the American media.) It was this, among other legacies of the war, which made progress towards a full normalization of diplomatic and commercial relations such a drawn-out process.

The normalization of trade relations between the two countries was agreed in a meeting between Vietnamese and US officials in July 1999 and marked the culmination of three years' discussions. But conservatives in the politburo prevented the agreement being signed into law worried, apparently, about the social and economic side effects of such reform. This did not happen until 28 November 2001 when Vietnam's National Assembly finally ratified the treaty. It has led to a substantial increase in bilateral trade. In 2003 the USA imported US$4.5 billion worth of Vietnamese goods, roughly four times more than it exported to Vietnam. And not only goods: by 2004 the US Consulate General in Ho Chi Minh City handled more applications for American visas than any other US mission in the world.

Recent progress More good news came for Vietnam when it became the 150th member of the World Trade Organization in January 2007. The immediate effect was the lifting of import quotas from foreign countries thereby favouring Vietnamese exporters. Full benefits are expected to be realised when Vietnam hope to gains full market economy status in 2020. In June 2007 President Nguyen Minh Triet became the first president of Vietnam to visit the US. He met with George W Bush in Washington to discuss relations between the two countries; trade between the two former enemies now racks up US$9 billion a year. And, in October 2007, Vietnam was elected to the UN Security Council from 1 January 2008 as a non-permanent member for two years. In 2009, the International Bank for Reconstruction and Development loaned the country US$500 million, a sign that Vietnam's economic growth is good.

The future of Communism in Vietnam
In his book *Vietnam at the Crossroads*, BBC World Service commentator Michael Williams asks the question: "Does Communism have a future in Vietnam?" He answers that "the short answer must be no, if one means by Communism the classical Leninist doctrines and central planning". Instead some bastard form of Communism has been in the process of evolving. As Williams adds: "Even party leaders no longer appear able to distinguish between Communism and Capitalism".

There is certainly **political opposition** and disenchantment in Vietnam. At present this is unfocused and dispersed. Poor people in the countryside, especially in the north, resent the economic gains in the cities, particularly those of the south (see the section on serious disturbances, page 216, in Thai Binh). But this rump of latent discontent has little in common with those intellectual and middle class Vietnamese itching for more political freedom or those motivated entrepreneurs pressing for accelerated economic reforms or those Buddhist monks and Christians demanding freedom of worship and respect for human rights. Unless and until this loose broth of opposition groups coalesces, it is hard to see a coherent opposition movement evolving.

Nonetheless, each year a small number of brave, foolhardy or committed individuals challenge the authorities. Most are then arrested, tried, and imprisoned for various vaguely defined crimes including anti-government activity (see page 217). There is always the possibility that cataclysmic, and unpredictable, political change will occur.

The tensions between reform and control are constantly evident. A **press law** which came into effect in mid-1993 prohibits the publication of works "hostile to the socialist homeland, divulging state or [Communist] party secrets, falsifying history or denying the gains of the revolution". The Party's attempts to control the flow of information have extended to the internet. In 1997 a National Internet Control Board was established and all internet and email usage is strictly monitored. The authorities attempt to firewall topics relating to Vietnam in a hopeless attempt to censor incoming information. By 2004 a number of 'cyber-activists' were held on charges of disseminating information deemed injurious to national interests, see www.hrw.org/en/news/2010/05/26/vietnam-stop-cyber-attacks-against-online-critics. The government continues to crack down on blogs and websites it sees critical of the government, according to Human Rights Watch. Facebook has also been blocked.

People

Vietnam is home to a total of 54 ethnic groups including the Vietnamese themselves. The ethnic minorities vary in size from the Tay, with a population of about 1.3 million, to the Odu, who number only 300 individuals. Life has been hard for many of the minorities who have had to fight not only the French and Vietnamese but often each other in order to retain their territory and cultural identity. Traditions and customs have been eroded by outside influences such as Roman Catholicism and Communism although some of the less alien ideas have been successfully accommodated. Centuries of Viet population growth and decades of warfare have taken a heavy toll on minorities and their territories; increasingly, population pressure from the minority groups themselves poses a threat to their way of life.

Highland people: the Montagnards of Vietnam

The highland areas of Vietnam are among the most linguistically and culturally diverse in the world. In total, the highland peoples number around seven million. As elsewhere in Southeast Asia, a broad distinction can be drawn in Vietnam between the peoples of the lowlands and valleys and the peoples of the uplands. The former tend to be settled, cultivate wet rice and are fairly closely integrated into the wider Vietnamese state; in most instances they are Viet. The latter are often migratory, cultivate upland crops often using systems of shifting cultivation and are comparatively isolated from the state. The generic term for these diverse peoples of the highlands is Montagnard (from the French, Mountain People), in Vietnamese *nguoi thuong* (highland citizen) or, rather less politely, *moi* (savage or slave). As far as the highland peoples themselves are concerned, they identify with their village and tribal group and not as part of a wider grouping, as highland inhabitants.

The French attitude towards the Montagnards was often inconsistent. The authorities wanted to control them and sometimes succumbed to the pressure from French commercial interests to conscript them into the labour force, particularly on the plantations. But some officials were positively protective; one, Monsieur Sebatier, refused missionaries access to the territory under his control, destroyed bridges to prevent access and had three tribal wives. He recommended total withdrawal from their lands in order to protect their cultural integrity. In *A Dragon Apparent*, Norman Lewis provides a wonderful account of the Montagnards and their way of life and perceptively examines the relationship between them and the French.

Relations between the minorities and the Viet have not always been as good as they are officially portrayed. Recognizing and exploiting this mutual distrust and animosity, both the French and American armies recruited from among the minorities. In 1961 US Special Forces began organizing Montagnards into defence groups to prevent Communist infiltration into the Central Highlands from the north. Since 1975, relations between minorities and Viet have improved but there is still hostility and in recent years this has flared into vicious fighting. Official publications paint a touching picture portraying the relationship between Viet and minority peoples. Thus we read "successive generations of Vietnamese, belonging to 54 ethnic groups, members of the great national community of Vietnam, have always stood side by side with one another, sharing weal and woe, shedding sweat and blood to defend and build up their homeland". This illusion has been shattered by recent events so the government is keen to stress its role in improving health, eradicating poverty and introducing a settled rather than a nomadic existence among the minorities. But one serious consequence of a sedentary way of life has been the narrowing, blunting and elimination of cultural differences. In recent years the government has come to regard the minorities as useful 'tourist fodder' – with a splash of colour, primitive villages and ethnic dances, they provide a taste of the 'mystical East', which much of the country otherwise lacks.

Potentially tourism is a more serious and insidious threat to the minorities' way of life than any they have yet had to face. A great deal has been written about cultural erosion by tourism and any visitor to a minority village should be aware of the extent to which he or she contributes to this process. Traditional means of livelihood are quickly abandoned when a higher living standard for less effort can be obtained from the tourist dollar. Long-standing societal and kinship ties are weakened by the intrusion of outsiders. Young people may question their society's values and traditions that may seem archaic, anachronistic and risible by comparison with those of the modern tourist. And dress and music lose all cultural significance and symbolism if they are allowed to become mere tourist attractions.

Nevertheless, this is an unavoidable consequence of Vietnam's decision to admit tourists to the highland areas. Perhaps fortunately, however, for the time being at least, many of the minorities are pretty inaccessible to the average traveller. Visitors can minimize their impact by acting in a sensitive way; it is, for example, perfectly obvious when someone does not want their photograph taken. See also box, page 21 for general advice on visiting minority villages. In addition, you can report to provincial tourism authorities on arrival to check the latest on areas where travel is permitted. But the minority areas of Vietnam are fascinating places and the immense variety of colours and styles of dress add greatly to the visitor's enjoyment.

Bahnar (Ba-na)

This is a Mon-Khmer-speaking minority group concentrated in the central highland provinces of Gia Lai-Kon Tum, numbering about 174,000. Locally powerful from the 15th to 18th centuries, they were virtually annihilated by neighbouring groups during the 19th century. Roman Catholic missionaries influenced the Bahnar greatly and they came to identify closely with the French. Some conversions to Roman Catholicism were made but Christianity, where it remains, is usually just an adjunct to Bahnar animism. Bahnar houses are built on stilts and in each village there is a communal house, or *rông*, which is the focus of social life. When a baby reaches his or her first full month he or she has their ears pierced in a village ceremony equivalent to the Vietnamese *day thang*; only then is a child considered a full member of the community. Their society gives men and women relatively equal status. Male and female heirs inherit wealth and the families of either husband or wife can arrange marriage. Bahnar practise both settled and shifting cultivation.

Coho (Co-ho, also Kohor, K'Ho, Xre, Chil and Nop)

These are primarily found on the Lam Dong Plateau in Lam Dong Province (Dalat) with a population of about 100,000. Extended family groups live in longhouses or *buon*, sometimes up to 30-m long. Unusually, society is matrilineal and newly married men live with their wives' families. The children take their mother's name; if the wife dies prematurely her younger sister will take her place. Women wear tight-fitting blouses and skirts. Traditional shifting cultivation is giving way to settled agriculture.

Yao (Dao, also Mán)

The Yao live in northern Vietnam in the provinces bordering China, particularly in Lao Cai and Ha Giang. They number 6210,000 and include several sub-groupings, notably the Dao Quan Chet (Tight Trouser Dao), the Dao Tien (Money Dao) and the Dao Ao Dai (Long Dress Dao). As these names suggest, Yao people wear highly distinctive clothing although sometimes only on their wedding day. The **Dao Tien** or Money Dao of Hoa Binh and Son La provinces are unique among the Yao in that the women wear black skirts and leggings rather than trousers. A black jacket with red embroidered collar and cuffs, decorated at the back with coins (hence the name) together with a black red-tasselled turban and silver jewellery are also worn. By contrast men look rather plain in black jacket and trousers. Headgear tends to be elaborate and includes a range of shapes (from square to conical), fabrics (waxed hair to dried pumpkin fibres) and colours.

The women of many branches of Yao shave off their eyebrows and shave back their hair to the top of their head before putting on the turban; a hairless face and high forehead are traditionally regarded as attributes of feminine beauty.

Yao wedding customs are as complex as Yao clothing and vary with each group. Apart from parental consent, intending marriage partners must have compatible birthdays and the groom has to provide the bride's family with gifts worthy of their daughter. If he is unable to do this, a temporary marriage can take place but the outstanding presents must be produced and a permanent wedding celebrated before *their* daughter can marry.

The Yao live chiefly by farming: those in higher altitudes are swidden cultivators growing maize, cassava and rye. In the middle zone, shifting methods are again used to produce rice and maize, and on the valley floors sedentary farmers grow irrigated rice and rear livestock.

Spiritually the Yao have also opted for diversity; they worship *Ban Vuong*, their mythical progenitor, as well as their more immediate and real ancestors. The Yao also find room for elements of Taoism, and in some cases Buddhism and Confucianism, in their elaborate metaphysical lives. Never enter a Yao house unless invited; if tree branches are suspended above the gate to a village, guests are not welcome – reasons might include a post-natal but pre-naming period, sickness, death or special ceremony. Since the Yao worship the kitchen god, guests should not sit or stand immediately in front of the stove.

Ede (also Rhadê)

Primarily concentrated in the Central Highlands province of Dac Lac and numbering nearly 270,000, they came into early contact with the French and are regarded as one of the more 'progressive' groups, adapting to modern life with relative ease. Traditionally the Ede live in longhouses on stilts; accommodated under one roof is the matrilineal extended family or commune. The commune falls under the authority of an elderly, respected woman known as the *khoa sang* who is responsible for communal property, especially the gongs and jars, which feature in important festivals. Ede society is matrilocal in that after the girl's family selects a husband, he then comes to live with her. As part of the wedding festivities the two families solemnly agree that if one of the partners should break the wedding vow they will forfeit a minimum of one buffalo, a maximum of a set of gongs. Wealth and property are inherited solely by daughters. Shifting cultivation is the traditional subsistence system, although this has given way in most areas to settled wet rice agriculture. Spiritually the Ede are polytheist: they number animism (recognizing the spirits of rice, soil, fire and water especially) and Christianity among their beliefs.

Giarai (Gia-rai, also Chó Ray)

Primarily found in Gia Lai and Kon Tum provinces (especially near Play Ku) and numbering 317,557, these are the largest group in the Central Highlands. They are settled cultivators and live in houses on stilts in villages called *ploi* or *bon*. The Giarai are animist and recognize the spiritual dimension of nature; ever since the seventh century they have had a flesh and blood King of Fire and King of Water whose spirit is invoked in rain ceremonies.

Hmong (Hmông, also Mèo and Mieu)

These are widely spread across the highland areas of the country, but particularly near the Chinese border down to the 18th parallel. The Hmong number about 787,600 (over 1% of Vietnam's population) and live at higher altitudes, above 1500 m, than all other hill people. Comparatively recent migrants to Vietnam, the Hmong began to settle in the country during the 19th century after moving south from China. The Hmong language in its various dialects remained oral until the 1930s when a French priest attempted to Romanize it with a view to translating the Bible. A more successful attempt to create a written Hmong language was made in 1961 but has since fallen into disuse. Nevertheless – or perhaps because of this failure – the Hmong still preserve an extraordinarily rich oral tradition of legends, stories and histories. Hmong people are renowned for their beautiful folk songs. Each branch of the Hmong people preserves its own corpus of songs about love, work and festivals that are sung unaccompanied or with the accompaniment of the *khène*, a small bamboo pipe organ, a two-stringed violin, flutes, drums, gongs and jew's harps. Numerous Hmong dances also exist to celebrate various dates in the social calendar and to propitiate animist spirits.

They have played an important role in resisting both the French and the Vietnamese. Living at such high altitudes they tend to be one of the most isolated of all the hill people. Their way of life does not normally bring them into contact with the outside world – the Hmong traders at Sapa are an exception. High in the hills, flooding is not a problem so their houses are built on the ground, not raised up on stilts. Hmong villages are now increasingly found along the river valleys and roads as the government resettlement schemes aim to introduce them to a more sedentary form of agriculture. The Hmong practice slash-and-burn cultivation growing maize and dry rice. Traditionally opium has been a valuable cash crop. Although fields are often cleared on very steep and rocky slopes, the land is not terraced. There are a number of different groups among the Hmong including the White, Black, Red and Flower Hmong that are distinguishable by the colour of the women's clothes. Black Hmong wear almost entirely black clothing with remarkable pointed black turbans. White Hmong women wear white skirts and the Red Hmong tie their heads in a red scarf while the Flower Hmong wrap their hair (with hair extensions) around their head like a broad-brimmed hat. However, such numerous regional variations occur that even experts on ethnic minority cultures sometimes have problems trying to identify which branch of Hmong they have encountered. Serious social problems have occurred among the Hmong owing to opium addiction; with over 30% of the male population of some Hmong villages addicted, the drug has rendered many incapable of work, causing misery and malnutrition for their families and with the drug finding its way on to the streets of Vietnam's cities, the authorities have resolved to clamp down hard on opium production. This has had tragic consequences when the Hmong have tried to protect their livelihoods.

Muong (Mường)

Numbering more than one million the Muong are the fourth largest ethnic minority in Vietnam. They live in the area between northern Thanh Hoa Province and Yen Bai but mainly in Hoa Binh Province. It is thought that the Muong are descended from the same stock as the Viets: their languages are similar and there are also close similarities in culture and religion. But whereas the Vietnamese came under strong Chinese cultural influence from the early centuries of the Christian era, the Muong did not. The Muong belong to the Viet-Muong language group; their language is closest to Vietnamese of all the ethnic minority languages. Muong practise wet and dry rice cultivation where possible, supplementing their income with cash crops such as manioc, tobacco and cotton. Weaving is still practised; items produced include pillowcases and blankets. Culturally the Muong are akin to the Thai Vietnamese ethnic minority and they live in stilt houses in small villages called *quel*; groupings of from three to 30 quel form a unit called a *muong*. Muong society is feudal in nature with each *muong* coming under the protection of a noble family (*lang*). The common people are not deemed worthy of family names so are all called Bui. Each year the members of a *muong* are required to labour for one day in fields belonging to the lang.

Marriages are arranged: girls, in particular, have no choice of spouse. Muong cultural life is rich, literature has been translated into Vietnamese and their legends, poems and songs are considered particularly fine.

Mnong (Mnông)

The Mnong number some 92,000 people and predominantly live in Dak Lak, Binh Phuoc and Binh Duong province with a smaller group living in Lam Dong province. The Mnong are hunter-gatherers and grow rice. The Mnong village is characterised by a longhouse on stilts although some groups live in normal sized stilt houses. Families are matrilineal and tradition sees the women bare topped and with distended earlobes. It is the Mnong who are the elephant catchers at Ban Don.

Nung (Nùng)

Concentrated in Cao Bang and Lang Son provinces, adjacent to the Chinese border, the Nung number approximately 860,000 people. They are strongly influenced by the Chinese and most are Buddhist, but like both Vietnamese and Chinese the Nung practise ancestor worship too. In Nung houses a Buddhist altar is placed above the ancestor altar and, in deference to Buddhist teaching, they refrain from eating most types of meat. The Nung are settled agriculturalists and, where conditions permit, produce wet rice; all houses have their own garden in which fruit and vegetables are grown.

Tay (Tày, also Tho)

The Tay are the most populous ethnic minority in Vietnam; they number about 1.5 million and are found in the provinces of northwest Vietnam stretching from Quang Ninh east to Lao Cai. Tay society was traditionally feudal with powerful lords able to extract from the free and semi-free serfs' obligations such as droit de seigneur. Today Tay society is male dominated with important decisions being taken by men and eldest sons inheriting the bulk of the family's wealth.

Economically the Tay survive by farming and are highly regarded as wet rice cultivators, they are also noted for the production of fruits (pears, peaches, apricots and tangerines), herbs and spices. Diet is supplemented by animal and fish rearing and cash is raised by the production of handicrafts. The Tay live in houses on stilts, located in the river valleys. Tay architecture is quite similar in design to that of the Black Thai, but important differences may be identified, most notably the larger size of the Tay house, the deeper overhang of the thatched or (among more affluent Tay communities) tiled roof and the extent of the railed balcony which often encircles the entire house.

Like the Thai, Tay ancestors migrated south from southern China along with those of the Thai and they follow the three main religions of Buddhism, Confucianism and Taoism in addition to ancestor worship and animist beliefs. While Tay people have lived in close proximity to the Viet majority over a period of many centuries, their own language continues to be their primary means of communication. They hail from the Austro-Asian language family and specifically the Thai-Kadai language group. Tay literature has a long and distinguished history and much has been translated into Vietnamese. During the French colonial period, missionaries Romanized Tay script.

Thai (Thái, also Tày DmTày)

Numbering more than one million this is the second largest ethnic minority in Vietnam and ethnically distinct from the Thais of modern-day Thailand. There are two main sub-groups, the Black (Thai Den), who are settled mainly in Son La, Lai Chan, Lao Cai and Yen Bai provinces and the White Thái, who are found predominantly in Hoa Binh, Son La, Thanh Hoa and Vinh Phu provinces, as well as many others, including the Red Thai (Thai Do). The use of these colour-based classifications has usually been linked to the colour of their clothes, particularly the colour of women's shirts. However, there has been some confusion over the origins of the terms and there is every reason to believe that it has nothing to do with the colour of their attire and is possibly linked to the distribution of the sub-groups near the Red and Black rivers. The confusion of names becomes even more perplexing when the Vietnamese names for the sub-groups of Thai people are translated into Thai. Some scholars have taken Thai Den (Black Thai) to be Thai Daeng – *daeng* being the Thai word for red, thereby muddling up the two groups. With the notable exception of the White Thai communities of Hoa Binh, traditional costume for the women of both the Black and White Thai generally features a coloured blouse with a row of silver buttons down the front, a long black skirt, a coloured waist sash and a black headscarf embroidered with intricate, predominantly red and yellow designs.

The traditional costume of the White Thai women of Hoa Binh comprises a long black skirt with fitted waistband embroidered with either a dragon or chicken motif together with a plain pastel coloured blouse and gold and maroon sash.

Being so numerous the Thai cover a large part of northwest Vietnam, in particular the valleys of the Red River and the Da and the Ma rivers, spilling over into Laos and Thailand. They arrived in Vietnam between the fourth and 11th centuries from southern China and linguistically they are part of the wider Thai-Kadai linguistic grouping. Residents of Lac village in Mai Chau claim to have communicated with visitors from Thailand by means of this shared heritage.

The Thai tend to occupy lowland areas and they compete directly with the Kinh (ethnic Vietnamese) for good quality farmland that can be irrigated. They are masters of wet rice cultivation producing high yields and often two harvests each year. Their irrigation works are ingenious and incorporate numerous labour-saving devices including river-powered water wheels that can raise water several metres. Thai villages (*ban*) consist of 40-50 houses on stilts; they are architecturally attractive, shaded by fruit trees and surrounded by verdant paddy fields. Commonly located by rivers, one of the highlights of a Thai village is its suspension footbridge. The Thai are excellent custodians of the land and their landscapes and villages are invariably very scenic.

Owing to their geographical proximity and agricultural similarities with the Kinh it is not surprising to see cultural assimilation – sometimes via marriage – and most Thai speak Vietnamese. It's also interesting to note the extent to which the Thai retain a distinctive cultural identity, most visibly in their dress.

When a Thai woman marries, her parents-in-law give her a hair extension (*can song*) and a silver hair pin (*khat pom*) that she is expected to wear (even in bed) for the duration of the marriage. There are two wedding ceremonies, the first at the bride's house where the couple live for one to three years, followed by a second when they move to the husband's house.

Sedang (Xó-dang)

Concentrated in Gia Lai and Kon Tum provinces and numbering about 127,000, the Sedang live in extended family longhouses and society is patriarchal. The Sedang practise both shifting agriculture and the cultivation of wet rice. A highly war-like people, they almost wiped out the Bahnar in the 19th century. Sedang thought nothing of kidnapping neighbouring tribesmen to sacrifice to the spirits; indeed the practice of kidnapping was subsequently put to commercial use and formed the basis of a slave trade with Siam (Thailand). Sedang villages, or *ploi*, are usually well defended (presumably for fear of reprisal) and are surrounded by thorn hedges supplemented with spears and stakes. Complex rules designed to prevent in-breeding limit the number of available marriage partners, sometimes resulting in late marriages.

Other groups

These are Hre (Hrê), in Quang Ngai and Binh Dinh provinces, numbering 113,000 and Stieng/Xtieng (Xtiêng) in Song Be province, with 66,788.

Viet (Kinh)

The 1999 census revealed that 86.2% of the population were ethnic Vietnamese. But with a well-run family planning campaign beginning to take effect in urban areas and higher fertility rates among the ethnic minorities it is likely that this figure will fall. The history of the Kinh is marked by a steady southwards progression from the Red River basin to the southern plains and Mekong Delta. Today the Kinh are concentrated into the two great river deltas, the coastal plains and the main cities. Only in the central and northern highland regions are they outnumbered by ethnic minorities. Kinh social cohesion and mastery of intensive wet rice cultivation has led to their numerical, and subsequently political and economic, dominance of the country. Ethnic Vietnamese are also in Cambodia where some have been settled for generations; recent Khmer Rouge attacks on Vietnamese villages have, however, caused many to flee to Vietnam.

Cham

With the over-running of Champa in 1471 (see page 198) Cham cultural and ethnic identity was diluted by the more numerous ethnic Vietnamese. The Cham were dispossessed of the more productive lands and found themselves in increasingly marginal territory. Economically eclipsed and strangers in their own land, Cham artistic creativity atrophied, their sculptural and architectural skills, once the glory of Vietnam, faded and decayed like so many Cham temples and towers. It is estimated that there are, today, 132,873 Cham people in Vietnam, chiefly in central and southern Vietnam in the coastal provinces extending south from Quy Nhon. Small communities are to be found in Ho Chi Minh City and in the Mekong Delta around Chau Doc. They are artistically the poor relations of their forebears but skills in weaving and music live on.

The Cham of the south are typically engaged in fishing, weaving and other small-scale commercial activities; urban Cham are poor and live in slum neighbourhoods. Further north the Cham are wet or dry rice farmers according to local topography; they are noted for their skill in wet rice farming and small-scale hydraulic engineering.

In southern Vietnam the majority of Cham are Muslim, a comparatively newly acquired religion although familiar from earlier centuries when many became acquainted with Islamic tenets through traders from India and the Indonesian isles. In central Vietnam most Cham are Brahminist and the cult of the linga remains an important feature of spiritual life.

Hoa: ethnic Chinese

There are nearly one million ethnic Chinese or Hoa in Vietnam, 80% living in the south of the country. Before reunification in 1975 there were even more; hundreds of thousands left due to persecution by the authorities and a lack of economic opportunities since the process of socialist transformation was initiated. There are now large Vietnamese communities abroad, particularly in Australia, on the west coast of the US and in France. It has been estimated that the total Viet-Kieu population numbers some two million. With the reforms of the 1980s, the authorities' view of the Chinese has changed; they now appreciate the crucial role they played, and could continue to play, in the economy. Before 1975, the Hoa controlled 80% of industry in the south and 50% of banking and finance. Today, ethnic Chinese in Vietnam can own and operate businesses and are once again allowed to join the Communist party, the army and to enter university. The dark days of the mid to late 1970s seem to be over.

Viet Kieu: overseas Vietnamese

Since 1988, overseas Vietnamese or Viet Kieu (most of whom are of Chinese extraction) have been allowed back to visit their relatives, in some cases helping to spread stories of untold wealth in the US, Australia and elsewhere. The largest community of overseas Vietnamese, about 1.1 million, live in the US. The next largest populations are resident in France (250,000) and Australia (160,000), with much smaller numbers in a host of other countries. In 1990, 40,000 returned to visit; in 2003, 340,000 returned 'home'. Amusingly, many from America come back for dental treatment as it is much cheaper in Vietnam.

Many Viet Kieu are former boat people, while others left the country as part of the UN-administered Orderly Departure Programme that began in earnest in the late 1980s. A smaller number (and one wonders whether they are strictly classed as Viet Kieu) left

Vietnam for one of the former COMECON countries at some point between the 1950s and 1980s either to study or to work. The largest number appear to have gone to East Germany from where many have returned to take up important political positions. Those fortunate enough to find themselves in dour East Germany at the time of reunification suddenly found themselves privileged to be citizens of one of the world's richest countries. In the upheavals occasioned by ridding Eastern Europe of Communism they showed sound business acumen and carved out a pivotal position in the German tobacco smuggling industry.

In America the Viet Kieu have often shown enormous perseverance and grit. Take the small Texan shrimping town of Palacios. Today there are around 300 Americans of Vietnamese extraction, mostly Roman Catholics, living in and around Palacios. When the first settlers arrived in 1976 escaping from the defeated South, most had nothing. Many faced bigotry from racist elements in the local community who feared competition from foreigners. But they worked and saved and by the early 1980s some families had managed to buy shrimping boats for themselves. Another 10 years on and the most successful boats were owned and operated by Vietnamese. By that time, many of their children had been born and raised in the local community, they had gone through local schools (often winning the top scholastic prizes) and few questioned their credentials to be counted as Americans. There are Little Saigons in many countries but the most famous is in Los Angeles. From this social and economic hub the Vietnamese diaspora has set about cornering several industries. The nail manicure business is now virtually synonymous with the Vietnamese. In California and increasingly in other parts of the world, nail bars are Vietnamese owned; 'Hollywood Nails' appears to be the name of choice. In California, it seems, almost every block has a Vietnamese pharmacy and a *pho* restaurant selling noodles. And now shoppers in malls from Virginia to San José can sit down to a good bowl of *pho bo* (beef noodle soup), surely one of the more surprising outcomes of the Vietnam War.

As the Viet Kieu have discovered some measure of prosperity in the West, the Vietnamese government is anxious to welcome them back – or rather, welcome their money. So far, however, flows of investment for productive purposes have been rather disappointing and largely concentrated in the service sector, particularly in hotels and restaurants. Far more is thought to have been invested in land and property as overseas Vietnamese have, since 2000, been able to purchase property in their own name. (This, incidentally, has contributed to property speculation and a dizzy spiral of price increases that have made land prices in Ho Chi Minh City and Hanoi some of the most expensive in Asia.) Part of the problem is that many Viet Kieu were escaping from persecution in Vietnam and of all people continue to harbour doubts about a government that is, in essence, the same as the one they fled. On the government's side, they worry that the Viet Kieu may be a destabilizing influence, perhaps even a Fifth Column intent on undermining the supremacy of the Communist Party. Again the leadership have cause for concern as the most vocal opponents of the US policy of rapprochement have been Viet Kieu. Nor are the Overseas Vietnamese quite as rich as their ostentatious displays of wealth on the streets of Ho Chi Minh City and Hanoi would indicate. They do not have the economic muscle of the Overseas Chinese, for example, and in most cases have only been out of the country for less than 20 years, many having lost everything in their attempt to escape. Many young Viet Kieu have, however, equipped themselves with qualifications and skills overseas – often much needed in Vietnam – and can find lucrative employment back in Vietnam.

Religion

Vietnam supports followers of all the major world religions, as well as those religions that are peculiarly Vietnamese: Theravada and Mahayana Buddhism, Protestant and Roman Catholic Christianity, Taoism, Confucianism, Islam, Cao Daism, Hoa Hao and Hinduism. In addition, spirit and ancestor worship (*To Tien*) are also practised. Confucianism, although not a formal religion, is probably the most pervasive doctrine of all. Nominal Christians and Buddhists will still pay attention to the moral and philosophic principles of Confucianism and it continues to play a central role in Vietnamese life.

Following the Communist victory in 1975, the authorities moved quickly to curtail the influence of the various religions. Schools, hospitals and other institutions run by religious organizations were taken over by the state and many clergy either imprisoned and/ or sent to re-education camps. The religious hierarchies were institutionalized, and proselytizing severely curtailed.

During the late 1980s and into the early 1990s some analysts identified an easing of the government's previously highly restrictive policies towards religious organizations. At the beginning of 1993, former General Secretary of the Vietnamese Communist Party, Do Muoi, even went so far as to make official visits to a Buddhist monastery and a Roman Catholic church. However it is clear the Communist hierarchy is highly suspicious of priests and monks. They are well aware of the prominent role they played in South Vietnamese political dissension and are quick to crack down on any religious leader or organization that becomes involved in politics. In recent years this religious intolerance has been particularly manifest in the repression of the Montagnards in the Central Highlands, the closure of churches and imprisonment of church leaders, particularly protestant sects.

There is no question that more people today are attending Buddhist pagodas, Christian churches and Cao Dai temples. However, whether this rise in attendance at temples and churches actually means some sort of religious rebirth is questionable. Dang Nghiem Van, head of Hanoi's Institute of Religious Studies, poured scorn on the notion that young people are finding religion. They "are not religious", he said, "just superstitious. This isn't religion. It's decadence".

Mahayana Buddhism

Although there are both Theravada (also known as Hinayana) and Mahayana Buddhists in Vietnam, the latter are by far the more numerous. Buddhism was introduced into Vietnam in the second century AD: Indian pilgrims came by boat and brought the teachings of Theravada Buddhism, while Chinese monks came by land and introduced Mahayana Buddhism. In particular, the Chinese monk Mau Tu is credited with being the first person to introduce Mahayana Buddhism in AD 194-195.

Initially, Buddhism was very much the religion of the elite and did not impinge upon the common Vietnamese man or woman. It was not until the reign of Emperor Ly Anh Tong (1138-1175) that Buddhism was promoted as the state religion, nearly 1000 years after Mau Tu had arrived from China to spread the teachings of the Buddha. By that time it had begun to filter down to the village level, but as it did so it became increasingly syncretic; Buddhism became enmeshed with Confucianism, Taoism, spirituality, mysticism and animism. In the 15th century it also began to lose its position to Confucianism as the dominant religion of the court.

There has been a resurgence of Buddhism since the 1920s. It was the self- immolation of Buddhist monks in the 1960s which provided a focus of discontent against the government in the south, and since the Communist victory in 1975, monks have remained an important focus of dissent, hence the persecution of Buddhists during the early years following reunification. Mahayana Buddhists are concentrated in the centre and north of the country and the dominant sect is the Thien (Zen) meditation sect. Of the relatively small numbers of Theravada Buddhists, the majority are of Cambodian stock and are concentrated in the Mekong Delta. In Vietnam, Buddhism is intertwined with Confucianism and Taoism.

Confucianism

Although Confucianism is not strictly a religion, the teachings of the Chinese sage and philosopher Confucius (551-479 BC) form the basis on which Vietnamese life and government were based for much of the historic period. Even today, Confucianist perspectives are, possibly, more strongly in evidence than Communist ones. Confucianism was introduced from China during the Bac Thuoc Period (111 BC-AD 938) when the Chinese dominated the country. The 'religion' enshrined the concept of imperial rule by the mandate of heaven, constraining social and political change.

In essence, Confucianism stresses the importance of family and lineage and the worship of ancestors. Men and women in positions of authority were required to provide role models for the 'ignorant', while the state, epitomized in the emperor, was likewise required to set an example and to provide conditions of stability and fairness for his people. Crucially, children had to observe filial piety. This set of norms, which were drawn from the experience of the human encounter at the practical level, were enshrined in the *Forty-seven Rules for Teaching and Changing* first issued in 1663. A key element of Confucianist thought is the Three Bonds (*tam cuong*) – the loyalty of ministers to the emperor, obedience of children to their parents and submission of wives to their husbands. Added to these are mutual reciprocity among friends and benevolence towards strangers. Not surprisingly the Communists are antipathetic to such a hierarchical view of society although ironically Confucianism, which inculcates respect for the elderly and authority, unwittingly lends support to a politburo occupied by old men. In an essay entitled 'Confucianism and Marxism', Vietnamese scholar Nguyen Khac Vien explains why Marxism proved an acceptable doctrine to those accustomed to Confucian values: "Marxism was not baffling to Confucians in that it concentrated man's thoughts on political and social problems. By defining man as the total of his social relationships, Marxism hardly came as a shock to the Confucian scholar who had always considered the highest aim of man to be the fulfilment of his social obligations ... Bourgeois individualism, which puts personal interests ahead of those of society and petty bourgeois anarchism, which allows no social discipline whatsoever, are alien to both Confucianism and Marxism."

Taoism

Taoism was introduced from China into Vietnam at about the same time as Confucianism. It is based on the works of the Chinese philosophers Lao Tzu (circa sixth-fifth centuries BC) and Chuang Tzu (fourth century BC). Although not strictly a formal religion, it has had a significant influence on Buddhism (as it is practised in Vietnam) and on Confucianism. In reality, Taoism and Confucianism are two sides of the same coin: the Taoist side is poetry and spirituality; the Confucianist side, social ethics and the order of the world. Together they form a unity. Like Confucianism, it is not possible to give a figure to the number of followers of Taoism in Vietnam. It functions in conjunction with Confucianism and Buddhism and also often with Christianity, Cao Daism and Hoa Hao. Of all the world's religions, Taoism is perhaps the hardest to pin down. It has no formal code, no teachings and no creed. It is a cosmic religion. Even the word Tao is usually left untranslated or merely translated as 'The Way'. The inscrutability of it all is summed up in the writings of the Chinese poet Po Chu-i: "Those who speak know nothing, Those who know keep silence. These words, as I am told, were spoken by Lao Tzu. But if we are to believe that Lao Tzu was himself one who knew, how comes it that he wrote a book of five thousand words?"

Or to quote Chuang Tzu even more inscrutably: "Tao is beyond material existence ... it may be transmitted, but it cannot be received [possessed]. It may be attained, but cannot be seen. It exists prior to Heaven and Earth, and, indeed, for all eternity ... it is above the Zenith, but is not high; it is beneath the Nadir, but it is not low. It is prior to Heaven and Earth, but it is not ancient. It is older than the most ancient, but it is not old."

Central to Taoist belief is a world view based upon yin and yang, two primordial forces on which the creation and functioning of the world are based. The yin-yang is not specifically Taoist or Confucianist, but predates both and is associated with the first recorded Chinese ruler, Fu-hsi (2852-2738 BC). The well-known yin-yang symbol symbolizes the balance and equality between the great dualistic forces in the universe: dark and light, negative and positive, male and female. JC Cooper explains in *Taoism: the Way of the Mystic*, the symbolism of the black and white dots: "There is a point, or embryo, of black in the white and white in the black. This ... is essential to the symbolism since there is no being which does not contain within itself the germ of its opposite. There is no male wholly without feminine characteristics and no female without its masculine attributes." Thus the dualism of the yin-yang is not absolute, but permeable.

To maintain balance and harmony in life it is necessary that a proper balance be maintained between yin (female) and yang (male). This is believed to be true both at the scale of the world and the nation, and also for an individual, for the human body is the world in microcosm. The root cause of illness is imbalance between the forces of yin and yang. Even foods have characters: 'hot' foods are yang and 'cold', yin. Implicit in this is the belief that there is a natural law underpinning all of life, a law upon which harmony ultimately rests. Taoism attempts to maintain this balance and thereby harmony. In this way, Taoism is a force promoting inertia, maintaining the status quo. Traditional relationships between fathers and sons, between siblings, within villages, and between the rulers and the ruled, are all rationalized in terms of maintaining balance and harmony. Forces for change – like Communism and democracy – are resisted on the basis that they upset this balance.

Christianity

Christianity was first introduced into Vietnam in the 16th century by Roman Catholic missionaries from Portugal, Spain and France. The first Bishop of Vietnam was appointed in 1659 and by 1685 there were estimated to be 800,000 Roman Catholics in the country. For several centuries Christianity was discouraged, and at times, outlawed. Many Christians were executed and one of the reasons the French gave for annexing the country in the late 19th century was religious persecution (see page 199). Today, 8-10% of the population are thought to be Roman Catholic; less than 1% are Protestant. This Christian population is served by around 2000 priests. Following reunification in 1975, many Roman Catholics in the former south were sent to re-education camps. They were perceived to be both staunchly pro-American and anti-Communist and it was not until 1988 that many were returned to normal life.

Today, Roman Catholics are still viewed with suspicion by the state and priests felt to be drifting from purely religious concerns into any criticism of the state (seen as anti-government activity) are detained, such as Father Nguyen Van Ly. And this is the key point: the Vietnamese remain tolerant and open in matters of religion and spirituality. It is the political overtones that come with any established religion that the authorities find impossible to accept. While memories of the role of the Roman Catholic church in the downfall of Polish Communism linger, relations between Hanoi and the Vatican are not warm and often strained and Rome finds it difficult to appoint bishops. However, in 2007 the prime minister became the first head of government to be received at the Vatican to discuss relations. More generally, the authorities have been slow to permit Vietnamese men to become ordained, and they have limited the production and flow of religious literature. Nevertheless centuries of existence in what for the Roman Catholic church has been the hostile environment of Vietnam has enabled it to reach a degree of acceptance. Doubtless the brighter of the Communist leaders realize the Roman Catholic church will be around long after their Party has disappeared.

Protestant sects have a much tougher time. This is partly due to the evangelical nature of much Protestantism that makes the authorities distinctly uneasy. Evangelical protestants have faced the brunt of the crackdowns in the last couple of years.

Islam and Hinduism
The only centres of Islam and Hinduism are among the Cham of the central coastal plain and Chau Doc. The Cham were converted to Islam by Muslim traders. There are several mosques in Ho Chi Minh City and Cholon, some of them built by Indians from Kerala.

Cao Daism
Cao Dai took root in southern Vietnam during the 1920s after Ngo Van Chieu, a civil servant, was visited by 'Cao Dai' or the 'Supreme Being' and was given the tenets of a new religion. Ngo received this spiritual visitation in 1919 on Phu Quoc Island. The Cao Dai later told Ngo in a seance that he was to be symbolized by a giant eye. The religion quickly gained the support of a large following of dispossessed peasants. It was both a religion and a nationalist movement. In terms of the former, it claimed to be a synthesis of Buddhism, Christianity, Taoism, Confucianism and Islam. Cao Dai 'saints' include Joan of Arc, the French writer Victor Hugo, Sir Winston Churchill, Sun Yat Sen, Moses and Brahma. Debates over doctrine are mediated through the spirits who are contacted on a regular basis through a strange wooden contraption called a *corbeille-à-bec* or planchette. The five Cao Dai commandments are: do not kill any living creature; do not covet; do not practise high living; do not be tempted; and do not slander by word. But, as well as being a religion, the movement also claimed that it would restore traditional Vietnamese attitudes and was anti-colonial and modestly subversive. Opportunist to a fault, Cao Dai followers sought the aid of the Japanese against the French, the Americans against the Viet Minh and the Viet Minh against the south. Following reunification in 1975, all Cao Dai lands were confiscated and their leadership emasculated. The centre of Cao Daism remains the Mekong Delta where – and despite the efforts of the Communists – there are thought to be perhaps two million adherents and perhaps 1000 Cao Dai temples. The Cao Dai Great Temple is in the town of Tay Ninh, 100 km from Ho Chi Minh City (see page 169).

Hoa Hao
Hoa Hao is another Vietnamese religion that emerged in the Mekong Delta. It was founded by Huynh Phu So in 1939, a resident of Hoa Hao village in the province of Chau Doc. Effectively a schism of Buddhism, the sect discourages temple building and

worship, maintaining that simplicity of worship is the key to better contact with God. There are thought to be perhaps 1-1.5 million adherents of Hoa Hao, predominantly in the Chau Doc area.

Land and environment

The regions of Vietnam

The name Vietnam is derived from that adopted in 1802 by Emperor Gia Long: Nam Viet. This means, literally, the Viet (the largest ethnic group) of the south (Nam), and substituted for the country's previous name, Annam. The country is S-shaped, covers a land area of 329,600 sq km and has a coastline of 3000 km. The most important economic zones, containing the main concentrations of population, are focused on two large deltaic areas. In the north, there are the ancient rice fields and settlements of the Red River, and in the south, the fertile alluvial plain of the Mekong. In between, the country narrows to less than 50 km wide, with only a thin ribbon of fertile lowland suited to intensive agriculture. Much of the interior, away from the coastal belt and the deltas, is mountainous. Here ethnic minorities (Montagnards), along with some lowland Vietnamese resettled in so-called New Economic Zones since 1975, eke out a living on thin and unproductive soils. The rugged terrain means that only 25% of the land is actually cultivated. Of the rest, 20-25% is forested and some of this is heavily degraded.

The French subdivided Vietnam into three regions, administering each separately: Tonkin or Bac Ky (the north region), Annam or Trung Ky (the central region) and Cochin China or Nam Ky (the south region). Although these administrative divisions have been abolished, the Vietnamese still recognize their country as consisting of three regions, distinct in terms of geography, history and culture. Their new names are Bac Bo (north), Trung Bo (centre) and Nam Bo (south).

Northern Highlands

Vietnam consists of five major geographical zones. In the far north are the northern highlands which ring the Red River Delta and form a natural barrier with China. The rugged mountains on the west border of this region – the Hoang Lien Son – exceed 3000 m in places. The tributaries of the Red River have cut deep, steep-sided gorges through the Hoang Lien Son, which are navigable by small boats. The eastern portion of this region, bordering the Gulf of Tonkin, is far less imposing; the mountain peaks of the west have diminished into foothills, allowing easy access to China. It was across these hills that the Chinese mounted their successive invasions of Vietnam, the last of which occurred as recently as 1979, see page 215.

Red River Delta

The second region lies in the embrace of the hills of the north. This, the Red River Delta, can legitimately claim to be the cultural and historical heart of the Viet nation. Hanoi lies at its core and it was here the first truly independent Vietnamese polity was established in AD 939 by Ngo Quyen. The delta covers almost 15,000 sq km and extends 240 km inland from the coast. Rice has been grown on the alluvial soils of the Red River for thousands of years. Yet despite the intricate web of canals, dykes and embankments, the Vietnamese have never been able to completely tame the river, and the delta is the victim of frequent and sometimes devastating floods. The area is very low-lying, rarely more than 3 m above sea level and often less than 1 m. The highwater mark is nearly 8 m above land level in some places. During the monsoon season, the tributaries of the Red River quickly become torrents rushing through the narrow gorges of the Hoang Lien Son, before emptying into the main channel that then bursts its banks. Although the region supports one of the highest agricultural population densities in the world, the inhabitants have frequently had to endure famines, most recently in 1989.

South of the Red River Delta

South of the Red River Delta region lie the central lowlands and the mountains of the Annamite Chain. The **Annam Highlands**, now known as **Truong Son Mountain Range**, form an important cultural divide between the Indianized nations of the west and the Sinicized cultures of the east. Its northern rugged extremity is in Thanh Hoa Province. From here the Truong Son stetches over 1200 km south, to peter out 80 km north of Ho Chi Minh City.

The highest peak is Ngoc Linh Mountain in Kon Tum Province at 2598 m. The Central Highlands form an upland plateau on which the hill resorts of **Buon Ma Thuot** and **Dalat** are situated. On the plateau, plantation agriculture and hill farms are interspersed with stands of bamboo and tropical forests. Once rich in wildlife, the plateau was a popular hunting ground during the colonial period.

Central coastal strip

To the east, the Annamite Chain falls off steeply, leaving only a narrow and fragmented band of lowland suitable for settlement: the central coastal strip. In places the mountains advance all the way to the coast, plunging into the sea as dramatic rock faces and making north-south communication difficult. At no point does the region extend more than 64 km inland, and in total it covers only 6750 sq km. The soils are often rocky or saline, and irrigation is seldom possible. Nonetheless, the inhabitants have a history of sophisticated rice culture and it was here that the Champa Kingdom was established in the early centuries of the Christian era. These coastal lowlands have also formed a conduit along which people have historically moved. Even today, the main north-south road and rail routes cut through the coastal lowlands.

Mekong Delta

Unlike the Red River Delta this region is not so prone to flooding and consequently rice production is more stable. The reason why flooding is less severe lies in the regulating effect of the Great Lake of Cambodia, the Tonlé Sap. During the rainy season, when the water flowing into the Mekong becomes too great for even this mighty river to absorb, rather than overflowing its banks, the water backs up into the Tonlé Sap, which quadruples in area. The Mekong Delta covers 67,000 sq km and is drained by five branches of the Mekong, which divides as it flows towards the sea. The vast delta is one of the great rice bowls of Asia producing nearly half of the country's rice and over the years has been cut into a patchwork by the canals that have been dug to expand irrigation and rice cultivation. Largely forested until the late 19th century, the French supported the settlement of the area by Vietnamese peasants, recognizing that it could become enormously productive. The deposition of silt by the rivers that cut through the delta, means that the shoreline is continually advancing, by up to 80 m each year in some places. To the north of the delta lies Ho Chi Minh City.

Climate

Vietnam stretches more than 1800 km from north to south and the weather patterns in the two principal cities, Hanoi in the north and Ho Chi Minh City in the south, are very different. Average temperatures tend to rise the further south you go, while the seasonal variation in temperature decreases. The exceptions to this general rule of thumb are in the interior highland areas where the altitude means it is considerably colder.

North Vietnam

The seasons in the north are similar to those of South China. The winter is November to April, with temperatures averaging 16°C and little rainfall. The summer begins in May and lasts until October. During these months it can be very hot, with an average temperature of 30°C, along with heavy rainfall and the occasional violent typhoon.

Central Vietnam

Central Vietnam experiences a transitional climate, halfway between that in the south and in the north. Hué has a reputation for poor weather: it's often overcast and an umbrella is needed whatever the month, even in the short 'dry' season from February to April. Hué's annual rainfall is 3250 mm. See page 18 for the best time to visit.

South Vietnam

Temperatures in the south are fairly constant through the year (25°C-30°C) and the seasons are determined by the rains. The dry season runs from November to April (when there is virtually no rain whatsoever) and the wet season from May to October. The hottest period is during March and April, before the rains have broken. Typhoons are quite common in coastal areas between July and November.

Highland Areas

In the hill resorts of Dalat (1500 m), Buon Ma Thuot and Sapa nights are cool throughout the year and in the 'winter' months between October to March it can be distinctly chilly with temperatures falling to 4°C. Even in the hottest months of March and April the temperature rarely exceeds 26°C.

Flora and fauna

Together with overseas conservation agencies such as the Worldwide Fund for Nature (WWF), Vietnamese scientists have, in recent years, been enumerating and protecting their fauna and flora. The establishment of nature reserves began in 1962 with the gazetting of the Cuc Phuong National Park. Today there are a total of 87 reserves covering 3.3% of Vietnam's land area. However, some of them are too small to sustain sufficiently large breeding populations of endangered species and many parks are quite heavily populated. For instance 80,000 people live, farm and hunt within the 22,000 ha Bach Ma National Park. Vietnamese scientists with support from outside agencies, in particular the WWF, have begun the important task of cataloguing and protecting Vietnam's wildlife.

The **Javan rhinoceros** is one of the rarest large mammals in the world and until recently was thought only to survive in the Ujung Kulon National Park in West Java, Indonesia. However in November 1988 it was reported that a Stieng tribesman had shot a female Javan rhino near the Dong Nai River around 130 km northeast of Saigon. When he tried to sell the horn and hide he was arrested and this set in train a search to discover if there were any more of the animals in the area. Researchers discovered that Viet Cong soldiers operating in the area during the war saw – and killed – a number of animals. One former revolutionary, Tran Ngoc Khanh, reported that he once saw a herd of 20 animals and that between 1952 and 1976 some 17 animals were shot by the soldiers. With the Viet Cong shooting the animals whenever they chanced upon them, and the Americans spraying tonnes of defoliant on the area, it is a wonder than any survived through to the end of the war. However, a study by George Schaller and three Vietnamese colleagues in 1989 found tracks, also near the Dong Nai River, and estimated that a population of 10 to 15 animals probably still survived in a 750 sq km area of bamboo and dipterocarp forest close to and including Nam Cat Tien National Park.

This remarkable find was followed by, if anything, an even more astonishing discovery: of two completely new species of mammal. In 1992 British scientist Dr John MacKinnon discovered the skeleton of an animal now known as the **Vu Quang ox** (*Pseudoryx nghetinhensis*) but known to locals as *sao la*. The Vu Quang ox was the first new large mammal species to be found in 50 years; scientists were amazed that a large mammal could exist on this crowded planet without their knowledge. In June 1994 the first live specimen (a young calf) was captured and shortly afterwards a second one was caught and taken to the Forestry Institute in Hanoi. Sadly, both died in captivity but in early 1995 a third was brought in alive. The animals look anything but ox-like, and have the appearance, grace and manner of a small deer. The government responded to the discovery by extending the Vu Quang Nature Reserve and banning hunting of *sao la*. Local ethnic minorities, who have long regarded *sao la* as a tasty and not uncommon animal, have therefore lost a valued source of food and no longer have a vested interest in the animal's survival. *Sao la* must rue the day they were 'discovered'. In 1993 a new species of deer that has been named the **giant muntjac** was also found in the Vu Quang Nature Reserve. The scientists have yet to see it alive but villagers prize its meat and are reported to trap it in quite large numbers.

Large rare mammals are confined to isolated pockets where the government does its best to protect them from hunters. On Cat Ba Island, the national park is home to the world's last wild troops of white-headed langur. In North Vietnam tigers have been hunted close to extinction and further south territorial battles rage between elephants and farmers. Rampaging elephants sometimes cause loss of life and are in turn decimated by enraged villagers.

Among the **larger mammals**, there are small numbers of tiger (around 200), leopard, clouded leopard, Indian elephant, Malayan sun bear, Himalayan black bear, sambar deer, gibbon and gaur (wild buffalo). These are rarely seen, except in zoos. There are frequent news reports of farmers maiming or killing elephants after their crops have been trampled or their huts flattened. The larger reptiles include two species of crocodile, the estuarine (*Crocodilus porosus*) and Siamese (*Crocodilus siamensis*). The former grows to a length of 5 m and has been reported to have killed and eaten humans. Among the larger snakes are the reticulated python (*Python reticulatus*) and the smaller Indian python (*Python molurus*), both non-venomous constrictors. Venomous snakes include two species of cobra (the king cobra and common cobra), two species of krait and six species of pit viper.

Given the difficulty of getting to Vietnam's more remote areas, the country is hardly a haven for amateur naturalists. Professional photographers and naturalists have been escorted to the country's wild areas but this is not an option for the average visitor. Getting there requires time and contacts. A wander around the markets of Vietnam reveals the variety and number of animals that end up in the cooking pot, including deer, bear, snakes, monkeys and turtles. The Chinese penchant for exotic foods (such gastronomic wonders as tigers' testicles and bear's foot) has also become a predilection of the Vietnamese and most animals are fair game.

Birds

Birds have, in general, suffered rather less than mammals from over-hunting and the effects of the war. There have been some casualties however: the eastern sarus crane of the Mekong Delta – a symbol of fidelity, longevity and good luck – disappeared entirely during the war. However, in 1985 a farmer reported seeing a single bird, and by 1990 there were over 500 pairs breeding on the now pacified former battlefields. A sarus crane reserve has been established in Dong Thap Province. The best time of year for birding is November to May.

Among the more unusual birds are the snake bird (named after its habit of swimming with its body submerged and only its snake-like neck and head above the surface), the argus pheasant, which the Japanese believe to be the mythical phoenix, the little bastard quail of which the male hatches and rears the young.

But what may come as the real surprise to many visitors to Vietnam is that it has the highest number of endemic bird species of any country in mainland Southeast Asia. There are currently 12 endemic species of bird that can only be seen in Vietnam which is one reason it is becoming a popular destination for overseas birdwatchers. In addition to these 12 endemics there are many more near endemics, bird species restricted to Vietnam and a few neighbouring countries, and other distinct subspecies that may well be considered endemic species in the future.

An incredible diversity of birds live in the forest and wetland habitats of **Nam Cat Tien National Park**, including an estimated 230 species of birds. Endangered birds that can be found here include Germain's peacock pheasant, green peafowl and the highly elusive orange-necked partridge. You can hire a jeep at the park headquarters to visit areas further afield such as Bird Lake to look for visiting waders or Crocodile Lake where grey-headed fish eagle, lesser adjutant and Asian golden weaver may be seen, as well as the reintroduced Siamese crocodiles. During the walk through the forest to Crocodile Lake look out for bar-bellied and blue-rumped pitta, red-and-black and banded broadbill and orange-breasted trogon. Other interesting species at Cat Tien include scaly-breasted partridge, Siamese fireback, woolly-necked stork and grey-faced tit-babbler and white-bellied, great slaty, pale-headed and heart-spotted woodpecker. On the trails or the headquarters road, green-eared, blue-eared, lineated and – if you're lucky – red-vented barbet can often be seen perched high up in the roadside trees.

Twenty minutes by road from Dalat at **Langbian Mountain**, the evergreen forests are home to many interesting birds including several endemic species. Key species to be found here include the silver pheasant, Indochinese cuckooshrike, Eurasian jay, mugimaki flycatcher, yellow-billed nuthatch and red crossbill. This is also the place to see three of Vietnam's most sought-after endemics: collared laughingthrush, Vietnamese cutia and Vietnamese greenfinch. Mount Langbian is best avoided at weekends and holidays when it is a popular destination for local tourists.

Tuyen Lam Lake, only 3 km from the centre of Dalat, is another hotspot for birders. Take a boat to far side of the lake where a track leads through the pines to areas of remnant tropical evergreen forest. With luck, the rare and endemic grey-crowned crocias, rediscovered in 1994 after not being seen for nearly 60 years, can be found. Other interesting species here include slender-billed oriole, maroon oriole, rufous-backed sibia, black-crowned parrotbill and orange-breasted, black-hooded and white-cheeked laughingthrush.

Ta Nung Valley, around 10 km from Dalat, holds pockets of remnant evergreen forest where many of the Dalat specialities can still be found including orange-breasted, black-hooded and white-cheeked laughingthrush, blue-winged minla, grey-crowned crocias, black-crowned parrotbill and black-throated sunbird.

In **Cuc Phuong National Park**, see page 81, an area of limestone hills covered with large tracts of primary forest, key bird species include silver pheasant, red-collared woodpecker, pied falconet, white-winged magpie and limestone wren- babbler and bar-bellied, blue-rumped and eared pitta.

Books and films

Art and archaeology

Hejzlar, J, *The Art of Vietnam* (Hamlyn: London, 1973). The text is rather heavy going, but there are numerous photos.
Le Brusq, Arnauld and **de Selva, Léonard**, *Vietnam, A Travers L'Architecture Coloniale* (Patimoines et Medias, 1999). Available in German but not in English. A meticulously researched and fascinating guide to Vietnam's colonial architecture chronicling the evolution of the colonial cities and describing the history of many of Vietnam's

public buildings erected during French rule. Superbly illustrated with contemporary colour photos, archive pictures and plans.
Parmentier, Henri with **Mus, Paul** and **Aymonier, Etienne** *Cham Sculpture in the Tourane Museum: Religious Ceremonies and Superstitions of Champa* (White Lotus, 2001). Reprint of a classic 1922 text by Parmentier who was responsible for assembling the Cham sculptures and after whom the museum in Danang was originally named.

Biography and autobiography

Fenn, Charles, *Ho Chi Minh: A Biographical Introduction* (Studio Vista: London, 1973).
Greene, Graham, *Ways of Escape* (1980). Autobiographical.
Ho Chi Minh, *Prison Diary* (Hanoi: Foreign Languages Publishing House). A collection of poems by Ho while he was incarcerated in China in 1942. They record his prison experiences and his yearning for home.
Page, Tim, *Derailed in Uncle Ho's Victory*

Garden (Touchstone Books, 1995). War photojournalist Tim Page makes a return visit to Vietnam, amusing in places.
Tin, Bui, *Following Ho Chi Minh* (Hurst: London, 1995). Autobiographical account of a North Vietnamese Colonel's disillusionment with the communist regime following Ho Chi Minh's death. Western readers may find it rather self-congratulatory in tone but it's still an interesting read.

Culture

Hickey, Gerald, *Village in Vietnam* (Yale University Press: New Haven, 1964). Classic

village study, only available second-hand.

Economics, politics and development

Beresford, Melanie, *Vietnam: Politics, Economics and Society* (Pinter: London, 1988). Academic account of social, economic and political developments to the mid-

1980s; too early to include much discussion of economic reform programme.
Hayton, Bill, *Vietnam–Rising Dragon* (Yale University Press: 2010). A new,

well-researched insightful account into Vietnam today that seeks to enlighten readers about the current economic and political structures and issues in this rapidly growing country. Hayton spent time as a BBC reporter in Hanoi.

Kemf, Elizabeth, *Month of Pure Light: The Re-greening of Vietnam* (The Women's Press: London, 1990). Account of the attempts to overcome the after-effects of US defoliation and replant the Vietnamese countryside; more light travelogue than objective book.

Nugent, Nicholas, *Vietnam: The Second Revolution* (In Print: London, 1996). A good summary of the main changes in Vietnam's economy and society. Also covers the more recent changes dating from the early 1990s.

Popkin, Samuel L, *The Rational Peasant: The Political Economy of Rural Society in Vietnam* (Berkeley: University of California Press, 1979). This book was written in response to James Scott's *The Moral Economy of the Peasant*. Popkin contests the view that traditional Southeast Asia (here, Vietnam) was a moral economy where village solidarity and community spirit were dominant.

Scott, James C, *The Moral Economy of the Peasant: Rebellion and Subsistence in Southeast Asia* (New Haven: Yale University Press, 1976). The classic historical study of the 'moral' economy of the peasant. Available as a portable paperback.

Templer, Robert, *Shadows and Wind: A View of Life in Modern Vietnam* (London: Little Brown, 1998). Templer was an Agence France Presse correspondent and this is his account of modern Vietnam and where it is headed. It is a downbeat picture of the country, one where bureaucratic inertia and political heavy handedness constrain progress, but is a fascinating read.

Turner, Robert F, *Vietnamese Communism: Its Origins and Development* (Hoover Institution Press: Stanford, 1975). Academic study of the rise of communism in Vietnam.

Williams, Michael C, *Vietnam at the Crossroads* (Pinter: London, 1992). Most recent survey of political and economic reforms by a senior BBC World Service commentator; lucid and informed.

Young, Marilyn, *The Vietnam Wars 1945-1990* (Harper Collins: New York, 1990). Good account of the origins, development and aftermath of the Vietnam wars.

History

Elliott, Mai, *Sacred Willow: Four Generations in the Life of a Vietnamese Family* (OUP: Oxford, 1999). Recounts the history of Vietnam through the life of the Duong family from the 19th century to the tragedy of Boat People. A story of Vietnam through Vietnamese eyes.

Marriott, Edward, *Claude and Madeline: A True Story of War, Espionage and Passion* (Picador 2005). This is an unputdownable tale of madness and bravado set in Vietnam and France.

Osborne, Roger, *The Deprat Affair: Ambition, Revenge and Deceit in French Indochina* (Jonathan Cape, 1999). An account of

the extraordinary pickle into which Jacques Deprat, a brilliant young geologist, got himself. Whether he was guilty of professional deceit or not the book gives a useful insight into colonial society and mores in the first two decades of the 20th century.

Taylor, Keith Weller, *The Birth of Vietnam* (University of California Press: Berkeley, 1983) Academic history of early Vietnam from the third century BC to 10th century.

Wintle, Justin, *The Vietnam Wars* (Weidenfeld and Nicholson: London, 1991). Not just about *the* War, but about all of Vietnam's interminable conflicts.

Novels

Duras, Marguerite, *The Lover* (London: Flamingo, 1984). Now a film starring Jane March; this is the story of the illicit relationship between an expat French girl and a Chinese from Cholon set in the 1930s.

Greene, Graham, *The Quiet American* (Heinemann: London, 1954). What is remarkable about this novel is the way that it predicts America's experience in Vietnam. The two key figures are Alden Pyle, an idealistic young American, and Thomas Fowler, a hard-bitten and cynical British journalist. It is set in and around Saigon as the war between the French and the Viet Minh intensifies.

Grey, Anthony, *Saigon* (Pan: London, 1983). An entertaining novel.

Travel and geography

Garstin, Crosbie, *The Voyage from London to Indochina* (Heinemann, 1928). Hilarious and rather irreverent account of a journey through Vietnam.

Lewis, Norman, *A Dragon Apparent: Travels in Cambodia, Laos and Vietnam* (1951). One of the finest of all travel books.

Theroux, Paul, *The Great Railway Bazaar* (Penguin: London, 1977). Theroux describes a graphic account of one American's attempt to travel by rail between Saigon and Hué.

Vu Tu Lap and **Taillard, Christian,** *An Atlas of Vietnam* (Reclus – La Documentation Française, 1994). Summary of the population and economy of Vietnam in maps.

Wintle, Justin, *Romancing Vietnam. Inside the Boat Country* (Penguin 1992). A humorous and unusual account of a writer's attempts to see as much of the real Vietnam as possible whilst surrounded and monitored by bureaucratic officials. It also gives an insight into a very changed Vietnam – in the 1980s – which a recent traveller may find hard to comprehend.

Vietnamese literature in English

Nguyen Du, *The Tale of Kieu* (also known as *Truyen Kieu*) (Yale University Press: New Haven, 1983), translated by Huynh Sanh Thong. This is an early 19th-century Vietnamese classic and, for many, the masterpiece of Vietnamese poetry. It is also published in Vietnam (in English) by the Foreign Languages Publishing House. It tells the story of a beautiful girl and her doomed love affair with a soldier.

Vietnamese wars

Cawthorne, Nigel, *The Bamboo Cage* (Leo Cooper, 1992). The story of MIAs and POWs.

Doyle, Jeff with **Grey, Jeffrey** and **Pierce, Peter,** *Australia's Vietnam War*, (A&M University Press, 2002). Australia's role in the Vietnam War is little known and this book examines Australia's motives for joining and contribution to America's war effort.

Fall, Bernard B, *Hell in a Very Small Place: The Siege of Dien Bien Phu* (Pall Mall Press, 1967).

Fitzgerald, Francis, *Fire in the Lake* (Vintage Books: New York, 1972). Pulitzer prize winner; a well-researched and readable account of the US involvement.

Harrison, James P, *The Endless War: Fifty Years of Struggle in Vietnam* (Free Press: New York, 1982).

Herr, Michael, *Dispatches* (Knopf: New York, 1977). An acclaimed account of the war written by a correspondent who experienced the conflict first hand.

Kaiser, David, *American Tragedy: Kennedy, Johnson and the Origins of the Vietnam War* (Harvard University Press, 1999). This account is based on newly opened archives and provides a penetrating insight into America's involvement in Vietnam.

Karnow, Stanley, *Vietnam: A History* (Viking Press: New York, 1983 and 1991). A comprehensive and readable history; the best there is.

Kissinger, Henry, *The White House Years* (Little, Brown, 1979). Part one of the memoirs of America's best known diplomat. This covers the first Nixon term and ends with the Paris Peace Accord of 1973. Also, *Years of Upheaval* (Little, Brown, 1982). This covers the turbulent months from his visit to Hanoi in February 1973 to Nixon's resignation in August 1974. And, *Years of Renewal* (Simon and Schuster, 1999). The third and concluding volume of the memoirs covers the end of the Vietnam war and collapse of the South.

Lunn, Hugh, *Vietnam: A Reporter's War* (University of Queensland Press: St Lucia, Australia, 1985). Account of Australian reporter Hugh Lunn's year in Vietnam with Reuters between 1967 and 1968, including an account of the Tet Offensive.

McNamara, Robert S and Mark, Brian Van de, *In Retrospect: The Tragedy and Lessons of Vietnam* (Times/Random House: New York, 1995). McNamara was Secretary for Defense from 1961 to 1968 and this is his cathartic account of the war. Informed from the inside, he concludes that the war was a big mistake.

Mangold, Tom and Penycate, John, *The Tunnels of Cu Chi* (1985). Compelling account of the building of the tunnels and the Viet Cong who fought in them.

Mason, Robert, *Chickenhawk* (Penguin: Harmondsworth, 1984). Excellent autobiography of a helicopter pilot.

Ninh, Bao, *The Sorrow of War* (Secker & Warburg, London, 1993). Wartime novel by a North Vietnamese soldier, a wonderful account of emotions during and after the war.

Roth, Philip, *The Human Stain* (Jonathan Cape, 2000). Not, ostensibly, about the Vietnam war at all but it has an excellent account of American war vets coming to terms with their traumas and the country that shuns them.

Sheehan, Neil, *A Bright Shining Lie* (Jonathan Cape: London, 1989). A meticulously researched 850-page account of the Vietnam War, based around the life of John Paul Vann. Recommended.

Sheehan, Neil, *Two Cities: Hanoi and Saigon* (in US *After the War was Over*) (Jonathan Cape: London, 1992). A short but fascinating book that tries to link the past with the present in a part autobiography, part travelogue, part contemporary commentary.

SIPRI, *Ecological Consequences of the Second Indochina War* (Almqvist & Wiksell: Stockholm, 1976). Academic study of environmental side effects of war.

Swain, Jon, *River of Time* (Heinemann, 1996). A gripping account of this war correspondent's time throughout the Vietnam War. He expounds the interesting hypothesis that the reason the American generals were willing to sacrifice so many men was that they saw it as a rehearsal for a future war in Europe against the Red Army.

Turley, William S, *The Second Indochina War: A Short Political and Military History 1954-75* (Westview: Boulder, 1986). A clear, well-balanced academic account of the war.

Windrow, Martin, *The Last Valley: Dien Bien Phu and the French Defeat in Vietnam* (De Capo Press, 2004). A new, detailed and well regarded account of the battle in the north that heralded the end of French involvement in Indochina.

Young, Gavin, *A Wavering Grace: A Vietnamese Family in War and Peace* (London: Viking, 1997). An account of the war – Young was a reporter – told through the lives of a Vietnamese family.

Cambodia

Contents

Footprint features

Border crossings

Cambodia–Vietnam, *page 262*
Cambodia–Thailand, *page 278*
Cambodia–Laos, *page 280*

At a glance

⊖ **Getting around** Major towns have daytime bus services. *Song-thaews* and trucks cover remote areas. Domestic flights available.

⊘ **Time required** 1-4 weeks

☼ **Weather** Nov-Mar is best, although it can be cool at higher elevations. Temperatures peak in Apr. Rainy season May-Sep/Oct.

⊗ **When not to go** Mar-May can be hot, humid and hazy. Outdoor activities such as hiking can be tricky in the wet season.

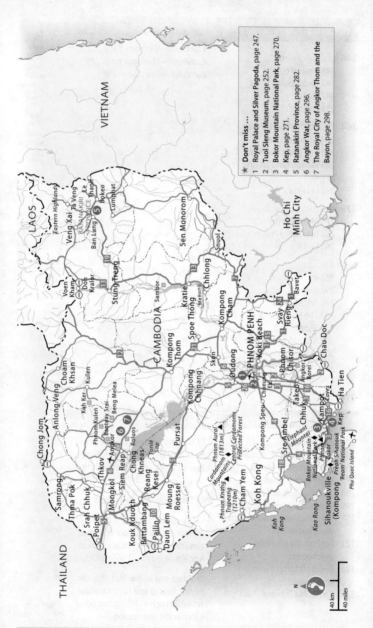

Don't miss ...
1 Royal Palace and Silver Pagoda, page 247.
2 Tuol Sleng Museum, page 252.
3 Bokor Mountain National Park, page 270.
4 Kep, page 271.
5 Ratanakiri Province, page 282.
6 Angkor Wat, page 296.
7 The Royal City of Angkor Thom and the
  Bayon, page 298.

VIETNAM

LAOS

Ho Chi
Minh City

CAMBODIA

THAILAND

PHNOM PENH

Siem Reap

Battambang

Sihanoukville

N

40 km
40 miles

Introduction

Impenetrable jungles; abandoned temples smothered in centuries of foliage; arcing white-sand beaches fringed with swaying palms; exotic, smiling locals – in almost every respect Cambodia satisfies the hackneyed expectations of Southeast Asia. And, if you get off the beaten track, Cambodia also offers that increasingly elusive feeling of discovery; the feeling that you are entering into arcane and unknown worlds where few Westerners have been before. But this is a country that is still trying to make sense of itself after the horrors of the genocidal Khmer Rouge rule. While the UN-sponsored trial of the former leaders finally got underway in 2007, many of its minor officials still hold positions of influence and power in Cambodia and you don't have to spend long in the country to see the gulf between the indifferent rich and the absolute poor.

Yet, without doubt, ancient Cambodia produced one of the world's greatest civilizations at Angkor. This temple complex near Siem Reap is truly breathtaking. But don't just stop there; Angkor Wat is merely one temple at the heart of a thousand others.

Today's capital, Phnom Penh, with its charming riverside setting is rapidly shedding its laid-back dusty charm and becoming a dynamic city complete with Hummer-driving Khmer yuppies, chic bars serving cocktails, clubs with designer interiors and hangouts filled with the great and the gorgeous.

On the beaches to the south you can find relaxed resort towns on the coast, such as Kep. In the northeastern provinces, tracts of red earth cut through hills carpeted in jungle. At Ban Lung you won't be disappointed by the waterfalls, boat rides and the stunning, bottle-green waters of Yaek Lom Lake.

Phnom Penh

→ *Colour map 6, B3.*

It is not hard to imagine Phnom Penh in its heyday, with wide, shady boulevards, beautiful French buildings and exquisite pagodas. They're still all here but are in a derelict, dust-blown, decaying state surrounded by growing volumes of cars, pickup trucks and motorcyclists. It all leaves you wondering how a city like this works. But it does, somehow.

Phnom Penh is a city of contrasts: East and West, poor and rich, serenity and chaos. Although the city has a reputation as a frontier town, due to drugs, gun ownership and prostitution, a more cosmopolitan character is being forged out of the muck. Monks' saffron robes are once again lending a splash of colour to the capital's streets, following the reinstatement of Buddhism as the national religion in 1989, and stylish restaurants and bars line the riverside. However, the amputees on street corners are a constant reminder of Cambodia's tragic story. Perhaps the one constant in all the turmoil of the past century has been the monarchy – shifting, whimsical, pliant and, indeed, temporarily absent as it may have been. The splendid royal palace, visible to all, was a daily reminder of this ultimate authority whom even the Khmer Rouge had to treat with caution. The royal palace area, with its glittering spires, wats, stupas, national museum and broad green spaces, is perfectly situated alongside the river and is as pivotal to the city as the city is to the country.
‣‣ *For listings, see pages 253-263.*

Ins and outs

Getting there

Air Phnom Penh International airport lies approximately 10 km west of the city on Road No 4. There are flights to Phnom Penh from Bangkok, Ho Chi Minh City, Vientiane and Siem Reap. A taxi from the airport to town costs US$7 and a moto about US$3. The journey takes between 40 minutes and one hour, although at peak times the roads are often gridlocked, so be prepared for delays in the morning and late afternoon.

Boat and bus It is possible to get to Phnom Penh by boat and bus from Chau Doc in Vietnam and by road crossing at Moc Bai. ‣‣ *See box, page 262.*

Getting around

Fleets of tuk-tuks (*lomphata* in Khmer) provide the nearest thing to taxis in Phnom Penh. Hotels can arrange car hire around town and surrounding areas. Motorbikes are ubiquitous. Most visitors use the local *motodops* (motorbike taxis where you ride on the back) as a quick, cheap and efficient way of getting around. Be advised that riding a moto can be risky; wear a helmet. There are cyclos too, which undoubtedly appeal to many tourists but for regular journeys they prove to be just too slow and expensive. At present there is no public transport system in Phnom Penh. A bus network has been mooted and there's even talk of a futuristic 'Skytrain' to link the river with the airport but without any concrete plans in place at this stage both projects seem years away. When travelling on any form of public transport in Phnom Penh, be wary of bag snatchers.

Tourist information

Ministry of Tourism ① *3 Monivong Blvd, T023-427130.*

Background

Phnom Penh lies at the confluence of the Sap, Mekong and Bassac rivers and quickly grew into an important commercial centre. Years of war have taken a heavy toll on the city's infrastructure and economy, as well as its inhabitants. Refugees first began to flood in from the countryside in the early 1950s during the First Indochina War and the population grew from 100,000 to 600,000 by the late 1960s. In the early 1970s there was another surge as people streamed in from the countryside again, this time to escape US bombing and guerrilla warfare. On the eve of the Khmer Rouge takeover in 1975, the capital had a population of two million, but soon became a ghost town. On Pol Pot's orders it was forcibly emptied and the townspeople frog-marched into the countryside to work as labourers. Only 45,000 inhabitants were left in the city in 1975 and a large number were soldiers. In 1979, after four years of virtual abandonment, Phnom Penh had a population of a few thousand. People began to drift back following the Vietnamese invasion (1978-1979) and as hopes for peace rose in 1991, the floodgates opened yet again: today the population is approaching one million.

Phnom Penh has undergone an economic revival since the Paris Peace Accord of 1991. Following the 1998 coup, however, there was an exodus of businesses and investors for whom this bloody and futile atrocity was the final straw. The relative stability since the coup has seen a partial revival of confidence but few are willing to risk their capital in long-term investments.

Sights

Royal Palace and Silver Pagoda
① *Entrance on Samdech Sothearos Blvd. Daily 0730-1100, 1400-1700. US$3, plus US$2 for camera or US$5 for video camera.*

The Royal Palace and Silver Pagoda were built mainly by the French in 1866, on the site of the old town. The **Throne Hall**, the main building facing the Victory Gate, was built in 1917 in Khmer style; it has a tiered roof and a 59-m tower, influenced by Angkor's Bayon Temple. The steps leading up to it are protected by multi-headed nagas. It is used for coronations and other official occasions: scenes from the *Ramayana* adorn the ceiling. Inside stand the sacred gong and French-style thrones only used by the sovereign. Above the thrones hangs Preah Maha Svetrachatr, a nine-tiered parasol, which symbolizes heaven. There are two chambers for the king and queen at the back of the hall, which are used only in the week before a coronation when the royal couple are barred from sleeping together. The other adjoining room is used to house the ashes of dead monarchs before they are placed in a royal stupa.

The **Royal Treasury** and the **Napoleon III Pavilion** (summer house), built in 1866, are to the south of the Throne Room. The latter was presented by Napoleon III to his Empress Eugenie as accommodation for the princess during the Suez Canal opening celebrations. She later had it dismantled and dispatched it to Phnom Penh as a gift to the king.

The **Silver Pagoda** is often called the Pagoda of the Emerald Buddha or Wat Preah Keo Morokat after the statue housed here. The wooden temple was originally built by King Norodom in 1892 to enshrine royal ashes and then rebuilt by Sihanouk in 1962. The pagoda's steps are Italian marble, and inside, its floor comprises of more than 5000 silver blocks which together weigh nearly six tonnes. All around are cabinets filled with presents from foreign dignitaries. The pagoda is remarkably intact, having been granted

1 Phnom Penh

To Boat Piers & Route 5

French
Embassy

British Embassy

International
Mosque

Calmette
Hospital

US Embassy

Boeng Kak Lake
Lake being filled in (not complete)

Tropical & Travellers
Medical Clinic

Psar Thmei
(Central
Market)

Confederation de Russie Blvd

Kampuchea Krom Blvd

Nehru Blvd

Charles de Gaulle Blvd

O Russei

Wat Koh

Croix Rouge

Olympic
Stadium

Preah Sihanouk Blvd

Lucky
Supermarket

Wat Moha
Montrei

Dragon
Air

Thai

Tuol Sleng
Museum

To Cheoung Ek

To Phnom Penh Water Park, Airport & Routes 3 & 4

Monireth Blvd

Mao Tse Tung Blvd

Moniyong Blvd

To Wat Tuol Tom Pong, Psar Tuol
Tom Pong(Russian Market) Rajana &

To Vietnamese Embassy

To **5** & Route 6

Japanese
Friendship
Bridge

To Siem Reap

N

200 metres
200 yards

Wat Phnom

Tonlé Sap

Sisowath Quay

Psar Chas
(Old Market)

Wat Ounalom

National
Museum of
Cambodia

Samdech Sothearos Blvd

Royal
Palace

Silver
Pagoda

Sisowath Quay

Norodom Blvd

Vietnam
Airlines

Monument Books

International SOS
Medical & Dental Clinic

Silk Air

Independence
Monument

Air France

Lao Airlines

Khmer
Web

Wat Lang Ka

Vietnam Airlines

To Lao
Embassy

To **17**, Former US Embassy, Route 1 & Vietnam

→ **Phnom Penh maps**
1   Phnom Penh, page 248
2   Sisowath Quay, page 251

Sleeping 🛏
Almond **23** E5
Amber Villa **24** D4
Anise **20** E4
Aram **28** D5

Billabong **1** C3
Boddhi Tree Umma **2** E3
Capitol **5** D3
Golden Gate **10** D4
Grandview
  Guesthouse **12** A3
Juliana **19** C2
KIDS **7** C4
Lazy Fish Guesthouse **21** B3
Le Royal **22** B3
New York **25** C3
Palm Resort **17** E4
Pavilion **38** D5
Regent Park **31** D5
Royal Guesthouse **39** C4
Scandinavia **32** E4
Simon 2 Guesthouse **34** B3
Sunway **36** B3
Velkommen Inn **40** B4
Walkabout **37** C4

Eating 🍴
Asia Europe Bakery **1** D3
Baan Thai **2** E4
Boeung Bopha **5** A4
Elsewhere **6** D4
Family **7** B3
Garden Centre Café **4** E4
Gasolina **8** E4
Green Vespa **18** B4
Jars of Clay **11** E2
Java **10** D5
K'NYAY **20** D5
La Marmite **13** B4
Lazy Gecko **14** B3
Le Gourmandise
  Bleu **31** E3
Living Room **29** E4
Mount Everest **15** D4
Origami **16** D5
Pyong Yang **19** E3
Romdeng **37** C4
Sam Doo **21** C3
The Deli **36** C4
The Shop **24** D4

Bars & clubs 🍸
Blue Chilli **39** C4
Cathouse **26** C4
Heart of Darkness **27** C4
Manhattan **30** A3
Meta House **39** D5
Pontoon **40** B4
Sharkys **9** C4
Zepplin **34** C3

Phnom Penh's inhabitants

Of the original population of Phnom Penh, thousands died during the Pol Pot era so the population of the city now seems rural in character. The population tends to vary from season to season: in the dry season people pour into the capital when there is little work in the countryside but go back to their farms in the wet season when the rice has to be planted.

Phnom Penh has long faced a housing shortage – two-thirds of its houses were damaged by the Khmer Rouge between 1975 and 1979 and the rate of migration into the city exceeds the rate of building. Apart from the sheer cost of building

new ones and renovating the crumbling colonial mansions, there has been a severe shortage of skilled workers in Cambodia: under Pol Pot 20,000 engineers were killed and nearly all the country's architects.

Exacerbating the problem is the issue of land ownership as so many people were removed from their homes. These days there are many more qualified workers but sky-rocketing property prices coupled with the confusing issue of land title has created a situation where a great land grab is occuring with people being tossed out of their homes or having them bulldozed to make way for profitable developments.

special dispensation by the Khmer Rouge, although 60% of the Khmer treasures were stolen from here. In the centre of the pagoda is a magnificent 17th-century emerald Buddha statue made of Baccarat crystal. In front is a 90-kg golden Buddha studded with 9584 diamonds, dating from 1906. It was made from the jewellery of King Norodom and its vital statistics conform exactly to his – a tradition that can be traced back to the god-kings of Angkor.

National Museum of Cambodia

ⓘ *Entrance is on the corner of streets 13 and 178. Daily 0700-1130, 1400-1730. US$2, plus US$3 for camera or video; photographs only permitted in the garden. French- and English-speaking guides are available, mostly excellent.*

The National Museum of Cambodia was built in 1920 and contains a collection of Khmer art – notably sculpture – throughout the ages (although some periods are not represented). Galleries are arranged chronologically in a clockwise direction. Most of the exhibits date from the Angkor period but there are several examples from the pre-Angkor era (that is from the kingdoms of Funan, Chenla and Cham). The collection of Buddhas from the sixth and seventh centuries includes a statue of Krishna Bovardhana found at Angkor Borei showing the freedom and grace of early Khmer sculpture. The chief attraction is probably the pre-Angkorian statue of Harihara, found at Prasat Andat near Kompong Thom. There is a fragment from a beautiful bronze statue of Vishnu found in the West Baray at Angkor, as well as frescoes and engraved doors.

The riverside and Wat Ounalom

Sisowath Quay is Phnom Penh's Left Bank. A broad pavement runs along the side of the river and on the opposite side of the road a rather splendid assemblage of colonial buildings looks out over the broad expanse of waters. The erstwhile administrative buildings and merchants' houses today form an unbroken chain – almost a mile long – of bars and restaurants, with the odd guesthouse thrown in. While foreign tourist commerce fills the street, the quayside itself is dominated by local Khmer families who stroll and sit in the cool of the evening, served by an army of hawkers.

Phnom Penh's most important wat, **Wat Ounalom**, is north of the national museum, at the junction of Street 154 and Samdech Sothearos Boulevard, facing the Tonlé Sap. The first building on this site was a monastery, built in 1443 to house a hair of the Buddha. Before 1975, more than 500 monks lived at the wat but the Khmer Rouge murdered the Patriarch and did their best to demolish the capital's principal temple. Nonetheless it remains Cambodian Buddhism's headquarters. The complex has been restored since 1979 although its famous library was completely destroyed. The stupa behind the main sanctuary is the oldest part of the wat.

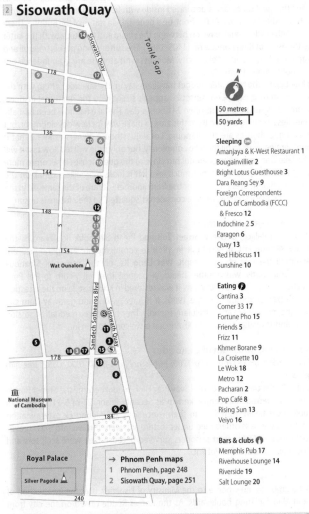

2 Sisowath Quay

50 metres
50 yards

Sleeping
Amanjaya & K-West Restaurant **1**
Bougainvillier **2**
Bright Lotus Guesthouse **3**
Dara Reang Sey **9**
Foreign Correspondents
  Club of Cambodia (FCCC)
  & Fresco **12**
Indochine 2 **5**
Paragon **6**
Quay **13**
Red Hibiscus **11**
Sunshine **10**

Eating
Cantina **3**
Corner 33 **17**
Fortune Pho **15**
Friends **5**
Frizz **11**
Khmer Borane **9**
La Croisette **10**
Le Wok **18**
Metro **12**
Pacharan **2**
Pop Café **8**
Rising Sun **13**
Veiyo **16**

Bars & clubs
Memphis Pub **17**
Riverhouse Lounge **14**
Riverside **19**
Salt Lounge **20**

→ **Phnom Penh maps**
1 Phnom Penh, page 248
2 Sisowath Quay, page 251

Central Market, Wat Phnom and Boeng Kak Lake

The stunning Central Market (Psar Thmei) is a perfect example of artdeco styling and one of Phnom Penh's most beautiful buildings. Inside a labyrinth of stalls and hawkers sell everything from jewellery through to curios. Those who are after a real bargain are better off heading to the Russian Market where items tend to be much cheaper.

Wat Phnom stands on a small hill and is the temple from which the city takes its name. It was built by a wealthy Khmer lady called Penh in 1372. The sanctuary was rebuilt in 1434, 1890, 1894 and 1926. The main entrance is to the east; the steps are guarded by nagas and lions. The principal sanctuary is decorated inside with frescoes depicting scenes from Buddha's life and the *Ramayana*. At the front, on a pedestal, is a statue of the Buddha. There is a statue of Penh inside a small pavilion between the vihara and the stupa, with the latter containing the ashes of King Ponhea Yat (1405-1467). The surrounding park is tranquil and a nice escape from the madness of the city. Monkeys with attitude are in abundance but they tend to fight among themselves.

Boeng Kak Lake is the main area budget travellers stay in. The lakeside setting with the all important westerly aspect – eg sunsets – appeals strongly to the nocturnal instincts of guests. Some bars and restaurants open 24 hours a day. The lake has now been partially filled and families are being evicted from this area to make way for new development, but many bars and guesthouses are still standing. Local guesthouse owners estimate that it will take another two years to fill the lake completely, but only time will tell how fast it will develop. The lake was once quite beautiful but close to the guesthouses it becomes more like a floating rubbish tip and with not much lake left it looks more like a canal. On the water not much differentiates one guesthouse from another – all are of the same ilk. In the eyes of the law, the places on the lake are considered 'squatted' so their future is unsure.

Around Independence Monument

South of the Royal Palace, between Street 268 and Preah Sihanouk Boulevard, is the **Independence Monument**. It was built in 1958 to commemorate independence but has now assumed the role of a cenotaph. **Wat Lang Ka**, on the corner of Sihanouk and Norodom boulevards, was another beautiful pagoda that fell victim to Pol Pot's architectural holocaust. Like Wat Ounalom, it was restored in Khmer style on the direction of the Hanoi-backed government in the 1980s. It is a really soothing getaway from city madness and the monks here are particularly friendly. They hold a free meditation session every Monday and Thursday night at 1800; anyone is welcome to join in.

Tuol Sleng Museum (Museum of Genocide)

ⓘ *Street 113, Tue-Sun 0800-1100, 1400-1700; public holidays 0800-1800. US$2; free film at 1000 and 1500.*

After 17 April 1975 the classrooms of Tuol Svay Prey High School became the Khmer Rouge main torture and interrogation centre, known as Security Prison 21 or S-21. More than 20,000 people were taken from S-21 to their executions at Choeung Ek extermination camp, see below. Countless others died under torture and were thrown into mass graves in the school grounds. Only seven prisoners survived because they were sculptors and could turn out countless busts of Pol Pot.

Former US Embassy

The former US Embassy, now home to the Ministry of Fisheries, is at the intersection of Norodom and Mao Tse Tung boulevards. As the Khmer Rouge closed on the city from the north and the south in April 1975, US Ambassador John Gunther Dean pleaded with Secretary of State Henry Kissinger for an urgent airlift of embassy staff. But it was not until the very last minute (just after 1000 on 12 April 1975, with the Khmer Rouge firing mortars from across the Bassac River onto the football pitch near the compound that served as a landing zone) that the last US Marine helicopter left the city. Flight 462, a convoy of military transport helicopters, evacuated the 82 remaining Americans, 159 Cambodians and 35 other foreigners to a US aircraft carrier in the Gulf of Thailand. Their departure was overseen by 360 heavily armed marines. Despite letters to all senior government figures from the ambassador, offering them places on the helicopters, only one, Acting President Saukham Khoy, fled the country. The American airlift was a deathblow to Cambodian morale. Within five days, the Khmer Rouge had taken the city and within hours all senior officials of the former Lon Nol government were executed on the tennis courts of the embassy.

Choeung Ek

ⓘ *Southwest on Monireth Blvd, about 15 km from town. US$2. Return trip by moto US$2-5. A shared car (US$10) is more comfortable.*

In a peaceful setting, surrounded by orchards and rice fields, Choeung Ek was the execution ground for the torture victims of Tuol Sleng, the Khmer Rouge extermination centre, S-21 (see above). It is referred to by some as 'The killing fields'. Today a huge glass tower stands on the site, filled with the cracked skulls of men, women and children exhumed from 129 mass graves in the area (which were not discovered until 1980). To date 8985 corpses have been exhumed. Rather disturbingly, rags and crumbling bones still protrude from the mud.

◉ Phnom Penh listings

Hotel and guesthouse prices

LL over US$200	L US$151-200	AL US$101-150
A US$66-100	B US$46-65	C US$31-45
D US$21-30	E US$12-20	F US$7-11
G US$6 and under		

Restaurant prices

₮₮₮ over US$12	₮₮ US$6-12	₮ under US$6

● Sleeping

Phnom Penh *p246, maps p248 and p251*
Boeung Kak Lake, which is likely to be completely redeveloped in the next couple of years, has become something of a Khaosan Rd, with most backpackers opting to stay there. Street 182 also offers a selection of cheaper alternatives. The majority of hotels organize airport pickup and most of them for free.
LL Le Royal, St 92, T023-981888, www. raffles-hotelleroyal.com. A wonderful colonial-era hotel built in 1929 that has been superbly renovated by the Raffles Group. The renovation was done tastefully, incorporating many of the original features and something of the old atmosphere. The hotel has excellent bars, restaurants and a delightful tree-lined pool. 2 for 1 cocktails 1600-2000 daily at the Elephant Bar is a must.
AL Amanjaya, corner St 154 and Sisowath Quay, T023-214747, www.amanjaya.com. Gorgeous rooms full of amenities, beautiful furniture and creative finishing touches. The balconies have some of the best views on the river. Service can be a little ragged – you'll be asked to pay in full when you check-in – but they get enough right to make this probably the best place by the river. Free Wi-Fi and awesome breakfast are both included in the room rate. Good location. Recommended.
AL-A The Quay, 277 Sisowath Quay, T023-224894, www.thequayhotel.com. Brand new hotel from the FCC people set on the riverfront in a remodelled colonial property.

It aspires to create a designer feel, which it partly pulls off, although this is undone by a patchy cheap finish. Big tubs, colour flatscreen TVs, a/c, free Wi-Fi and a good location. Also claims to be an 'eco-hotel' though it's not certain if these claims can be substantiated.

AL-A Sunway, No 1 St 92, T023-430333, asunway@online.com.kh. Overlooking Wat Phnom, this is an adequate hotel in an excellent location. 140 ordinary though well-appointed rooms, including 12 spacious suites, provide comfort complemented by facilities and amenities to cater for the international business and leisure traveller.

A Aram, St 244, T012-565509, www.boddhi tree.com. Nice little guesthouse tucked away in a small street near the palace. The stylish rooms are a bit small and overpriced.

A Bougainvillier Hotel, 277G Sisowath Quay, T023-220528, www.bougainvillierhotel. com. Lovely riverside boutique hotel, rooms decorated in a very edgy, modern Asian theme, with a/c, safe, cable TV and minibar. Good French restaurant.

A Foreign Correspondents Club of Cambodia (FCCC), 363 Sisowath Quay, T023-210142, www.fcccambodia.com. Known locally as the FCC. 3 decent sized rooms are available in this well-known Phnom Penh landmark.

A Juliana, No 16, St 152, T023-880530, www.julianacambodia.com.kh. A very attractive resort-style hotel with 91 rooms, and decent-sized pool in a secluded garden that provides plenty of shade; several excellent restaurants.

A The Pavilion, 227 St 19, T023-222280, www.pavilion-cambodia.com. A popular and beautiful small, 10-room hotel set in an old French colonial villa. Each room is unique with a/c, en suite and TV. The restaurant also serves decent food. However, the management has a reputation for being extremely prickly and a penchant for banning organizations and individuals. Children are completely banned (unless friends of the owner) – we've had several reports of the management abruptly and unceremoniously asking women with children to leave the restaurant.

A-B Almond Hotel, 128F Sotheoros Bvld. T023-220822, www.almondhotel.com.kh. Stylish, new hotel in upmarket part of town that still offers good value for facilities. The more expensive rooms offer the best deal and come with huge balconies – the cheaper ones have no windows. A/c, en suite and TV throughout. Breakfast and Wi-Fi included.

A-D Regent Park, 58 Samdech Sotheoros Blvd, T023-427131, regentpark@online. com.kh. The well-designed lobby belies a collection of ordinary rooms and apartment-style suites. Still, it's reasonable value and in a good location. Thai and European restaurant. Price includes breakfast.

B-C Amber Villa, 1a St 57, T023-216303, www.amber-kh.com. This friendly, family-run small hotel is often full so book ahead – rooms include breakfast, laundry and internet – all have a/c, en suite facilities. The best have TV/DVD and balconies.

B-C Billabong, No 5, St 158, T023-223703, www.thebillabonghotel.com. Reasonably new hotel with well-appointed rooms. Breakfast included. Swimming pool, poolside bar and de luxe rooms with balconies overlooking the pool. Internet.

C-D Red Hibiscus, No 277c Sisowath Quay, T023-990691, www.redhibiscus.biz. Stylish rooms, some with river views, in an excellent location. A/c, en suite and with TV.

C-D Scandinavia Hotel, 4 St 282, T023-214498, www.hotel-scandinavia-cambodia. com. Very friendly service is married to stylish, well-designed rooms (some are a bit dark, though), all with a/c, en suite facilities, internet, cable TV. The rooftop restaurant serves decent food and the small pool, filled with huge inflatable toys, is as funky as they come. The owner has also turned much of the public space into a gallery for international and contemporary art. Recommended.

C-E Anise, 2c St 278, T023-222522, www. anisehotel.com. Excellent value in the heart of a busy area. All rooms are en suite with cable TV and a/c. Pay a little more and you'll get a room with a bath and private balcony. Included in the price is laundry, internet and breakfast. Recommended.

C-E Boddhi Tree Umma, No 50, St 113, T016-865445, www.boddhitree.com. A tranquil setting. Lovely old wooden building with guest rooms offering simple amenities, fan only, some rooms have private bathroom. Great gardens and fantastic food. Very reasonable prices.

C-E Golden Gate Hotel, No 9 St 278 (just off St 51), T023-721161, goldengatehtls@ hotmail.com. Very popular and comparatively good value for the facilities offered. Clean rooms with TV, fridge, hot water and a/c. Within walking distance to restaurants and bars. Visa/MasterCard.

C-E New York Hotel, 256 Monivong Blvd, T023-214116, www.newyorkhotel.com.kh. The rooms aren't going to set the world on fire but the facilities are good for the price – massage centre, sauna, restaurant and in-room safe.

C-E Palm Resort, on Route 1, 5 km out of Phnom Penh, T023-308 6881. Beautiful bungalows surrounded by lush gardens and a very large swimming pool. A/c rooms with very clean bathrooms. Excellent French restaurant. Recommended.

C-F Paragon Hotel, 219b Sisowath Quay, T023-222607, info_paragonhotel@yahoo. com. The Paragon gets the simple things right – it's a well-run and friendly hotel. The best and priciest rooms have private balconies overlooking the river. The cheaper rooms at the back are dark but still some of the best value in this part of town. Colour TV, hot water and private shower or bath, a/c or fan. Recommended.

D Dara Reang Sey Hotel, 45 Corner St of St 13 and 118 Phsar Chas, T023-428181, darareangsey@cannet.com. Busy hotel with popular local restaurant downstairs, clean rooms with hot water and some rooms have baths.

D-E Velkommen Inn, 23 St 104, T092-177710, www.velkommeninn.com. A friendly Norwegian and his Khmer wife run **Velkommen Inn**. It's located 50 m from Angkor Express and Mekong Express bus stations near the riverside and boat docks and has clean rooms.

D-F Bright Lotus Guesthouse, No 22 St 178 (near the museum), T023-990446, sammy_ lotus@hotmail.com. Fan and a/c rooms with private bathroom and balconies. Restaurant.

D-F Indochine 2 Hotel, No 28-30 St 130, T023-211525. Great location and good, clean, comfortable rooms.

D-F KIDS Guesthouse, No 17A, St 178, T012-410406, ryan@ryanhem.com. Guest-house of the Khmer Internet Development Service (KIDS) set in a small tropical garden, spotted with a couple of cabana-style internet kiosks. A couple of rooms are a decent size, quite clean and equipped with a huge fridge. Discount on internet use for guests. Welcoming, safe and free coffee.

D-G Sunshine, No 253 Sisowath Quay, T023-725684. With 50 rooms, a few with a glimpse of the river. Facilities, from a/c to fan, in accordance with price.

D-G Walkabout Hotel, corner of St 51 and St 174, T023-211715, www.walkabouthotel. com. A popular Australian-run bar, café and guesthouse. 23 rooms ranging from small with no windows and shared facilities to large with own bathroom and a/c. Rooms and bathrooms are OK but lower-end rooms are a little gloomy and cell-like. 24-hr bar.

E-F Royal Guesthouse, 91 St 154, hou_heng@yahoo.com. Small family-run guesthouse. Some rooms are much better than others. Ask for the top floor balcony rooms with a/c at US$12; they're worth paying extra for.

E-G Capitol, No 14, St 182, T023-217627, www.capitolkh.com. As they say, 'a Phnom Penh institution'. What, in 1991, was a single guesthouse has expanded to 5 guesthouses all within a stone's throw. All aim at the budget traveller and offer travel services as well as a popular café and internet access. There are a number of other cheap guesthouses in close proximity, such as **Happy Guesthouse** (next door to Capitol Guesthouse) and **Hello Guesthouse** (No 24, 2 St 107) – all about the same ilk.

F-G Grandview Guesthouse, just off the lake, T023-430766. This place is streets ahead of local competition. Clean, basic rooms. A few extra bucks gets you a/c. Nice rooftop restaurant affording good sunset views, with large breakfast menu, pizza, Indian and Khmer food. Travel services and internet.

G Lazy Fish Guesthouse and Restaurant, No 16 St 93, lakeside, T012-703358 or T016533913, lazyfishlakeside@hotmail.com (although the owner admits he's lazy and never checks it). Very basic guesthouse with shared bathroom facilities. Has small veranda area but no lake left outside to look at.

G Simon 2 Guesthouse, on the road in front of the lake, T012-608892. This place has the largest, cleanest rooms.

● Eating

Phnom Penh *p246, maps p248 and p251*
Most places are relatively inexpensive – US$3-6 per head. There are several cheaper cafés along Monivong Blvd, around the lake, Kampuchea Krom Blvd (St 128) in the city centre and along the river. Generally the food in Phnom Penh is good and the restaurants surprisingly refined.

♥♥♥ Bougainvillier Hotel, 277G Sisowath Quay, T023-220528. Upmarket French and Khmer food. Superb foie gras and you can even find truffles here. Fine dining by the river. Recommended.

♥♥♥ Elsewhere, No 175, St 51, T023-211348. An oasis in the middle of the city offering delectable modern Western cuisine. Seats are speckled across wonderful tropical gardens, all topped off by a well-lit pool.

♥♥♥ Foreign Correspondents Club of Cambodia (FCCC), No 363 Sisowath Quay, T023-724014. A Phnom Penh institution that can't be missed. Superb colonial building, 2nd floor bar and restaurant that overlooks the Tonlé Sap. Extensive menu with an international flavour – location excellent, food patchy.

♥♥♥ K-West, Amanjaya Hotel, corner of St 154 and Sisowath Quay, T023-219579. Open 0630-2200. Beautiful, spacious restaurant offering respite from the outside world. Khmer and European food plus extensive cocktail list. Surprisingly, the prices aren't that expensive considering how upmarket it is. Come early for the divine chocolate mousse – it sells out quickly. Free Wi-Fi. Recommended.

♥♥♥ Origami, No 88 Sothearos Blvd, T012-968095. Best Japanese in town, fresh sushi and sashimi. Pricey – one local describes it as where "good things come in very small, expensive packages".

♥♥♥ Pacharan, 389 Sisowath Quay, T023-224394. Open 1100-2300. Excellent Spanish tapas and main courses in a old colonial villa with views across the river and an open kitchen. Stylish Mediterranean feel to it. While the tapas are good value the prices of the main courses are about the highest in town. Part of the FCC empire. Recommended.

♥♥♥ Yi Sang, ground floor of **Almond Hotel** (see Sleeping), daily. Serving up excellent Cantonese food in 3 sittings: 0630-1030 dim sum and noodles, 1130-1400 dim sum and à la carte, 1730-2200 seafood and à la carte – the newly opened Yi Sang is hoping to offer some of the best grub in town. Very good quality and great value.

♥♥♥-♥♥ Corner33, 33 Sothearos Blvd, T092-998850, www.corner33.com. Daily 0700-2200. Set on the upper floors of a building on the corner of St 178, the big sofas and large windows are perfect for views of the palace. Thai and Asian food along with some pasta, coffee and cakes. Free Wi-Fi/internet with coffee.

♥♥ Baan Thai, No 2, St 306, T023-362991. Open 1130-1400 and 1730-2200. Excellent Thai food and attentive service. Popular restaurant. Garden and old wooden Thai house setting with sit-down cushions.

♥♥ **Boddhi Tree**, No 50, St 113, T016-865445, www.boddhitree.com. A delightful garden setting and perfect for lunch, a snack or a drink. Salads, sandwiches, barbecue chicken. Very good Khmer food.

♥♥ **Cantina**, No 347 Sisowath Quay T023-222502. Great Mexican restaurant and bar opened by long-time local identity, Hurley Scroggins III. Fantastic food made with the freshest of ingredients. The restaurant attracts an eclectic crowd and can be a source of great company.

♥♥ **The Deli**, near corner of St 178 and Norodom Blvd T012-851234. Great cakes, bread, salads and lunch at this sleek little diner. Sandwich fillings, for the price, are a bit light, though.

♥♥ **Gasolina**, 56/58 St 57, T012-373009. Open 1100-late. Huge garden and decent French-inspired food await in this friendly, relaxed restaurant. The owner also arranges t'ai chi and capoeira classes. They normally have a barbecue at the weekends.

♥♥ **Green Vespa**, No 95 Sisowath Quay, T012-877228. Open 0630-late. Serving the best Sunday roast dinners in Cambodia, the best you are going to get away from home.

♥♥ **Khmer Borane**, No 389 Sisowath Quay, T012-290092. Open until 2300. Excellent Khmer restaurant just down from the FCC. Wide selection of very well prepared Khmer and Thai food. Try the Amok.

♥♥ **K'NYAY**, 25k Soramit Blvd (St 268), T023-225225, www.knyay.com. Tue-Fri 1200-2100, Sat 0700-2100 and Sun 0700-1500. One of the only places in Phnom Penh that advertises itself as selling vegan food and set in a villa, complete with stylish interior, **K'NYAY** even has a pretentious name. Unfortunately, despite creating a hip image the food doesn't match. Very average but if you're a veggie, a godsend.

♥♥ **La Croisette**, No 241 Sisowath Quay, T023-882221. Authentically French and good value hors d'oeuvres and steak. Good selection of wines.

♥♥ **La Marmite**, No 80 St 108 (on the corner with Pasteur), T012-391746. Wed-Mon.

Excellent-value French food – some of the best in town. Extremely large portions.

♥♥ **Le Wok**, 33 St 178, T09-821857. Daily 0900-2300. French-inspired Asian food served in this friendly little restaurant located on fashionable street 178. Daily fixed lunch menus and à la carte.

♥♥ **Living Room**, No 9 St 306, T023-726139. Tue-Thu 0700-1800 and Fri-Sun 0700-2100. The Japanese owner has done a superlative job at this pleasant hangout spot. The food and coffee is spot-on and the set plates are great value but it's the laid back, calming vibe that is the clincher. There's a purpose-built kids' play area downstairs. Free Wi-Fi if you spend over US$3. Highly recommended.

♥♥ **Metro**, corner of Sisowath and St 148. Open 1000-0200. Huge, affordable tapas portions make this a great spot for lunch or dinner. Try the crème brûlée smothered in passion fruit. Free Wi-Fi. Recommended.

♥♥ **Mount Everest**, 98 Sihanouk Blvd, T023-213821. Open 1000-2300. Has served acclaimed Nepalese and Indian dishes for 5 years, attracting a loyal following. There's also a branch in Siem Reap.

♥♥ **Pop Café**, 371 Sisowath Quay, T012-562892. Open 1100-1430 and 1800-2200. Almost perfect, small, Italian restaurant sited next door to the FCC. Owned and managed by Italian expat Giorgio, the food has all the panache you'd expect from an Italian. The home-made lasagne is probably one of the best-value meals in town. Recommended.

♥♥ **Pyong Yang Restaurant**, 400 Monivong Blvd, T023-993765. This North Korean restaurant is an all-round experience not to be missed. The food is exceptional but you need to get there before 1900 to get a seat before their nightly show starts. All very bizarre: uniformed, clone-like waitresses double as singers in the nightly show, which later turns into open-mic karaoke.

♥♥ **Rising Sun**, No 20, St 178 (just round the corner from the FCC). English restaurant with possibly the best breakfast in town. Enormous roasts and excellent iced coffee.

Romdeng, No 74 St 174 T092-2153 5037, romdeng@mithsamlanh.org. Open 1100-2100. Sister restaurant to **Friends** (see below), helping out former street kids. Serves just Khmer foods. Watch out for specials like fried tarantula with chilli and garlic. Highly recommended.

Veiyo (River Breeze), No 237 Sisowath Quay, T012-847419. Pizza and pasta, along with Thai and Khmer cuisine.

Boeung Bopha, Highway 6 (over the Japanese Friendship Bridge), T012-928353. Open until 2300. Large Khmer restaurant with huge menu and buffet.

Family Restaurant, St 93, lakeside. Small, unassuming family-run, Vietnamese restaurant serving brilliant (and quite adventurous) food at ridiculously low prices. Great service, lovely owners.

Fortune Pho, St 178, just behind the FCC. Open 0800-2100. This small shop offers great Vietnamese, with an authentic and amusingly brusque service.

Friends, No 215, St 13, T023-426748. Non-profit restaurant run by street kids being trained in the hospitality industry. The food is delicious and cheap.

Frizz, 335 Sisowath Quay, T023-220953. Awesome Khmer food. Friendly service and great location. One of the best spots to eat local food on the riverside. Incredibly cheap as well. Offers cooking classes too. Recommended.

Lazy Gecko, St 93, lakeside. Popular, chilled out restaurant/café/bar offering a good selection of sandwiches, burgers and salads in large portions. Good home-cooked Sun roast. Affable owner, Juan, is a good source of information. Selection of new and used books for sale. Good trivia night on Thu.

Sam Doo, 56 Kampuchea Krom Blvd, T023-218773. Open until 0200. Late night Chinese food and the best and cheapest dim sum in town.

The Shop, No 39, St 240, T012-901964. 0900-1800. Deli and bakery serving sandwiches, juices, fruit teas, salads and lunches.

Cafés and bakeries

Asia Europe Bakery, No 95 Sihanouk Blvd, T012-893177. One of the few Western-style bakery/cafés in the city. Delicious pastries, cakes and excellent breakfast and lunch menu. Recommended.

Fresco, 365 Sisowath Quay, T023-217041. Just underneath the FCC and owned by the same people. They have a wide selection of sandwiches, cakes and pastries of mixed quality and high price.

Garden Centre Café, No 23, St 57, T023-363002. Popular place to go for lunch and breakfast, perhaps not surprisingly, the garden is nice too.

Jars of Clay, No 39 St 155 (beside the Russian Market). Fresh cakes and pastries.

Java, No 56 Sihanouk Blvd. Contenders for best coffee in town. Good use of space, with open-air balcony and pleasant surroundings. Delightful food. Features art and photography exhibitions on a regular basis.

La Gourmandise Bleue, 159 St 278, T023-994019. Tue-Sun 0700-2000. Sweet little French-North African bakery serving up almost perfect cakes and coffee. Famous for its macaroons and also does couscous dishes.

T&C Coffee World, numerous branches – 369 Preah Sihanouk Blvd; Sorya Shopping Centre; 335 Monivong Blvd. Vietnamese-run equivalent of **Starbucks**, but better. Surprisingly good food and very good coffee. Faultless service.

Bars and clubs

Phnom Penh *p246, maps p248 and p251* The vast majority of bars in Phnom Penh attract prostitutes.

Blue Chilli, No 36 St 178, T012-566353. Open 1800-late. Gay bar with DJ and dancing. Drag show on Sat.

The Cathouse, corner of St 51 and St 118. Open until 2400. Around since the UNTAC days of the early 1990s and one of the oldest running bars in the city. Not a bad place to have a beer.

Elephant Bar, Le Royal Hotel. Open until 2400. Stylish and elegant bar in Phnom Penh's top hotel, perfect for an evening gin. 2 for 1 happy hour every day with unending supply of nachos, which makes for a cheap night out in sophisticated surroundings. Probably the best drinks in town.

Elsewhere, No 175, St 51. Highly atmospheric, upmarket bar set in garden with illuminated pool. Great cocktails and wine. Very popular with the expats, who have been known to strip off for a dip. Livens up on the last Sat of every month for parties.

Foreign Correspondents Club of Cambodia (FCCC), 363 Sisowath Quay. Satellite TV, pool, *Bangkok Post* and *The Nation* both available for reading here, happy hour 1700-1900. Perfect location overlooking the river.

Heart of Darkness, No 26, St 51. Reasonable prices, friendly staff and open late. Has been Phnom Penh's most popular hangout for a number of years. Full of prostitutes, but your best bet for a night of dancing. There have been many violent incidents here, so it is advisable to be on your best behaviour in the bar as they do not tolerate any provocation.

Manhattan, in the rather dubious **Holiday International Hotel**, St 84, T023-427402. One of Phnom Penh's biggest discos. Security check and metal detectors at the door prevent you from bringing in small arms.

Memphis Pub, St 118 (off Sisowath Quay). Open till 0200. Small bar off the river. Very loyal following from the NGO crowd. Live rock and blues music from Tue to Sat.

Metro, corner Sisowath and St 148, T023-217517. Open 1000-0200. Serves fine grub and is home to a fabulous bar. Popular with rich Khmers and expats. Recommended.

Pontoon, on the river at end of St 108, T012-572880. Weekdays 1200-2330, until late at weekends. Great little spot for a drink and dance. Hosts international DJs and serves good cocktails. Gay nights Thursdays and Fridays. Saturday Club night. Recommended.

Riverhouse Lounge, No 6, St 110 Sisowath Quay. Open 1600-0200. Upmarket, cocktail bar and club. Views of the river and airy open balcony space. Live music (Sun) and DJs (Sat).

Riverside Bar, 273a Sisowath Quay. Great riverfront bar. Tasty food. Recommended.

Salt Lounge, No 217, St 136, T012-289905, www.thesaltlounge.com. Funky minimalist bar. Atmospheric and stylish. Gay friendly.

Sharkys, No 126 St 130. "Beware pickpockets and loose women" it warns. Large, plenty of pool tables and food served until late. Quite a 'blokey' hangout.

Talking to a Stranger, No 21 St 294, T012-798530. Great cocktails, relaxed atmosphere. Recommended.

Zepplin Bar aka Rock Bar, No 128, St 136 (just off Monivong beside the Central Market), open until late. Hole in the wall bar owned by a Taiwanese man named Joon who has more than 1000 records for customers to choose from. Cheap beer and spirits.

⊕ Entertainment

Phnom Penh *p246, maps p248 and p251* Pick up a copy of the *Cambodia Daily* and check out the back page, it details up-and-coming events.

Dance
National Museum of Cambodia, St 70. Folk and national dances are performed by the National Dance group as well as shadow puppets and circus. Fri and Sat 1930, US$4.

Live music
Memphis Pub, St 118 (off Sisowath Quay), open until 0200. Small bar off the river, very loyal following from the NGO crowd. Live rock and blues music from Tue-Sat.

Riverhouse Lounge, No 6, St 110 (Sisowath Quay). Usually has a guest DJ on the weekends and live jazz on Tue and Sun.

⚙ Shopping

Phnom Penh *p246, maps p248 and p251*
Art galleries
Reyum Institute of Arts and Culture, No 4, St 178, T023-217149. Open 0800-1800 www.reyum.org. This is a great place to start for those interested in Cambodian modern art. Some world-class artists have been mentored and exhibit here.

Handicrafts
Many non-profit organizations have opened stores to help train or rehabilitate some of the country's under-privileged.
Bare Necessities, No 46 St 322, T023-996664. Selling a range of bras and underwear which fit Western sizes, from maternity to sporty to sexy. A social enterprise raising money to support awareness and treatment of breast cancer for poor, rural Cambodian women.
Disabled Handicrafts Promotion Association, No 317, St 63. Handicrafts and jewellery made by people with disabilities.
Nyemo, No 71 St 240 between St 63 and Monivong Boulevard, www.nyemo.com.
The National Centre for Disabled People, 3 Norodom, T023-210140. Great store with handicrafts such as pillow cases, tapestries and bags made by people with disabilities.
Orange River, 361 Sisowath Quay (under FCCC), T023-214594, has a selection of beautifully designed decorative items and a very good stock of fabrics and silks which will leave many wishing for more luggage allowance. Pricier than most other stores.
Rajana, No 170, St 450, next to the Russian Market. Traditional crafts.
Silk & Pepper, 33 St 178 (next door to Le Wok, see Eating). Contemporary, sleek, Khmer-inspired fashions and silks, Also sells Kampot pepper in little china pots.

Markets
Psar Thmei (Central Covered Market), just off Monivong Blvd, distinguished by its central art deco dome (built 1937), is mostly full of stalls selling silver and gold jewellery.
Tuol Tom Pong, between St 155 and St 163 to east and west, and St 440 and St 450 to north and south. Known to many as the Russian Market. Sell huge range of goods, fabrics and an immense variety of tobacco – an excellent place for buying souvenirs, especially silk. Most things at this market are about half the price of the Central Market.

Shopping centres
Sorya Shopping Centre, St 63, besides the Central Market. 7-floor, a/c shopping centre. It even has a skating rink.

Silverware and jewellery
Old silver boxes, belts, antique jewellery along Monivong Blvd (the main thorough-fare), Samdech Sothearos Blvd just north of St 184, has a good cluster of silver shops.

Supermarkets
Sharky Mart, No 124, St 130 (below Sharkys Bar), T023-990303. 24-hr convenience store.

⚙ Activities and tours

Phnom Penh *p246, maps p248 and p251*
Cookery courses
Cambodia Cooking Class, No 14, St 285, T023-882314, www.cambodia-cooking- class.com.

Language classes
The Khmer School of Language, No 529, St 454, Tuol Tumpung 2, Chamcar Morn, T023-213047, www.camb comm.org.uk/ksl.

Tour operators
Asia Pacific Travel, 19-20 EO, St 371, T023-884432, www.asia-pacifictravel.com. Operates tours throughout the region.
Asian Trails, No 22, St 294, Sangkat Boeng Keng Kong I, Khan Chamkarmorn, PO Box 621, T023-216555, www.asiantrails.travel. Offers a broad selection of tours: Angkor, river cruises, remote tours, biking trips.

Capitol Tours, No 14AE0, St 182 (see **Capitol Guesthouse**), T023-217627, www.bigpond. com.kh/users/capitol. Cheap tours around Phnom Penh's main sites and tours around the country. Targeted at budget travellers.
Exotissimo Travel, 6th floor, SSN Center No 66 Norodom Blvd, T023-218948, www.exotissimo.com. Wide range of day trips and classic tours covering mainstream destinations.
PTM Tours, No 333B Monivong Blvd, T023-219161, www.ptm-travel.com. Reasonably priced package tours to Angkor and around Phnom Penh. Offers cheap hotel reservations.
RTR Tours, No 54E Charles de Gaulle Blvd, T023-210468, www.rtrtours.com.kh. Tours and travel services. Friendly and helpful.

⊖Transport

Phnom Penh *p246, maps p248 and p251*
Air
Siem Reap Airways and new national carrier, **Cambodia Angkor Air** have connections with **Siem Reap**. Book in advance.

Airline offices Most airline offices are open Mon-Fri 0800-1700, Sat 0800-1200.
AirAsia, Room T6 Phnom Penh Airport, T023-890035, www.airasia.com. **Asiana Airlines**, Room A16, Domestic Arrival Terminal, Phnom Penh Airport, T023-890441, www.flyasiana. com. **Bangkok/Siem Reap Airways**, No 61A St 214, T023-722545, www.bangkokair.com. **China Airlines**, 32 Norodom, T023-222056, www.china-airlines.com. **Cambodia Angkor Air**, 1-2/294, Mao Tse Tung, T023-6666786, www.cambodiaangkorair.com. **Dragon Air**, Unit A3, 168 Monireth Blvd, T023-424300, www.dragonair.com. **Jet Star Asia**, 333b Monivong, T023-220909, www. jetstarasia.com. **Lao Airlines**, 111 Sihanouk Blvd, T023-222956. **Malaysian Airlines**, 35-37 Samdech Pan, St 214, T023-218923, www.malaysiaairlines.com. **Silk Air**, 219B Himawari Hotel, T023-426806, www.silkair. net. **Thai** T023-214359, www.thaiairways. com. **Vietnam Airlines**, No 41 St 214, T023-990840, www.vietnamairlines.com.vn.

Bicycle
Hire from guesthouses for about US$1 per day. Cycling is probably the best way to explore the city as it's mostly flat.

Boat
Fast boats to **Siem Reap** depart from the tourist boat dock on Sisowath Quay at the end of 106 St. Ferries leave from wharves on the river north of the Japanese Friendship Bridge. Fast boat connections (5 hrs) with **Siem Reap**, US$35 1 way. All boats leave early, 0700 or earlier. Most hotels will supply ferry tickets.

Bus
Most buses leave southwest of Psar Thmei (Central Market) by the Shell petrol station. All the companies mentioned here run a service between **Siem Reap** and **Phnom Penh**. **Capitol Tours**, T023-217627, departs from its terminal, No 14, St 182. **GST**, T012-895550, departs from the southwest corner of the Central Market (corner of St 142). **Phnom Penh Public Transport Co** (formerly Ho Wah Genting Bus Company), T023-210359, departs from Charles de Gaulle Blvd, near the Central Market. To **Kratie**, 1 bus per day (US$4); **Capitol Tours** runs a bus to **Kampot**, 0700 and 1300, US$3.50. There are also frequent departures from the Central Market (Psar Thmei) bus terminal. **Phnom Penh Bus Co** to **Sihanoukville**, 5 times daily. GST buses leave 4 times daily, 4 hrs. To **Siem Reap**, see page 313. **Virak Buntham Express Travel**, Street 106, on the riverfront opposite the Night Market, T012-322302, run buses to and from **Koh Kong**, 0800. To **Stung Treng** the Soyra bus, Central Bus Station, T023-210359, leaves Phnom Penh at 0715, US$10. The Soyra bus also leaves for **Banlung, Ratanakiri** at 0700.

Buses from **Phnom Penh** to **Ho Chi Minh City** depart daily (Phnom Penh Public Transport Co, Capitol Tour, Soyra, Mekong Express), 8 hrs, US$9-12 per 1-way ticket. The **Soyra bus company** and **Mekong Express** run a daily bus to **Bangkok** from

Border essentials: Cambodia–Vietnam

If travelling to Vietnam by road, ensure that your visa is appropriately stamped with the correct entry point or you will be turned back at the border. Don't forget visas for Vietnam are not available at the border.

Bavet (Cambodia)–Moc Bai (Vietnam)

There is a road crossing at Moc Bai on Highway 1 connecting Phnom Penh in Cambodia with Ho Chi Minh City via Tay Ninh Province. Travellers taking the bus from Phnom Penh to Ho Chi Minh City will cross at Bavet in Cambodia.

Kaam Samnor (Cambodia)–Vinh Xuong (Vietnam)

Further south, there is a crossing at Kaam Samnor to Vinh Xuong via Chau Doc in the Mekong Delta by boat. Capitol and Narin guesthouses organize buses to the Neak Luong ferry crossing on the Mekong from where a fast boat transports passengers to the Vietnamese border. After the border crossing there is a boat to Chau Doc. Departs 0800, arrive Chau Doc 1400, US$12.

Phnom Den (Cambodia)–Tinh Bien (Vietnam)

Further south still there is a road crossing into Vietnam at Phnom Den, approximately 22 km south of Chau Doc.

Kep (Cambodia)–Ha Tien (Vietnam)

Right at the very south of the country there is a new scenic border open at Ha Tien between Cambodia and Vietnam. As this exit/entry point is so new, fares have not been decided on. They should settle at roughly US$5 for a moto and US$10 for a tuk-tuk. Sok Lim tours are now also offering shared-car transport from US$4.

Phnom Penh, 0630 and 0730, US$9. The **Soyra** bus company also run frequent routes to **Laos** and leaves **Phnom Penh** for **Pakse** every morning at 0645, US$27.

Car

Car Rental, T012-950950. Chauffeur-driven cars are available at most hotels from US$25 per day upwards. Several travel agents will also hire cars. Prices increase if you're venturing out of town.

Mr Vanny, a local English-speaking guide and driver, offers an excellent fast and safe service to pretty much anywhere in Cambodia – T09-285 0989/T01-197 7328.

Cyclo

Plentiful but slow. Fares can be bargained down but are not that cheap – a short journey should be no more than 1000 riel.

A few cyclo drivers speak English or French. They are most likely to be found loitering around the big hotels and can also be hired for the day (around US$5).

Moto

'Motodops' are 50-100cc motorbike taxis and the fastest way to get around Phnom Penh. Standard cost per journey is around US$0.50 for a short hop but expect to pay double after dark. If you find a good, English-speaking moto driver, hang on to him and he can be yours for US$8-10 per day.

Shared taxi

These are either Toyota pickups or saloons. For the pickups the fare depends upon whether you wish to sit inside or in the open; vehicles depart when the driver has enough fares. **Psar Chbam Pao**, just over Monivong Bridge on Route 1, for **Vietnam**. For **Sihanoukville** and **Siem Riep**, take a shared taxi from the Central Market (Psar Thmei). Leave early 0500-0600. Shared taxi to **Kampot** takes 2-3 hrs, US$4, leaving from Doeum Kor Market on Mao Tse Tung Blvd.

Taxi
There are only a few taxis in Phnom Penh as the risk of being held up at gunpoint is too high. It is possible to get a taxi into town from the airport and 1 or 2 taxi companies can be reached by telephone but expect to see no cabs cruising and no meter taxis. **Taxi Vantha**, T012-855000/T023-982542, 24 hrs.

Phnom Penh hotels will organize private taxis to **Sihanoukville** for around US$25.

Train
The railway station is a recently restored, fine old 1930s art deco French edifice. These days the station's main function is to provide a place for the homeless to sleep. The station is on Monivong Blvd between 106 and 108 streets. There are 2 lines: the southern line to **Sihanoukville** and the northern line to **Battambang**. In mid-2010 there were no rail services running in Cambodia though plans are emerging for routes to reopen.

⊙ Directory

Phnom Penh *p246, maps p248 and p251*
Banks ANZ Royal Bank, Russian Blvd, 20 Kramuon Sar (corner of street 67), has opened ATMs throughout Phnom Penh; near the Independence Monument; 265 Sisowath Quay. **Canadia Bank**, No 126 Charles de Gaulle Blvd, T023-214668; 265-269 Ang Duong St, T023-215286. Cash advances on credit cards. **Cambodia Commercial Bank** (CCB), No 130 Monivong Blvd (close to the Central Market), T023-426208. Cash advance on credit cards, TCs and currency exchange. **Union Commercial Bank** (UCB), No 61, St 130, T023-724931. Most banking

services, charges no commission on credit card cash advances. **Embassies and consulates** Australia, No 11, St 254, T023-213470, australia.embassy.cambodia@ dfat.gov.au. Canada, No 11, St 254, T023-213470, pnmpn@dfait-maeci.gc.ca. China, 156 Mao Tse Tung Blvd, T023-720920, kh.china-embassy.org. France, 1 Monivong Blvd, T023-430020, www.ambafrance-kh.org. Laos, 15-17 Mao Tse Tung Blvd, T023-997931. Thailand, 196 Norodom Blvd, T023-7263 0610, www.mfa.go.th. UK, No 29, St 75, T023-427124, ukincambodia.fco.gov.uk. USA, 1, St 96 Sangkat Wat, T023-728000, cambodia. usembassy.gov. Vietnam, 436 Monivong Blvd, T023-362531, embvnpp@camnet.com.kh. **Emergency services** Ambulance, T119 (from 023 phones) or T023-723840. Fire, T118 (from 023 phones) or T023-723555 or T012-786693. Police, T117, T112 (from 023 phones) and T012-999999 or for tourist police T097-7780002. To report child abuse, T023-720555. **Immigration** Opposite the international airport. Visa extensions, photograph required, 1 month US$30. **Internet** Nearly every café, restaurant, guesthouse and hotel now has free Wi-Fi. In addition, Phnom Penh has an excellent mobile 3G network which can often be quicker than fixed line, cable internet. Internet cafés/shops are also extremely cheap and ubiquitous. Rates can be as low as US$0.50 per hr although in many places they are higher. **Medical services** It is highly advisable to try and get to Bangkok if you are seriously ill or have injured yourself as Cambodia's medical services are not up to scratch. Bumrungrad Hospital Office, 113 Mao Tse Tung Blvd, T023-221103, is the local service office for the private hospital in Bangkok. Calmette Hospital, 3 Monivong Blvd, T023-426948, is generally considered the best, 24-hr emergency. Tropical and Travellers Medical Clinic, No 88 St 108, T023-306802. English doctor. Pharmacy de la Gare, 81 Monivong Blvd, T023-526855. **Post office** Main post office, St 13, possible to make international telephone calls from here.

Southern Cambodia

With the opening of the Vietnamese border near Kampot at Ha Tien, southern Cambodia is now firmly grasping its tourist potential as a staging post for overland travellers. Yet, in many ways it manages to encompass the worst and best of what tourism can offer to a developing country such as Cambodia. Take Sihanoukville, which not so long ago was a sleepy port offering idyllic beaches. Now, with human waste pouring directly into the sea from dozens of generic backpacker shanty bars and flophouses, this town could almost offer a textbook study in environmental catastrophe.

Travel down the coast to Kep and Kampot, and things couldn't be more different. An old French trading port overlooking the Prek Kamping Bay River and framed by the Elephant Mountains, low-key Kampot is filled with decrepit dusty charm. Just outside Kampot is Kep, the resort of choice for France's colonial elite, which is now slowly reasserting its position as a place for rest and recuperation. Don't go to Kep expecting wild nights or even a great beach, but perfect views, good seafood and serenity are on offer here.

Northwest from Sihanoukville is Koh Kong province, a vast and untamed expanse of jungle that smothers the stunning Cardamom Mountain range in a thick green blanket. There's a sealed road through here linking Sihanoukville with Thailand. With logging companies waiting in the wings, this area is facing an uncertain future. ▸▸ *For listings, see pages 272-279.*

Sihanoukville →*For listings, see pages 272-279. Colour map 6, C2.*

If Sihanoukville was being tended with care it would occupy a lovely site on a small peninsula whose knobbly head juts out into the Gulf of Thailand. The first-rate beaches, clean waters, trees and invigorating breezes are slowly being replaced with human effluvia, piles of rubbish and nasty flophouses. Cambodia's beaches could be comparable to those in Thailand but are slowly being horribly degraded. Most people head for beaches close to the town which, starting from the north, are Victory, Independence, Sokha, Ochheauteal and, a little further out, Otres. Sihanoukville's layout is unusual, with the 'town' itself acting as a satellite to the roughly equidistant main beaches. The urban area is pretty scattered and has the distinct feel of a place developing on an ad hoc basis.

Ins and outs

There are regular departures from Phnom Penh in comfortable, well-maintained, air-conditioned coaches, costing US$3-4. Buses generally leave every 30 minutes from 0700 until 1330. Taxis cost US$20-30. There is now a fledgling bus service linking Sihanoukville to Kampot and Kep, but this can depend on season and demand making the journey along the shoreline not always the easiest (though there are plentiful buses from Phnom Penh to these coastal jewels). You can also travel to Koh Kong via the brand new road from Sihanoukville or Hat Lek, Thailand. With the new road and bridges finally completed the boat from Sihanoukville to Koh Kong is very likely to disappear. Departing from Sihanoukville there are taxis to Kampot and Phnom Penh at around 0700-0800, US$5-6. You can travel to Koh Kong from Sihanoukville or Hat Lek, Thailand. ▸▸ *See Transport, page 277.*

Background

Sihanoukville, or Kompong Som as it is called during the periods the king is in exile or otherwise 'out of office', was founded in 1964 by Prince Sihanouk to be the nation's sole

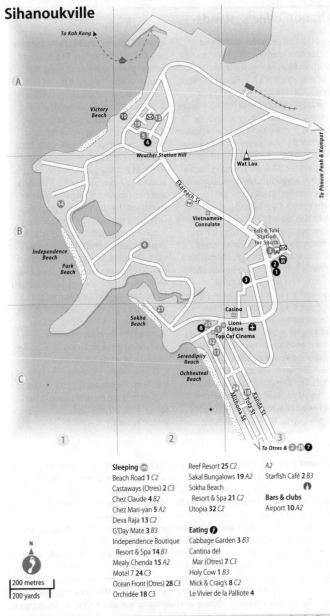

Sihanoukville

To Koh Kong ▶

Victory Beach

Weather Station Hill

Wat Lau

Ekareach St

Vietnamese Consulate

Bus & Taxi Station for South

Independence Beach

Park Beach

Sokha Beach

Casino

Lions Statue

Top Cat Cinema

Serendipity Beach

Ochheutal Beach

Mithona St

Tola St

Tanida St

To Phnom Penh & Kampot

To Otres & ② ㉘ ❼

N

200 metres
200 yards

Sleeping
Beach Road **1** C2
Castaways (Otres) **2** C3
Chez Claude **4** B2
Chez Mari-yan **5** A2
Deva Raja **13** C2
G'Day Mate **3** B3
Independence Boutique
  Resort & Spa **14** B1
Mealy Chenda **15** A2
Motel 7 **24** C3
Ocean Front (Otres) **28** C3
Orchidée **18** C3

Reef Resort **25** C2
Sakal Bungalows **19** A2
Sokha Beach
  Resort & Spa **21** C2
Utopia **32** C2

Eating
Cabbage Garden **3** B3
Cantina del
  Mar (Otres) **7** C3
Holy Cow **1** B3
Mick & Craig's **8** C2
Le Vivier de la Palliote **4**

A2
Starfish Café **2** B3

Bars & clubs
Airport **10** A2

Sihanoukville's islands

More than 20 beautiful islands and pristine coral reefs lie off Sihanoukville's coastline. Most of the islands are uninhabited except Koh Russei (Bamboo Island), Koh Rong Salaam and a few others that contain small fishing villages.

Diving and snorkelling around the islands is pretty good. The coast offers an abundance of marine life including star fish, sea anemones, lobsters and sponge and brain coral. Larger creatures such as stingrays, angel fish, groupers, barracuda, moray eels and giant clams are ubiquitous. Baby whale sharks and reef sharks also roam the waters. More elusive are the black dolphins, pink dolphins, common dolphins and bottle-nosed dolphins but they are sighted from time to time. It is believed that further afield (closer to Koh Kong) are a family of dugongs (sea cows). No one has sighted these rare creatures except for one hotel owner who sadly saw a dugong head for sale in Sihanoukville's market.

The islands are divided into three separate groups: the Kampong Som Group, the Ream Group and the Royal Islands. The Kampong Som Islands are the closest to Sihanoukville and have quite good beaches. Here the visibility stretches up to 40 m. Koh Pos is the closest island to Sihanoukville, located just 800 m from Victory Beach. Most people prefer Koh Koang Kang also known as Koh Thas, which is 45 minutes from shore. This island has two beautiful beaches (with one named after Elvis) and the added attraction of shallow rocky reefs, teeming with wildlife, which are perfect for snorkelling. More rocky reefs and shallow water can be found at the Rong Islands. Koh Rong is about two hours west of Sihanoukville and has a stunning, 5-km-long sand beach (on the southwest side of the island). To the south of the Koh Rong is Koh Rong Salaam, a smaller island that is widely considered Cambodia's most beautiful. There are nine fantastic beaches spread across this island and on the east coast, a lovely heart-shaped bay. It takes about 2½ hours to get to Koh Rong from Sihanoukville. Koh Kok, a small island off Koh Rong Salaam, is one of the firm favourite dive sites, warranting it the nickname 'the garden' and takes 1¾ hours to get there.

During winter (November to February) the Ream Islands are the best group to visit as they are more sheltered than some of the other islands but they are a lot further out.

deep-water port. It is also the country's prime seaside resort. In its short history it has crammed in as much excitement as most seaside towns see in a century – but not of the sort that resorts tend to encourage. Sihanoukville was used as a strategic transit point for weapons used in fighting the US, during the Vietnam War. In 1975, the US bombed the town when the Khmer Rouge seized the container ship *SS Mayaguez*.

Sihanoukville has now turned a corner, however, and with rapid development has firmly secured its place in Cambodia's 'tourism triangle', alongside Phnom Penh and Angkor Wat. Not much of this development is sustainable and incredibly tacky and overpriced resorts have already being built. While a liberal attitude towards the smoking of marijuana attracts a youthful crowd, no amount of intoxicants can cover up the fact that Sihanoukville is rapidly becoming an environmental stain on this already horribly scarred country. By late 2009 massive offshore sand-dredging was also having an impact on this

The Ream Islands encompass those islands just off the Ream coast: Prek Mo Peam and Prek Toek Sap, which don't offer the clearest waters. The islands of Koh Khteah, Koh Tres, Koh Chraloh and Koh Ta Kiev are best for snorkelling. Giant mussels can be seen on the north side of Koh Ta Kiev island. Some 50 km out are the outer Ream Islands which, without a doubt, offer the best diving in the area. The coral in these islands though has started to deteriorate and is now developing a fair bit of algae. Kondor Reef, 75 km west of Sihanoukville, is a favorite diving spot. A Chinese junk filled with gold and other precious treasures is believed to have sunk hundreds of years ago on the reef and famous underwater treasure hunter, Michael Archer, has thoroughly searched the site but no one can confirm whether he struck gold.

Koh Tang, Koh Prins and Paulo Wai are seven hours away to the southwest. These islands are believed to have visibility that stretches for 40 m and are teeming with marine life; they are recommended as some of the best dive sites. It is believed that Koh Prins once had a modern shipwreck and sunken US helicopter but underwater scavengers looking for steel and US MIA guys have completely cleared the area. Large schools of yellow fin tuna are known to inhabit the island's surrounding waters. Koh Tang is worth a visit but is quite far from the mainland so an overnight stay on board might be required. Many local dive experts believe Koh Tang represents the future of Cambodia's diving. The island became infamous in May 1975 when the US ship SS Mayaguez was seized by the Khmer Rouge just off here. The area surrounding Paulo Wai is not frequently explored, so most of the coral reefs are still in pristine condition.

Closer to Thailand lies Koh Sdach (King's Island), a stop off on the boat ride between Sihanoukville and Koh Kong. This undeveloped island is home to about 4000 people, mostly fishing families. The beaches are a bit rocky but there is some fabulous snorkelling. At the time of publication a guesthouse was being built on the island.

The Cambodian diving industry is still in its fledgling years; most of the islands and reefs are still in relatively pristine condition and the opportunities to explore unchartered waters limitless.

Some of the islands mentioned above now have guesthouses and hotels, see page 273 for details.

see page 273 for details.

fragile coastline; the beaches here were slowly being eroded with high tides swamping many of the beachside bars and restaurants. If it all becomes too much there is the coastal Preah Sihanouk 'Ream' National Park close by.

Sights

Victory Beach is a thin, 2-km-long beach on the north of the peninsula, just down from the port, and at its extremes offers reasonably secluded beaches. Beach hawkers are ubiquitous and outnumber tourists at a ratio of about three to one. The area does afford a good sunset view, however. **Independence Beach** was at one time the sole preserve of the once bombed and charred – and now beautifully restored – **Independence Hotel**. The location of the hotel is magnificent and the grounds are a reminder of the place's former grandeur. With the restoration of this sleek hotel complete, its re-opening will do a lot to revive Independence Beach's fortunes. **Sokha Beach** is arguably Sihanoukville's most beautiful beach. The shore laps around a 1-km arc and even though the large **Sokha Beach Resort** has taken up residence it is very rare to see more than a handful of people on the beach. It is stunning and relatively hassle-free. **Ochheauteal Beach** lies to the south and, bizarrely, is the most popular with hordes of backpackers. What was once a sparkling stretch of white sand has been reduced to an unending dustbin of rickety, badly planned budget bars, restaurants and accommodation. Several of these places have now been cleared out and this stretch of beach is attempting to move upmarket. Along the beach front road here keep a look out for Hun Sen's massive and impregnable residence. Watch your stuff as theft is also common here. The beach commonly referred to as **Serendipity Beach** is at the very north end of Ochheauteal and is basically Ochheauteal-like. This little strand has gained flavour with travellers due in part to being the first beach in Sihanoukville to offer a wide range of budget accommodation. At the time of publication, the many guesthouses and restaurants lining the shore of Serendipity and the extended Ochheauteal Beach area were at the centre of a land dispute with developers hankering to clear the budget accommodation to make way for large Thai-style resorts.

Otres Beach is a couple of kilometres south of Ochheauteal and is, at least for the moment, relatively quiet and undeveloped. The stretch of sand here is probably Sihanoukville's longest and it is easy to find a spot for yourself. There are now a number of budget guesthouses opening up should you wish to stay here (see Sleeping, page 272). To reach Otres you'll need to take a moto or tuk-tuk (US$3-4). Be careful of walking the long road out here or passing through the local fishing village, as several tourists have been robbed, threatened and even a stabbing has been reported.

Preah Sihanouk 'Ream' National Park → Colour map 6, C2.

ⓘ T012-875096, daily 0700-1715. Boat trip US$30 for 4 people. Nature trek with a guide (3-5 hrs), US$5 per person.

This beautiful park is a short 30-minute drive from Sihanoukville, hugging the coastline of the Gulf of Thailand. It includes two islands and covers 21,000 ha of beach, mangrove swamp, offshore coral reef and the Prek Tuk Sap Estuary. Samba deer, endangered civet species, porcupines and pangolin are said to inhabit the park, as well as dolphins. To arrange a guided tour visit the park office or arrange one through a guesthouse in Sihanoukville.

Koh Kong and around → For listings, see pages 272-279. Colour map 6, B1.

Dusty Koh Kong is better known for its brothels, casinos and 'Wild West' atmosphere than for lying at the heart of a protected area with national park status (granted by Royal Decree in 1993). It is also often confused with its beautiful offshore namesake Koh Kong Island. The town is also reputed to have the highest incidence of HIV infection of anywhere in Cambodia and is a haven for members of the Thai mafia trying to keep their heads down and launder large sums of money through the casino. The place is only really used by travellers as a transit stop on the way to and from Thailand or two of the most scenic places in Cambodia – Koh Kong Island and the Cardamom Mountains. Due to its border location most people in Koh Kong will accept Thai baht as well as the usual US dollars and Cambodian riel.

Footprint Mini Atlas
Vietnam, Cambodia & Laos

Map symbols

□	Capital city	▨	Building
○	Other city, town	▪	Sight
⌁	International border	♰♰	Cathedral, church
⌁	Regional border	⌂	Chinese temple
⊖	Customs	⚑	Hindu temple
⬭	Contours (approx)	⚲	Meru
▲	Mountain, volcano	⌁	Mosque
⇌	Mountain pass	⌂	Stupa
⊔⊔⊔	Escarpment	✡	Synagogue
⌁	Glacier	ℹ	Tourist office
⌁	Salt flat	🏛	Museum
⌁	Rocks	⊠	Post office
⌁	Seasonal marshland	ⓟ	Police
⌁	Beach, sandbank	Ⓢ	Bank
⚑	Waterfall	@	Internet
⌁	Reef	♪	Telephone
═══	National highway	ⓜ	Market
───	Paved road	✚	Medical services
───	Unpaved or *ripio* (gravel) road	Ⓟ	Parking
⌁	Track	⛽	Petrol
⋯⋯	Footpath	⚑	Golf
───	Railway	⁖	Archaeological site
⊢▪	Railway with station	♦	National park,
✈	Airport		wildlife reserve
🚌	Bus station	✻	Viewing point
Ⓜ	Metro station	⚑	Campsite
─ ─ ─	Cable car	⌂	Refuge, lodge
╬╬╬	Funicular	🏰	Castle, fort
⛴	Ferry	⚑	Diving
⌁	Pedestrianized street	♠♣	Deciduous, coniferous,
Σ ⊂	Tunnel		palm trees
→	One way-street	⚘	Mangrove
⫿⫿⫿	Steps	⌂	Hide
⨝	Bridge	⚑	Vineyard, winery
▲▲▲	Fortified wall	⚑	Distillery
⌁	Park, garden, stadium	⌁	Shipwreck
●	Sleeping	✕	Historic battlefield
❶	Eating	⬀	Related map
❶	Bars & clubs		

Map 1

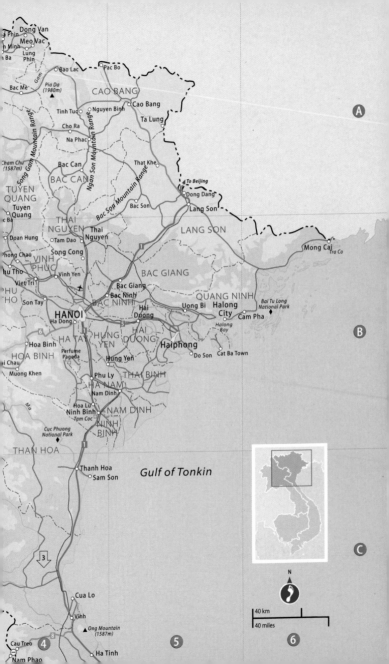

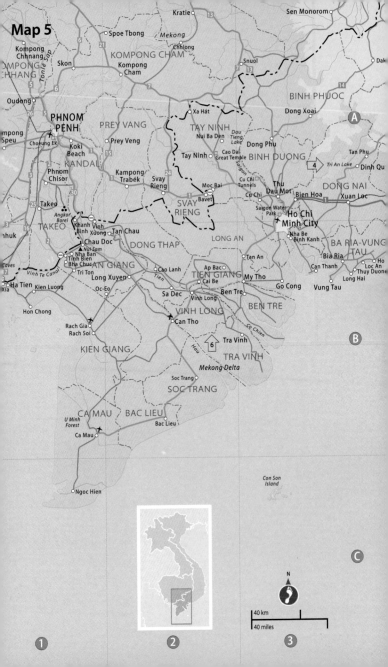

Map 6

Join us online...

Follow us on **Twitter** and **Facebook** – ask us questions, speak to our authors, swap your stories, and be kept up to date with travel news and exclusive discounts and competitions.

Upload your travel pics to our **Flickr** site – inspire others on where to go next, and have your photos considered for inclusion in Footprint guides.

And don't forget to visit us at   footprinttravelguides.com

Central Cardamoms Protected Forest → *Colour map 6, B2.*

① *The area remains relatively inaccessible but over the next few years it is anticipated that ecotourism operators will flock to the area. For now, it is best to make short trips into the park as the area is sparsely populated and heavily mined (so stay on clearly marked paths). Take a motorbike (with an experienced rider) or a boat. The latter option is more convenient in Koh Kong. There are usually several men with boats willing to take the trip down the Mohaundait Rapids, cutting through the jungled hills and wilderness of the Cardamoms. The cost of the trip is between US$25-30.*

In 2002, the government announced the creation of the **Central Cardamoms Protected Forest**, a 402,000-ha area in Cambodia's Central Cardamom Mountains. With two other wildlife sanctuaries bordering the park, the total land under protection is 990,000 ha – the largest, most pristine wilderness in mainland Southeast Asia. The extended national park reaches widely across the country, running through the provinces of Koh Kong, Pursat, Kompong Speu and Battambang. Considering that Cambodia has been severely deforested and seen its wildlife hunted to near-extinction, this park represents a good opportunity for the country to regenerate flora and fauna. The Cardamoms are home to most of Cambodia's large mammals and half of the country's birds, reptiles and amphibians. The mountains have retained large populations of the region's most rare and endangered animals, such as the Indochinese tigers, Asian elephants and sun bears. Globally threatened species like the pileated gibbon and the critically endangered Siamese crocodile, which has its only known wild breeding population here, exist. Environmental surveyors have identified 30 large mammal species, 30 small mammal species, more than 500 bird species, 64 reptile species and 30 amphibian species. Conservationists are predicting they will discover other animals that have disappeared elsewhere in the region such as the Sumatran rhinoceros. With virgin jungles, waterfalls, rivers and rapids this area has a huge untapped ecotourism potential. However, tourist services to the area are still quite limited.

Koh Kong Island → *Colour map 6, B1*

About 1-1½ hours by boat from Koh Kong town. Boats from town usually charge ฿1000 per round trip. Koh Kong Divers offer diving and snorkelling trips to Koh Kong, see page 277.

The island (often called Koh Kong Krau) is arguably one of Cambodia's best. There are six white powdery beaches each stretching kilometre after kilometre, while a canopy of coconut trees shade the glassy-smooth aqua waters. It's a truly stunning part of the country and has been ear-marked by the government for further development, so go now, while it's still a little utopia. There are a few frisky dolphin pods that crop up from time to time. Their intermittent appearances usually take place in the morning and in the late afternoon. You could feasibly camp on the island though would likely need to bring all supplies with you, including drinking water. ▶▶ *For the border with Thailand, see box, page 278.*

Kampot and around → *For listings, see pages 272-279. Colour map 6, C2.*

Kampot is a charming riverside town that was established in the 19th century by the French. The town lies at the base of the Elephant Mountain Range, 5 km inland on the river Prek Thom and was for a long time the gateway to the beach resort at Kep (see page 271). On one side of the river are tree-lined streets, crumbling mustard yellow French shop fronts and a sleepy atmosphere, while on the other side you will find locals working in the salt pans.

The town has the feel of another era – with a dabbling of Chinese architecture and overall French colonial influence – which, with a bit of restoration work, could easily be compared to UNESCO World Heritage Sites such as Hoi An in Vietnam and Luang Prabang in Laos. Life is laid-back in Kampot and the town has become an expat retreat with Phnom Penh-ites ducking down here for the fresh air and cooler climate.

Bokor Mountain National Park → Colour map 6, C2.

ⓘ 42 km (90 minutes) from Kampot, US$5. Park rangers can speak some English and have a small display board on the flora and fauna in the park at their office. There are dorms (US$5) and double rooms (US$20) and a few basic dishes available. A moto and driver for the day will cost around US$15 or a car around US$30.

Note: In 2009 work began on a new road to Bokor and a new Korean-owned casino project on the plateau top. At present the roadbuilders are allowing some road traffic through though this is intermittent and likely to be with local tour operators only. This situation could also change and you should check with locals when you arrive in Kampot. The old abandoned French-built resort complex (see below) is likely to be demolished.

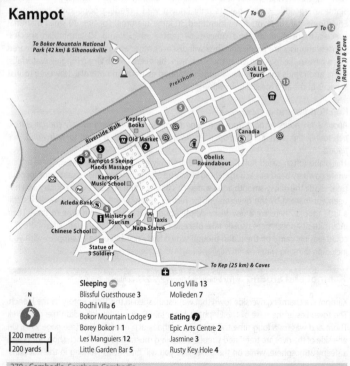

Kampot

To Bokor Mountain National Park (42 km) & Sihanoukville

To Phnom Penh (Route 3) & Caves

To 6
To 12

Prekthom

Sok Lim Tours

Riverside Walk

Kepler's Books

Old Market

Canadia

Kampot 5 Seeing Hands Massage

Kampot Music School

Obelisk Roundabout

Acleda Bank

Ministry of Tourism

Taxis

Naga Statue

Chinese School

Statue of 3 Soldiers

To Kep (25 km) & Caves

N

200 metres
200 yards

Sleeping 😴
Blissful Guesthouse **3**
Bodhi Villa **6**
Bokor Mountain Lodge **9**
Borey Bokor 1 **1**
Les Manguiers **12**
Little Garden Bar **5**

Long Villa **13**
Molieden **7**

Eating 🍴
Epic Arts Centre **2**
Jasmine **3**
Rusty Key Hole **4**

Bokor Mountain National Park's plateau, at 1040 m, peers out from the southernmost end of the Elephant Mountains with a commanding view over the Gulf of Thailand and east to Vietnam. Bokor Hill (Phnom Bokor) is densely forested and in the remote and largely untouched woods scientists have discovered 30 species of plant unique to the area. Not for nothing are these called the Elephant Mountains and besides the Asian elephant there are tigers, leopards, wild cows, civets, pigs, gibbons and numerous bird species. At the peak of the mountain is Bokor Hill Station, where eerie, abandoned, moss-covered buildings sit in dense fog. The buildings were built by the French, who attracted by Bokor's relative coolness, established a 'station climatique' on the mountain in the 1920s. In 1970 Lon Nol shut it down and Bokor was quickly taken over by Communist guerrillas; it later became a strategic military base for the Khmer Rouge. In more recent years there was a lot of guerrilla activity in the hills, but the area is now safe, with the exception of the danger, ever-present in Cambodia, of landmines. The ruins are surprisingly well preserved but bear evidence of their tormented past. There is a double waterfall called Popokvil Falls, a 2-km walk from the station, which involves wading through a stream, though in the wet season this is nigh on impossible.

Kbal Romeas caves and temple → *Colour map 6, C3.*

Ten kilometres outside Kampot, on the roads to both Phnom Penh and to Kep, limestone peaks harbour interesting caves with stalactites and pools. It is here that you can find one of Cambodia's hidden treasures – an 11th-century temple slowly being enveloped by stalactites and hidden away in a cave in Phnom Chhnok, next to the village of Kbal Romeas. The temple, which is protected by three friendly monks, was discovered by Adhemer Leclere in 1866. Many motos (US$3-4) and cars (US$10) now do trips.

Kep → *For listings, see pages see pages 272-279. Colour map 6, C3.*

ⓘ *From Jul to Oct Kep is subject to the southeast monsoon, occasionally rendering the beach dangerous for swimming because of the debris brought in.*

Tucked in on the edge of the South China Sea, Kep was established in 1908 by the French as a health station for their government officials and families. The ruins of their holiday villas stand along the beachfront and in the surrounding hills. They were largely destroyed during the civil war under Lon Nol and by the Khmer Rouge and were then further ransacked during the famine of the early 1980s when starving Cambodians raided the villas for valuables to exchange for food.

At the time of publication, Kep still hadn't hit the radar of many international tourists. It is very popular on weekends with holidaying Cambodians who have managed to keep this idyllic town one of the country's best-kept secrets. Beautiful gardens and lush green landscape juxtaposed against the blue waters make it one of the most wonderfully relaxing places in the country. The town itself only has one major beach, a pebbly murky water pool that doesn't really compare with Sihanoukville beaches but they can be found at almost all of the 13 outlying islands where you can snorkel and dive although this is better around the islands off Sihanoukville; Kep is considerably more beautiful than Sihanoukville and much more relaxing. It is famous for the freshly caught crab that is best eaten on the beach (US$1.50 per kilo) and the *tik tanaout jiu*, palm wine. From Kep it is possible to hire a boat to **Rabbit Island** (Koh Toensay). Expect to pay about US$10 to hire a boat for the day. There are four half-moon beaches on this island which have finer, whiter sand than Kep beach.

For Sleeping and Eating price codes and other relevant information, see pages 40 - 43.

◉ Sleeping

Sihanoukville *p264, map p265*

L-AL The Independence Boutique Resort and Spa, Independence Beach, T034-934300, www.independcehotel.net. The most gorgeous hotel in town, beautifully restored to all its modernist glory. The rooms are minimalist, chic and complete with a/c, TV, bath and other luxuries. Great sea views from the hilltop perch, it's also set in some pleasing gardens with a pool. This is exactly the kind of thing Sihanoukville needs to pull itself out of its current malaise. You can also haggle the rates down when it is quiet. Highly recommended.

L-A Sokha Beach Resort and Spa, St 2 Thnou, Sangkat 4, Sokha Beach, T034-935999, www.sokhahotels.com. A de luxe, 180-room beachfront resort and spa, set amid an expansive 15 ha of beachfront gardens and fronting a pristine white sandy beach. Guests have a choice between hotel suites or private bungalows dotted in the tropical gardens. The hotel has fantastic facilities including a landscaped pool, tennis court, archery range, children's club and in-house Filipino band at night. Rooms are impressive. The hotel has very low occupancy, so check if it can offer a discount as it's always running special deals.

B-E Beach Road Hotel, Serendipity Rd, T017-827677, www.beachroad-hotel.com. Excellent value, well-run and maintained hotel with a large range of rooms to fit most budgets; prices drop during low season. All rooms are en suite, with TV, a/c, free Wi-Fi and hot water. The clincher is the gorgeous pool. There's a reasonable and decent bar attached.

C-D Chez Claude, between Sokha Beach and Independence Beach, T012-824870. A beautiful hillside spot with 9 bungalows

representing a cross-section of indigenous housing. The restaurant has fantastic views.

C-D Deva Raja Villa and Bungalows, Serendipity Beach, T012-160 0374, www.devarajavilla.com. Stylish rooms, en suite facilities with nice baths, a/c. Good restaurant. Recommended.

C-D Reef Resort, Serendipity Beach, T012- 315338, www.reefresort.com.kh. Well run, small hotel at the top of the hill near the garish golden lions roundabout. Rooms are a touch overpriced but there is a nice pool and breakfast included. Bar and restaurant. Probably the best mid-range place in town. Book ahead. Recommended.

D-F Chez Mari-yan, Sankat 3, Khan Mittapheap, T01-291 6468. Currently the best bungalow-style place to stay in this end of town. Offers a block of hotel rooms and simple wooden and concrete bungalows perched on stilts at the top of a hill affording nice sea views. Restaurant sports a short menu that features fish, squid and crab.

D-F Orchidée Guesthouse, Tola St, T034-933639, www.orchideeguesthouse.com. Well run, clean and well-aired rooms, with a/c and hot water. Restaurant with Khmer and Western seafood. Nice pool area, a 5-min walk to the Ochheauteal Beach.

E Ocean Front, Otres Beach, T012-478531. Reasonably well-run place with the glass fronted rooms laid-out looking onto the beach. The rooms are a bit dingy though. Claims to have electricity all day in high season. Every room has fan and cold water en suite bathrooms.

E-F Castaways, Otres Beach. Friendly place with basic bungalows and rooms directly on the beach. All are en suite and have fans. Good electricity supply that should be 24 hrs in high season.

E-F G'Day Mate, Ekareach St, T012-280947. Decent enough rooms, fan and a/c, all with TV and fridge. They run a good bar and restaurant and also a (sporadic) bus service to Kampot and Kep.

E-F Motel 7, Ochheuteal Beach, T015-207719. Set just back from the beach on the road, this is a brand new, stylish and simple guesthouse. All rooms have en suite facilities, cable TV and free Wi-fi; the pricier ones also have a/c and hot water. Friendly owners were planning to set up a small coffee and ice cream parlour.

E-G Mealy Chenda, on the crest of Weather Station Hill, T034-933472, www.mealy chenda.com. Very popular hotel offering accommodation to suit a wide range of budgets from dorm rooms through to a/c double rooms. Sparkly clean with fantastic views from the restaurant.

E-G Sakal Bungalows, near the end of Weather Station Hill, T012-806155, www.sakalbungalows.com. A mix of fan and a/c rooms and bungalows available in this spotless and well-run mini-resort. Restaurant, bar and cheap internet also available. Closest bungalows to Victory Beach. Popular and cheap.

G Utopia, Serendipity Rd, T034-934319, www.utopiacambodia.com. It's hard to figure out if this is a new concept in budget travel – the bunks in the dorm rooms are completely free (they also have private rooms for US$5) – or if it's the beginning of some kind of Beach-like cult. The avowed aim here is partying with poolside raves and an endless supply of fries and burgers. There's nothing remotely Khmer about the experience on offer here but it might indicate one possible future for budget travel.

Sihanoukville islands

D Lazy Beach, Koh Rung Samloem, booking office is just past **Seahorse Bungalows**, T016-214211, www.lazybeachcambodia.com. Simple, clean bungalows set by a stunning beach. They charge US$10 per person per single boat transfer to reach the island. Serve up a good array of food as well.

D-G Jonty's Jungle Camp, Koh Ta Kiev Island, T092-502374, www.jontysjungle camp.com. Basic, hammock-style camping accommodation in this gorgeous island retreat. They also have a few treehouses if you don't fancy a hammock. Don't come expecting any mod cons but you will be given a mosquito net. Price drops if you stay for more than 1 night. Great snorkelling nearby, idyllic if you like this sort of thing. Serve their own basic food. Price includes long-tail to and from the island.

E-G Koh Ru, Koh Russie Island, booking office just past **Sea Horse Bungalows**, T012-388860. This is a quaint collection of simple fan bungalows and dorm rooms in a lovely beachside location. Totally relaxed and quiet, this is a decent spot to really get away from it all. Also serves food and drinks. Boat transfers US$10.

Koh Kong and around *p268*

With the road to Phnom Penh and Sihanoukville now completed, accommodation and other facilities in Koh Kong are improving.

D-E Apex Koh Kong, Street 8, T016-307919, www.apexkohkong.com. With a pool, free Wi-fi, friendly staff and good food this is easily one of the best places to stay in Koh Kong. The bright, fresh rooms, all set around a courtyard, have cable TV, hot water and a/c. Excellent value. Recommended.

D-E Asean Hotel, riverfront, T012-936667. Good rooms with a/c, bathtubs, cable TV. The ones at the front have balconies and river views. There's a decent internet café downstairs. Friendly owners and well run. Recommended.

D-E Koh Kong City Hotel, riverfront, T035-936777, kkcthotel.netkhmer.com. This biggish hotel by the river has decent, clean rooms, the best of which have great river views. Staff are a little indifferent but it makes for a good place to stay. Rooms are a/c with cable TV and hot-water en suite facilities throughout.

Kampot and around *p269, map p270*
There's a good range of accommodation.
B-D Bokor Mountain Lodge, T017-071 2062, www.bokorlodge.com. Old colonial property on the river front that has had several incarnations and was once even an HQ for the Khmer Rouge. It has bags of atmosphere and is probably the best spot in town for an icy sundowner. All rooms en suite with a/c, cable TV.
B-D Les Manguiers, 2 km north of town, T092-330050, www.mangokampot.com. Cute little French-run guesthouse. Set by the river amidst paddies and swaying tropical trees this is a relaxing place to spend a couple of days. Good bungalows with fans or a/c; some rooms also in main building. Offers free bicycles to guests.
D-E Little Garden Bar, T012-427572, www. littlegardenbar.com. Basic, clean rooms, fan and bathroom. Restaurant offering panoramic views of Mount Bokor.
D-F Borey Bokor Hotel 1, T092-978168, boreybokorhotel@yahoo.com. In an ostentatious style with all rooms offering a/c, fridge and comfy beds.
E-G Bodhi Villa, 2 km northwest of town on Teuk Chhou Rd, T012-728884, www. bodhivilla.com. Cheap, friendly, well-run and popular budget guesthouse in a good location just outside town, set on the river bank. Owners seem well-intentioned, linking into local volunteer projects, though some might consider that the hedonistic atmosphere and roaring speedboat which they've introduced to the peaceful river detracts from their efforts. Basic rooms, simple bungalows and US$1 a night dorm.
E-G Molieden, a block from the main bridge, T012-820779, chuy_seth@yahoo.com. A surprisingly good find, its hideous façade gives way to a very pleasant interior. Large, tastefully decorated modern art deco rooms with TV and fan. The rooftop restaurant also serves some of the best Western food in town. Very good value with free Wi-Fi.
G Blissful Guesthouse, next to Acleda Bank, T092-494331, www.blissfulguesthouse.com.

Converted colonial building with lovely surrounding gardens. Rooms are simple with mosquito net, fan and attached bath. High on atmosphere and very popular with locals and expats. Recommended.
G Long Villa, T092-251418 or T012-731400, www.longvillaguesthouse.com. Very friendly, well-run guesthouse. The unspectacular though functional rooms vary from en suite with a/c and TV through to fan with shared facilities. Recommended.

Bokor Mountain National Park *p270*
The park rangers run a simple guesthouse at the hill station – youth-hostel style. There are bunk beds (US$5) and doubles (US$20), with clean shared toilets and showers. Bring your own food: there is a large kitchen available for guests. Pack warm clothes and waterproofs.

Kep *p271*
Accommodation in Kep is better and cheaper than in the rest of the country.
L-AL Knai Bang Chatt, T012-349742, www.knaibangchatt.com. Set in a restored 20th-century modernist villa, this property seeks to recreate an elitist and colonial atmosphere. Some people will love the banality of exclusivity – others may judge that their money would be better spent elsewhere. Rooms come with all the usual luxury amenities.
A-D La Villa, T012-1702648, www.lavilla kep.com. An interesting old French villa forms the centrepiece of this bungalow operation set by the sea. The bungalows are well-appointed with verandas, a/c, en suite bathrooms, Wi-Fi and cable TV. There are plans to open a restaurant and art space in the villa. Recommended.
A-F Veranda Resort and Bungalows, next door to N4, further up Kep Mountain, T012-888619, www.veranda-resort.com. Superb accommodation. Large wooden bungalows, each with a good-sized balcony, fan, mosquito net and nicely decorated mosaic bathroom. The more expensive of

these include very romantic open-air beds. The restaurant offers the perfect vista of the ocean and surrounding countryside. Epicureans will love the variety of international cuisines including poutine of Quebec, smoked ham linguini, fish fillet with olive sauce (all under US$3). Recommended.

C-D The Beach House, T012-240090, www. thebeachhousekep.com. Arguably the nicest spot to stay in Kep. Great rooms, nearly all of which look out onto the mesmeric ocean – all have a/c, hot water, TV. They have a small pool and soothing chill-out area. Unpretentious and good value. The staff can sometimes appear to be half-asleep but are very friendly when provoked. Recommended.

E The Vana Guesthouse, TT012-755038, www.vannabungalows.com. On the hill before Le Bout Du Monde, this guesthouse comprises 4 attractive thatch-roofed bungalows with attached bathrooms and Western toilet. They are clean but simple with double beds, mosquito nets and little more. The open, thatched restaurant and eating terrace has a friendly and sedate atmosphere and the food is also good. Staff are friendly and more than willing to organize boat trips to the offshore islands.

⦿ Eating

Sihanoukville p264, map p265
Chez Mari-yan, Victory Beach area. Has a good seafood restaurant with probably the nicest setting in Sihanoukville.
Le Vivier de la La Paillote, top of Weather Station Hill. This is the finest dining establishment in town and one of the best in the country. The service can't be surpassed and it is high on atmosphere.
Holy Cow, Ekareach St, on the way out of town. Ambient restaurant offering a selection of healthy, Western meals – pasta, salads, baked potatoes. The English owner is a long-term resident and very good source of local information. To his credit

he has created a lovely atmosphere and provides impeccable working conditions for his staff.
Mick and Craig's, Ochheauteal Beach. Thankfully, the menu here is a lot more creative than the venue's name. Sufficiently large meals with a bit of pizzazz – pizzas, burgers, hummus, etc. The restaurant also offers 'themed food nights', Sun roast, barbecue and 'all you can eat' nights.
Starfish Café, behind **Samudera Super market**, T034-952011. Small café-cum-bakery in a very peaceful garden setting. Here you can eat great food, while knowing that you are supporting a good cause. The organization was originally established to help rehabilitate people with disabilities and has extended its services to cover a range of poverty-reducing schemes. A very positive place that oozes goodness in its food, environment and service – good Western breakfasts, cakes, sandwiches, salads and coffees. A non-profit massage business has also opened on premises.
Cabbage Garden, T011-940171, down a back lane between Golden Lions and town centre; see map, page 265. Open 1000-2300. This restaurant is rightly famous with both locals and resident expats for its incredible Khmer food. The spicy shrimp mango salad is essential. It's a little tricky to find but a real discovery when you do. Highly recommended.
Cantina del Mar, Otres Beach, owned by the same people who run the restaurant of the same name in Phnom Penh. You should find authentic Mexican food and cold Mexican beer here.

Koh Kong and around p268
There are several places around town that sell Thai food – most of the Khmer-owned hotels listed in Sleeping, above, also serve food or have a restaurant attached. The market is also a good place to pick up fruit and street food.
Café Laurent, next to Koh Kong City Hotel, T011-590168. Mon-Sat 0700-0000. This new bistro serves excellent breakfasts,

pastas and pizzas. The coffee and bread are also superb and the pastries are not bad either. Highly recommended.

† Aqua Sunset Bar and Restaurant, riverfront, T035-6378626. Open 0700-2400. Average Thai, Western and Khmer food served here. They also plan to run river sunset cruises every day at 1700. It's still a great spot to sip a sundowner even if the boat is not running.

† Dug Out. Great Western breakfasts. Also serve other meals but it's at its best first thing.

Kampot and around *p269, map p270*
† Molienden Restaurant, see Sleeping. On the roof of the guesthouse. Extensive selection of pastas, spaghetti, soup and Italian seafood dishes. Fantastic food. Recommended.

† Bokor Mountain Lodge, see Sleeping. Great sandwiches made with the best ingredients – the fish and chicken *amok* is also divine. Recommended.

† Jasmine, is a riverside eatery set up by a Khmer woman (Jasmine) and her American photographer partner. They offer a slightly more up-market experience than many of the other places along the riverfront, Khmer and Western dishes. Recommended.

† Rusty Key Hole Bar and Restaurant, River Rd, past **Bamboo Light**. Run by the very down-to-earth Mancunian, Christian, **Rusty's** is now something of a local legend. Western food served. Friendly and the best place to watch football in town. The barbecue seafood and ribs come highly recommended.

† Little Garden Bar, T012-994161. This is an attractive and relaxed bar and restaurant on the riverfront offering delicious Khmer and Western food for reasonable prices. The rooftop bar is the place to be for spectacular sunsets over the Elephant Mountains.

† Epic Arts Café, is a brilliant little NGO-run establishment in the centre of Kampot. Set up as a project to employ local disabled people, they produce delicious cakes.

Kep *p271*
There are scores of seafood stalls on the beach, just before the tourist centre, that specialize in cooking freshly caught crab. At the tourist office itself there is also a row of restaurants serving crab, shrimp and fish. Nearly every hotel or guesthouse serves food – see also Sleeping entries.

† The Riel, T017-902771, www.kep-riel-bar.com. This is now Kep's only proper restaurant-cum-café-cum bar. Great friendly atmosphere and decent food should make this establishment a winner. Good rock 'n' roll stories from the owner as well.

🍷 Bars and clubs

Sihanoukville *p264, map p265*
Most resorts, guesthouses and hotels are also home to some kind of bar. In the Serendipity/Ochheuteal beach area, 2 of the most infamous night time hangouts are **Monkey Republic** and **Utopia**. For a Khmer alternative head to one of the Khmer restaurants near the Golden Lions where you will very likely be serenaded by Khmer singers.

Airport, Victory Beach. Set up by the same Russians who own **Snake House** this massive nightclub is located inside a fake aircraft hangar which is home to an actual, real aircraft. Decent beachside spot and free entry make this place doubly popular when Sihanoukville is busy.

🎣 Activities and tours

Sihanoukville *p264, map p265*
Diving
Scuba Nation Diving Centre, Weather Station Hill, T012-604680, www.dive cambodia.com. This company has the best reputation in the town and is the longest-established PADI dive centre. Prices vary depending on what you want. An Open Water course is US$350, dive trips are US$70.

Fishing
Tradewinds Charters at The Fishermen's Den Sports Bar, T01-270 2478, a couple of blocks opposite from the Marlin Hotel on Ekareach St, runs daily fishing trips. If you have caught something worth eating, the proprietor, Brian, will organize the restaurant to prepare a lovely meal from the catch.

Massage
Seeing Hands Massage, next to Q&A Book Café on Ekareach St. Open 0900-2100. US$6 per hour. Have a soothing Japanese-style shiatsu massage from the trained blind masseurs.

Koh Kong and around *p268*
Diving and tours
Koh Kong Divers, 243 Riverfront Rd. T035-690 0073, www.kohkongdivers. com. The only dive shop in Koh Kong is a professional and well-run operation offering the usual PADI courses, diving and snorkelling trips. They also offer several day trips to local islands, 4WD vehicle sojourns into the nearby Cardamom Mountains and numerous other boat excursions up river to waterfalls and into mangroves. Recommended.

Kampot *p269, map p270*
Massage
There are a couple of great blind masseuse places in town, the best being the **Kampot 5 Seeing Hands**, just back from the river near the Bokor Mountain Lodge. The people here are incredibly warm and friendly and at US$4 an hour, it's a great way to relax.

Tour operators **Cheang Try** is a local Khmer who runs both a motorcycle rental outlet in the centre of Kampot town (T012-974698) and also does guided tours. At 17 Mr Try's entire family was murdered by the Khmer Rouge and he was forced to live alone in the jungle on Elephant Mountain, near Bokor for 18 months. He then returned to fight the Khmer Rouge. If you take a tour

with Mr Try to Bokor his experiences really bring the place alive – rather than getting some wooden tourist tour you'll come away with some redolent and powerful memories. Highly recommended.

⊖ Transport

Sihanoukville *p264, map p265*
Bus
All buses depart from the main bus station near the new market unless otherwise stated. Many guesthouses and local tour operators may also offer minibus services but these vary in price and scheduling according to season. Around Khmer New Year and during the peak season you will need to book tickets the day before travel. **Phnom Penh Sorya** and **Paramount** both run several services between 0700 and 1400, US$4 to US$5; **Mekong Express** at 0745, 1430, US$6. Route 4 is quick and comfortable and the trip takes about 4 hrs.

Bus services to **Koh Kong** are developing but there are roughly 2 morning departures a day, 4 hrs, US$13. The Thai border is open until 2000 and buses depart until 2330 from Trat to Bangkok.

Minibuses to/from **Kampot** are presently run on a somewhat ad hoc basis by the **G'Day Mate** guesthouse (see Sleeping, page 272) US$7.50, 0830 departure and the **Peppercorn Express** (T017-921990), 0830, US$7.50. Both will also pick you up from your guesthouse and need to be booked in advance.

Taxi
Seats in shared taxis are available to **Phnom Penh** (US$7), **Koh Kong** (US$9) and **Kampot** (US$5). All depart from the taxi stand near the bus station. Private taxis are available and according to the quality of the car vary: Phnom Penh (US$35-US$50), Koh Kong (US$60) and Kampot (US$20-US$25).

Border essentials: Cambodia–Thailand

Cham Yem (Cambodia)–Hat Lek (Thailand)

The border crossing is 12 km from Koh Kong, across the river (15-20 minutes). The trip to the border at Cham Yem inside Cambodia costs ฿60 by moto, ฿50 by shared taxi and US$6 with own taxi. The border is open 0700-2000. There are public minibuses on the Thai side to Trat (84 km, 1¼ hrs, until 1800, ฿150). You can find private taxis after 1800 but bidding will start at ฿1000. From Trat buses run to Pattaya, Bangkok and Bangkok airport.

Poipet (Cambodia)–Aranya Prathet (Thailand)

The border crossing between Poipet and Thailand is open daily 0730-1700 and is a very popular route for budget-conscious foreigners entering Cambodia. The immigration officials at the Poipet border can be difficult.

Transport from Thailand Bus: four to five hours, air-conditioned bus ฿160-200, non-air conditioned bus ฿100, leave from the northern bus station in Bangkok. Take a motorbike, ฿25, or tuk-tuk, ฿40-50, the 7 km from Aranya Prathet to the Cambodian border.

Train: six to eight hours, ฿100, from Bangkok to Aranya Prathet.

There are two other minor crossings at Pailin and Anglong Veng but neither town is covered in this guide.

Koh Kong and around *p268*
Boat

At time of publication the boat service between Koh Kong and Sihanoukville was suspended and unlikely to be reinstated.

Bus

Bus tickets are available from most main guesthouse and hotels with buses departing from bus station 1 km out of town down Street 3. There are presently about 2-3 departures a day to/from **Sihanoukville** (US$13, 4 hrs) and **Phnom Penh** (US$8-US$10, 5 hrs). There are also numerous minibus services to destinations in **Thailand** including Trat, Pattaya and Bangkok, but almost all require a change of bus at the border.

Taxi

To **Sihanoukville**, 5-6 hrs, leaves from market, US$9 person in shared taxi (6 per

car), from 0600 onwards, leaves when full. Private taxi, US$60

Kampot and around *p269, map p270*
Bus

There are 2 buses in both directions run by the **Phnom Penh Sorya Transport Co** between Kampot and **Phnom Penh**. These services also stop in **Kep**. They depart the bus station on Blvd Charles de Gaulle near the central market in Phnom Penh at 0730 and 1315, returning at 0730 and 1230 from Kampot bus stand, US$4.

For buses to/from Sihanoukville see Sihanoukville bus listings, page 277.

Taxi

From **Phnom Penh**, 3 hrs to Kampot. Leaving from Doeum Kor Market on Mao Tse Tung Blvd and not the central market in Phnom Penh, US$3-4, 3 hrs. To **Phnom Penh**, vehicles leave from the truck station next to the **Total** gas station at 0700-1400, US$3.50, private taxi US$20. To **Sihanoukville**, US$4, private US$20-25, 2 hrs. To **Kep**, US$8, return US$14-15.

Kep *p271*

Kep is only 25 km from Kampot. The road is good and the journey can be made in 30-45 mins. A large white horse statue marks the turn-off to Kep. Buses now run twice a day between Kep/Kampot and Phnom Penh (see above).

⊙ Directory

Sihanoukville *p264, map p265*
Banks 4 banks in town (often shut):

Acleda, UCB, Canadia and the **Mekong Bank**, all on Ekareach St. UCB and **Canadia** offer Visa/ MasterCard cash advances. Cash advances at **Samudera Supermarket. Lucky Web**, on Weather Station Hill, charges 4% commission. **Internet** Several places around town, particularly near beaches. 3000-8000 riel per hr.

Kampot and around *p269, map p270*
Banks Canadia Bank, close to the Borey Bokor 1 Hotel. Cash advances on Visa and MasterCard. **Internet** On the road between the river and central roundabout, US$1 per hr. International calls around 600-900 riel per min.

Northeast Cambodia

A wild and rugged landscape, consisting of the three provinces of Ratanakiri, Mondulkiri and Stung Treng, greets any visitor to Cambodia's remote northeast region. Vast forested swathes of sparsely inhabited terrain spread north and eastwards toward Vietnam and Laos and are home to several distinct ethnic groups. The thick jungles also provide sanctuary to the majority of Cambodia's few remaining tigers.

During the civil war, the Northeast was cut off from the rest of the country. Then came years of bad transport links, with only the most committed making the arduous run up from up Phnom Penh. Yet the Northeast, much like the rest of the country, is now developing. A new Chinese-built road, including a road bridge over the river in Stung Treng, forms a strong link between Cambodia and Laos, cutting hours off the journey time.

Framing its western edge, and cutting it off from the rest of the country, is the Mekong River. It bifurcates, meanders and braids its way through the country and represents in its width a yawning chasm and watery superhighway that connects the region with Phnom Penh. Stung Treng and Kratie are located on this mighty river and despite the lack of any kind of riverboat service are still excellent places to view the elusive Irrawaddy River Dolphin.

The dust-blown and wild frontier town of Ban Lung, the capital of Ratanakiri, is slowly emerging as a centre of trekking and adventure travel. ▶▶ *For listings, see pages 283-287.*

Mekong Provinces → *For listings, see pages 283 -287.*

Kompong Cham, Kratie and Stung Treng make up the Mekong Provinces. Despite the Mekong River, its waterway and perpetual irrigation, these provinces are surprisingly economically unimportant and laid back. But with the new Chinese-built road now open and fully functioning – its easily one of the best in the country – the Northeast's provincial charms may soon be eradicated.

Border essentials: Cambodia–Laos

The official border crossing is Don Kralor–Voem Kham (Laos), an hour north of the town of Stung Treng (see page 281). Visas for both Laos and Cambodia are now available at the border. For Cambodia the usual entry requirements apply: two passport photos and US$20. For Laos, fees vary: US$20 for Chinese nationals, US$30 for Australians, US$35 for most EU nationals including the UK and US$42 for Canadians; you will need a passport photo as well. The border is open 0800-1700, but they may open before/after for a fee.

Transport Most travellers pass directly through the border on bus services as the crossing point is at a remote location and few facilities are available there. All buses wait for travellers to acquire visas. At present **Sorya** (see www.ppsoryatransport.com) runs the best direct service from Phnom Penh to 4000 Islands and Pakse, in Laos. This bus also stops in Stung Treng where you can hop on if there any seats left. From Stung Treng, the tour company **Xplore Asia** (see page 286) also offers minibus tickets to 4000 Islands and Pakse. It should be noted that there is little point arranging your own travel to the border in the hope of picking something else up on the other side as this will work out much more expensive.

Kompong Cham and around → *Colour map 6, B4.*

Kompong Cham is the fourth largest town in Cambodia and is a town of some commercial prosperity owing to its thriving river port and also, it is said, as a result of preferential treatment received from local boy made good, the Prime Minister, Hun Sen. Town and province have a combined population of more than 1.5 million people.

There is nothing in or around Kompong Cham to detain the visitor for long, most merely pass through, en route for Stung Treng and the northeast, but it is a pleasant enough town to rest awhile.

The small town of **Chhlong**, between Kompong Cham and Kratie, is one of Cambodia's best-kept secrets. The small town, nestled on the banks of the Mekong, 41 km from Kratie and 82 km from Kompong Cham, is one of the few places that survived the Khmer Rouge's ransacking and contains a multitude of French colonial buildings and traditional wooden Khmer houses. Of particular interest are the foundations of 120 antique houses and a 19th-century wooden Khmer house supported by 100 columns. Formerly a base for workers to surrounding rubber plantations, it is easy to feel nostalgic for a bygone era in Chhlong, with its wats and monasteries, an old school and charming market set in a colonial-style building. There's a couple of basic guesthouses on the riverfront road should you want to stop here for a night or two: **E Penh Chet** T012-690354, with simple clean rooms and **E Mekong Guesthouse**, T012-203896, which is a lovely old atmospheric wooden house, though rooms are a bit dirty. There's also a small market with a few stalls selling noodle and rice dishes. At the time of going to press a new road linking Kompong Cham and Kratie, and passing just outside Chhlong, is near completion. This would not only shave about 90 minutes off the original journey time but could place Chhlong on a new travellers' route.

Kratie → *Colour map 6, B4.*

Kratie (pronounced 'Kratcheay') is a port town on the Mekong roughly half way between Phnom Penh and Laos. In many ways it is a delightful place with a relaxed atmosphere and some good examples of shophouse architecture, but there is a discernible nefarious undercurrent due to Kratie's reputation as a centre of organized crime and corruption. Yet with the murky majesty of the Mekong dominating the town, sunset is a real highlight in Kratie, as the burning red sun descends slowly below the shore line.

Koh Trong Island, directly opposite Kratie town, has a lovely 8-km stretch of sandy dunes (in the dry season) where you can swim and relax. Aside from the beach, the island consists of small market farms and a simple, laid-back rural life – highly recommended for those who want to chill out. On the south side is a small Vietnamese floating village.

Kratie's main claim to some modicum of fame are the **Irrawaddy dolphins** that inhabit this portion of the Mekong (Kampi pool), 15 km north of the town on the road to Stung Treng. The best time to glimpse these rare and timid creatures is at sunrise or sunset when they are feeding. Motos from the town are US$4-US$5 return, boats then cost US$9 per person or US$7 per person if there is three or more.

Kampi Rapids ① *3 km north of Kampi Dolphin Pool, also known as Kampi resort, 1000 riel*, provides a refreshing and picturesque area to take a dip in the clear Mekong waters (during the dry season). A bridge leads down to a series of scenic thatched huts which provide shelter for the swimmers.

Twenty one kilometres further north of the Kampi pool is **Sambor**, a pre-Angkorian settlement, but today, unfortunately, not a single trace of this ancient heritage exists. The highpoint of a trip to Sambor is more in the getting there, as you pass through beautiful countryside, than in the temples themselves. Replacing the ancient ruins are two temples. The first and most impressive is the 100-column pagoda, rumoured to be the largest new pagoda in the country. It is a replica of the 100-column wooden original, which was built in 1529. During the war, Pol Pot based himself out of the complex, killing hundreds of people and destroying the old pagoda. The new one was built in 1985 (perhaps the builders were slightly overzealous – it features 116 columns). Some 300 m behind the gigantic pagoda sits a much smaller and arguably more interesting temple. The wat still contains many of its original features including a number of wooden pylons that date back 537 years.

Stung Treng → Colour map 6, A4.

Yet another eponymous provincial capital set at the point where the Sekong River cuts away from the Mekong, Stung Treng is just 40 km from Laos and a stopping-off place

Kratie

To Snuol & Stung Treng

Street 5
Street 6
Pagoda Wat
Taxis
Street 7
Ferry Port
Street 8
Street 9   Phnom Penh Public Transport Co
Street 10
Food Stalls   Hour Lean Bus Station
Street 11
Acleda
Street 12
To Phnom Penh

To Koh Trong Island & Vietnamese Floating Village

Mekong

Preah Soramarth St

N

Not to scale

Sleeping
Balcony Guesthouse 9
Oudom Sambath 4
Santhepheap 3
Star Guesthouse 1
You Hong Guesthouse 8

Eating
Red Sun Falling 1

on the overland route to Ratanakiri. The town still maintains a wild frontier feel despite losing much of its edge due to the building of the mammoth Chinese road and a striking bridge that has created good links to Laos (see Transport, page 286, for more details on how to reach Laos). Pigs, cows and the odd ox-cart still wander through the town's busy streets but there isn't a lot for tourists around Stung Treng. Tour guides can organize boat runs to a local river dolphin project, cycling trips along the river banks and excursions to some waterfalls making it a friendlier alternative to Kratie. **Lbak Khone**, the 26 km rocky area that the Mekong rapids flow through en route to the Laos border, is one of the country's most stunning areas.

Ratanakiri Province → *For listings, see pages 283 -287.*

Ratanakiri is like another planet compared to the rest of Cambodia – dusty, red roads curl through the landscape in summer, while in the rainy season the area becomes lush and green turning the roads into slippery mush. Adventure enthusiasts won't be disappointed, with waterfalls to discover, ethnic minorities to meet, elephants to ride, river trips to take and the beautiful Yaek Lom volcanic lake to take a dip in. Be warned: get there soon as a major new road linking Ban Lung to the outside world is now under construction. Once this has been completed Ban Lung is likely to obscure into just another provincial town.

Ban Lung and around → *Colour map 6, A5.*
Ban Lung has been the dusty provincial capital of Ratanakiri Province ever since the previous capital Lumphat was flattened by US bombers trying to 'destroy' the foot- paths and tracks that made up the Ho Chi Minh Trail. The dirt tracks that used to suffocate the town with their dry season dust and wet season mud have now been mostly paved, making a visit here more amenable. The town is situated on a plateau dotted with lakes and hills, many of great beauty, and serves as a base from which visitors can explore the surrounding countryside. With the Vietnamese in the east building a road from the nearby Le Thanh/O Yadao border crossing, plans to pave the existing roads into and out of Ban Lung, and a burgeoning tourist market, mark this part of Cambodia for dramatic change. At present you'll find basic guesthouse accommodation, and food and drink can be obtained in town.

Ins and outs Ban Lung is 13 hours from Phnom Penh. It is better to break your journey in Kratie and Stung Treng and take a pickup/taxi from there. The chief mode of transport is the motorbike, which comes with a driver, or not, as required (usually US$5 without driver and US$15 with, but you'll have to haggle). Bus services are sporadic. Cars with driver can be hired for US$40-50 a day.

Sights around Ban Lung The name Ratanakiri means 'jewel mountains' in Pali, and presumably comes from the wealth of gems in the hills, but it could just as easily refer to the beauty of the landscape. **Yaek Lom** ① *US$1 and a parking charge of 500 riel*, is a perfectly circular volcanic lake about 5 km east of town and easily reached by motorbike. The crystalline lake is rimmed by protected forest dominated by giant emergents (diptero-carps and shoreas) soaring high into the sky. It takes about one hour to walk around the lake: in doing so you will find plenty of secluded bathing spots, a couple of small jetties and, given the lack of water in town, it is not surprising that most locals and visitors bathe in the wonderfully clear and cool waters of the lake. There is a small 'museum' of ethnography and a couple of minority stilt houses to be seen.

There are three **waterfalls** ① *2000 riel each*, in close proximity to Ban Lung town. **Kachaang Waterfall** is 6 km away. The 12-m high waterfall flows year round and is surrounded by magnificent, pristine jungle and fresh mist rising from the fall. **Katien Waterfall** is a little oasis 7 km northwest of Ban Lung. Believed to have formed from volcanic lava hundreds of years ago, the 10-m plunging falls are sheltered from the outside world by a little rocky grotto. It is one of the better local falls to swim in as it is very secluded (most people will usually have the area to themselves); the water is completely clean. The best waterfall is arguably **Chaa Ong Falls**, with the 30-m falls plunging into a large pool. Those game enough can have a shower behind the crescent-shaped ledge. To get to the waterfalls, follow Highway 19 out of town and branch off 2 km out on the main road in the first village out of Ban Lung: Chaa Ong Falls are 9 km northwest at the intersection, turn right at the village and head for about 5 km to head to Katien Waterfall (follow the signs), the same road heads to Kachaang Waterfall.

The trip to **Ou'Sean Lair Waterfall**, 35 km from Ban Lung, is a wonderful day excursion offering a fantastic cross-section of what is essentially Ratanakiri's main attractions (without the riverside element). From Ban Lung, fields of wind-bent, spindly rubber trees provide a canopy over the road's rolling hills, a legacy left from the French in the 1960s. Punctuating the mottled natural vista is an equally diverse range of ethnic minority settlements. Tampeun and Kreung villages are dotted along the road and about half way (17 km from Ban Lung), in a lovely valley, is a tiny Cham village. The perfect end to the journey is the seven-tiered **Ou'Sean Lair falls**. The falls were reportedly 'discovered' by a Tampeun villager five years ago, who debated as to whether he should tell the Department of Tourism of their existence. In return for turning over the falls, they were named after him. The falls are most spectacular in the wet season but are still pretty alluring during the dry season.

◉ Northeast Cambodia listings

For Sleeping and Eating price codes and other relevant information, see pages 40 - 43.

◉ Sleeping

Kompong Cham and around *p280*
D-E Monorom 2 VIP Hotel, Mort Tunle St, waterfront, T092-777102, www.monoromviphotel.com. With a perfect Mekong setting this brand-new hotel is easily the best in town. Get a room at the front and you'll have a balcony overlooking the river – each comes with bathtub, hot water, cable TV, tea-making facilities and there's free Wi-Fi/internet for guests on the ground floor. Recommended.
D-G Leap Viraksar Hotel, big yellow building on right just before bridge on way to Kratie, T042-633 7778. Range of rooms

from grim-looking fan rooms through to accommodation replete with a/c, TV and bathtubs. Friendly; mini-mart attached.
E-F Rana, T012-696340. Set in a small village just outside Kampong Cham, this is a well-run and engaging homestay programme run by Kheang and her American husband, Don. Set up more for educational purposes than as a business; you can get a real insight into rural life here. Rates include full-board but accommodation is basic. They offer free moto pickup from Kampong Cham if you book for 2 or more nights. Recommended.

Kratie *p280, map p281*
E-F Santepheap Hotel, on the river road, T072-971537. Rooms are adequate in this reasonable hotel. It has a quiet atmosphere

and the clean and airy rooms come with attached bathrooms, fridge, fan or a/c.

E-G Balcony Guesthouse, riverfront road, T01-604036, www.balconyguesthouse.net. There are several airy, clean and basic rooms in this villa overlooking the river. There is, of course, a giant, communal balcony which is a great place to lounge and watch Mekong sunsets. Bar, restaurant and internet as well.

E-G Oudom Sambath Hotel, 439 River Rd, T072-971502. Well-run place with a friendly English speaking Chinese-Khmer owner. The rooms are huge, with a/c, TV, hot water, etc. The more expensive rooms have large baths and regal-looking furniture. The huge rooftop balcony has the best views of the Mekong in town – they have rooms up here as well but these fill quickly. Also has a decent and very cheap restaurant. Recommended.

G Star Guesthouse, beside the market, T072-971663. This has gained the reputation of being the friendliest guesthouse in town. It is very popular with travellers and its rooms are nicely appointed.

G You Hong Guesthouse, between the taxi rank and the market, T012-957003. Clean rooms with attached bathroom and fan. US$1 extra gets you cable TV. Friendly, helpful owners. The restaurant is often filled with drunk backpackers.

Stung Treng p281

C-E Hotel Gold River, riverfront, T012-980678. Brand new 4-storey hotel with splendid river views and the only lift in northeastern Cambodia. Each spotless and comfortable room has a hot-water bathtub, cable TV and a/c; the ones at the front offer the river as backdrop. Friendly service and a bargain given the location. Recommended.

D-F Nature Lodge, a few kilometres north of Stung Treng town, T074-637 7767. Gorgeous location set in a nook of the Mekong River is offset by the tired-looking rooms and bungalows. It's just been taken over by a local community group who hope to help this wonderfully sited resort-type set-up reach its full potential. Check in Stung

Treng at the **XploreAsia** office (see Activities and Tours, page 286) for more details.

D-G Ly Ly Guesthouse, opposite the market, T012-937859. Decent Chinese-style hotel with varying types of rooms – all come with private shower/toilet and cable TV. The ones at the back of the building have balconies and are the best value – you have the option of a/c or fan throughout. Friendly with some English spoken. Recommended.

D-G Stung Treng Hotel and Guest House, on main road near the river, T016-888335. Decent enough rooms in a good location – a reasonable second option.

Ban Lung and around p282

C-E Borann Lodge, 800 m east of market, T012-959363, www.yaklom.com. This huge chalet-style villa set down a Ban Lung side street comes with 6 rooms of varying sizes though each has a/c and fan and en suite bathroom with hot water. The owners and staff are very friendly and Borann feels more like a homestay than a guesthouse. Massive wooden model of Angkor and various over-the-top wooden furniture items add to the character. Affiliated with **Yaklom Hill Lodge**. Recommended.

C-E NorDen House, on road to Yaklom Lake, T012-880327, www.nordenhouseyaklom. com. The nearest accommodation to the Yaklom Lake. You'll find a collection of spotless, well-appointed bungalows here each with a/c, TV and en suite hot-water facilities. There are some attractive gardens, a decent restaurant, free Wi-Fi plus they can arrange bus tickets. Owner also rents out the best motorbikes in town. Swedish and Khmer owners. Recommended.

D-F Yaklom Hill Lodge, near Yaklom Lake, 6 km east of Ban Lung, T012-644240, www.yaklom.com. Set in a private forest this rustic ecolodge is a bit out of town. Bungalows have balconies and hammocks and are well decorated with local handicrafts and fabrics. Fan, mosquito net, attached bathroom, shower; power is supplied via generator and solar panels.

The friendly owner, Sampon, arranges all manner of tours and treks and is the only operator in the area who uses local ethnic minority peoples as guides. Affiliated with **Borann Lodge**. The food is a bit ropey but still this place is recommended.

E-F Sopheap Guest House, next to the market, T012-958746. Clean rooms come complete with hot water, fan or a/c, cable TV and a noisy and lively central location. Get one with a balcony and you'll have a great view of the market life unfolding below you.

F-G Tree Top Eco Lodge, Phum Nol, Laban Seak commune, T011-600381, www. treetop-ecolodge.com. Lovely set of large wooden bungalows overlooking a valley on the edge of town. Interiors are well decorated and each room comes complete with adjacent huge balconies and en suite hot-water bathrooms. There are some good communal areas and verandas, a restaurant/bar and free transfers to the bus station. Recommended.

🍴 Eating

Kompong Cham and around p280
🍴 **Ho An Restaurant**, Monivong St, T042-941234. Large, Chinese restaurant with a good selection of dishes. Friendly service.
🍴-🍴 **Lazy Mekong Daze**, on the riverfront. British owner Simon provides alcohol, cakes, fish and chips, and Khmer food from this friendly riverside establishment. He also has a free pool table and you can watch the latest football on his TV.
🍴 **Fresh Coffee**, same block as **Monorom 2 VIP Hotel** on riverfront. Open 0700-2100. Small new coffee shop selling burgers, cakes and some Khmer food.
🍴 **Smile Restaurant**, same block as **Monorom 2 VIP Hotel** on riverfront. Open 0630-2200. Huge Khmer menu with some Western dishes in this new and excellent NGO-connected eatery that helps orphans and kids with HIV. Free Wi-Fi. Recommended.

Kratie p280, map p281
There are a number of foodstalls along the river at night serving fruit shakes. The market also sells simple dishes during the day.
🍴-🍴 **Balcony Guesthouse**, (see Sleeping above). Serves up an excellent fried British breakfast and various other Western and Khmer dishes from its huge balcony overlooking the river. Good spot for a drink as well. Recommended.
🍴-🍴 **Red Sun Falling**, on the river road. Open Mon-Sat. Probably the best restaurant in town, it offers a variety of excellent Western dishes and a few Asian favourites. The full monty breakfast is fantastic. Good cocktails. The very friendly proprietor, Joe, also runs a very good bookshop on the premises. Recommended.
🍴-🍴 **Star Guesthouse**. See Sleeping, above. A decent enough menu but sometimes the prices (almost US$1 for a squeeze of honey) and quality let the place down. Western food, and the home-made bread is excellent.

Stung Treng p281
🍴 **Prochum Tonle Restaurant**, at the Sekong Hotel on the riverfront. Some of the best Khmer food in town at this locally renowned restaurant.
🍴 **Sophakmukal**, near the market. Beer garden-style restaurant with very good, cheap Cambodian food, curry, amok, soup (all under US$1). Very friendly owner. Recommended.
🍴 **Stung Treng Burger**, in a side street near the market. Daily 0630-2100. Very friendly owners, fresh decor and good food make this place one of the best spots in town. Great burgers and pizza supplement excellent Khmer food; decent breakfasts too. Recommended.

Ban Lung and around p282
Food options are now improving in Ban Lung with a greater range of fresh fruit and other produce on sale at the market and various small bakeries offering Khmer-style cakes and breads opening up.

A' Dam, on the same road as **Borann Lodge** and **Tree Top Eco Lodge**. Open 1100(ish)-2400. It's understandable why A'Dam is a popular with both Ban Lung locals and expat NGO workers. Great Khmer and Western food is piled high and served cheap by the friendly Khmer owners. Also doubles as a bar. Recommended.

Apocalypse Bar (near Borann Lodge). You can get decent coffee and tea plus breakfasts at this small eatery attached to the **Dutch Couple** tour agency.

Ratanak Hotel Restaurant. Quite popular, serves a spectacular barbecue that you cook at your table. Cambodian food US$1-2.

Tree Top Eco Lodge, see Sleeping, above. Great location for both dinner and a drink but the food isn't all that it could be. Best setting but you can eat better at other places.

◑ Activities and tours

Stung Treng p281

XploreAsia, on the riverfront near the Hotel Gold River. This tour company opened a small office in late 2009. They are working in conjunction with various local community projects and offer a variety of tours including river excursions, trips to see the dolphins, and cycling and kayaking tours. You should also be able to find out about other tours at the **Riverside Guesthouse** (see Sleeping, above).

Ban Lung and around p282

Dutch Couple, on road east of the market, T099-531745, www.ecotourismcambodia.info. This is a small and recently opened eco-tourism outfit offering well-equipped, upmarket and pricey tours to various destinations in northeast Cambodia.

Yaklom Hill Lodge, see Sleeping, above. Offer a variety of tours and other adventures. They use their own local ethnic minority guides.

◉ Transport

Kompong Cham and around p280
Bus

The town is 120 km northeast of Phnom Penh via the well-surfaced Routes 5, 6 and 7. There are regular connections with **Phnom Penh** by shared taxi and numerous bus companies run regular services. Buses also connect to all points north including **Chhlong**, **Kratie**, **Stung Treng** and **Ban Lung**.

Moto/tuk-tuk/taxi

Local transport is by moto, tuk-tuk or taxi. A moto for a day is between US$6-8 and between 500-1000 riel for short trips. Local tuk-tuk driver and guide Mr Vannat has an excellent reputation and is fluent in French and English, T012-995890. US$20 a day for a boat ride.

Kratie p280, map p281
Bus

Roughly 4 buses a day run to **Phnom Penh**, US$5/US$8, 4-5 hrs, stopping off at **Kompong Cham** en route. **Stung Treng** is served by regular minibuses 0800-1400, US$6, 2 hrs, and at least 1 daily bus, US$4, 2½ hrs; while there is at least 1 minibus a day to **Ban Lung**, US$12, 6 hrs. Many of these buses depart from the bus stand near the river, but you might want to ask at your accommodation if this has changed. You can also find shared taxis plying routes to all destinations though prices fluctuate according to season, road condition and fuel prices.

Motodop

Local transport by *motodop* US$1 per hr or US$6-7 per day.

Stung Treng p281

Before the bridge opened in 2008, Stung Treng used to be the staging post for travel to Laos with regular boats plying the few kilometres upriver to the border. This situation, however, has now completely changed with most travellers heading south from Pakse in Laos (see box on page 280 for details of this border crossing), no longer stopping in Stung Treng, preferring instead to take through buses directly to Kratie and Phnom Penh.

Most hotels (**Sekong**, **Riverside**, etc) can organize tickets. Alternatively, you can go directly to the taxi/bus rank. At present there is at least 1 bus a day to **Pakse**, 4½ hrs, US$6, in Laos and through ticketing to **Vientiane** (change in Pakse) is also available, US$35, should you wish to connect directly to the Laos capital. There are a couple of buses to **Phnom Penh** daily, 9 hrs, US$7.50; and the same bus will stop at **Kratie**, US$5. Plenty of minibuses also ply this route. Pickups and shared taxis connect regularly with **Phnom Penh** via **Kratie**, and with recent road construction the roads should be OK to travel along (if a little bumpy). Shared taxis to **Phnom Penh** leave at 0600 from the taxi rank near the river, 7 hrs, US$15. To **Ban Lung** at 0700 from the taxi rank and the trip takes 4-5 hrs, US$10.

Ban Lung and around *p282*
Bus

With the route from Kompong Cham to Kratie being both shortened and improved plus the plans to upgrade the road into Ban Lung, journey times between **Ratanakiri** and **Phnom Penh** (and places en route) could be significantly reduced in the near future.

Regular daily buses to **Stung Treng**, 3 hrs, ; US$6; **Kratie**, 5-6 hrs, US$7, ; **Kompong Cham**, 6-8 hrs, US$9, ; **Siem Reap** (14 hrs, change in Skon, US$16), ; **Phnom Penh**, 9-11hrs, US$9-US$14; and to the **Vietnamese border**, see box, page 262, 2½ hrs, US$10, are all available in a variety of mini and larger buses. Share and private taxis are also available with prices fluctuating depending on season, road conditions and price of fuel; ask at your guesthouse/hotel for price approximations on arrival.

Motorbike
Den Norden guesthouse (see Sleeping, above) has a few top-class 250cc and 400cc dirtbikes for rent, from US$25 to US$50 per day.

ⓘ Directory

Kompong Cham and around *p280*
Banks There are 2 banks in town - **Acleda** and **Canadia Bank**. Acleda, 0800-1600, will do Western Union transfers and Canadia will do advances on Visa and MasterCard. **Internet** ABC computers, in the centre of town, was the only internet shop operating at the time of writing, US$1 per hr, overseas phone calls.

Kratie *p280, map p281*
Banks There is an **Acleda Bank** half way down St 11. It does not offer advances on Visa or MasterCard but is a subsidiary for Western Union. **Internet** You Hong Guesthouse offer a good, cheap connection. **Three Star Internet** US$4 per hr. There is another internet café near **Phnom Penh Transport** bus office but at the time of writing it was US$4 per hr.

Stung Treng *p281*
Banks There are no banks in town. **Internet** Available at the computer shop opposite the market and the **Sekong Hotel**, US$4 per hr. **Telephone** There are telephone shops all over town.

Ban Lung and around *p282*
Banks Amazingly **ANZ** bank have opened an ATM near the airport. Details are sketchy if foreign bank cards are being accepted by this machine so it's best not to rely on it for a source of cash. The **Mountain Guesthouse** and the **Ratanak Hotel** both change TCs but allow at least 3 days for your cheques to clear. **Internet** CIC near Sovannikiri Hotel. **Medical services** The hospital is on the road north towards O Chum. Dr Vannara, T012-970359, speaks very good English. **Post office** In the centre of town.

Angkor

The huge temple complex of Angkor, the ancient capital of the powerful Khmer Empire, is one of the archæological treasures of Asia and the spiritual and cultural heart of Cambodia. Angkor Wat is arguably the greatest temple within the complex, both in terms of grandeur and sheer magnitude. After all, it is the biggest religious monument in the world, its outer walls clad with one of the longest continuous bas-relief ever created. The diverse architectural prowess and dexterity of thousands of artisans is testified by around 100 brilliant monuments in the area. Of these the Bayon, with its beaming smiles; Banteay Srei, which features the finest intricate carvings; and the jungle temple of Ta Prohm are unmissable. Others prefer the more understated but equally brilliant temples of Neak Pean, Preah Khan and Pre Rup.

The petite town of Siem Reap sits nearby the Angkor complex, and is home to a gamut of world-class hotels, restaurants and bars. A hop, skip and a jump from the town is Southeast Asia's largest lake, the Tonlé Sap, with floating villages, teeming with riverine life. ▸▸ *For listings, see pages 306-314.*

Ins and outs

Getting there

Air The **airport** ① *T063-963148*, is 7 km from Siem Reap, the town closest to the Angkor ruins (see Transport, page 313), with flights from Phnom Penh, Ho Chi Minh City, Bangkok and Vientiane. A moto into town is US$1, a taxi US$7. Guesthouse owners often meet flights. Visas can be issued upon arrival US$20 (฿1000), photo required. Departure airport tax is US$25.

Boat From Phnom Penh, US$35, five to six hours. The trip is a good way to see the mighty Tonlé Sap Lake. It is a less appealing option in the dry season when low water levels necessitate transfers to small, shallow draft vessels. In case of extremely low water levels a bus or pickup will need to be taken for part of the trip. The mudbank causeway between the lake and the outskirts of Siem Reap is hard to negotiate and some walking may be necessary (it's 12 km from Bindonville harbour to Siem Reap). Boats depart from the Phnom Penh Port on Sisowath Quay (end of 106 Street) 0700, departing Siem Reap 0700 from Chong Khneas on the Tonlé Sap Lake. Tickets and enquiries, T012-581358.

Bus The air-conditioned buses are one of the most convenient and comfortable ways to go between Phnom Penh and Siem Reap, US$6-11, six hours. Almost every guesthouse or hotel sells tickets although it is easy enough to pick up from the bus stations/terminal. In peak periods, particularly Khmer New Year, it is important to purchase tickets a day or two prior to travel. A shared taxi from Phnom Penh will cost you US$10.

Getting around

Most of the temples within the Angkor complex (except the Roluos Group) are located in an area 8 km north of Siem Reap, with the area extending across a 25 km radius. The Roluos Group are 13 km east of Siem Reap and further away is Banteay Srei (32 km).

Cars with drivers and guides are available from larger hotels from around US$25 to US$30 per day plus US$25 for a guide. An excellent guiding service by car is provided by **Mr Hak** ① *T012-540336, www.angkortaxidriver.com*, who offers a variety of packages and tours around

Angkor and the surrounding area. The Angkor Tour Guide Association and most other travel agencies can also organize this. Expect to pay around US$10-12 per day for a moto unless the driver speaks good English, in which case the price will be higher. This price will cover trips to the Roluos Group of temples but not to Banteay Srei. No need to add more than a dollar or two to the price for getting to Banteay Srei unless the driver is also a guide and can demonstrate to you that he is genuinely going to show you around. Tuk-tuks and their ilk have appeared in recent years and a trip to the temples on a motorbike-drawn cart is quite a popular option for two people, U$14-17 a day (maximum two people).

Bicycle hire, US$2-3 per day from most guesthouses, represents a nice option for those who feel reasonably familiar with the area. The White Bicycles scheme, set up by Norwegian expats (see Transport, page 313), offers bikes for US$2 per day with US$1.50 of that going straight into local charities and no commission to the hotels and is recommended. If you are on a limited schedule and only have a day or two to explore you won't be able to cover an awful lot of the temples on a pedal bike as the searing temperatures and sprawling layout can take even the most advanced cyclists a considerable amount of time. Angkor Wat and Banteay Srei have official parking sites, 1000 riel and at the other temples you can quite safely park and lock your bikes in front of a drink stall. You can also charter a helicopter, see page 312. Elephants are stationed near the Bayon or at the South Gate of Angkor Thom during the day. In the evenings, they are located at the bottom of Phnom Bakheng, taking tourists up to the summit for sunset. ▶▶ *See Activities and tours, page 312.*

Best time to visit
Angkor's peak season coincides with the dry season, November-February. Not only is this the driest time of year it is also the coolest (which can still be unbearably hot). The monsoon lasts from June to October or November. At this time it can get very muddy.

Tourist information
Guides can be invaluable when navigating the temples, with the majority being able to answer most questions about Angkor as well as providing additional information about Cambodian culture and history. Most hotels and travel agents will be able to point you in the direction of a good guide. The **Khmer Angkor Tour Guide Association** ① *on the road to Angkor, T063-964347, www.khmerangkortourguide.com*, has pretty well-trained guides. Most of the guides here are well briefed and some speak English better than others. The going rate is US$20-25 per day. There is a new **tourist office** ① *at the far end of Sivatha Street (towards the crocodile farm), 0730-1100 and 1430-1700.*

Temple fees and hours A one-day pass costs US$20, three-day pass US$40, seven-day pass US$60. The seven-day pass is valid for any seven days (they don't have to be consecutive) one month from the purchase date. Most people will be able to cover the majority of the temples within three days. If you buy your ticket after 1715 the day before, you get a free sunset thrown in. The complex is open daily 0530-1830. You will need to pay additional fees if you wish to visit Beng Melea (US$5), Phnom Kulen (US$20) or Koh Ker (US$10); payable at the individual sites.

Safety Landmines were planted on some outlying paths to prevent Khmer Rouge guerrillas from infiltrating the temples; they have pretty much all been cleared by now, but it is safer to stick to well-used paths. Be wary of snakes in the dry season. The very poisonous Hanuman snake (lurid green) is fairly common in the area.

Photography A generalization, but somewhat true, is that black and white film tends to produce better-looking tourist pictures than those in colour. The best colour shots usually include some kind of contrast against the temples, a saffron-clad monk or a child. Don't forget to ask if you want to include people in your shots. In general, the best time to photograph the great majority of temples is before 0900 and after 1630.

① Angkor, Siem Reap & Roluos

→ **Angkor maps**
1 Angkor, Siem Reap & Roluos, page 290
2 Angkor Wat, page 296
3 Angkor Thom, page 299
4 Siem Reap, page 304
5 Siem Reap market area, page 307

Itineraries

The temples are scattered over an area in excess of 160 sq km. A half-day would only allow enough time to visit the South Gate of Angkor Thom, Bayon and Angkor Wat. There are three so-called 'circuits'. The Petit Circuit takes in the main central temples including Angkor Wat, Bayon, Baphuon and the Terrace of the Elephants. The Grand Circuit takes a wider route, including smaller temples like Ta Prohm, East Mebon and Neak Pean. The Roluos Group Circuit ventures further afield still, taking in the temples near Roluos – Lolei, Preah Ko and Bakong. Here are some options for visiting Angkor's temples:

One day Angkor Wat (sunrise or sunset), South Gate of Angkor Thom, Angkor Thom Complex (Bayon, Elephant Terrace, Royal Palace) and Ta Prohm. This is a hefty schedule for one day; you'll need to arrive after 1615 and finish just after 1700 the following day.

Two days The same as above but with the inclusion of the rest of the Angkor Thom, Preah Khan, Srah Srang (sunrise), and at a push, Banteay Srei.

Three days Day 1 Sunrise at Angkor Wat; morning South Gate of Angkor Thom, Angkor Thom complex (aside from Bayon); Ta Prohm; late afternoon-sunset at the Bayon. **Day 2** Sunrise Srah Srang; morning Banteay Kdei and Banteay Srei; late afternoon Preah Khan; sunset at Angkor Wat. **Day 3** Sunrise and morning Roluos; afternoon Ta Keo and sunset either at Bakheng or Angkor Wat. Those choosing to stay one or two days longer should try to work Banteay Samre, East Mebon, Neak Pean and Thomannon into their itinerary. A further two to three days warrants a trip to Prasat Kravan, Ta Som, Beng Melea and Kbal Spean.

Beating the crowds

These days avoiding traffic within the Angkor complex is difficult but still moderately achievable. As it stands, there is a pretty standard one-day tour itinerary that includes: Angkor Wat (sunrise), Angkor Thom, the Bayon, etc (morning), break for lunch, Ta Prohm (afternoon), Preah Khan (afternoon) and Phnom Bakheng (sunset). If you reverse the order, peak hour traffic at major temples is dramatically reduced. As many tour groups troop into Siem Reap for lunch this is an opportune time to catch a peaceful moment in the complex, just bring a packed lunch or eat at 1100 or 1400.

To avoid the masses at the draw-card attraction, Angkor Wat, try to walk around the temple, as opposed to through it. Sunset at Phnom Bakheng has turned into a circus fiasco, so aim for Angkor or the Bayon at this time as they are both quiet in comparison.

Sunrise is still relatively peaceful at Angkor, grab yourself the prime position behind the left-hand pond (you need to depart Siem Reap no later than 0530), though there are other stunning early morning options, such as Srah Srang or Bakong. Bakheng gives a beautiful vista of Angkor in the early-mid morning.

Background

Khmer Empire

Under Jayavarman VII (1181-1218) the complex stretched more than 25 km east to west and nearly 10 km north to south, approximately the same size as Manhattan. For five centuries (ninth-13th), the court of Angkor held sway over a vast territory. At its height Khmer influence spanned half of Southeast Asia, from Burma to the southernmost tip of Indochina and from the borders of Yunnan to the Malay Peninsula. The only threat to this great empire was a river-borne invasion in 1177, when the Cham used a Chinese navigator to pilot their canoes up the Mekong. Scenes are depicted in bas-reliefs of the Bayon temple.

Jayavarman II (AD 802-835) founded the Angkor Kingdom, then coined Hariharalaya to the north of the Tonlé Sap, in the Roluos region (Angkor), in AD 802. Later he moved the capital to Phnom Kulen, 40 km northeast of Angkor, where he built a Mountain Temple and Rong Shen shrine. After several years he moved the capital back to the Roluos region. Jayavarman III (AD 835-877) continued his father's legacy and built a number of shrines at Hariharalaya. Many historians believe he was responsible for the initial construction of the impressive laterite pyramid, Bakong, considered the great precursor to Angkor Wat. Bakong, built to symbolize Mount Meru, was later embellished and developed by Indravarman. Indravarman (AD 877-889) overthrew his predecessor violently and undertook a major renovation campaign in the capital Hariharalaya. The majority of what stands in the Roluos Group today is the work of Indravarman. A battle between Indravarman's sons destroyed the palace and the victor and new king Yasovarman I (AD 889-900) moved the capital from Roluos and laid the foundations of Angkor itself. He dedicated the temple to his ancestors. His new capital at Angkor was called Yasodharapura, meaning 'glory-bearing city', and here he built 100 wooden ashramas, retreats (all of which have disintegrated today). Yasovarman selected Bakheng as the location for his temple-mountain and after flattening the mountain top, set about creating another Mount Meru. The temple he constructed was considered more complex than anything built beforehand, a five-storey pyramid with 108 shrines. A road was then built to link the former and present capitals of Roluos and Bakheng. Like the Kings before him, Yasovarman was obliged to construct a major waterworks and the construction of the reservoir – the East Baray (now completely dry) – was considered an incredible feat. After Yasovarman's death in AD 900 his son Harshavarman (AD 900-923) assumed power for the next 23 years. During his brief reign, Harshavarman is believed to have built Baksei Chamkrong (north-east of Phnom Bakheng) and Prasat Kravan (the 'Cardamom Sanctuary'). His brother, Ishanarvarman II (AD 923-928), resumed power upon his death but no great architectural feats were recorded in this time. In 928, Jayavarman IV moved the capital 65 km away to Koh Ker. Here he built the grand state temple Prasat Thom, an impressive seven-storey, sandstone pyramid. Following the death of Jayavarman, things took a turn for the worst. Chaos ensued under Harshavarman's II weak leadership and over the next four years, no monuments were known to be erected. Jayavarman's IV nephew, Rajendravarman (AD 944-968), took control of the situation and it's assumed he forcefully relocated the capital back to Angkor. Rather than moving back into the old capital Phnom Bakheng, he marked his own new territory, selecting an area south of the East Baray as his administrative centre. Here, in AD 961 he constructed the state temple, Pre Rup, and constructed the temple, East Mebon (AD 953), in the middle of the baray. Srah Srang, Kutisvara and Bat Chum were also constructed, with the help of his chief architect, Kavindrarimathana. It was towards the end of his reign that he started construction on Banteay Srei, considered one of the finest examples of Angkorian craftsmanship in the country. Rajendravarman's son Jayavarman V (AD 968-1001) became the new king in 968. The administrative centre was renamed Jayendranagari and yet again, relocated. More than compensating for the unfinished Ta Keo was Jayavarman's V continued work on Banteay Srei. Under his supervision the splendid temple was completed and dedicated to his father.

Aside from successfully extending the Khmer Empire's territory King Suryavarman I (1002-1049), made a significant contribution to Khmer architectural heritage. He presided over the creation of a new administrative centre – the Royal Palace (in Angkor Thom) – and the huge walls that surround it. The next in line was Udayadityavarman II (1050-1066), the son of Suryavarman I. The Baphuon temple-mountain was built during his relatively short appointment. After overthrowing his Great-Uncle Dharanin- dravarman, Suryavarman II (1112-1150), the greatest of Angkor's god-kings, came to power. His rule marked the highest point in Angkorian architecture and civilization. Not only was he victorious in conflict, having beaten the Cham whom couldn't be defeated by China, he was responsible for extending the borders of the Khmer Empire into Myanmar, Malaya and Siam. This aside, he was also considered one of the era's most brilliant creators. Suryavarman II was responsible for the construction of Angkor Wat, the current-day symbol of Cambodia. Beng Melea, Banteay Samre and Thommanon are also thought to be the works of this genius. He has been immortalized in his own creation – in a bas-relief in the South Gallery of Angkor Wat the glorious King Suryavarman II sitting on top of an elephant. After a period of political turmoil, which included the sacking of Angkor, Jayavarman VII seized the throne in 1181 and set about rebuilding his fiefdom. He created a new administrative centre – the great city of Angkor Thom. The mid-point of Angkor Thom is marked by his brilliant Mahayana Buddhist state temple, the Bayon. It is said that the Bayon was completed in 21 years. Jayavarman took thousands of peasants from the rice fields to build it, which proved a fatal error, for rice yields decreased and the empire began its decline as resources were drained. The temple, which consists of sculptured faces of Avolokiteshvara (the Buddha of compassion and mercy) are often said to also encompass the face of their great creator, Jayavarman VIII. He was also responsible for restoring the Royal Palace,

The Churning of the Sea

The Hindu legend, the Churning of the Sea, relates how the gods and demons resolved matters in the turbulent days when the world was being created. The elixir of immortality was one of 13 precious things lost in the churning of the cosmic sea. It took 1000 years before the gods and demons, in a joint dredging operation – aided by Sesha, the sea snake, and Vishnu – recovered them all.

The design of the temples of Angkor was based on this ancient legend. The moat represents the ocean and the gods use the top of Mount Meru – represented by the tower – as their churning stick. The cosmic serpent offered himself as a rope to enable the gods and demons to twirl the stick.

Paul Mus, a French archaeologist, suggests that the bridge with the naga balustrades which went over the moat from the world of men to the royal city was an image of the rainbow. Throughout Southeast Asia and India, the rainbow is alluded to as a multi-coloured serpent rearing its head in the sky.

renovating Srah Srang and constructing the Elephant Terrace, the Terrace of the Leper King and the nearby baray (northeast of Angkor Thom), Jayatataka reservoir. At the centre of his reservoir he built Neak Pean. Jayavarman VII adopted Mahayana Buddhism; Buddhist principles replaced the Hindu pantheon, and were invoked as the basis of royal authority. This spread of Buddhism is thought to have caused some of the earlier Hindu temples to be neglected. The king paid tribute to his Buddhist roots through his monastic temples – Ta Prohm and Preah Khan.

The French at Angkor

Thai ascendency and eventual occupation of Angkor in 1431, led to the city's abandonment and the subsequent invasion of the jungle. Four centuries later, in 1860, Henri Mouhot – a French naturalist – stumbled across the forgotten city, its temple towers enmeshed in the forest canopy. Locals told him they were the work of a race of giant gods. Only the stone temples remained; all the wooden secular buildings had decomposed in the intervening centuries. In 1873 French archaeologist Louis Delaporte removed many of Angkor's finest statues for 'the cultural enrichment of France'. In 1898, the École Française d'Extrême Orient started clearing the jungle, restoring the temples, mapping the complex and making an inventory of the site. Delaporte was later to write the two-volume Les Monuments du Cambodge, the most comprehensive Angkorian inventory of its time, and his earlier sketches, plans and reconstructions, published in Voyage au Cambodge in 1880 are without parallel.

Angkor temples → Colour map 6, A2.

The temples at Angkor were modelled on those of the kingdom of Chenla (a mountain kingdom centred on northern Cambodia and southern Laos), which in turn were modelled on Indian temples. They represent Mount Meru – the home of the gods of Indian cosmology. The central towers symbolize the peaks of Mount Meru, surrounded by a wall representing the earth and moats and basins representing the oceans. The devaraja, or god-king, was enshrined in the centre of the religious complex, which acted as the spiritual axis of the kingdom. The people believed their apotheosized king communicated directly with the gods.

Motifs in Khmer sculpture

Apsaras These are regarded as one of the greatest invention of the Khmers. The gorgeous temptresses – born, according to legend, 'during the churning of the Sea of Milk' – were Angkor's equivalent of pin-up girls and represented the ultimate ideal of feminine beauty. They lived in heaven where their sole raison d'être was to have eternal sex with Khmer heroes and holy men. The apsaras are carved in seductive poses with splendidly ornate jewellery and clothed in the latest Angkor fashion. Different facial features suggest the existence of several races at Angkor. Together with the five towers of Angkor Wat they have become the symbol of Khmer culture. The god-king himself possessed an apsara-like retinue of court dancers – impressive enough for Chinese envoy Chou Ta-kuan to write home about it in 1296.

Garuda Mythical creature – half-man, half-bird – was the vehicle of the Hindu god, Vishnu, and the sworn enemy of the nagas. It appeared relatively late in Khmer architecture.

Kala Jawless monster commanded by the gods to devour his own body – made its first appearance in lintels at Roluos. The monster represented devouring time and was an early import from Java.

Makara Mythical water-monster with a scaly body, eagles' talons and an elephantine trunk.

Naga Sacred snake. These play an important part in Hindu mythology and the Khmers drew on them for architectural inspiration. Possibly more than any other single symbol or motif, the naga is characteristic of Southeast Asia and decorates objects throughout the region. The naga is an aquatic serpent and is intimately associated with water (a key component of Khmer prosperity). In Hindu mythology, the naga coils beneath and supports Vishnu on the cosmic ocean. The snake also swallows the waters of life, these only being set free to reinvigorate the world after Indra ruptures the serpent with a bolt of lightning. Another version has Vishnu's servants pulling at the serpent to squeeze the waters of life from it (the so-called churning of the sea, see box, opposite).

Singha Lion in stylized form; often the guardians to temples.

The central tower sanctuaries housed the images of the Hindu gods to whom the temples were dedicated. Dead members of the royal and priestly families were accorded a status on a par with these gods. Libraries to store the sacred scriptures were also built within the ceremonial centre. The temples were mainly built to shelter the images of the gods – unlike Christian churches, Moslem mosques and some Buddhist pagodas, they were not intended to accommodate worshippers. Only priests, the servants of the god, were allowed into the interiors. The 'congregation' would mill around in open courtyards or wooden pavilions.

The first temples were of a very simple design, but with time they became more grandiose and doors and galleries were added. Most of Angkor's buildings are made from a soft sandstone which is easy to work. It was transported to the site from Phnom Kulen, about 30 km to the northeast. Laterite was used for foundations, core material, and enclosure walls, as it was widely available and could be easily cut into blocks. A common feature of Khmer temples was false doors and windows on the sides and backs of sanctuaries and other buildings. In most cases there was no need for well-lit rooms and corridors as hardly anyone ever went into them. That said, the galleries round the central towers in later temples, such as Angkor Wat, indicate that worshippers did use the temples for ceremonial circumambulation when they would contemplate the inspiring bas-reliefs from the important Hindu epic, *Ramayana* and *Mahabharata* (written between 400 BC and AD 200).

Despite the court's conversion to Mahayana Buddhism in the 12th century, the architectural ground-plans of temples did not alter much – even though they were based on Hindu cosmology. The idea of the god-king was simply grafted onto the new state religion and statues of the Buddha rather than the gods of the Hindu pantheon were used to represent the god-king (see page 343). One particular image of the Buddha predominated at Angkor in which he wears an Angkor-style crown, with a conical top encrusted with jewellery.

Angkor Wat → *Colour map 6, A2.*

The awe-inspiring sight of Angkor Wat, first thing in the morning, is something you're not likely to forget. Angkor literally means 'city' or 'capital' and it is the biggest religious monument ever built and certainly one of the most spectacular. The temple complex covers 81 ha. Its five towers are emblazoned on the Cambodian flag and the 12th-century masterpiece is considered by art historians to be the prime example of classical Khmer art and architecture. It took more than 30 years to build and is dedicated to the Hindu god Vishnu, personified in earthly form by its builder, the god-king Suryavarman II, and is aligned east to west.

2 Angkor Wat

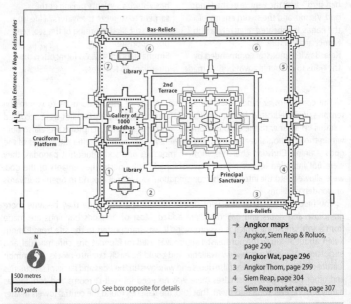

Bas-Reliefs

To Main Entrance & Naga Balustrades

⑥ ⑥
⑦ ⑤
Library
2nd Terrace

Gallery of 1000 Buddhas

Cruciform Platform

Library
Principal Sanctuary
① ④
② ③

Bas-Reliefs

N

500 metres
500 yards

◯ See box opposite for details

→ **Angkor maps**
1 Angkor, Siem Reap & Roluos, page 290
2 **Angkor Wat, page 296**
3 Angkor Thom, page 299
4 Siem Reap, page 304
5 Siem Reap market area, page 307

Anti-clockwise around Angkor Wat's bas-reliefs

1 Western gallery The southern half represents a scene from the Mahabharata of a battle between the Pandavas (with pointed head dresses, attacking from the right) and the Kauravas. The two armies come from the two ends of the panel and meet in the middle. The southwest corner has been badly damaged – some say by the Khmer Rouge – but shows scenes from Vishnu's life.

2 Southern gallery The western half depicts Suryavarman II (builder of Angkor Wat) leading a procession. He is riding a royal elephant, giving orders to his army before leading them into battle against the Cham. The rank of the army officers is indicated by the number of umbrellas. The undisciplined, outlandishly dressed figures are the Thais.

3 Southern gallery The eastern half was restored in 1946 and depicts the punishments and rewards one can expect in the after life. The damned are depicted in the bottom row, while the blessed, depicted in the upper two rows, are borne along in palanquins surrounded by large numbers of bare-breasted apsaras.

4 Eastern gallery The southern half is the best-known part of the bas-relief – the churning of the sea of milk by gods and demons to make ambrosia (the nectar of the gods which gives immortality). In the centre, Vishnu commands the operation. Below are sea animals and above, apsaras.

5 Eastern gallery The northern half is an unfinished representation of a war between the gods for the possession of the ambrosia. The gate in the centre was used by Khmer royalty and dignitaries for mounting and dismounting elephants.

6 Northern gallery Represents a war between gods and demons. Siva is shown in meditation with Ganesh, Brahma and Krishna. Most of the other scenes are from the Ramayana, notably the visit of Hanuman to Sita.

7 Western gallery The northern half has another scene from the Ramayana depicting a battle between Rama and Ravana who rides a chariot pulled by monsters and commands an army of giants.

Angkor Wat differs from other temples, primarily because it is facing westward, symbolically the direction of death, leading many to originally believe it was a tomb. However, as Vishnu is associated with the west, it is now generally accepted that it served both as a temple and a mausoleum for the king. Like other Khmer temple-mountains, Angkor Wat is an architectural allegory, depicting in stone the epic tales of Hindu mythology. The central sanctuary of the temple complex represents the sacred Mount Meru, the centre of the Hindu universe, on whose summit the gods reside. Angkor Wat's five towers symbolize Meru's five peaks; the enclosing wall represents the mountains at the edge of the world and the surrounding moat, the ocean beyond.

The temple complex is enclosed by a square moat – more than 5 km in length and 190 m wide – and a high, galleried wall, which is covered in epic bas-reliefs and has four ceremonial tower gateways. The main gateway faces west and the temple is approached by a 475-m-long road, built along a causeway, which is lined with naga balustrades. At the far end of the causeway stands a **cruciform platform**, guarded by stone lions, from which the devaraja may have held audiences; his backdrop being the three-tiered central sanctuary. Commonly referred to as the Terrace of Honour, it is entered through the colonnaded processional gateway of the outer gallery. The transitional enclosure beyond it is again cruciform in shape. Its four quadrants formed galleries, once stocked full of statues of the Buddha. Only a handful of the original 1000-odd images remain.

The cluster of **central towers**, 12 m above the second terrace, is reached by 12 steep stairways, which represent the precipitous slopes of Mount Meru. Many historians believe that the upwards hike to this terrace was reserved for the high priests and king himself. Today, anyone is welcome but the difficult climb is best handled slowly by stepping sideways up the steep incline. The five lotus flower-shaped sandstone towers – the first appearance of these features in Khmer architecture – are believed to have once been covered in gold. The eight-storey towers are square, although they appear octagonal, and give the impression of a sprouting bud. The central tower is dominant, as is the Siva shrine and principal sanctuary, whose pinnacle rises more than 30 m above the third level and, 55 m above ground level. This sanctuary would have contained an image of Siva in the likeness of King Suryavarman II, as it was his temple-mountain. But it is now a Buddhist shrine and contains statues of the Buddha.

More than 1000 sq m of bas-relief decorate the temple. Its greatest sculptural treasure is the 2-m-high **bas-reliefs**, around the walls of the outer gallery. It is the longest continuous bas-relief in the world. In some areas traces of the paint and gilt that once covered the carvings can still be seen. Most famous are the hundreds of figures of deities and apsaras in niches along the walls.

The royal city of Angkor Thom

Construction of Jayavarman VII's spacious walled capital, Angkor Thom (which means 'great city'), began at the end of the 12th century: he rebuilt the capital after it had been captured and destroyed by the Cham. Angkor Thom was colossal: the 100-m-wide moat surrounding the city, which was probably stocked with crocodiles as a protection against the enemy, extended more than 12 km. Inside the moat was an 8-m-high stone wall, buttressed on the inner side by a high mound of earth along the top of which ran a terrace for troops to man the ramparts.

Four great gateways in the city wall face north, south, east and west and lead to the city's geometric centre, the Bayon. The fifth, Victory Gate, leads from the royal palace (within the Royal Enclosure) to the East Baray. The height of the gates was determined by the headroom needed to accommodate an elephant and howdah, complete with parasols. The flanks of each gateway are decorated by three-headed stone elephants, and each gateway tower has four giant faces, which keep an eye on all four cardinal points. Five causeways traverse the moat, each bordered by sculptured balustrades of nagas gripped, on one side, by 54 stern-looking giant gods and on the other by 54 fierce-faced demons. The balustrade depicts the Hindu legend of the churning of the sea (see box, page 294).

The **South Gate** provides the most common access route to Angkor Thom, predominantly because it sits on the path between the two great Angkor complexes. The gate is a wonderful introduction to Angkor Thom, with well-restored statues of asuras (demons) and gods lining the bridge. The figures on the left, exhibiting serene expression, are the gods, while those on the right, with grimaced, fierce-looking heads, are the asuras.

The **Bayon** was Jayavarman VII's own temple-mountain, built right in the middle of Angkor Thom; its large faces have now become synonymous with the Angkor complex. It is believed to have been built between the late 12th century to early 13th century, around 100 years after Angkor Wat. The Bayon is a three-tiered, pyramid-temple with a 45-m-high tower, topped by four gigantic carved heads. These faces are believed to be the images of Jayavarman VII as a Bodhisattra, and face the four compass points. They are crowned with lotus flowers, symbol of enlightenment, and are surrounded by 51 smaller towers each with heads facing north, south, east and west. There are more than 2000 large faces carved throughout the structure. The first two of the three levels feature galleries of bas-relief (which should be viewed clockwise); a circular central sanctuary dominates the third level. The **bas-reliefs** which decorate the walls of the Bayon are much less imposing than those at Angkor Wat. The sculpture is carved deeper but is more naive and less sophisticated than the bas-reliefs at Angkor Wat. The relief on the outside depicts historical events; those on the inside are drawn from the epic world of gods and legends, representing the creatures who were supposed to haunt the subterranean depths of Mount Meru. In fact the reliefs on the outer wall illustrating historical scenes and derring-do with marauding Cham were carved in the early 13th century during the reign of Jayavarman; those on the inside which illuminate the Hindu cosmology were carved after the king's death when his successors turned from Mahayana Buddhism

3 Angkor Thom

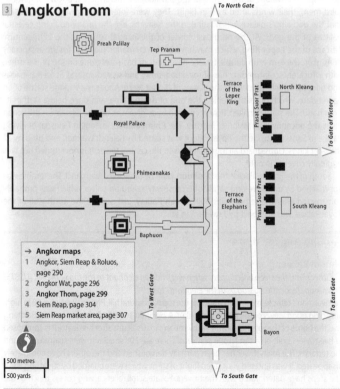

Preah Palilay

Tep Pranam

To North Gate

Royal Palace

Terrace of the Leper King

Prasat Suor Prat

North Kleang

To Gate of Victory

Phimeanakas

Terrace of the Elephants

Prasat Suor Prat

South Kleang

Baphuon

To East Gate

To West Gate

→ Angkor maps
1 Angkor, Siem Reap & Roluos, page 290
2 Angkor Wat, page 296
3 Angkor Thom, page 299
4 Siem Reap, page 304
5 Siem Reap market area, page 307

Bayon

To South Gate

500 metres
500 yards

back to Hinduism. Two recurring themes in the bas-reliefs are the powerful king and the Hindu epics. Jayavarman is depicted in the throes of battle with the Cham – who are recognizable thanks to their unusual and distinctive headdress, which looks like an inverted lotus flower. The other bas-reliefs give a good insight into Khmer life at the time – the warrior elephants, ox carts, fishing with nets, cockfights and skewered fish drying on racks. Other vignettes show musicians, jugglers, hunters, chess players, palm-readers and scenes of Angkor citizens enjoying drinking sessions. In the naval battle scenes, the water around the war-canoes is depicted by the presence of fish, crocodiles and floating corpses.

The **Royal Palace**, to the north of the Bayon, had already been laid out by Suryavarman I: the official palace was in the front with the domestic quarters behind, its gardens surrounded by a laterite wall and moat. Suryavarman I also beautified the royal city with ornamental pools. Jayavarman VII simply improved his designs. In front of the Royal Palace, at the centre of Angkor Thom, Suryavarman I laid out the first Grand Plaza with the **Terrace of the Elephants** (also called the Royal Terrace). The 300-m-long wall derives its name from the large, life-like carvings of elephants in a hunting scene, adorning its walls. The 2.5-m wall also features elephants flanking the southern stairway. It is believed it was the foundations of the royal reception hall. Royalty once sat in gold-topped pavilions at the centre of the pavilion, and here there are rows of garudas (bird-men), their wings lifted as if in flight. They were intended to give the impression that the god-king's palace was floating in the heavens, like the imagined flying celestial palaces of the gods. At the northeast corner of the 'central square' is the 12th-century **Terrace of the Leper King**, which may have been a cremation platform for the aristocracy of Angkor. The 7-m-high double terrace has bands of bas-reliefs, one on top of the other, with intricately sculptured scenes of royal pageantry and seated apsaras as well as nagas and garudas which frequented the slopes of Mount Meru. Above is a strange statue of an earlier date, which probably depicts the god of death, Yama, and once held a staff in its right hand. The statue's naked, lichen-covered body gives the terrace its name – the lichen gives the uncanny impression of leprosy. The **Phimeanakas** (meaning Celestial or Flying Palace in Sanskrit) inside the Royal Palace was started by Rajendravarman and used by all the later kings. Lions guard all four stairways to the central tower. It is now ruined but was originally covered in gold.

South of the Royal Palace is the **Baphuon**, built by Udayadityavarman II. The temple was approached by a 200-m-long sandstone causeway, raised on pillars, which was probably constructed after the temple was built. **Preah Palilay**, just outside the north wall of the Royal Palace, was also built by Jayavarman VII.

Around Angkor Thom

Phnom Bakheng

ⓘ *Either climb the steep hill (slippery when wet), ride an elephant to the top of the hill (US$15) or walk up the gentle zig-zag path the elephants take.*

Yasovarman's temple-mountain stands at the top of a natural hill, Phnom Bakheng, 60 m high, affording good views of the plains of Angkor. A pyramid-temple dedicated to Siva, Bakheng was the home of the royal linga and Yasovarman's mausoleum after his death. It is composed of five towers built on a sandstone platform. There are 108 smaller towers scattered around the terraces. The main tower has been partially demolished and the others have completely disappeared. It was entered via a steep flight of steps which were guarded by squatting lions. The steps have deteriorated with the towers. Foliate scroll relief carving covers much of the main shrine – the first time this style was used. This strategically placed hill served as a camp for various combatants, including the Vietnamese, and suffered accordingly.

Ta Pro

The temple of Ta Prohm is the perfect lost-in-the-jungle experience. Unlike most of the other monuments at Angkor, it has been only minimally cleared of its undergrowth, fig trees and creepers. It is widely regarded as one of Angkor's most enchanting temples.

Ta Prohm was consecrated in 1186 – five years after Jayavarman VII seized power. It was built to house the divine image of the Queen Mother. The outer enclosures of Ta Prohm are somewhat obscured by foliage but reach well beyond the temple's heart (1 km by 650 m). The temple proper consists of a number of concentric galleries, featuring corner towers and the standard gopuras. Other buildings and enclosures were built on a more ad hoc basis.

Within the complex walls lived 12,640 citizens. It contained 39 sanctuaries or prasats, 566 stone dwellings and 288 brick dwellings. Ta Prohm literally translates to the 'Royal Monastery' and that is what it functioned as, home to 18 abbots and 2740 monks. By the 12th century, temples were no longer exclusively places of worship – they also had to accommodate monks, so roofed halls were increasingly built within the complexes.

The trees burgeoning their way through the complex are predominantly the silk-cotton tree and the aptly named strangler fig. Naturally, the roots of the trees have descended towards the soil, prying their way through the temples foundations in the process. As the vegetation has matured, growing stronger, it has forced its way further into the temples structure, damaging the man-built base and causing untold destruction.

Banteay Kdei, Srah Srang, Prasat Kravan and Pre Rup

The massive complex of **Banteay Kdei**, otherwise known as 'the citadel of cells', is 3 km east of Angkor Thom. Some archaeologists think it may be dedicated to Jayavarman VII's religious teacher. The temple has remained in much the same state it was discovered in – a crowded collection of ruined laterite towers and connecting galleries lying on a flat plan, surrounded by a galleried enclosure. It is presumed that the temple was a Buddhist monastery and in recent years hundreds of buried Buddha statues were excavated from the site. Like Ta Prohm it contains a Hall of Dancers (east side), an open-roof building with four separate quarters. The second enclosure runs around the perimeters of the inner enclosure. The third inner enclosure contains a north and south library and central sanctuary. The central tower was never finished. The square pillars in the middle of the courtyard still cannot be explained by scholars. There are few inscriptions here to indicate either its name or purpose, but it is almost certainly a Buddhist temple built in the 12th century, about the same time as Ta Prohm. The Lake (baray) next to Banteay Kdei is called **Srah Srang** – 'Royal Bath' – and was used for ritual bathing. The steps down to the water face the rising sun and are flanked with lions and nagas. This sandstone landing stage dates from the reign of Jayavarman VII but the Lake itself is thought to date back two centuries earlier. A 10th-century inscription reads 'this water is stored for the use of all creatures except dyke breakers', eg elephants. The baray (700 m by 300 m), has been filled with turquoise-blue waters for more than 1300 years. With a good view of Pre Rup across the lake, some archaeologists believe that this spot affords the best vista in the whole Angkor complex.

Prasat Kravan, built in AD 921, means 'Cardamom Sanctuary' and is unusual in that it is built of brick. By that time brick had been replaced by laterite and sandstone. It consists of five brick towers arranged in a line. The Hindu temple, surrounded by a moat, consists of five elevated brick towers, positioned in a north-south direction. Two of the five decorated brick towers contain bas-reliefs (the north and central towers). The central tower is probably the most impressive and contains a linga on a pedestal. The sanctuary's three walls all contain pictures of Vishnu.

Northeast of Srah Srang is **Pre Rup**, the State Temple of King Rajendravarman's capital. Built in AD 961, the temple-mountain representing Mount Meru is larger, higher and artistically superior than its predecessor, the East Mebon, which it closely resembles. Keeping with tradition of state capitals, Pre Rup marked the centre of the city, much of which doesn't exist today. The pyramid-structure, which is constructed of laterite with brick prasats, sits at the apex of an artificial, purpose-built mountain. The central pyramid-level consists of a three-tiered, sandstone platform, with five central towers sitting above. Its modern name, 'turning the body', derives from local legend and is named after a cremation ritual in which the outline of a body was traced in the cinders one way and then the other. The upper levels of the pyramid offer a brilliant, panoramic view of the countryside.

Preah Khan

The 12th-century complex of Preah Khan, one of the largest complexes within the Angkor area, was Jayavarman VII's first capital before Angkor Thom was completed. Preah Khan means 'sacred sword' and is believed to have derived from a decisive battle against the Cham, which created a 'lake of blood', but was invariably won by Jayavarman VII. It is similar in ground-plan to Ta Prohm but attention was paid to the approaches: its east and west entrance avenues leading to ornamental causeways are lined with carved-stone boundary posts. Evidence suggests that it was more than a mere Buddhist monastery but most likely a Buddhist university. Nonetheless an abundance of Brahmanic iconography is still present on site. Around the rectangular complex is a large laterite wall, surrounded by large garudas wielding the naga (each more than 5 m in height), the theme continues across the length of the whole 3-km external enclosure, with the motif dotted every 50 m. Within these walls lies the surrounding moat.

Preah Neak Pean

To the east of Preah Khan is the Buddhist temple Preah Neak Pean built by Jayavarman VII. The temple of Neak Pean is also a fountain, built in the middle of a pool and representing the paradisiacal Himalayan mountain-lake, Anaavatapta, from Hindu mythology. It is a small sanctuary on an island in the baray of Preah Khan. Two nagas form the edge of the island, and their tails join at the back. The temple pools were an important part of the aesthetic experience of Preah Khan and Neak Pean – the ornate stone carving of both doubly visible by reflection.

Outlying temples

The Roluos Group → Colour map 6, B2.

The Roluos Group receives few visitors but is worth visiting if time permits. Jayavarman II built several capitals including one at Roluos, at that time called Hariharalaya. This was the site of his last city and remained the capital during the reigns of his three successors. The three remaining Hindu sanctuaries at Roluos are **Preah Ko**, **Bakong** and **Lolei**. They were finished in AD 879, AD 881 and AD 893 respectively by Indravarman I and his son Yashovarman I and are the best-preserved of the early temples. All three temples are built of brick, with sandstone doorways and niches. Sculptured figures which appear in the Roluos group are the crouching lion, the reclining bull (Nandi – Siva's mount) and the naga (snake).

Preah Ko, meaning 'sacred ox', was named after the three statues of Nandi (the mount of the Hindu god, Siva) which stand in front of the temple. Orientated east-west, there is a cluster of six brick towers arranged in two rows on a low brick platform, the steps up to which are guarded by crouching lions while Nandi, looking back, blocks the way. The front row of towers was devoted to Indravarman's male ancestors and the second row to the female. Indravarman's temple-mountain, **Bakong**, is a royal five-stepped pyramid-temple with a sandstone central tower built on a series of successively receding terraces with surrounding brick towers. Indravarman himself was buried in the temple. Bakong is the largest and most impressive temple in the Roluos Group by a long way. A bridge flanked by a naga balustrade leads over a dry moat to the temple. The central tower was built to replace the original one when the monument was restored in the 12th century and is probably larger than the original. The Bakong denotes the true beginning of classical Khmer architecture and contained the god-king's Siva linga. **Lolei** was built by Yashovarman I in the middle of Indravarman's baray. The brick towers were dedicated to the king's ancestors, but they have disintegrated; of the four, two have partly collapsed.

Banteay Srei → Colour map 6, A2.

Banteay Srei, 25 km from Ta Prohm along a decent road, was built by the Brahmin tutor to King Rajendravarman, Yajnavaraha, grandson of Harshavarman, and founded in AD 967. Banteay Srei translates to 'Citadel of Women', a title bestowed upon it in relatively recent years due to the intricate apsara carvings that adorn the interior. The temple is considered by many historians to be the highest achievement of art from the Angkor period. The explicit preservation of this temple reveals covered terraces, of which only the columns remain, which once lined both sides of the primary entrance. In keeping with tradition, a long causeway leads into the temple, across a moat, on the eastern side. The main walls, entry pavilions and libraries have been constructed from laterite and the carvings from pink sandstone. The layout was inspired by Prasat Thom at Koh Ker. Three beautifully carved tower-shrines stand side by side on a low terrace in the middle of a quadrangle, with a pair of libraries on either side enclosed by a wall. Two of the shrines, the southern one and the central one, were dedicated to Siva and the northern one to Vishnu; both had libraries close by, with carvings depicting appropriate legends. The whole temple is dedicated to Brahma. Having been built by a Brahmin priest, the temple was never intended for use by a king, which goes some way towards explaining its small size – you have to duck to get through the doorways to the sanctuary towers. Perhaps because of its modest scale Banteay Srei contains some of the finest examples of Khmer sculpture. Finely carved and rare pink sandstone replaces the plaster-coated carved-brick decoration, typical of earlier temples. All the buildings are covered in carvings: the jambs, the lintels, the balustered windows. Banteay Srei's ornamentation is exceptional – its roofs, pediments and lintels are magnificently carved with tongues of flame, serpents' tails, gods, demons and floral garlands.

Siem Reap → For listings, see pages 306-314. Colour map 6, A2.

The nearest town to Angkor, Siem Reap is a bustling tourism hub with a growing art and fashion crowd; however, it's still true to say that without the temples few people would ever find themselves here. Siem Reap is also an easy place to stay for volunteers looking to do a stint in saving the world, but perhaps too many nights spent in crowded bar street distracts from the task in hand. Visitors exhausted by the temple trail might care to while away a morning or afternoon in Siem Reap itself. The town has developed quite

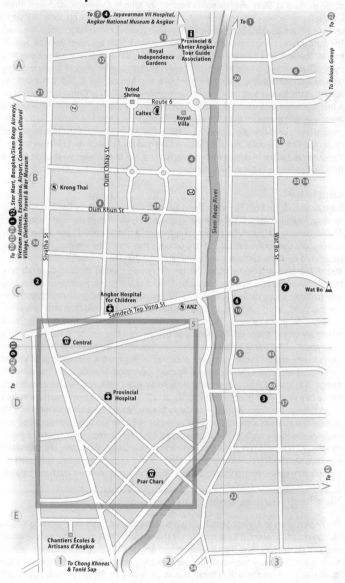

To 7 4, Jayavarman VII Hospital,
Angkor National Museum & Angkor

To 1

To 22

13

Provincial &
Khmer Angkor
Tour Guide
Association

Royal
Independence
Gardens

A

32

26

6

To Roluos Group

21

Yoted
Shrine

Route 6

Caltex

18

Pol

Royal
Villa

B

Krong Thai

4

Oum Chhay St

30 14

8

Oum Khun St

Wat Bo St

38

27

Siem Reap River

36

Sivatha St

C

2

3

7

Wat Bo

Angkor Hospital
for Children

6

Samdech Tep Vong St

ANZ

10

5

Central

D

Provincial
Hospital

5

41

40

3

37

To 22

Psar Chars

To

22

E

Chantiers Écoles &
Artisans d'Angkor

1

To Chong Khneas
& Tonlé Sap

2

3

34

To 10 12 15 16 19, Star Mart, Bangkok/Siem Reap Airways,
Vietnam Airlines, Exotissimo, Airport, Cambodian Cultural
Village, Diethelm Travel & War Museum

substantially in the past couple of years and, with the blossoming of hotels, restaurants and bars, it is now a pleasant place in its own right. Hotel building has pretty much kept pace with tourist arrivals so the town is a hive of activity.

The town is laid out formally and because there is ample land on which to build, it is pleasantly airy. Buildings are often set in large overgrown grounds resembling mini wildernesses. The current level of unprecedented growth and development is set to continue, so this may not be the case five years from now. The growth spurt has put a great strain on the city's natural resources.

The Old Market area is the most touristy part of the town. Staying around here is recommended for independent travellers and those staying more than two or three days. A sprinkling of guesthouses are here but a much greater selection is offered just across the river, in the Wat Bo area. This part of Siem Reap has recently become a popular place to stay with a range of accommodation available. It's not so crowded as the old market area and less traffic than airport road.

The **Angkor National Museum** ⓘ on the road to the temples, www.angkornationalmuseum.com, daily 0830-1800, US$12, is a short walk from the town centre. Due to the high entry price this museum is usually empty and it does seem rather incongruous that the artefacts on display here are not actually still in-situ at the temples themselves. Having said that, it isn't a bad museum and you can gather a lot of useful information about the development of Angkor. There are also some intriguing background details such as the 102 hospitals built during the reign of Jayavarman VII and the 1960 boxes of haemorrhoid cream that were part of their annual provisions. There are also some displays on the clothes the average Angkorian wore but it's a shame there isn't more about the daily lives of these ancients.

100 metres
100 yards

Sleeping 😴
Angkor Village Resort 1 *A3*
Bopha 5 *D3*
Bou Savy 19 *A1*
Borann 6 *A3*
Casa Angkor 8 *B1*
Earthwalkers 10 *C1*
FCC Angkor 4 *B2*
Golden Banana B&B 34 *E2*
Heritage Suites 23 *A3*
Home Sweet Home 14 *B3*
Jasmine Lodge 15 *B1*
La Noria 26 *A3*
La Residence D'Angkor 3 *C3*
Le Meridien Angkor 7 *A2*
Mahogany Guesthouse 18 *B3*
Mekong Angkor Palace 36 *C1*
Ombrelle & Kimono 37 *D3*
Passaggio 22 *E2*
Raffles Grand d'Angkor 13 *A2*
Royal Bay Inn Angkor Resort 38 *B2*
Sala Bai 39 *C1*
Shadow of Angkor II 40 *D3*
Shinta Mani 27 *B2*

Sokha Angkor 21 *A1*
Soria Moria 41 *D3*
Two Dragons Guesthouse 30 *B3*
Victoria Angkor 32 *A1*
The Villa 42 *C1*
Villa Kiara 43 *E3*

Eating 🍴
Abacus 1 *A1*
Barrio 2 *C1*
Butterfly Garden 3 *D3*
Chez Sophea 4 *A2*
Moloppor 6 *C3*
Paul Dubrule 12 *C1*
Sugar Palm 9 *C1*
Viroth's 7 *C3*

Bars & clubs 🍸
Fresh at Chilli Si Dang 10 *C3*
Zone One 11 *C1*

→ **Angkor maps**
1 Angkor, Siem Reap & Roluos, page 290
2 Angkor Wat, page 296
3 Angkor Thom, page 299
4 Siem Reap, page 304
5 Siem Reap market area, page 307

For Sleeping and Eating price codes and other relevant information, see pages 40-43.

⊜ Sleeping

It is not uncommon for taxi, moto and tuk-tuk drivers to tell new arrivals that the guesthouse they were booked into is now 'closed' or full. They will try to take you to the place where they get the best commission. One way around this is to arrange for the guesthouse or hotel to pick you up from either the bus station or other arrival point – many offer this service for free or a small fee.

Siem Reap *p303, maps p304 and p307*
LL Heritage Suites, behind Wat Po Lanka, T063-969100, www.heritage.com.kh. Super luxurious and exclusive villas, rooms and suites in this stylish property secreted away behind a temple. Much is made with traditional materials and the top-end rooms come with private steam baths and gardens. A super-splurge but well worth it. Expect all the usual amneties for such a top-end establishment.
LL-A Steung Siem Reap Hotel, Street 9, T063-965167, www.steungsiemreaphotel. com. This new-build colonial-era-styled hotel is an excellent addition to the central market area of Siem Reap. The pleasant rooms come with cooling wooden floors and many overlook a verdant and very quiet pool. There are all the trimmings you'd expect in this price range, including gym, sauna, free Wi-Fi, free breakfast, a/c, huge bathtubs and good, friendly service. Recommended.
LL-A Villa Kiara, just outside eastern edge of town, Sala Kamroeuk village, T063-764156, www.villakiara.com. Set in a very peaceful, private garden compound a couple of kilometres east of town this 17-room/suite 'boutique' resort is unpretentious yet stylish. There's free breakfast, Wi-Fi,

a restaurant and complimentary transfers to and from town. The pool is cute as well. All rooms are, of course, a/c with TV and en suite hot-water facilities. Recommended.
L-AL Hotel de la Paix, corner of Achemean and Sivatha, T063-966000, www.hoteldela paixangkor.com. Owned by the same company that also runs Bangkok's famous **Bed Supper Club**, this is probably Siem Reap's best-value luxury hotel. The rooms offer simple contemporary design with giant bathtubs and plump bedding – all with a/c and cable TV. The pool is a maze of plinths and greenery and makes for a perfect spot to laze. Can feel a bit urban for Siem Reap but still a great hotel. Recommended.
L-AL Le Meridien Angkor, main road towards temples, T063-963900, www. lemeridien.com/angkor. From the outside this 5-star hotel resembles a futuristic prison camp – severe, angled architecture with small, dark slits for windows. Walk into the lobby and it is immediately transformed into space and light. Rooms are nicely designed and sized and all come with a/c, en suite and cable TV. Other facilities include spa, restaurants and pool. The garden is a lovely spot to take breakfast. Recommended.
L-AL Raffles Grand Hotel d'Angkor, 1 Charles de Gaulle Blvd, T063-963888, www. raffles.com. Certainly a magnificent period piece from the outside, Siem Reap's oldest (1930) hotel fails to generate ambience, the rooms are sterile and the design of the huge new wings is uninspired (unforgivable in Angkor). Coupled with this is a history of staff lock-outs and mass sackings that have caused the Raffles brand damage. However, it does have all the mod cons, including sauna, tennis, health and beauty spa, lap pool, gym, 8 restaurants and bars, nightly traditional performances, landscaped gardens, 24-hr valet service and in-house movie channels. Considering its astronomical rates, guests have every right to feel disappointed.

L-AL Sokha Angkor, Sivatha St, T063-969999, www.sokhahotels.com. One of the few Cambodian-owned 5-star hotels in the country, the rooms and services here are top notch, even if the decor is a little gaudy (if you can't afford to stay here, come and check out the incredibly over-the-top swimming pool, complete with faux temple structures and waterfalls). Also home to an excellent Japanese restaurant. Recommended.

L-AL Victoria Angkor Hotel, Route 6, T063-760428, www.victoriahotels-asia.com. Perfection. A beautiful hotel, with that 1930s east-meets-west style that exemplifies the French tradition of *art de vivre*. The superb decor makes you feel like you are staying in another era. Each room is beautifully decorated with local fabrics and fantastic furniture. Swimming pool, open-air salas, jacuzzi and spa. It's the small touches and attention to detail that stands this hotel apart from the rest. Highly recommended.

5 Siem Reap market area

→ **Angkor maps**
1 Angkor, Siem Reap & Roluos, page 290
2 Angkor Wat, page 296
3 Angkor Thom, page 299
4 Siem Reap, page 304
5 Siem Reap market area, page 307

Sleeping 🛏
Hotel de la Paix **5**
Molly Malone's **3**
Neth Socheata **4**
Steung Siem Reap **7**

Eating 🍴
Blue Pumpkin **1**
Dead Fish Tower **5**

Khmer Kitchen **3**
Le Malraux **4**
Red Piano **7**
Singing Tree **8**
Soup Dragon **11**
Tell **12**

Bars & clubs 🍸
Angkor What? **13**

Laundry **14**
Linga **15**
Miss Wong **9**
Temple Club **16**
Warehouse **10**
X Rooftop Bar **17**

AL Angkor Village Resort, T063-963561, www.angkorvillage.com. Opened in 2004, the resort contains 40 rooms set in Balinese-style surroundings. Traditional massage services, 2 restaurants, theatre shows and lovely pool. Elephant, boat and helicopter rides can be arranged. Recommended.

AL La Residence D'Angkor Hotel, River Rd, T063-963390, www.residenceangkor.com. This is a hotel to aspire to. With its beautifully laid out rooms all lavishly furnished with marble and hardwoods, it is reassuringly expensive. Each room has a huge, free-form bath – which is the perfect end to a day touring the temples.

AL Shinta Mani, junction of Oum Khun and 14th St, T063-761998, www.shintamani.com. This 18-room boutique, luxury hotel is wonderful in every way: the design, the amenities, the food and the service. The hotel also offers a beautiful pool, library and has mountain bikes available. Provides vocational training to underprivileged youth.

AL-A FCC Angkor, near the post office on Pokambor Av, T063-760280, www.fcc cambodia.com. The sister property of the famous FCC Phnom Penh, this hotel is set in the grounds of a restored, modernist villa. Rooms offer contemporary luxury and plenty of space but be warned – there is a massive generator at one end of the complex running 24/7 so make sure you are housed well away from here. Also tends to trade more on its reputation so service, food, etc can be ropey.

AL-A Royal Bay Inn Angkor Resort, Oum Khon St, T063-760500, www.royalbayinnangkor.com. All rooms have balconies facing onto a huge swimming pool in this new resort, set in nice gardens. Expect the usual upmarket trimmings of a/c, multi-channel TV and good service.

A-B Ombrelle & Kimono, 557 Wat Bo Rd, T09-277 4313, www.ombrelle-et-kimono.com. There are only 5 rooms in this minute villa complete with pool and arty gardens. The rooms are a little pretentious but the welcome is friendly. All en suite, a/c and with private terrace.

A-D Casa Angkor, corner of Chhay St and Oum Khun St, T063-966234, www.casa angkorhotel.com. This is a good-looking, pleasant and well-managed 21-room hotel. 3 classes of room, all a decent size, well appointed and with cool wooden floors. Friendly reception and efficient staff. Restaurant, beer garden and reading room.

A-D Molly Malone's, Old Market area, T063-963533. Fantastic rooms with 4-poster beds and good clean bathrooms. Irish pub downstairs. Lovely owners. Recommended.

A-D Passaggio, near the Old Market, T063-760324, www.passaggio-hotel.com. 15 double and 2 family rooms, spacious, a/c, minibar and cable TV, internet, laundry service, bar and restaurant, outdoor terrace.

A-D Soria Moria, Wat Bo Rd, T063-964768, www.thesoriamoria.com. Excellent, well-run small hotel that has a roof-top bar and

a decent restaurant. Rooms – all en suite, with contemporary Asian flourishes, a/c and colour TVs – are quiet; the upper ones have nice airy views over the town. Highly recommended.

B-D La Noria, on road running on east side of the river, just past the 'stone' bridge, T063-964242, www.lanoriaangkor.com. Almost perfect riverside setting for this gorgeous small resort. Tranquil gardens, a small pool and a real away-from-it-all vibe seduces guests who stay in brightly coloured a/c and en suite rooms each with their own balcony. No TV, very quiet and decent restaurant. Recommended.

C-D Borann, T063-964740, borann@ pigpond.com.kh. This is an attractive hotel in a delightful garden with a swimming pool. It is secluded and private. 5 small buildings each contain 4 comfortable rooms. Some have a/c, some fan only: price varies.

C-D The Villa, 153 Taphul St, T063-761036, www.thevillasiemreap.com. From the outside this place looks like a funky little guesthouse but some of the rooms are small and dark. All have a/c, TV and shower while the more expensive de luxe rooms are spacious and spotless.

C-E Bopha, on the east side of the river, T063-964928, bopharesa@everyday.com. kh. Stunning hotel. Good rooms with all the amenities, decorated with local furniture and fabrics. Brilliant Thai-Khmer restaurant. Highly recommended.

D Mekong Angkor Palace Hotel, 21 Sivatha Rd, T063-963636, www. mekongangkorpalaces.com. Excellent mid-range, great-value hotel in a good central location. All the spotless rooms are trimmed with a contemporary Khmer vibe, free Wi-Fi, a/c, hot-water bathrooms and TVs. Room rates also include breakfast and there's an excellent pool as well. Recommended.

D Shadow of Angkor II, Wat Bo Rd, T063-760363, www.shadoworangkor.com. Set on a quiet road this is the sister guesthouse of **Shadow of Angkor I** located on the

market side of the river. This is another place offering well-located, good-value, well-run mid-range accommodation. As well as being clean and comfortable most rooms have balconies and all have a/c, free Wi-Fi, TV and hot water.

D-E Home Sweet Home, T063-963245, sweethome@camintel.com. Popular, and a favourite of the moto drivers (who get a kickback). Regardless, it's still got quite good, clean rooms, some with TV and a/c.

D-E Sala Bai, 155 Taphul Rd, T063-963329, www.salabai.com. Part of an NGO programme that trains disadvantaged young Cambodians to work in the hospitality industry. The rooms are decent enough, in a good location and the suite is an excellent deal. Cheaper rooms have fan, pricier ones a/c, and have private hot-water showers. Gets booked up so reserve in advance. See also Eating, page 310.

D-F Golden Banana Bed and Breakfast, Wat Damnak Area (past **Martini Bar**), T012-885366, info@golden-banana.com. Good, clean rooms and decent restaurant.

D-F Two Dragons Guesthouse, Wat Bo Village, T012-868551. Very pleasant, cleanrooms. Good little Thai restaurant. Gordon, the owner of this place, is one of the well-briefed guys in Siem Reap and runs www. talesofasia.com. He can organize a whole range of exciting tours around the area.

D-G Jasmine Lodge, Airport Rd near to town centre, T012-784980, www. jasminelodge.com. One of the best budget deals in town, Jasmine is often fully booked, and with good reason. The super-friendly owner Kunn and his family go out of their way to make this a superlative place to stay; there's free internet and Wi-Fi, breakfast can be included in the rate on request, there are huge shared areas for sitting, a book exchange, tour bookings, bus tickets, etc. There is a huge spread of rooms from basic ones with a fan and shared facilities to sparkling new accommodation with a/c, TV and hot-water bathrooms. Highly recommended.

E Neth Socheata, 10 St Thnou, T063-963294, www.angkorguesthousenethsocheata. com. One of the Siem Reap's best deals, this small newly built budget guesthouse, tucked away down a quiet small alley opposite the market, has very nice, clean, pleasantly decorated rooms. All have en suite hot-water facilities and the price varies according to if you choose a/c or fan. The best rooms have small balconies while others are windowless. There's free Wi-Fi and a friendly welcome. Recommended.

E-G Bou Savy, just outside town off the main airport road, T063-964967, www. bousavy guesthouse.com. One of the best budget options in town this tiny and very friendly family-owned guesthouse is set in soothing gardens and offers a range of rooms with fan or a/c. They also offer breakfast, internet and have some nice public areas. Recommended.

E-G Earthwalkers, just off the airport road, T012-967901, mail@earthwalkers.no. Popular European-run budget guesthouse. Good gardens and pool table. Bit far out of town.

G Mahogany Guesthouse, Wat Bo St, T063-963417/012-768944, proeun@bigpond. com.kh. Fan and some a/c. An attractive and popular guesthouse, lovely wooden floor upstairs (try to avoid staying downstairs), coffee-making facilities and friendly guests.

🍴 Eating

Angkor *p288, map p290*
Near the moat there are a number of cheap food and drink stalls, bookshops and a posse of hawkers selling film, souvenirs, etc. Outside the entrance to Angkor Wat is a larger selection of cafés and restaurants including the sister restaurant to **Blue Pumpkin**, serving good sandwiches and breakfasts, ideal for takeaway.

Siem Reap *p303, maps p304 and p307*
₸₸₸ Abacus, Oum Khun St, off Sivatha St, T012-644286. A little further out from the main Old Market area, this

place is considered one of the best restaurants in town. Offering French and Cambodian, everything is fantastic here. The fish is superb, the steak is to die for. Recommended.

₸₸₸ Barrio, Sivatha St, away from the central area. Fantastic French and Khmer food. A favourite of the expats. Recommended.

₸₸₸ Chez Sophéa, outside Angkor Wat, T012-858003. A unique place in the evening serving Khmer and French cuisine. Romantic setting. It closes around 2100, but later if you want to stay for a digestif or two.

₸₸₸ Le Malraux, Sivatha Bvld, T063-966041, www.le-malraux-siem-reap.com. Daily 0700-2400. Sophisticated French cuisine served in this excellent restaurant. Also do some Khmer and Asian dishes, great wine list and good cognacs. Patio or indoor seating. Recommended.

₸₸₸-₸₸ Sala Bai Restaurant School. See Sleeping, page 309. Open for breakfast and lunch only. Taking in students from impoverished backgrounds from the poorest areas of Cambodia, Sala Bai trains them in catering skills and places them in establishments around town. Service is not the best as students are quite shy practising their English, but a little bit of patience will help them through. Highly recommended.

₸₸₸-₸₸ Soria Moria Fusion Kitchen, Wat Bo Road, T063-964768. Open 0700-2200. Serves a range of local, Scandinavian and Japanese specialities. Wed night is the popular US$1 night where all tapas dishes and drinks, including cocktails, cost US$1 each.

₸₸ The Blue Pumpkin, Old Market area, T063- 963574. Western and Asian food and drinks. Sandwiches, ice cream, pitta, salads and pasta. Candidate for 'least likely eatery to find in Siem Reap' with its white minimalist decor reminiscent of the finest establishments in New York or London. Good breakfasts and cheap cocktails. Eat on the 2nd level. Branches at both the international and domestic terminals at the airport and across from Angkor. Recommended if you need a retreat for 30 mins.

¶ **Bopha**, on the east side of the river, slightly up from Passagio, T063-964928. Fantastic Thai-Khmer restaurant in lovely, tranquil garden setting. One of the absolute best in town. Highly recommended.

¶ **Butterflies Gardens**, just off Wat Bo Rd, T063-761211, www.butterfliesofangkor. com. Daily 0800-2200. Tropical butterflies flit around a koi-filled pond in this slightly odd eatery. The food is Khmer/Asian and is average but the setting is well worth a visit.

¶ **Dead Fish Tower**, Sivatha Blvd, T063-963060. Thai and Khmer restaurant in a fantastically eclectic modern Thai setting. Multiple platforms, quirky decorations, sculptures, apsara dance shows, small putting green and a crocodile farm all add to the atmosphere of this popular restaurant.

¶ **Molly Malone's**, T063-963533. Lovely Irish bar offering classic dishes like Irish lamb stew, shepherd's pie, roasts, and fish and chips.

¶ **Red Piano**, northwest of the Old Market, T063-963240. An institution in Siem Reap, based in a 100-year-old colonial building. Coffee, sandwiches, salad and pastas. Cocktail bar offering a range of tipples, including one dedicated to Angelina Jolie (who came here while working on Tomb Raider).

¶ **Singing Tree**, Wat Bo Rd, T09-263 5500, www.singingtreecafe.com. Tue-Sun 0800-2100. Brilliant diner-cum-community centre with tasty European and Khmer home cooking, with plenty of veggie options. Also host a DVD library and a fairtrade shop.

¶ **Soup Dragon**, T063-964933. Serves a variety of Khmer and Vietnamese dishes but its speciality is soups in earthenware pots cooked at the table. Breezy and clean, a light and colourful location. Upstairs bar, happy hour 1600-1930.

¶ **The Sugar Palm**, Taphul Road, T012-818143. Closed Sun. Sophisticated Khmer restaurant, with immaculate service with casual ambience.

¶ **Teli**, 374 Sivatha St, T063-963289. Swiss, German, Austrian restaurant and bar. Branch of the long-established Phnom Penh restaurant. Serves excellent fondue and raclette, imported beer and sausages. Reasonable prices and generous portions.

¶ **Viroth's Restaurant**, No 246 Wat Bo St, T016-951800. Upmarket place offering very good modern Khmer cuisine plus a few Western staples. Looks more expensive than it actually is, and is good value.

¶ **Khmer Kitchen**, opposite Old Market and Alley West, T063-964154. Tasty cheap Khmer dishes service can be a little slow, but the food is worth waiting for. Sit on the alley side for good people-watching. Recommend their pumpkin pies (more of an omelette than a pie!).

¶ **Moloppor**, east of the river, near **Bopha Hotel**. Good cheap Japanese and pizzas.

¶ **Paul Dubrule Hotel and Tourism School**, airport road, about 3 km from town centre, T063-963672, www.ecolepauldubrule.org. Offers a pretty good set lunch. It can be hit and miss but the quality is often very high and they are always eager to keep their guests happy. Your money will also go to support an excellent vehicle for development: some of the school's graduates have gone on to be well-paid chefs at some of Asia's top hotels and restaurants.

Bars and clubs

Siem Reap *p303, maps p304 and p307*
Angkor What?, Bar St, T012-490755. Friendly staff, popular with travellers and young expats.

Fresh at Chilli Si Dang, East River Rd, T017 875129. Open 0800-late. Laid back atmosphere, friendly service away from the tourist drag. Happy hour between 1700 and 2100.

Laundry, near the Old Market, turn right off 'Bar St', T012-246912. Open till late. Funky little bar.

Linga, Laneway behind 'Bar St', T012-246912. Gay-friendly bar offering a wide selection of cocktails. Great whiskey sours.

Miss Wong, The Lane (behind Pub St) T092-428332. Open 1700-0100. Cute little bar serving sharp cocktails in an Old Shanghai setting.

Temple Club, on 'Bar St', T015-999909. Popular drinking hole, dimly lit, good music. Not related to its seedier counterpart in Phnom Penh.

The Warehouse, opposite Old Market Area, T063-964600. Open 1000-0300. Popular bar, good service and Wi-Fi.

X Rooftop Bar, top of Sivataha St (you'll see the aluminous X from most high-rise buildings in town), T092-207842. Open 1600-sunrise. The latest closing bar in town. Happy hour 1600-1730.

Zone One, Taphul Village, T012-912347. Open 1800-late. The place to go to experience local nightlife.

Entertainment

Siem Reap *p303, maps p304 and p307*
Shadow puppetry

This is one of the finest performing arts of the region. The **Bayon** Restaurant, Wat Bo Rd, has regular shadow puppet shows in the evening. Local NGO, Krousar Thmey, often tour its shadow puppet show to Siem Reap. The show is performed by underprivileged children (who have also made the puppets) at **La Noria Restaurant** (Wed, 1930 but check as they can be irregular). Donations accepted.

A popular Sat evening attraction is the one-man concert put on by **Dr Beat Richner** (Beatocello), founder of the Jayavarman VII hospital for children. Run entirely on voluntary donations the 3 hospitals in the foundation need US$9 million per year in order to treat Cambodian children free of charge. He performs at the hospital, on the road to Angkor, at 1915, 1 hr, free admission but donations gratefully accepted. An interesting and worthwhile experience.

Shopping

Siem Reap *p303, maps p304 and p307*
Outside Phnom Penh, Siem Reap is about the only place whose markets are worth browsing in for genuinely interesting souvenirs. **Old Market** (Psar Chars) is not a large market but stallholders and keepers of the surrounding shops have developed quite a good understanding of what tickles the appetite of foreigners: Buddhist statues and icons, reproductions of Angkor figures, silks, cottons, kramas, sarongs, silverware, leather puppets and rice paper rubbings of Angkor bas-reliefs are unusual mementos. In the night market area, off Sivatha St, you'll find bars, spas and cafés. The original night market, towards the back, has more original stalls, but is slightly more expensive.

Chantiers Écoles, down a short lane off Sivatha St, T063-963330. School for orphaned children that trains them in carving, sewing and weaving. Products are on sale under the name **Les Artisans d'Angkor** and raise 30% of the school's running costs.

Senteurs d'Angkor, opposite Old Market, T063-964801. Sells a good selection of handicrafts, carvings, silverware, silks, handmade paper, cards, scented oils, incense, pepper and spices.

Activities and tours

Siem Reap *p303, maps p304 and p307*
Helicopter and balloon rides

For those wishing to see Angkor from a different perspective it is possible to charter a helicopter. In many ways, it is only from the air that you can really grasp the size and scale of Angkor and a short flight will certainly be a memorable experience. Try **Helicopters Cambodia**, T063-963316, www.helicopterscambodia.com, who offer flights from US$75 per person.

A cheaper (but not nearly as fun) alternative for a good aerial view is to organize a balloon ride above the temples. The tethered balloons float 200 m above Angkor Wat for about 10 mins, US$10 per trip. The balloon company is based about 1 km from the main gates from Angkor Wat, on the road from the airport to the temples.

Therapies

Khmer, Thai, reflexology and Japanese massage are readily available. Many masseuses will come to your hotel.

Frangipani, Hup Guan St near Angkor Hospital for Children, T063-964391, www.frangipanisiemreap. Professional masseuse offers aromatherapy, reflexology and other treatments.

Mutita Spa, at Borei Angkor Resort and Spa on route 6, T63-964406. Offers unique J'Pong therapy, which is a traditional Cambodian heat and relaxation treatment using herbal steam.

Seeing Hands, Massage by sight-impaired individuals. US$3 per hr. Highly recommended.

Tour operators

Asia Pacific Travel, 100 Route No 6, T063-760862, www.angkortravelcambodia.com. Tours of Angkor and the region.

Buffalo Tours, 556 Tep Vong St, Khum Svay Dangkom, T063-965670, www.buffalotours.com. Wide range of customised tours.

Exotissimo Travel, No 300, Highway 6, T063- 964323, www.exotissimo.com. Tours of Angkor and sites beyond.

Hidden Cambodia Adventure Tours, T012-655201, www.hiddencambodia.com. Specializing in dirt-bike tours to remote areas and off-the-track temple locations. Recommended for the adventurous.

Journeys Within, on the outskirts of Siem Reap towards the temples, T063-966463, www.journeys-within.com. Customized tours, visiting temples and experiencing the everyday lives of Cambodians.

Terre Cambodge, on Huap Guan St near Angkor Hospital for Children, T092-476682, www.terrecambodge.com. Offers tours with a twist, including cruises on an old sampan boat. Not cheap but worth it for the experience.

Two Dragons Guesthouse, see page 309. Ccan also organize some off-the-beaten-track tours. Owner Gordon Sharpless is a very knowledgeable and helpful fellow.

WHL Cambodia, Wat Bo Road, T063-963854, www.angkorhotels.org. Local website booking hotels and tours with a responsible tourism approach.

World Express Travel, Street No11 (Old Market area), T063-963600. Can organize tours all over Cambodia. Also books local and international air/bus tickets. A good place to extend visas. Friendly service.

⊖ Transport

Siem Reap p303, maps p304 and p307
Air

Airline offices can be found in Siem Reap.
Bangkok Airways, Airport Rd, www.bangkokair.com, 6 flights a day to **Bangkok**. Jetstar Asia, www.jetstarasia.com, flies to **Singapore** 3 times a week. Malaysian budget airlines AirAsia, T023-890035, www.airasia.com, to **Kuala Lumpur** daily. Helicopters Cambodia, 658 St Hup Quan, near Old Market, T063 963316, is a New Zealand company offering chartered flights around the temples. Lao Airlines, T/F063-963283, Mon-Fri 0800-1700 and Sat 0800-1200, flies to **Vientiane**, 3 times a week via **Pakse**. Malaysia Airlines, T063-964135, flies 3 times a week to **Kuala Lumpur**. Vietnam Airlines, Airport Rd, T063-964488, www.vietnamairlines.com, flies to **Ho Chi Minh City**. Silkair, T063-426 808, www.silkair.com, has daily flights to **Singapore**.

Bicycle

White Bicycles, www.thewhite bicycles.org, can be found at several hotels and guesthouses throughout Siem Reap. The White Bicycles scheme has been set up by expat Norwegian NGO workers as a way to provide not only a source of income and work for locals but also to develop a charitable fund that supports children and teenagers in Cambodia. The bikes cost US$2 a day to rent with US$1.50 going to the charitable fund and US$0.50 going to sustain and repair the bikes by employing and training locals. **Khemara**, opposite the Old Market, T063- 964512, rents bicycles for US$2 per day.

Bus

Neak Krorhorm Travel, GST, Mekong Express and **Capitol** go to and from Siem Reap. Most buses depart Phnom Penh bus station between 0630 and 0800 and the same from Siem Reap (departing near the Old Market). The best bus service is the **Mekong Express**, US$11, 5 hrs.

Directory

Siem Reap *p303, maps p304 and p307*
Banks   ATMs can be found all over town. **ANZ Royal**, Old Market and Tep Vong St, T063-969700. Efficient friendly service. **Cambodia Commercial Bank**, 130 Sivatha St, currency and TC exchange, advance on Visa, MasterCard, JCB, AMEX. **Mekong Bank**, 43 Sivatha, Mon-Fri, Sat morning, US dollar TCs cashed, 2% commission,

cash advance on Visa and JCB cards only. **Union Commercial Bank**, north of Old Market, Mon-Fri and Sat morning, cash advance on MasterCard and Visa (no commission), cash TCs. **Internet**   Rates vary but should be around 3000 riel per hr. Most internet cafés now offer internet calls while most bars, restaurants, cafés and guesthouses have complimentary Wi-Fi for those using their services. **Medical services**   Medical facilities are OK here and improving but by no means of an international standard. In most cases it's probably best to fly to Bangkok. **Royal International Hospital**, Airport Rd, T063-39911. Good standard and costs can be claimed back from most international insurance companies. **Naga International Clinic**, Highway 6 (airport road), T063-965988. International medical services. 24-hr emergency care. **Post office**   Pokamber Av, on the west side of Siem Reap river, 0700-1700, but can take up to a month for mail to be delivered.

Background

Pre-history

Archaeological evidence suggests that the Mekong Delta and the lower reaches of the river – in modern-day Cambodia – have been inhabited since at least 4000 BC. But the wet and humid climate has destroyed most of the physical remains of the early civilizations. Excavated remains of a settlement at Samrong Sen on the Tonlé Sap show that houses were built from bamboo and wood and raised on stilts – exactly as they are today. Where these people came from is uncertain but anthropologists have suggested that there were two waves of migration; one from the Malay peninsula and Indonesia and a second from Tibet and China.

Rise of the Lunar and Solar dynasties

For thousands of years Indochina was isolated from the rest of the world and was virtually unaffected by the rise and fall of the early Chinese dynasties. India and China 'discovered' Southeast Asia in the first millennium AD and trade networks were quickly established. The Indian influence was particularly strong in the Mekong basin. The Khmers adopted and adapted Indian script as well as their ideas about astrology, religion (Buddhism and Hinduism) and royalty (the cult of the semi-divine ruler). Today, several other aspects of Cambodian culture are recognizably Indian in origin, including classical literature and dance. Religious architecture also followed Indian models. These Indian cultural influences that took root in Indochina gave rise to a legend to which Cambodia traces its historical origins. An Indian Brahmin called Kaundinya, travelling in the Mekong Delta area, married Soma, daughter of the Naga (the serpent deity), or Lord of the Soil. Their union, which founded the 'Lunar Dynasty' of Funan (a pre-Angkorian Kingdom), symbolized the fertility of the kingdom and occupies a central place in Khmer cosmology. The Naga, Soma's father, helpfully drank the floodwaters of the Mekong, enabling people to cultivate the land.

Funan

The kingdom of Funan – the forerunner of Kambuja – was established on the Mekong by tribal people from South China in the middle of the third century AD and became the earliest Hindu state in Southeast Asia. Funan was known for its elaborate irrigation canals which controlled the Mekong floodwaters, irrigated the paddy fields and prevented the incursion of seawater. By the fifth century Funan had extended its influence over most of present-day Cambodia, as well as Indochina and parts of the Malay peninsula. Leadership was measured by success in battle and the ability to provide protection, and in recognition of this fact, rulers from the Funan period onward incorporated the suffix 'varman' (meaning protection) into their names. Records of a third-century Chinese embassy give an idea of what it was like: "There are walled villages, places and dwellings. The men ... go about naked and barefoot ... Taxes are paid in gold, silver and perfume. There are books and libraries and they can use the alphabet." Excavations conducted in the last 100 years or so suggest a seafaring people engaged in extensive trade with both India and China, and elsewhere.

The 'Solar Dynasty' of Chenla was a vassal kingdom of Funan, probably first based on the Mekong at the junction with the Mun tributary, but it rapidly grew in power, and was centred in the area of present-day southern Laos. It was the immediate predecessor of

Kambuja and the great Khmer Empire. According to Khmer legend, the kingdom was the result of the marriage of Kambu, an ascetic, to a celestial nymph named Mera. The people of Chenla – the Kambuja, or the sons of Kambu – lent their name to the country. In AD 540 a Funan prince married a Chenla princess, uniting the Solar and Lunar dynasties. The prince sided with his wife and Funan was swallowed by Chenla. The first capital of this fusion was at **Sambor**. King Ishanavarman (AD 616-635) established a new capital at Sambor Prei Kuk, 30 km from modern Kompong Thom, in the centre of the country (the monuments of which are some of the best preserved of this period). His successor, Jayavarman I, moved the capital to the region of Angkor Borei near Takeo.

Quarrels in the ruling family led to the break-up of the state later in the seventh century: it was divided into 'Land Chenla', a farming culture located north of the Tonlé Sap (maybe centred around Champassak in Laos), and 'Water Chenla', a trading culture based along the Mekong. Towards the end of the eighth century Water Chenla became a vassal of Java's powerful Sailendra Dynasty and members of Chenla's ruling family were taken back to the Sailendra court. This period, from the fall of Funan until the eighth century, is known as the pre-Angkorian period and is a somewhat hazy time in the history of Cambodia. The Khmers remained firmly under Javanese suzerainty until Jayavarman II (AD 802-850) returned to the land of his ancestors around AD 800 to change the course of Cambodian history.

Angkor and the god-kings

Jayavarman II, the Khmer prince who had spent most of his life at the Sailendra court, claimed independence from Java and founded the Angkor Kingdom to the north of the Tonlé Sap in AD 802, at about the same time as Charlemagne became Holy Roman Emperor in Europe. They were men cast in the same mould, for both were empire builders. His far-reaching conquests at Wat Phou (Laos) and Sambhupura (Sambor) won him immediate political popularity on his return and he became king in AD 790. In AD 802 he declared himself a World Emperor and to consolidate and legitimize his position he arranged his coronation by a Brahmin priest, declaring himself the first Khmer devaraja, or god-king, a tradition continued today. From then on, the reigning monarch was identified with Siva, the king of the Hindu gods. In the centuries that followed, successive devaraja strove to outdo their predecessors by building bigger and finer temples to house the royal linga, a phallic symbol which is the symbol of Siva and the devaraja. The god-kings commanded the absolute allegiance of their subjects, giving them control of a vast pool of labour that was used to build an advanced and prosperous agricultural civilization. For many years historians and archaeologists maintained that the key to this agricultural wealth lay in a sophisticated hydraulic – that is irrigated – system of agriculture which allowed the Khmers to produce up to three harvests a year. However, this view of Angkorian agriculture has come under increasing scrutiny in recent years and now there are many who believe that flood-retreat – rather than irrigated – agriculture was the key. Jayavarman II installed himself in successive capitals north of the Tonlé Sap, secure from attack by the Sailendras, and he ruled until AD 850, when he died on the banks of the Great Lake at the original capital, Hariharalaya, in the Roluos area (Angkor).

Jayavarman III (AD 850-877) continued his father's traditions and ruled for the next 27 years. He expanded his father's empire at Hariharalaya and was the original founder of the laterite temple at Bakong. **Indravarman** (AD 877-889), his successor, was the first of the great temple-builders of Angkor and somewhat overshadowed the work of Jayavarman III. His means to succession are somewhat ambiguous but it is generally agreed that he overthrew Jayavarman III violently. Unlike his predecessor, Indravarman was not the son of a king but more than likely the nephew of Jayavarman's II Queen. He expanded and renovated the capital, building Preah Ko Temple and developing Bakong. Indravarman is considered one of the key players in Khmer history. Referred to as the "lion among kings" and "prince endowed with all the merits", his architectural projects established precedents that were emulated by those that followed him. After Indravarman's death his sons fought for the King's title. The victor, at the end of the ninth century was **Yasovarman I** (AD 889-900). The battle is believed to have destroyed the palace, thus spurring a move to Angkor. He called his new capital Yasodharapura and copied the water system his father had devised at Roluos on an even larger scale, using the waters of the Tonlé Sap. After Yasovarman's death in 900 his son **Harshavarman** (AD 900-923) took the throne, until he died 23 years later. Harshavarman was well regarded, one particular inscription saying that he "caused the joy of the universe". Upon his death, his brother **Ishanarvarman II**, assumed the regal status. In AD 928, **Jayavarman IV** set up a rival capital about 65 km from Angkor at Koh Ker and ruled for the next 20 years. After Jayavarman IV's death there was a period of upheaval as **Harsharvarman II** tried unsuccessfully to lead the empire. **Rajendravarman** (AD 944-968), Jayarvarman's nephew, managed to take control of the empire and moved the court back to Angkor, where the Khmer kings remained. He chose to build outside of the former capital Bakheng, opting instead for the region south of the East Baray. Many saw him as the saviour of Angkor with one inscription reading: "He restored the holy city of Yashodharapura, long deserted, and rendered it superb and charming." Rajendravarman orchestrated a campaign of solidarity – bringing together a number of provinces and claiming back territory, previously under Yasovarman I. From the restored capital he led a successful crusade against the Champa in what is now Vietnam. A devout Buddhist, he erected some of the first Buddhist temples in the precinct. Upon Rajendravarman's death, his son **Jayavarman V** (AD 968-1001), still only a child, took the royal reigns. Once again the administrative centre was moved, this time to the west, where Ta Keo was built. The capital was renamed Jayendranagari. Like his father, Jayavarman V was Buddhist but was extremely tolerant of other religions. At the start of his tenure he had a few clashes with local dissidents but things settled down and he enjoyed relative peace during his rule. The next king, **Udayadityavarman I**, lasted a few months before being ousted. For the next few years Suryavarman I and Jayaviravarman battled for the King's title.

The formidable warrior **King Suryavarman I** (1002-1049) won. He was a determined leader and made all of his officials swear a blood oath of allegiance. He undertook a series of military campaigns geared towards claiming Mon territory in central and southern Thailand and victoriously extended the Khmer empire into Lower Menam, as well as into Laos and established a Khmer capital in Louvo (modern day Lopburi in Thailand). Suryavarman holds the record for the greatest territorial expansion ever achieved in the Khmer Empire. The Royal Palace (Angkor Thom), the West Baray and the Phimeanakas pyramid temples were Suryavarman's main contributions to Angkor's architectural heritage. He continued the royal Hindu cult but also tolerated Mahayana Buddhism.

On Suryavarman's death, the Khmer Kingdom began to fragment. His three successors had short, troubled reigns and the Champa kingdom captured, sacked and razed the capital. When the king's son, **Udayadityavarman II** (1050-1066), assumed the throne, havoc ensued as citizens revolted against him and some of his royal appointments.

When Udayadityavarman II died, his younger brother, **Harsharvarman III** (1066-1080), last in the line of the dynasty, stepped in. During his reign, there were reports of discord and further defeat at the hands of the Cham.

In 1080 a new kingdom was founded by a northern provincial governor claiming aristocratic descent. He called himself **Jayavarman VI** (1080-1107) and is believed to have led a revolt against the former king. He never settled at Angkor, living instead in the northern part of the kingdom. He left monuments at Wat Phou in southern Laos and Phimai, in Thailand. There was an intermittent period where Jayavarman's IV brother, **Dharanindravarman** (1107-1112) took the throne but he was overthrown by his grand-nephew **Suryavarman II** (1113-1150), who soon became the greatest leader the Angkor Empire had ever seen. He worked prolifically on a broad range of projects and achieved some of most impressive architectural feats and political manoeuvres seen within the Angkorian period. He resumed diplomatic relations with China, the Middle Kingdom, and was held in the greatest regard by the then Chinese Emperor. He expanded the Khmer Empire as far as Lopburi, Siam, Pagan in Myanmar, parts of Laos and into the Malay peninsula. He attacked the Champa state relentlessly, particularly Dai Vet in Northern Vietnam, eventually defeating them in 1144-1145, and capturing and sacking the royal capital, Vijaya. He left an incredible, monumental legacy behind, being responsible for the construction of Angkor Wat, an architectural masterpiece that represented the height of the Khmer's artistic genius, Phnom Rung temple (Khorat) and Banteay Samre. A network of roads was built to connect regional capitals.

However, his success was not without its costs – his widespread construction put serious pressure on the general running of the kingdom and major reservoirs silted up during this time; there was also an intensified discord in the provinces and his persistent battling fuelled an ongoing duel between the Cham and Khmers that was to continue (and eventually be avenged) long after his death.

Suryavarman II deposed the King of Champa in 1145 but the Cham regained their independence in 1149 and the following year, Suryavarman died after a disastrous attempt to conquer Annam (northern Vietnam). The throne was usurped by **Tribhuvanadityavarman** in 1165, who died in 1177, when the Cham seized their chance of revenge and sacked Angkor in a surprise naval attack. This was the Khmer's worst recorded defeat – the city was completely annihilated. The 50-year-old **Jayavarman VII** – a cousin of Suryavarman – turned out to be their saviour. He battled the Cham for the next four years, driving them out of the Kingdom. In 1181 he was declared king and seriously hit back, attacking the Chams and seizing their capital, Vijaya. He expanded the Khmer Kingdom further than ever before; its suzerainty stretched from the Malay peninsula in the south to the borders of Burma in the west and the Annamite chain to the northeast.

Jayavarman's VII's first task was to plan a strong, spacious new capital – Angkor Thom; but while that work was being undertaken he set up a smaller, temporary seat of government where he and his court could live in the meantime – Preah Khan meaning 'Fortunate City of Victory' (see page 302). He also built 102 hospitals throughout his kingdom, as well as a network of roads, along which he constructed resthouses. But because they were built of wood, none of these secular structures survive; only the foundations of four larger ones have been unearthed at Angkor.

Angkor's decline

As was the case during Suryavarman II's reign, Jayavarman VII's extensive building campaign put a large amount of pressure on the kingdom's resources and rice was in short supply as labour was diverted into construction.

Jayavarman VII died in 1218 and the Kambujan Empire fell into progressive decline over the next two centuries. Territorially, it was eroded by the eastern migration of the Siamese.

The Khmers were unable to prevent this gradual incursion but the diversion of labour to the military rice farming helped seal the fate of Angkor. Another reason for the decline was the introduction of Theravada Buddhism in the 13th century, which undermined the prestige of the king and the priests. There is even a view that climatic change disrupted the agricultural system and led to Kambuja's demise. After Jayavarman VII, no king seems to have been able to unify the kingdom by force of arms or personality – internal dissent increased while the king's extravagance continued to place a crippling burden on state funds. With its temples decaying and its once-magnificent agricultural system in ruins, Angkor became virtually uninhabitable. In 1431 the royal capital was finally abandoned to the Siamese, who drove the Khmers out and made Cambodia a vassal of the Thai Sukhothai Kingdom.

Explaining Angkor's decline

Why the Angkorian Empire should have declined has always fascinated scholars in the West – in the same way that the decline and fall of the Roman Empire has done. Numerous explanations have been offered, and still the debate remains unresolved. As Anthony Barnett argued in a paper in the *New Left Review* in 1990, perhaps the question should be "why did Angkor last so long? Inauspiciously sited, it was nonetheless a tropical *imperium* of 500 years' duration."

There are essentially five lines of argument in the 'Why did Angkor fall?' debate. First, it has been argued that the building programmes became simply so arduous and demanding of ordinary people that they voted with their feet and moved out, depriving Angkor of the population necessary to support a great empire. Second, some scholars present an environmental argument: the great irrigation works silted up, undermining the empire's agricultural wealth. (This line of argument conflicts with recent work that maintains that Angkor's wealth was never based on hydraulic – or irrigated – agriculture.) Third, there are those who say that military defeat was the cause – but this only begs the question: why they were defeated in the first place? Fourth, historians with a rather wider view, have offered the opinion that the centres of economic activity in Southeast Asia moved from land-based to sea-based foci, and that Angkor was poorly located to adapt to this shift in patterns of trade, wealth and, hence, power. Lastly, some scholars argue that the religion that demanded such labour of Angkor's subjects became so corrupt that it ultimately corroded the empire from within.

After Angkor – running scared

The next 500 years or so, until the arrival of the French in 1863, was an undistinguished period in Cambodian history. In 1434 the royal Khmer court under Ponheayat moved to Phnom Penh, where a replica of the cosmic Mount Meru was built. There was a short-lived period of revival in the mid-15th century until the Siamese invaded and sacked the capital again in 1473. One of the sons of the captured King Suryavarman drummed up enough Khmer support to oust the invaders and there were no subsequent invasions during the 16th century. The capital was established at Lovek (between Phnom Penh and Tonlé Sap) and then moved back to the ruins at Angkor. But a Siamese invasion in 1593 sent the royal court fleeing to Laos; finally, in 1603, the Thais released a captured prince to rule over the Cambodian vassal state. There were at least 22 kings between 1603 and 1848.

Politically, the Cambodian court tried to steer a course between its powerful neighbours of Siam and Vietnam, seeking one's protection against the other. King **Chey Chetta II** (1618-1628), for example, declared Cambodia's independence from Siam and in order to back up his actions he asked Vietnam for help. To cement the allegiance he was forced to marry a Vietnamese princess of the Nguyen Dynasty of Annam, and then obliged to pay tribute to Vietnam. His successors – hoping to rid themselves of Vietnamese domination – sought Siamese assistance and were then forced to pay for it by acknowledging Siam's suzerainty. Then in 1642, **King Chan** converted to Islam, and encouraged Malay and Javanese migrants to settle in Cambodia. Considering him guilty of apostasy, his cousins ousted him – with Vietnamese support. But 50 years later, the Cambodian **Ang Eng** was crowned in Bangkok. This see-saw pattern continued for years; only Siam's wars with Burma and Vietnam's internal disputes and long-running conflict with China prevented them from annexing the whole of Cambodia, although both took territorial advantage of the fragmented state.

By the early 1700s the kingdom was centred on Phnom Penh (there were periods when the king resided at Ondong). But when the Khmers lost their control over the Mekong Delta to the Vietnamese in the late 18th century, the capital's access to the sea was blocked. By 1750 the Khmer royal family had split into pro-Siamese and pro-Vietnamese factions. Between 1794-1811 and 1847-1863, Siamese influence was strongest; from 1835-1837 the Vietnamese dominated. In the 1840s, the Siamese and Vietnamese armies fought on Cambodian territory, devastating the country. This provoked French intervention – and cost Cambodia its independence, even if it had been nominal for several centuries anyway. On 17 April 1864 (the same day and month as the Khmer Rouge soldiers entered Phnom Penh in the 20th century) King Norodom agreed to French protection as he believed they would provide military assistance against the Siamese. The king was to be disappointed: France honoured Siam's claim to the western provinces of Battambang, Siem Reap and Sisophon, which Bangkok had captured in the late 1600s. And in 1884, King Norodom was persuaded by the French governor of the colony of Cochin China to sign another treaty that turned Cambodia into a French colony, along with Laos and Vietnam in the Union Indochinoise. The establishment of Cambodia as a French protectorate probably saved the country from being split up between Siam and Vietnam.

French colonial period

The French did little to develop Cambodia, preferring instead to let the territory pay for itself. They only invested income generated from tax revenue to build a communications network and from a Cambodian perspective, the only benefit of colonial rule was that the French forestalled the total disintegration of the country, which would otherwise have been divided up between its warring neighbours. French cartographers also mapped Cambodia's borders for the first time and in so doing forced the Thais to surrender the northwestern provinces of Battambang and Siem Reap.

For nearly a century the French alternately supported two branches of the royal family, the Norodoms and the Sisowaths, crowning the 18-year-old schoolboy **Prince Norodom Sihanouk** in 1941. The previous year, the Nazis had invaded and occupied France and French territories in Indochina were in turn occupied by the Japanese – although Cambodia was still formally governed and administered by the French. It was at this stage that a group of pro-independence Cambodians realized just how weak the French control of their country actually was. In 1942 two monks were arrested and accused of preaching anti-French sermons; within two days this sparked demonstrations by more than 1000 monks in Phnom Penh, marking the beginning of **Cambodian nationalism**.

In March 1945 Japanese forces ousted the colonial administration and persuaded King Norodom Sihanouk to proclaim independence. Following the Japanese surrender in August 1945, the French came back in force; Sihanouk tried to negotiate independence from France and they responded by abolishing the absolute monarchy in 1946 – although the king remained titular head of state. A new constitution was introduced allowing political activity and a National Assembly elected.

Independence and neutrality

By the early 1950s the French army had suffered several defeats in the war in Indochina. Sihanouk dissolved the National Assembly in mid-1952, which he was entitled to do under the constitution, and personally took charge of steering Cambodia towards independence from France. To publicize the cause, he travelled to Thailand, Japan and the United States, and said he would not return from self-imposed exile until his country was free. His audacity embarrassed the French into granting Cambodia independence on 9 November 1953 – and Sihanouk returned, triumphant.

The people of Cambodia did not want to return to absolute monarchy, and following his abdication in 1955, Sihanouk became a popular political leader. But political analysts believe that despite the apparent popularity of the former king's administration, different factions began to develop at this time, a process that was the root of the conflict in the years to come. During the 1960s, for example, there was a growing rift between the Khmer majority and other ethnic groups. Even in the countryside, differences became marked between the rice-growing lands and the more remote mountain areas where people practised shifting cultivation, supplementing their diet with lizards, snakes, roots and insects. As these problems intensified in the late 1960s and the economic situation deteriorated, the popular support base for the Khmer Rouge was put into place. With unchecked population growth, land ownership patterns became skewed, landlessness grew more widespread and food prices escalated.

Sihanouk managed to keep Cambodia out of the war that enveloped Laos and Vietnam during the late 1950s and 1960s by following a neutral policy – which helped attract millions of dollars of aid to Cambodia from both the West and the Eastern Bloc. But when a civil war broke out in South Vietnam in the early 1960s, Cambodia's survival – and Sihanouk's own survival – depended on its outcome. Sihanouk believed the rebels, the National Liberation Front (NLF) would win; and he openly courted and backed the NLF. It was an alliance which cost him dear. In 1965-1966 the tide began to turn in South Vietnam, due to US military and economic intervention. This forced NLF troops to take refuge inside Cambodia. When a peasant uprising in northwestern provinces in 1967 showed Sihanouk that he was sailing close to the wind his forces responded by suppressing the rebellion and massacring 10,000 peasants.

Slowly – and inevitably – he became the focus of resentment within Cambodia's political elite. He also incurred American wrath by allowing North Vietnamese forces to use Cambodian territory as an extension of the **Ho Chi Minh Trail**, ferrying arms and men into South Vietnam. This resulted in his former army Commander-in-Chief, **Marshal Lon Nol** masterminding Sihanouk's removal as Head of State while he was in Moscow in 1970. Lon Nol abolished the monarchy and proclaimed a republic. One of the most auspicious creatures in Khmer mythology is the white crocodile. It is said to appear 'above the surface' at important moments in history and is said to have been sighted near Phnom Penh just before Lon Nol took over.

Pol Pot – the idealistic psychopath

Prince Norodom Sihanouk once referred to Pol Pot as "a more fortunate Hitler". Unlike his erstwhile fascist counterpart, the man whose troops were responsible for the deaths of perhaps two million fellow Cambodians has managed to get away with it. He died on 15 April 1998, either of a heart attack or, possibly, at his own hands or somebody else's.

Pol Pot's real name was Saloth Sar – he adopted his nom de guerre when he became Secretary-General of the Cambodian Communist Party in 1963. He was born in 1928 into a peasant family in Kompong Thom, central Cambodia, and is believed to have lived as a novice monk for nine months when he was a child. His services to the Democrat Party won him a scholarship to study electronics in Paris. But he became a Communist in France in 1949 and spent more time at meetings of Marxist revolutionary societies than in

classes. In his 1986 book *Sideshow Story*, William Shawcross notes that at that time the French Communist Party, which was known for its dogmatic adherence to orthodox Marxism, "taught hatred of the bourgeoisie and uncritical admiration of Stalinism, including the collectivization of agriculture". Pol Pot finally lost his scholarship in 1953.

Returning to newly independent Cambodia, Pol Pot started working as a school teacher in Phnom Penh and continued his revolutionary activities in the underground Cambodian Communist Party (which, remarkably kept its existence a secret until 1977). In 1963, he fled the capital for the countryside, fearing a crackdown of the left by Sihanouk. There he rose to become Secretary-General of the Central Committee of the Communist Party of Kampuchea. He was trained in guerrilla warfare and he became

Third Indochina War and the rise of the Khmer Rouge

On 30 April 1970, following the overthrow of Prince Norodom Sihanouk, US President Richard Nixon officially announced **Washington's military intervention in Cambodia** – although in reality it had been going on for some time. The invasion aimed to deny the Vietnamese Communists the use of Sihanoukville port through which 85% of their heavy arms were reaching South Vietnam. The US Air Force had been secretly bombing Cambodia using B-52s since March 1969. In 1973, facing defeat in Vietnam, the US Air Force B-52s began carpet bombing Communist-controlled areas to enable Lon Nol's inept regime to retain control of the besieged provincial cities.

Historian David P Chandler wrote: "When the campaign was stopped by the US Congress at the end of the year, the B-52s had dropped over half a million tons of bombs on a country with which the United States was not at war – more than twice the tonnage dropped on Japan during the Second World War.

The war in Cambodia was known as 'the sideshow' by journalists covering the war in Vietnam and by American policy-makers in London. Yet the intensity of US bombing in Cambodia was greater than it ever was in Vietnam; about 500,000 soldiers and civilians were killed over the four-year period. It also caused about two million refugees to flee from the countryside to the capital."

As Henry Kamm suggested, by the beginning of 1971 the people of Cambodia had to face the terrifying realisation that nowhere in the country was safe and all hope and confidence a leader of the Khmer Rouge forces, advocating armed resistance to Sihanouk and his 'feudal entourage'. In 1975 when the Khmer Rouge marched into Phnom Penh, Pol Pot was forced out of the shadows to take the role of leader, 'Brother Number One'. Although he took the title of prime minister, he ruled as a dictator and set about reshaping Cambodia with his mentor, Khieu Samphan, the head of state. Yet, during the years he was in power, hardly any Cambodians – save those in the top echelons of the Khmer Rouge – had even heard of him.

The Vietnam-backed Hun Sen government, which took over the country after the overthrow of the Khmer Rouge in December 1978, calculated that by demonizing Pol Pot as the mastermind of the genocide, it would avert the possibility of the Khmer Rouge ever making a comeback.

The Hun Sen regime showed no interest in analysing the complex factors that combined to bring Pol Pot to power. Within Cambodia, he has been portrayed simply as a tyrannical bogey-man. During the 1980s, 20 May was declared National Hate Day, when everyone reaffirmed their hatred of Pol Pot.

In a review of David Chandler's biography of Pol Pot (*Brother Number One: A Political Biography of Pol Pot*, Westview Press, 1992), Peter Carey – the co-director of the British-based Cambodia Trust – was struck by what he called "the sinister disjunction between the man's evident charisma ... and the monumental suffering wrought by his regime". Carey concludes: "one is left with the image of a man consumed by his own vision, a vision of empowerment and liberation that has little anchorage in Cambodian reality".

in Cambodia's future during the war was lost. A year after the coup d'etat the country was shattered: guerrilla forces had invaded Angkor, Lol Non had suffered a stroke and had relocated to Hawaii for months of treatment, Lol Non's irregularly paid soldiers were pillaging stores at gunpoint, and extreme corruption was endemic.

By the end of the war, the country had become totally dependent on US aid and much of the population survived on American rice rations. Confidence in the Lon Nol government collapsed as taxes rose and children were drafted into combat units. At the same time, the **Khmer Rouge** increased its military strength dramatically and began to make inroads into areas formerly controlled by government troops. Although officially the Khmer Rouge rebels represented the Beijing-based Royal Government of National Union of Cambodia (Grunc), which was headed by the exiled Prince Sihanouk, Grunc's de facto leaders were Pol Pot, Khieu Samphan (who, after Pol Pot's demise, became the public face of the Khmer Rouge), Ieng Sary (later foreign minister) and Son Sen (Chief of General Staff) – all Khmer Rouge men. By the time the American bombing stopped in 1973, the guerrillas dominated about 60% of Cambodian territory, while the government clung tenuously to towns and cities. Over the next two years the Khmer Rouge whittled away Phnom Penh's defence perimeter to the point that Lon Nol's government was sustained only by American airlifts into the capital.

Some commentators have suggested that the persistent heavy bombing of Cambodia, which forced the Communist guerrillas to live in terrible conditions, was partly responsible for the notorious savagery of the Khmer Rouge in later years. Not only were they brutalized by the conflict itself, but they became resentful of the fact that the city-dwellers had no inkling of how unpleasant their experiences really were. This, writes US political scientist Wayne Bert, "created the perception among the Khmer Rouge that the bulk of the population did not take part in the revolution, was therefore not enthusiastic about it and could not be trusted to support it. The final step in this logic was to punish or eliminate all in these categories who showed either real or imagined tendencies toward disloyalty". And that, as anyone who has watched The Killing Fields will know, is what happened.

'Pol Pot time': building year zero

On 1 April 1975 President Lon Nol fled Cambodia to escape the advancing Khmer Rouge. Just over two weeks later, on 17 April, the victorious Khmer Rouge entered Phnom Penh. The capital's population had been swollen by refugees from 600,000 to over two million. The ragged conquering troops were welcomed as heroes. None in the crowds that lined the streets appreciated the horrors that the victory would also bring. Cambodia was renamed Democratic Kampuchea (DK) and Pol Pot set to work establishing a radical Maoist-style agrarian society. These ideas had been first sketched out by his longstanding colleague Khieu Samphan, whose 1959 doctoral thesis – at the Sorbonne University in Paris – analysed the effects of Cambodia's colonial and neo-colonial domination. In order to secure true economic and political independence he argued that it was necessary to isolate Cambodia completely and to go back to a self-sufficient agricultural economy.

Within days of the occupation, the revolutionaries had forcibly evacuated many of the inhabitants of Phnom Penh to the countryside, telling citizens that the Americans were about to bomb the capital. A second major displacement was carried out at the end of the year, when hundreds of thousands of people from the area southeast of Phnom Penh were forced to move to the northwest.

Prior to the Khmer Rouge coming to power, the Cambodian word for revolution (bambahbambor) had a conventional meaning, 'uprising'. Under Pol Pot's regime, the word pativattana was used instead; it meant 'return to the past'. The Khmer Rouge did this by obliterating everything that did not subscribe to their vision of the past glories of ancient Khmer culture. Pol Pot wanted to return the country to '**Year Zero**' – he wanted to begin again. One of the many revolutionary slogans was "we will burn the old grass and new will grow"; money, modern technology, medicine, education and newspapers were outlawed. Khieu Samphan, who became the Khmer Rouge Head of State, following Prince Sihanouk's resignation in 1976, said at the time: "No, we have no machines. We do everything by mainly relying on the strength of our people. We work completely self-sufficiently. This shows the overwhelming heroism of our people. This also shows the great force of our people. Though bare-handed, they can do everything".

The Khmer Rouge, or Angkar Loeu ('The Higher Organization') as they touted themselves, maintained a stranglehold on the country by dislocating families, disorientating people and sustaining a persistent fear through violence, torture and death. At the heart of their strategy was a plan to unfurl people's strongest bonds and loyalties: those that existed between family members. The term kruosaa, which traditionally means 'family' in Khmer, came to simply mean 'spouse' under the Khmer Rouge. In Angkar, family no longer existed. Krusosaa niyum, which loosely translated to 'familyism' (or pining for one's relatives) was a criminal offence punishable by death. Under heinous interrogation procedures people were intensively probed about their family members (sisters, brothers, grandparents and in-laws) and encouraged to inform on them. Those people who didn't turn over relatives considered adversaries (teachers, former soldiers, doctors, etc) faced odious consequences, with the fate of the whole family (immediate and extended) in danger.

Memoirs from survivors detailed in the book *Children of Cambodia's Killing Fields* repeatedly refer to the Khmer Rouge dictum "to keep you is no benefit to destroy you is no loss." People were treated as nothing more than machines. Food was scarce under Pol Pot's inefficient system of collective farming and administration was based on fear, torture and summary execution. A veil of secrecy shrouded Cambodia and, until a few desperate refugees began to trickle over the border into Thailand, the outside world was largely ignorant of what was going on. The refugees' stories of atrocities were, at first, disbelieved. Jewish refugees who escaped from Nazi occupied Poland in the 1940s had encountered a similarly disbelieving reception simply because (like the Cambodians) what they had to say was, to most people, unbelievable. Some left-wing academics initially viewed the revolution as an inspired and brave attempt to break the shackles of dependency and neo-colonial domination. Others, such as Noam Chomsky, dismissed the allegations as right wing press propaganda.

It was not until the Vietnamese 'liberation' of Phnom Penh in 1979 that the scale of the Khmer Rouge carnage emerged and the atrocities witnessed by the survivors became known. The stories turned the Khmer Rouge into international pariahs – but only until 1982 when, remarkably, their American and Chinese sympathizers secured them a voice at the United Nations. During the Khmer Rouge's 44-month reign of terror, it had hitherto been generally accepted that around a million people died. This is a horrendous figure when one considers that the population of the country in 1975 was around seven million. What is truly shocking is that the work undertaken by a team from Yale University indicates that this figure is far too low.

Although the Khmer Rouge era in Cambodia may have been a period of unprecedented economic, political and human turmoil, they still managed to keep meticulous records of what they were doing. In this regard the Khmer Rouge were rather like the Chinese during the Cultural Revolution, or the Nazis in Germany. Using Australian satellite data, the team was expecting to uncover around 200 mass graves; instead they found several thousand. The Khmer Rouge themselves have claimed that around 20,000 people died because of their 'mistakes'. The Vietnamese have traditionally put the figure at two to three million, although their estimates have generally been rejected as too high and politically motivated (being a means to justify their invasion of the country in 1978/1979 and subsequent occupation). The Documentation Center of Cambodia, involved in the heavy mapping project, said that 20,492 mass graves were uncovered containing the remains of 1,112,829 victims of execution. In addition, hundreds of thousands more died from famine and disease; frighteningly, the executions are believed to only account for about 30-40% of the total death toll.

How such a large slice of Cambodia's people died in so short a time (1975-1978) beggars belief. Some were shot, strangled or suffocated; many more starved; while others died from disease and overwork. The Khmer Rouge transformed Cambodia into what the British journalist, William Shawcross, described as: "a vast and sombre work camp where toil was unending, where respite and rewards were non-existent, where families were abolished and where murder was used as a tool of social discipline. The manner of execution was often brutal. Babies were torn apart limb from limb, pregnant women were disembowelled. Men and women were buried up to their necks in sand and left to die slowly. A common form of execution was by axe handles to the back of the neck. That saved ammunition".

The Khmer Rouge revolution was primarily a class-based one, fed by years of growing resentment against the privileged elites. The revolution pitted the least-literate, poorest rural peasants (referred to as the 'old' people) against the educated, skilled and foreign-influenced urban population (the 'new' people). The 'new' people provided an endless flow of numbers for the regime's death lists. Through a series of terrible purges, the members of the former governing and mercantile classes were liquidated or sent to work as forced labourers. But Peter Carey, Oxford historian and Chairman of the Cambodia Trust, argues that not all Pol Pot's victims were townspeople and merchants. "Under the terms of the 1948 Genocide Convention, the Khmer Rouge stands accused of genocide," he wrote in a letter to a British newspaper in 1990. "Of 64,000 Buddhist monks, 62,000 perished; of 250,000 Islamic Chams, 100,000; of 200,000 Vietnamese still left in 1975, 100,000; of 20,000 Thai, 12,000; of 1800 Lao, 1000. Of 2000 Kola, not a trace remained." American political scientist Wayne Bert noted that: "The methods and behaviour compare to that of the Nazis and Stalinists, but in the percentage of the population killed by a revolutionary movement, the Khmer Rouge holds an unchallenged record."

It is still unclear the degree to which these 'genocidal' actions were controlled by those at the centre. Many of the killings took place at the discretion of local leaders, but there were some notably cruel leaders in the upper echelons of the Khmer Rouge and none can have been ignorant of what was going on. Ta Mok, who administered the region southwest of Phnom Penh, oversaw many mass executions for example. There is also evidence that the central government was directly involved in the running of the Tuol Sleng detention centre in which at least 20,000 people died. It has now been turned into a memorial to Pol Pot's holocaust (see page 252).

In addition to the legacy left by centres such as Tuol Sleng, there is the impact of the mass killings upon the Cambodian psyche. One of which is – to Western eyes – the startling openness with which Khmer people will, if asked, matter-of-factly relate their family history in detail: this usually involves telling how the Khmer Rouge era meant they lost one or several members of their family. Whereas death is talked about in hushed terms in Western society, Khmers have no such reservations, perhaps because it touched, and still touches, them all.

Vietnamese invasion

The first border clashes over offshore islands between Khmer Rouge forces and the Vietnamese army were reported just a month after the Khmer Rouge came to power. These erupted into a minor war in January 1977 when the Phnom Penh government accused Vietnam of seeking to incorporate Kampuchea into an Indochinese federation. Hanoi's determination to oust Pol Pot only really became apparent however, on Christmas Day 1978 when 120,000 Vietnamese troops invaded. By 7 January (the day of Phnom Penh's liberation) they had installed a puppet government which proclaimed the foundation of the People's Republic of Kampuchea (PRK): Heng Samrin, a former member of the Khmer Rouge, was appointed president. The Vietnamese compared their invasion to the liberation of Uganda from Idi Amin – but for the Western world it was unwelcome. The new government was accorded scant recognition abroad, while the toppled government of Democratic Kampuchea retained the country's seat at the United Nations.

The country's 'liberation' by Vietnam did not end the misery; in 1979 nearly half Cambodia's population was in transit, either searching for their former homes or fleeing across the Thai border into refugee camps. American political scientist Wayne Bert wrote:

"The Vietnamese had long seen a special role for themselves in uniting and leading a greater Indochina Communist movement and the Cambodian Communists had seen with clarity that such a role for the Vietnamese could only be at the expense of their independence and prestige."

Under the Lon Nol and Khmer Rouge regimes, Vietnamese living in Cambodia were expelled or exterminated. Resentment had built up over the years in Hanoi – exacerbated by the apparent ingratitude of the Khmer Rouge for Vietnamese assistance in fighting Lon Nol's US-supported Khmer Republic in the early 1970s. As relations between the Khmer Rouge and the Vietnamese deteriorated, the Communist superpowers, China and the Soviet Union, polarized too – the former siding with the Khmer Rouge and the latter with Hanoi. The Vietnamese invasion had the full backing of Moscow, while the Chinese and Americans began their support for the anti-Vietnamese rebels.

Following the Vietnamese invasion, three main anti-Hanoi factions were formed. In June 1982 they banded together in an unholy and unlikely alliance of convenience to fight the PRK and called themselves the Coalition Government of Democratic Kampuchea (CGDK), which was immediately recognized by the United Nations. The Communist **Khmer Rouge**, whose field forces recovered to at least 18,000 by the late 1980s were supplied with weapons by China and were concentrated in the Cardamom Mountains in the southwest and were also in control of some of the refugee camps along the Thai border. The National United Front for an Independent Neutral Peaceful and Co-operative Cambodia (Funcinpec) – known by most people as the **Armée Nationale Sihanoukiste** (ANS) was headed by Prince Sihanouk although he spent most of his time exiled in Beijing. The group had fewer than 15,000 well-equipped troops – most of whom took orders from Khmer Rouge commanders. The anti-Communist **Khmer People's National Liberation Front** (KPNLF), headed by Son Sann, a former prime minister under Sihanouk. Its 5000 troops were reportedly ill-disciplined in comparison with the Khmer Rouge and the ANS.

The three CGDK factions were ranged against the 70,000 troops loyal to the government of President Heng Samrin and Prime Minister Hun Sen (previously a Khmer Rouge cadre). They were backed by Vietnamese forces until September 1989. Within the forces of the Phnom Penh government there were reported to be problems of discipline and desertion. But the rebel guerrilla coalition was itself seriously weakened by rivalries and hatred between the different factions: in reality, the idea of a 'coalition' was fiction. Throughout most of the 1980s the war followed the progress of the seasons: during the dry season the PRK forces with their tanks and heavy arms took the offensive but during the wet season this heavy equipment was ineffective and the guerrilla resistance made advances.

Road towards peace

In the late 1980s the Association of Southeast Asian Nations (ASEAN) – for which the Cambodian conflict had almost become a raison d'être – began steps to bring the warring factions together over the negotiating table. ASEAN countries were united primarily in wanting the Vietnamese out of Cambodia. While publicly deploring the Khmer Rouge record, ASEAN tacitly supported the guerrillas. Thailand, an ASEAN member-state, which has had a centuries-long suspicion of the Vietnamese, co-operated closely with China to ensure that the Khmer Rouge guerrillas over the border were well-supplied with weapons.

After Mikhail Gorbachev had come to power in the Soviet Union, Moscow's support for the Vietnamese presence in Cambodia gradually evaporated. Gorbachev began leaning on

Vietnam as early as 1987, to withdraw its troops. Despite saying their presence in Cambodia was 'irreversible', Vietnam completed its withdrawal in September 1989, ending nearly 11 years of Hanoi's direct military involvement. The withdrawal led to an immediate upsurge in political and military activity, as forces of the exiled CGDK put increased pressure on the now weakened Phnom Penh regime to begin power-sharing negotiations.

Modern Cambodia

In September 1989, under pressure at home and abroad, the Vietnamese withdrew from Cambodia. The immediate result of this withdrawal was an escalation of the civil war as the rebel factions tried to take advantage of the supposedly weakened Hun Sen regime in Phnom Penh. The government committed itself to liberalizing the economy and improving the infrastructure in order to undermine the political appeal of the rebels – particularly that of the Khmer Rouge. Peasant farmers were granted life tenancy to their land and collective farms were substituted with agricultural co-operatives. But because nepotism and bribery were rife in Phnom Penh, the popularity of the Hun Sen regime declined. The rebel position was further strengthened as the disparities between living standards in Phnom Penh and those in the rest of the country widened. In the capital, the government became alarmed; in a radio broadcast in 1991 it announced a crackdown on corruption claiming it was causing a "loss of confidence in our superb regime ... which is tantamount to paving the way for the return of the genocidal Pol Pot regime".

With the withdrawal of Vietnamese troops, the continuing civil war followed the familiar pattern of dry season government offensives, and consolidation of guerrilla positions during the monsoon rains. Much of the fighting focused on the potholed highways – particularly Highway 6, which connects the capital with Battambang – with the Khmer Rouge blowing up most of the bridges along the road. Their strategy involved cutting the roads in order to drain the government's limited resources. Other Khmer Rouge offensives were designed to serve their own economic ends – such as their capture of the gem-rich town of Pailin.

The Khmer Rouge ran extortion rackets throughout the country, even along the strategic Highway 4, which ferried military supplies, oil and consumer goods from the port of Kompong Som (Sihanoukville) to Phnom Penh. The State of Cambodia – or the government forces, known as SOC – was pressed to deploy troops to remote areas and allot scarce resources, settling refugees in more secure parts of the country. To add to their problems, Soviet and Eastern Bloc aid began to dry up.

Throughout 1991 the four warring factions were repeatedly brought to the negotiating table in an effort to hammer out a peace deal. Much of the argument centred on the word 'genocide'. The Prime Minister, Hun Sen, insisted that the wording of any agreement should explicitly condemn the former Khmer Rouge regime's 'genocidal acts'. But the Khmer Rouge refused to be party to any power-sharing deal which labelled them in such a way. Fighting intensified as hopes for a settlement increased – all sides wanted to consolidate their territory in advance of any agreement.

Rumours emerged that China was continuing to supply arms – including tanks, reportedly delivered through Thailand – to the Khmer Rouge. There were also accusations that the Phnom Penh government was using Vietnamese combat troops to stem Khmer Rouge advances – the first such reports since their official withdrawal in 1989. But finally, in June 1991, after several attempts, Sihanouk brokered a permanent ceasefire during a meeting of the Supreme National Council (SNC) in Pattaya, South Thailand. The SNC had been proposed by the United Nations Security Council in 1990 and formed in 1991, with an equal number of representatives from the Phnom Penh government and each of the resistance factions, with Sihanouk as its chairman. The following month he was elected chairman of the SNC, and resigned his presidency of the rebel coalition government in exile. Later in the year, the four factions agreed to reduce their armed guerrillas and militias by 70%. The remainder were to be placed under the supervision of the United Nations Transitional Authority in Cambodia (UNTAC), which supervised Cambodia's transition to multi-party democracy. Heng Samrin decided to drop his insistence that reference should be made to the former Khmer Rouge's 'genocidal regime'. It was also agreed that elections should be held in 1993 on the basis of proportional representation. Heng Samrin's Communist Party was promptly renamed the Cambodian People's Party, in an effort to persuade people that it sided with democracy and capitalism.

Paris Peace Accord

On 23 October 1991, the four warring Cambodian factions signed a peace agreement in Paris which officially ended 13 years of civil war and more than two decades of warfare. The accord was co-signed by 15 other members of the International Peace Conference on Cambodia. There was an air of unreality about the whole event, which brought bitter enemies face-to-face after months of protracted negotiations. There was, however, a notable lack of enthusiasm on the part of the four warring factions. Hun Sen said that the treaty was far from perfect because it failed to contain the word 'genocide' to remind Cambodians of the atrocities of the former Khmer Rouge regime and Western powers obviously agreed. But in the knowledge that it was a fragile agreement, everyone remained diplomatically quiet. US Secretary of State James Baker was quoted as saying "I don't think anyone can tell you there will for sure be lasting peace, but there is great hope."

Political analysts ascribed the successful conclusion to the months of negotiations to improved relations between China and Vietnam – there were reports that the two had held secret summits at which the Cambodia situation was discussed. China put pressure on Prince Norodom Sihanouk to take a leading role in the peace process, and Hanoi's new understanding with Beijing prompted Hun Sen's participation. The easing of tensions between China and Moscow – particularly following the Soviet Union's demise – also helped apply pressure on the different factions. Finally, the United States had shifted its position: in July 1990 it had announced that it would not support the presence of the Khmer Rouge at the UN and by September US officials were talking to Hun Sen.

On 14 November 1991, Prince Norodom Sihanouk returned to Phnom Penh to an ecstatic welcome, followed, a few days later, by Son Sen, a Khmer Rouge leader. On 27 November Khieu Samphan, who had represented the Khmer Rouge at all the peace negotiations, arrived on a flight from Bangkok. Within hours mayhem had broken out, and a lynch mob attacked him in his villa. Rumours circulated that Hun Sen had orchestrated the demonstration, and beating an undignified retreat down a ladder into a waiting armoured personnel carrier, the bloodied Khmer Rouge leader headed back to Pochentong Airport. The crowd had sent a clear signal that they, at least, were not happy to see him back. There were fears that this incident might derail the entire peace process – but in the event, the Khmer Rouge won a small public relations coup by playing the whole thing down. When the Supreme National Council (SNC) finally met in Phnom Penh at the end of December 1991, it was unanimously decided to rubberstamp the immediate deployment of UN troops to oversee the peace process in the run-up to a general election.

UN peace-keeping mission

Yasushi Akashi, a senior Japanese official in the United Nations, was assigned the daunting task of overseeing the biggest military and logistical operation in UN history. UNTAC comprised an international team of 22,000 peacekeepers – including 16,000 soldiers from 22 countries; 6000 officials; 3500 police and 1700 civilian employees and electoral volunteers. The first 'blue-beret' UN troops began arriving in November 1991, even before the SNC had agreed to the full complement of peacekeepers. The UN Advance Mission to Cambodia (UNAMIC) was followed four months later by the first of the main peacekeeping battalions. The odds were stacked against them. Shortly after his arrival, Akashi commented: "If one was a masochist one could not wish for more."

UNTAC's task

UNTAC's central mission was to supervise free elections in a country where most of the population had never voted and had little idea of how democracy was meant to work. The UN was also given the task of resettling 360,000 refugees from camps in Thailand and of demobilizing more than a quarter of a million soldiers and militiamen from the four main factions. In addition, it was to ensure that no further arms shipments reached these factions, whose remaining forces were to be confined to cantonments. In the run-up to the elections, UNTAC also took over the administration of the country, taking over the defence, foreign affairs, finance, public security and information portfolios as well as the task of trying to ensure respect for human rights.

Khmer Rouge pulls out

At the beginning of 1993 it became apparent that the Khmer Rouge had no intention of playing ball, despite its claim of a solid rural support base. The DK failed to register for the election before the expiry of the UN deadline and its forces stepped up attacks on UN personnel. In April 1993 Khieu Samphan and his entire entourage at the Khmer Rouge compound in Phnom Penh left the city. It was at this stage that UN officials finally began expressing their exasperation and anxiety over the Khmer Rouge's avowed intention to disrupt the polls. It was well known that the faction had procured fresh supplies of Chinese weapons through Thailand – although there is no evidence that these came from Beijing – as well as large arms caches all over the country.

By the time of the elections, the group was thought to be in control of between 10% and 15% of Cambodian territory. Khmer Rouge guerrillas launched attacks in April and May 1993. Having stoked racial antagonism, they started killing ethnic Vietnamese villagers and settlers, sending up to 20,000 of them fleeing into Vietnam. In one particularly vicious attack, 33 Vietnamese fishermen and their families were killed in a village on the Tonlé Sap. The Khmer Rouge also began ambushing and killing UN soldiers and electoral volunteers.

The UN remained determined that the elections should go ahead despite the Khmer Rouge threats and mounting political intimidation and violence between other factions, notably the Cambodian People's Party and Funcinpec. In the event, however, there were remarkably few violent incidents and the feared coordinated effort to disrupt the voting failed to materialize. Voters took no notice of Khmer Rouge calls to boycott the election and in fact, reports came in of large numbers of Khmer Rouge guerrillas and villagers from areas under their control, turning up at polling stations to cast their ballots.

UN-supervised elections

The days following the election saw a political farce – Cambodian style – which, as Nate Thayer wrote in the Far Eastern Economic Review "might have been comic if the implications were not so depressing for the country's future". In just a handful of days, the Phnom Penh-based correspondent went on, Cambodia "witnessed an abortive secession, a failed attempt to establish a provisional government, a royal family feud and the manoeuvres of a prince [Sihanouk] obsessed with avenging his removal from power in a military coup more than 20 years [previously]". The elections gave Funcinpec 45% of the vote, the CPP 38% and the BLDP, 3%. The CPP immediately claimed the results fraudulent, while Prince Norodom Chakrapong – one of Sihanouk's sons – announced the secession of the country's six eastern provinces. Fortunately, both attempts to undermine the election dissolved. The CPP agreed to join Funcinpec in a power-sharing agreement while, remarkably, the Khmer Rouge were able to present themselves as defenders of democracy in the face of the CPP's claims of vote-rigging. The new Cambodian constitution was ratified in September 1993, marking the end of UNTAC's involvement in the country. Under the new constitution, Cambodia was to be a pluralistic liberal-democratic country. Seventy-year-old Sihanouk was crowned King of Cambodia, reclaiming the throne he relinquished in 1955. His son Norodom Ranariddh was appointed First Prime Minister and Hun Sen, Second Prime Minister, a situation intended to promote national unity but which instead lead to internal bickering and dissent.

An uncivil society?

Almost from day one of Cambodia's rebirth as an independent state espousing the principles of democracy and the market, cracks began to appear in the rickety structure that underlay these grand ideals. Rampant corruption, infighting among the coalition partners, political intrigue, murder and intimidation all became features of the political landscape – and have remained so to this day. There are three bright spots in an otherwise pretty dismal political landscape. First of all, the Khmer Rouge – along with Pol Pot – is dead and buried. Second, while there have been coups, attempted coups, murder, torture and intimidation, the country does still have an operating political system with an opposition of sorts. And third, the trajectory of change in recent years has been upwards. But, as the following account shows, politics in Cambodia makes Italy seem a model of stability and common sense.

From the elections of 1993 through to 1998, relations between the two key members of the ruling coalition, the CPP and Funcinpec, went from bad to quite appalling. At the end of 1995 Prince Norodom Sirivudh was arrested for plotting to kill Hun Sen and the prime minister ordered troops and tanks on to the streets of Phnom Penh. For a while the capital had the air of a city under siege. Sirivudh, secretary-general of Funcinpec and King Norodom Sihanouk's half brother, has been a vocal critic of corruption in the government, and a supporter of Sam Rainsy, the country's most outspoken opposition politician and the bane of Hun Sen's life. The National Assembly voted unanimously to suspend Sirivudh's immunity from prosecution. Few commentators really believed that Sirivudh had plotted to kill Hun Sen. In the end Hun Sen did not go through with a trial and Sirivudh went into self-imposed exile.

In 1996, relations between the CPP and Funcinpec reached another low. First Prime Minister Prince Norodom Ranariddh joined his two exiled brothers – princes Chakkrapong and Sirivudh – along with Sam Rainsy, in France. Hun Sen smelled a rat and when Ranariddh threatened in May to pull out of the coalition his worries seemed to be confirmed.

Only pressure from the outside prevented a meltdown. Foreign donors said that continuing aid was contingent on political harmony, and ASEAN sent the Malaysian foreign minister to knock a few heads together. Some months later relations became chillier still following the drive-by killing of Hun Sen's brother-in-law as he left a restaurant in Phnom Penh.

Things, it seemed, couldn't get any worse – but they did. In February 1997, fighting between forces loyal to Ranariddh and Hun Sen broke out in Battambang. March saw a grenade attack on a demonstration led by opposition leader Sam Rainsy outside the National Assembly leaving 16 dead and 150 injured – including Rainsy himself who suffered minor injuries. In April, Hun Sen mounted what became known as the 'soft coup'. This followed a complicated series of defections from Ranariddh's Funcinpec party to the CPP which, after much to-ing and fro-ing overturned Funcinpec's small majority in the National Assembly. In May, Hun Sen's motorcade was attacked and a month later, on 16 June, fighting broke out between Hun Sen and Ranariddh's bodyguards leaving three dead. It was this gradual decline in relations between the two leaders and their parties which laid the foundations for the coup of 1997.

In July 1997 the stage was set for Cambodia to join ASEAN. This would have marked Cambodia's international rehabilitation. Then, just a month before the historic day, on 5-6 June, Hun Sen mounted a coup and ousted Norodom Ranariddh and his party, Funcinpec, from government. It took two days for Hun Sen and his forces to gain full control of the capital. Ranariddh escaped to Thailand while the United Nations Centre for Human Rights reported that 41 senior military officers and Ranariddh loyalists were hunted down in the days following the coup, tortured and executed. In August the National Assembly voted to withdraw Ranariddh's immunity from prosecution. Five months later, in January 1998, United Nations High Commissioner for Human Rights Mary Robinson visited Cambodia and pressed for an investigation into the deaths – a request that Hun Sen rejected as unwarranted interference. ASEAN, long used to claiming that the Association has no role interfering in domestic affairs, found it had no choice but to defer Cambodia's accession. The coup was widely condemned and on 17 September the UN decided to keep Cambodia's seat vacant in the General Assembly.

Following the coup of 1997 there was some speculation that Hun Sen would simply ignore the need to hold elections scheduled for 26 July. In addition, opposition parties threatened to boycott the elections even if they did occur, claiming that Hun Sen and his henchmen were intent on intimidation. But despite sporadic violence in the weeks and months leading up to the elections, all parties ended up participating. It seems that intense international pressure got to Hun Sen who appreciated that without the goodwill of foreign aid donors the country would simply collapse. Of the 4.9 million votes cast – constituting an impressive 90% of the electorate – Hun Sen's Cambodian People's Party won the largest share at just over 41%.

Hun Sen offered to bring Funcinpec and the SRP into a coalition government, but his advances were rejected. Instead Rainsy and Ranariddh encouraged a series of demonstrations and vigils outside the National Assembly – which quickly became known as 'Democracy Square', à la Tiananmen Square. At the beginning of September 1998, following a grenade attack on Hun Sen's residence and two weeks of uncharacteristic restraint on the part of the Second Prime Minister, government forces began a crack down on the demonstrators. A week later the three protagonists – Ranariddh, Sam Rainsy and Hun Sen – agreed to talks presided over by King Sihanouk in Siem Reap. These progressed astonishingly well considering the state of relations between the three men and two days later the 122-seat National Assembly opened at Angkor Wat on 24 September.

In mid-November further talks between the CPP and Funcinpec led to the formation of a coalition government. Hun Sen became sole prime minister and Ranariddh chairman of the National Assembly. While the CPP and Funcinpec took control of 12 and 11 ministries respectively, with Defence and Interior shared, the CPP got the lion's share of the key portfolios. **Sam Rainsy** was left on the opposition benches. It was only after the political détente that followed the elections that Cambodia was given permission to occupy its UN seat in December 1998. At a summit meeting in Hanoi around the same time, ASEAN also announced that they had agreed on the admission of Cambodia to the grouping – which finally came through on 30 April 1999.

A return to some kind of normality

The year 1997 was the low point in Cambodia's stuttering return to a semblance of normality. The Asian economic crisis combined with the coup (see above) to rock the country back on its heels. On 3 February 2002 free, fair and only modestly violent local commune elections were held. The CPP won the vote by a landslide and although there is little doubt that Hun Sen's party used a bit of muscle here and there, foreign election observers decided that the result reflected the will of the 90% of the electorate who voted. The CPP, despite its iron grip on power, does recognize that democracy means it has to get out there and make a case. Around one third of the CPP's more unpopular commune chiefs were replaced prior to the election. Funcinpec did badly, unable to shake off the perception that it sold out its principles to join the coalition in 1998. The opposition Sam Rainsy Party did rather better, largely for the same reason: the electorate viewed it as standing up to the might of the CPP, highlighting corruption and abuses of power.

In July 2002 Hun Sen took on the rotating chairmanship of ASEAN and used a round of high-profile meetings to demonstrate to the region, and the wider world, just how far the country has come. Hun Sen, who hardly has an enviable record as a touchy-feely politician, used the chairmanship of ASEAN to polish his own as well as his country's credentials in the arena of international public opinion. But despite the PR some Cambodians are concerned that Hun Sen is becoming a little like Burma's Ne Win. Like Ne Win, Hun Sen seems to be obsessed with numbers. His lucky number is nine; in 2002 he brought the local elections forward by three weeks so that the digits in the date would add up to nine. In 2001 he closed down all Cambodia's karaoke bars. With over 20 years as prime minister there is no one to touch Hun Sen and he seems to revel in his strongman reputation. Judges bow to his superior knowledge of the judicial system; kings and princes acknowledged his unparalleled role in appointing the new king; many journalists are in thrall to his power. If even the most fundamental of rights are negotiable then it would seem that only Cambodia's dependence on foreign largesse constrains his wilder impulses.

Compared to its recent past, the last 10 years has been a period of relative stability for Cambodia. Political violence and infighting between parties continues to be a major problem – by international standards the elections were borderline unacceptable, although most of the major parties were reasonably satisfied with the results which saw Hun Sen's landslide victory. The 2003 election wasn't smooth-sailing either. Prior to the June 2003 election the alleged instructions given by representatives of the CPP to government controlled election monitoring organizations were: "If we win by the law, then we win. If we lose by the law, we still must win." Nonetheless a political deadlock arose, with the CPP winning a majority of votes but not the two-thirds required under the constitution to govern alone. The incumbent CPP-led administration assumed power and took on a caretaker role, pending the creation of a coalition that would satisfy the required number of National Assembly seats to form government. Without a functioning legislature, the course of vital legislation was stalled. After almost a year-long stalemate, the National Assembly approved a controversial addendum to the constitution, which allowed a new government to be formed by vote. The vote took place on July 15 2004, and the National Assembly approved a new coalition government, an amalgam of the CPP and FUNCINPEC, with Hun Sen at the helm as prime minister and Prince Norodom Ranariddh as president of the national assembly.

The government's democratic principles came under fire once again in February 2005, when opposition leader Sam Rainsy fled the country after losing his parliamentary immunity from prosecution. Rainsy is perceived as something of a threat due to his steadily gaining popularity with young urban dwellers, whose growing disenchantment with the current government he feeds off. On the one hand, his 'keep the bastards honest' style of politics has added a new dimension of accountability to Cambodian politics, but on the other, his nationalist, racist rantings, particularly his anti-Vietnamese sentiments, could be a very bad thing for the country. In May, 2005 Hun Sen said that Sam Rainsy would have to wait until the "next life" before he would guarantee his safety. However, having received a pardon in February 2006, he returned to the political fray soon after.

The lingering death of the Khmer Rouge

What many outsiders found hard to understand was how the Khmer Rouge enjoyed such popular support among Cambodians – even after the massacres and torture.

The Khmer Rouge was not, of course, just a political force. Its political influence was backed up and reinforced by military muscle. And it has been the defeat of the Khmer Rouge as an effective fighting force that seems to have delivered the fatal blow to its political ambitions.

In mid-1994 the National Assembly outlawed the Khmer Rouge, offering a six-month amnesty to rank-and-file guerrillas. By the time the six months was up in January 1995, 7000 Khmer Rouge had reportedly defected to the government, leaving at that time somewhere between 5000 and 6000 hardcore rebels still fighting. A split in this core group can be dated to 8 August 1996 when Khmer Rouge radio announced that former 'brother number two', Ieng Sary, had betrayed the revolution by embezzling money earned from mining and timber contracts, and branded him a traitor.

This was the first evidence available to Western commentators that a significant split in the Khmer Rouge had occurred. In retrospect, it seems that the split had been brewing for some years – ever since the UN-sponsored elections had revealed a division between 'conservatives' and 'moderates'. The latter, apparently, wished to co-operate with the UN, while the former group desired to boycott the elections. In 1996 the moderate faction, headed by Ieng Sary, finally broke away from the conservatives led by Pol Pot and hardman General Ta Mok. Hun Sen announced soon after the radio broadcast in August 1996 that two Khmer Rouge commanders, Ei Chhien and Sok Pheap had defected to the government. At the end of September Ieng Sary held a press conference to declare his defection. On 14 September King Norodom Sihanouk granted Ieng Sary a royal pardon.

The Cambodian government's conciliatory line towards Ieng Sary seemed perplexing given the man's past. Although he cast himself in the mould of 'misguided and ignorant revolutionary', there are few who doubt that he was fully cognisant of what the Khmer Rouge under Pol Pot were doing even if, as Michael Vickery argues, he was not Brother Number Two, just Brother Number Four or Five. Indeed he has admitted as much in the past. Not only is he, as a man, thoroughly unpleasant – or so those who know him have said – but he was also a key figure in the leadership and was sentenced to death in absentia by the Phnom Penh government. Stephen Heder of London's School of Oriental & African Studies was quoted as saying after the September press conference: "It's totally implausible that Ieng Sary was unaware that people were being murdered [by the Khmer Rouge]". The split in the Khmer Rouge and the defection of Ieng Sary deprived the Khmer Rouge of 3000-5000 men – halving its fighting force – and also denied the group important revenues from key gem mining areas around Pailin and many of the richest forest concessions.

The disintegration of the Khmer Rouge continued in 1997 after a complicated deal involving Pol Pot, Khieu Samphan, Son Sen and Ta Mok, as well as members of Funcinpec, collapsed. In early June Khieu Samphan, the nominal leader of the Khmer Rouge, was thought to be on the verge of brokering an agreement with Funcinpec that would give Pol Pot and two of his henchmen immunity from prosecution. This would then provide the means by which Khieu Samphan might enter mainstream Cambodian politics. It seems that Hun Sen, horrified at the idea of an alliance between Khieu Samphan and Funcinpec, mounted the coup of June 1997 to prevent the deal coming to fruition. Pol Pot was also, apparently, less than satisfied with the terms of the agreement and pulled out – killing Son Sen in the process. But before Pol Pot could flee, Ta Mok captured his erstwhile leader on June 19th at the Khmer Rouge stronghold of Anlong Veng.

A little more than a month later the 'Trial of the Century' began in this jungle hideout. It was a show trial – more like a Cultural Revolution lynching. A crowd of a few hundred people were on hand. Pol Pot offered the usual Khmer Rouge defence: the revolution made mistakes, but its leaders were inexperienced. And, in any case, they saved Cambodia from annexation by Vietnam. (There is an argument purveyed by some academics that the Khmer Rouge was essentially involved in a programme of ethnic cleansing aimed at ridding Cambodia of all Vietnamese people and influences.) Show trial or not, few people had any sympathy for Pol Pot as he was sentenced by the Khmer Rouge 'people's' court to life imprisonment for the murder of Son Sen. A Khmer Rouge radio station broadcast that with Pol Pot's arrest and sentencing, a 'dark cloud' had been lifted from the Cambodian people.

Confirmation of this bizarre turn of events emerged in mid-October when journalist Nate Thayer of the *Far Eastern Economic Review* became the first journalist to interview Pol Pot since 1979. He reported that the former Khmer Rouge leader was "very ill and perhaps close to death". Even more incredibly than Ieng Sary's defence, Pol Pot denied that the genocide had ever occurred and told Nate Thayer that his 'conscience was clear'.

In March 1998 reports filtered out of the jungle near the Thai border that the Khmer Rouge was finally disintegrating in mutinous conflict. The end game was at hand. The government's amnesty encouraged the great bulk of the Khmer Rouge's remaining fighters to lay down their arms and in December 1998 the last remnants of the rebel army surrendered to government forces, leaving just a handful of men under hardman 'The Butcher' Ta Mok still at large. But even Ta Mok's days of freedom were numbered. In March 1999 he was captured near the Thai border and taken back to Phnom Penh.

The death of Pol Pot

On 15 April 1998 unconfirmed reports stated that Pol Pot – a man who ranks with Hitler, Stalin and Mao in his ability to kill – had died in a remote jungle hideout in the north of Cambodia. Given that Pol Pot's death had been announced several times before, the natural inclination among journalists and commentators was to treat these reports with scepticism. But it was already known that Pol Pot was weak and frail and his death was

Buddhist temple wars and beyond

The stunning temple complex at Preah Vihear, pressed up tight on the remote regions of northern Cambodia, has long been a source of contention between Thailand and the Khmers. Since the colonial-era borders were established back in the early 20th century, Thailand has made repeated attempts to annex the area. However, in 1962, the argument was arbitrated by the International Court of Justice in The Hague, which ruled that the temple fell within the boundaries of Cambodia. Unfortunately this was proved to be far from the last the international community saw of the dispute and over the years Preah Vihear has been at the centre of tensions between these neighbours.

In the 1990s Thailand suddenly closed access to the site, citing the illegal use of the border. In January 2003 there was further escalation of tensions after the misinterpretation of remarks allegedly made by a Thai actress insinuating that Thailand should regain control of the area. The Thai embassy in Phnom Penh was badly damaged in rioting along with many Thai-owned businesses. In May 2005 the two countries both deployed troops on the border surrounding Preah Vihear and while the troops, at that point, stood down, the situation remained testy.

Fast forward to 2008 and a longstanding application for Preah Vihear to be placed on the UNESCO World Heritage Site list came to fruition. Initially the Thai government supported the move, even though this meant accepting the contested areas were inside Cambodian territory. The thinking at the time was that the site could now benefit both nations.

With huge pressure coming to bear on the then Peoples' Power Party (PPP) goverment from the extreme fascistic nationalists of the Peoples' Alliance for Democracy (PAD), Thailand withdrew its support for UNESCO status and reneged on its promise to finally recognize Cambodia's claims. Nonetheless, UNESCO declared Preah Vihear a World Heritage Site in July 2008. Much sabre rattling ensued, with shots fired and military units mobilized. Thai nationalists were arrested by the Cambodians as they tried to plant a Thai flag in the Preah Vihear's grounds and bizarre black magic rituals were claimed

confirmed when journalists were invited to view his body the following day. Pol Pot was reported to have died from a heart attack. He was 73.

A new era?

The question of what to do with Ieng Sary was the start of a long debate over how Cambodia – and the international community – should deal with former members of the Khmer Rouge. The pragmatic, realist line is that if lasting peace is to come to Cambodia, then it may be necessary to allow some people to get away with – well – murder. As one Western diplomat pondered: "Do you owe fealty to the dead for the living?" This would seem to be Hun Sen's preferred position.

By late 1998, with the apparent end of the Khmer Rouge as a fighting force, the government seemed happy to welcome back the rank and file into mainstream Cambodian life while putting on trial key characters in the Khmer Rouge like Ta Mok, to have been enacted by both sides. With the Thai foreign minister forced to resign and Thailand completely entrenched, a conflict seemed inevitable.

In October 2008 the fighting started in earnest with a mini-battle taking place that left several soldiers on both sides dead or injured. Thai nationals were advised to leave Cambodia by the Thai government and war seemed imminent. Fortunately, after intervention by the international community, both sides saw sense and pulled back from the brink.

In 2009 the situation continued to be tense, not least because the extremists of the PAD once again entered the fray holding a series of violent protests at the border. At one point they even threatened to attempt to storm the temple but the Cambodian government made it very clear they would shoot to kill if this took place. Skirmishes between both nations' armies then took place in April with several soldiers being killed. The PAD backed down and the situation was temporarily relieved.

Yet, there was worse to come. In late 2009 Cambodian PM Hun Sen declared the Thai PM, Thaksin Shinawatra, who was deposed in a 2006 military coup,

an economic adviser to Cambodia. For the ruling Thai Democrat Party government and their PAD allies, both of whom supported the military coup in 2006, this was a deliberate provocation by Hun Sen. Thailand recalled its ambassador, trade agreements were ripped up and the right wing Thai press went into hysterics. For a short while it seemed like full-blown war might take place but, once again, both parties, amid calls for restraint from the international community, pulled back from the brink.

In mid-2010 the relationship between Thailand and Cambodia was still a long way from normalised. Thailand's ongoing internal political problems have the potential to stir things up between the nations and there have been continued skirmishes throughout the year.

Quite clearly visiting Preah Vihear is not advisable until this entire situation is at least partially resolved. Most foreign governments are also advising against travel to the temple. If you do plan to visit we would recommend, at the very least, you take good advice from locals about the situation at time of travel and also use the services of a reputable tour operator or guide.

Khieu Samphan and Nuon Chea. While the government was considering what to do, former leaders of the Khmer Rouge were busy trying to rehabilitate their muddied reputations. After years of living pretty comfortable lives around the country, particularly in and around Pailin, by the end of 2007 the old guard of the Khmer Rouge were finally being brought to book. This turn of events was finally set in motion in March 2006 with the nomination of seven judges by the then Secretary General of the United Nations, Kofi Annan for the much anticipated Cambodia Tribunal. With Ta Mok dying in prison in early July 2006 the first charges were laid against the notorious head of the Tuol Sleng prison, Khang Khek Ieu – aka 'Comrade Duch'. Indicted on 31 July with crimes against humanity and after spending eight years behind bars, Duch is due to go on trial soon. Yet it was with the arrests in late 2007 of Ieng Sary, Nuon Chea and Khieu Samphan that the tribunal finally began to flex its muscles. Each of these arrests made international news and it seems, almost 30 years after the Vietnam invasion ended the abhorrent Khmer Rouge regime, that Cambodia may finally be coming to terms with its horrific past.

However, with only the few living key Khmer Rouge figures standing trial most of the minor – and probably equally murderous – cadre are still in circulation. It could be argued that the Tribunal is purely a diversion that allows this coterie of killers and Hun Sen's nefarious past to remain hidden from scrutiny.

What is obvious is that as the Tribunal progressed, many of the old divisions that have riven Cambodian society for generations where taking hold again. In late 2007 Cambodia was officially and internationally recognised as one of the most corrupt countries in history. Spend five minutes in Phnom Penh and this air of corruption is staring you in the face – Toyota Land Cruisers, giant, black Lexus SUVs and Humvees plough through the streets without regard for anyone or anything. When these vehicles do crush or kill other road users, the driver's well-armed body guards hop out, pistols waving, and soon dissuade any eager witnesses. This kind of event is commonplace and the poorer locals know this. Speak to a moto or tuk-tuk driver and you'll soon sense the resentment, "We hate the corrupt and we'd be happy to see them die", is a frequent comment reminiscent of Cambodia's darker times. The establishment of a new, rich elite is not leading to the trickle-down of wealth but the entrenchment of certain groups who have no regard at all for building a new society. Even the aid community is complicit in this – one senior worker made this damning off-the-record comment, "We view corruption as the only stabilising factor in Cambodian society. It is awful but what else is there?"

The July 2008 general election changed little. Hun Sen was returned with an enlarged majority after a campaign that drew both praise and criticism from EU observers. On the upside the election was seen as being 'technically proficient' and possibly the best-run vote in Cambodia's history. Not that that's saying much – Hun Sen's ruling CPP was seen to have abused its position and not only dominated the media but also disenfranchised tens of thousands of opposition voters. Yet the same EU observers also felt the CPP would have won despite any machinations by Hun Sen and the vote was accepted in the international community. At the same time the election was taking place a row began to brew with Thailand over the contested Preah Vihear temple near the Thai/Cambodian border (see box, page 336). In early July the Cambodian-led effort to turn the revered Preah Vihear into a UNESCO World Heritage Site was greeted by huge celebrations in Phnom Penh. For the Cambodians this meant that the long-contested temple was now firmly recognized as being in their territory. By early October 2008 a troop build-up escalated into an exchange of fire that led to a tense two-week stand-off and resulted in several deaths. Eventually, after pressure from the international community, both sides backed down but the dispute is still not settled and, at present, one of the region's most spectacular sites is off-limits.

It wasn't all bad news though as on 17 February 2009, 30 years after the fall of the Khmer Rouge regime, the first trial finally began against one of its former commanders began when Comrade Duch, the infamous commander of the Tuol Sleng death camp. As it progressed on through 2009, Duch's trial attracted a huge amount of international attention, not least for the plea the accused made in November 2009 to be released. While it must be said Duch has been one of the few senior Khmer Rouge leaders to have expressed any regret, this was still a staggering moment. With this book going to press in mid-2010 it is impossible to comment on the final verdict and sentencing for Duch's case due to be delivered on 26 July 2010 but there is little doubt of his guilt (he made full and frank admissions of his crimes) and he is likely to face the rest of his natural life in prison. Furthermore, by the end of 2009 it wasn't only Duch facing trial – several of the other cases

Cambodia Tribunal

In 1997, with the country's interminable civil war set to end, the Cambodian government made an official approach to the UN to establish a court to prosecute the senior members of the Khmer Rouge. The thinking at the time was that Cambodia lacked the institutions and know-how to handle such a big trial and that outside expertise would be needed.

At first, things for the prosecution looked promising, with an agreed handing over of Pol Pot (holed up in northern Cambodia in Anlong Veng), set to take place in April 1998. But he never made it to court, mysteriously dying the night before his supposed arrest. Some say from a heart attack, others that he took his own life.

In 1999, Kaing Guek Eav aka ' Comrade Duch', the commandant of the infamous Tuol Sleng prison camp in Phnom Penh, surrendered to the Cambodian authorities. In the same year, Ta Mok, another blood-soaked Khmer Rouge leader, was also arrested (he died in custody seven years later in 2006). Initially, however, no power or legal authority existed to try them and it wasn't until 2001 that the Cambodian government agreed to pass a law setting up what came to be known as the 'Extraordinary Chambers in the Courts of Cambodia for the Prosecution of Crimes Committed during the Period of Democratic Kampuchea' or, for short, the Cambodia Tribunal.

Several more years passed, with the sometimes indifferent Cambodians stating that they had no money to finance the trials and the international community unwilling to fund a process in a country where corruption was so rampant. But despite this, in early 2006, buildings just outside Phnom Penh were requisitioned, the UN nominated its judges and by July of the same year a full panel of 30 Cambodian and UN judges were fully sworn in. A list of five main suspects was drawn up in July 2007 and the first person formally charged was the already incarcerated Comrade Duch on 31 July 2007.

Then, in late 2007, after years of snail-like progress, and with the main protagonists approaching their twilight years, a flurry of dramatic arrests occurred. Former Khmer Rouge ideologue and Foreign Minister Ieng Sary and his wife, the Minister of Social Affairs, Ieng Thirith, former Chief of State and Pol Pot's number two, Khieu Samphan, were all taken into custody and charged with war crimes and crimes against humanity.

The first trial of Extraordinary Chambers in the Courts of Cambodia for the Prosecution of Crimes Committed during the Period of Democratic Kampuchea began with Comrade Duch in February 2009. By the end of the same year his trial was over and trials against many other senior Khmer Rouge figures also began. In July 2010, Duch was found guilty of crimes against humanity and sentenced to 35 years in jail.

There's no doubt that Duch's public trial marked a turning point for Cambodia. For the first time the Khmer Rouge's crimes were aired in the cold, calculated and unambiguous efficiency of a courtroom. Victims confronted their tormentor with Duch expressing remorse and, more bizarrely, asking to be released by the court. With the first trial completed a giant psychological hurdle was taken in its stride by the Cambodian people. Finally, after almost 40 years, it seems like justice will be delivered – this can only bode well for Cambodia's future.

of remaining senior Khmer Rouge figures also began, with pre-trial hearings continuing on through 2010 (see box, page 339).

The other main issue that has dominated Cambodia over the last period has been its relations with its neighbour, Thailand. Ostensibly focused on the disputed Preah Vihear temple (see box, page 336), this dispute has already reached the shooting stage on several occasions with soldiers on both sides being killed. There's also little doubt that the appointment of deposed Thai PM Thaksin – who is loathed by the controlling Thai elite and has been defined as a wanted 'criminal' by the Thai state – as an economic adviser by Hun Sen only exacerbated the situation. After Thaksin arrived in Cambodia in late 2009 the Thais withdrew their ambassador, threatened to tear up long-standing trade agreements and demanded that Cambodia, an ASEAN partner, arrest Thaksin and extradite him to Thailand to face a prison cell.

Hun Sen, with some justification, refused, citing that Thaksin's criminal conviction in Thailand was politicised and that Cambodia could choose who it wanted as an economic adviser. After the Thais threw a few more toys out of the pram, things calmed down enough for Hun Sen to visit Thailand for an ASEAN meeting and by mid-2010 it seemed as though the Thaksin element in Thai/Cambodia relations was no longer a defining factor.

Yet the Preah Vihear issue remains, as does the need for both governments to have an issue around which they can raise nationalistic sentiment and support. While Cambodia under Hun Sen's rule has made huge advances in recent years, and the Khmer Rouge trials clearly point to the nation finally coming to terms with itself, there is still a strong warrior streak running the Cambodian leader's character – maintaining peaceful relations with its turbulent and troublesome neighbour is key to Cambodia's ongoing development.

People and society

Before 1975, Cambodia had a population of about 7.2 million; within four years this had dropped to around six million (some were the victims of genocide, others became refugees). The population topped 10 million in 1995 and a UN estimate from 2005 suggested that the figure stood at around 14.8 million. The Khmers are the dominant group (about 85% of the total population) but there are significant Chinese and Vietnamese minorities as well as a small percentage of tribal groups – most of whom suffered badly during the Pol Pot years.

Khmers

The Khmers are believed to have lived in the region from about the second century AD but there is some argument as to where they migrated from. Some anthropologists suggest that they are a fusion of Mongul and Melanesian elements. They have been mainly influenced over the centuries by the powerful Indian and Javanese kingdoms.

Khmer Loeu

The Khmer Loeu, or Upland Khmer (divided into the Saoch, Pear, Brao and Kui), are one of the main tribal groups and live in the forested mountain zones, mainly in the northeast. The Saoch live in the Elephant Mountains to the southwest; the Pear occupy the Cardamom Mountains to the west; while the Brao are settled along the Lao border to the northeast. Traditionally the Khmer Loeu were semi-nomadic and practised slash and burn agriculture. Like many tribal groups in Southeast Asia they were also mainly animist. In recent years, however, increasing numbers have turned to settled agriculture and adopted many of the customs of the lowland Khmers.

Chinese

In the 18th and 19th centuries large numbers of ethnic Chinese migrated to Southeast Asia, where most became involved in commerce. Until the Khmer Rouge take-over in 1975, the Chinese played a central role in the economy, controlling trade, banking and transport. As in neighbouring Thailand, they assimilated to a greater degree than in other parts of Southeast Asia. In recent decades, most of Cambodia's urban and governing élite has had at least some Chinese blood – Lon Nol, for example had a Chinese grandparent. The Chinese started leaving the country when civil war broke out in 1970 – and many of those who did not get out before 1975 were killed during the Pol Pot years. The few who survived the Khmer Rouge era emigrated during the first months of the pro-Vietnam PRK rule. Officially, the Chinese population of Cambodia today constitutes around 1% of the total.

Vietnamese

The southern part of Cambodia, particularly along the Mekong, has always had many inhabitants of Vietnamese descent, as well as the area around Phnom Penh. The Vietnamese live very separate lives to the Cambodians due to centuries of mistrust and animosity between the two groups. They are known by the Khmers as 'youn', a derogatory term meaning 'people from the north' and it is hard to find other Cambodians who have anything positive to say about Vietnamese settlers in the country. One human rights official was quoted as saying "Given a choice, a lot of people in this country would expel every single Vietnamese". And if the nationalistic fervour of Sam Rainsy ever comes to fruition, this could potentially happen. This dislike of the Vietnamese stems partly from historical fears – Vietnam absorbed large areas of the former Cambodian Empire in the 18th and 19th centuries; partly from Vietnam's role in Cambodia between 1979 and 1989; and partly from the sheer size of Vietnam – some 70 million inhabitants – when set against Cambodia's population of 10 million. As a result, anti-Vietnamese sentiment is mainstream politics in the country. Inventing fanciful stories about Vietnamese commandos infiltrating the country, or Vietnamese control of the economy, is never likely to do harm to a budding populist politician. Many Vietnamese (and Cham) live in floating villages due to the foreign ownership laws relating to property.

Cham-Malays

There are about 200,000 Cham-Malays, descended from the Cham of the royal kingdom of Champa based in present-day central Vietnam. They now constitute the single largest ethnic minority in the country. In the 15th century the Vietnamese moving south drove many of the Cham living in the lower Mekong area into Cambodia. They now mainly live along the Mekong, north of Phnom Penh. The Chams were badly persecuted during the Pol Pot years and their population more than halved. They are Muslim and their spiritual centre is Chur-Changvra near Phnom Penh. They adopted their faith and script from Malays who settled in Kampot and interior regions on the invitation of the Muslim Khmer King Chan in 1642, after he had converted to Islam. The Cham are traditionally cattle traders, silk weavers and butchers – Theravada Buddhism forbids the Khmer to slaughter animals. Their batik sarongs are very similar to those found in Malaysia.

Although the Cham are now free to pursue their faith largely free from persecution, they still suffer from the stigma of being viewed, by many Cambodians, as second-class citizens. Strangely perhaps, there is a close affinity between Christians and Muslims in Cambodia – in the face of an overwhelmingly dominant Buddhist faith.

Other groups

There are also a small number of Shans, Thai and Lao, most who live near Battambang, the descendants of miners and jewellers who came to work the ruby mines of Pailin during the French colonial era.

Language and literature

The Khmer language

The Khmer language belongs to the Mon-Khmer family, enriched by the Indian Pali and Sanskrit languages and peppered with Thai and French influences. The use of Sanskrit in royal texts became more widespread after the introduction of Mahayana Buddhism in the 12th century (although there are inscriptions dating from the sixth century) and the Pali language spread into Cambodia via Siam with Theravada Buddhism. Khmer is related to languages spoken by hill tribe people of Laos, Vietnam and even Malaysia – but is very different to Thai or Lao. Khmer has no tones, no tenses, and has words attached to the masculine or feminine genders. But Khmer does have 23 vowel-sounds and 33 consonants; it is also a very specific language – for instance, there are 100 different words for types of rice. The Khmer language is written from left to right often with no separation between words.

French was widely spoken by the intelligentsia before 1975 and is still spoken by a few elderly Cambodians. But these days most people seem to want to learn English, and there are informal pavement English schools setting up on Phnom Penh's streets. This has led to some Franco-Anglophone friction. Understandably, the French government – one of Cambodia's largest aid donors – would like to see the French language sustained, perhaps even developed. In 1995 this led to the strange spectacle of language riots on the campus of Phnom Penh's Cambodian University of Technology as students burnt French text books in protest at being forced to learn a language which, they said, 'got them nowhere'.

Religion

The god-kings of Angkor

Until the 14th century Buddhism and Hinduism existed side-by-side in Kambuja. In the pre-Angkor era, the Hindu gods Siva and Vishnu were worshipped as a single deity, Harihara. The statue of Harihara from Phnom Da (eighth century) is divided in half: the 'stern' right half is Siva (with wild curly hair) and the 'sublime' left half, Vishnu (who wears a mitre). The first city at Angkor, built by Jayavarman II in the early ninth century, was called Hariharalaya after this god. Early Angkor kings promoted various Hindu sects, mainly dedicated to Siva and Vishnu. During the Angkor period, Siva was the most favoured deity but by the 12th century Vishnu replaced him. Jayavarman VII introduced Mahayana Buddhism as the official court religion at the end of the 12th century. The constant chopping, changing and refining of state religion helped sustain the power of the absolute monarch – each change ushered in a new style of rule and refinements and historians believe refinements and changes of religion were deliberately imported to consolidate the power of the kings.

One reason the Khmer Empire was so powerful was its basis on the Hindu concept of the god-king or devaraja. Jayavarman II (802-850) crowned himself as a reincarnation of Siva and erected a Siva lingam (a phallic monument to the god) at Phnom Kulen, the source of power for the Khmer Dynasty. Siva-worship was not originally introduced by Jayavarman II, however – it had been previously practised in the old kingdom of Funan.

The investiture of power was always performed by a Brahmin priest who also bestowed divinity on the king as a gift from Siva. This ceremony became an essential rite of kingship which was observed continuously into the 20th century. The king's spirit was said to reside in the lingam, which was enshrined in the centre of a monumental religious complex, representing the spiritual axis of the kingdom. Here the divinely ordained king communicated with the gods. Succeeding monarchs followed Jayavarman II's example and continued to install themselves as god-kings, evoking the loyalty of their subjects.

Very few of the statues of Vishnu and Siva and other gods left by the Khmer Empire were traditional representations of the deities. The great majority of the images were portraits of kings and princes and high dignitaries, each represented as the god into whom they would be absorbed at the end of their earthly existence.

The installation of the devaraja cult by Jayavarman II took place on the summit of Phnom Kulen. Under subsequent kings, it was transferred, in turn, to Bakong, Phnom Bakheng, Koh Ker and Phimeanakas. At the end of the 11th century, the Baphuon was constructed to house the golden lingam. The tradition of the god-king cult was so deeply rooted in the court that even Theravada Buddhism introduced in the 14th century bowed to its influence. Following the adoption of Mahayana Buddhism in the second half of the 12th century, the god-king left his lingam to enter the statue of the Buddha. Jayavarman VII built the Bayon to shelter the statue of the Buddha-king in the centre of the city of Angkor.

Temple-mountains were built as microcosms of the universe, with Mount Meru, the home of the gods, at the centre, surrounded by oceans (followed most perfectly at Angkor Wat, see page 296). This concept was not invented by the Khmers but was part of an inherited tradition from India. At the summit of the cosmic mountain, at the centre of the city, the king, embodied by his own sacred image, entered into contact with the world of gods. Each temple was the personal temple of an individual king, erected by him during his life. When, after his death, his ashes or remains were deposited there (to animate the statue and give the cult a living image), the temple became his mausoleum. His successor always built another sanctuary to house the image of the god-king. During the Angkor period the Khmers did not seem to question this system. It ordered their lives, regulating everything from agriculture to birth and death rites. But the temples were not the products of a popular faith, like Christian cathedrals – they were strictly the domain of royalty and high priests and were reserved for the worship of kings and members of the entourage deified in the form of one of the Hindu or Buddhist gods.

Theravada Buddhism

Despite the powerful devaraja cult, most Khmers also practised an amalgam of ancestor worship and animism. As Theravada Buddhism swept through Southeast Asia (well after the adoption of Mahayana Buddhism), propagated by missionary monks, its message of simplicity, austerity and humility began to undermine the cult of the god-king. As a popular religion, it had great attractions for a population which for so many centuries had been denied access to the élitist and extravagant devaraja cult. By the 15th century Theravada Buddhism was the dominant religion in Cambodia.

Buddhism shares the belief, in common with Hinduism, in rebirth. A person goes through countless lives and the experience of one life is conditioned by the acts in a previous one. This is the Law of Karma (act or deed, from Pali kamma), the law of cause and effect. For most people, nirvana is a distant goal, and they merely aim to accumulate merit by living good lives and performing good deeds such as giving alms to monks.

In this way the layman embarks on the Path to Heaven. It is also common for a layman to become ordained, at some point in his life (usually as a young man), for a three month period during the Buddhist Rains Retreat.

Monks should endeavour to lead stringently ascetic lives. They must refrain from murder, theft, sexual intercourse, untruths, eating after noon, alcohol, entertainment, ornament, comfortable beds and wealth. They are allowed to own only a begging bowl, three pieces of clothing, a razor, needle, belt and water filter. They can only eat food that they have received through begging. Anyone who is male, over 20, and not a criminal can become a monk.

The 'Way of the Elders', is believed to be closest to Buddhism as it originally developed in India. It is often referred to by the term 'Hinayana' (Lesser Vehicle), a disparaging name foisted onto Theravadans by Mahayanists. This form of Buddhism is the dominant contemporary religion in the mainland Southeast Asian countries of Thailand, Cambodia, Laos and Burma.

In Theravadan Buddhism, the historic Buddha, Sakyamuni, is revered above all else and most images of the Buddha are of Sakyamuni. Importantly, and unlike Mahayana Buddhism, the Buddha image is only meant to serve as a meditation aid. In theory, it does not embody supernatural powers, and it is not supposed to be worshipped. But the popular need for objects of veneration has meant that most images are worshipped. Pilgrims bring flowers and incense, and prostrate themselves in front of the image. This is a Mahayanist influence which has been embraced by Theravadans.

Buddhism in Cambodia

The Cambodian Buddhist clergy divide into two groups: the Mahanikay and Thommayuth (or Dhammayuttikanikay) orders. The latter was not introduced from Thailand until 1864, and was a reformist order with strong royal patronage. Theravada Buddhism remained the dominant and unchallenged faith until 1975.

It was a demonstration by Buddhist monks in Phnom that which first kindled Cambodian nationalism in the wake of the Second World War. According to historians, one of the reasons for this was the intensifying of the relationship between the king and the people, due to the founding of the Buddhist Institute in Phnom Penh in 1930. The Institute was under the joint patronage of the kings of Laos and Cambodia as well as the French. It began printing and disseminating Buddhist texts – in Pali and Khmer. Historian David P Chandler wrote: "As the Institute's reputation grew, enhanced by frequent conferences, it became a rallying point for an emerging intelligentsia." The institute's librarian founded a Khmer-language newspaper (*Nagaravatta* – or 'Angkor Wat') in 1936, which played a critical role in articulating and spreading the nationalist message.

Before 1975 and the arrival of the Khmer Rouge, there were 3000 monasteries and 64,000 monks (*bonzes*) – many of these were young men who had become ordained to escape conscription – in Cambodia and rural life was centred around the wat (Buddhist monastery). Under Pol Pot, all monks were 'defrocked' and, according to some sources, as many as 62,000 were executed or died in the ricefields. Monasteries were torn down or converted to other uses, Pali – the language of Theravada Buddhism – was banned, and former monks were forced to marry. Ironically, Saloth Sar (Pol Pot) himself spent some time as a novice when he was a child. Buddhism was revived in 1979 with the ordination of monks by a visiting delegation of Buddhists from Vietnam; at the same time, many of the wats – which were defiled by the Khmer Rouge – were restored and reconsecrated. The two orders of Theravada Buddhism – the Thommayuth (aristocratic) and Mahanikay (common)

– previously practised in Cambodia have now merged. The Hun Sen government softened the position on Buddhism to the degree that it was reintroduced as the national religion in 1989 and young men were allowed to be ordained (previously restricted to men over 45 that were no longer able to serve in the army).

Today 90% of Cambodian citizens are Buddhist. In 2004, the country had almost 59,500 monks spread across the country's 3980 wats. Cambodian Buddhism is an easy-going faith and tolerates ancestor and territorial spirit worship, which is widely practised. The grounds usually consist of a *vihara* (Buddhist temple), Sala Thoama *saphea* (the hall where Dharma is taught) and *kods* (the quarters where the monks live). Traditionally, the vihara and the Buddha statues contained within them will face east in order to express gratitude to Lord Buddha for enlightenment and guide others toward the path of enlightenment. There are often small rustic altars to the guardian spirits (*neak ta*) in the corner of pagodas. Cambodians often wear *katha* – or charms – which are believed to control external magical forces. Most important ceremonies – weddings, funerals, coming of age – have both Buddhist and animist elements. Wats play an important role in education and it is fairly common to find schools built inside or beside wats.

Other religions
There are around 60,000 Roman Catholics in Cambodia, mainly Vietnamese, and about 2000 Protestants. Islam, of the Sunni sect, is practised by many of the 200,000 (some commentators would say 500,000) Cham. During the Khmer Rouge period it was reported that Cham were forced to eat pork while most Cham mosques were destroyed, and only now are they being slowly rebuilt. A new International Mosque in Phnom Penh, built with Saudi money, was opened in 1994. Almost all the Chinese in Cambodia are Taoist/Confucianist.

Land and environment

Geography
Cambodia is all that remains of the once mighty Khmer Empire. Covering a land area of 181,035 sq km – about the size of England and Wales combined – the country is squeezed in between Thailand to the west, Vietnam to the east and Laos to the north. Cambodia holds many features of international conservation significance. The country has one of the highest proportions of land as natural habitat (forest and wetlands) in the world, and one of the least disturbed coastlines in continental Asia. The coastline stretches along the Gulf of Thailand for 435 km, supports 64 islands and extensive mangroves and coral reefs. The **Mekong** is as central to life in Cambodia as the Nile is to life in Egypt. The river runs through Cambodia for about 500 km, bisecting the east lowlands, north to south. It is navigable by cargo ships from the delta in Vietnam, right up to Phnom Penh and beyond. Near the centre of the country is the **Tonlé Sap** – the 'Great Lake' – the largest freshwater lake in Southeast Asia. It is connected to the Mekong via the short channel-like Tonlé Sap River. The Tonlé Sap basin includes all or part of eight of Cambodia's 24 provinces and covers 80,000 sq km (44% of Cambodia's total area) and is estimated to be home to 3.6 million people, one-third of Cambodia's total population. When the Mekong floods between June and October – sometimes these floods can be devastating, as they were in 1991 – the Tonlé Sap River reverses its flow and the floodwaters fill the Great Lake, which doubles in size, covering the surrounding countryside.

North of Phnom Penh, the Mekong is known as the Upper Mekong – or just the Mekong; downriver from the capital it divides into the Lower Mekong and the Bassac rivers. These two tributaries then swing to the southeast across the fertile alluvial plain, towards the sprawling delta and the sea. The broad valley of the Mekong is a centuries-old trade route and its fertile central flood-plain is densely populated. The alluvial soils are irrigated but have an even greater potential for agricultural production than is presently being realized. Throughout most of its course in Cambodia the river averages more than 1.6 km in width. There are viscous rapids at Kratie, northeast of Phnom Penh, and a succession of dramatic waterfalls – Li Phi and Khong Phapheng Falls – on the border with Laos.

The **central lowlands** are surrounded by savannah; in south Cambodia these plains run all the way to the Vietnamese border. But to the north, east and west, Cambodia is enclosed by mountain chains: the Cardamom Mountains and Elephant Range to the west and southwest, while the sandstone escarpment of the Dangrek Range forms a natural border with Thailand. The **Cardamom Mountains** (named after the spice) run in a gentle curve from just south of Battambang towards Phnom Penh. Phnom Aoral, in the Cardamoms, is Cambodia's highest peak at 1813 m and in 2004 Global Witness detected a large amount of illegal logging in the area. The **Elephant Mountains** run along the south coastline. All these mountains are densely forested and sparsely inhabited, making them perfect operational bases for Cambodia's rebel guerrilla factions, who fought the Phnom Penh government throughout the 1980s. On the south coast around Kompong Som is a lowland area cut off from the rest of the country by mountains. Because the Mekong was a major thoroughfare, the **coastal region** never developed into a centre of trade until a road was built with American aid from Kompong Som to Phnom Penh in the 1960s.

Climate

The monsoons determine rainfall and temperature patterns in Cambodia. The southwest monsoon, from May to October, brings heavy rain throughout the country. This period accounts for between 75% and 80% of the total annual rainfall. The northeast monsoon blows from October to April and ushers in the dry season. In the mountain areas the temperature is markedly cooler and the dry season only lasts three months. Between the heat and rains there are transitional periods and the best time to visit the country is between November and January, before it gets too hot. Rainfall varies considerably from region to region. The Cardamom Mountains are the wettest. The mean temperature for Cambodia is 27.5°C. It is cooler – around 24°C – from November to January and hotter – around 32°C – between February and April. Humidity is generally high.

Flora and fauna

The central plains are a predominantly agricultural area and are sparsely wooded but most of the rest of Cambodia – until recently – was still forested. In 1970, 73% of Cambodia's land area was thought to be forested but by 1995 the figure was less than 40%, and a paper published at the end of 1998 put the area at 30%. So the trend is rapidly down. The reasons for the alarming decline in Cambodia's forests are pretty clear – illegal logging (see below). In the southwest, around the Cardamom and Elephant Mountains, there are still large tracts of primary forest where teak predominates. There are also tracts of virgin rainforest in the west and the northeast. At higher elevations in these mountains there are areas of pine forest and in the north and east highlands, temperate forest.

Cambodia has a wide variety of fauna and, before war broke out in the 1970s, was on the international game-hunters' circuit; there were tigers (now an endangered species), buffalo, elephants, wild oxen, majestic birds, clouded leopards (also endangered) and bears, including Malaysian sun bears. Today, there are 630 types of protected wildlife, including 122 mammal species, 537 bird species, 114 are from the rodent family, 40 are aquatic animals and 300 are insects and butterflies.

Even after all the fighting, game is still said to be abundant in forested areas, particularly in north-eastern provinces of Mondulkiri and Ratanakiri. Smaller animals include monkeys, squirrels, tree rats and shrews, flying foxes and numerous species of reptile, including several varieties of poisonous snake, the most common being Russell's viper, the banded krait, cobra and king cobra. Even around Phnom Penh one can see herons, cranes, grouse, pheasant, wild duck, pelicans, cormorants and egrets. The kouprey (meaning 'jungle cow') is Cambodia's most famous animal and a symbol of the Worldwide Fund for Nature. A wild ox, it was first identified in 1939 but is now virtually extinct worldwide. In 1963, King Sihanouk declared the animal Cambodia's national animal. Small numbers are thought to inhabit the more remote areas of the country, although some experts fear that the last specimens were either killed by guerrillas for meat or are being fatally maimed after treading on anti-personnel mines laid by the Khmer Rouge. An effort to capture and breed the kouprey is underway in Vietnam.

The Tonlé Sap area is particularly rich in fish-eating waterfowl and marine life. It supports possibly the largest inland fishing industry in the world. The lake is the lifeline for about 40% of the Cambodian population and provides almost 60% of the country's protein. In 1997 the government applied to UNESCO seeking the nomination of the great lake as a Biosphere Reserve, covering 300,000 ha including both the lake and its surrounding shores. Around 1.36 million Khmers are estimated to be wholly dependent on inland waterways for transport.

The lower reaches of the Mekong, marking the border between Cambodia and Laos, is also the last place in Indochina where the rare Irrawaddy dolphin (*Orcaella brevirostris*) is to be found. Unfortunately, fishermen in the area took to fishing using dynamite and this threatens the survival of the mammal. Countless numbers were also killed under the Khmer Rouge regime. It was also once found in Thailand's Chao Phraya River, but pollution put paid to that population years ago.

The poverty of most of Cambodia's population has made the trade in exotic fauna an attractive proposition. By 1997 the trade in wildlife had become 'rampant', according to the environmental NGO Global Witness. A case in point is the plight of the Malayan sun bear (*Helarctos malayanus*), which has been protected in Cambodia since 1992. But its paws and gall bladder are treasured by many Chinese and bear bile is said to command a price of US$100 per gramme in China due to its perceived medicinal properties. The animals are captured and caged and the bile siphoned off through a steel tube inserted into the gall bladder. There is also documentary footage of animals having their paws amputated while still alive. Once again, the failure to protect the sun bear, and many other wild animals, is not due to an absence of environmental legislation but due a lack of commitment to its implementation. Giant ibis and black-necked storks are sold for US$400-500 a pair, rewards are put out for black cranes, turtles and pythons are sold to Chinese and Korean restaurants, and the eggs and chicks of water birds are collected for sale in markets. Cambodia's fauna is being caught, sold and slaughtered on a truly grand scale.

Timber tragedy

In 1995 the Cambodian government, to much fanfare, introduced a new environment law. This was heralded as the first step in the sustainable exploitation of Cambodia's forests and other natural resources. The introduction of the law was accompanied by other legislation, including a new Environmental Impact Assessment Law. At the end of 1996 the government seemed to go one step further when they outlawed the export of whole logs. But even in 1995 experts were sceptical about the ability of the Cambodian government to deliver on its environmental promises. The lack of transparency in many of the regulations, and the ease with which companies and individuals with political and economic power could – and still can – circumvent those regulations, makes environmental protection difficult to achieve in any systematic sense.

This scepticism was borne out later, in 1998, when the UK-based environmental group Global Witness claimed that, unless the rate of logging was reduced substantially, Cambodia was "heading toward deforestation of all saleable timber within three to five years". Patrick Alley, who has done much to highlight the plight of Cambodia's wild areas, claimed at a press conference that "the logging situation is out of control". Although Cambodia still has forests, it is believed 40-50% of the country's forests have been logged.

With foreign donors becoming increasingly frustrated at the Cambodian government's lack of commitment to protecting the environment, Prime Minister Hun Sen ordered a crack-down on illegal loggers in March 1999. The fact that some donors were moving towards making further aid dispersal contingent on forestry reform no doubt concentrated the mind of the Prime Minister. The difficulty for one of the poorest countries in the world is that forestry is one of Cambodia's major industries, accounting for 43% of foreign trade and contributing 15% of GDP in 1997. But even more crucial than the fact that forestry is important to the nation is that fact that timber is valuable to individuals.

The problem is that apparently just about everyone from senior government ministers through to senior army officers and foreign governments or their representatives are involved in illegal logging activities. As Ly Thuch, Under-Secretary for State for the Environment, told a meeting at the Foreign Correspondents Club in Phnom Penh, "the main destroyers of the environment are the Khmer Rouge and the rich and powerful". It is doubtful that even Cambodia's aid donors can make a difference. In mid-1996 international aid donors had become so worried about the failure of the Cambodian government to control logging that the IMF suspended a US$20 million budget-support payment. But Cambodia's two prime ministers continued to sign logging contracts – without cabinet discussion and in contravention of their own environmental laws.

In early 2000, Hun Sen vouched: "If I cannot put an end to the illegal cutting of trees, I will resign from my position of prime minister in the first quarter of 2001." True to his word? No. Needless to say the Cambodian government was still entering into illegal logging concessions in 2004-2005, breaking an international moratorium on logging that was due to expire in late 2005. Furthermore, those critical of the government's illegal activities have been threatened and hassled. In April 2002, a senior official with the independent forestry monitor Global Witness was beaten near her office. The next day she was sent an email instructing her to quit. The forestry monitor, Global Witness, was later sacked by Hun Sen.

There are major ecological side effects of deforestation, particularly in a country where 80% of the population rely on subsistence agriculture. The ongoing rice crop failure and siltation of the waterways, effecting the valuable fisheries can largely be contributed to the rampant deforestation.

In an interview published in November 1996, William Shawcross suggested that illegal logging was "perhaps the most serious crisis of corruption in the regime". Nothing much has changed in the intervening years.

National parks

Cambodia was the first country in Southeast Asia to establish protected areas, with the forests surrounding the Angkor temples declared a national park in 1925. By 1969, six wildlife sanctuaries had been established covering 2.2 million hectares or 12% of the country for the protection of wildlife, in particular large mammals. Towards the end of 1993, King Sihanouk signed a decree to create 23 protected areas, now covering over 21% of the country. Cambodia has one of the highest percentages of national territory within protected areas in the world and had the goal to increase that area to 25% by the end of 2005.

It may be rather ironic, but the dislocations caused by Cambodia's long-running civil war probably helped to protect the environment, rather than destroy it. Although larger animals like the kouprey may have suffered from the profusion of land mines that dot the countryside, other animals have benefited from the lack of development. Unlike Thailand and Vietnam, forest has not been cleared for agriculture and many regions became 'no-go' areas to all except for the foolhardy and the well-armed. This created conditions in which wildlife could survive largely undisturbed by the forces of 'development'. Now wildlife experts and environmentalists are arguing that Cambodia has a unique asset that should be preserved at all costs – and not just because it might be the morally 'right' thing to do. In addition, the growth in eco-tourism worldwide could create a considerable money-spinner for the country.

Books

Novels

Cixous, Helene *The Terrible but Unfinished Story of Norodom Sihanouk, King of Cambodia*. (University of Nebraska Press, 1994.) Avant-garde 20th-century literature associated with recent political history.

Dith Pran *Children of Cambodia's Killing Fields*. (Yale University Press, 1998.) Eyewitness accounts of the Khmer Rouge regime by Cambodian survivors.

Documentation Centre of Cambodia *The Khmer Rouge – From Victory to Destruction*. The compilation of reports, orders and chronological details helps to give an insight into how the Khmer Rouge operated during this period.

Drabble, Margaret *The Gates of Ivory*. (London: Penguin, 1992.) The third part of a trilogy which deals with Cambodia during the period of the civil war while the Vietnamese 'occupied' Phnom Penh and the Khmer Rouge controlled much of the countryside.

Ho, Minfong *Brother Rabbit: A Cambodian Tale*. (Lothrop, Lee and Shepard Books, 1997.) Traditional legend translated into English along with a discussion on the place of folklore in Cambodia, relating themes to Cambodian history.

Koch, Christopher *Highways to War*. (Minerva, 1996.) New novel about wartime Cambodia and Vietnam – part thriller, part mystery, part heroic epic by the author of *The Year of Living Dangerously*.

Ngor, Haing S *Surviving the Killing Fields*. One of the best, first-hand accounts of this terrible period. Recommended.

Ryan, Paul Ryder *Khmer Rouge End Game*. (Munewata Press, 1999.) Work of 'faction' relating the kidnapping of six foreigners by the one-legged guerrilla leader Ta Mok.

History

Affonco, Denise *To the End of Hell: One Woman's Struggle to Survive Cambodia's Khmer Rouge.* (Reportage Press, 2007.) A bestseller in France, this is the first English translation of the French-born author's time living with her Communist husband in Khmer Rouge-ruled-Cambodia.

Bizot, Francois *The Gate.* (Vintage Press, 2004.) This is the author's true story of his capture by the Khmer Rouge guerrilla force in 1971. An archaeologist studying the Angkor temples, Bizot was held and interrogated by Comrade Duch, the notorious commandant of Tuol Sleng who is now awaiting trial at the UN Cambodia Tribunal. Bizot charts his relationship with Duch, becoming the only Westerner to be released alive by the Khmer Rouge.

Chandler, David P *Brother Number One: a political biography of Pol Pot.* (Colorado: Westview Press, 1992.) Chandler is considered one of the most authoritative academics in the field of Cambodian history.

Chanda, Nayan *Brother Enemy: the war after the war.* (New York: Macmillan, 1986.) Exhaustive and engrossing account of 'the third Indochina war' puts Cambodian conflict into regional perspective: vivid journalistic style.

Chou Ta-kuan *The Customs of Cambodia.* (Bangkok: Siam Society, 1993.) Written in 1296-1297 by Chou Ta-kuan, a Chinese emissary to the kingdom of Angkor. It is a potted, first hand account of life and livelihoods in the 13th century. Widely available in Bangkok.

May, Someth *Cambodian Witness.* (London: Faber and Faber, 1986.) A chilling personal account of the Pol Pot period. Of Someth May's family of 14 only four survived the terrible years of the Khmer Rouge.

Osborne, Milton *Sihanouk.* (Allen and Unwin, 1996.) A biography of the controversial Asian leader chronicling his evolution from a dilettante king to rigorous and ruthless politician.

Shawcross, William *Sideshow: Kissinger, Nixon and the destruction of Cambodia.* (London: Chatto & Windus, 1979, revised 1986.) Excellent, balanced and very readable investigative work on American involvement in the Cambodian 'sideshow'; it runs through to cover the Pol Pot period.

Shawcross, William *Cambodia's New Deal* (1994.) A book by Shawcross examining the UN-brokered peace deal and the country's progress since the elections.

Swain, Jon *River of Time.* (London: Minerva, 1995.) Jon Swain was a journalist in Indochina during the Vietnam War and then stayed on to be one of the few foreigners to witness the fall of Phnom Penh to the Khmer Rouge. The chapters on Cambodia are excellent and Swain's account of Indochina during this traumatic period is enthralling.

Szymusiak, Moldya *The stones cry out: a Cambodian childhood.* (London: Jonathan Cape, 1986.) An account of the recent tragedy of Cambodia from a personal perspective.

Ung, Loung *First They Killed My Father: A Daughter Of Cambodia Remembers.* (Harper Perennial, 2001.) The devastatingly sad and true story of what Loung and her family experienced during the Khmer Rouge period.

General

Basan, Ghillie *The Food and Cooking of Cambodia: Over 60 Authentic Classic Recipes from an Undiscovered Cuisine.* (Southwater, 2007.) A Frenchman, Basan is one of the leading experts on Khmer cuisine. This was a bestseller in the author's home country.

Gilboa, Amit *Off the rails in Phnom Penh: into the Dark Heart of Guns, Girls and Ganja.* (1997) Slightly breathless account of some of Phnom Penh's well known vices.

Gray, Spalding *Swimming to Cambodia* (Theatre Communications Group, 2005.) A re-issue of Gray's cult classic where he charts his involvement in the Oscar-winning movie, *The Killing Fields*.

Jacob, Judith M. *The Traditional Literature of Cambodia: A Preliminary Guide*. (OUP, 1996.) Comprehensive survey of ancient Cambodian writing.

Livingston, Carol *Gecko Tails*. (Orion Paperbacks, 1997.) A humorous chronicle of the new wave of tourism that followed the demise of the Khmer Rouge.

Oeur, U. Sam *Sacred Vows*. (Coffee House Press, 1998.) Collection of poems recalling the horror of the author and his family's spell in six different concentration camps.

Page, Tim *Derailed in Uncle Ho's Victory Garden*. (Scribner Paperback, 1999.) Page's odyssey, 20 years after the liberation of Vietnam, through the land that dominated his life as a wartime photographer.

Poole, Colin (Author) and **Briggs, Eleanor** (Photographer) *Tonlé Sap: The Heart of Cambodia's Natural Heritage*. (River Books, 2005.) A stunning collection of photos that charts the lives of people living on the incredible Tonlé Sap river and lake.

Venn, Savat and Downie, Sue *Down Highway One: Journeys Through Vietnam and Cambodia*. (Allen and Unwin, 1993.) Highway One is one of the longest and most historic roads in Asia. This recounts the author's travels there.

Travel, geography and guides

Hoskins, John *The Mekong*. (Bangkok: Post Publishing, 1991.) A large-format coffee table book with good photographs and a modest text. Widely available in Bangkok.

Jacobson, Matt *Adventure Cambodia*. (Silkworm Books, 2005, 2nd edition.) A good guide for people interested in motorcycling through Cambodia.

Jensen, Carsten and Haveland, Barbara *I Have Seen the World Begin*. (Harvill Press, 2000.) Collection of travel writings with insights into local households, lives and personal points of view.

Lewis, Norman *A Dragon Apparent: travels in Indochina*. (London: Jonathan Cape, 1951.) Possibly Norman Lewis' best known travel book. Witty and perceptive, about a fifth is based on his travels in Cambodia. Gives a good feel of Cambodia 'before the fall'.

Art and architecture

le Bonheur, Albert *Of Gods, Kings, and Men: Bas-reliefs of Angkor Wat and Bayon*. (Serindia Publications, 1995.)

Dumarcay, Jaques and Smithies, Michael *Cultural Sites of Burma, Thailand and Cambodia*. (OUP SE Asia, 1996.) An investigation of the most important historic sites in these countries.

Dumarcay, Jaques and Smithies, Michael *The Site of Angkor*. (OUP SE Asia, 1998.) An introduction to this amazing complex's history and construction.

Giteau, Madeleine and **Gueret, Danielle** and **Renaut, Thomas** and **Keo, Pich** *L'Art Khmer/Khmer Art*. (ASA Editions, 1998.) A representation of more than a millennium of Cambodian art.

Ibbitson Jessup, Helen *Sculpture of Angkor and Ancient Cambodia: Millennium of Glory*. (Thames and Hudson, 1997.) 1000- year artistic legacy of Cambodia displayed in an extensively illustrated volume.

Mannikka, Eleanor *Angkor Wat: Time, Space and Kingship*. (University of Hawaii Press, 1996.) An attempt to understand the temple in terms of the measurement systems used by its original builders and uncovering a sophisticated system of philosophical and religious principles within them.

Roveda, Vittorio *Khmer Mythology*. (Thames and Hudson, 1997.) The thousands of temples and shrines erected by the Khmer people were carved with stone reliefs and this volume studies these..

Werly, Richard, Renaut, Thomas and **Lacouture, Jean** *Eternal Phnom Penh*. (ASA Editions, 1998.) Photographs and descriptions of Phnom Penh of today.

Economics, politics, society and development
Brady, Christopher *United States Foreign Policy towards Cambodia, 1977-1992*. (Macmillan Press Ltd, 1999.) A study of US foreign policy that delves into decision-making theory and foreign-policy analysis. Widely considered one of the best accounts of this historical period. Recommended.
Curtis, Grant *Cambodia Reborn? The transition to Democracy and Development*. (Brookings Institution Press, 1998.) This book examines Cambodia's uneasy renaissance from years of conflict, isolation and authoritarian rule following the UN-

Zephir, Thierry *Khmer*. (Thames and Hudson, 1998.) The Khmer Empire's art and architecture, its influences, rise and fall explained.

sponsored elections of 1993.
Findlay, Trevor *Cambodia*. (Macmillan Press, 1997.) This is an account and analysis of the UN peacekeeping operation mounted in Cambodia between 1991 and 1993.
Heininger, Janet E *Peacekeeping in Transition: The United Nations in Cambodia*. (Brookings Institution Press, 1994.) This book investigates the UN Transitional Administration in Cambodia's experiences in their entirety arguing that they can make future UN peace-keeping efforts more effective.

Contents

Border crossings

Laos-Thailand, *page 381*
Laos-Vietnam, *pages 408, 421, 433, 441*
Laos-Cambodia, *page 457*

At a glance

○ **Getting around** Major towns have bus services. *Songthaews* and trucks cover remote areas. Domestic flights available. Riverboats ply the Mekong in the north.

◐ **Time required** 1-4 weeks

☀ **Weather** Nov-Mar is best, although it can be cool at higher elevations. Temperatures peak in Apr. Rainy season May-Sep/Oct.

✕ **When not to go** Mar-May can be hot, humid and hazy. Outdoor activities such as hiking can be tricky in the wet season.

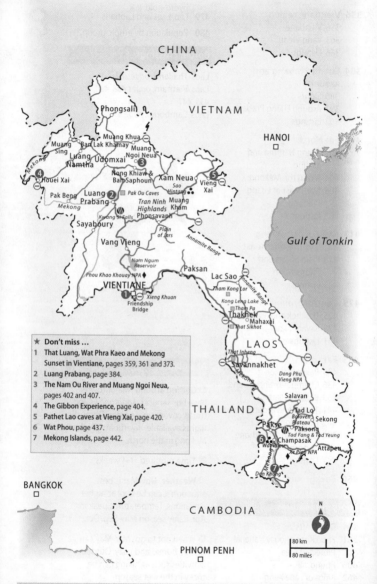

CHINA

VIETNAM

Phongsali

HANOI

Muang Khua
Muang Sing   Ban Lak Khamay
Muang   Muang
Namtha   Ngoi Neua
Udomxai
Houei Xai   Nong Khiaw &   Xam Neua   Vieng
Ban Saphoun   Sao   Xai
Pak Beng   Hintang
Luang   Pak Ou Caves   Muang
Prabang   Tran Ninh   Kham
Highlands
Kwang Si Falls   Phonsavanh
Sayaboury   Plain
of Jars   Annamite Range
Vang Vieng   Gulf of Tonkin

Nam Ngum
Reservoir   Paksan
Phou Khao Khouay NPA   Lac Sao
VIENTIANE   Tham Kong Lor
Xieng Khuan   Kong Leng Lake
Friendship   Tham Pa
Bridge   Thakhek
Mahaxei
That Sikhot

LAOS

That Inheng
Savannakhet

Dong Phu
Vieng NPA

Salavan

THAILAND   Tad Lo
Boloven
Plateau   Sekong
Pakse
Paksong
Champasak   Tad Fang & Tad Yeung
Wat Phou   Attapeu
Xe Pian NPA

Don Khong

★ Don't miss ...
1 That Luang, Wat Phra Kaeo and Mekong
   Sunset in Vientiane, pages 359, 361 and 373.
2 Luang Prabang, page 384.
3 The Nam Ou River and Muang Ngoi Neua,
   pages 402 and 407.
4 The Gibbon Experience, page 404.
5 Pathet Lao caves at Vieng Xai, page 420.
6 Wat Phou, page 437.
7 Mekong Islands, page 442.

BANGKOK

CAMBODIA

N

80 km
80 miles

PHNOM PENH

Introduction

Laos is fast becoming the darling of Southeast Asia, satisfying all the romantic images of perfumed frangipani trees, saffron-robed monks, rusty old bicycles and golden temples, all set among a rich tapestry of tropical river islands, ethnic minority villages, cascading waterfalls and vivid green rice paddies, and bound together by the mighty Mekong River, the country's lifeline. The vernacular architecture, which other countries have swept away in a maelstrom of redevelopment, survives in Laos. Simple wooden village homes, colonial-era brick-and-stucco shophouses and gently mouldering monasteries mark Laos out as different. Traditional customs are also firmly intact: incense wafts out of streetside wats, monks collect alms at daybreak and the clickety-clack of looms weaving richly coloured silk can be heard in most villages.

As compelling as these sights and sounds are, the lasting impression for most visitors is of the people and their overwhelming friendliness. Many believe the best thing about Laos is the constant chime of *sabaidee* ringing out from schoolchildren, monks and other passers by, extending an invitation to join their meal. This is a land that endures the terrible legacy of being the most bombed country per capita in the world, yet its people transform bomb casings into flower pots and bomb craters into fish ponds. Regardless of their history and their poverty, people here radiate a sunny, happy disposition.

Life is simple in Laos but the people share with their former French colonists an infectious joie de vivre that ensures that good food and great company are the pinnacle of enjoyment. If you're seeking a relaxed lifestyle and a warm welcome, you've come to the right place.

Vientiane region

Vientiane's appeal lies in its largely preserved fusion of Southeast Asian and French colonial culture. Baguettes, plunged coffee and Bordeaux wines coexist with spring rolls, pho soup and papaya salad. Colourful tuk-tuks scuttle along tree-lined boulevards, past old Buddhist temples and cosmopolitan cafés. Hammer-and-sickle flags hang at ten-pin bowling discos, locals carry sacks of devalued currency and green and pink chickens wander the streets. But, as in the rest of Laos, the best thing about Vientiane is its people. Take the opportunity to stroll around some of the outlying bans *(villages) and meet the wonderful characters who make this city what it is.*

Close to the city is Xieng Khuan, popularly known as the Buddha Park, a bizarre collection of statues and monuments, while, to the north, Vang Vieng, the adventure capital of Laos, attracts backpackers with a multitude of outdoor activities. » For listings, see pages 366-383.

Ins and outs → *Colour map 1, C3.*

Getting there

Air Most visitors arrive in Vientiane by air, the great bulk on one of the daily connections from Bangkok, with **Thai Air** (www.thaiair.com) or **Lao Airlines** (www.laoairlines.com), which also runs international flights from Thailand, Cambodia, Vietnam and China. **Vietnam Airlines** (www.vietnamairlines.com) runs flights from Hanoi and Ho Chi Minh City. **AirAsia** (www.airasia.com) flies from Kuala Lumpur. **Wattay International Airport** ① *T021-512012,* lies 6 km west of the town centre. Vientiane is the hub of Laos' domestic airline system and to travel from the north to the south or vice versa it is necessary to change planes here. Only taxis are allowed to pick up passengers at the airport, although tuk-tuks can drop off here. But tuk-tuks can be taken from the main road and sometimes lurk at the far side of the airport parking area, near the exit (40,000 kip to the centre).

A cheaper alternative from Thailand is to fly from Bangkok to **Udon Thani** on a budget airline such as NokAir (www.nokair.com) or AirAsia (www.airasia.com) and then continue by road to Vientiane via the Friendship Bridge, which lies just 25 km downstream from the capital (allow three hours). Shuttle buses from Udon Thani, ฿800, run between the bus station and Vientiane. to the border after every flight. There are several flights a day between Udon Thani and Bangkok.

Bus There are three public bus terminals in Vientiane. The **Southern bus station** (T021-740521) for destinations in the south of the country is 9 km north of the city centre on Route 13. Most international buses bound for Vietnam depart from here as well as buses to southern and eastern Laos. The station has a VIP room, restaurants, a few shops, mini-mart and there's a guesthouse nearby.

The **Northern bus station** (T021-261905) is on Route T2, about 3 km northwest of the centre before the airport, and serves destinations in northern Laos. Most tuk-tuks will take you there from the city for 10,000-20,000 kip; ask for *Bai Thay Song*. There are English-speaking staff at the help desk.

A third **bus station** (T021-216507) is across the road from the Morning Market, in front of Talaat Kudin, on the eastern edge of the city centre. This station serves destinations within Vientiane Province, buses to and from the Thai border and international buses to Nong Khai and Udon Thani in Thailand. It is also a good place to pick up a tuk-tuk » *See Transport, page 378.*

Getting around

Vientiane is small and manageable and is one of the most laid-back capital cities in the world. The local catch phrase '*bopenyang*' (no worries) has permeated through every sector of the city, so much so that even the mangy street dogs look completely chilled out. The core of the city is negotiable on foot and even outlying hotels and places of interest are accessible by bicycle. Cycling remains the most flexible way to tour the city. It can be debilitatingly hot at certain times of year but there are no great hills to struggle up. If cycling doesn't appeal, a combination of foot and tuk-tuk or small 110-125cc scooters take the effort out of sightseeing.

Vientiane can be rather confusing for the first-time visitor as there are few street signs and most streets have two names, pre- and post-revolutionary but, because Vientiane is so small and compact, it doesn't take long to get to grips with the layout. The names of major streets or *thanon* usually correspond to the nearest wat, while traffic lights, wats, monuments and large hotels serve as directional landmarks. When giving directions to a tuk-tuk it is better to use these landmarks, as street names leave them a little bewildered.

Tourist information

Lao National Tourism Authority ① *Lane Xang (towards Patuxai), T021-212251 for information, www.tourismlaos.org*, can provide information regarding ecotourism operators and trekking opportunities. The **Tourist Police** ① *0830-1200, 1300-1600*, are upstairs.

Background

Vientiane is an ancient city. There was probably a settlement here, on a bend on the left bank of the Mekong, in the 10th century but knowledge of the city before the 16th century is sketchy. From the chronicles, scholars do know that King Setthathirat decided to relocate his capital here in the early 1560s. It seems that it took him four years to build the city, constructing a defensive wall (hence 'Wiang', meaning a walled or fortified city), along with Wat Phra Kaeo and a much enlarged That Luang. Vieng Chan remained intact until 1827 when it was ransacked by the Siamese; this is why many of its wats are of recent construction.

The city was abandoned for decades and erased from the maps of the region. It was only conjured back into existence by the French, who commenced reconstruction at the end of the 19th century. They built rambling colonial villas and wide tree-lined boulevards, befitting their new administrative capital, Vientiane. At the height of American influence in the 1960s, it was renowned for its opium dens and sex shows.

For the moment, the city retains its unique innocence: DJs are officially outlawed (although this is not enforced); there is a 2330 curfew; a certain percentage of music played at restaurants and bars every day is supposed to be Lao (overcome by banging out the Lao tune quota at 0800 in the morning) and women are urged to wear the national dress, the *sinh*. However, to describe the Lao government as autocratic is unfairly negative. Vientiane's citizens are proud of their cultural heritage and are usually very supportive of the government's attempts to promote it. The government has tried, by and large, to maintain the national identity and protect its citizens from what it sees as harmful outside influences. This is already starting to change with the government reshuffle in 2006 came a gradual loosening of the cultural stranglehold.

Sights

Most of the interesting buildings in Vientiane are of religious significance. All tour companies and many hotels and guesthouses will arrange city tours and excursions to surrounding sights but it is just as easy to arrange a tour independently with a local tuk-tuk driver; the best English speakers (and thus the most expensive tuk-tuks) can be found in the parking lot beside Nam Phou. Those at the Morning Market (Talaat Sao) are cheaper. Most tuk-tuk drivers pretend not to carry small change, so make sure you have the exact fare with you before taking a ride.

Vientiane

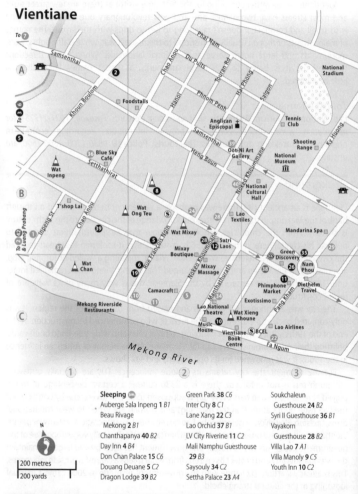

Sleeping 🛌
Auberge Sala Inpeng **1** *B1*
Beau Rivage
  Mekong **2** *B1*
Chanthapanya **40** *B2*
Day Inn **4** *B4*
Don Chan Palace **15** *C6*
Douang Deuane **5** *C2*
Dragon Lodge **39** *B2*

Green Park **38** *C6*
Inter City **8** *C1*
Lane Xang **22** *C3*
Lao Orchid **37** *B1*
LV City Riverine **11** *C2*
Mali Namphu Guesthouse
  29 *B3*
Saysouly **34** *C2*
Settha Palace **23** *A4*

Soukchaleun
  Guesthouse **24** *B2*
Syri II Guesthouse **36** *B1*
Vayakorn
  Guesthouse **28** *B2*
Villa Lao **7** *A1*
Villa Manoly **9** *C5*
Youth Inn **10** *C2*

That Luang

ⓘ *That Luang Rd, 3.5 km northeast of the city centre; daily 0800-1200, 1300-1600 (except 'special' holidays), 5000 kip. A booklet about the wat is on sale at the entrance.*

That Luang is Vientiane's most important site and the holiest Buddhist monument in the country. The golden spire looks impressive at the top of the hill, overlooking the city.

According to legend, a stupa was first built here in the third century AD by emissaries of the Moghul Emperor Asoka. Excavations on the site, however, have only located the remains of an 11th- to 13th-century Khmer temple, making the earlier provenance doubtful in the extreme. The present monument, encompassing the previous

Eating 🍴

Aria **5** *B2*

Chinese Liao-ning
  Dumplings **2** *A1*

Delight House of Fruit
  Shakes **4** *B4*

Fathima **10** *C2*

Full Moon
  Café **6** *C2*

Indochina Old House
  Antique Café **8** *B2*

Joma **11** *C3*

Khop Chai Deu **26** *C3*

La Terrasse **28** *B2*

Le Croissant d'Or **12** *B2*

Le Nadao **1** *A6*

Le Silapa **3** *A1*

Makphet **39** *B1*

Scandinavian Bakery **35** *B3*

Sticky Fingers **19** *C2*

Tamnak Lao **40** *A6*

Bars & clubs 🍸

Jazzy Brick **38** *C3*

Spirit House **42** *B1*

Wind West **6** *A1*

buildings, was built in 1566 by King Setthathirat, whose statue stands outside. Plundered by the Thais and the Chinese Haw in the 18th century, it was restored by King (Chao) Anou at the beginning of the 19th century.

The reliquary is surrounded by a square cloister, with an entrance on each side, the most famous on the east. There is a small collection of statues in the cloisters, including one of the Khmer king Jayavarman VII. The cloisters are used as lodgings by monks who travel to Vientiane for religious reasons and especially for the annual **That Luang Festival** (see page 374). The base of the stupa is a mixture of styles, Khmer, Indian and Lao -- and each side has a *hor vay* or small offering temple. This lowest level represents the material world, while the second tier is surrounded by a lotus wall and 30 smaller stupas, representing the 30 Buddhist perfections. Each of these originally contained smaller golden stupas but they were stolen by Chinese raiders in the 19th century. The 30-m-high spire dominates the skyline and resembles an elongated lotus bud, crowned by a stylized banana flower and parasol. It was designed so that pilgrims could climb up to the stupa via the walkways around each level. It is believed that originally over 450 kg of gold leaf was used on the spire.

Patuxai (Victory Monument)

ⓘ *Junction of That Luang Rd and Lane Xang Av, daily 0800-1200, 1300-1630, 3000 kip.*

At the end of That Luang is the Oriental answer to Paris's Arc de Triomphe and Vientiane's best-known landmark, the Victory Monument or Patuxai. It was built by the former regime in memory of those who died in the wars before the Communist takeover, but the cement ran out before its completion. Refusing to be beaten, the regime diverted hundreds of tonnes of cement, part of a US aid package to help with the construction of runways at Wattay Airport, to finish off the monument in 1969.

Wat Sisaket

ⓘ *Junction of Lane Xang Av and Setthathirat Rd, daily 0800-1200, 1300-1600, 5000 kip. No photographs in the sim.*

Further down Lane Xang is the **Morning Market** or **Talaat Sao** (see page 375) and beyond, is one of Vientiane's two national museums, Wat Sisaket. Home of the head of the Buddhist community in Laos, **Phra Sangka Nagnok**, it is one of the most important buildings in the capital and houses over 7000 Buddha images. Wat Sisaket was built in 1818 during the reign of King Anou. A traditional Lao monastery, it was the only temple that survived the Thai sacking of the town in 1827-1828, making it the oldest building in Vientiane.

The main sanctuary, or **sim**, with its sweeping roof, shares many stylistic similarities with Wat Phra Kaeo (see below): window surrounds, lotus-shaped pillars and carvings of deities held up by giants on the rear door. The sim contains 2052 Buddha statues (mainly terracotta, bronze and wood) in small niches in the top half of the wall. There is little left of the Thai-style *jataka* murals on the lower walls but the depth and colour of the originals can be seen from the few remaining pieces.

The **cloisters** were built during the 1800s and were the first of their kind in Vientiane. They shelter 120 large Buddhas in the attitude of subduing Mara, plus a number of other images in assorted *mudras*, and thousands of small figures in niches, although many of the most interesting Buddha figures are now in Wat Phra Kaeo.

The whole ensemble is washed in a rather attractive shade of caramel and, combined with the terracotta floor tiles and weathered roof, is a most satisfying sight.

Phou Khao Khouay National Protected Area

Phou Khao Khouay National Protected Area (pronounced *poo cow kway*) is one of Laos' premier national protected areas. The area extends across 2000 sq km and incorporates an attractive sandstone mountain range. It is crossed by three large rivers, smaller tributaries and two waterfalls at Tad Leuk and Tad Sae, which weave their way in to the Ang Nam Leuk reservoir, a stunning man-made dam and lake that sits on the outskirts of the park. Within the protected area is an array of wildlife, including wild elephants, gibbons, tigers, clouded leopards and Asiatic black bears.

Around the village of Ban Na the village's sugar cane plantations and river salt deposits attract a herd of wild elephants (around 30), which have, in the past, destroyed the villagers' homes and even killed a resident. This has limited the villagers' ability to undertake normal tasks, such as collecting bamboo, fearing that they may come across the wild elephants. To help compensate, the village, in conjunction with some NGOs, has constructed an elephant observation tower and has started running trekking tours to see these massive creatures in their natural habitat. The elephant tower is the primary attraction and it possible to stay over at the tower, 4 km from Ban Na, to try and catch a glimpse of the giant pachyderms who come to lap up salt from the nearby salt lick in the early evening hours. One-to three-day treks through the national park cross waterfalls, pass through pristine jungle and, with luck, offer the opportunity to hear or spot the odd wild elephant. It is too dangerous to get close. This is an important ecotour that contributes to the livelihood of the Ban Na villagers and helps conserve the elephant population. Advance notice is required so it's advisable to book with a tour operator in Vientiane. If you are travelling independently you will need to organize permits, trekking and accommodation with the village directly. To do this, contact Mr Bounthanam, T020-220 8286. Visit www.trekkingcentrallaos.com and contact the **National Tourism Authority** in Vientiane or **Green Discovery Laos** (see page 377). Visitors will need to bring drinking water and snacks. Do not try to feed the elephants, they are dangerous.

Ban Hat Khai is home to 90 families from the Lao Loum and Lao Soung ethnic groups. It is also a starting point for organized treks through mountain landscapes, crossing the Nam Mang River and the Phay Xay cliffs. Most treks take in the Tad Sae Falls. Homestay accommodation is available.

The park is northeast of Vientiane along Route 13 South. To get to Ban Na you need to stop at Tha Pabat Phonsanh, 80 km northeast of Vientiane; the village is a further 2 km. For Ban Hat Khai, 100 km northeast of Vientiane, continue on Route 13 to Thabok, where a *songthaew* or boat can take you 7-8 km to the village. Buses to Paksan from Vientiane's Talaat Sao bus station and That Luang market stop at Thabok.

Wat Phra Kaeo

ⓘ *Setthathirat Rd, daily 0800-1200, 1300-1600, closed public holidays, 5000 kip. No photographs in the sim.*

Almost opposite Wat Sisaket is Wat Phra Kaeo. It was originally built by King Setthathirat in 1565 to house the Emerald Buddha (Phra Kaeo), now in Bangkok, which he had brought from his royal residence in Chiang Mai. It was never a monastery but was kept instead for royal worship. The Emerald Buddha was removed by the Thais in 1779 and Wat Phra Kaeo was destroyed by them in the 1827 sacking of Vientiane. (The Thais now claim the Emerald Buddha as their most important icon in the country.) The whole building was in a bad state of repair after the sackings, the only thing remaining fully intact was the floor. The building was expertly reconstructed in the 1940s and 1950s and is now surrounded by a garden. During renovations, the interior walls of the wat were restored using a plaster made of sugar, sand, buffalo skin and tree oil.

The sim stands on three tiers of galleries, the top one surrounded by majestic, lotus-shaped columns. The tiers are joined by several flights of steps and guarded by nagas. The main, central (southern) door is an exquisite example of Lao wood sculpture with carved angels surrounded by flowers and birds; it is the only notable remnant of the original wat. (The central door at the northern end, with the larger carved angels supported by ogres, is new.) The sim now houses a superb assortment of Lao and Khmer art and some pieces of Burmese and Khmer influence, mostly collected from other wats in Vientiane. Although people regularly come and pray here, the wat's main purpose is as a quasi-museum.

Lao National Museum
ⓘ *Samsenthai Rd, opposite the Cultural Centre Hall, daily 0800-1200, 1300-1600, 10000 kip. No photography allowed.*

Formerly called the Revolutionary Museum, in these post-revolutionary days it has been redesignated the National Museum. The museum's collection has grown over the last few years and now includes a selection of historical artefacts from dinosaur bones and pre-Angkorian sculptures to a comprehensive photographic collection on Laos' modern history. The rhetoric of these modern collections has been toned down from the old days, when photographic descriptions would refer to the 'running dog imperialists' (Americans). The museum features a dazzling array of personal effects from the revolutionary leader Kaysone, including his exercise machine and a spoon he once used. Downstairs there are ancient artefacts, including stone tools and poignant burial jars. Upstairs the museum features a range of artefacts and busts, as well as a small exhibition on various ethnic minorities. The final section of the museum comprises mostly photographs which trace, chronologically, the country's struggle against the 'brutal' French colonialists and American 'imperialists'.

Xieng Khuan
ⓘ *Route 2 (25 km south of Vientiane), daily 0800-1630, 5000 kip, plus 5000 kip for cameras. Food vendors sell drinks and snacks.*

Otherwise known as the **Garden of the Buddhas** or **Buddha Park**, Xieng Khuan is close to the border with Thailand. It has been described as a Laotian Tiger Balm Gardens, with reinforced concrete Buddhist and Hindu sculptures of Vishnu, Buddha, Siva and various other assorted deities and near-deities. There's also a bulbous-style building with three levels containing smaller sculptures of the same gods.

The garden was built in the late 1950s by a priest-monk-guru-sage-artist called Luang Pu Bunleua Sulihat, who studied under a Hindu *rishi* in Vietnam and then combined the Buddhist and Hindu philosophies in his own very peculiar view of the world. He left Laos because his anti-communist views were incompatible with the ideology of the Pathet Lao (or perhaps because he was just too weird) and settled across the Mekong near the Thai town of Nong Khai, where he proceeded to build an equally revolting and bizarre concrete theme park for religious schizophrenics, called Wat Khaek. With Luang Pu's forced departure from Laos his religious garden came under state control and it is now a public park.

To get there take the No 14 bus (one hour) from the Talaat Sao bus station, a tuk-tuk (100,000 kip), hire a private vehicle (US$15), or take a motorbike or bicycle because the road follows the river and is reasonably level the whole way.

Vang Vieng → *For listings, see pages 366-383.*

The drive from Vientiane to Vang Vieng, on the much-improved Route 13, follows the valley of the Nam Ngum north and then climbs steeply onto the plateau where Vang Vieng is located, 160 km north of Vientiane. The surrounding area is inhabited by the Hmong and Yao hill peoples and is particularly picturesque: craggy karst limestone scenery, riddled with caves, crystal-clear pools and waterfalls. In the early morning the views are reminiscent of a Chinese Sung Dynasty painting.

The town itself is nestled in a valley on the bank of the Nam Song River, amid a misty jungle. It enjoys cooler weather and offers breathtaking views of the imposing mountains of Pha Tang and Phatto Nokham.

The town's laid-back feel has made it a popular haunt for the backpacker crowd, while the surrounding landscape has helped to establish Vang Vieng as Laos' premier outdoor activity destination, especially for rock climbing, caving and kayaking. Its popularity in many ways has also become its downfall: neon lights, pancake stands, 'happy' this and 'happy' that, and pirated *Friends* DVDs now pollute this former oasis. Nevertheless, the town and surrounding area is still full of wonderful things to do and see.

Ins and outs

Safety Laos is a very safe country for tourists but a disproportionate number of accidents and crimes seem to happen in Vang Vieng. Theft is routinely reported, ranging from robberies by packs of kids targeting tubers on the river to the opportunist theft of items from guests' rooms. Most guesthouses won't take responsibility for valuables left in rooms, instead it is usually advisable to hand in valuables to the management. Otherwise, you will need to padlock your bag. Another major problem is the sale of illegal drugs. Police often go on sting operations and charge fines of up to US$600 for possession. Legal issues aside, numerous travellers have become seriously ill from indulging in the 'happy' supplements supplied by the restaurants. **▸▸** *For details of the significant safety risks involved in adventure activities, see Activities and tours, page 377.*

Vang Vieng has become synonymous with tubing down the Nam Song. Tubes can be picked up from the Old Market area where the tubing company has formed a cartel. Without stops the 3 km tubing trip from the Organic Farm to town can take one to two hours if done quickly, but most people do it in three to four hours or take all day, choosing to stop along the way and drink, play volleyball or use the flying fox swings at the many bars dotted along the river. **▸▸** *See also Tubing, page 378.*

Many tour operators organize kayaking trips as well. Popular routes include kayaking down the Nam Song to incorporate the caves (especially Tham Nam – water cave), or the trip back to Vientiane via the drop-off point at Nam Lik. If you want to break the journey, there are several nice guesthouses at Nam Lik including the Nam Lik eco-village, south of the town. **▸▸** *See also Kayaking and rafting, page 377.*

Caves

ⓘ Many caves have stalls where you can buy drinks and snacks. You can buy hand-drawn maps from the town but all the caves are clearly signposted in English from the main road so these are not really necessary.

Vang Vieng is best known for its limestone caves, sheltered in the mountains flanking the town. Pretty much every guesthouse and tour operator offers tours to the caves (the best of these is **Green Discovery**, page 377) and, although some caves can be accessed independently, it is advisable to take a guide to a few as they are dark and difficult to navigate. Often children from surrounding villages will take tourists through the caves for a small fee. Don't forget to bring a torch, or even better a head-lamp, which can be picked up cheaply at the market both in Vang Vieng and Vientiane.

Of Vang Vieng's myriad caves, **Tham Chang** is the most renowned of all. Tham Chang penetrates right under a mountain and is fed by a natural spring: perfect for an early morning dip. From the spring it is possible to swim into the cave for quite a distance (bring a waterproof torch, if possible). The cave is said to have been used as a refuge during the 19th century from Chinese Haw bandits and this explains its name: *chang* meaning 'loyal' or 'steadfast'. Entrance is via Vang Vieng resort south of town. Although the cave is not the most magnificent, it serves as a superb lookout point.

Another popular cavern is **Tham Poukham** *ⓘ 7 km from Vang Vieng, 10000 kip*. The cave is often referred to as the cave of the Golden Crab and is highly auspicious. It's believed that if you catch a golden crab you will have a lifetime of fortune. To get there you need to cross the foot-bridge near the **Villa Nam Song**, and then follow the road for a further 6 km until you reach the village of Ban Nathong. From the village the cave is 1-km walk and a short climb up quite a steep hill. Mossy rocks lead the way into the main cavern area where a large bronze reclining Buddha is housed. Here there is an idyllic lagoon, with glassy green-blue waters, great for a swim.

Tham None *ⓘ 4 km north of Vang Vieng, 10,000 kip*, is known locally as the 'Sleeping Cave' because 2000 villagers took refuge there during the war. The large cave is dotted with stalagmites and stalactites, including the 'magic stone of Vang Vieng', which reflects light. Lots of bats reside in the grotto.

Tham Xang *ⓘ 14 km north of Vang Vieng on the banks of the Nam Song, 2000 kip*, also known as the 'Elephant Cave', is named after the stalagmites and stalactites that have created an elephant formation on a ledge. The cave also contains some Buddha images, including the Footprint of Buddha. Although the cave itself is relatively non-descript the bell used by monks is made of a former bomb. From this cave there is a signposted path that leads to **Tham Nam** (water cave) *ⓘ 15 km from town, 10000 kip*, a long spindly cave that is believed to stretch for at least 7 km. It takes about two hours to explore the cavern and at the entrance there is a crystal-clear pool. This is one of Vang Vieng's most interesting caves and in the wet season needs to be explored with an inner tube or by wading, while pulling yourself along a rope, although tour operators will also take you beyond the roped area. It's not an easy task and should not be attempted alone. At times the cavern is an extremely tight fit and commando-type crawling is required; a hard helmet with lamp attached is necessary. However, this is an incredible caving experience. To get to these two caves follow Route 13 north and turn left at Km 14, follow this dirt road for 1 km until you reach the river. Boats charge 10,000 kip to cross the river to see Tham Xang; from there you can walk to Tham Nam.

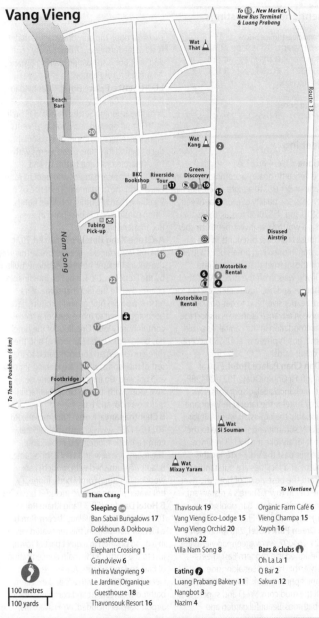

Vang Vieng

To **15**, *New Market,*
New Bus Terminal
& Luang Prabang

Wat That

Route 13

Beach Bars

20

Wat Kang **2**

BKC Bookshop

Riverside Tour **11**

Green Discovery **1** **16**

S

15

3

S

Nam Song

6

4

Tubing Pick-up

@

Disused Airstrip

19 **12**

22

6

Motorbike Rental

9

4

Motorbike Rental

17

1

16

To Tham Poukham (6 km)

Footbridge

8 **18**

Wat Si Souman

Wat Mixay Yaram

To Vientiane

Tham Chang

N

100 metres
100 yards

Sleeping
Ban Sabai Bungalows **17**
Dokkhoun & Dokboua
  Guesthouse **4**
Elephant Crossing **1**
Grandview **6**
Inthira Vangvieng **9**
Le Jardine Organique
  Guesthouse **18**
Thavonsouk Resort **16**

Thavisouk **19**
Vang Vieng Eco-Lodge **15**
Vang Vieng Orchid **20**
Vansana **22**
Villa Nam Song **8**

Eating
Luang Prabang Bakery **11**
Nangbot **3**
Nazim **4**

Organic Farm Café **6**
Vieng Champa **15**
Xayoh **16**

Bars & clubs
Oh La La **1**
Q Bar **2**
Sakura **12**

Hotel and guesthouse prices

LL over US$200	**L** US$151-200	**AL** US$101-150
A US$66-100	**B** US$46-65	**C** US$31-45
D US$21-30	**E** US$12-20	**F** US$7-11
G US$6 and under		

Restaurant prices

♦♦♦ over US$12	♦♦ US$6-12	♦ under US$6

● Sleeping

Vientiane *p356, map p358*

There is very little quality accommodation in Vientiane under US$10 a night. There is a big difference in the quality of rooms between the US$10 and US$20-30 rooms, the extra US$10 is a worthwhile investment. Cheaper guesthouses will offer discounts in the wet season. Higher-end hotels offer better rates on the internet than the rack rate given if you walk in off the street. All of the guesthouses and boutique hotels, except for the most expensive, tend to get booked up, so reserve in advance as there is a shortage of accommodation in the capital. As a rule of thumb, hotels priced over US$50 accept major credit cards.

LL-L Don Chan Palace Hotel, Piawat Village (off Fa Gnum Quay) T021-244288, www.donchanpalacelaodpdr.com. This 14-storey hotel is the largest in Vientiane and probably the ugliest. It was built for the ASEAN summit and is so close to the river that locals joke it may fall in. Once you can get past the ugly exterior, the 230 rooms and facilities are outstanding and afford the best views of both the river and the city in town. There's a restaurant, private karaoke rooms, bar, poolside massage, gym and Wi-Fi.

LL-AL Green Park Hotel, 248 Khou Vieng Rd, T021-264097, www.greenparkvientiane. com. Designed in a modern East-meets-West style, this hotel is set alongside Vientiane's primary park. Beautiful rooms with all the mod cons, Wi-Fi and super-duper bathtubs. Beautiful garden and excellent pool. The only drawback is that it is set alittle further out from the city centre and river, but is still within walking distance. A fantastic luxury option.

LL-AL Settha Palace Hotel, 6 Pang Kham Rd, T021-217581/2, www.sethapalace. com. The stunning **Settha Palace** was built in 1936 and opened as a hotel in 1999. Its French architecture, impressive colonial decor, period furniture, plush rooms with black marble sinks and bathtubs and beautiful tropical gardens and pool more easily with the fundamental essence of Vientiane than the other top-level hotels. Often considered the best hotel in town. Recommended.

A-C Lane Xang Hotel, Fa Ngum Rd, T021-214100, www.lanexanghotel.com.la This was the original 'luxury' hotel in Vientiane, built by the French in 1964. It has an indefinable charm, despite the fact that some of its retro-hip Soviet fittings and furniture have been ripped out to make way for a more contemporary look. One floor of the hotel has been remodelled (38 rooms) and the difference is remarkable compared to the rest of the rooms, which are looking shoddy and unloved. Go for a a junior suite de luxe room, with its own bar. Other facilities include a pool and bar.

B Chanthapanya, Nokeo Khoummane Rd, T021-244284, www.chanthapanyahotel. com. Fantastic modern Asian building. The rooms are new and very comfortable. Beautifully furnished with modern Lao wooden furniture, comfy beds, fridge, TV, hot water, phone and a/c. Includes breakfast.

B Hotel Day Inn, 59/3 Pang Kham Rd, T021-222985, dayinn@laopdr.com. Run by a friendly Cambodian, this renovated villa is in a good position in a quiet part of town, just to the north of the main concentration of bars and restaurants. Attractive, airy, clean, large rooms, with a/c and excellent bathrooms; breakfast and complimentary airport transfer included. Wi-Fi available.

B Lao Orchid Hotel, Chao Anou. T021-264134, www.lao-orchid.com. Beautiful spacious rooms with stunning modern furnishings, polished floorboards and large showers. Outstanding value for the price and very popular with business travellers. 4½-star accommodation for a 3½-star price. Very busy so advanced bookings essential. Includes breakfast and Wi-Fi. Café and zen fish pond. Visa and MasterCard accepted. Recommended.

B-C Beau Rivage Mekong, Fa Ngum Rd, T021-243350, www.hbrm.com. One of the first Western-style boutique hotels in Vientiane, it is beautifully furnished, with artistic decoration and fantastic bathtubs. The pink exterior does not sit well with its surroundings but nonetheless this is a great hotel with superb Mekong river views. Its location, just out of the centre of town on the river, ensures peace and quiet but it's still only a 5-min walk to the hustle and bustle. Garden view rooms are cheaper. Includes breakfast.

B-C Inter City Hotel, 24-25 Fa Ngum Rd, T021-242842, www.ramayana-laos.com. This Singaporean-owned hotel is one of the oldest in Vientiane and has been operating for over 30 years. Renovations have made it sparkle: mosaics, relief sculptures and murals adorn the walls, and traditional shutters, silk hangings and furniture feature in every room. The a/c rooms are light and spacious, with slick bathrooms and fantastic balconies overlooking the Mekong. Lovely atrium and excellent gift shop with beautiful antique costumes. Wi-Fi available.

B-C LV City Riverine Hotel, 48 Fa Ngum Rd, Mixay, T021-214643, www.lvcitylaos.com. A good central choice in the heart of town. The suite is sweet and cosy with a 4-poster bed, textile decor and a good-sized bathroom and stand-alone sink. The de luxe rooms have beds raised on small platforms but with smaller bathrooms; standard rooms are very nice with thoughtful extras like a clothes stand. Wi-Fi and breakfast is included.

C Villa Manoly, Ban Phyavat, T021-218907, manoly20@hotmail.com. This is a wonderful ramshackle French colonial villa crowded with objet d'art, curios, books and ancient TV sets. It's like a rambling private house. There's a pool too in the garden. 12 rooms are in the main building and 8 rooms in a new block with small patios out front overlooking the pool. Monthly rates are US$650. Recommended.

C-D Auberge Sala Inpeng, 063 Unit 06, Inpeng St, T021-242021, www.salalao.com. 9 very attractive bungalows set in a small garden in a quiet street. The economy rooms don't come with TV. Opt for a standard or superior if available for the space and decor. Breakfast is included.

C-D Mali Namphu Guesthouse, 114 Pang Kham Rd , T021-215093, www.malinamphu.com. Difficult to spot as it looks like a small shopfront but the façade is deceiving, the foyer opens onto a beautifully manicured courtyard surrounded by quaint, terraced rooms. Clean, bright rooms are traditionally decorated with a modern twist and come with a/c, hot water, cable TV and a fantastic breakfast. The twin rooms are much nicer than the doubles. Friendly staff. Highly recommended. One of the best guesthouses in Laos in this price range.

D Douang Deuane, Nokeo Khoummane Rd, T021-222301, dd_hotel@hotmail.com. From the exterior, this dilapidated building looks like a classic Communist edifice, but the a/c rooms have charm and character: parquet wood floors, art deco furniture, excellent bathrooms with bathtubs (showers in single rooms) and satellite TV. Try and get a balcony room for lovely patchwork views of the roofs of the city. Although the room rates are no longer competitive, it is a good centrally located option B if the others within this price range are fully booked. Good-value motorbike rentals, 70,000 kip per day.

D Vayakorn Guesthouse, 91 Nokeo Khoummane Rd, T021-241911, www.vayakorn.com. The rooms are clean, beautifully decorated with modern furniture and very comfortable. Polished floors, hot water, a/c and TV. Sadly breakfast is no longer included with rooms but it is still excellent value. Great value and centrally located. The new **Vayakorn Inn** has opened around the corner. Wi-Fi.

D-E Dragon Lodge, 311-313 Samsenthai Rd, T021-250114, dragonlodge2002@yahoo. com. Somewhere between a guesthouse and a hotel. Fun, colourful downstairs restaurant area – good for a party; if you're looking for quiet this probably isn't the best choice. Nice, simply decorated rooms, with hot water, TV and a/c. 5-star service. Visa accepted. Fan rooms are cheaper.

D-E Villa Lao (formerly **Thongbay Guesthouse**), off Luang Prabang Rd, turn right before the **Novotel**, Ban Non Douang, T021-242292, www.villalao.com. Lovely traditional Lao house set in a lush tropical garden. Rooms have traditional-style fittings, mosquito nets and fan or a/c. Rooms with shared bath are cheapest. The guesthouse also runs cooking classes on request (150,000 kip), which include buying ingredients at the local market. The only drawback of this place is the distance from the city centre. Perfect if you want to relax.

E Youth Inn, 29 Fa Ngum Rd and on Francois Ngin Rd, T021-217130, youthinn@ hotmail.com. A Vietnamese-run operation with 2 locations in the heart of things and a new addition to the budget scene. The standard-sized rooms are spotlessly clean and are compact with a/c. The owners are sometimes friendly and sometimes not!

E-F Saysouly, 23 Manthaturath Rd, T021-218383. A variety of rooms, a bit on the musty side. Parquet floors, cheap single fan rooms with shared bathroom. The shared bathrooms are excellent with powerful showers. Extra for a/c. The more expensive en suite rooms are quite good value.

E-F Soukchaleun Guesthouse, 121 Setthathirat Rd, T021-218723, soukchaleun_ gh@yahoo.com. Quaint guesthouse with a variety of rooms ranging from fan rooms

with shared bathroom through to a/c en suite. Comfy, homely and very clean. The views are not scenic but the guesthouse is friendly and relatively good value.

E-F Syri II Guesthouse, 63/6-7 Setthathirat Rd, T021-223178, syri2@hotmail.com. This is probably one of the best options within the cheaper price range. 3-storey guesthouse with a variety of rooms including fan rooms with shared bathroom and private bathroom. Clean and simply decorated with wooden furniture. Decorated with quirky curios from around Asia, with lounges and shared communal areas. Helpful staff. Recommended.

Vang Vieng p363, map p365

The town's popularity has ensured a uniformity among almost all places catering to budget tourists: most restaurants feature the same menu and there isn't much individuality in the cheaper guesthouses either. The majority are geared to the needs of travellers and offer a laundry service, guides and bicycles. However, in the last 2 years a couple of higher-end hotels have cropped up, providing more attractive options. Although the accommodation in the centre of town is usually cheaper, try and get a room with a view of the river as it is simply stunning. A couple of new bamboo bridges have been constructed across the river to new bungalow developments; note though, that during the rainy season, the only bridge in operation is the Namsong bridge (4000 kip return, 6000 kip for bikes, 10,000 kip for motorbikes) as well as the high bridge leading past the Vang Vieng Orchid to the island bars.

A-B Villa Nam Song, T023-511637, www. villanamsong.com. Quaint terracotta villas set in manicured gardens overlooking the Nam Song with parquet floors, hot water and separate shower compartments. Fan-cooled restaurant attached; breakfast included. Although this is an attractive hotel there is better value for money in town. Cheaper rooms lack river view. 2 rooms have wheelchair access.

A-D Thavonsouk Resort, on the river, T023-511096, www.thavonsouk.com. Offers 5 different styles of accommodation across a sprawling riverfront premises. Rooms are much more attractive on the outside than in; standard rooms come with tacky wood-imitation tiles. Some mid-range bungalows are great value with massive balconies fitted with sunbeds. There is a traditional Lao house, decorated with Lao furnishings, suitable for a family or big group, plus suites (TV, fridge, bath, a/c) and standard accommodation. Fantastic restaurant. Keep your eye out for local home-grown pop star, Aluna and her father, Alom, who run this family business.

B-D Elephant Crossing, on the Nam Song river, T023-511232, www.theelephant crossinghotel.com. A great, , attractive mid-range option. Australian-owned riverfront hotel classically decorated with modern wooden furnishings. The big bathtub and sliding window between the bedroom and bathroom will be a big hit with romantics. All rooms except 6, have view, fridge, Wi-Fi and a/c. Breakfast included. There's a set of kids' swings in the garden. The owners are really lovely.

C Ban Sabai Bungalow, on the banks of the river, T023-511088, www.xayohgroup. com. A lovely complex of bungalows with balconies in a spectacular location, with all the modern fittings but the rooms are not well-lit, the water is not very hot, the bathroom is badly designed with the sink in the shower compartment and the breakfast service is very unpolished. Rooms 1-4 are near the laundry room and although not too noisy, light sleepers will be disturbed. Bungalows closer to the river are a bit more expensive.

C Vansana, by the river, T023-511598, www.vansanahotel-group.com. Despite its soulless exterior this hotel boasts the best rooms and facilities in town. Large bedrooms fitted with all the mod cons have stunning mountain and river views. Modern wooden furniture, minibar and local handicrafts decorate the room. Beautiful pool and bar by the river with deckchairs.

Ask for a room with a view; breakfast included. Recommended. Non-guests can use the pool for 20,000 kip per day.

C-D Inthira Vangvieng, T023-511070, www.inthirahotel.com. Opened in November 2009 with 28 rooms in a rather narrow slot on the main street. Well-furnished rooms with medium-sized bathrooms and small balconies.

E-F Grandview, on the river, T023-511474, grandviewguesthouse@gmail.com. A 2007 newcomer offers spotless rooms with attached hot-water bathroom. The cheaper rooms don't have a view or a/c. Excellent value. Highly recommended.

E-F Le Jardine Organique Guesthouse, on the river, about 900 m from the centre of town, T023-511420. This set of bungalows and a guesthouse has been surrounded by 2 other properties owned by family members thus Le Jardine now offers no river view. The raised bungalows are smart and lovely with balconies attached. The guesthouse rooms are plain and clean. The **Bansuan Riverview** with rattan bungalows now hog the view while the **Vilayvong** facing **Le Jardine** bungalows offers smart wooden, floor-height bungalows with balconies. It is, thus, now like a compound of rooms but not unattractive with it. Cheaper rooms have fan only. The owners are lovely and don't suffer from the Vang Vieng jadedness quite often found in these cheaper bungalows.

E-F Vang Vieng Orchid, on the river road, T023-511172. Comfortable fan or more expensive a/c rooms. Hot water in the bathrooms, clean tiled floors, very comfortable rooms. The rooms with the private balconies are well worth the few extra dollars because you will have your own personal piece of the phenomenal view. Unfortunately, they're not as friendly as they used to be.

F-G Dokboua Guesthouse, T020-5614 4933. This newcomer, close to **Dokkhoun**, offers some of the best budget rooms in town. Sparklingly clean rooms with taut white linens and good mattresses with huge attached bathrooms right in the centre. A/c rooms are more expensive; older rooms are cheaper. Friendly family owners. Highly recommended.

G Thavisouk, in the centre of town, T023-511658. If you are looking for a budget option in town, this is perfect. No frills but very clean. Rooms with en suite bathrooms and hot water, US$3-4. While the accommodation is good value, their tours, tickets and other services aren't.

Out of town

The places on the outskirts of town are great for those who wish to escape into a more natural landscape. The lack of facilities and transport in the area ensures tranquillity but also makes it quite difficult to get to town.

D-E Vang Vieng Eco-Lodge, 7 km north of town, T021-413370, www.vangvieng-eco-lodge.com. Although this isn't an eco-lodge it is still an exceptionally beautiful place to stay. Set on the banks of the river with stunning gardens and beautiful rock formations, it is a perfect place to get away from it all. The 11 chalet-style bungalows, which have been nicely decorated, with beautiful balconies, comfortable furnishings and a big hot-water bathtub; a bungalow of 4 rooms with sliding doors with great riverside views but small double bed and shower room; and a rattan longhouse (cheaper still, **G**) with 8 rooms and shared bath; breakfast included. Good Lao restaurant. Also arranges activities.

G Vang Vieng Organic Farm, 3 km north of town in Ban Sisavang, T023-511174, www.laofarm.org. This mulberry farm has basic rooms with mosquito net, dorm accommodation and full board. If you volunteer (building a mudhouse, English teaching, working on the farm) you get a 20,000 kip per night discount. A new guesthouse with unappealing, very overpriced rooms with hard mattresses has opened (**E**). Hugely popular restaurant, serving great starfruit wine and famous mulberry pancakes (0600-2130). It is a very popular drop-off spot for tubers. The farm supports the **Equal Education for All** project (www.eefaproject.com).

● Eating

Vientiane p356, map p358

The absolutely best place to get Lao food is from the open-air stalls that line the banks of the Mekong along **Fa Ngum**. The restaurants are ridiculously low in price and high in atmosphere, particularly at night with their flickering candles. From time to time the government kicks all the eateries off the patch but they usually return with a vengeance. By the time this book goes to press they might all be gone as the park project to redesign the riverfront is well underway. The **Dong Palane Night Market**, on Dong Palane, and the night markets near the corner of **Chao Anou** and **Khoun Boulom Rd** are also good places to go for Lao stall food. There are various other congregations of stalls and vendors around town, most of which set up shop around 1730 and close down by 2100. Be sure to sample Lao ice cream with coconut sticky rice.

The **Chinese quarter** is around Chao Anou, Heng Boun and Khoun Boulom and is a lively spot in the evenings. There are a number of noodle shops here, all of which serve a palatable array of vermicelli, *muu daeng* (red pork), duck and chicken.

The **Korean-style barbeque**, *sindat*, is extremely popular, especially among the younger Lao, as it is a very social event and very cheap. It involves cooking finely sliced meat on a hot plate in the middle of the table, while forming a broth with vegetables around the sides of the tray. Reminiscent of a 1970s fondue evening. Seendat (see below) is a favourite amongst the older Lao.

¶¶¶-¶¶ Le Nadao, Ban Donmieng (on the right-hand side of the Patuxai roundabout), T021-213174. Mon-Fri 1200-1330 and 1900-2230, Sat-Sun 1900-2230. This place is difficult to find but definitely worth every second spent searching the back streets of Vientiane in the dark. Sayavouth, who trained in Paris and New York, produces delectable French cuisine: soups, venison, lamb and puddings. The set lunch menu is one of the best lunches you will get in town. Fantastic.

⏶⏶-⏶ Le Silapa, 17/1 Sihom Rd , T021-219689. Daily 1130-1400 and 1800-2200; closed for 1 month a year in the rainy season and for a week over Lao New Year. Anthony and Frederick provide a fantastic French-inspired menu (tilapia with a vegetable marmalade, lime and black olive sauce). and intimate atmosphere for fine dining without blowing the budget. Innovative modern meals that would be as at home in the fine dining establishments of New York and London as they are here. Great value set lunch menu. Part of the profits (5000 kip per bottle of wine) are donated to disadvantaged families, usually for expensive but life-saving surgical procedures. Wine degustation evenings are occasionally held, US$75.

⏶⏶ Tamnak Lao Restaurant, That Luang Rd, T021-413562. 1200-2200. It's well worth deviating from the main Nam Phou area for a bite to eat here. This restaurant and its sister branch in Luang Prabang have a reputation for delivering outstanding Lao and Thai food, usually prepared with a modern twist.

⏶⏶-⏶ Aria, 8 Rue François Ngin, T021-222589. An outstanding addition to the Vientiane dining scene. Divine ice cream, a wine list 16 pages long, and a long mouth-watering menu of homemade pastas, ravioli, risottos and pizzas with real buffalo mozzarella. Dishes include mountain hunter's ravioli stuffed with slow fire-braised deer and mountain cheeses, barbera red wine and herb sauce. Service is ultra efficient and the owner, who is so friendly and welcoming, is an Italian returnee to Vientiane.

⏶⏶-⏶ La Terrasse, 55/4 Nokeo Koummane Rd, T021-218550. Mon-Sat 1100-1400, 1800-2200. This is the best European restaurant in terms of variety and price. Large fail-safe menu offering French, European, Lao and Mexican food. Good desserts, especially the rich chocolate mousse, and a good selection of French wine. Fantastic service. Reasonable prices with an excellent 'plat du jour' each day. Great 1970s-style comfort food.

⏶ Chinese Liao-ning Dumpling Restaurant, Chao Anou Rd, T021-240811. Daily 1100- 2230. This restaurant is a firm favourite with the expats and it isn't hard to see why: fabulous steamed or fried dumplings and a wide range of vegetarian dishes. The place is spotlessly clean but the birds in cages outside are a bit off-putting. No one is ever disappointed by the meals here. Highly recommended.

⏶ Fathima, Th Fa Gnum, T021-219097. Without a doubt the best-value Indian in town. Ultra-friendly service and a large menu with a range of excellent curries.

⏶ Full Moon Café, Rue François Ngin, T021-243373. Daily 1000-2300. Delectable Asian fusion cuisine and Western favourites. Huge pillows, good lighting and great music make this place very relaxing. Fantastic chicken wrap and some pretty good Asian tapas. The Ladybug shake is a winner. Also a book exchange and music and movie shop for iPods. Free Wi-Fi available.

⏶ Khop Chai Deu, Setthathirat Rd, on the corner of Nam Phou Rd. Daily 0800-2330, www.khopchaideu.com. This lively place housed in a former colonial building is one of the city's most popular venues. Garden seating, good atmosphere at night with soft lantern lighting, and an eclectic menu of Indian, Italian, Korean and international dishes (many of which come from nearby restaurants). While the food is okay most come for the bustling atmosphere. The best value are the local Lao dishes though, which are made on site and toned down for the falang palate. Also serves draft or bottled beer at a pleasant a/c bar. Excellent lunch buffet. Live performances.

⏶ Makphet, in a new location behind Wat Ong Teu, T021-260587, www.friends-international.org. Fantastic Lao non-profit restaurant that helps raise money for street kids. Run by the trainees, who are former street kids, and their teachers. Modern Lao cuisine with a twist. Selection of delectable drinks such as the iced hibiscus with lime juice. Beautifully decorated with modern furniture and painting by the kids.

Also sells handicrafts and toys produced by the parents from vulnerable communities.

Seendat, Sihom Rd, T021-213855. Daily 1730-2200. This restaurant has been in existence for well over 20 years and is a favourite amongst the older Lao for its clean food (*sindat*) and good atmosphere. About US$1 per person more expensive than most other places but this is reflected in the quality.

Sticky Fingers, François Ngin Rd, T021-215972. Tue-Sun 1000-2300. Very popular small restaurant and bar serving Lao and international dishes, including fantastic salads, pasta, burgers and such like. Everything from Middle Eastern through to modern Asian on offer. Fantastic comfort food and the best breakfast in town. Great cocktails, lively atmosphere, nice setting. Deliveries available. Stickies should be the first pit-stop for every visitor needing to get grounded quickly as, food aside, the expats who frequent the joint are full to the brim with local knowledge.

Cafés, cakeshops and juice bars

Pavement cafés are 10 a penny in Vientiane. You need not walk more than half a block for some hot coffee or a cold fruit shake.

Delight House of Fruit Shakes, Samsenthai Rd, opposite the Asian Pavilion Hotel, T021-212200. Daily 0700-2000. A wonderful selection of fresh shakes and fruit salads for next to nothing.

Indochina Old House Antique Café, 86/11 Setthathirat Rd, T021-223528. A delightful curio store where upstairs you can sip wholesome juices or coffee amid the artful clutter of antiques, propaganda work and knick-knacks. A real treat.

Joma, Setthathirat Rd, T021-215265. Mon-Sat 0700-2100. A very modern, chic bakery with efficient service. Wi-Fi and arctic-style a/c. However, it is starting to get a bit pricey and the iced coffee is better next door at Dao Fa.

Le Croissant d'Or, top of Nokeo Khoummane Rd, T021-223741. Daily 0700-2100. French bakery, great for pastries.

Scandinavian Bakery, 71/1 Pang Kham Rd, Nam Phou Circle, T021-215199. Daily 0700-2000. Delicious pastries, bread, sandwiches and cakes. Great place for a leisurely coffee. Pricey for Laos but a necessary European fix for many expats. The Nam Phou Circle outlet is much better value and has a wider selection of cakes and sandwiches.

Vang Vieng *p363, map p365*

There is a string of eating places on the main road through town. Generally, the cuisine available are hamburgers, pasta, sandwiches and basic Asian dishes. Most of the restaurants offer 'happy' upgrades – marijuana or mushrooms in your pizza, cake or lassi, or opium tea. Although many people choose the 'happy' offerings, some wind up very ill.

Luang Prabang Bakery Restaurant, just off the main road, near BCEL. Excellent pastries, cakes and shakes and delicious breakfasts. Make sure you ask for the freshest batch as they have a tendency to leave cakes on the shelf well past their use-by date. Recommended.

Nangbot, on the main road, T023-511018. This proper sit-down restaurant is one of the oldest tourist diners in town and serves a few traditional dishes, such as bamboo shoot soup and *laap* with sticky rice, alongside the usual Western fare. However, the main road entrance is closed. Walk through to the disused airstrip side where all the action is taking place.

Nazim, on the main road, T023-511214. The largest and most popular Indian restaurant in town. Good range of South Indian and buriyani specialities, plus a selection of vegetarian meals.

Organic Farm Café, further down the main road. Small café offering over 15 tropical fruit shakes and a fantastic variety of food. Mulberry shakes and pancakes are a must and the harvest curry stew is absolutely delicious. Try the fresh spring rolls with pineapple dipping sauce as a starter. The food is highly recommended, the service could do with a little work. The sister branch is at the **Organic Mulberry Farm**.

¶ **Vieng Champa Restaurant**, on the main road, T023-511370. Refreshingly, this family-run restaurant seems to have a greater selection of Lao food than most other places on the street. Most meals are between 15,000 and 20,000 kip.

¶ **Xayoh**, Luang Prabang Rd, T023-511088. Restaurant with branches in Vientiane and Luang Prabang offering good Western food in a comfy environment. Pizza, soups and roast dinners. **Xayoh** may have moved location by the time you read this.

🌙 Bars and clubs

Vientiane *p356, map p358*
Bars

There are a number of bar stalls, which set up in the evening along **Quai Fa Ngum** (the river road); at least until the new park opens when they may be cleared away; a good place for a cold beer as the sun sets. Most bars will close at 2300 in accordance with the local curfew laws; some places seem to be able to stay open past this time although that varies on a day-to-day basis. Government officials go through phases of shutting down places and restricting curfews. **Jazzy Brick**, Setthathirat Rd, near Phimphone Market. Very sophisticated, modern den, where delectable cocktails are served with jazz cooing in the background. Garish shirts banned. Decorated with an eclectic range of quirky and kitsch artefacts. Very upmarket. Head here towards the end of the night.

Khop Chai Deu, Setthathirat Rd (near the corner with Nam Phou). Probably the most popular bar for tourists in Vientiane. Casual setting with a nightly band.

Spirit House, follow Fa Ngum Rd until it turns into a dirt track, past the Mekong River Commission, T021-243795, www. thespirithouselaos.com. Beautiful wooden bar in perfect river location. Range of snacks and burgers but salads are overpriced. Good for those wanting to catch the sunset in style with some of the best cocktails in the city. Wi-Fi.

Sticky Fingers, Rue François Ngin, opposite the **Tai Pan Hotel**. A fantastic bar and restaurant run by 2 Australian women. Brilliant cocktails, especially the renowned Tom Yum. Also serves food (see page 372).

Sunset Bar, end of Fa Ngum Rd. Although this run-down wooden construction isn't much to look at, it is a firm favourite with locals and tourists hoping to have a quiet ale and take in the magnificent sunset.

Wind West, by traffic lights, Luang Prabang Rd. Usually stays open after 2300. Seedier than others; many wild nights happen here.

Vang Vieng *p363, map p365*
The latest hotspot in Vang Vieng changes week to week.

Oh La La Bar, off the main street. Very popular, open bar with pool table.

Sakura Bar, between the main road and the river. Big open bar with loud, blaring and often live music. A new addition is Q Bar on the main road diagonally opposite to Xayoh.

🎭 Entertainment

Vientiane *p356, map p358*
Films and exhibitions

Blue Sky Café, on the corner of Setthathirat and Chao Anou roads. Movies are shown on a 29-in TV on the 2nd floor.

COPE Visitors' Centre, National Rehabilitation Centre, Khou Vieng Rd (sign-posted), www.copelaos.org. Open 0900-1800, free. COPE (Cooperative Orthotic and Prosthetic Enterprise) has set up an exhibition on UXO (unexploded ordnance) and its effects on the people of Laos. The exhibition is very interesting and includes a small movie room, photography, UXO and a range of prosthetic limbs (some that are actually crafted out of UXO). The exhibition helps raise money for the work of COPE, which includes the production of prosthetic limbs and rehabilitation of patients.

French Cultural Centre, Lang Xang Rd, T021-215764, www.centredelangue.org. Shows exhibitions, screens French films and also hosts the Southeast Asian film festival. Check the *Vientiane Times* for up-to-date details or pick up its quarterly programme. **Lao-International Trade Exhibition & Convention Center (ITECC)**, T4 Rd – Ban Phonethane Neua, T021-416002, www.laoitecc. info. Shows a range of international films. Keep an eye in the *Vientiane Times* for international performances at the **Lao Cultural Centre** (the building that looks like a big cake opposite the museum).

Karaoke

Could almost be the Lao national sport and there's nothing like bonding with the locals over a heavy-duty karaoke session. Karaoke places are everywhere. The more expensive, up-market **Don Chan Palace**, see page 366, lets you hire your own room.

Traditional dance

Lao National Theatre, Manthaturath Rd, T020-5550 1773. Daily shows of Lao dancing, from 1730. Tickets, US$7. Performances represent traditional dance of lowland Lao as well as some minority groups. Performances are less regular in the low season. Temporarily closed at publication time.

⊛ Festivals and events

Vientiane *p356, map p358*
1st weekend in Apr Pi Mai (Lao New Year) is celebrated with a 3-day festival and a huge water fight.
12 Oct Freedom from the French Day.
Oct Boun Souang Heua is a beautiful event on the night of the full moon at the end of Buddhist Lent. Candles are lit in all the homes and a candlelit procession takes place around the city's wats and through the streets. Then, thousands of banana-leaf boats holding flowers, tapers and candles are floated out onto the river. The boats signify your bad luck floating away. On the 2nd day, boat races take place, with 50 or so men in each boat; they power up the river in perfect unison. Usually, a bunch of foolhardy

expats also tries to compete, much to the amusement of the locals.
Nov (movable) Boun That Luang is celebrated in all of Vientiane's *thats* but most notably at That Luang (the national shrine). Originally a ceremony in which nobles swore allegiance to the king and constitution, it amazingly survived the Communist era. On the festival's most important day, **Thak Baat**, thousands of Lao people pour into the temple at 0600 and again at 1700 to pay homage. Monks travel from across the country to collect alms from the pilgrims. It is a really beautiful ceremony, with monks chanting and thousands of people praying. Women who attend should invest in a traditional *sinh*. A week-long carnival surrounds the festival with fireworks, music and dancing.

○ Shopping

Vientiane *p356, map p358*
Bookshops
Kosila Books, Nokeo Khoummane Rd, T021-241352. Small selection of second-hand books.
Monument Books, 124/1 Nokeo Khoummane Rd, T021-243708, www. monument-books.com. The largest selection of new books in Vientiane, **Monument** stock a range of Southeast Asian speciality books as well as coffee-table books. Good place to pick up Lao-language children's books to distribute to villages on your travels.
Vientiane Book Center, 32/05 Fa Ngum Rd, T021-212031, vientianebookcenter@ yahoo.com. A limited but interesting selection of used books in a multitude of languages.

Clothing and textiles
Couleur d'Asie, Nam Phou Circle. Modern-style Asian clothing. Pricey but high-quality fusion fashion.
Lao Textiles by Carol Cassidy, Nokeo Koummane Rd, T021-212123, www.

laotextiles.com. Mon-Fri 0800-1200, 1400-1700, Sat 0800-1200. Exquisite silk fabrics, including *ikat* and traditional Lao designs, made by an American in a beautifully renovated colonial property. Dyeing, spinning, designing and weaving all done on site (and can be viewed). It's expensive, but many of the weavings are real works of art; custom-made pieces available on request.

Mixay Boutique, Nokeo Khoummane, T021-25717943, contact@mixay.com. Exquisite Lao silk in rich colours. Clothing and fantastic photographs and artefacts.

Satri Laos, Setthathirat, T021-244387. If Vientiane had a Harrods this would be it. Upmarket boutique retailing everything from jewellery, shoes, clothes, furnishings and homewares. Beautiful stuff, although most of it is from China, Vietnam and Thailand.

Handicrafts and antiques

The main shops are along Setthathirat, Samsenthai and Pang Kham. The **Talaat Sao** (Morning Market) is also worth a browse, with artefacts, such as appliquéd panels, decorated hats and sashes, basketwork both old and new, small and large wooden tobacco boxes, sticky-rice lidded baskets, axe pillows, embroidered cushions and a wide range of silver work.

Camacraft, Nokeo Khoummane, T020-5556 1660. NGO which retails handicrafts produced by the Hmong people. Beautiful embroidery, mulberry tea, Lao silk.

Oot-Ni Art Gallery, Samsenthai Rd, T021-21 4359. An Aladdin's Cave of serious objets d'art.

T'Shop Lai, Vat Inpeng St (behind Wat Inpeng), T021-223178, www.artisanslao.com. Mon-Sat 0800-2000, Sun 0800-1500. has exhibitions of crafts made by disadvantaged people, as well as a shop.

Jewellery

Tamarind, Manthathurath, T021-243564. Great innovative jewellery designs, nice pieces. Also stocks a range of beautiful clothes made in stunning silk and organza.

Markets and shopping malls

Vientiane has several excellent markets. **Talaat Sao**, off Lane Xang Av. It's busiest in the mornings (from around 1000), but operates all day. There are money exchanges here (quite a good rate), and a good selection of foodstalls selling Western food, soft drinks and ice cream sundaes. It sells imported Thai goods, electrical appliances, watches, DVDs and CDs, stationery, cosmetics, a selection of handicrafts, an enormous choice of Lao fabrics, and upstairs there is a large clothing section, silverware, some gems and gold and a few handicraft stalls.

There is also the newer addition to the Morning Market – a modern shopping centre-style market. This is not as popular as it is much pricier and stocked with mostly Thai products sold in baht. Next to it, the most enormous shopping mall should be open by the time you read this. The **Talat Sao Mall**, www.talatsaomall.com, will be 8 storeys of shops, restaurants, cinema, gym, disco and hotel.

There is an interesting produce section at **Talaat Kudin**, the ramshackle market on the other side of the bus stop. This market offers many of the same handicrafts and silks as the morning market but is a lot cheaper.

Supermarkets

Phimphone Market, Setthathirath Rd, opposite **Khop Chai Deu Restaurant**. This supermarket has everything a foreigner could ask for in terms of imported food, drink, magazines, translated books, personal hygiene products, household items and much more (and the price to go with it).

Simuang Minimart, Samsenthai Rd, opposite Wat Simuang. Supermarket with a great selection of Western products. Great place to pick up wine but check it is not past its use-by-date.

ⓞ Activities and tours

Vientiane p356, map p358

Cooking

Villa Lao (formerly **Thongbay Guesthouse**) (see page 368), T021-242292. Cooking classes, covering all of meal preparation, from purchasing the ingredients to eating the meal.

Cycling

Bicycles are available for hire from several places in town, see Transport, page 378. A good outing is to cycle downstream along the banks of the Mekong. Cycle south on Tha Deua Rd until Km 5 (watch the traffic) and then turn right down one of the tracks (there are a number) towards the riverbank. A path, suitable for bicycles, follows the river beginning at about Km 4.5. There are monasteries and drinks sellers en route to maintain interest and energy.

Gym

Sengdara, 77/5 Phonthan Rd, T021-414058. This is a very modern, well-equipped gym, with pool, sauna and massage.

Every afternoon at 1700 there is a free aerobics session in the outdoor gymnasium on the river. Completely bizarre but lots of fun.

Kickboxing

Soxai Boxing Stadium, 200 m past the old circus in Baan Dong Paleb. Kickboxing is every Sat between 1400-1600.

Massage, saunas and spas

The best massage in town is given by the blind masseuses in a little street off Samsenthai Rd, 2 blocks down from Simuang Minimart (across from Wat Simuang). There are 2 blind masseuse businesses side-by-side and either one is fantastic: **Traditional Clinic**, T020-5565 9177, and **Porm Clinic** (no English spoken). They are marked by blue signs off both Khou Vieng and Samsenthai roads.
Mandarina, 74 Pang Kham, T021-218703. A range of upmarket treatments between US$5-30. Massage, facials, body scrubs, mini-saunas, oils, jacuzzi.
Papaya Spa, opposite Wat Xieng Veh, T020-5561 0565, www.papayaspa.com. Daily 0900-2000. Surrounded by beautiful gardens. Massage, sauna, facials. They also have a new branch that is more accessible on Lane Xang Avenue just up from the Morning Market.

Shooting

There is a shooting range in the Southern corner of the national stadium US$1-2 for a few rounds.

Swimming and waterparks

Nongchan Water Park, Khou Vieng St, T021-219386. Open 1000-1800. 30 000 kip, children 20 000 kip.
Several hotels in town permit non-residents to use their fitness facilities for a small fee, including the **Tai Pan Hotel** (rather basic), the **Lao Hotel Plaza**, the **Lane Xang Hotel** and the luxurious **Settha Palace** (with a hefty entrance price to boot). The **Australian Embassy Recreation Club** Km 3, Tha Deua Rd, T021-314921, has a fantastic saltwater pool with superb Mekong views.

Ten-pin bowling

Bowling is a very popular local pastime. Although it might sound quite sedate, the bowling alleys are often the only bars that are open after curfew.
The Lao Bowling Center, behind the Lao Plaza Hotel, T021-218661. Good value, shoe hire is included but bring your own socks.

Thak Baat

Every morning at day-break (around 0530-0600) monks flood out of the city's temples, creating a swirl of orange on the streets, as they collect alms. It is truly beautiful to see the misty, grey streets come alive with the robe-clad monks. Foreigners are more than welcome to participate, just buy some sticky rice or other food from the vendors and kneel beside others.

Tour operators

For general travel information for Phou Khao Khouay, visit the **National Tourism Authority**. Most agents will use 'eco' somewhere in their title but this doesn't necessarily mean anything.

Asian Trails, Unit 10, Ban Khounta Thong, Sikhottabong District, T021-263936, www.asiantrails.travel.

Christophe Kittirath, No 15, Unit 01, Ban Savang, Chanthaboury District, T020-5550 4604, laowheels@yahoo.co.uk. Christophe runs tours all over the country with or without public transport, speaks English and French and is very helpful.

Diethelm Travel, Nam Phou Circle, T021-215129, www.diethelmtravel.com. Flight agent only.

Exotissimo, 6/44 Pang Kham Rd, T021-241861, www.exotissimo.com. Tours and travel services. Excellent but pricey.

Green Discovery, Setthathirat Rd, next to Kop Chai Deu T021-223022, www.greendiscoverylaos.com. Specializes in ecotours and adventure travel.

Yoga

Vientiane Yoga Studio, Sokpaluang Rd, Soi 1 (first *soi* on the right after you turn onto Sokpaluang from Khou Vieng Rd), www.vientianeyoga.com. Yoga and Pilates classes, 50,000 kip.

Vang Vieng *p363, map p365*

Tour guides are available for hiking, rafting, visiting the caves and minority villages and can be booked at most travel agents and guesthouses. Safety issues need to be considered when taking part in any adventure activity. There have been fatalities in Vang Vieng from boating, trekking and caving accidents. The Nam Song River can flow very quickly during the wet season (Jul and Aug) and tourists have drowned here. Make sure you wear a life jacket during all water-borne activities and time your trip so you aren't travelling on the river after dark. A price war between tour operators has led

to cost cutting, resulting in equipment that is not well maintained or does not exist at all. With all tour operators it is imperative you are given safety gear and that canoes, ropes, torches and other equipment are in a good state of repair. The more expensive, reputable companies are often the best option (see also Vientiane Tour operators, above). Reliable tour operators include:

Green Discovery, attached to **Xayo`h Café**, T023-511440, www.greendiscoverylaoscom. By far the best tour operator in town. Caving, kayaking, hiking and rock climbing plus motorbike tours and mountain-bike tours from US$22-40 for 1 day. Very professional and helpful. Recommended. Also rents motorbikes from US$25-30 for 1 day. The office may have moved location by the time you read this.

Riverside Tour T020-2225 4137, www.riversidetourlaos.com. Kayaking and adventure tours. Also tour agency; friendly.

VLT Natural Tours, T023-511369, T020-55208283, www.vangviengtour.com. As well as all the usual tours, this company also offers cooking tours, fishing, camping trips, slow boat to Vientiane and a sunset barbecue on the river. Combined trekking, caving, tubing, kayaking is around 150,000 kip; a similar trip with **Green Discovery** is from US$52.

Kayaking and rafting

See also tour operators, above. Kayaking is a very popular activity around Vang Vieng and competition between operators is fierce. There are a wide variety of trips available, ranging from day trips (with a visit to the caves and surrounding villages), to kayaking all the way to Vientiane via the stop-off point at Nam Lik, US$33-87, about 6 hrs, including a 40-min drive at the start and finish. All valuables are kept in a car, which meets kayakers at the end of their paddle. Be wary of intensive rafting or kayaking trips through risky areas during the wet season, as it can be very dangerous. Check equipment thoroughly before committing.

Rock climbing

Vang Vieng is the only really established rock climbing area in the country, with over 50 sites in the locality, ranging from grade 5 to 8A+. Almost all of these climbs have been 'bolted'. There are climbing sites suitable for beginners through to more experienced climbers. **Green Discovery** (see Tour operators, page 377) runs climbing courses almost every day in high season (US$20-45 per day, including equipment rental). The best climbing sites include: Sleeping Cave, Sleeping Wall and Tham Nam Them.

Trekking

Almost all guesthouses and agents offer hiking trips, usually incorporating a visit to caves and minority villages and, possibly, some kayaking or tubing. The best treks are offered through the major tour operators who will provide an English-speaking guide, all transport and lunch for US$10-15 per day.

Tubing

No trip to Vang Vieng is complete without tubing down the Nam Song. Floating slowly along the river is an ideal way to take in the stunning surroundings of limestone karsts, jungle and rice paddies. The drop-off point is 3 km from town near the **Organic Farm**, where several bars and restaurants have been set up along the river. Try and start early in the day as it's dangerous to tube after dark and the temperature of the water drops sharply. Women should take a sarong and avoid walking through town in a bikini, it is culturally unacceptable and highly offensive to the locals.

Since July 2009, tube operators have formed a cartel to benefit the 1555 families in town who have a stake in this activity. Thus there is only 1 place where you can pick up the tubes (marked on map, page 365). Tube collection is from 0830-1530 and costs 55,000 kip including the tuk-tuk ride to the drop-off point and a life jacket. A deposit of 60,000 kip is required. A rented dry bag costs 20,000 kip. For a lost tube the fine is US$7, a lost life jacket US$20 and a lost dry bag US$15. The tube must be returned by 1800 or a fine of 20,000 kip is imposed (people may offer to return the tubes for you; it is best to decline this offer).

It is essential that you wear a life jacket as people have drowned on the river, particularly in the wet season (Jul and Aug) when the river swells and flows very quickly. Without stopping, expect the journey to take 2 hrs in the dry season and 1 hr in the wet season. Most people stop along the way and make a day of it.

☉ Transport

Vientiane *p356, map p358*
Air
Lao Airlines, 2 Pang Kham Rd , T021-212054, www.laoairlines.com, also at Wattay Airport; T021-212051

Phongsavanh Airlines (T021-513 0000) flies to **Xam Neua, Phongsali and Sayaboury.** Thai Airways, Head Office, Luang Prabang Rd, not far past the Novotel, T021-222527, www.thaiairways.com, Mon-Fri 0830-1200, 1300-1500, Sat 0830-1200. At Wattay Airport, 1st floor, Room 106, T021-512024, daily 0700-1200, 1300-1600. Vietnam Airlines, Lao Plaza Hotel, T021-217562, www.vietnamairlines.com.vn, Mon-Fri 0800-1200, 1330-1630.

Prices and schedules are constantly changing, so always check in advance.

Lao Airlines to **Bangkok** (80 mins) and **Chiang Mai** in Thailand; to **Siem Reap** and **Phnom Penh** (1½ hrs); **Kunming** and **Nanning** in China. In Vietnam to **Hanoi** and **Ho Chi Minh City**. Domestic services include **Luang Prabang** (40 mins); and **Pakse** (50 mins). To **Oudomxay** and **Luang Nam Tha**, **Xieng Khouang** (Phonsavan), Phongsavanh Airlines operates flights to **Xam Neua** (50 mins), **Sayaboury** and **Phongsaly** (1 hr).

Bicycle and motorbike
For those energetic enough in the hot season, **bikes** are the best way to get

around town. Many hotels and guesthouses have bikes available for their guests, expect to pay about 10,000 kip per day. There are also many bike hire shops around town. Markets, post offices and government offices usually have 'bike parks' where it is advisable to leave your bike. A small minding fee is charged.

Motorbikes are available for hire from US$5-10 per day and leave your passport as security. Insurance is seldom available anywhere in Laos on motorbikes but most places will also hire out helmets, a necessity. PVO also has a reliable selection of motorbikes from 70,000-250,000 kip per day. Often a driving licence can be used in lieu of a motorbike licence if the police pull you over.

Bus

Vientiane has 3 main public bus terminals: Northern, Southern and Talaat Sao (Morning Market).

Southern bus station Route 13, 9 km north of the city centre (T021-740521). Public buses depart daily for destinations in southern Laos. Prices change around every 3 months and also fluctuate (yes, they go down!) according to gas prices, so these prices are just a guide. The southern bus station has a range of stores, pharmacy and massage. To **Paksan**, at 0730, 1030, 1100, 1200, 1330, 150 km, 1 hr 30 mins, 25,000-40,000 kip. To **Lak Sao** (for the Vietnamese border), 335 km, 8 hrs, 50,000 kip, 3 daily at 0500, 0600, 0700, continuing to **Thakhek**, 360 km, 3 daily, 5-6 hrs, 50,000 kip; 1 VIP bus at 1300, 75,000 kip or take any southbound bus. To **Savannakhet**, 483 km, 8 daily (early morning), 8 hrs, 65,000 kip. Taking the overnight southbound VIP bus to Pakse costs 95,000 kip. To **Pakse**, 736 km, 8 daily, 13 hrs, 100,000 kip; express buses, 5 buses, 130,000 kip; there are also overnight express buses to Pakse, 11 hrs, 150,000 kip at 2030. **Thongli**, T021-242657, operates an overnight VIP service daily at 2030, which takes about the same time but has beds, water, snacks, etc, 135,000 kip. **KVT**, T021-213043, also runs VIP buses to Pakse at 2030.

Banag Saigon, T021-720175, runs buses to **Hanoi**, 24 hrs, 130,000 kip, **Vinh**, 1900, 160,000 kip, **Thanh Hoa**, 1900, 180,000 kip, **Hué**, 1900-1930, 150,000 kip, and **Danang**, 1900-1930, 200,000 kip. These services run on odd days so check in advance.

Northern bus station Route 2, towards the airport 3.5 km from the centre of town, T021-261905. Northbound buses are regular and have a/c. For the more popular routes, there are also VIP buses, which will usually offer snacks and service. To **Luang Prabang**, 400 km, standard buses, 8 daily, 10 hrs, 95,000 kip; VIP buses daily at 0800 and 0900, 8 hrs, 115,000 kip. To **Udomxai**, 550 km, standard buses 0645 and 1345, 13 hrs, 110,000 kip; a/c bus at 1700 daily, 130,000 kip; VIP bus at 1600, 155,000 kip. To **Luang Namtha**, 698 km, 0830 daily, 19 hrs, 140,000 kip. To **Phongsali**, 815 km, 0715 daily, 26 hrs, 160,000 kip. To **Houei Xai**, 895 km, daily 1730, 25-30 hrs, 180,000 kip. To **Sayaboury**, 485 km, standard at 0900 and 1630 daily, 12-15 hrs, 90,000 kip; a/c at 1830 daily, 110,000 kip. To **Xam Neua**, 850 km, at 0700, 0945, 1245, 30 hrs (it may go via Phonsavanh), 150,000 kip. To **Phonsavanh**, 365 km, standard at 0630, 0930, 1600, 10 hrs, 80,000 kip; a/c at 0800 and 1840 daily, 95,000 kip; VIP bus at 2000 daily, 115,000 kip.

Talaat Sao bus station (T021-216507) Across the road from Talaat Sao, in front of Talaat Kudin, on the eastern edge of the city centre. Destinations, distances and fares are listed on a board in English and Lao. Most departures are in the morning and can leave as early as 0400, so many travellers on a tight schedule have regretted not checking departure times the night before. There is a useful map at the station, and bus times and fares are listed clearly in Lao and English. However, it's more than likely you will need a bit of direction at this bus station: staff at the ticket office only speak a little English so a better option is to chat to the friendly chaps in the planning office, who love a visit, T021-216506. The times listed below vary depending on the weather and the number of stops en route.

To the **Southern bus station**, every 30 mins, 0600-1800, 2000 kip. To the **Northern bus station**, catch the Nongping bus (5 daily) and ask to get off at '*Thay song*' (1500 kip). To **Wattay Airport**, every 30 mins, 0640-1800, 3000 kip. Buses to Vang Vieng 5 daily, 3½ hrs, 15,000 kip.

There are numerous buses criss-crossing the province; most aren't very useful for tourists. To the **Friendship Bridge** (Laoside), every 30 mins, 0650-1710, 5000 kip. To **Nong Khai** (Thai side of the Friendship Bridge), 6 daily 0730-1800, about 1 hr including immigration, 15,000-80,000 kip.

Other private bus services To **Vang Vieng**, Green Discovery, from their office on Setthathirat, www.greendiscoverylaos.com, it also runs to Luang Prabang and Pakse. There is also **Sabaidee Bus** for the same price. Both services will pick you up from your guesthouse if you arrange in advance. Other tour companies also offer this service. Sabaidee Bus to **Luang Prabang**, Tue and Thu, 130,000 kip, with a stopover in **Vang Vieng** on the way. Sabaidee also runs international buses to **Bangkok**, ฿800 at 1700 with a change at Nong Khai leaving at 2000, arriving Bangkok 0600. **Green Discovery**, www.greendiscoverylaos.com, also runs international buses to **Udon Thani**, **Bangkok**, **Nong Khai**, **Chiang Mai** and **Pattaya** in Thailand and **Hanoi**, **Vinh**, **Hué**, **Danang** and **Ho Chi Minh City** in Vietnam.

Car hire
Europcar Laos (Asia Vehicle Rental), 354-356 Samsenthai Rd, T021-223 867, www.europcarlaos.com, hires cars.

Taxi
These are mostly found at the **Morning Market** (Talaat Sao) or around the main hotels. Newer vehicles have meters but there are still some ageing jalopies. Flag fall is 8000-12000 kip. A taxi from the Morning Market to the **airport**, US$5-6; to **Tha Deua** (for the Friendship Bridge and Thailand), US$10-12, although you can usually get the trip much cheaper but some taxis are so decrepit that you may as well take a tuk-tuk, 95,000 kip (see below). To hire a taxi for trips outside the city costs around US$20-30 per day. **Lavi Taxi**, T021-350 000 is the only reliable call-up service in town but after 2000 you may not get an answer.

Train
In spring 2009 a new train station opened in Laos, Thanaleng, beyond the Friendship Bridge, where trains cross the border into Thailand and run to Bangkok thus avoiding the need to get on and off transport to cross the border, but you still need to change trains in Nong Khai. See box on the Friendship Bridge border, page 381.

Tuk-tuks
Tuk-tuks usually congregate around **Nam Phou**, **Talaat Sao** and **Talaat Kudin**.

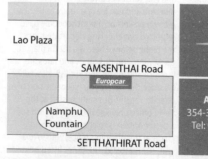

Border essentials: Friendship Bridge

The bridge is 20 km southeast of Vientiane; catch the Thai–Lao International bus from the Talaat Sao terminal (15,000 kip) 90 minutes at 0730, 0930, 1240, 1430, 1530 and 1800 to Nong Khai bus station (see page opposite). Or take one of the Friendship Bridge tuk-tuks from the corner of Setthathirat and Gallieni (close to the French embassy), which run 0700-1800, 30 minutes, 5000 kip to the border, and arrange transport across. The border is open daily 0730-1800. Shuttle minibuses take punters across the bridge every 20 minutes, stopping at the Thai and Lao immigration posts where an overtime fee is charged at weekends and on public holidays.

There are good facilities at the Lao border, including a telephone box, a couple of duty-free shops, some drinks and snack stalls and a post office. Allow up to 1½ hours to get to the bridge and through formalities on the Lao side. The paperwork is pretty swift, unless you are arriving in Lao and require a visa or are leaving the country and have overstayed your visa. Thirty-day visas are processed in about 15 minutes and cost US$30-42 depending on your nationality. You will require a passport-sized photograph and the name of a guesthouse or hotel you are staying at. You will need to bargain hard, but in a friendly way, for a good price on private transport from the border. Coming into Lao the taxis can be a bit sharkish and charge up to US$15 into the centre of Vientiane; it should be no more than US$7-10.

The Thai side is über-efficient but not nearly as friendly. Tuk-tuks wait to take punters to Nong Khai (10 minutes), ฿50 per person; Udon Thani is another hour further on; taxis from the Thai side of the border charge about ฿700 to get you there; add another ฿300 if you organize the Thai taxi from the Lao side. If you get stuck in Nong Khai, Mut Mee Guesthouse (www.mutmee.com) is recommended. From Udon Thani you can get to Bangkok easily by budget airline. Discount airlines (AirAsia and Nok Air) fly several times daily. From Udon Thani, you can catch a minibus or taxi to the Lao border or a bus directly to the border for ฿200. Taking the Udon/Friendship Bridge option between Bangkok and Vientiane will probably only add one hour to your journey, since immigration at Wattay Airport tends to be slow.

Another option is to catch the new overnight train (T021-820228) from Thanaleng near the Friendship Bridge that crosses into Thailand. You must change trains at Nong Khai though for the Bangkok-bound train which goes to Bangkok's Hualamphong Station (฿750-800 for a fan sleeper, ฿950-1050 for an air-conditioned sleeper and ฿1550-1650 for a first-class air-conditioned sleeper) and leaves at 1500 arriving at 0625. Thanaleng to Nong Khai at 1040 and 1700, 15 minutes, ฿20-50. Nong Khai to Bangkok at 1820 arriving 0625 from ฿253 for third class up to ฿1317 for air-conditioned lower bunk first-class sleeper. From Nong Khai to Thanaleng at 1000 and 1600.

Buses also run from both Udon Thani and Nong Khai to Bangkok.

Tuk-tuks can be chartered for longer out-of-town trips (maximum 25 km) or for short journeys of 2-3 km within the city (from 100,000-40,000 kip per person). Printed official prices are 55,000 kip to the airport; 40,000 kip to That Luang and Northern Bus Station; 60,000 kip to the Southern Bus Station; 95,000 kip to the Friendship Bridge; 150,000 kip return to the Beer Lao Factory; 195,000 kip return to the Buddha Park and 80,000 kip per hr sightseeing. An 8-hr charter is officially quoted at US$30. There are also shared tuk-tuks, which run on regular routes along the city's main streets.

For shared tuk-tuks to the Friendship Bridge, see border box, page 381.

Tuk-tuks are available around Nam Phou until 2330 but are quite difficult to hire after dark in other areas of town. The tuk-tuks that congregate on the city corners are generally part of a quasi cartel, it is thus much cheaper to travel on one that is passing through.

To stop a vehicle, simply flag it down. A good, reliable driver is **Mr Souk**, T020-7771 2220, who speaks good English and goes beyond the call of duty.

Vang Vieng *p363, map p365*
Bicycle and motorbike
There are many bicycles for rent in town (10,000 kip per day). There are also a few motorbike rental places (60,000 kip per day); the best of these is diagonally opposite the **Organic Farm Café** in town.

Bus
Buses now leave from the new bus terminal at the New Market, 2 km north of town, T023-511657. Ticket office open daily 0530-1630; English is spoken and staff are helpful. There are toilets, shops and cafés. A tuk-tuk into town should cost around 5000-10,000 kip per person. Minibuses leave from most guesthouses to both Vientiane and Luang Praban. To **Vientiane** on local bus at 0530-0600, 0630, 0700, 1230 and 1400, 30,000 kip, 4 hrs; express bus at 1000, 1300, 60,000 kip, 3½ hrs; pick-ups every 20 mins, 30,000 kip, 4 hrs. To **Luang Prabang** express bus at 1000, 80,000 kip. To **Phonsovan** at 0930, 90,000 kip, 7 hrs.

Private minivan transport and VIP buses Tickets are usually sold by guesthouses and will include a pickup at your hotel to the bus. Minivan to **Vientiane** 0900, 80,000 kip, 3½-4 hrs; drop off at Mekong riverside restaurants. Minibus to **Luang Prabang** 0900 and 1400, 90,000 kip (5-6 hrs). Every guesthouse and travel agent can book the VIP/minivans and they will pick up from your guesthouse.

Tour companies sell through tickets to **Pakse** and international tickets to **Vietnam** and **Bangkok** but there are better, more efficient and cost-effective ways to get back to the Thai capital.

Tuk-tuks
A day trip to the caves should cost US$10 but there have been reports of some drivers offering trips to the caves for 10,000 kip per person and then demanding an outrageous fee for the return leg.

Make sure all prices are set in stone before setting off.

❶ Directory

Vientiane *p356, map p358*
Banks
See Money, page 55 , for details on changing money in Laos. There are now around a dozen or more multicard Visa and MasterCard ATMs in the city. The **Banque Pour le Commerce Exterieur (BCEL)**, corner of Fa Ngum and Pang Kham roads, takes all the usual credit cards (maximum withdrawal 700,000 kip; much less on Sun). Other multicard ATMs can be found in front of the **Novotel**, and next to **Green Discovery** on and beside the petrol station near Wat Simuang. BCEL, 1 Pang Kham Rd, traditionally offers the lowest commission (1.5%) on changing US$ TCs into US$ cash; there is no commission on changing US$ into kip. **Joint Development Bank**, Lane Xane Ave, T021-213535, offers good rates on cash advances and has an ATM.

Embassies and consulates
Australia, Km 4 Thadeua Rd, T021-353800,www.laos.embassy.gov.au. **Britain**, no embassy; served by the Australian Embassy. **Cambodia**, Tha Deua Rd, Km3, T021-314952, visas daily 0730-1030. Cambodian visas US$20. **Canada**, no embassy; served by the Australian Embassy. **China**, Thanon Wat Nak Nyai T021-315105. Visas take 4 days. **France**, Setthathirat Rd,

T021-2126 7400, www.ambafrance-laos.org.
Germany, 26 Sok Paluang Rd, T021-312110.
Japan, Sisavangvong Rd, T021-414400, www.
la.emb-japan.go.jp. **Malaysia,** 23 Singha
Rd, T021-414205. **Myanmar (Burma),** Lao
Thai St, Watnak, T021-314910, daily 0800-
1200, 1300-1630. **Sweden,** Sok Paluang
Rd, T021-315003, www.swedenabroad.se/
vientiane. **Thailand,** Kaysone Phomivane Rd,
T021-214581 (consular section has moved
to Unit 15, Ban Phonsinaun, T021-415335
ext 605, www.consular.go.th, 0830-1200
for visa extensions), Mon-Fri 0830-1200. If
crossing by land, 30-day visas are also issued
at the Friendship Bridge, see page 381. **USA,**
Bartolonies St, Xieng Nyuen, T021-267000,
www.laos.usembassy.gov. **Vietnam,** 85, 23
Singha Rd, T021-413401, www.mofa.gov.
vn/vnemb.la, visas 0800-1045, 1415-1615.
1-month visa costs US$45 and you must wait
3 days. An extra US$5 for the visa in 1 day.

Immigration
Immigration office, Phai Nam Rd (near
Morning Market), Mon-Thu 0800-1200,
1300-1800. Visa extensions can be organized
for US$2 per day. Overstay, US$10 per day.
For visa information, see Essentials, page 63.

Internet
Internet cafés have opened up all over the
city, many on Setthathirat and Samsenthai
roads. You shouldn't have to pay more than
100 kip per min. Internet phones are now
very popular, with most cafés providing this
service for under US$1 per min. Also, most
major internet cafés are fitted with Skype and
headphones. **Apollo Internet,** Setthathirat Rd,
Mon-Fri 0830-2300, Sat and Sun 0900-2300.

Medical services
There are 2 pretty good pharmacies close
to the Talaat Sao Bus Station. **Australian
Embassy Clinic,** Australian Embassy, KM 4
Thadeua Rd, T021-353800/840, Mon-Fri
0830-1230, 1330-1700. **Mahosot Hospital,**
Fa Gnum, T021-214018, suitable for minor
ailments only. For anything major it is

advisable to cross the border to Nong Khai
and visit **AEK Udon International Hospital,**
T+66-4234 2555. In cases of emergency
where a medical evacuation is required,
contact **Lao West Coast Helicopter,** Hangar
703, Wattay International Airport, T021-
512023, www.laowestcoast.com. A charter
to Udon Thani costs from US$1550, subject
to availability and government approval.

Police
Tourist Police Office, Lang Xang Av (in
the same office as the National Tourism
Authority of Laos), T021-251128.

Post
Post Office, Khou Vieng Rd/Lane Xang Av
(opposite market), T021-216425, offers
local and international telephone calls.
Also a good packing service and a philately
counter. To send packages, use **DHL,** Nong
No Rd, near the airport, T021-214868, or
TNT Express, Thai Airways Building, Luang
Prabang Rd, T021-261918.

Telephone
The international telephone office is on
Setthathirat Rd, near Nam Phou Rd, 24 hrs.

Vang Vieng and around
p363, map p365
Banks BCEL, T021-511480, exchanges
cash, TCs and will also do cash advances on
Visa and MasterCard, 0830-1530. Visa and
MasterCard ATM. There are now a number of
ATMs in town. **Internet** There are a number
of internet cafés along the main drag; most
offer international internet calls from 3000
kip per min. **Magnet** is the best of the internet
cafés and offers internet as well as music/
movie transfer to iPod and cash advances
from the EFTPOS facility for 3% commission.
Medical services Vang Vieng Hospital is
located on the road that runs parallel to the
river; it's terribly under-equipped. In most
cases it is better to go to Vientiane. **Post
office** The post office is next to the former
site of the old market, 0830-1600.

Luang Prabang and around

Anchored at the junction of the Mekong and Nam Khan rivers, the former royal capital of Lane Xang is now a UNESCO World Heritage Site. It is home to a spellbinding array of gilded temples, weathered French colonial façades and art deco shophouses. In the 18th century there were more than 65 wats in the city. Yet for all its magnificent temples, this royal 'city' feels more like an easy-going provincial town: at daybreak, scores of monks in saffron robes amble silently out of the monasteries bearing gold-topped wooden boxes in which to collect offerings from the town's residents; in the early evening women cook, old men lounge in wicker chairs and young boys play takraw in the streets. The famous Pak Ou Caves and the Kuang Si Falls are located near the town. ⊂ For listings, see pages 392-401.

▣ Luang Prabang

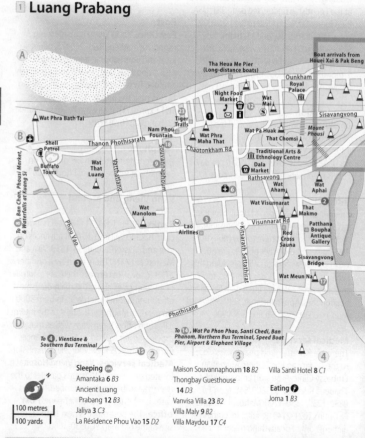

Sleeping ⊜
Amantaka 6 B3
Ancient Luang
  Prabang 12 B3
Jaliya 3 C3
La Résidence Phou Vao 15 D2

Maison Souvannaphoum 18 B2
Thongbay Guesthouse
  14 D3
Vanvisa Villa 23 B2
Villa Maly 9 B2
Villa Maydou 17 C4

Villa Santi Hotel 8 C1

Eating ◑
Joma 1 B3

Ins and outs → *Colour map 1, B2.*

Getting there Flying is still the easiest option with daily connections from Vientiane, plus flights from Bangkok and Chiang Mai to **Luang Prabang International Airport (LPQ)** ① *4 km northeast of town, T071-212172/3.* The airport has a phone box, a couple of restaurants and handicraft shops. There is a standard US$6 charge for a tuk-tuk ride from the airport to the centre.

Route 13 is now safe, with no recent bandit attacks reported, and the road has been upgraded, shortening the journey from Vientiane to eight or nine hours. There are also overland connections with other destinations in northern Laos. Luang Prabang has two main bus stations: **Kiew Lot Sai Neua** (northern bus station), located on the northeast side of Sisavangvong Bridge, for traffic to and from the north; and **Naluang** (southern bus station) for traffic to and from the south. Occasionally buses will pass through the opposite station to what you would expect, so be sure to double-check. The standard tuk-tuk fare to/from either bus station is 10,000 kip. If there are only a few passengers, it's late at night or you are travelling to/from an out-of-town hotel, expect to pay 20,000 kip. These prices tend to fluctuate with the international cost of petroleum. Another option is to travel by river: a firm favourite is the two-day trip between Luang Prabang and Houei Xai (close to the Thai border), via Pak Beng (see page 404). Less frequent are the boats to Muang Ngoi Neua and Nong Khiaw, and Muang Khua.
▶▶*See Transport, page 399.*

Getting around Luang Prabang is a small town and the best way to explore is either on foot or by bicycle. Bicycles can be hired from most guesthouses for US$1 per day. Strolling about this beautiful town is a real pleasure but there are also tuk-tuks and *saamlors* for hire. Depending on the prevailing mood of the local government, motorbikes may or may not be available for hire. Motorbikes can be rented for about $15-20 per day.

Best time to visit Luang Prabang lies 300 m above sea level on the upper Mekong, at its confluence with the Nam Khan. The most popular time to visit the town is during the comparatively cool months of November and December but the best time to visit is from December to February. After this the weather is hotting up and the views are often shrouded in a haze, produced by

Mekong River

Tourist Boats to Pak Ou

Souvanna Khampong

Sakkaline

Nam Khan

Nam Khan

To Pak Ou, Northern Bus Terminal & Xang Hai

To Airport, & Ban Hat Hien

Wat Tao Hai

→ **Luang Prabang maps**
1 Luang Prabang, page 384
2 Luang Prabang detail, page 388

⑤   ⑥

Bars & clubs 🎵
Dao Fao Nightclub **4** *D1*
Muang Swa **2** *C4*
Utopia **3** *C1*

shifting cultivators using fire to clear the forest for agriculture. This does not really clear until May or, sometimes, June. During the months of March and April, when visibility is at its worst, the smoke can cause soreness of the eyes, as well as preventing planes from landing.

In terms of festivals, on the October full moon, the delightful Lai Heua Fai fireboat festival takes place, see page 397.

Tourist information **Luang Prabang Tourist Information Centre** ① *Sisavang-vong, T071-212487*, provides provincial information and offers a couple of good ecotourism treks (which support local communities), including one to Kuang Si and one in Chompet District. The Chompet trek receives quite good reviews and includes visits to hot springs, villages and the chance to watch a traditional performance from Hmong performers.

Background

According to legend, the site of Luang Prabang was chosen by two resident hermits and was originally known as Xieng Thong – 'Copper Tree City'. Details are sketchy regarding the earliest inhabitants of Luang Prabang but historians imply the ethnic Khmu and Lao Theung groups were the initial settlers. They named Luang Prabang, Muang Sawa, which literally translates as Java, hinting at some kind of cross-border support. By the end of the 13th century, Muang Sawa had developed into a regional hub.

A major turning point in the city's history came about in 1353, when the mighty Fa Ngum travelled up the Mekong River, backed by a feisty Khmer army, and captured Muang Sawa. Here, the warrior king founded Lane Xang Hom Khao (Kingdom of a Million Elephants, White Parasol) and established a new Lao royal lineage, which was to last another 600 years. The name of the city refers to the holy Pra Bang, Laos' most sacred image of the Buddha, which was given to Fa Ngum by his father-in-law, the King of Cambodia.

The city had been significantly built up by the time King Visounarat came to power in 1512 and remained the capital until King Setthathirat, fearing a Burmese invasion, moved the capital to Vieng Chan (Vientiane) in 1563.

Luang Prabang didn't suffer as greatly as other provincial capitals during the Indochina wars, narrowly escaping a Viet Minh capture in 1953. During the Second Indochina War, however, the Pathet Lao cut short the royal lineage, forcing King Sisavang Vatthana to abdicate and sending him to a re-education camp in northeastern Laos where he, his wife and his son died from starvation. Despite the demise of the monarchy and years of revolutionary rhetoric on the city's tannoy system, Luang Prabang's dreamy streets have somehow retained the aura of old Lane Xang.

Sights

The sights are conveniently close together but, to begin with, it is worth climbing Phousi or taking a stroll along the river roads to get a better idea of the layout of the town. Most of Luang Prabang's important wats are dotted along the main road, Phothisarath.

Mount Phousi

① *The western steps lead up from Sisavangvong Rd, daily 0700-1800, admission at western steps 20,000 kip. If you want to watch the sun go down, get there early and jostle for position – don't expect to be the only person there.*

Directly opposite the Royal Palace is the start of the steep climb up Mount Phousi, the spiritual and geographical heart of the city and a popular place to come to watch the sunset over the Mekong, illuminating the hills to the east. Phousi is a gigantic rock with sheer forested sides, surmounted by a 25 m-tall *chedi*, **That Chomsi**. The *chedi* was constructed in 1804, restored in 1914 and is the designated starting point for the colourful Pi Mai (New Year) celebrations in April. Its shimmering gold-spired stupa rests on a rectangular base, ornamented by small metal Bodhi trees. Next to the stupa is a little sanctuary, from which the candlelit procession descends at New Year, accompanied by effigies of Nang Sang Kham, the guardian of the New Year, and Naga, protector of the city.

Royal Palace
ⓘ *Sisavangvong Rd, daily 0800-1100, 1330-1600 (closed Tue), 80,000 kip, including a new audio tour and a map. Shorts, short-sleeved shirts and strappy dresses are prohibited; shoes should be removed and bags must be put in lockers. No photography.*

Also called the **National Museum**, the Royal Palace is right in the centre of the city on the main road and close enough to the Mekong to allow royal guests ready access by river. Unlike its former occupants, the palace survived the 1975 revolution and was converted into a museum the following year.

It was built by the French for the Lao King Sisavang Vong in 1904 in an attempt to bind him and his family more tightly into the colonial system of government. Later work saw the planting of the avenue of palms and the filling in of one of two fish ponds. Local residents regarded the ponds as the 'eyes' of the capital, so the blinding of one eye was taken as inviting bad fortune by leaving the city unprotected. The subsequent civil war seemed to vindicate these fears. The palace is Khmer in style, cruciform in plan and mounted on a small platform of four tiers. The only indication of French involvement can be seen in the two French lilies represented in stucco on the entrance, beneath the symbols of Lao royalty. There are a few Lao motifs but, in many respects, the palace is more foreign than Lao: it was designed by a French architect, with steps made from Italian marble; built by masons from Vietnam; embellished by carpenters from Bangkok, and funded by the largesse of the colonial authorities.

The small ornate pavilion of **Wat Ho Prabang** is located in the northeast corner of the palace compound, to the right of the entrance to the Royal Palace. The chapel contains four Khmer Buddhas, ivories mounted in gold, bronze drums used in religious ceremonies and about 30 smaller Buddha images from temples all over the city. The Pra Bang, see below, is due to be moved here.

The main **entrance hall** of the palace was used for royal religious ceremonies, when the Supreme Patriarch of Lao Buddhism would oversee proceedings from his gold-painted lotus throne. It now contains a collection of 15th- to 17th-century Buddha statues. The room to the immediate right of the entrance was the King's reception room, also called the **Ambassadors' Room**. It contains French-made busts of the last three Lao monarchs, a model of the royal hearse (which is kept in Wat Xieng Thong) and a mural by French artist Alex de Fontereau, depicting a day in the life of Luang Prabang in the 1930s.

In comparison to the state rooms, the royal family's **private apartments** are modestly decorated. They have been left virtually untouched since the day the family left for exile in Xam Neua Province. To the rear of the entrance hall, the **Coronation Room** was decorated between 1960 and 1970 for Crown Prince Sisavong Vatthana's coronation, an event which was interrupted because of the war. The walls are a brilliant red with Japanese glass mosaics embedded in a red lacquer base with gilded woodwork and depict scenes from Lao festivals.

To the left of the entrance hall is the reception room of the **King's Secretary**, and beyond it, the **Queen's reception room**, which together house an eccentric miscellany of state gifts from just about every country except the UK.

To the far right of the entrance to the palace is a room (viewed from the outside) in which sits the **Pra Bang**, or **Golden Buddha**, from which the city derived its name. The Buddha is in the attitude of Abhayamudra or 'dispelling fear'. Some believe that the original image is kept in a bank vault, though most dispel this as rumour. It is 90% solid gold. Reputed to have originally come from Ceylon, and said to date from any time between the first and ninth centuries, the statue was moved to Cambodia in the 11th century, given to King Phaya Sirichanta, and was then taken to Lane Xang by King Fa Ngum, who had spent some time in the courts of Angkor and married into Khmer royalty. An alternative story has the Pra Bang following Fa Ngum to the city: it is said he asked his father-in-law, the King of Angkor, to send a delegation of holy men to assist him in spreading the Theravada Buddhist faith in Lane Xang. The delegation arrived bringing with them the Pra Bang as a gift from the Cambodian King. The Pra Bang's arrival heralded the capital's change of name, from Xieng Thong to Nakhon Luang Prabang, 'The city of the great Buddha'. In 1563 King Setthathirat took the statue to Lane Xang's new capital at Vientiane. Two centuries later in 1779 the Thais captured it but it was returned to Laos in 1839. The Pra Bang is revered in Laos as its arrival marked the beginnings of Buddhism in Lane Xang.

② Luang Prabang detail

Sleeping
3 Nagas 14 *B3*
Ammata Guesthouse 20 *A3*
Apsara Rive Droite 15 *B4*
The Belle Rive 3 *A3*
Le Calao Inn 5 *A4*
Oui's Guesthouse 21 *B5*
Pa Phai 8 *A2*
Pack Luck 7 *A3*
Sala Luang Prabang 9 *A1*
Sayo Guesthouse 11 *A1*
Silichit Guesthouse 12 *A2*

Eating
Blue Lagoon 21 *A1*
Café Ban Vat Sene 1 *B2*
Coconut Garden 13 *B1*
Couleur Café 6 *A2*
Dao Fa 3 *B2*
Dyen Sabai 12 *B2*
Khemkhan Food
 Garden 5 *B2*
L'Éléphant 7 *A3*
L'Étranger 8 *B1*
Morning Glory 23 *B3*
Tamarind 22 *A3*
Tamnak Lao 15 *B3*
View Khaem Khong 4 *A1*

100 metres
100 yards

Wat Mai

ⓘ *Sisavangvong Rd, daily 0800-1700, 10,000 kip.*

Next to the Royal Palace is Wat Mai. This royal temple, inaugurated in 1788, has a five-tiered roof and is one of the jewels of Luang Prabang. It took more than 70 years to complete. It was the home of the Buddhist leader in Laos, Phra Sangkharath, until he moved to That Luang in Vientiane. During Pi Mai (New Year), the Pra Bang is taken from the Royal Palace and installed at Wat Mai for its annual ritual cleansing, before being returned to the palace on the third day.

The façade is particularly interesting: a large golden bas-relief tells the story of Phravet (one of the last reincarnations of the Gautama or historic Buddha), with several village scenes, including depictions of wild animals, women pounding rice and people at play. Inside, the interior is an exquisite amalgam of red and gold, with supporting pillars similar to those in Wat Xieng Thong.

Wat Sene (Wat Saen)

Further up the promontory, Wat Sene was built in 1718 and was the first sim in Luang Prabang to be constructed in Thai style, with a yellow and red roof. The exterior may lack subtlety, but the interior is delicate and rather refined, painted red, with gold patterning on every conceivable surface. Sen means 100,000 and the wat was built with a local donation of 100,000 kip from someone who discovered 'treasure' in the Khan River.

→ **Luang Prabang maps**
1 Luang Prabang, page 384
2 Luang Prabang detail, page 388

Bars & clubs 🍸
Hive **18** *B1*
Icon Klub **14** *B2*
Khily Wine Bar **24** *B5*
Lao Lao Garden **26** *B1*
Lao Lao Sports Bar **19** *B1*
Pack Luck **25** *B2*

Wat Xieng Thong

ⓘ *Xiengthong Rd, daily 0800-1700, 20,000 kip.*

Wat Xieng Thong Ratsavoraviharn, usually known as just Wat Xieng Thong, is set back from the road, at the top of a flight of steps leading down to the Mekong. It is arguably the finest example of a Lao monastery, with graceful, low-sweeping eaves, beautiful stone mosaics and intricate carvings. The wat has several striking chapels, including one that houses a rare bronze reclining Buddha and another sheltering a gilded wooden funeral chariot. Inside, resplendent gold-stencilled pillars support a ceiling with *dharma* wheels. The striking buildings in the tranquil compound are decorated in gold and post-box red, with imposing tiled roofs and mosaics, making this the most important and finest royal wat in Luang Prabang. It was built by King Setthathirat in 1559, and is one of the few buildings to have survived the successive Chinese raids that marked the end of the 19th century.

The **sim** is a perfect example of the Luang Prabang style. Locals believe the roof has been styled to resemble a bird, with wings stretched out to protect her young.

The eight central wooden pillars have stencilled motifs in gold and the façade is finely decorated. The beautiful gold-leaf inlay is predominantly floral in design but a few images illustrate *Ramayana*-type themes and the interior frescoes depict *dharma* wheels and the enigmatic King Chantaphanit. At the rear of the sim is a mosaic representation of the thong copper 'Tree of Life' in glass inlay.

Behind the sim are two red *haw song phra* (**side chapels**): the one on the left is referred to as **La Chapelle Rouge** (the Red Chapel) and houses a rare Lao reclining Buddha in bronze, dating from the 16th century. The exterior mosaics which relate local tales, were added in 1957 to honour the 2500th anniversary of the Buddha's birth, death and enlightenment. The other *haw song phra*, to the right of the sim, houses a standing image of the Buddha which is paraded through the streets of the city each New Year and doused in water.

The **Chapel of the Funeral Chariot** is diagonally across from the sim and was built in 1962. The centrepiece is the grand 12-m-high gilded wooden hearse, with its seven-headed serpent, which was built for King Sisavang Vong, father of the last sovereign, and used to carry his urn to the stadium next to Wat That Luang where he was cremated in 1959. It was built on the chassis of a six-wheel truck by the sculptor, Thid Tan. On top of the carriage sit several sandalwood urns, none of which contain royal ashes. Originally the urns would have held the bodies of the deceased in a foetal position until cremation. The mosaics inside the chapel were never finished but the exterior is decorated with some almost erotic scenes from the *Phalak Phalam* (the local version of the *Ramayana*), sculpted in enormous panels of teak wood and covered with gold leaf.

Wat Visunnarat (Wat Wisunarat) and That Makmo
① *Daily 0800-1700, 20,000 kip.*

This is better known as Wat Visoun and is on the south side of Mount Phousi. It is a replica of the original wooden building, constructed in 1513, which had been the oldest building in Luang Prabang, until it was destroyed by marauding Chinese tribes. The sim is virtually a museum of religious art, with numerous 'Calling to the Rain' Buddha statues: most are more than 400 years old and have been donated by locals. Wat Visoun also contains the largest Buddha in the city and old stelae engraved with Pali scriptures (called *hin chaleuk*). The big stupa, commonly known as That Makmo ('melon stupa'), was built by Queen Visounalat in 1504. It is of Sinhalese influence with a smaller stupa at each corner, representing the four elements.

Wat Phra Maha That

Close to the **Hotel Phousi** on Phothisarath, this is a typical Luang Prabang wat, built in the 1500s and restored at the beginning of this century. The ornamentation of the doors and windows of the sim merit attention, with their graceful, golden figures from the Phalak phalam (the *Ramayana*). The pillars, ornamented with massive nagas, are also in traditional Luang Prabang style and reminiscent of certain styles adopted in Thailand.

Wat Manolom

South of Wat That Luang, Wat Manolom was built by the nobles of Luang Prabang to entomb the ashes of King Samsenthai (1373-1416) and is notable for its large armless bronze Buddha statue, one of the oldest Lao images of the Buddha, which dates back to 1372 and weighs two tonnes. Locals maintain that the arm was removed during a skirmish between Siamese and French forces during the latter part of the 19th century.

While it is not artistically significant, the temple – or at least the site – is thought to be the oldest in the city, dating back, so it is said, to 1375 and the reign of Fa Ngum.

Wat Pa Phon Phao and Santi Chedi
① *3 km northeast of town, near Ban Phanom, daily 0800-1000, 1300-1630, donation expected.*
Outside town, Wat Pa Phon Phao is a forest meditation centre renowned for the teachings of its famous abbot, Ajahn Saisamut, one of the most popular monks in Lao history. More famous to tourists, though, is Santi Chedi, known as the Peace Pagoda. It looks as though it is made of pure gold from a distance but is rather disappointing close up. The wat was started in 1959 but was only completed in 1988; the names of donors are inscribed on pillars inside. It is modelled on the octagonal Shwedagon Pagoda in Yangon (Rangoon) and its inner walls are festooned with gaily painted frescoes of macabre allegories. Less grotesque paintings, extending right up to the fifth floor, document the life of the Buddha. On the second level, it is possible to duck through a tiny opening to admire the Blue Indra statues and the view of Luang Prabang.

Traditional Arts and Ethnology Centre
① *Ban Khamyong, T071-253364, www.taeclaos.org, Tue-Sun 0900-1800, 20,000 kip.*
A fantastic museum dedicated to the various ethnic groups in Laos. This non-profit centre has a permanent exhibition featuring fantastic photographs, religious artefacts, clothing, household objects and handicrafts. Within the exhibition there is a focus on the Hmong and their New Year celebrations; the Khmu and their baskets and art of backstrap looms; the Mien Yao embroidery and Lanten Taoist religious ceremonies, the Tai Dam bedding and Tai Lue culture. Truly this museum is a must-see in Luang Prabang – particularly for those that are venturing further north to go trekking. Attached to the centre is a handicraft shop that directly supports ethnic artisan communities. There's also a café and a small library.

Around Luang Prabang

Pak Ou caves → *Colour map 1, B3.*
① *20,000 kip, free for children. Torches are available but candles make it possible to see reasonably well after your eyes have become accustomed to the dark. A boat trip from Luang Prabang is the best way to reach the caves. Rest houses, tables and a basic toilet are available.*
The Pak Ou Caves are perhaps the most popular excursion from Luang Prabang and are located 25 km upstream from the city, set in the side of a limestone cliff opposite the mouth of the Mekong's Nam Ou tributary (Pak Ou means 'Mouth of the Ou'). The two caves are studded with thousands of wooden and golden Buddha images – 2500 in the lower cave and 1500 in the upper – and are one of the main venues for Pi Mai in April, when hundreds make the pilgrimage upriver from Luang Prabang.

The two sacred caves were supposedly discovered by King Setthathirat in the 16th century but it is likely that the caverns were associated with spirit (*phi*) worship before the arrival of Buddhism in Laos. For years the caves, which locals still believe to be the home of guardian spirits, were inhabited by monks.

Kuang Si Falls → *Colour map 1, B3.*
① *30 km south Luang Prabang, 20,000 kip, parking 2500 kip. There are public toilets and changing rooms. Travel agents run tours or you can charter a tuk-tuk for about US$15 return.*

Slow boats take 1 hr down and 2 hrs back upriver, via Ban Ou (a pretty little village), where it is necessary to take a tuk-tuk for the last 6 km or so to the falls.

These waterfalls are on a tributary of the Mekong. The trip to the falls is almost as scenic as the cascades themselves, passing through small Hmong and Khmu villages and vivid, green, terraced rice paddies. The falls are stunningly beautiful, misty cascades flowing over limestone formations, which eventually collect in several tiered, turquoise pools. Best of all, and despite appearances, it's still possible to take the left-hand path halfway up the falls and strike out through the pouring torrents and dripping caves to the heart of the waterfall. Note that swimming is only permitted in designated pools and, as the Lao swim fully clothed, you should wear modest swimwear and bring a sarong.

Hoy Khoua Waterfall (Tad Hoy Khoua)
ⓘ *14 km west of Luang Prabang in Ban Pakleung.*

Beautiful two-tiered cascades that plummet 50 m, with a deep pool at the bottom. There are several Hmong and Khmu villages in the vicinity. To get to the falls cross the Mekong by boat at Tha Heua (boat station) in Luang Prabang to Xiang Men Village and then travel the rest by road. There are three bungalows here at **Tad Hoy Khoua Guesthouse**, T020-5557 0825.

◉ Luang Prabang and around listings

For Sleeping and Eating price codes and other relevant information, see Essentials pages 40-43.

⊜ Sleeping

Luang Prabang *p384, maps p384 and p388*

Accommodation in Luang Prabang continues to expand at the rate of knots. There were a few new places in development at the time of publication worth keeping an eye out for, in particular a new luxury riverfront hotel built in a former palace next to Wat Xieng Thong that will probably be completed in late 2011.

LL Amantaka, Kingkitsarath Rd, T071-860333, www.amanresorts.com. For those on the ultimate splurge, slip into one of the Pool Villas (complete with private plunge pool) in this latest addition to the Aman Resort chain. Minimalist decor and top-notch gym and spa now grace the old buildings of the French colonial hospital at the foot of Phousi hill. Try the Four Hands Massage for a supremely relaxing experience.

LL La Résidence Phou Vao, T071-212 5303, www.residencephouvao.com. Best hotel

in town by a mile. Every little detail in this plush hotel is perfect, from the fragrance of frangipani that wafts through the foyer, to the carefully lit pool with lines of lamps. Massive, beautiful rooms with lounge area, fresh fruit and a simply divine bathroom. A luxury hotel through and through. In the low season they drop their rates by about US$200.

LL-L Villa Maly, T071-253902, www.villa-maly.com. This is a gorgeous boutique hotel set around a pool with ivory umbrellas in a leafy garden. The former royal residence has been lavished with attention: it's stylish and petite and the rooms are plush; the bathrooms, however, are small with serious practical flaws. Service is impeccable.

L 3 Nagas by Alila, Sakkaline Rd, T071-253888, www.alilahotels.com/3nagas. Housed in a beautifully restored building, with an annexe across the road, this boutique hotel is a running contender for best room in town. Attention to detail is what sets this hotel apart: from the 4-poster bed covered with local fabrics, to the large deep-set bathtub with natural handmade beauty products. Private balconies or rooms leading onto a stunning courtyard. There's a lovely sitting area in each room, plus traditional *torchis* walls and teak floors. Breakfast (included) is served in the fantastic café downstairs. Internet facilities available for those travelling with laptop.

L-AL The Belle Rive, Souvannakhamphong Rd, T071-260733, www.thebellerive.com. Elegant rooms occupy refurbished structures facing the Mekong on a quiet end of the peninsula. The hotel's restaurant garden patio offers fine views of boats drifting by. The attraction of this hotel lies in its charm; you would almost expect to find Graham Greene or Noel Coward staying here.

AL-A Villa Maydou, set very close to the grounds of Wat Meun Na, T071-254601, www. villamaydou.com. Slightly on the expensive side but beautiful nonetheless. The hotel has a very evocative Buddhist feel due to its location right on the doorstep of Wat Meun Na. The French-owned hotel is set in restored government buildings, originally built in 1925. Spacious airy a/c rooms simply decorated in a modern style with bathtub and minibar.

AL-A Villa Santi Hotel, Sisavangvong Rd, T071-252157, www.villasantihotel.com. Almost an institution in Luang Prabang, this is a restored house from the early 20th century that served as the private residence of the first King Sisavangvong's wife and then Princess Manilai. It's a charming place, full of character and efficiently run and has just received a much-needed facelift. There are 6 heavenly suites in the old building, and 14 newer rooms, with baths and showers, in a stylishly built annexe. The daughter of the official royal cook rustles up mouthwatering French cuisine in the **Princess Restaurant** and there are attractive seating areas in the garden, lobby or on the balcony.

A Ancient Luang Prabang, Sisavangvong Rd, T071-212264, www. ancientluangprabang.com. 12 fantastically designed open-plan rooms featuring a big modern bathtub (separate toilet). The perfect romantic retreat for couples but not the place to bunk down with your mother. Rooms facing the road can be a bit noisy as the night market carries on down below.

These rooms represent good value though. Lovely wooden furnishings. Café downstairs with Wi-Fi and a good range of coffees including frappés.

A Le Calao Inn, river road, T071-212100, www.calaoinn.laopdr.com. Enclosed by yellow walls, this Portuguese/French colonial (1902) building boasts beautiful rooms in an incomparable position overlooking the Mekong. The balcony view is a real plus, so ensure you ask for a room with water views.

A Maison Souvannaphoum, Phothisarath, T071-212200, www.angsana.com. Formally Prince Souvannaphouma's residence, this place really is fit for royalty. There are 4 spacious suites and 23 rooms, with a/c, aromatherapy burners and special treats left in the rooms. The service is top-notch.

A-B Sala Luang Prabang, 102/6 Ounkham Rd, T071-252460, www.salalao.com. Very chic, renovated 100-year-old building several of which overlook the Mekong. Nice use of exposed beams and stone inlay in communal areas. Rooms have a minimalist, up-to-date edge with a/c, modern bathrooms, and doors either opening onto a small courtyard or river balcony (more expensive). Bus, car and bicycle hire available.

A-C The Apsara, Kingkitsarath, T071-254670, www.theapsara.com. Ivan Scholte, wine connoisseur and antique collector, has done a perfect job on this establishment. It oozes style. The stunningly beautiful rooms are themed by colour, with 4-poster beds, changing screen, big bathtub and lovely balcony. Very romantic with a modern twist. The rooms in the 2nd building are equally magnificent and have large terrazzo showers you could fit an elephant in. The foyer and lovely restaurant (see Eating) are decorated with Vietnamese lanterns, Burmese offering boxes and modern art. Room rate includes breakfast. Get in early, this popular place gets booked up in advance.

A-C The Apsara Rive Droite, Ban Phanluang, T071-254670, www.theapsara. com. The Apsara's 9-room cousin across the Khan River is accessible by boat from the other Apsara. Spacious, well appointed rooms sport a unique French-Lao vibe and have balconies that have striking views of the city. This hotel also has the first salt-water pool in Luang Prabang, if not the country.

A-C Sayo Guesthouse, Sotikoumman Rd, T071-252614, sayo@laotel.com. A lovely hotel set in colonial mansion. The front rooms are beautifully and tastefully decorated with local fabrics and woodwork, polished wooden floors and furniture, and they boast a fantastic view over Wat Xieng Mouan – you can watch the monks carving, painting and woodworking. The back rooms aren't as good value but are still recommended. This hotel also has branches on the Mekong and near the post office.

B Pack Luck, opposite L'Éléphant, T071-253373, packluck@hotmail.com. This boutique hotel has 5 rooms that you couldn't swing a cat in but are tastefully decorated with beautiful fabrics and have bathrooms with deep slate bathtubs.

C Ammata Guesthouse, T071-212175, phetmanyp@yahoo.com.au. Very popular guesthouse with largish rooms decorated simply and stylishly with wooden furniture and polished floorboards. Hot water and en suite bathroom.

C Oui's Guesthouse, at the end of the peninsula in Ban Khili on Sukkaserm, T071-252374, ouisguesthouse@gmail.com. Charming little guesthouse with sparkling new rooms with polished floorboards, hot water, TV and fridge. Nicely decorated with local artefacts. Fantastic wine bar next door.

C Riverside Guesthouse, T071-212664, www.villariverside.com. Small, attractive guesthouse in a quiet part of town. There are 5 rooms on the 1st floor (1 with a great balcony) but walls are thin and so the concrete ground floor rooms are a better option. The owner is really friendly and helpful. Wi-Fi available.

D-E Silichit Guesthouse, just off Ounkham Rd, T071-212758. Despite the dubious sounding name, this clean guesthouse is excellent value and well located.

Comfortable rooms with fan, en suite bathroom and hot water. The very friendly owners speak English and French, and often invite guests to sit down for a family dinner or have a Beer Lao. As with most budget places, prices drop dramatically in the low season.

E Jaliya, Phamahapasaman Rd, T071-252154. The ever-popular **Jaliya** has a range of bungalow-type rooms on offer, with varied facilities, from shared bathrooms and fan through to a/c and TV, so take a look around. Relaxing garden area. Bicycle and motorbike rental.

E Vanvisa Villa, T071-212925, vandara1@hotmail.com. Brightly coloured guesthouse down a quaint street. This is a little gem, with teak floors, large, characterful and immaculate rooms and friendly owners. The downstairs has beautiful handicrafts and antiques. It's a bit run down but has a homely feel.

E-F Pa Phai, opposite Wat Pa Phai. This guesthouse is run by an elderly lady who speaks good English and French. It is a bit run down but classic Laos: an attractive little wooden place with a shady garden and a veranda on the first floor. 10 clean rooms (separated only by rattan walls – which don't leave much to the imagination), very clean bathrooms, bikes for rent and same day laundry service. Recommended.

Hotels out of Luang Prabang

D Thongbay Guesthouse, Ban Vieng May, 3 km southeast of the centre of Luang Prabang, T071-253234, www.thongbbay-guesthouses.com. Absolutely stunning set-up of modern bungalows overlooking the Nam Khan. 12 bungalows including 2 extra large family-sized ones. Beautiful tropical garden with a small pond as a centrepiece. The rooms overlooking the river are the best, affording fantastic views of the laid-back rural life. Bungalows have a fridge, 4-poster bed and hot water. Popular with tour groups so advanced booking is necessary. Recommended.

❼ Eating

Luang Prabang p384, maps p384 and p388

Note that, as Luang Prabang has a curfew; most places won't stay open past 2200.

The most famous local delicacy is *khai pehn*, dried river weed, mainly from the Nam Khan, which is mixed with sesame, fried and eaten nationwide. *Cheo bong*, a spicy, smoky purée made with buffalo hide, is also popular throughout the country. Other delicacies include: *phak nam*, a watercress that grows around waterfalls and is commonly used in soups and salads; *mak kham kuan*, tamarind jam, and *mak nat kuan*, pineapple jam.

One of the best local culinary experiences is to grab some Lao takeaway food from the night market that runs off **Sisavangvong Rd**, 1600-2200. Here you can pick up fresh spring rolls (*nem dip*), papaya salad (*tam som*), sticky rice (*khao niao*), the local delicacy Luang Prabang sausage (*Sai Oua*), barbecue chicken on a stick (*gai*) or fish (*pa*), dried buffalo (*sin savanh*) and dried river weed. There are also a number of cheap buffets where you can get a selection of local curries and dishes. If you don't want your food too spicy ask for '*bo pet*'.

℣℣℣-℣℣ L'Éléphant, Ban Vat Nong, T071-252482, contact@elephantrestau.com. About as fine as dining gets in Luang Prabang. Very upmarket and utterly delectable cuisine. Pan-fried fillet of snapper, with capers and basil-flavoured mash is delicious, as are the simmered scallops. Also a number of Lao dishes. There are 3 set menus and an extensive wine list.

℣℣-℣ The Apsara, see Sleeping. Beautifully decorated restaurant offering modern Lao/Thai/Western fusion cuisine. Try their delicious red curry cream soup with lentils and smoked duck or braised beef shin Chinese style. Great fish cakes. Good value.

℣℣-℣ Blue Lagoon, beside the Royal Palace, www.blue-lagoon-cafe.com, T071-253698. This restaurant offers a great selection of delicious hearty European meals – especially Swiss-inspired meals such as the fondue

chinoise. Great steaks, beef stroganoff, pasta and ice creams. Indoor and outdoor seating in comfortable candlelit garden setting.

℣℣-℣ Coconut Garden, Sakkaline Rd, T071-252482. A hip spin-off of L'Elephant and centrally located on main street. Similar French and Lao menu but affordable prices. The chic bar and excellent service make this a place not to miss.

℣℣-℣ Couleur Café/Restaurant, Ban Vat Nong, T020-5562 1064. The French expats in town have nothing but praise for this place with its French and Lao meals and ambient setting. Good wine. This is the place for the carnivores as it has become renowned for its steaks.

℣℣-℣ Dyen Sabai, Ban Phan Luang, T020-5510 4817. In the dry season, this cosy, prettily lit spot is accessible via bamboo bridge (4000 kip 0800-1700, 1700-2330 free) across the Khan River (around mid-Nov to late May). From late May to mid-Nov the restaurant offers free paddle boat rides to and fro across the river. The original cocktails (happy hour 1200-1900) and Lao food are not to be missed. Amazing sunset views! This is a highly recommended spot.

℣ Dao Fa, Sisavangvong Rd, T071-215651, www.daofa-bistro.com. Great selection of teas and coffees, fab ice creams and tasty home-made pasta. The latter is the real draw and is recommended. Brightly decorated space with pavement seating.

℣ Morning Glory, Sakkaline Rd, 0800-1600. Small but cosy Thai restaurant decorated with the proprietor's photographs and paintings. Intimate open-style kitchen serving up fantastic home-style meals – great juices, breakfasts and curries. Try the *Tom Kha Gai* and zesty juice.

℣ Tamarind, facing Wat Nong, T020-7777 0484, www.tamarindlaos.com. Mon-Sat 1100-1800. Brilliant restaurant offering modern Lao cuisine; an utterly exceptional dining experience. Try the 5-bites (the Lao equivalent to tapas), the pumpkin soup is to die for and the tamarind juice is exceptional. Even better than their à la carte menu are the 'dining experiences' such as the traditional

Lao Celebration meal *Pun Pa*, which includes succulent marinated fish and purple sticky rice dessert, or the Adventurous Lao Gourmet degustation menu, which comes with clear explanations of what each dish is. They also do **market tours** with in-depth explanations of Lao delicacies (advance booking is essential) and can organize picnics. You also can't go wrong drinking a chilli-watermelon granita, watching the colours of the temple take on a surreal glow at sunset. The owners Joy and Caroline have been receiving accolades from around the region.

¶ **Tamnak Lao**, Sisavangvong Rd, opposite **Villa Santi**, T071-252525. Brilliant restaurant, serving modern Lao cuisine, with a strong Thai influence. Very popular with tour groups. The freshest ingredients are used: try fish and coconut wrapped in banana leaf or pork-stuffed celery soup. Atmospheric surroundings, particularly upstairs, yet service can be a bit spotty. Best for dinner.

¶ **View Khaem Khong**, Ounkham Rd, T071-212726. The most popular of the dining establishments along the river with consistently excellent food. Good for a beer at sunset. Tasty Luang Prabang sausage, curry spaghetti and *laap*.

Cafés and bakeries

Café Ban Vat Sene, Sakkaline Rd. Great French food, more of a restaurant than a café, upmarket, great for breakfast.

Joma, Sisavangvong Rd, T071-252292. Serves an utterly delicious array of comfort foods. If you're planning a trek or boat trip get yout picnic food here.

L'Étranger, Kingkitsarath Rd, T020-5547 17036. This is a great little bookshop-cum-café. Outstanding breakfasts. Books are rented here for 5000 kip per day. A movie is shown daily at 1900.

⊕ Bars and clubs

Luang Prabang *p384, maps p384 and p388*
Dao Fa nightclub on the way to the South Bus Station. Extremely popular with locals, plays Asian dance music.

Hive Bar, Kingkitsarath Rd, next to L'Étranger. Luang Prabang's most happening bar-club is good for a dance, though it has become quieter now that the competition around it has started to grow.

Icon Klub, Just off of Sisavangvong Rd near the Khan River. For bohemians, poets and lovers, this Hungarian-owned bar is perfect for an eclectic drink. Signature cocktails and a worldly clientele make for interesting evenings of conversation. Open from 1730 until the bar runs dry!

Khily Wine Bar, tucked away next door to **Oui's Guesthouse** at the end of the peninsula. A secret hotspot for locals. This intimate bar has high chairs and a long bar stocked with an extensive selection of *lao-lao* and wine. Great for a quiet drink.

L'Éléphant, **La Résidence Phou Vao** and **Apsara**, provide attractive settings for a drink. A sunset beer at the restaurants overlooking the river is divine. After everything closes between 2200 and 2300 most locals either head to Dao Fa or have a bowl of soup and a cold beverage on Phou Vao Rd at one of the many *pho* noodle shops.

Lao Lao Garden, Kingkitsarath Rd. A tiered landscaped terrace, with low lighting, that's become a favourite backpacker haunt with cheap, delicious cocktails. A bonfire keeps you cozy in the winter months. The Lao-style barbecue is the best in town.

Lao Lao Sports Bar, Kingkitsarath Rd, opposite **Hive Bar** (formerly known as **Khob Jai**). This bar fills up during football matches, televised on a big screen.

Muang Swa, Phouvao Rd. Local style nightclub decked out with low couches and alternates between Thai pop, Lao traditional music and occasional western oldies. Practice your Lamvong (circle dance) moves. Part 50s prom, part 70s disco and highly recommended.

Pack Luck, Sisavangvong Rd. For a more upmarket drink, this cosy wine bar has a great selection of tipples and well-selected wines. This modern establishment is high on atmosphere, with comfy beanbags, modern art adorning its walls and candlelit tables.

Utopia, on the Khan River in Ban Aphay. Landscaped gardens, a sand volleyball court and a long wooden deck overlook the Khan. Great for a drink at sunset, but there are better places in town for food.

◎ Entertainment

Luang Prabang *p384, maps p384 and p388*
Theatre and dance
Traditional dance performances are held Mon, Wed and Sat at 1800, at the **Royal Palace**; US$6-15.

◎ Festivals and events

Luang Prabang *p384, maps p384 and p388*
Apr Pi Mai (Lao New Year; movable) is the time when the tutelary spirits of the old year are replaced by those of the new. It has special significance in Luang Prabang, with certain traditions celebrated in the city that are no longer observed in Vientiane. It lasts 11 days.
May Vien Thiene (movable). Candlelit festival.
Sep Boat races. Boats are raced by the people living in the vicinity of each wat.
Oct Lai Heua Fai (Fireboat Festival). Each village creates a large boat made of bamboo and paper and decorated with candles and offerings. These are paraded down main street to Wat Xieng Thong where they are judged and sent down into the Mekong to bring atonement for sins. All of the temples and most houses are decorated with paper lanterns and candles. People also make their own small homemade floats, similar to Loy Krathong in Thailand, to release in the Mekong River.
Dec Luang Prabang Film Festival, www.lpfilmfest.org. The country's 1st and only major film festival, this new annual event held in early Dec showcases Southeast Asian cinema. The project also produces ongoing educational activities for young Lao relating to media literacy.

◎ Shopping

Luang Prabang *p384, maps p384 and p388*
Caruso Gallery, Sisavangvong Rd (towards the **Three Nagas Boutique Hotel**) stunning but expensive wood furniture and artefacts.
Naga Creations, Sisavangvong Rd, T071-212775. A large collection of jewellery and trinkets, combining Lao silver with quality semi-precious stones. Both contemporary and classic pieces. Some truly innovative work by the jeweller **Fabrice**, including beautiful use of beetle wings (the same style that were once used to adorn royal clothing).
Ock Pop Tok, near L'Éléphant restaurant, T071-253219. **Ock Pop Tok**, which literally translates as 'East meets West', truly incorporates the best of both worlds in beautiful designs and fabrics. It specializes in naturally dyed silk, which is of a much better quality than synthetically dyed silk as it doesn't run. Clothes, household items, hangings and custom-made orders are also available (if ordered well in advance). Check out the **Fibre2Fabric** gallery next door to see the stories behind the fabulous creations.
Patthana Boupha Antique Gallery, Ban Visoun, T071-212262. This little gem can be found in a partitioned-off area in a fantastic colonial building. Antique silverware and jewellery, Buddhas, old photos and fine textiles. Less common are furniture and household items. Reasonable prices. Often closed, so ring beforehand.
Satri Lao Silk, Sisavangvong Rd, T071-219295. Truly beautiful silks and handicrafts for sale. Can sometimes be slightly over-priced, but definitely worth a look.

Markets
Night market, sprawls down several blocks off Sisavangvong Rd (this market has been moving around the last few years but is expected to return to Sisavangvong Rd).

Daily 1700-2230. Hundreds of villagers flock to the market to sell their handicrafts, ranging from silk scarves through to embroidered quilt covers and paper albums. The market shouldn't be missed.

Phousy market, 1.5 km from the centre of town. This market is a real gem: aside from the usual fruit and vegetables, it is a fantastic place to pick up quality silk garments. Pre-made silk clothes are sold here for a fraction of the price of the shops in town. Make sure that you are very detailed with instructions and ensure the same colour thread is used.

Talat Dala, housed in a market building in the middle of town on the corner of Setthathirat and Chao Sisophon roads, has been recently revamped to become a major market for artisans and jewellers to sell their wares.

Silver

There are several Lao silversmiths around the Nam Phou area (fountain), where you can watch the artisans ply their trade. **Thit Peng**, signposted almost opposite Wat That, is a workshop and small shop.

⏱ Activities and tours

Luang Prabang *p384, maps p384 and p388*
Cookery classes

There are a number of classes offered in Luang Prabang. The cooking classes are ordered in preference below.

Tamarind, www.tamarindlaos.com, facing Wat Nong, T020-7777 0484. This successful restaurant has been running specialized classes for groups in their enchanting jungle garden school outside of town. Recommended.

Tamnak Lao, T071-252525, www.laocookingcourse.com, US$25 per person for 1-day cooking class, including shopping at the markets.

Tum Tum Cheng, Sakkaline Rd, T071-253388, www.tumtumcheng.com. Mon-Sat. Popular cooking classes operating since 2001. 1 day, US$25; 2 days, US$45; 3 days, US$60. Advanced bookings are required.

Elephants tours and activities

Elephant Village, 15 km from Luang Prabang (visits and activities can be organized through their office on Sisavangvong Rd, www.elephantvillage-laos.com, T071-252417).This was originally established in conjunction with **Tiger Trails** in Luang Prabang. They have bought old elephants that were chained up in Hongsa as they were no longer useful for hauling timber. In order to keep the old elephants active, the operators run a number of activities. Tourists can participate in up to 25 activities at the elephant park, including experiencing life as a *mahout* (elephant keeper), washing the elephants or trekking with them. There are a few other similar elephant park projects but these are pale imitations.

Exhibitions and galleries

Fibre2Fabric, 71 Ban Vat Nong (next door to **Ock Pop Tok**), T071-254761, www.fibre2fabric.org. A fantastic gallery exhibiting textiles and a display on the culture surrounding the textiles of different ethnic groups. Exhibition with photography, weaving and explanations of local ethnic customs and cultures associated with textile production. Local weavers often on hand to explain.

Kinnaly Gallery, Sakkaline Rd, T020-5555 7737. Gallery featuring black and white photographic work.

Kop Noi, Ban Aphay, www.kopnoi.com. This little shop has a rotating exhibition. They also exhibit photographs from renowned Lao photographer Sam Sisombat.

Spa and massage

Aroma Spa, Sisavangvong Rd, T020-77611255. Another mid-priced spa offering aromatherapy, facials, body scrubs, etc.

Khmu Spa, Sisavangvong Rd, T071-212092. A range of cheaply priced massages including the Khmu massage (gentler, lighter strokes), Lao massage (stretching, cracking and pressure points) and foot massage. Also has herbal sauna. Open until 2200.

Maison Souvannaphoum (see Sleeping).
A spa with a range of luxurious and
expensive treatments. For sheer indulgence.
Red Cross Sauna, opposite Wat Visunnarat,
reservations T071-212303. Daily 0900-2100
(1700-2100 for sauna). Massage 30,000
kip per hr, traditional Lao herbal sauna
10,000 kip. Bring your own towel or sarong.
Profits go to the Lao Red Cross.
The Spa at La Residence Phou Vao www.
residencephouvao.com, T071-212530.
Offers 3-hr massage courses, US$190 for
2 people. This includes a 1-hr massage for
each person, the class, a handbook and oils.
Spa Garden, Ban Phonheauang, T071-
212325, spagardenlpb@hotmail.com.
More upmarket. Offers a wide selection of
massage and beauty treatments including
aromatherapy massage US$12 per hr,
sports body massage, facial treatments,
skin detox US$25 per hr. The best value
for money in luxury massages, pedicure,
manicure all set in a relaxing building with
oil burners, wind chimes and dolphin-
esque sounds playing in the background.
Packages between US$5 and US$38.

Tour operators
Asia Pacific Travel, 88/07 Ban Phonpheng
Rd, T071-224473, www.laosvoyage.com.
Good operator running tours throughout
the region.
All Laos Service, Sisavangvong Rd. Large
successful travel agency organizing
ticketing and travel services.
Buffalo Tours, 8/40 Ban Nongkham,
T071-254395, www.buffalotours.com. New
player on the block organizes tours that
delve into local culture in conjunction with
tours around Southeast Asia. Very helpful,
knowledgable and very efficient.
Green Discovery, T071-212093, www.
greendiscoverylaos.com. Rafting and
kayaking trips on grade 1 and 2 rapids.
Cycling trips around Luang Prabang.
Homestays, trips to Pak Ou caves, etc.
Tiger Trail, Sisavangvong Rd, T071-252655,
www.laos-adventures.com. Adventure

specialists: elephant treks, trekking, rafting,
mountain biking tours, rock climbing, etc.

Weaving
Weaving Centre, 2 km out of town on the
river (bookings at **Ban Vat Nong Gallery**,
T071-253219, info@ockpoptok.com).
The team behind the fabulous creations
at **Ock Pop Tok** have opened a weaving
centre. Half-day dyeing classes introduce
students to the world of silk dyes (US$35).
A variety of 1- to 3-day weaving classes are
offered at US$35 per day. Classes are run by
professional weavers and their English-
speaking assistants. A small café is also open,
serving amazing renditions of Lao favorites
as well as some original signatures, such as
Silkworm Poo Tea.

⊖ Transport

Luang Prabang p384, maps p384
and p388
Air
Luang Prabang International Airport (LPQ)
about 4 km from town, T071-212172/3. **Lao
Airlines**, Phamahapasaman Rd, T071-212172,
has daily connections with **Vientiane**,
40 mins, and a service to **Chiang Mai**, **Siem
Reap** and **Hanoi**, Pakse and Phonsavanh.
It also runs daily flights to **Bangkok**. These
flights are notoriously prone to change so
check schedule well in advance. **Bangkok
Airways** runs daily flights to **Bangkok**.

Early morning departures are often
delayed during the rainy and cool seasons,
as dense cloud can make the airport
inoperable until about 1100. Airline tickets
are more often than not substantially
cheaper from travel agents (see Tour
operators, above) than from the actual
airline. Confirm bookings a day in advance
and arrive at the airport early, as flights have
been known to depart as soon as they're full.

Bicycle
Bikes can be rented for about US$1 per day
from most guesthouses.

Boat

Tha Heua Mea Pier is the most popular departure point and has a blackboard listing all the destinations and prices available (daily 0730-1130 and 1300-1600). Prices are largely dependent on the price of gasoline. There is also a dock at **Ban Don** (15 mins north of town by tuk-tuk, US$1-2).

To Houei Xai/Pak Beng The 2-day boat trip down the Mekong between Houei Xai and Pak Beng has become a rite of passage for travellers in Southeast Asia. There are a range of boat options to suit the flashpacker to the backpacker.

The **slow boat** to Houei Xai, leaves from the boat pier on Khem Khong Rd called the Tha Heua Mea pier, 2 days, with a break in Pak Beng after 6-7 hrs on the 1st day. It is US$25 for each leg of the trip and almost all travel agents sell tickets. It's often packed to the brim so wear something comfortable and bring some padding to sit on. Seats are usually basic wooden benches though you may luck out with one that has bus seats. The trip from Luang Prabang to Houei Xai (via Pak Beng overnight) is usually less busy than in the other direction. (If the boat to Pak Beng is full, you can charter your own for about US$400-500.) Tickets for the onward trip to Houei Xai, can be purchased in Pak Beng. Take a good book and a grab some goodies from one of the bakeries to take on board. Most boats will have a vendor selling basic drinks. The boat usually leaves between 0800 and 0900 (changeable so check) but it is necessary to get there early to secure yourself a good seat.

The most luxurious way to make the trip is on the **Luangsay Cruise**, office on Sisavangvong Rd, T071-252 553, www.luangsay.com, which makes the trip in 2 days and 1 night, stopping over at Pak Ou Caves en route and staying overnight at their luxurious lodge in Pak Beng (see page 409). The boat is extra comfortable and has lounges and a well-stocked bar and small library. Food and drinks are more than ample. Very popular in high season and will need to be booked 6 months in advance. In low season the boat runs from Houei Xai to Luang Prabang on Mon and Fri and in the opposite direction on Wed and Sat (US$348 twin/US$427 single). In the high season the boat runs from Houei Xai to Luang Prabang on Mon, Thu and Fri, and in the opposite direction Luang Prabang–Houei Xai on Tue, Wed and Sat (US$546 twin/US$630 single). In the low season it may be possible to get a standby rate if there is availability. The Luangsay Lodge, off Phouvao, in the southwest of town should be open by the time you read this.

Speedboats (which are not recommended) depart from Ban Don to **Houei Xai** (on the Thai border; see page 404), US$30, around 6 hrs, with a short break in **Pak Beng**. Tickets are available from most travel agents. The boats are horribly noisy and dangerous (numerous fatalities have been reported from boats jack-knifing when hitting waves). Ear plugs are recommended and ensure boatmen provide a helmet and life jacket.

A few boats travel up the Nam Ou to **Nong Khiaw**. However, these are infrequent, especially when the river is low. The journey usually takes 6 hrs to Nong Khiaw, 150,000 kip. The Nam Ou joins the Mekong near the Pak Ou Caves, so it is possible to combine a journey with a visit to the caves en route. The irregular travel dates to Nong Khiaw are posted on a board outside the boat pier or ask one of the travel agents on Sisavangvong Rd when the next departure is. It is possible to charter a boat for 1-6 people for US$200. Speedboats to Nong Khiaw sometimes leave from Ban Don, expect to pay 200,000 kip. These boats are hazardous, uncomfortable and not environmentally friendly.

Bus/truck

The northern bus terminal is for north-bound traffic and the southern for traffic to/from the south. Always double-check which terminal your bus is using, as unscheduled changes are possible.

From the northern terminal To **Luang Namtha**, daily 0900 and 1730, 10 hrs, usually via Udomxai, 80,000 kip. The roads are reasonable and paved but quite hilly. The 1730 bus has usually come from Vientiane and is often full. An alternative is to break the journey by catching the bus to **Udomxai**, 0900 and 1130 daily, 5 hrs, 50,000 kip, and then continuing on to Luang Namtha in the afternoon. There are also daily departures (usually in the morning) to **Houei Xai** on the Thai/Lao border, 110,000 kip, 11-12 hrs. A VIP bus to Houei Xai passes through daily, 1000, 10 hrs, 155,000 kip. There is a very long bus journey to **Xam Neua**, 1630, they say it takes 14 hrs but it can be up to 20 hrs, 120,000 kip. **Phongsali**, 1600, 13-15 hrs 110,000 kip. To Nong Khiaw, by *songthaew*, regular departures usually in the morning 35,000 kip.

From the southern terminal There are up to 8 daily buses to **Vientiane**, although scheduled departures tend to decline in the low season, 10-11 hrs, 950,000 kip; most of these services stop in **Vang Vieng**, 6 hrs, 80,000 kip. VIP buses to Vientiane depart 0800 and 0900, 9 hrs, 115,000 kip; both these services stop in Vang Vieng, 115,000 kip.

To **Phonsavanh**, daily 0830, 8-9 hrs, 75,000 kip. It should cost 10,000-15,000 kip to get to the centre of town from the station.

Minibus
Minibuses with driver are available from several hotels and the tour companies, US$50 per day around Luang Prabang, US$60 per day if travelling further afield. Check out the notice boards for services to **Vang Vieng**, 5 hrs, and **Vientiane**, 7 hrs; quicker than the bus, but more expensive. If you have a big group you can organize independent minivan rental.

Saamlor and tuk-tuk
Lots around town which can be hired to see the sights or to go to nearby villages. A short stint across town should cost about 10,000 kip per person, but expect to pay 20,000 kip for anything more than 1 km. Most of the nearby excursions will cost US$5-10.

Directory

Luang Prabang *p384, maps p384 and p388*
There's now a healthy scattering of ATMs around Luang Prabang.
Banks Lao Development Bank, 65 Sisavangvong Rd, Mon-Sat 0830-1200, 1330-1530, will change US$/Thai TCs into kip, but doesn't accept credit cards. **Banque pour le Commerce Exterieur Lao** (BCEL), Sisavangvong Rd, Mon-Sat 0830-1200, 1330-1530; all transactions in kip, will exchange Thai baht, US$, AU$, UK£, Euros and TCs, also offers cash advances on Visa cards. They also have an ATM. Many of the jewellery stalls in the old market, plus restaurant and tourist shop owners, will change US$ and Thai baht. Many of the travel agencies will do credit card advances if you get stuck after hours without money but charge a whopping 6-8% commission. **Internet** There are a concentration of places on Sisavangvong Rd. Wi-Fi is now available in a good number of hotels, guesthouses and cafés. Non-guests can access Wi-Fi for a fee in certain areas; in other places, it's free. **Medical services** The main hospital, is about 3 km outside of town, T071-252049, and is only useful for minor ailments. For anything major you're better off getting a flight to Bangkok. There are a few reasonably well-equipped pharmacies towards Villa Santi on Sisavangvong Rd. **Post and telephone** The post and telephone office is on the corner of Chau Fa Ngum and Setthathirat, Mon-Fri 0830-1730, Sat 0830-1200, express mail service, international telephone facilities. Hotels and some guesthouses allow international calls from reception (about US$5 a min). It is dramatically cheaper to make international calls from one of the internet cafés, which usually have Skype.

Far north

The misty, mountain scenery of the far north conjures up classic Indochina imagery of striking rice terraces, golden, thatched huts and dense, tropical forests, all dissected by a cross-hatching of waterways. Here life is beautifully interwoven with the ebb and flow of the rivers. The mighty Mekong forges its way through picturesque towns, such as Pak Beng and Houei Xai, affording visitors a wonderful glimpse of riverine life, while, to the east, the Nam Ou attracts visitors to Nong Khiaw and, the latest traveller hot spot, Muang Ngoi Neua. The wonderful upland areas are home to around 40 different ethnic groups, including the Akha, Hmong, Khmu and Yao, and it's not surprising that the country's best trekking is also found here. ▶▶ For listings, see pages 408-416.

Luang Namtha and around → For listings, see pages 408-416. Colour map 1, A2.

This area has firmly established itself as a major player in Laos' ecotourism industry, primarily due to the **Nam Ha Ecotourism Project**, which was established in 1993 by NTA Lao and UNESCO to help preserve Luang Namtha's cultural and environmental heritage in the Nam Ha National Protected Area. The Nam Ha NPA is one of the largest protected areas in Laos and consists of mountainous areas dissected by several rivers. It is home to at least 38 species of large mammal, including the black-cheeked crested gibbon, tiger and clouded leopard, and over 300 bird species, including the stunning Blythe's kingfisher.

Udomxai → Colour map 1, B2.
Heading northwest from Luang Prabang, travellers will reach Udomxai, the capital of Udomxai Province. It's a hot and dusty town that is used as a pit-stop and a brothel stop but the local tourist board, with the help of a German NGO are keen to promote the area's other attractions. However, the town does make a decent stop-off point at a convenient junction; it's one of the biggest settlements in northern Laos and has excellent facilities. One only has to look around at the presence of Chinese flags on shop fronts to get an inkling of the large presence of Chinese workers and businesses in town.

Luang Namtha → Colour map 1, A2.
Luang Namtha Province has witnessed the rise and decline of various Tai Kingdoms and now more than 35 ethnic groups reside

Luang Namtha

Sleeping 🛏
Boat Landing Guesthouse
 & Restaurant 12
Manychan Guesthouse 4
Thoulasith Guesthouse 3
Zuela Guesthouse 5

Eating 🍴
Banana 3
Coffee House 6
Yamuna 4

100 metres
100 yards

in the province, making it the most ethnically diverse in the country. Principal minorities include Tai Lu, Tai Dam, Lanten, Hmong and Khmu. The provincial capital was obliterated during the war and the concrete structures erected since 1975 have little charm but there are a number of friendly villages in the area. As with all other minority areas it is advisable to visit villages with a local guide or endorsed tourism organization.

The **Luang Namtha Museum** ⓘ *near the Kaystone Monument, Mon-Fri 0800-1130, 1300-1600, 10,000 kip,* houses a collection of indigenous clothing and artefacts, agricultural tools, weapons, textiles and a collection of Buddha images, drums and gongs.

In the centre of town is a **night market** with a range of food stalls. It is only in its infancy but the local authorities have aspirations to expand the market to include ethnic handicrafts, making it similar to the one in Luang Prabang.

Surrounding villages

Ban Nam Chang is a Lanten village, 3 km along a footpath outside town; **Ban Lak Khamay** is quite a large Akha village 27 km from Luang Namtha on the road to Muang Sing. The settlement features a traditional Akha entrance; if you pass through this entrance you must visit a house in the village, or you are considered an enemy. Otherwise you can simply pass to one side of the gate but don't touch it. Other features of interest in Akha villages are the swing, located at the highest point in the village and used in the annual swing festival (you must not touch the swing), and the meeting house, where unmarried couples go to court and where newly married couples live until they have their own house. **Ban Nam Dee** is a small bamboo papermaking Lanten village about 6 km northeast of town. The name of the village means 'good water' and not surprisingly, if you continue on 1 km from Ban Nam Dee there's a waterfall. The trip to the village is stunning, passing through verdant rice paddies dotted with huts. A motorbike rather than a bicycle will be necessary to navigate these villages and sights, as the road can be very rocky. Villagers usually charge 5000 kip for access to the waterfall.

The small Tai Lue village of **Ban Khone Kam** is also worth a visit. The villagers offer **homestays** here (30,000 kip per night, includes meals), for one or two nights.

Ban Vieng Nua is a Tai Kolom village, 3 km from the centre of town, famous for its traditional house where groups can experience local dancing and a good luck *baci* ceremony (150,000 kip per person). Contact the tourist information office to make a booking. Dinner can also be organized here at a cost of 42,000 kip per head.

Nam Ha National Protected Area

Both Luang Namtha and Vieng Phouka are great bases from which to venture into the Nam Ha National Protected Area, one of a few remaining places on earth where the rare black-cheeked gibbon can be found. If you're lucky you can hear the wonderful singing of the gibbons in the morning. See also the Gibbon Experience, page 404. The 222,400-sq-km conservation area encompasses more than 30 ethnic groups and 37 threatened mammal species. Organizations currently lead two- and three-day treks in the area for small groups of four to eight culturally sensitive travellers. Treks leave three to four times a week; check with the Luang Namtha Guide Service Unit or Vieng Phouka Eco Guide Service or **Green Discovery** (see Tour operators, page 412) for departure days; an information session about the trek is given at the Guide's Office. The price will cover the cost of food, water, transportation, guides, lodging and the trekking permit. All the treks utilize local guides who have been trained to help generate income for their villages. Income for conservation purposes is also garnered from the fees for trekking permits into the area. ⟫ *See Activities and tours, page 412.*

Muang Sing and around → *Colour map 1, A2.*

Many visitors consider this peaceful valley to be one of the highlights of the north. The only way to get to Muang Sing is by bus or pickup from Luang Namtha. The road is asphalt and the terrain on this route is mountainous with dense forest. Muang Sing itself is situated on an upland plateau among misty, blue-green peaks. The town features some interesting old wooden and brick buildings and, unlike nearby Luang Namtha and several other towns in the north, it wasn't bombed close to oblivion during the struggle for Laos. Numerous hill peoples come to the market to trade, including Akha and Hmong tribespeople, along with Yunnanese, Tai Dam and Tai Lu. The **Muang Sing Tourism Office** ⓘ *T086-400015, www.luangnamtha-tourism.org*, offers treks.

Muang Sing Ethnic Museum ⓘ *in the centre of town, daily 0800-1200 and 1300-1600, 5000 kip*, is a beautiful building housing a range of traditional tools, ethnic clothes, jewellery, instruments, religious artefacts and household items. The building was once the royal residence of the Cao Fa (Prince), Phaya Sekong.

The population of the district is said to have trebled between 1992 and 1996, due to the resettlement of many minorities, either from refugee camps in Thailand or from highland areas of Laos and, as a result, it is one of the better places in northern Laos to visit ethnic villages. The town is predominantly Tai Lu but the district is 50% Akha, with a further 10% Tai Nua. The main activity for visitors is to hire bicycles and visit the villages that surround the town; several guesthouses have maps of the surrounding area and trekking is becoming increasingly popular. However, do not undertake treks independently as it undermines the government's attempts to make tourism sustainable and minimize the impact on local villages. ▸▸ *See Activities and tours, page 412.*

From Muang Sing, trek uphill past **Stupa Mountain Lodge** for 7 km up an 886-m hill to reach **That Xieng Tung**, the most sacred site in the area. The stupa was built in 1256 and is believed to contain Buddha's Adam's apple. It attracts lots of pilgrims in November for the annual full moon festival. There is a small pond near the stupa, which is also believed to be very auspicious: if it dries up it is considered very bad luck for Muang Sing. It is said that the pond once dried up and the whole village had no rice and starved.

Along the Mekong → *For listings, see pages 408-416. Colour map 1, B1/2.*

The slow boat along the Mekong between Houei Xai and Luang Prabang is a favourite option for visitors travelling to and from the Thai border. It's a charming trip through lovely scenery.

Houei Xai → *Colour map 1, B1.*

Located southwest of Luang Namtha on the banks of the Mekong, Houei Xai is a popular crossing point to and from Thailand. Few people spend more than one night in the town. Boats run between here and Luang Prabang, two days' journey downstream, via Pak Beng. Most passengers arrive close to the centre at the passenger ferry pier. The vehicle ferry pier is 750 m further north (upstream). Although the petite, picturesque town is growing rapidly as links with Thailand intensify, it is still small and easy enough to get around on foot.

Most visitors who do stick around in Houei Xai do so to visit the **Gibbon Experience** ⓘ *T084-212021, www.gibbonx.org, from €180 (price includes tree house accommodation, transport, food, access to Bokeo Nature Reserve and well-trained guides)*. This is a thrilling, exciting and unmissable three-day trip into Bokeo Nature Reserve, where a number of tree houses have been built high up in the jungle canopy and linked by interconnected zip-lines. Staying in the trees and waking to the sound of singing gibbons is a truly awe-inspiring experience, as is zip-lining high above the jungle canopy, through the mist. In the morning well-trained guides take visitors hiking to see if they can spot the elusive gibbons as well as other plant and animal species. Others to look out for are the giant squirrel, one of the largest rodents in the world, and the Asiatic black bear, whose numbers are in decline as they are hunted for their bile and gall bladders. First and foremost this is a very well-run conservation project. The Gibbon Experience was started to help reduce poaching, logging, slash-and-burn farming and the destruction of primary forest by working with villagers to transform the local economy by making a non-destructive living from their unique environment. Already the project has started to pay dividends: the forest conservation and canopy visits generate as much income year on year as the local logging company could do only once.

Pak Beng → *Colour map 1, B2.*
This long thin strip of a village is perched halfway up a hill, with fine views over the Mekong. Its importance lies in its location at the confluence of the Mekong and the Nam Beng. There is not much to do here but it's the obligatory place to stop en route between Houei Xai and Luang Prabang (or vice versa). The village is worth a visit for its traditional atmosphere and the friendliness of the locals, including various minorities. There are also a couple of monasteries in town. The locals are now organizing guided treks to nearby villages; check with the guesthouses.

Northeast of Luang Prabang → *For listings, see pages 408-416. Colour map 1, B3.*

In recent years the settlements of Nong Khiaw and Muang Ngoi Neua in the north of Luang Prabang Province have become firm favourites with the backpacker set. In fact, idyllic Muang Ngoi Neua is often heralded as the new Vang Vieng, surrounded by stunning scenery and the fantastic ebb of life on the river. It is far more pleasant to travel between Luang Prabang and Nong Khiaw/Ban Saphoun, just south of Muang Ngoi Neua, by long boat, than by bus. The Nam Ou passes mountains, teak plantations, dry rice fields and a movable waterwheel mounted on a boat, which moves from village to village and is used for milling. But with the improvements that have been made to Route 13, road travel has now become the preferred option for many – partly because it is cheaper, and partly because it is quicker. Route 13 north runs parallel with the river for most of the journey to Nam Bak. There are trekking and activities around Nong Khiaw and Muang Ngoi Neua.

Nong Khiaw and Ban Saphoun → *Colour map 1, B3.*
Nong Khiaw lies 22 km northeast of Nam Bak and is a delightful, remote little village on the banks of the Nam Ou, surrounded by limestone peaks and flanked by mountains, the largest aptly named Princess Mountain. It is one of Laos' prettiest destinations. There are, in fact, two settlements here: Ban Saphoun on the east bank of the Nam Ou and Nong Khiaw on the west. Of the two, Ban Saphoun offers the best views and has the best riverside accommodation. Confusingly, the combined village is sometimes called one name, sometimes the other and sometimes Muang Ngoi, which is actually another town to the north (see below) and the name of the district.

One reason why the area has become a popular stopping place for travellers is because of its pivotal position on the Nam Ou, affording river travel from Luang Prabang to the north. It is also on the route between Udomxai and Xam Neua, which is one of the most spectacular in Laos, passing through remote villages. Despite its convenience as a staging

Phongsali

High up in the mountains at an altitude of about 1628 m, this northern provincial capital provides beautiful views and an invigorating climate. It is especially stunning from January to March, when wildflowers bloom in the surrounding hills. The town can be cold at any time of the year, so take some warm clothes. Mornings tend to be foggy and it can also be very wet. There is an end of an earth feel in the areas surrounding the main centre, with dense pristine jungle surrounded by mountains.

Phongsali was one of the first areas to be liberated by the Pathet Lao in the late 1940s. The old post office (just in front of the new one), is the sole physical reminder of French rule. The town's architecture is a strange mix of Chinese post-revolutionary concrete blocks, Lao wood-and-brick houses, with tin roofs, and bamboo or mud huts, with straw roofs. The most attractive part of town is a series of shophouses that wind around away from the Phongsaly hotel towards Hat Xa. The town itself is home to about 20,000 people, mostly Lao, Phou Noi and Chinese, while the wider district is a mixture of ethnicities, with around 28 minorities inhabiting the area.

It is not possible to hire bikes, tuk-tuks or even ponies here so walking is the only way to explore the fantastic landscapes of this region. Many paths lead out of town over the hills; the walking is easy and the panoramas are spectacular. Climb the 413 steps to the top of Mount Phoufa for humbling views of the surrounding hills. The Provincial Tourism Office ⓘ *signposted as 60 m off the main road, T088-210098, www.phongsali.net, Oct-Apr Mon-Fri 0800-1200, 1330-1630, May-Sept Mon-Fri 0730-1130, 1300-1600*, can arrange guided ecotreks, including village homestays, for up to five nights. The rates depend on the number of people. Some people trek north from Phongsali to Uthai, staying in Akha villages en route. Uthai is probably as remote and unspoilt as it gets.

● Sleeping

E-F Phongsaly Hotel, around the corner from the Kaysone Monument, T088-210042. This Chinese 4-storey monstrosity is one of the tallest buildings in town. There are 2 floors of large and

post, this village is a destination in its own right. It is a beautiful spot, the sort of place where time stands still, journals are written, books read and stress is a deeply foreign concept. It is possible to swim in the river (women should wear sarongs) or walk around the town or up the cliffs. If you go to the boat landing it is also possible to organize a fishing trip with one of the local fishermen for very little money. You might need someone to translate for you. The bridge across the Nam Ou offers fine views and photo opportunities. There are caves in the area and the Than Mok waterfall.

Tham Pha Thok cave ⓘ *2.5 km southeast of the bridge, 10,000 kip*, was a Pathet Lao regional base during the civil war. It was divided into sections – the hospital section, a police section and a military section. Old remnants exist like campfires and ruined beds but other than that there is little evidence of it being the PT headquarters until you see the bomb crater at the front. To get there you walk through beautiful rice paddies. There is a second cave about 300 m further down on the left, **Tham Pha Kwong**, which was the Pathet Lao's former banking cave. The cave is a tight squeeze and is easier to access with help from a local guide. It splits into two caves, one of which was the financial office and the other the accountant's office. A further 2 km along the road, at Ban Nokien airy double and twin rooms with hot-water bathrooms. Excellent views from the roof and a good restaurant. The more expensive of the 19 rooms come with a/c.

F-G Sensaly Guesthouse, up the hill and around the bend from the market, T088-210165. A new building houses comfortable rooms with hot water showers, TV and fan. Worn but comfortable rooms in a concrete building, with squat toilets and scoop showers at the back. The friendly owners will bring you hot water in the evening for the Lao tea provided in your room or, if you prefer, to shower with. If you end up in the cheaper rooms, opt for the first floor as the floorboards are paper thin.

🍴 Eating

🍴 **Phongsaly Hotel** is also a good bet and has a larger variety of dishes, including a few Thai, Chinese and Lao ones.

🍴 **Yu Houa Guesthouse**, across the road from the market. Has a short Lao and Chinese section on an English menu; cheap and good.

🚍 Transport

You can travel from Muang Khua to Phongsali either by truck or by boat or by plane. Trucks also depart from Pak Nam Noi (near Muang Khua); buy lunch from the market before departure. The ride is long and difficult when the pickup is full, but it's a great experience and the scenery near Phongsali is utterly breathtaking. Alternatively, catch a boat from Muang Khua to Hat Xa, 20 km or so to the northeast of Phongsali, 5-6 hrs, 90,000 kip. In the low season there may not be any scheduled boats so it might be necessary to gather a few extra tourists and charter a boat, US$110. Depending on the season, the river is quite shallow in places, with a fair amount of white water. It can be cold and wet so wear waterproofs and take a blanket. Note that you may find yourself stuck in Hat Xa, as there are no onward buses to Phongsali after mid-afternoon. Alternative routes to Phongsali are by bus to/from Udomxai, 9-10 hrs, or by plane to/from Vientiane, with Phongsavanh Airlines Group (T021-513 0000) which flies to and from Boun Neua airport (PSL), a 1½-hr bus ride from Phongsali.

is the **Than Mok** waterfall, also accessible by boat.

Muang Ngoi Neua → *Colour map 1, B3.*

The town of Muang Ngoi Neua lies 40 km (one hour) north of Nong Khiaw, along the Nam Ou. This small town surrounded by ethnic villages has become very popular with backpackers over the last few years. The town is a small slice of utopia, set on a peninsula at the foot of Mount Phaboom, shaded by coconut trees, with the languid river breeze wafting through the town's small paths. Most commonly known as Muang Ngoi, the settlement has had to embellish its name to distinguish it from Nong Khiaw, which is also often referred to as Muang Ngoi (see above). It's the perfect place to go for a trek to surrounding villages, or bask the day away swinging in your hammock. A market is held every 10 days and villagers come to sell produce and handicrafts. There are also caves and waterfalls in the area.

Muang Khua → *Colour map 1, A3.*

Muang Khua is nestled into the banks of the Nam Ou, close to the mouth of the Nam Phak, in the south of Phongsali Province. Hardly a destination in itself, it's usually just a stopover

Border essentials: Sop Hun-Tay Trang (Vietnam)

The border linking Dien Bien Phu with Laos in this part of the country is now open. The border at Sop Hun is open daily 0800-1700. A Lao visa is obtainable on arrival. Vietnamese visas are not available on arrival. There is little transport on the Laos side to Muang Khua and the road may still be under construction so expect delays. There is a direct bus from Muang Khua to Dien Bien Phu, costing 50,000 kip, which lets you off for border formalities. It leaves from the opposite side of the river bank to Muang Khua at 0600.

between Nong Khiaw and Phongsali and the first town of significance for those crossing in from Vietnam from Dien Bien Phu, a relatively new border crossing. It only has electricity from 1900 to 2200 nightly. The Akha, Khmu and Tai Dam are the main hilltribes in the area. The nearest villages are 20 km out of town and you will need a guide if you want to visit them (tourist office, T020-2284 8020). Trekking around Muang Khua is fantastic and still a very authentic experience, as this region remains largely unexplored by backpackers. The friendly villages are very welcoming to foreigners, as they don't see as many here as in somewhere like Muang Sing. For these reasons, it is very important to tread lightly and adopt the most culturally sensitive principles: don't hand out sweets and always ask before taking a photograph. Treks usually run for one to three days and involve a homestay at a villager's house (usually the Village Chief).

⦿ Far north listings

For Sleeping and Eating price codes and other relevant information, see Essentials pages 40-43.

⦿ Sleeping

Udomxai *p402*
E-F Litthavixay Guesthouse, about 100 m before the turning onto the airport road, T081-212175, litthavixay@yahoo.com. This place has some of the best rooms in town, large single, double and triple rooms and all very clean. Rooms with lots of facilities. Hot-water shower attached; bathrooms on the small side. Opt for the nicer upstairs rooms. Fan rooms are cheaper. Best-value internet (Wi-Fi available) in town. The restaurant has a small but good selection of foreign breakfast dishes. Car hire possible.
E-F Villa Keoseumsack, 2 doors down from the Siinphet restaurant, T081-312170, seumsack@hotmail.com. Not quite a villa but this is definitely the classiest place to stay in town and extremely good value with

17 rooms with polished floors, large comfy double beds, desks, wardrobes and spacious hot-water showers. Fan rooms are cheaper. Recommended.

Luang Namtha *p402, map p402*
B-C Boat Landing Guesthouse & Restaurant, T086-312398, www. theboatlanding.com. Further out of town than most, this place is right on the river. Time stands still here. It's an eco-resort that's got everything just right: pristine surroundings, environmentally friendly rooms, helpful service and a brilliant restaurant serving traditional northern Lao cuisine. Recommended.
F Manychan Guesthouse, on main road in centre opposite the smaller bus station, T086-312209, ath.phongsavanh@yahoo. com. One of the most popular places, probably due to the location and restaurant. Decent, clean rooms with fan and hot-water bathrooms. The staff are very friendly.

F Thoulasith Guesthouse, T086-212166, thoulasithguesthouse@gmail.com. The newbie in town set off the main road in a compound with a garden, tables and chairs. Rooms come with TV, desk, hot-water bathrooms (3 rooms have bathtubs) and free Wi-Fi. Friendly management. Restaurant too.

F Zuela Guesthouse, T020-5588 6694. Fantastic value guesthouse in a beautiful, modern, wooden building with immaculate fan rooms. Extremely comfortable beds, en suite hot-water bathrooms and linen provided. This family-run guesthouse is truly a league apart from other budget options in town. Restaurant attached. Highly recommended.

Muang Sing p404

E Phou lu Bungalows, at the southern end of town, T030-5511 0326, www.muang-sing. com. This is the best accommodation in town by a long way. There are great spacious double ground-floor bungalows with 4-poster beds, small balconies with bamboo seats, set around a grassy compound with restaurant and massage service.

G Taileu Guesthouse, on the main road, T030-511 0354. Above the restaurant, 8 very basic rattan rooms with bamboo-style, 4-poster beds (the rickety backpacker version not the romantic type), squat toilets and temperamental hot water via solar power. The owners are lovely, lovely people.

Houei Xai p404

E-F BAP Guesthouse, on the main Sekhong Rd, T084-211083, bapbiz@live.com. One of the oldest guesthouses in town consisting of a labyrinth of additions and add-ons as their business has grown over the years. A range of rooms, though the newer tiled ones with hot-water bathrooms are the best. Rooms with TV are more expensive; rooms with shared bath are cheaper. The female proprietor here is hard as nails but has loads of charisma and a wily sense of humour. She's also super helpful.

E-F Taveensinh Guesthouse, northwest end of the town, T084-211502. The best value in town with fan, TV hot-water bathrooms; a/c costs more. Great communal balconies overlooking the river and friendly family in charge.

Pak Beng p405

During peak season, when the slow boat arrives from Luang Prabang, about 60 people descend on Pak Beng at the same time. As the town doesn't have an endless supply of great budget guesthouses, it is advisable to get someone you trust to mind your bags, while you make a mad dash to get the best room in town.

A Pakbeng Lodge, T081-212304, www. pakbenglodge.com. A wooden and concrete construction, built in Lao style, this stunning guesthouse sits perched on a hillside above the Mekong and includes 20 rooms with fan, toilet and hot water. Good restaurant and wonderful views. Breakfast is included. 10 new de luxe rooms were due to open. Wi-Fi available.
Elephant activities arranged.

F Salika, T081-212306. This is an elegant structure on the steep cliff overlooking the river. 15 big, clean rooms with toilet and shower en suite (mostly cold), tiled floors. There is a great restaurant, serving reasonably priced meals (see Eating). Fantastic service.

Nong Khiaw and Ban Saphoun p405

C-E Nong Kiau Riverside, turn-off left just over the bridge in Ban Saphoun, T020-5570 5000, www.nongkiau.com. Stunning bungalows and restaurant. Beautifully decorated rooms with 4-poster beds, mosquito nets and hot-water bathrooms. For those looking for something upmarket this exquisite place fits the bill perfectly. The restaurant has a great selection of wines and access to the internet. Book in advance as it is a favourite with tour groups. Recommended.

E Sunset Guesthouse, down a lane about 100 m past the bridge, Ban Saphoun, T071-810033, sunsetgh2@hotmail.com. Slap bang on the bank of the river – you couldn't ask for a more picturesque setting from which to watch the sunset. The charming, sprawling bamboo structure looks out onto tables and sun umbrellas liberally arranged over the various levels of decking that serve as a popular restaurant in the evenings. 13 wood and brick bungalows with decent bathrooms with Western toilet and hot water shower outside. The twins are more attractive than the doubles; breakfast included. Internet access.

G CT Guesthouse (formerly Phanoy Guesthouse), just past the bridge, Ban Saphoun, T071-253919. Guesthouse has 7 basic but clean and comfortable thatched bungalows with mosquito nets and squat toilets. Inside bathroom. Fantastic verandas overlooking the river. Very nice family-owned business with a great atmosphere.

Muang Ngoi Neua *p407*

The accommodation in town is dirt cheap and of the same standard: bungalows with extremely welcoming hammocks on their balconies. Most offer a laundry service for around 10,000 kip per kg and all have electricity 1800-2200. Theft has become a bit of a problem in Muang Ngoi Neua. Secure all windows and doors and do not leave any valuables in your room. Bring earplugs for the wat gong at 0500 and the cockerels from 0400.

E Ning Ning Guesthouse, T030-514 0863, behind the boat landing with a restaurant with a great ringside view for sunset. Double and twin bungalows, with separate Western toilet and hot shower; the smarter rooms have large comfy double beds and super-white linens and mosquito nets; breakfast included. The food in the adjoining restaurant is great and the owner speaks good English. A popular spot.

G Lattanavongsa Guesthouse 2, T030-514 0770. Close to the river, these 4 bungalows are fenced in around a small garden, cluster bomb and picnic table and are just beyond the main Lattanvongsa restaurant near the dock. Decent-sized bathrooms.

G Phet Davanh Guesthouse, T020-2214 8777, on the main road, near the boat landing. Concrete guesthouse, with 7 double and twin rooms. Comfy mattresses on the floor; 3 shared Western toilets and shower. There's a well-positioned balcony on the 2nd floor complete with hammocks.

Muang Khua *p407*

E-F Sernnali Hotel, in the middle of town, near the top of the hill, T021-414214. By far the most luxurious lodging in town. 18 rooms with large double and twin beds, hot-water scoop showers and Western-style toilets, immaculately clean. Balconies overlook the Nam Ou. Chinese, Vietnamese and Lao food served in the restaurant.

G Nam Ou Guesthouse & Restaurant, follow the signs at the top of the hill, T081-210844. Looking out across the river where the boats land, this guesthouse is the pick of the ultra-budget bunch in Muang Khua. Singles, twins and doubles, some with hot-water en suites, and 3 newer rooms with river views. Good food (see Eating, below). A popular spot. Go for an upstairs room.

🍴 Eating

Udomxai *p402*

🍴 **Sinphet Restaurant**, opposite Linda Guesthouse. One of the best options in town. English menu, delicious iced coffee with ovaltine, great Chinese and Lao food. Try the curry chicken, *kua-mii* or yellow noodles with chicken.

🍴 **Litthavixay Guesthouse** (see Sleeping.) Can whip up some good dishes, including Western-style pancakes and breakfasts.

Luang Namtha *p402, map p402*

The night market, though small, offers an interesting array of local cuisine.

♙♙-♙ Boat Landing Guesthouse & Restaurant (see Sleeping), T086-312398. The best place to eat in town, with innovative cuisine. Serves a range of northern Lao dishes made from local produce, thereby supporting nearby villages. Highly recommended.

♙ Banana Restaurant, main road, T020-5558 1888. This restaurant is gaining favour with the locals and tourists for its good fruit shakes and Lao food. Also serves a few Western dishes.

♙ Coffee House, off the main road around the corner from **Green Discovery**, T030-525 7842. This fantastic little Thai restaurant with a range of delicious meals all under 12,000 kip. The meals are served on brown rice imported from Thailand and include Massaman curry, Tom Yum soup and a variety of other Thai staples. Fantastic coffees. Mr Nithat, the owner's husband, is good for a chat. Recommended.

♙ Yamuna Restaurant, on the main road, T020-5557 1579. Delicious Indian restaurant with vegetarian, non-vegetarian and halal dishes. Extensive, predominantly south Indian menu.

Muang Sing *p404*

♙ Muang Sing View Restaurant. A bamboo walkway leads to this rustic restaurant which enjoys the best views in Muang Sing overlooking the paddy fields and the valley. All the usual Lao staples are served.

♙ Sengdeuane Guesthouse & Restaurant. Korean barbecue only (*sindat*). Popular with the locals.

♙ Taileu Guesthouse & Restaurant (see Sleeping), T081-212375. The most popular place to eat due to its indigenous Tai Leu menu. Tasty meals, including baked aubergine with pork, soy mash and fish soup. One of the few places in the country where you can sample northern cuisine. Try their local piña colada with *lao-lao*, their *sa*

lo (Muang Sing's answer to a hamburger) or one of the famous *jeow* (chilli jam) dishes. The banana flower soup is fantastic. Stand-out option in town and an eating experience you won't find elsewhere in Laos. Noi, the owner, is very friendly. Highly recommended.

Houei Xai *p404*

♙ Bar How? A cute little place with fresh spring rolls, soups, sarnies, and other Western and Lao offerings. There's a warm atmosphere with paper lanterns and wooden tables. Breakfasts are a little expensive.

♙ Khemkhong Restaurant, across from the immigration stand. Good option for those who want a drink after the cross-border journey. Lao and Thai food.

♙ Nutpop, on the main road, T084-211037. The fluorescent lights and garish beer signs don't give a good impression. However, this is a pleasant little garden restaurant, set in an atmospheric lamp-lit building, with good Lao food including fried mushrooms and curry. The fish here is excellent.

♙ Riverview Garden Restaurant. There's no river view but its streetside view and tables have become a firm favourite with the backpacker set. There's a mixed menu of sandwiches, pizzas, stir fries, barbecue and noodles. It's conveniently next to the **Gibbon Experience** office.

Pak Beng *p405*

There are dozens of restaurants lining the main road towards the river; all seem to have the same English menu, basic Lao dishes, eggs and freshly made sandwiches.

♙ Kopchaideu Restaurant, overlooking the Mekong. This restaurant has a large selection of Indian dishes with a few Lao favourites thrown in. Great shakes and fantastic service.

Nong Khiaw and Ban Saphoun *p405*

Most of the guesthouses have cafés attached. For some fine dining the restaurant at the **Riverside** is absolutely fantastic, with an extensive wine menu. For those on a budget the **CT Guesthouse** does reasonably good food. Ask for dishes to be served with *jeow*, which is delicious.

Muang Ngoi Neua *p407*
♥-♥ **Sainamgoi Restaurant & Bar**, centre of town. Tasty Lao food in a pleasant atmosphere, with good background music. The bar, the only one in town, is in the next room.
♥ **Nang Phone Keo Restaurant**, on the main road. All the usual Lao food, plus some extras. Try the 'Falang Roll' for breakfast (a combination of peanut butter, sticky rice and vegetables).
♥ **Sengdala Restaurant & Bakery**, on the main road. Very good, cheap Lao food, terrific pancakes and freshly baked baguettes.

Muang Khua *p407*
The **Nam Ou Guesthouse & Restaurant** (see Sleeping) is up the mud slope from the beach. An incomparable location for a morning coffee overlooking the river; it has an English menu and friendly staff.

⏱ Activities and tours

Luang Namtha and around *p402, map p402*
Tour operators
Green Discovery, T086-211484, www. greendiscoverylaos.com. Offers 1- to 7-day kayaking/rafting, cycling and trekking excursions into the Nam Ha NPA.
Luang Namtha Provincial Tourism Office and Eco Guide Unit, T086-211534, www. luangnamtha-tourism.org. Information on treks to Nam Ha NPA.
Vieng Phouka Eco Guide Service Unit, T084-212400, mpvpk@laotel.com.

Muang Sing *p404*
Trekking
This activity has become a delicate issue around Muang Sing as uncontrolled tourism was beginning to have a detrimental effect

on some of the surrounding minority villages. Some sensible procedures and protocols have been put in place to ensure low impact tourism which still benefits the villages concerned.
Exotissimo, www.exotissimo.com (T086-400016, akhaexp@gmail.com in Muang Sing). In cahoots with **GTZ**, a German aid agency, have launched more expensive but enjoyable treks such as the **Akha Experience**, which include tasty meals prepared by local Akha people. Closed on weekends.
Muang Sing Tourism Office, T086-400015, www.luangnamtha-tourism.org. Mon-Fri 0800-1130 and 1330-1700, Sat-Sun 0800-1000 and 1500-1700. Offers 1-, 2- and 3-day treks from 300,000 kip per person (minimum 2 people). Most treks have received glowing reports from tourists, particularly the **Laosee Trek**.

Nong Khiaw *p405*
Check out www.nongkiauclimbing.com in association with **Green Discovery**.
Lao Youth Travel, www.laoyouthtravel.com, at the boat landing offer trekking, fishing, tubing, boat trips and kayaking.
Tiger Trails, www.laos-adventure.com. Runs trips to the 100 waterfalls and organizes trekking.

Muang Ngoi Neua *p407*
Trekking, hiking, fishing, kayaking, trips to the waterfalls and boat trips can be organized through most of the guesthouses.
Lao Youth Travel, T030-514 0046, www. laoyouthtravel.com. Daily 0730-2000. Half-day, day, overnight or 2-night treks. Also kayaking trips.

⏣ Transport

Udomxai *p402*
Air
There are flights to **Vientiane**, 3 times a week. **Lao Airlines** has an office at the airport, T081-312047.

Bus/truck/songthaew

Udomxai is the epicentre of northern travel. If arriving into Udomxai to catch a connecting bus, it's better to leave earlier in the day as transport tends to peter out in the afternoon.

The bus station is 1 km east of the town centre. Departures east to **Nong Khiaw**, 3 hrs, trucks are fairly frequent, most departing in the morning. If you get stuck on the way to Nong Khiaw it is possible to stay overnight in **Pak Mong** where there are numerous rustic guesthouses. The bus to **Nong Khiaw** leaves at 0900. **Pak Mong**, 1400 and 1600, 2 hrs, 22,000 kip. To **Luang Prabang**, 0800, 1100 and 1400, 5 hrs direct, 48,000 kip. Direct bus to **Vientiane**, 1530 and 1800, 15 hrs, 100,000 kip. Vientiane VIP bus, 1600 and 1800, 121,000 kip (also runs via **Luang Prabang**). **Xam Neua**, Tue-Sat 1230, 100,000 kip. **Luang Namtha**, 0800, 1130 and 1500, 4 hrs, 32,000 kip. **Boten** (the Chinese border), 0800, 28,000 kip. It is possible for some nationalities to obtain Chinese visas at the border, check eligibility in advance (at the time of publication UK citizens could, but US citizens could not).

There are services north on Route 4 to **Phongsali**, 0800, 9 hrs, 60,000 kip; this trip is long so bring something soft to sit on and try to get a seat with a view.

There are plenty of *songthaew*s waiting to make smaller trips to destinations like **Pak Mong** and **Nong Khiaw**, if you miss one of the earlier buses it is worth bargaining with the drivers, as if they can get enough money or passengers they will make the extra trip.

Luang Namtha *p402, map p402*
Air

The airport is 6 km south of town There are flights 3 times a week to **Vientiane**. Lao Airlines, T086-212072, has an office south of town on the main road.

Bicycle/motorbike

Bicycles for hire from Namtha Vehicle Rental Service, next door to the **Manychan**

Guesthouse, T086-312172 for 8000-20,000 kip a day. Motorbikes for hire for US$30-50 a day from **Zuela guesthouse**.

Boat

Slow boats are the best and most scenic option but their reliability will depend on the tide and in the dry season (Jan-May) they often won't run. There isn't really a regular boat service from Luang Namtha, so you will have to either charter a whole boat and split the cost or hitch a ride on a boat making the trip already. If you organize a boat it should cost around 1,900,000 kip to **Houei Xai**. It is cheaper to go from Luang Namtha to Houei Xai than vice versa. The **Boat Landing Guesthouse** is a good source of information; if arrangements are made for you, a courtesy tip is appreciated.

Bus/truck/songthaew

The main inter-provincial bus station and its ticket office have moved to 10 km south of town. A new intra-provincial bus station is close to the **Panda Restaurant**, on the main road.

To **Udomxai**, 0830, 1200, 1430, 100 km, 4 hrs, 32,000 kip, additional services will leave in the early afternoon if there is demand, otherwise jump on a bus to Luang Prabang.

To **Houei Xai**, 0900 and 1330, 55,000 kip, 4 hrs. Take this service for Vieng Phouka. To **Luang Prabang**, 0930 daily, 8 hrs, 65,000 kip. To **Vientiane**, 0830, 1430, 21 hrs, 140,000 kip. To get to **Nong Khiaw**, you need to go via Udomxai (leave early).

From the intra-provincial (unsigned) bus station: to **Muang Sing**, 3 daily, 1½ hrs, 20,000 kip, additional pickups may depart throughout the rest of the day, depending on demand.

Muang Sing *p404*
Bicycle

Available for rent from **Tiger Man** trekking agency on the main road.

Bus/truck

The bus station is across from the new morning market, 500 m from the main road. To **Luang Namtha**, by bus or pickup, 0800, 0930, 1100, 1300, 1400, 1500, 2 hrs, 20,000 kip. To charter a *songthaew* or tuk-tuk to Luang Namtha costs at least 250,000 kip.

Houei Xai *p404*

Lao National Tourism State Bokeo, on the main street up from immigration, T084-211162, can give advice on the sale of boat, bus, pickup and other tickets. Numerous travel agencies congregate around the immigration centre offering bus and boat ticket sales. See page 400 for information on boat travel between Houei Xai and Luang Prabang.

Air

Houei Xai airport is located 2 km south of town and has flights to **Vientiane**, 3 times a week.

Boat

The BAP Guesthouse in Houei Xai is a good place to find out about boat services.

The 2-day trip to Luang Prabang has become part of the Southeast Asian rite of passage. The slow boat to **Pak Beng** is raved about by many travellers. However, in peak season the boat can be packed extremely uncomfortable. Bring something soft to sit on, a good book and a packed lunch. The boat leaves from a jetty 1.5 km north of town, daily 1100, 6-7 hrs, 250,000 kip for the 2-day trip (usually you buy the ongoing ticket at Pak Beng). If you can get enough people together it is possible to charter a boat, 1,765,000 kip although ask for advice at the tourist office as they quote much cheaper. The trip, done in reverse, usually has fewer passengers.

For those looking for a luxury option there is the **Luangsay Cruise**, T084-212092, www.luangsay.com, which undertakes a 2-day/1-night cruise down the river in extreme comfort with cushioned deckchairs, a bar and games on board. Guests stay at the beautiful **Luangsay Lodge** in Pak Beng.

Speedboats are a noisy, nerve-wracking, dangerous alternative to the slow boats; they leave from the jetty south of town, to **Pak Beng**, 0900, 3 hrs, 180,000 kip and to **Luang Prabang**, 360,000-400,000kip. There have been reports of unscrupulous boatmen claiming there are no slow boats in the dry season to encourage travellers to take their fast boats. This is usually untrue. To **Luang Namtha** by longtail boat, 1,750,000 kip, max 5 people, 2 days.

Bus/truck/songthaew

The bus station is located at the Morning Market, 3 km out of central Houei Xai, a tuk-tuk to the centre costs 10,000 kip. Trucks, buses and minivans run to **Vieng Phouka**, daily 0830, 1230, 5 hrs, 35,000 kip; to **Luang Namtha**, daily 0830, 1230, 1700, 170 km, 7 hrs, 55,000 kip (there are also more regular minivans to Luang Namtha); to **Udomxai**, daily 0900, 1200, 1700, 12 hrs, 120,000 kip; to **Luang Prabang**, 0900, 1200, 1700, 12 hrs, 120,000 kip; to **Vientiane**, daily 1130, 20 hrs, 200,000 kip.

Pak Beng *p405*
Boat

The times and prices for boats are always changing so check beforehand. The slow boat to **Houei Xai** leaves 0900 from the port and takes all day, 110,000 kip. The slow boat to **Luang Prabang** leaves around the same time. Get in early to get a good seat. Speedboats to Luang Prabang (2-3 hrs) and Houei Xai leave in the morning, when full.

Bus/truck/songthaew

Buses and *songthaews* leave about 2 km from town in the morning for the route to **Udomxai**, 6-7 hrs, 40,000 kip. Direct *songthaews* to **Udomxai** are few, so an alternative is to take one to **Muang Houn** to catch the more frequent service from there.

Nong Khiaw and Ban Saphoun *p405*
Boat

Boat services have become irregular following road improvements, although you may find a service to **Muang Noi Neua**, 1 hr, 20,000 kip, from the boat landing. Likewise, boats to Luang Prabang only run if there are enough people, so you might find yourself waiting a couple of days. 100,000 kip per person, minimum 10 people or charter the whole boat, 7-8 hrs. Some vessels also head upriver to **Muang Khua**, 5 hrs, 100,000 kip per person, minimum 10 people. The river trips from Nong Khiaw are spectacular.

Bus/truck

Buses en route from surrounding destinations stop in Nong Khiaw briefly. As they usually arrive from Vientiane or Luang Prabang, the timetables are unreliable. Basic timetables are offered but buses can be early or late, so check details on the day. It is often a matter of waiting at the bus station and catching the bus on its way. Waiting in a restaurant on the main road usually suffices but you will need to flag down the bus. To **Luang Prabang**, 0830 and 1100, 3-4 hrs, by *songthaew* at 0900 and 1100, 35,000 kip; minibus at 1300, 50,000 kip. Also several departures daily to **Nam Bak**, 30 mins, 10,000 kip and on to **Udomxai** 1100, 4 hrs, 40,000 kip. Alternatively, there are more regular *songthaews* to **Pak Mong**, 1 hr, 20,000 kip, where there is a small noodle shop-cum-bus station on the west side of the bridge, and from there travel on to Udomxai/Vientiane.

Travelling east on Route 1, there are buses to **Vieng Kham**, 0900, 2 hrs, 25,000kip, and a village 10 km from **Nam Nouan**, where you can change and head south on Route 6 to **Phonsavanh** and the **Plain of Jars**. There are direct buses north to **Xam Neua** and the village near Nam Nouan, which can be caught from the toll gate on the Ban Saphoun side of the river when it comes through from Vientiane at around

2000-2200, 100,000 kip; it's usually quite crowded. If you miss a bus to/from Nong Khiaw you can always head to **Pak Mong** which is a junction town sitting at the crossroads to Luang Prabang, Nong Khiaw and Udomxai. Aim to get here earlier in the day to catch through traffic otherwise you may have to stay overnight. (If you do, try the **Pak Mong Guesthouse Restaurant**, T020-5579 5860, or any of the other places in town.)

Muang Ngoi Neua *p407*
Boat

From the landing at the northern end of town, slow boats travel north along the beautiful river tract to **Muang Khua**, 5 hrs, per person, minimum 10 people. Slow boats also go south (irregularly) to **Nong Khiaw**, 1 hr, 25,0000 kip per person (minimum 10 people), and **Luang Prabang**, 8 hrs, US$100 per boat. Departure times vary and whether they depart at all depends on demand. For more information and tickets, consult the booth at the landing.

Muang Khua *p407*
Boat

Road travel is now more popular but irregular boats still travel south to **Muang Ngoi Neua/Nong Khiaw**, 3 hrs to Muang Ngoi Neua, 100,000 kip. Also north to **Phongsali** via Hat Xa, 100,000 kip. Boats can be charted to Phongsali 4-6 hrs, 90,000-100,000 kip per person, minimum 10 people at 0900 and 1000. A truck transports travellers on from Hat Xa to Phongsali, 20 km, 2 hrs along a very bad road, 10,000 kip at 1000 and 1430. Alternatively, charter what other limited transport is available.

Songthaew/truck

To get to **Phongsali**, take a *songthaew* to **Pak Nam Noi**, 0800, 1 hr, 10,000 kip, then the *songthaew* or bus that passes through from Udomxai at around 1000, 50,000 kip.

To **Udomxai**, buses leave 0800, 1200 and 1530 from the bus station alongside the market, 3 hrs, 30,000 kip and **Luang Prabang**, 8 hrs, US$7.

Buses also now travel to **Sop Hun** for the border crossing to Vietnam at Tay Trang. See border box page 408.

❶ Directory

Udomxai *p402*
Banks Lao Development Bank, Udomxai, just off the road on the way to Phongsali, changes US$, Thai ฿ and Chinese ¥. The BCEL Bank, on the main road, offers the same services. ATM available. **Internet** Litthavixay Guesthouse.

Luang Namtha *p402, map p402*
Banks Mon-Fri only. Lao Development Bank, changes US$ and Thai ฿, also TCs but charges a sizeable commission. The BCEL changes US$ and Thai ฿ and does cash advances on Visa. ATM available. **Internet** KNT Computers. **Telephone** Lao Telecom.

Muang Sing *p404*
Banks The small Lao Development Bank opposite the market will exchange Thai ฿, US$ and Chinese ¥. **Internet** Muang Sing Tourism Office, offers internet.

Houei Xai *p404*
Banks Mon-Fri only. BCEL, and has an ATM. **Immigration** At the boat terminal, daily 0800-1800, a small overtime fee is charged Sat and Sun and after 1600. Quite possibly the most friendly immigration post in the country. **Internet** There is internet opposite **Sabaydee** hotel.

Pak Beng *p405*
Bank There is no bank in Pak Beng, but most of the guesthouses and restaurants will exchange Thai ฿ and US$ cash at a hefty commission. **Internet** Available at the ferry office.

Nong Khiaw and Ban Saphoun *p405*
Internet Sunset Guesthouse and Riverside Guesthouse.

Muang Khua *p407*
Bank Lao Development Bank, near the truck stop, Mon-Fri 0800-1130, 1300-1630, changes US$, Thai ฿ and Chinese ¥ at bad rates. Won't change TCs or do cash advances, so make sure you have plenty of cash before you come here. **Electricity** 1830-2200. **Telephone** International calls from the Telecom office, a small hut with a huge satellite, halfway up the road, behind the bank.

Plain of Jars, Vieng Xai and the northeast

Apart from the historic Plain of Jars, Xieng Khouang Province is best known for the pounding it took during the war. Many of the sights are battered monuments to the plateau's violent recent history. Given the cost of the return trip and the fact that the jars themselves aren't that spectacular, some consider the destination oversold. However, further east, and near border crossings with Vietnam, are the Vieng Xai caves, the Pathet Lao subterranean headquarters during the Secret War. For those interested in modern history, it's the most fascinating area of Laos and helps one to gain an insight into the resilient nature of the Lao people. The countryside, particularly towards the Vietnam frontier, is beautiful – among the country's best – and the jars, too, are interesting by dint of their very oddness: as if a band of carousing giants had been suddenly interrupted, casting the jars across the plain in their hurry to leave. The cave history is fascinating and brought to life by brand new audio tours. ▸▸ *For listings, see pages 422-424.*

Background

Xieng Khouang Province has had a murky, blood-tinted, war-ravaged history. The area was the most bombed province in the most bombed country, per capita, in the world as it became a very important strategic zone that both the US and Vietnamese wanted to retain control of. The town of Phonsavanh has long been an important transit point between China to the north, Vietnam to the east and Thailand to the south and this status made the town a target for neighbouring countries. What's more, the plateau of the Plain of Jars is one of the flatter areas in northern Laos, rendering it a natural battleground for the numerous conflicts that ensued from the 19th century to 1975. While the enigmatic Plain of Jars is here, this region will also hold immense appeal for those interested in the modern history of the country.

Once the French departed from Laos, massive conflicts were waged in 1945 and 1946 between the Free Lao Movement and the Viet Minh. The Pathet Lao and Viet Minh joined forces and, by 1964, had a number of bases dotted around the Plain of Jars. From then on, chaos ensued, as Xieng Khouang got caught in the middle of the war between the Royalist-American and Pathet Lao-Vietnamese. The extensive US bombing of this area was to ensure it did not fall under the Communist control of the Pathet Laos. The Vietnamese were trying to ensure that the US did not gain control of the area from which they could launch attacks on North Vietnam.

During the 'Secret War' (1964-1974) against the North Vietnamese Army and the Pathet Lao, tens of thousands of cluster bomb units (CBUs) were dumped by the US military on Xieng Khouang Province. Other bombs, such as the anti-personnel plastic 'pineapple' bomblets were also used but by and large cluster bombs compromised the majority dropped. The CBU was a carrier bomb, which held 670 sub-munitions the size of a lemon. As the CBU was dropped each of these smaller bombs was released. Even though they were the size of a tennis ball, they contained 300 metal ball-bearings that were propelled hundreds of metres. As 30% of the original bombs did not explode, these cluster bombs continue to kill and maim today. The Plain of Jars was also hit by B-52s returning from abortive bombing runs to Hanoi, who jettisoned their bomb loads before heading back to the US air base at Udon Thani in northeast Thailand. Suffice it to say that, with over 580,944 sorties flown (one-and-a-half times the number flown in Vietnam), whole towns were obliterated and the area's geography was permanently altered. Today, as the Lao Airlines plane begins its descent towards the plateau, the meaning of the term 'carpet bombing' becomes clear. On the final approach to the town of Phonsavanh, the plane banks low over the cratered paddy fields, affording a T-28 fighter-bomber pilot's view of his target, which in places has been pummelled into little more than a moonscape. Some of the craters are 15 m across and 7 m deep. Testament to the Lao people's resilience, symbolically, many of these craters have been turned into tranquil fish ponds; the bombs transformed into fences and the CBU carriers serving as planter pots. Because the war was 'secret', there are few records of what was dropped and where and, even when the unexploded ordnance (UXO) have been uncovered, their workings are often a mystery – the Americans used Laos as a testing ground for new ordnance so blueprints are unavailable. The UK-based **Mines Advisory Group (MAG) UXO Visitor Information Centre** ⓘ *on the main road in the centre of town, Mon-Fri 0800-2000, Sat and Sun 1600-2000,* is currently engaged in clearing the land of UXO. They have an exhibition of bombs, photographs and information on the bombing campaign and ongoing plight of Laos with UXO. Usually there are staff on hand to explain exactly how the bombs were used. All T-shirts sold here help fund the UXO clearance of the area and are a very worthwhile souvenir.

Xieng Khouang remains one of the poorest provinces in an already wretchedly poor country. The whole province has a population of only around 250,000, a mix of different ethnic groups, predominantly Hmong, Lao and a handful of Khmu.

Trekking and biking opportunities have opened up in the area with the help of a German NGO. Contact the **Xieng Khouang Provincial Tourism Department**, 2 km from the town centre, T061-312217, xkgtourism@yahoo.com, for the Xieng Khouang Discovery Guide or local tour operators.

Plain of Jars and Phonsavanh → *For listings, see pages 422-424. Colour map 2, C2.*

The undulating plateau of the Plain of Jars (also known as Plaine de Jarres or **Thong Hai Hin**) stretches for about 50 km east to west, at an altitude of 1000 m. In total there are 136 archaeological sites in this area, containing thousands of jars, discs and deliberately placed stones, but at the moment only three principal sites are open to tourists. The plateau can be cold from December to March. **Phonsavanh** is the main town of the province today – old Xieng Khouang having been flattened – and its small airstrip is a crucial transport link in this mountainous region. It's the only base from which to explore the Plain of Jars, so it has a fair number of hotels and guesthouses. Note that travel agents and airlines tend to refer to Phonsavanh as Xieng Khouang, while the nearby town of 'old' Xieng Khouang is usually referred to as Muang Khoune.

Ins and outs
Getting there Phonsavanh Airport (aka Xieng Khouang airport) is 4 km west of Phonsavanh – there are flights from Vientiane. A tuk-tuk to town costs 20,000 kip per person. The most direct route by road from Luang Prabang to Xieng Khouang is to take Route 13 south to Muang Phou Khoun and then Route 7 east. An alternative, scenic, albeit convoluted, route is via Nong Khiaw (see page 405), from where there are pickups to Pak Xeng and Phonsavanh via Vieng Thong on Route 1 or Nam Nouan.

The bus station is 4 km west of Phonsavanh on Route 7; a tuk-tuk to/from the centre costs 10,000 kip.

Getting around Public transport is limited and sporadic. Provincial laws have occasionally banned tuk-tuks and motorbikes from ferrying customers around the area. It should be possible to drive from Phonsavanh to the Plain of Jars, see Site one below, and return to town in two hours. Expect to pay in the region of US$30 for an English-speaking guide and vehicle for four people, or US$60 for seven people and a minivan. A tuk-tuk to Site one costs approximately US$7 per person. Alternatively, guesthouses and tour companies in Phonsavanh run set tours to the Plain of Jars. If you arrive by air, the chances are you'll be inundated with official and unofficial would-be guides as soon as you step off the plane. Note that it is not possible to walk from the airport to Site one, as there is a military base in between. It is recommended that you hire a guide, for at least a day, to get an insight into the history of the area. The cost of admission to each site is 10000 kip. The sites are open October-February 0800-1600, March-September 0700-1700. ▸▸ *See Activities and tours and Transport, page 423*

Background
Most of the jars are between 1 m and 2.5 m high, around 1 m in diameter and weigh about the same as three small cars. The largest are about 3 m tall. The jars have long presented an archaeological conundrum, leaving generations of theorists nonplussed by how they got there and what they were used for. Local legend relates that King Khoon Chuong and his troops from Southern China threw a stupendous party after their victory over the wicked Chao Angka and had the jars made to brew outrageous quantities of *lao-lao*. However, attractive as this alcoholic thesis is, it is more likely that the jars are in fact 2000-year-old stone funeral urns. The larger jars are believed to have been for the local aristocracy and the smaller jars for their minions. Tools, bronze ornaments, ceramics and other objects have been found in the jars, indicating that a civilized society was responsible for making them but no one has a clue which one, as the artefacts seem to bear no relation to those left behind by other ancient Indochinese civilizations. Some of the jars were once covered with round lids and there is one jar, in the group facing the entrance to the cave, which is decorated with a rough carving of a dancing figure.

The sites
More than 334 jars survive, mainly scattered on one slope at so-called 'Site one' or **Thong Hai Hin**, 10 km southwest of Phonsavanh, entry 10,000 kip. This site hosts the largest jars. A path, cleared by MAG, winds through the site, with a warning not to walk away from delineated areas as UXO are still around. Each of the jars weighs about a tonne, although the biggest, called **Hai Cheaum**, is over 2 m tall and weighs over six tonnes.

True jar lovers should visit Site two, known as **Hai Hin Phu Salatao** (literally 'Salato Hill Stone Jar Site') and Site three called **Hai Hin Laat Khai** – entry to both is 7,000 kip each

Site two is 25 km south of Phonsavanh and features 90 jars spread across two hills. The jars are set in a rather beautiful location, affording scenic 360 degree views. Most people miss this site but it is in fact the most atmospheric because of the hilltop location. On the second hill, trees have grown through the centre of the jars, splitting them four ways; butterflies abound.

A further 10 km south of Site two, Site three is the most peaceful, set in verdant green rolling hills, Swiss-cheesed with bomb craters. To get there you have to walk through some rice paddies and cross the small bamboo bridge. There are more than 130 jars at this site, which are generally smaller and more damaged than at the other sites. There's also a very small, basic restaurant, serving *feu* (noodle soup).

Tham Piu

① *The cave is to the west of the Muang Kham-Xam Neua Rd, just after the 183 km post, entry 5000 kip. A rough track leads down to an irrigation dam, built in 1981. To get there from Phonsavanh you can either go the easy way and hire a vehicle US$30-40, or go the hard way, by public transport. For the latter, take the bus to Nong Haet, and request to stop at the Tham Phiu turn-off. From here walk towards the towering limestone cliff and follow the small trails for the last kilometre. It is best to do this with a guide as UXOs still litter the area.*

This cave is more of a memorial than a tourist site but will be of interest to those fascinated by the war. More evidence of the dirty war can be seen here. The intensity of the US bombing campaign under the command of the late General Curtis Le May was such that entire villages were forced to take refuge in caves. If discovered, fighter bombers were called in to destroy them. In Tam Phiu, a cave overlooking the fertile valley near Muang Kham, 374 villagers from nearby Ban Na Meun built a two-storey bomb shelter and concealed its entrance with a high stone wall. They lived there for a year, working in their rice fields at night and taking cover during the day from the relentless bombing raids that killed thousands in the area. On the morning of 24 November 1968 two T-28 fighter-bombers took off from Udon Thani air base in neighbouring Thailand and located the cave mouth that had been exposed on previous sorties. It is likely that the US forces suspected that the cave contained a Pathet Lao hospital complex. Indeed, experts are at odds whether this was a legitimate target or an example of collateral damage. There are a few people still alive whose families died in the cave, and they certainly see it as innocent civilians being targeted. The first rocket destroyed the wall, the second, fired as the planes swept across the valley, carried the full length of the chamber before exploding. There were no survivors and 11 families were completely wiped out; in total 374 people died, many reportedly women and children. Local rescuers claim they were unable to enter the cave for three days, but eventually the dead were buried in a bomb crater on the hillside next to the cave mouth. You will need a torch to explore the cave but there isn't much inside, just eerily black walls. The interior of the cave was completely dug up by the rescue parties and relatives and today there is nothing but rubble inside. It makes for a poignant lesson in military history and locally it is considered a war memorial. Further up the cliff is another cave, **Tham Phiu Song**, which fortunately didn't suffer the same fate. Before the stairway to the caves there is a little memorial centre that displays photographs from the war and is usually attended by a relative of the victims. A poignant sculpture of a soldier carrying a dead child marks the site, free of the victory and glory of most other war monuments. Many bomb craters around the site have been turned into fish ponds now bearing beautiful lotus.

Vieng Xai (Viengsay) → *For listings, see pages 422-424. Colour map 2, B3.*

The village of Vieng Xai lies 31 km east of Xam Neua on a road that branches off Route 6 at Km 20. The trip from Xam Neua is possibly one of the country's most picturesque journeys, passing terraces of rice, pagodas, copper- and charcoal-coloured karst formations, dense jungle with misty peaks and friendly villages dotted among the mountains' curves. The area is characterized by lush tropical gardens, a couple of smallish lakes and spectacular limestone karsts, riddled with natural caves that proved crucial in the success of the left-wing insurgency in the 1960s and 1970s.

Getting there Tourists are often put off visiting Hua Phan Province by the long bus haul to get there but, considering the road passes through gorgeous mountain scenery, the

Border essentials: Na Maew–Nam Xoi (Vietnam)

Route 6A heads east from Xam Neua to the border crossing between Na Maew (Laos) and Nam Xoi (Vietnam), which was opened to tourists in 2004. You'll need to get your Laos and Vietnam visa in advance. The border is open 0730-1130 and 1330-1700. It may be necessary to pay a processing or overtime fee.

The trip to the border is two hours from Vieng Xai. *Songthaew* leave Vieng Xai at 0640 from the main Xam Neua–Na Maew road, 1km from the centre of Vieng Xai, 20,000 kip. It is also possible to take a *songthaew* from Xam Neua station at 0630-0715 (three to four hours), 30,000 kip, or to charter a *songthaew* to the border from Xam Neua for about US$50.

Footprint has received several complaints about difficulties with unethical tourism operators on the Vietnamese side of this border crossing, charging a fortune for transport. A motorbike taxi to Quan Son should cost around US$10. If you get really stuck on the Vietnam side contact Mr Pham Xuan Hop in Na Maew, T0084-9923 7425, who may be able to organize minivan rental (US$42-50 to Quan Son).

There are two guesthouses in Na Maew (Phucloc Nha Tru and Minhchien) offering rudimentary facilities for US$3-5 per night).

A bus runs from Na Maew to Thanh Hoa every Tuesday, Thursday and Saturday at 1130, US$8 but check all transport details in Xam Neua at the bus station or with the very helpful provincial tourism office.

---

trip is well worth the endeavour. There are three main sealed roads to Xam Neua: Route 6 from the south, linking Xam Neua with Phonsavanh; Route 1 from Vieng Thong and the west, and Road 6A from the Vietnamese border. Due to the upgrading of Route 6, it is now possible to make the journey between Phonsavanh and Xam Neua in a day without an overnight stop in Nam Nouan en route but always check on road conditions before setting off. There is an airport at Xam Neua, 3 km from the centre of town on the road to Vieng Xai and Vietnam. **Houa Phanh Provincial Tourist Office** ① *T064-312567, hp_pto@yahoo.com,* is run by the helpful Kaiphet and his team in Xam Neua.

Ins and outs

There are seven caves open to visitors. (By late 2010, the market cave will be open with a new bakery and garden with tea trees and mulberry bushes.) Five were formerly occupied by senior Pathet Lao leaders (Prince Souphanouvong, Kaysone Phomvihan, Nouhak Phounsavanh, Khamtai Siphandon and Phoumi Vongvichit). All the caves are within walking distance of the village. Tickets are sold at the **Viengxay Caves Visitor Centre** ① *T064-314321, www.visit-viengxay.com, daily 0800-1200, 1300-1600, guided tours are conducted in English at 0900 and 1300, 30,000 kip with compulsory guide.* If you pitch up out of these hours, tours are 50,000 kip. Tours are usually conducted on bikes which can be rented from the office (20,000-30,000 kip) if you don't have your own transport. Tours last between three-four hours A new set of excellent 90-minute audio tours with personal memories of local people included has launched (US$6.50). A taster can be heard on: www.visit-viengxay.com. If you plan on coming across from Xam Neua it is advisable to stay overnight.

From 1964 onwards, Pathet Lao operations were directed from the cave systems at Vieng Xai, which provided an effective refuge from furious bombing attacks. The village of Vieng Xai grew from four small villages consisting of less than 10 families into a thriving hidden city concealing over 20,000 people in in the 100 plus caves in the area. The Pathet Lao leadership renamed the area Vieng Xai, meaning 'City of Victory' and it became the administrative and military hub of the revolutionary struggle.

The caves have a secretive atmosphere, with fruit trees and frangipani decorating the exteriors. Each one burrows deep into the mountainside and features 60-cm-thick concrete walls, encompassing living quarters, meeting rooms, offices, dining and storage areas. The caves are lit but you may find a torch useful.

⊙ Plain of Jars and the northeast listings

For Sleeping and Eating price codes and other relevant information, see Essentials pages 40-43.

⊖ Sleeping

Phonsavanh *p418*
B Auberge de la Plaine des Jarres (aka Phu Pha Daeng Hotel), 1 km from the centre, T030-517 0282, www. plainedesjarres.com. In a spectacular position on a hill overlooking the town are 15 stone and wood chalets. Cosy and comfortable and the restaurant serves good food. Highly recommended.
B Vansana, on a hill about 1 km out of town, T061-213170, www.vansanahotel-group.com. Big, modern rooms with telephone, TV, minibar, and tea/coffee-making facilities. The best room is the smart suite with polished wooden floors and textile decoration. Phenomenal views of the countryside. Opt for the rooms upstairs, with free-form bathtub and picturesque balcony views. Restaurant offers Lao and foreign cuisine.
B-C The Hillside Residence, (aka Nearn Phou), T061-213300, www.thehillresidence. com. New, family-run guesthouse on the track to the Vansana Resort. Rooms are decorated with textiles and come with luggage racks and floral-tiled bathrooms; twins are larger and a couple of the doubles are tiny. The 1st-floor balcony is a great place to kick back.
D-E White Orchid, just off the main road in the centre of town, T061-312403. You can't miss this big green building.

Guesthouse, not quite at hotel standard but close enough to be good value. Rooms with TV, hot water, comfy beds and bath. Nicely decorated; twins are spacious and have bathtubs. Free breakfast and airport pickup (if you ring in advance).
E-F Kong Keo, just off the main road, T061-211354, www.kongkeojar.com. This popular hangout is run by the friendly Kong. 13 rooms; the modern rooms are small and basic with tiny bathrooms; the wooden bungalows are darker but larger and more atmospheric but the bathrooms are even smaller. The bonfire inside the cluster bomb case is a nightly draw in the restaurant.

Vieng Xai and Xam Neua *p420*
F Kheamxam Guesthouse, on the corner by the river, Xam Neua, T064-312111. Wide range of fairly well-appointed large rooms, with attached spacious hot-water bathroom, some with a/c and TV. These are some of the best rooms (soft pillows) in town by a long way.
F-G Naxay Guesthouse 2, opposite Vieng Xai Cave Visitor Centre, T064-314336. The best option with 11 clean, beautiful bungalows with tepid water, comfortable beds and Western toilet set in a leafy compound. Recommended.

❼ Eating

Phonsavanh *p418*
♥♥-♥ Auberge de la Plaine des Jarres, see Sleeping. Reasonable menu of Lao dishes

and some delicious French food; overpriced given the competition but the Asian menu is much better value. The dining room with roaring fire is a welcome retreat.

♥-♥ Craters, main street, T020-7780 5775. Modern, Western restaurant offering average burgers, pizza and sandwiches. Good music, attentive service. Delectable but pricey cocktails.

♥ Nisha Indian, on the main road. Good north and south Indian food. The sweet Indian chai is very moreish.

♥ Sangah, main street. Thai, Lao, Vietnamese and Western dishes. Huge portions.

♥ Simmaly, main street, T061-211013. Fantastic *feu* soup. Great service and immensely popular. Recommended.

Vieng Xai and Xam Neua *p420*
♥ Dannaomuangxam, a block back from the river, near the bridge, Xam Neua, T064-314126. A good option. The fried fish is excellent as is the *feu, laap* and French fries. Good service. Menu in English.

The *Xailomyen*, Vieng Xai, does a range of fish, pork, noodle and egg dishes and has a lovely view over the lake.

⊕ Festivals and events

Phonsavanh *p418*
Dec National Day on the 2 Dec is celebrated with horse-drawn drag-cart racing. Also in Dec is Hmong New Year (movable), which is celebrated in a big way in this area.

⊘ Activities and tours

Phonsavanh *p418*
There is no shortage of tour operators in Phonsavanh and most guesthouses can now arrange tours and transport. A full-day tour for 4 people should cost up to US$50-60, although you may have to bargain for it. Most travel agencies are located within a block of each other on the main road.

Amazing Lao Travel, on the main road, T061-312121, www.amazinglao.com. Offers tours to Xam Neua and can arrange other transport. Internet service too.

Indochina Travel, on the main road, T061-312409, www.indochinatravelco.com. Expensive but well-regarded minivan tours.

Inter-Lao Travel, on the main road, T061-211729, www.interlao.laopdr.com. Offers a range of minivan tours to the jars and outlying villages as well as motorbike and bicycle rent and transport to Vientiane.

Lao Youth Travel, on Route 7, T020-5576 1233, www.laoyouthtravel.com. Offers a wide range of tours to the jars and post-conflict sites.

⊖ Transport

Phonsavanh *p418*
Air
Lao Airlines runs flights to **Vientiane**, 30 mins and once a week to **Luang Prabang**.

Bus
Full up-to-date bus timetables are available at the tourist office.

From the main bus station outside of town (T030-517 0148): To **Luang Prabang**, 0830 daily (VIP bus), 265 km on a sealed road, 8 hrs, 75,000 kip. To **Vientiane**, 6 daily, 9-10 hrs, 95,000 kip, also a VIP bus (with a/c and TV) daily, 120,000 kip. Also north to **Vang Vieng**, 6 VIP buses daily, 80,000-120,000 kip. To **Xam Neua**, for Vieng Xai, daily 0800, 1900, 2200, 60,000 kip, a 10-hr haul through some of the country's most beautiful scenery and very windy roads towards the end (you may want to take travel sickness medicine).

Also north to **Nam Nouan**, 0900, 4 hrs, 35,000 kip (change here for transport west to **Nong Khiaw**).

Buses also travel to **Vinh**, Vietnam, Tue, Thu, Fri and Sat 0630, 10 hrs, 138,000 kip. A VIP bus heads for **Hanoi** on Mon at 0630, 185,000 kip. If you want to cross the Nam Khan border here you will need to organize a visa in advance as there is no consulate in

Border essentials: Na Phao-Cha Lo (Vietnam)

The border is east of Thakhek near Na Phao (Laos) and is open daily 0730-1730. There are buses to the border from Thakhek. Arriving from Vietnam, 30-day Lao visas are issued at the border (prices vary for different nationalities but expect to pay around US$30-45).

Phonsavanh or agencies that will send your passport to Vientiane.

Car/songthaew/minivan
A full car with driver to the **Plain of Jars** will cost US$20 (US$5 each) to Site one, or US$30-40 to all 3 sites. To hire a *songthaew* to go to **Tham Phiu** is US$30-40 for the day, a minivan costs US$60.

Vieng Xai and Xam Neua p420
Air
Phongsavanh Airlines (T021-513 0000) flies the route to **Vientiane**.

Bus/truck/songthaew
From the Nathong Bus station (T030-312238), regular *songthaew* from Xam Neua to **Vieng Xai**, 50 mins, 10,000 kip, from 0620-1640 every 50 mins. To **Na Meo** (the Vietnam border), 0710, 3 hrs, 20,000 kip. To **Xam Tai**, 0900, 5 hrs, 34,000 kip. To **Thanh Hoa** (Vietnam), 0800 daily, 180,000 kip, 11 hrs. From Phoutanou bus station up the hill (T030-516 0974) to **Vieng Thong**, 0710, 6 hrs, 43,000 kip. To **Phonsavanh**, 0800, 0830, 0900, 1230, 60,000-70,000 kip, 1400 (VIP bus) 165,000 kip (8 hrs). To **Luang Prabang**, 0730, 0800, 14 hrs, 120,000 kip (the Luang Prabang

bus goes via **Nong Khiaw**, 12 hrs, 80,000 kip). To **Vientiane**, 0800, 0900, and 1230, 24 hrs, 150,000 kip, VIP bus at 1400, 18 hrs, 165,000 kip.

🅓 Directory

Phonsavanh p418
Banks Lao Development Bank, Mon-Fri 0800-1530, near Lao Airlines Office, 2 blocks back from the dry market. Changes cash and TCs and advances on Visa and MC. There are 2 BCEL ATMs on the main road. **Indochine Travel** has an exchange booth with Visa advance, but they charge 6.9% commission. **Internet** A couple of places. **Medical services** Lao-Mongolian Hospital, T061-312166. Sufficient for minor ailments. **Pharmacies** are ubiquitous in town. **Post office and telephone** The post office is opposite the dry market and has IDD telephone boxes outside.

Vieng Xai and Xam Neua 420
Banks The Lao Development Bank, Xam Neua, will change Thai baht, US$ and Chinese ¥ into kip but will only accept TCs in US$. **Internet** Available from Tami. com, just ask the **Sam Neua hotel**, over the first crossroads.

Central provinces

The central provinces of Laos, sandwiched between the Mekong (and Thailand) to the west and the Annamite Mountains (and Vietnam) to the east, are the least visited in the country, which is a shame as the scenery here is stunning, with dramatic limestone karsts, enormous caves, beautiful rivers and forests. In particular, the upland areas to the east, off Route 8 and Route 12, in Khammouane and Bolikhamxai Province, are a veritable treasure trove of attractions, mottled with scores of caves, lagoons, rivers and rock formations. Visitors will require some determination in these parts, as the infrastructure is still being developed. The Mekong towns of Thakhek and Savannakhet are elegant and relaxed and are the main transport and tourist hubs in the region. Pakse is the optimum place to base yourself to explore the southern provinces. ▶▶ *For listings, see pages 431-434.*

Thakhek and around → *For listings, see pages 431-434. Colour map 3, B2.*

Located on the Mekong, at the junction of Routes 13 and 12, Thakhek is a quiet town, surrounded by beautiful countryside. This will inevitably change, though, with the opening of the third Friendship Bridge to Thailand due to be completed by 2012. It is the capital of Khammouane Province and was founded in 1911-1912, under the French. Apart from Luang Prabang, Thakhek is probably the most outwardly French-looking town in Laos, with fading pastel villas clustered around a simple fountain area. It has a fine collection of colonial-era shophouses, a breezy riverside position and a relaxed ambience. One of Laos' holiest sites, That Sikhot, the stunning caves of the region and beautiful Mahaxai can all be visited from here. This town is the most popular stopover point in the central provinces, attracting a range of tourists with its vast array of caves, rivers, lakes and other attractions. Despite encompassing some of the most beautiful scenery in Laos: imposing jagged mountains, bottle green rivers, lakes and caves, the region is still not considered a primary tourist destination. Tourism infrastructure is still quite limited but is improving and a trip to this area will prove the highlight of most visitors' holidays to Laos.

Ins and outs

Getting there There are two bus terminals: the main terminal is about 4 km from town and offers inter-provincial and international buses, and the small *songthaew* station, near Soksombook market, which services local regions.

Getting around Thakhek is small enough to negotiate on foot or by bicycle. A number of places organize motorbike hire, such as the Thakhek Travel Lodge and the Tourism Information Centre, which acts as an agent for motorcycle dealers ⊂ *See Transport, page 433.*

Tourist information **Tourism Information Centre** ① *Vientiane Rd, in a chalet-like building T052-212512, Mon-Fri 0800-1130 and 1330-1630 and Sat-Sun 0800-1130 and 1400-1700.* Mr Somkiad, the head of the centre, is extremely helpful and speaks good English, T020-5575 1791, somkiad@yahoo.com. Motorbike hire for the loop, 100,000 kip per day; for town 70,000 kip per day.

That Sikhot → *Colour map 3, B2.*
ⓘ *6 km south of Thakhek, daily 0800-1800; 5000 kip. Tuk-tuk 30,000 kip.*

That Sikhot or **Sikhotaboun** is one of Laos' holiest sites. It overlooks the Mekong and the journey downstream from Thakhek, along a quiet road, reveals bucolic Laos at its best. The *that* is thought to have been built by Chao Anou at the beginning of the 15th century and houses the relics of Chao Sikhot, a local hero, who founded the old town of Thakhek.

According to local legend, Sikhot was bestowed with Herculean strength after eating some rice he had stirred with dirty – but as it turned out, magic – sticks. At that time, the King of Vientiane was having a problem with elephants killing villagers and taking over the country (hard to believe now but Laos was once called Land of a Million Elephants). The King offered anyone who could save the region half his Kingdom and his daughter's hand in marriage. Due to his new-found strength, Sikhot was able to take on the pachyderms and secure most of the surrounding area as well as Vientiane, whereupon he married the King of Vientiane's daughter. The King was unhappy about handing over his kingdom and daughter to this man, and plotted with his daughter to regain control. Sikhot foolishly revealed to his new wife that he could only be killed through his anus, so the King of Vientiane placed an archer at the bottom of Sikhot's pit latrine and when the unfortunate Oriental Hercules came to relieve himself, he was killed by an arrow.

That Sikhot consists of a large gold stupa raised 29 m on a plinth, with a viharn upstream built in 1970 by the last King of Laos. A major annual festival is held here in July and during February.

Kong Leng Lake → *Colour map 3, A2.*
ⓘ *33 km northeast of Thakhek.*

This site is usually incorporated into hikes as there isn't direct road access to the lake. Steeped in legend, locals believe an underground Kingdom lies beneath the surface of the 100-m-deep lake. As a result, you must request permission to swim here from the local village authority and you can only swim in the designated swimming zone. Fishing is not permitted. The beautiful green waters of the lake morph into different shades season to season due to the dissolved calcium from the surrounding limestone crops. It is very difficult to get to on your own and the track is sometimes completely inaccessible except on foot. The tourism information centre organizes excellent treks to the lake.

Tham Pha (Buddha Cave) → *Colour map 4, A2.*
ⓘ *Ban Na Khangxang, off Route 12, 18 km from Thakhek, 2000 kip. A tuk-tuk will cost 100,000 kip, use of boat 5000 kip. Women will need to hire a sinh (sarong) at the entrance, 3000 kip.*

A farmer hunting for bats accidentally stumbled across the Buddha Cave (also known Tham Pa Fa, or Turtle Cave) in April 2004. On climbing up to the cave's mouth, he found 229 bronze Buddha statues, believed to be more than 450 years old, and ancient palm leaf scripts. These Buddhas were part of the royal collection believed to have been hidden here when the Thais ransacked Vientiane. Since its discovery, the cave has become widely celebrated, attracting pilgrims from as far away as Thailand, particularly around Pi Mai (Lao New Year). A wooden ladder and eyesore concrete steps have now been built to access the cave, but it is quite difficult to get to as the dirt road from Thakhek is in poor condition. It is recommended that you organize a guide through the **Thakhek Tourism Information Centre**, page 425, to escort you. In the wet season, it is necessary to catch a boat. The journey itself is half the fun as the cave is surrounded by some truly stunning karst formations sprawling across the landscape like giant dinosaur teeth.

Tham Kong Lor (Kong Lor cave)

ⓘ *Entrance fee at cave 5000 kip; US$12 for boat from Sala Kong Lor and US$17 from Sala Hin Boun; 100,000 kip to go through the cave (maximum 3 people per boat).*

Tham Kong Lor cave can only be described as sensational. The Nam Hinboun River has tunnelled through the mountain, creating a giant rocky cavern, 6 km long, 90 m wide and 100 m high, which opens out into the blinding bright light at Ban Natan on the other side. The cave is apparently named after the drum makers who were believed to make their instruments here. Although very rare, it is also home to the largest living cave-dwelling spiders in the world, though it is unlikely you will have a run in with the massive arachnid. Fisherman will often come into the cave to try their luck as it is believed that 20-kg fish lurk below the surface.

At the start of the cave, you will have to scramble over some boulders while the boatmen carry the canoe over the rapids, so wear comfortable shoes with a good grip. A torch or, better, a head-lamp, is also recommended. It is eerie travelling through the dark, cool cave, with water splashing and bats circulating. The cave can also be visited as part of the 400-km 'loop' from Thakhek, see below.

The best way to get there is by road and boat. There is a small transport terminus at the Route 13/Route 8 intersection in **Ban Lao** (also known as Tham Beng or Vieng Kham) for north-south buses between Vientiane and Pakse. *Songthaew* generally pass through here from early in the morning to well into the afternoon to **Ban Na Hin**, US$1-2. This trip along Route 8 is about 60 km. The drive between Ban Lao and Ban Na Hin is magical and passes through some truly amazing Gothic scenery; keep an eye out for the lookout at Km 54 from Route 13. Generally, a pick-up waits in Ban Na Hin to take passengers to Ban Kong Lor, where you can pick up a boat trip into the cave. There is also one public *songthaew* a day.

Alternatively, if the new road is flooded you can get a *songthaew*, as far as **Ban Napur**, or Na Phouak, and then catch a boat to Ban Phonyang, two to three hours, or **Ban Kong Lor** (closer to the cave), and onto the cave, a further one hour.

If you are staying at **Sala Hin Boun**, see Sleeping, they will send you a boat to Ban Napur to collect you, US$25.

Route 12 and the 'Loop' → *Colour map 3, A2/3.*

ⓘ *Contact Thakhek Travel Lodge (see Sleeping, page 431) for details of the 'Loop' route and for motorbike hire. Mr Ku who rents the motorbikes is based at the lodge from 0700-1100, 1500-1930 daily, T020-2220 5070. Motorbikes (100cc) cost 100,000 kip per day and come with a helmet and a good map. Mr Ku has contacts around the Loop. He recommends riders take 4 days. He will help out in an emergency and advises on no-go times; for example, in Sep and Oct during the rains.*

The impressive karst landscape of the Mahaxai area is visible to the northeast of town and can be explored on a popular motorbike tour from Thakhek, known as the **Loop**, which runs from Thakhek along Route 12 to Mahaxai, then north to Lak Sao, west along Route 8 to Ban Na Hin and then south back to Thakhek on Route 13, taking in caves and other beautiful scenery along the way. The circuit should take approximately three days but allow four to five, particularly if you want to sidetrack to Tham Kong Lor and the other caves.

The 'Loop' is mostly for motorcyclists, who pick up a bike in Thakhek and travel by road. The whole loop covers an area over 400 km (without the side-trips). This includes 50 km from Thakhek to the petrol station before the turn-off to Mahaxai; 45 km between the petrol station and Nakai; 75 km between Nakai and Lak Xao; 58 km between Lak Xao and Ban Na Hin; 41 km between Ban Na Hin and Ban Lao and then 105 km between Ban Lao and Thakhek. The trip between Ban Lao and Ban Na Hin offers some spectacular views.

If on a motorbike pack light: include a waterproof jacket, a torch, a few snacks, a long-sleeved shirt, sunglasses, sun block, closed-toe shoes, a sinh or sarong (to use as a towel, to stop dust and – for women – to bathe along the way), a phrase book and a good map. It is a bumpy, exhausting but enjoyable ride. All of the sites are now well signposted in English. Most sites charge a parking fee for motorbikes.

Note that this whole region is susceptible to change due to the Nam Theun II dam, a US$1.5 billion hydropower project, and other developments in the area. It is imperative that you check for up-to-date information before travelling. Check on the status of the roads at the Tourism Information Centre and with Mr Ku, see page 425, and check the logbook at the **Thakhek Lodge**. This trip is difficult in the wet season and will probably only be possible for skilled riders on larger dirt bikes. In the dry season it's very dusty.

The caves along Route 12 can also be visited on day trips from Thakhek, although some are difficult to find without a guide and access may be limited in the wet season. Many of the sights have no English signposts but locals will be more than obliging to confirm you are going in the right direction if you ask. Turn south off Route 12 at Km 7 to reach **Tham Xang** (Tham Pha Ban Tham), an important Buddhist shrine that contains some statues and a box of religious scripts. It is considered auspicious due to the 'elephant head' that has formed from calcium deposits and in the Lao New Year the locals sprinkle water on it. At Km 13, turn north on a track for 2 km to **Tha Falang** (Vang Santiphap – Peace Pool), a lovely emerald billabong on the Nam Don River, surrounded by pristine wilderness and breathtaking cliffs. It's a nice place to spend the afternoon or break your journey. In the wet season it may be necessary to catch a boat from the Xieng Liab Bridge to get here. Turn south off Route 12 at Km 14 and follow the track south to reach **Tham Xiang Liab**, a reasonably large cave at the foot of a 300-m-high limestone cliff, with a small swimming hole (in the dry season) at the far end. It is not easy to access the interior of the cavern on your own and, in the wet season, it can only be navigated by boat, as it usually floods. This cave, called 'sneaking around cave' derived its name from a legend of an old hermit who used to meditate in the cave with his beautiful daughter. A novice monk fell in love with the hermit's daughter and the two lovebirds planned their trysts sneakily around this cave and Tham Nan Aen. When the hermit found out he flew into a rage and did away with the novice monk; the daughter was banished to the cave for the rest of her life.

At Km 17, beyond the narrow pass, turn to the north and follow the path for 400 m to reach **Tham Sa Pha In**, a cave with a small lake and a couple of interesting Buddhist shrines. Swimming in the lake is strictly prohibited as the auspicious waters are believed to have magical powers. South of Route 12, at Km 18, a path leads 700 m to the entrance of **Tham Nan Aen** ① *7000 kip*. This is the giant of the local caverns at 1.5 km long and over 100 m high. It has multiple chambers and the entrances are illuminated by fluorescent lighting; it also contains a small underground freshwater pool.

Savannakhet → *For listings, see pages 431-434. Colour map 3, B2.*

Situated on the banks of the Mekong at the start of Route 9 to Danang in Vietnam, Savannakhet – or Savan as it is usually known – is an important river port and gateway to the south. The city has a sizeable Chinese population and attracts merchants from both Vietnam and Thailand, while the ubiquitous colonial houses and fading shopfronts are an ever-present reminder of earlier French influence. In 2010 authorities recognised the value of its historic core and 30 billion kip is to be spent on preserving the colonial-era architecture. Savannakhet Province has several natural attractions, although the majority are a fair hike from the provincial capital. For those short on time in Laos, Pakse makes a better stopover than Savannakhet.

Ins and outs
Getting there and around It is possible to cross into Vietnam by taking Route 9 east over the Annamite Mountains via Xepon. The border is at Dansavanh (Laos) and Lao Bao (Vietnam) (see border box, page 433) 236 km east of Savannakhet, with bus connections direct from Savannakhet to Danang, Dong Ha and Hué. It is possible to cross the border into Thailand near Mukdahan via the new Friendship Bridge (see box, page 381). The government bus terminal is near the Savan Xai market has connections with Vientiane, Thakhek, Pakse and Lao Bao; a tuk-tuk to the centre should cost about 10,000 kip. Just west of the bus station is the *songthaew* terminal, where vehicles depart to provincial destinations. Tuk-tuks, locally known as *Sakaylab*, criss-cross town. ▸▸ *See Transport, page 433.*

Tourist information The **Provincial Tourism Office** ⓘ *Chaleun Meuang Rd, T041-212755,* is one of the least helpful in the country with staff slumped on desks; 'too busy to help' apparently. Much better, much more helpful, more professional and much friendlier is the nearby **Eco Guide Unit** ⓘ *Rasphanit Rd, T041-214203, www.savannakhet-trekking.com,* which runs excellent ecotours and treks to Dong Natad and Dong Phu Vieng National Protected Areas, which should be organized in advance. Can also arrange guides and drivers for other trips.

Sights
Savan's colonial heritage can be seen throughout the town centre. Perhaps the most attractive area is the square east of the former immigration office between Khanthabouli and Phetsalath roads. **Wat Sounantha** has a three-dimensional raised relief on the front of the *sim*, showing the Buddha in the *mudra* of bestowing peace, separating two warring armies. **Wat Sayaphum** on the Mekong is rather more attractive and has several early 20th-century monastery buildings. It is both the largest and oldest monastery in town, although it was only built at the end of the 19th century. Evidence of Savan's diverse population is reflected in the **Chua Dieu Giac**, a Mahayana Buddhist pagoda that serves the town's Vietnamese population. The **Dinosaur Museum** ⓘ *Khanthabouli Rd, daily 0800-1200, 1300-1600, 5000 kip,* houses a collection of four different dinosaur and early mammalian remains, and even some fragments of a meteorite that fell to earth over 100 million years ago.

The **Provincial Museum** ⓘ *Khanthabouli Rd, Mon-Sat 0800-1200 and 1330-1600, 5000 kip,* offers plenty of propaganda-style displays but little that is terribly enlightening unless you are interested in the former revolutionary leader Kaysone Phomvihane.

That Inheng → *Colour map 3, B2.*
ⓘ *Any of the regular tuk-tuks will make the trip for 100,000 kip return, or take a shared songthaew to Xeno and ask to hop off at That Inheng. They will usually take you all the way there but if they drop you at the turning it is only a 3-km walk. Alternatively hire a bicycle in town and cycle.*

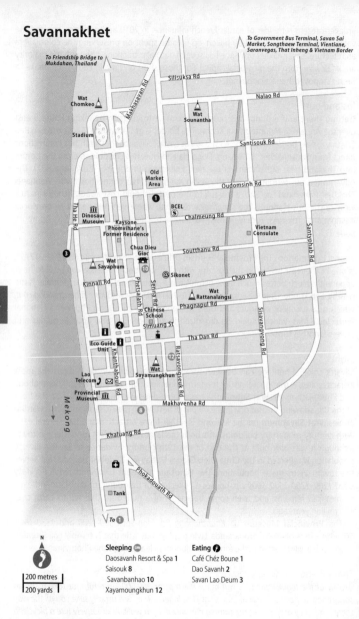

Savannakhet

To Friendship Bridge to
Mukdahan, Thailand

To Government Bus Terminal, Savan Sai
Market, Songthaew Terminal, Vientiane,
Saranvegas, That Inheng & Vietnam Border

Siliuksa Rd

Nalao Rd

Wat
Chomkeo

Wat
Sounantha

Stadium

Santisouk Rd

Old
Market
Area

Oudomsinh Rd

❶

BCEL
$

Chalmeung Rd

Tha He Rd

Dinosaur
Museum

Kaysone
Phomvihane's
Former Residence

Vietnam
Consulate

❸

Chua Dieu
Giac

Soutthanu Rd

Wat
Sayaphum

⑩

Sikonet

Chao Kim Rd

Kinnali Rd

Wat
Rattanalangsi

Santyphab Rd

Phetsalath Rd

Senna Rd

Chinese
School

Phagnapul Rd

Simuang St

Tha Dan Rd

Sisavangvong Rd

Eco Guide
Unit

❷

Khanthaboui Rd

Ratsavongseuk Rd

Lao
Telecom

Wat
Sayamungkhun

⑫

Provincial
Museum

Makhavenha Rd

Mekong

❽

Makhaavran Rd

Khaluang Rd

Phokadouath Rd

Tank

To ❶

N

200 metres
200 yards

Sleeping 🛏
Daosavanh Resort & Spa 1
Saisouk 8
Savanbanhao 10
Xayamoungkhun 12

Eating 🍴
Café Chéz Boune 1
Dao Savanh 2
Savan Lao Deum 3

This holy 16th-century *that* or stupa is 12 km northeast of Savannakhet and is the second-holiest site in Southern Laos after Wat Phou. It was built during the reign of King Sikhottabong at the same time as That Luang in Vientiane, although local guides may try to convince you it was founded by the Indian emperor Asoka over 2000 years ago. Needless to say, there is no historical evidence to substantiate this claim. The wat is the site of an annual festival at the end of November akin to the one celebrated at Wat Phou, Champasak (see page 437).

Dong Phou Vieng National Protected Area

The **Savannakhet Eco Guide Unit** (see page 429), runs excellent treks through the Dong Phou Vieng National Protected Area, home to wildlife such as Siamese crocodiles, Asian elephants, the endangered Eld's deer, langurs and wild bison (most of which you would be incredibly lucky to see). Located within the NPA is a **Song Sa Kae** (Sacred Forest and Cemetery), revered by the local Katang ethnic group, who are known for their buffalo sacrifices. The well-trained local guides show how traditional natural produce is gathered for medicinal, fuel or other purposes. The tours are exceptionally good value and homestay is included. Most only run during the dry season.

◉ Central provinces listings

For Sleeping and Eating price codes and other relevant information, see Essentials pages 40-43.

◉ Sleeping

Thakhek *p425*
D Inthira Sikhotabong Hotel, Chao Anou Rd, close to the fountain, T051-251237, www.inthirahotel.com. In a Lao nautical-style building, this small new hotel offers attractive rooms that are warmly decorated but twins are cramped, with a tiny toilet closet; doubles are better. Restaurant and Wi-Fi available.
E-F Southida Guesthouse, Chao Anou Rd (1 block back from the river), T051-212568. Very popular guesthouse in the centre of town. Clean comfortable rooms with a/c, TV, and hot water; cheaper with fan. Very helpful staff; often booked up.
E-F Thakhek Travel Lodge, 2 km from the centre of town, T030-530 0145, travell@laotel.com. Popular guesthouse set in a beautifully restored and decorated house. Fantastic outdoor seating area and with nightly open fire. The cheaper rooms are very basic but the 9-bed dorm (not bunk beds) is extremely nice (25,000 kip per person). The a/c rooms are huge with

large bathrooms and very comfortable. The restaurant food is not all good but recommended is the Hawaii curry, and barbecue (which needs to be ordered in advance); the service is ridiculously and unacceptably slow and haphazard. The Danish/Lao owners can provide travel advice, when they're around, and there's an excellent log-book for those intending to travel independently around the 'Loop'. Motorcycle hire.

Recommended for those planning adventure travel around the area; tours arranged. Ring them in advance if you're coming in on one of the midnight buses.

Tham Kong Lor
There are 2 guesthouses on Route 13 in **Ban Lao**, just past the Route 8 intersection, which are passable. Homestays are available in **Ban Kong Lor** and **Ban Natan**.
C-E Sala Hin Boun, Ban Phonyang, 10 km from Kong Lor cave, T020-7775 5220, www.salalao.com. The best option. It enjoys a scenic location on the riverbank amongst karst rock formations and has 10 well-equipped and very pleasant rooms in 2 bungalows. The manager will arrange for

a boat to pick you up in Napua for US$25, with advance notice. A tour to Kong Lor for 2-3 people is US$30 with picnic lunch. Discounts in low season.

E-G Sala Kong Lor Lodge, 1.5 km from Kong Lor cave, near Ban Tiou, T020-7776 1846. Lodge with 4 small huts with twin beds and several superior rooms.

Savannakhet *p428, map 430*

A-B Daosavanh Resort & Spa Hotel, 1 km south of the historic centre, T041-252188, www.daosavanhhtl.com. A brand new resort with attractive rooms (Mekong views cost more), super mattresses, rain shower in bathrooms, great pool and Wi-Fi; bathrooms need much better ventilation though. It's a little stuck out of the centre but great for the spa and pool. Let's hope they preserve the lovely French colonial building in the grounds that used to be the provincial museum.

F Savanbanhao, Senna Rd, T041-212202, sbtour@laotel.com. Centrally located hotel composed of 4 colonial-styles houses set around a quiet but large concrete courtyard, with a range of rooms. Cheaper rooms in '4th class' which are not musty, contrary to appearances. Most expensive have en suite showers and hot water.Some a/c. Large balcony. **Savanbanhao Tourism Co** is attached. Good for those who want to be in and out of Savannakhet, quickly, with relative ease.

F-G Saisouk, Makhavenha Rd, T041-212207. A real gem. This breezy new guesthouse has good-sized twin and double rooms, immaculately furnished and spotlessly clean, some a/c, communal bathrooms and cold water. Beautifully decorated with interesting *objets d'art* and what look like dinosaur bones. Plenty of chairs and tables on the large verandas. Very friendly staff, reasonable English. Very friendly and homely.

F-G Xayamoungkhun, 85 Rasavongseuk Rd, T041-212426. An excellent little guesthouse with 16 rooms in an airy colonial-era villa. Centrally positioned with

a largish compound. Range of very clean rooms available, more expensive have hot water, a/c and fridge. Very friendly owners. Second-hand books available. Recommended.

● Eating

Thakhek *p425*

There is the usual array of noodle stalls – try the one in the town 'square' with good fruit shakes. Warmed baguettes are also sold in the square in the morning. The best place to eat is at one of the riverside restaurants on either side of fountain square, where you can watch the sunset, knock back a Beer Lao and tuck into tasty barbecue foods. Otherwise, most restaurants are attached to hotels.

♥ Kaysone Restaurant, in the centre of town, T051-212563. Looks like someone's backyard, but once inside you discover a sprawling restaurant. Very popular with the locals. *Sindat*, Korean barbecue and an à la carte menu. The ice cream is fantastic. There's karaoke on site.

♥ Sabaidee Thakhek, T051-251245, is a refreshing addition to the restaurant scene serving up great backpacker fare (burgers, salads, sandwiches) plus Laos dishes on its cheery red-checked table cloths. Book exchange and CNN on TV. Closed between 1500-1700.

Savannakhet *p428, map p430*

Several restaurants on the riverside serve good food and beer. The market also sells good, fresh food, including Mekong river fish.

♥♥♥-♥ Dao Savanh, Simuang Rd, T041-260888. A new restaurant in a restored French colonial building with good but pricey food. It's worth splashing out for a set menu (65,000 kip-95,000 kip) for the charm and central location. Tables outside afford views of the central square.

♥♥-♥ Savan Lao Deum, T041-252125. This lovely restaurant has taken over the old ferry pier area. The attractive wooden restaurant juts out onto the river on a floating verandah. It's great for a sunset drink.

Border essentials: Dansavanh-Lao Bao

The Vietnam border is 236 km east of Savannakhet (45 km from Xepon). Getting through customs and dealing with potential obstacles on the other side means that it's impossible to state how long it may take to get into Vietnam itself.

Buses leave Savannakhhet for the border at 0630 and 0930 1200, four to five hours, 30,000 kip. There are buses that run from Savannakhet to Dong Ha, Hué and Danang, but for some you will need to change buses at the border.

The Lao border post is at Dansavanh, from where it is about 500 m to the Vietnamese immigration post and a further 3 km to Lao Bao, the first settlement across the border; motorbike taxis are available to carry weary travellers. We have received reports of long delays at this border crossing, as paperwork is scrutinized and bags are checked and double checked. Don't be surprised if formalities take one hour – and keep smiling! The problem seems to be at the Vietnamese end but those with a Vietnamese visa (required) should be OK. The closest Vietnamese consulate is in Savannakhet; see page 434 for visa application details and opening hours. Lao immigration can also issue 30-day tourist visas for US$45. Expect to pay 'overtime fees' on the Lao side if you come through on a Saturday or Sunday.

The food is delicious too - especially steamed fish and herbs. You could also try fried tree ant eggs, grilled buffalo skin and roasted cicadas. Service is exceptional. ¶ **Café Chéz Boune**, T041-215190. Open 0700-2300. Opposite the old market, this place provides good travellers' fare in attractive surrounds.

☺ Transport

Thakhek p425
Bus/truck
Thakhek's main bus station is 4 km northeast of town, T051-251519. Frequent connections from 0400-1200 to **Vientiane**, 346 km, 6 hrs, 50,000 kip; the VIP bus also dashes through town at 0915 daily, 70,000 kip. Get off at **Ban Lao**, 15,000 kip, for connections along Route 12. To **Savannakhet**, from 1030, every 30 mins daily, 139 km, 2½-3 hrs, 25,000 kip; to **Pakse**, every hour from 1030 until 2400 daily, 6-7 hrs, 50,000 kip; Pakse VIP bus leaves at 2400, 70,000 kip.

Buses to Vietnam. To Vinh, 0800 daily, 90,000 kip. To **Dong Hoi**, 0700 Mon, Wed, Sat and Sun, 85,000-130,000 kip; to **Hué**,

2000 Wed, Thu, Sat and Sun 90,000 kip. To Hanoi 0800 Sat and Sun, 160,000 kip.

The local bus station is at Talaat Lak Sarm. From here *songthaew* to **Na Phao** (Vietnam border) 142 km, 6-7 hrs, 40,000 kip; **Na Hin**, 45,000 kip. There is also a *songthaew* to **Kong Lor** village at 0830, 65,000 kip.

Motorbike
Can be rented from Thakhek Travel Lodge, 70,000 kip per day; and from Provincial Tourism Office 70,000 kip in town; 100,000kip per day for The Loop.

Savannakhet p428, map p430
Bus/truck
From the bus station (T041-213920) on the northern edge of town, daily to **Vientiane**, (0600-1130), 9 hrs, 80,000 kip. Most of the Vientiane- bound buses also stop at **Thakhek**, 125 km, 2½-3 hrs, 25,000 kip. To **Pakse** daily at 0700, 0900, 1030, 1230, 1730, 6-7 hrs, 35,000 kip; buses in transit from Vientiane to Pakse will also usually pick up passengers here. A VIP bus leaves at 2130, 8 hrs, 95,000 kip. To **Lao Bao** (Vietnam border, see page 433), 0630, 0900 and 1200 daily, 6 hrs, 40,000 kip. A bus also

departs at 2200 daily for destinations within Vietnam, including **Hué**, 13 hrs, 90,000 kip; **Danang**, 508 km, 13 hrs, 110,000 kip; and **Hanoi**, 24 hrs, 200,000 kip on Tue and Sat; there are additional services at 1000 (VIP bus to Hué). Luxury Vietnam-bound buses can also be arranged through the **Savanbanhao Hotel** (see Sleeping), 90,000 kip. Although all of these buses claim to be direct, a bus change is required at the border. Buses leave even days at 0800 and arrive in Hué at 1600.

Car/bicycle/motorbike
Car and driver can be hired from the **Savanbanhao Hotel**. Some of the guesthouses rent bicycles for 10,000 kip and motorbikes for 50,000-80,000 kip.

Tuk-tuk and saamlor
10,000 kip per person for a local journey.

● Directory

Thakhek *p425*
Banks Banque pour le Commerce Extérieur Lao (BCEL), Vientiane Rd, T051-212686, will change cash and TCs and does cash advances on Visa and MasterCard. It now also has a 24-hr Visa and MC ATM and there is one close to the fountain in the town centre too. **Lao Development Bank**, Kouvoravong Rd (eastern end), exchanges cash but doesn't do cash advances.

Internet Thakhek Travel Lodge and (expensive), Inthira Hotel, Mekong Hotel and Mukda internet café. Wi-Fi in the lobby of the Riveria and Inthira hotels. **Post office** Kouvoravong Rd (at crossroads with Nongbuakham Rd); international calls.

Savannakhet *p428, map 430*
Banks Lao Development Bank, Oudomsinh Rd, will change most major currencies. **Banque pour le Commerce Exterieur Lao (BCEL)**, Ratsavongseuk Rd, will exchange currency and has an ATM. **Embassies and consulates** Thai Consulate, Thahae Rd, T041-212373, Mon-Fri 0830-1200, 1300-1630. Visas are issued on the same day if dropped off in the morning. **Vietnam Consulate**, Sisavangvong Rd, T041-212182, Mon-Fri 0730-1100, 1330-1600. Provides Vietnamese visas in 3 days on presentation of 2 photos and US$45. **Internet** Sikonet, Chaluanmeung Rd, and others on this road. The **Hoongthip** hotel offers Wi-Fi in its lobby. **Medical services** Savannakhet Hospital, Khanthabuli Rd, T041-212051. **Police** A block back from the river, near the Tourist Office, T041-212069. **Post office** Makhasavanh Rd, Next to the new provincial museum, T020-22601993. **Telephone** Lao Telecom Office, next door to the post office, for domestic and international calls.

Far south

The far south is studded with wonderful attractions: from pristine jungle scenery to the cooler Bolaven Plateau and the rambling ruins of Wat Phou, once an important regional powerbase. The true gems of the south, however, are the Siphandon (4000 islands), lush green islets that offer the perfect setting for those wanting to kick back for a few days. This region, near the border with Cambodia, is an idyllic picture-perfect ending to any trip in Làos. The three main islands offer something for all tourists: the larger Don Khong is great for exploring and taking in the stunning vista and traditional Lao rural life; Don Deth is a backpacker haven and is good for those who want to while away the days in a hammock with a good book; and Don Khone is better for tourist sites such as the Li Phi falls or old colonial ruins. There are roaring waterfalls nearby and pakha, or freshwater dolphins, can sometimes be spotted here between December and May. ▸▸ *For listings, see pages 447-459.*

Pakse (Pakxe) → For listings, see pages 447-459. Colour map 3, C3.

Pakse is the largest town in the south and is strategically located at the junction of the Mekong and Xe Don rivers. It is a busy commercial town, built by the French early in the 20th century as an administrative centre for the south. The town has seen better days but the tatty colonial buildings lend an air of old-world charm. Pakse is a major staging post for destinations further afield such as the old royal capital of Champasak, famed for its pre-Angkor, seventh-century Khmer ruins of Wat Phou. Close to Pakse are ecotourism projects where elephant treks, bird watching and homestays are possible.

Ins and outs

Getting there Pakse is Southern Laos' transport hub. The upgraded airport is 2 km northwest of town; tuk-tuks will make the journey for around 20,000 kip. International flights from Bangkok and Siem Reap, as well as domestic flights to/from Vientiane, run several times a week. There are three official bus terminals in Pakse: the **Northern terminal** (Km 7 on Route 13 north, T031-251508) is for buses to and from the north; the **Southern terminal** (Km 8 south on Route 13, T031-212981) is for buses to and from the south; and the **VIP Khiang Kai and international bus terminal** (with neighbouring **Seangchaolearn terminal**) is for northbound VIP buses. VIP buses to Ubon in Thailand are available from the evening market; Laos visas are available on arrival at the Chongmek border crossing if you're coming in from Thailand, though, don't expect the bus to wait for you. Tuk-tuks wait to transport passengers from terminals to the town centre; you shouldn't have to pay more than 7000 kip if there are multiple passengers but they will wait until the vehicle is full. ▸▸ *See Transport, page 455.*

Getting around Tuk-tuks and *saamlors* are the main means of local transport and can be chartered for half a day for about US$5. The main tuk-tuk 'terminal' is at the Daoheung market. Cars, motorbikes and bicycles are available for hire from some hotels and tour companies. The town's roads are numbered as if they were highways: No 1 road through to No 46 road.

Tourist information **Champasak Provincial Department of Tourism** ⓘ *No 11 Rd, T031-212021, www.xepian.org, daily 0800-11300 and 1330-1630.* They have some fantastic ecotours on offer to unique destinations (some are offered in conjunction with local travel agents, such as **Green Discovery**, see Activities and tours, page 454.

Champasak and around → For listings, see pages 447-459. Colour map 3, C3.

The agricultural town of Champasak, which stretches along the right bank of the Mekong for 4 km, is the nearest town to Wat Phou and with enough comfortable accommodation, is a good base from which to explore the site and the surrounding area. It is about 40 km south of Pakse. The sleepy town is quaint and charming and a fantastic place to spend the night, though the trip can be done in a day. The town itself is dotted with simply stunning colonial buildings. Of these, the former residence of Champasak hereditary Prince Boun Oun and former leader of the right wing opposition, who fled the country in 1975 after the Communist takeover, is quite possibly the most magnificent colonial building in Laos. His daughter-in-law now resides there and although it is not open to tourists it is certainly worth a look from the outside. Champasak is known for its wood handicrafts, and vases, and other carved ornaments are available for sale near the jetty.

Pakse

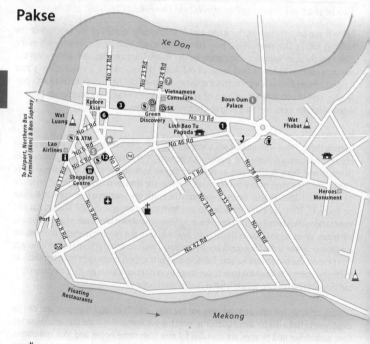

N

200 metres
200 yards

Sleeping 🛏
Champasak Palace **1**
Pakse **5**
Sabaidy 2 Guesthouse **7**
Salachampa **8**

Eating 🍴
Delta Coffee **1**
Jasmine **3**
Nazim's **6**
Xuan Mai **12**

Ins and outs

Getting there Most *songthaews* run from Pakse's Southern bus terminal on Route 13 to **Ban Lak Sarm Sip** (which translates as 'village 30 km'), where they take a right turn to **Ban Muang** (2-3 km). Here, people sell tickets for the ferry to Champasak (3000 kip; person and motorbike 10000 kip). The ferry runs from 0630-2000. Public boats from Pakse make the journey to Champasak in two hours (60,000 kip). A tuk-tuk from the ferry port into town costs 5000 kip. Public ferries run from Pakse to Champasak at 0800 daily. It is also possible to charter a boat, at quite a cost. A new road, due for construction, direct from Pakse, will make the little ferry crossing redundant.

Tourist information Champasak District Visitor Information Centre ① *Mon-Fri 0800-1230, 1400-1630 but daily in high season.* Can arrange boats to Don Daeng, guides to Wat Phou and tours to surrounding sites.

Wat Phou → Colour map 3, C3.

① *The site is officially open 0800-1630 but the staff are happy to let you in if you get there for sunrise, even as early as 0530, and you won't get thrown out until 1800. The admission fee of 30,000 kip goes towards restoration (entry to the Exhibition Centre is included). There is also the Wat Phu Exhibition Centre at the entrance; a surprisingly good museum with an array of artefacts such as the garuda and nandi bull. From the Champasak dock, you can catch a tuk-tuk to Wat Phou, 8-9 km, around 80,000 kip return. Most people prefer to hire a bicycle from one of the guesthouses in Champasak town and cycle to the ruins. Guides need to be arranged at the Champasak Tourist Information Centre with prices starting at US$15. There are several restaurants within the vicinity of the site. A new full moon event has been launched at Wat Phou, an atmospheric exploration of the site with lights from 1800-2100, 30,000 kip.*

The archaeological site of Wat Phou is at the foot of the Phou Pasak, 8 km southwest of Champasak. With its teetering, weathered masonry, it conforms exactly to the Western ideal of the lost city. The mountain behind Wat Phou is called **Linga Parvata**, as the Hindu Khmers thought it resembled a linga – albeit a strangely proportioned one. Although the original Hindu temple complex was built in the fifth and sixth centuries, most of what remains today is believed to have been built in the 10th to 11th centuries.

Wat Phou was a work in progress and was constructed and renovated over a period spanning several hundred years. Most of the ruins date back to the fifth and sixth centuries, making them at least 200 years older than Angkor Wat. At that time, the Champasak area was the centre of power on the lower Mekong. The Hindu temple only became a Buddhist shrine in later centuries.

Archaeologists and historians believe most of the building at Wat Phou was the work of the Khmer king, Suryavarman II (1131-1150), who was also responsible for starting work on Angkor Wat in Cambodia. The temple remained important for Khmer kings even after they had moved their capital to Angkor. They continued to appoint priests to serve at Wat Phou and sent money to maintain the temple until the last days of the Angkor Empire.

Exploring the site The king and dignitaries would originally have sat on a platform above the 'tanks' or *baray* and presided over official ceremonies or watched aquatic games. In 1959 a palace was built on the platform so the king had somewhere to stay during the annual Wat Phou Festival (see page 453). A long avenue leads from the platform to the pavilions. This **processional causeway** was probably built by Khmer King Jayavarman VI (1080-1107) and may have been the inspiration for a similar causeway at Angkor Wat.

The sandstone **pavilions**, on either side of the processional causeway, were added after the main temple and are thought to date from the 12th century. Although crumbling, with great slabs of laterite and collapsed lintels lying around, both pavilions are remarkably intact. The pavilions were probably used for segregated worship by pilgrims, one for women (left) and the other for men (right). The porticoes of the two huge buildings face each other. The roofs were thought originally to have been poorly constructed with thin stone slabs on a wooden beam-frame and later replaced by Khmer tiles. Only the outer

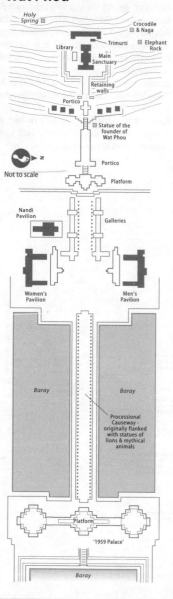

Wat Phou

Holy Spring

Crocodile & Naga

Trimurti

Elephant Rock

Library

Main Sanctuary

Retaining walls

Portico

Statue of the founder of Wat Phou

N

Not to scale

Portico

Platform

Nandi Pavilion

Galleries

Women's Pavilion

Men's Pavilion

Baray

Baray

Processional Causeway - originally flanked with statues of lions & mythical animals

Platform

'1959 Palace'

Baray

walls now remain but there is enough still standing to fire the imagination: the detailed carving around the window frames and porticoes is well-preserved. The laterite used to build the complex was brought from **Ou Mong**, also called Tomo Temple, another smaller Khmer temple complex a few kilometres downriver, but the carving is in sandstone. The interiors were without permanent partitions, although it is thought that rush matting was used instead, and furniture was limited – reliefs only depict low stools and couches. At the rear of the women's pavilion are the remains of a brick construction, believed to have been the queen's quarters.

Above the pavilions is a small temple, the **Nandi Pavilion**, with entrances on two sides. It is dedicated to Nandi, the bull (Siva's vehicle), and is a common feature in Hindu temple complexes. There are three chambers, each of which would originally have contained statues – these have been stolen. As the hill begins to rise above the Nandi temple, the remains of six brick temples follow the contours, with three on each side of the pathway. All six are completely ruined and their function is unclear. At the bottom of the steps is a portico and statue of the founder of Wat Phou, Pranga Khommatha.

The **main sanctuary**, 90 m up the hillside and orientated east-west, was originally dedicated to Siva. The rear section (behind the Buddha statue) is part of the original sixth-century brick building. Sacred spring water was channelled through the hole in the back wall of this section and used to wash the sacred linga. The water was then thrown out, down a chute in the right wall, where it was collected in a receptacle. Pilgrims would then wash in the holy water. The front of the temple was constructed later, probably in the eighth to ninth century, and has some fantastic carvings: apsaras, dancing Vishnu, Indra on a three-headed elephant and, above the portico of the left entrance, a carving of Siva, the destroyer, tearing a woman in two.

The Hindu temple was converted into a Buddhist shrine, either in the 13th century during the reign of the Khmer king Jayavarman VII or when the Lao conquered the area in the 14th century. A large Buddha statue now presides over its interior.

Don Daeng Island
ⓘ *An ecotour is the way to get here; contact the Provincial Tourism Office in Pakse or the Tourism Office in Champasak. A trip by boat from Champasak will cost around US$1.*
This idyllic river island sits right across from Champasak. It stretches for 8 km and is the perfect place for those wishing to see quintessential village life, with basket weaving, fishing and rice farming, and without the cars and hustle and bustle. There is a path around the island that can be traversed on foot or by bicycle. A crumbling ancient brick stupa, built in the same century as Wat Phu, is in the centre of the island and there are a few ancient remnants in **Sisak Village** from the construction. The local inhabitants of **Pouylao Village** are known for their knife-making prowess. There is a lovely sandy beach on the Champasak side of the island, perfect for a dip. The island has only recently opened up to tourism, so it is important to tread lightly. There is one upmarket hotel and homestay on the island, see Sleeping, page 448.

Xe Pian National Protected Area → *Colour map 3, C4.*
ⓘ *The provincial authorities are trying to promote ecotourism in this area: www.xepian.org. To organize an elephant trek go to the the Eco-Guide Unit at the tourism office in Pakse (T031-212021), the Kiet Ngong Visitor Centre or the Kingfisher Ecolodge, if you are staying there (see Sleeping, page 449).*
The Xe Pian National Protected Area (NPA) is home to large water birds, great hornbills, sun bears, Asiatic black bears and the yellow-cheeked crested gibbon. The area is rich in

bird-life and is one of the most threatened land-types in Laos. **Ban Kiet Ngong Village**, 1½ hours from Pakse, has a community- based project offering elephant trekking and homestay accommodation on the edge of the Xe Pian NPA. The village itself is at the **Kiet Ngong Wetland**, the largest wetland in Southern Laos. The villagers have traditionally been dependent on elephants for agricultural work and their treks can be organized to either the Xe Pian National Protected Area or the amazing fortress of **Phu Asa.** This ancient fortress is located 2 km from Kiet Ngong, at the summit of a small jungle-clad hill. It is an enigmatic site that has left archaeologists puzzled; it consists of 20 stone columns, 2m high, arranged in a semi-circle – they look a bit like a scaled-down version of Stonehenge. To reach the village from Pakse, follow Route 13 until you get to the Km48 junction with Route 18 at Thang Beng Village (the Xe Pian National Protected Area office is here). Follow route 18 east for 7 km, turn right at the signpost for the last 1.5 km to Ban Kiet Ngong (a 30,000 kip per person fee is now levied on entrance to the park).

There are several other two- to three-day trekking/homestay ecotours offered in the area, contact the **Provincial Tourism Information Office** in Pakse or the **Kingfisher Ecolodge**.

Bolaven Plateau → For listings, see pages 447-459. Colour map 3, C4.

The French identified the Bolaven Plateau, in the northeast of Champasak Province, as a prime location for settlement by hardy French farming stock. It is named after the Laven minority group that reside in the area. The soils are rich and the upland position affords some relief from the summer heat of the lowlands. However, their grand colonial plans came to nought and, although some French families came to live here, they were few in number and all left between the 1950s and 1970s as conditions in the area deteriorated. Today the plateau is inhabited by a mix of ethnic groups, such as the Laven, Alak, Tahoy and Suay, many of whom were displaced during the war. The premier attraction in the area is the number of roaring falls plunging off the plateau; Tad Lo and Tad Fan are particularly popular tourist destinations, while the grand Tad Yeung makes a perfect picnic destination. The plateau also affords excellent rafting and kayaking trips.

Ins and outs
Tourist infrastructure is limited. Trips to **Tad Fan** and other attractions can be organized in Pakse through **Sabaidy 2 Guesthouse** (see page 448), and **Green Discovery** (see page 454). Alternatively, the best base on the plateau is **Tad Lo** (see page 441), which can be reached by a bus or *songthaew* from Pakse, alighting at Ban Houa Set (2½ hours from Pakse). There is a sign here indicating the way to Tad Lo – a 1.5-km walk. You can usually get a tuk-tuk from Ban Houa Set to Tad Lo for around 10,000 kip. ➡ *See Activities and tours, page 454, and Transport, page 455.*

Paksong (Pakxong) and around → Colour map 3, C4.
The main town on the Bolaven Plateau is Paksong, a small town 50 km east of Pakse renowned for its large produce market. It was originally a French agricultural centre, popular during the colonial era for its cooler temperatures. The town occupies a very scenic spot, however, the harsh weather in the rainy season changes rapidly making it difficult to plan trips around the area.

Border essentials: Yalakhuntum-Bo Y (Vietnam)

The border crossing between Bo Y (Vietnam) and Yalakhuntum (Laos) on the 18B (113 km from Attapeu) is a relatively new crossing and is open daily 0800-1600. Lao 30-day visas are issued at the border. Vietnamese visas are not available at the border and will need to be obtained in advance. Buses leave Attapeu for Play Ku (Pleiku) in Vietnam daily at 0800-0900 (US$10, 12 hours).

On the way to Paksong, just past Km 38, is **Tad Fan**, a dramatic 120-m-high waterfall, which is believed to be one of the tallest cascades in the country. The fall splits into two powerful streams roaring over the edge of the cliff and plummeting into the pool below, with mist and vapour shrouding views from above.

Tad Yeung and around

Around 2 km from Tad Fan and 40 km from Pakse is Tad Yeung. The falls are about 1km from the main road. Set among beautiful coffee plantations and sprinkled with wooden picnic huts, these falls are possibly the best on offer on the plateau as they offer both height and accessibility. Packing a picnic in Pakse and bringing it along for an afternoon trip is recommended. The cascades plummet 50 m to a pool at the bottom, where it's possible to swim in the dry season. During the wet season the waterways create numerous little channels and islands around the cascades. Behind the main falls sits a cave, however it's best to get someone to guide you here. There is a slippery walkway from the top of the falls to the bottom, where you can swim. The falls can be reached by taking a local bus from the Southern Bus station in Pakse to a village at Km 40 (ask to go to **Lak See Sip**). The turn-off is on the right from Pakse (and on the left from Paksong). There is a sign on the main road which indicates **Sihom Sabaidy Guesthouse**, follow this road about 700 m to the falls. These falls are a great option if you are trying to avoid the backpacker hordes.

Just 17 km from Paksong are the twin falls of **Tad Mone** and **Tad Meelook**. Once a popular picnic spot for locals, the area is now almost deserted and the swimming holes at the base of the falls are an idyllic place for a dip.

Some 35 km northwest of Pakse is **Pasuam Waterfall** and **Utayan Bajiang Champasak** ⓘ *T031-251294, 5000 kip*, a strange ethnic theme park popular with Thai tourists. The large compound features small cascades, a model ethnic village, gardens and trails. There are bungalows, a tree house and rooms available for 1000. To get here from Pakse follow Route 13 towards Paksong and follow the left fork at 21 km and turn off at 30 km.

Tad Lo and around → *For listings, see pages 447-459. Colour maps 3, C4.*

Tad Lo is a popular 'resort' on the edge of the Bolaven Plateau, nestled alongside three rolling cascades. There are several places to stay in this idyllic retreat, good hiking, a river to frolic in (especially in the wet season) and elephant trekking. In the vicinity of Tad Lo there are also several villages, which can be visited in the company of a local villager. The guesthouses in Tad Lo can arrange guided treks to Ban Khian and Tad Soung.

The **Xe Xet** (or Houai Set) flows past Tad Lo, crashing over two sets of cascades nearby: **Tad Hang**, the lower series, is overlooked by the Tad Lo Lodge and Saise Guesthouse, while **Tad Lo**, the upper, is a short hike away.

A new Community Guides office has been established with a number of trained guides offering treks around the Tad Lo area and to nearby Ngai villages. Elephant treks can also be arranged from the Tad Lo Lodge for 85,000 kip per person for a 90-minute trek through the jungle and river.

There are two Alak villages, **Ban Khian** and **Tad Soung**, close to Tad Lo. Tad Soung is approximately 10 km away from the main resort area and are the most panoramic falls in the vicinity. The Alak are an Austro-Indonesian ethno-linguistic group. Most fascinating is the Alak's seeming obsession with death. The head of each household carves coffins out of hollowed logs for himself and his whole family (even babies), then stacks them, ready for use, under their rice storage huts. This tradition serves as a reminder that life expectancy in these remote rural areas is around 40 and infant mortality of around 100 per 1000 live births; the number-one killer is malaria.

Katou villages such as **Ban Houei Houne** (on the Salavan–Pakse road) are famous for their weaving of a bright cloth used locally as a *pha sinh* (sarong).

Don Khong → For listings, see pages 447-459. Colour map 3, C3.

Don Khong is the largest of the Mekong islands at 16 km long and 8 km wide. It's the place to relax or explore by bicycle. Visitors might be surprised by the smooth asphalt roads, electricity and general standard of amenities that exist on the island but two words explain it all – Khamtay Siphandone – Laos' former president, who has a residence on the island.

Ins and outs

Getting there and around The easiest way to get to all three major Siphandon islands from Pakse is by private minivan, 60,000 kip arranged by operators in Pakse. The luxurious way is aboard the **Vat Phou**, www.vatphou.com, a boutique riverborne hotel that does a three-day/two-night cruise from Pakse to Champasak and Wat Phou to Don Khong and then back to Pakse. *Songthaews* depart Pakse's Southern bus terminal hourly between 0800 and 1200. The occasional bus will also ply through but *songthaews* are the most common transport option. The journey to Ban Hat Xai Khoune (to catch a boat to Don Khong) should take between four and five hours and cost US$3; in most cases the bus/truck will board the car ferry at Ban Hat (1 km south of Ban Hat Xai Khoune) and take you right across to Ban Naa on Don Khong (1 km south of Muang Khong). Motorbikes on the car ferry from Ban Hat are charged 5,000 kip. There are also motorboats from Ban Hat Xai Khoune to Muang Khong (20,000 kip, depending on the number of passengers). Passenger boats run 24 hours but after 1800 the crossing costs 15,000 kip.

If there is not a bus directly to Don Khong, catch a bus bound for Ban Nakasang (the stop-off for Don Deth and Don Khone) and jump off at Ban Hat Xai Khoune. All local guesthouses are able to arrange bicycle hire. ▶▶ *See Transport, page 455.*

Around the island

Don Khong's 'capital' is **Muang Khong**, a small former French settlement. Pigs and chickens scrabble for food under the houses and just 50 m inland the houses give way to paddy fields. There are two wats in the town. **Wat Kan Khong**, also known as Wat Phuang Kaew, is visible from the jetty: a large gold Buddha in the *mudra* of subduing Mara garishly overlooks the Mekong. Much more attractive is **Wat Chom Thong** at the upstream extremity of the village, which may date from the early 19th century but which was much extended during the colonial period. The unusual Khmer-influenced sim may be gently decaying but it is doing so with style. The wat compound, with its carefully tended plants and elegant buildings, is very peaceful. The naga heads on the roof of the main sim are craftily designed to channel water, which issues from their mouths.

Most people come to Muang Khong as a base for visiting the **Li Phi** and **Khong Phapheng Falls** (see page 446) in the far south. However, these trips, alongside the dolphin-watching trips, are much easier to arrange from Don Deth or Don Khone. This island is a destination in itself and offers a great insight into Lao rural life without all the

Mekong islands

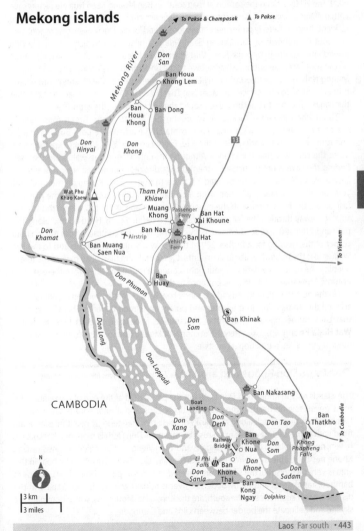

hustle and bustle found in more built-up areas. To a certain extent, except for electricity, a sprinkling of cars and a couple of internet terminals, time stands still in Dong Khong.

The island itself is worth exploring by bicycle and deserves more time than most visitors give it. It is flat – except in the interior where there are approximately 99 hills – the roads are quiet, so there is less risk of being mown down by a timber truck, and the villages and countryside offer a glimpse of traditional Laos. Most people take the southern 'loop' around the island, via **Ban Muang Saen Nua**, a distance of about 25 km (two to three hours by bike). The villages along the section of road south of **Ban Muang Saen Nua** are picturesque with buffalos grazing and farmers tending to their rice crops. Unlike other parts of Laos the residents here are fiercely protective of their forests and logging incurs very severe penalties.

About 6 km north of Ban Muang Saen Nua is a hilltop wat, which is arguably Don Khong's main claim to national fame. **Wat Phou Khao Kaew** (Glass Hill Monastery) is built on the spot where an entrance leads down to the underground lair of the nagas, known as **Muang Nak**. This underground town lies beneath the waters of the Mekong, with several tunnels leading to the surface – another is at That Luang in Vientiane. Lao legend has it that the nagas will come to the surface to protect the Lao whenever the country is in danger.

Tham Phou Khiaw is tucked away among the forests of the **Green Mountain** in the centre of the island. It's a small cave, containing earthenware pots. Buddha images and other relics and offerings litter the site. Every Lao New Year (April) townsfolk climb up to the cave to bathe the images. Although it's only 15 minutes' walk from the road, finding the cave is not particularly straightforward except during Lao New Year when it is possible to follow the crowds. Head 1.5 m north from Muang Khong on the road until you come to a banana plantation, with a couple of wooden houses. Take the pathway just before the houses through the banana plantation and at the top, just to the left, is a small gateway through the fence and a fairly well-defined path. Head up and along this path and, after 300 m or so, there is a rocky clearing. The path continues from the top right corner of the clearing for a further 200 m to a rocky mound that rolls up and to the left. Walk across the mound for about 20 m, until it levels out, and then head back to the forest. Keeping the rock immediately to your right, continue round and after 40 m there are two upturned tree trunks marking the entrance to the cave.

On the northern tip of the island is a sandy beach. Note that swimming is generally not advised due to parasites in the water and potentially strong currents. There is a rumour that Laos' former president, Khamtay Siphandone, is building a resort here. In nearby **Wat Houa Khong**, approximately 13 km north of Muang Khong, is the former President's modest abode set in traditional Lao style.

Don Deth, Don Khone and around → For listings, see pages 447-459. Colour map 6, A4.

The islands of Don Khone and Don Deth are the pot of gold at the end of the rainbow for most travellers who head to the southern tip of Laos, and it's not hard to see why. The bamboo huts that stretch along the banks of these two staggeringly beautiful islands are filled with contented travellers in no rush to move on. Don Deth is more of a backpacker haven, not dissimilar to the Koh Phangans and Vang Viengs of the region, meanwhile Don Khone has been able to retain a more authentically Lao charm. Travelling by boat in this area is very picturesque: the islands are covered in coconut palms, flame trees, stands of bamboo, kapok trees and hardwoods; the river is riddled with eddies and rapids. In the distance, a few kilometres to the south, are the Khong Hai Mountains, which dominate the skyline and delineate the border between Laos and Cambodia.

In the area are the **Li Phi** (or Somphamit) **Falls** and **Khong Phapheng Falls** – the latter are the largest in Southeast Asia and reputedly the widest in the world.

The French envisaged Don Deth and Don Khone as strategic transit points in their grandiose masterplan to create a major Mekong highway from China. In the late 19th century, ports were built at the southern end of Don Khone and at the northern end of Don Deth and a narrow-gauge railway line was constructed across Don Khone in 1897 as an important bypass around the rapids for French cargo boats sailing upriver from Phnom Penh. In 1920, the French built a bridge across to Don Deth and extended the railway line to Don Deth port. This 5-km stretch of railway has the unique distinction of being the only line the French ever built in Laos. On the southern side of the island lie the rusted corpses of the old locomotive and boiler car. Before pulling into Ban Khone Nua, the main settlement on Don Khone, Don Deth's original 'port' is on the right, with what remains of its steel rail jetty.

Don Deth & Don Khone

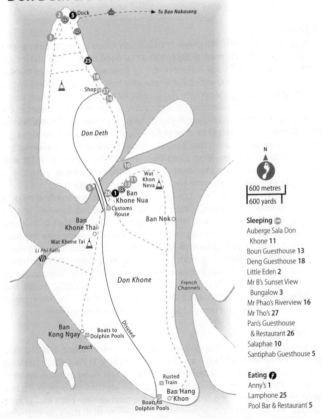

N

600 metres
600 yards

Sleeping 😴
Auberge Sala Don
 Khone **11**
Boun Guesthouse **13**
Deng Guesthouse **18**
Little Eden **2**
Mr B's Sunset View
 Bungalow **3**
Mr Phao's Riverview **16**
Mr Tho's **27**
Pan's Guesthouse
 & Restaurant **26**
Salaphae **10**
Santiphab Guesthouse **5**

Eating 🍴
Anny's **1**
Lamphone **25**
Pool Bar & Restaurant **5**

Ins and outs

A number of companies run tours to this area, especially from Pakse. To get to Don Deth or Don Khone independently from Pakse the bus/*songthaew* will need to drop you off at **Ban Nakasang**. This is not the most pleasant of Lao towns and several travellers have complained about being ripped off here. However, it has a thriving market, where most of the islanders stock up on goods, so it's worth having a look around before you head off, particularly if you need to pick up necessities like torches and batteries. It's a 500-m walk from the bus stop down to the dock. The 'ticket office' is located in a little restaurant to the right-hand side of the dock. However, you can ask anyone that's jumping across to the islands for a lift, at a dramatically reduced rate. The boats take about 15 to 20 minutes to make the easy trip to the islands and cost around 20,000 kip per person. Prices will be higher if you are travelling solo. A boat between Don Deth and Don Khone costs 30,000 kip; alternatively you can walk between the two islands, paying the 10000 kip charge to cross the bridge (also used as ticket to see Li Phi Falls). Both islands can easily be navigated on foot or bicycles can be rented from guesthouses for 10,000 kip per day. ▸▸ *See Activities and tours, page 454, and Transport, page 455.*

Don Deth → *Colour map 6, A4.*

The riverbank here is peppered with cheap-as-chips bamboo huts and restaurants geared to accommodate the growing wave of backpackers that flood south to stop and recoup in this idyllic setting. A good book, hammock and icy beverage is the order of the day here, but those with a bit more energy should explore the truly stunning surroundings. It's a great location for watching the sunrises and sunsets, for walking through shady palms and frangipani trees and for swimming off the beaches, which attract the hordes in the dry season. Away from the picturesque waterfront, the centre of the island comprises rice paddies and farms; you should take care not to harm crops when exploring the island.

The national tourism authorities have been coordinating with locals to ensure that the beautiful island doesn't become 'Vang Vieng-ified', so you'll find no *Friends* DVDs here, although 'happy' shakes have started appearing. The islands got 24-hour electricity in November 2009 although not everyone has signed up to the 24-hour connection, there are no cars (except for the odd truck and tourist open-sided buses) and few other modern conveniences. Internet has amazingly made its way to the island, however, and it's possible to get mobile phone coverage. Most guesthouses run tours to the falls/dolphins. A few entrepreneurial types are starting to promote adventure tourism here. Kayaking and rafting trips can be organized through **Xplore-asia** ① *T031-212893, www.xplore-asia. com.* Several guesthouses also have tubes for rent. It is definitely inadvisable to go tubing in the wet season and probably not a good idea all year round. It is also inadvisable to go alone; there are a huge set of falls at the bottom of Laos. Swimming, visiting the falls and other activities all need to be undertaken with the utmost caution here. The river's current is probably the strongest in all of Laos and several tourists have drowned here.

Don Khone → *Colour map 6, A4.*

From the railway bridge, follow the southwest path through **Ban Khone Thai** and then wind through the paddy fields for 1.7 km (20 minutes' walk) to Li Phi Falls ① *10000 kip paid at the bridge.* Also known as Somphamit or Khone Yai Falls, these are a succession of rapids, crashing through a narrow gorge. In the wet season, when the rice is green, the area is beautiful; in the dry season, it is scorching. From the main vantage point on a jagged, rocky outcrop, the falls aren't that impressive, as a large stretch of them are obscured.

'Phi' means ghost, a reference, it is believed, to the bodies that floated down the river from the north during the war. It's best to visit Li Phi around June or July, when all the fishermen are putting out their bamboo fish traps. These are dangerous waterfalls, do not swim here.

The Mekong, south of Don Khone, is one of the few places in the world where it is possible to see very rare freshwater dolphins. They can be spotted from December to May, from the French pier at the end of the island, not far from the village of **Ban Hang Khon**. The walk across Don Khone from the railway bridge is some 4 km and bicycles can be hired. (A much better bicycle route is to head north round the tip and down to Hang Khon, 45 minutes; the disused railway bridge is not a comfortable ride for bikes as it's rocky.) It is more likely, however, to catch a glimpse of the dolphins if you're in a boat (from **Ban Kong Ngay** or **Ban Hang Khon**), as they reside in deep-water pools. There are thought to be 80-120 dolphins. The Laos–Cambodia border transects the dolphin pool and the Lao boatman have to pay US$1 to the Cambodian authorities in order to access the waters in which the dolphins live. Cambodia gets a bit tetchy about these 'border incursions' and may, on the odd occasion, deny access. ▶ *See Activities and tours, page 454.*

Khong Phapheng Falls → *Colour map 6, A4.*
ⓘ *Near Ban Thatkho, 10,000 kip. Guesthouses organize trips for around 60,000 kip per person (minimum 4 passengers), usually booked in conjunction with a trip to see the dolphins (at extra cost).*

About 36 km south of Ban Hat Xai Khoune at Ban Thatkho, a road branches off Route 13 towards Khong Phapheng Falls, which roar around the eastern shore of the Mekong for 13 km. One fork of the road leads to a vantage point, where a large wooden structure, built up on stilts, overlooks the cascades for a fantastic head-on view of the falls. When you see the huge volume of white water boiling and surging over the jagged rocks below, it is hard to imagine that there is another 10 km width of river running through the other channels. A path leads down from the viewpoint to the edge of the water, be very careful here. Unsurprisingly, the river is impassable at this juncture. Another road leads down to the bank, 200 m away, just above the lip of the falls; at this deceptively tranquil spot, the river is gathering momentum before it plunges over the edge.

⊚ Far south listings

For Sleeping and Eating price codes and other relevant information, see Essentials pages 40-43.

⊜ Sleeping

Pakse *p83, map p436*
A-D Pakse Hotel, No 5 Rd , T031-212131, www.paksehotel.com. This is one of the best places to stay in town –and indeed in the country – with 65 rooms. The French owner, Mr Jérôme, has integrated local handicraft decorations, rosewood accents and tasteful furnishings into this slick hotel. The eco-rooms are good value and the deluxe rooms are a luxury in this part

of the country. Breakfast included. Wi-Fi. Good rooftop restaurant with a perfect view over the city and river; the dimly lit eatery oozes ambience. The chicken curry soup is a must - as are the lethal mojitos!
C-D Champasak Palace, No 13 Rd, T031-212263, www.champasak-palace-hotel.com. This is a massive chocolate box of a hotel with 55 rooms and lit up like a Christmas tree. It was conceived as a palace for a minor prince. There are some large rooms and 40 more modern, and very plain rooms. It is quite bizarre to see bellhops in traditional uniforms. Recent renovations have resulted in a loss of original character in favour of

modernity but some classic touches remain: wooden shutters, some art deco furniture and lovely tiles. The restaurant is one of the most atmospheric place to eat in town, set on a big veranda overlooking lovely frangipani trees. The friendly staff speak a smattering of English, there's a good terrace and the facilities are good, including a massage centre. It's a great position above the Xe Don and the views from higher levels are stunning. Splash out on the King suite for the kitsch factor, jacuzzi and private balcony.

C-E Salachampa, No 10 Rd, T031-212273, salachampa@yahoo.com. The most characterful place in town. Choose a room in the main 1920s building: huge with large en suite bathrooms with warm-water showers; the upstairs rooms with balconies are best. There are quaintly rustic rooms in a 'new' extension. Recommended for those looking for a touch of colonial elegance and friendly service. Exceptional value for money.

F-G Sabaidy 2 Guesthouse, No 24 Rd, T031-212992, www.sabaidy2tour.com. A range of rooms on offer, from dorms to rooms with private bathrooms and hot water. Quite basic but the service is exceptional. The proprietor, Mr Vong offers tours, information and visa extensions. Very popular, you may need to book in advance. Basic food available. Motorbike rental.

Champasak p84

B Inthira Champakone Hotel, diagonally opposite **Vong Pasued**, T031-214059, www.inthirahotels.com. This is a lovely hotel with a friendly US manager. The twins in the courtyard outback come with outdoor rain showers and wooden-floored spacious rooms. The double de luxe is a mini apartment with mezzanine bed area, balcony, shower room and bathroom. The twins are actually more homely. The colonial building opposite is due to open with 6 more rooms.

E-G Anouxa Guesthouse, 1 km north of the roundabout, T031-213272. A wide range of accommodation from wooden bungalows through to concrete rooms with hot water

and either a/c (pay extra) or fan and dingy bamboo structures with cold water. The concrete villas are the best, with a serene river vista from the balconies. The restaurant is probably one of the best in town, overlooking the river plus a shady cabaña. The only drawback is that it is a little out of town (although next to the new spa) and some of the staff can't be bothered to serve customers. Bikes (10,000 kip) and motorbikes (70,000 kip) for hire.

E-G Vong Pasued Guesthouse, 450 m south of the roundabout, T020-2271 2402. The grimy, dingy shop-front façade is deceiving, as out the back, beside the river, are a range of pleasant rooms for all budgets. Strange resident parrot that squawks 'cow' incessantly. The owners are very pleasant. A firm favourite with the backpacker set, this small family-run guesthouse offers pretty reasonable rooms. The rooms by the river are great value, clean with hot water, The more basic rooms do not face the river and are fan only. Good restaurant, perfect for a natter with fellow travellers. Rents bikes for 10,000 kip per day.

F-G Khamphouy Guesthouse, on the main road southwest of the roundabout, T031-252700. Delightful family-run place. Fine bright but basic rooms in the main house with en suite shower. Newer rooms, built in the garden, will cost more. Clean, comfortable, friendly, relaxed. The room facing the front room has a semi-private patio with tables and chairs out front and a larger bathroom than most. Bikes for hire (10,000 kip); book exchange. Good value for those on a budget.

Don Daeng Island p439

L-A La Folie Lodge, T030-534 7603, www.lafolie-laos.com. 24 rooms housed in lovely wooden bungalows, each with its own balcony overlooking the river. The lodge has a stunning pool surrounded by landscaped tropical gardens. Restaurant with good wine and cocktail selection. Bicycle hire and swimming pool use is available to non-guests for a fee. It's a luxurious base from where to explore the island. The German manager is efficient and entertaining.

G Homestays are offered in a community lodge and 17 homestays in Ban Hua Don Daeng. The wooden lodge has 2 common rooms, sleeping 5 people with shared bathrooms and dining area. Meals are 20,000 kip. The **Champasak Tourism office** can arrange the homestay or call direct to English-speaking Mr Khamfong, T020-5599 6609. Boat transfer 30,000 kip. The restaurant serves meals for 20,000 kip. Bicycle hire, 20,000 kip; boat to Tomo temple, 150,000 kip; guide 20,000 kip.

Xe Pian National Protected Area *p439*
A-D Kingfisher Ecolodge, 1km east of Kiet Ngong, T030-534 5016, www.kingfisherecolodge.com. A bonafide eco-lodge set facing wetlands. The set of 6 glass-fronted bungalows are lovely and romantic with 4-poster beds. There are also 4 attractive thatched rooms with nearby shared bathroom. The restaurant, set on the 2nd floor of the lodge, has simply stunning views over the Pha Pho wetlands. Elephant-related activities and massage can be arranged. The owners Massimo and Bangon are so helpful. Highly recommended.
G Homestay, Ban Kiet Ngong, www.xepian.org/accommodation. 27 villagers offer basic homestay. Meals are 20,000 kip per person. You can book at the **Village Information Center** but in Lao only T030-534 6547. If you cannot make yourself understoon on arrival, better to ask for Mr Ho who speaks a little bit of English: first house behind the wat.

Paksong and around *p440*
C-E Tad Fan Resort, T020-5553 1400, www.tadfane.com. Perched on the opposite side of the ravine from the falls is a series of wooden bungalows with nicely decorated rooms and en suite bathrooms (hot showers). The 2nd floor of the excellent open-air restaurant offers the best view of the falls and serves a wide variety of Lao, Thai and Western food. Great service.

Treks to the top of falls and the Dan-Sin-Xay Plain can be arranged.

Tad Yeung *p441*
G Sihom Sabaidy Guesthouse, T020-5667 6186. It is the only operational guesthouse in the vicinity of these falls. There are 8 basic rooms with shared hot-water bathrooms. There is an adjoining restaurant offering basic Lao meals, noodles, eggs and coffee. The guesthouse is set on a coffee plantation and tours are available to the waterfall as well as to nearby orchid areas and tours to see how coffee is made.

Tad Lo and around *p441*
B-F Saise Guesthouse & Resort (aka Sayse Guesthouse), T034-211886. This resort is scattered right across the falls area with varying prices for the accommodation. It is inconvenient to stay in the far-flung buildings (eg the Green and Blue Houses) if the restaurant (at the foot of Tad Hang) is of prime importance. The resort belongs to the Minister of Tourism and his son. It is beneath contempt, therefore, that a government minister houses in his garden two caged gibbons, two caged macaques, a caged civet and a caged bird.
C Tad Lo Lodge, T034-211889, souriyavincent@yahoo.com. Reception on the east side of the falls with chalet-style accommodation (some accommodation is built right on top of the waterfalls on the opposite side; it's a highly inconvenient hike from one to the other for the restaurant). Rates include breakfast and hot water. The location is attractive (during the wet season) and the accommodation is comfortable; cane rocking chairs on the balconies overlook the cascades on the left bank. Good restaurant serving plenty of Lao and Thai food.
F-G Tim Guesthouse & Restaurant, down the bridge road, T034-211885, www.geocities.com/tadlo_net. Five bungalows and 7 twin and double rooms with shared hot-water bathrooms, fans and lock boxes.

Also internet access (500 kip per minute with all proceeds to the local school), international calls, laundry, book exchange, a substantial music collection. He runs a good range of sevices. Motorbike hire, 80,000 kip per day.

Don Khong *p442*

A-C Senesothxeune Hotel, 100 m to the left of the main ferry point, T030-526 0577, www.ssxhotel.com. Tastefully designed, modern interpretation of colonial Lao architecture. Beautiful fittings, including carved wooden fish above each entrance and brass chandeliers. Rooms are fitted with mod cons like a/c, TV, hot water and minibar. Superior rooms have fantastic bathtubs. Splurge a little for the superior room with private balcony. The hotel has a modern internet café (Wi-Fi also available) and restaurant. The menu is mainly confined to Asian dishes; the chicken and vermicelli soup is good. A little English is spoken by waiters. This is the island's best accommodation by a long shot although Mr Pon's new hotel will give it a run for its money. The hotel is run by the gentle, softly spoken Mr Senesavath and his wife, both former mathematics professors from Don Dok University in Vientiane. Both speak English and French. Recommended.

B-C Pon's Arena Khong Island Hotel, 40m north of the main strip, T031-253065, pon_arena@hotmail.com. Mr Pon's has opened a new handsome hotel. You'll want one of the rooms with balconies overlooking the river. All tastefully decorated with high ceilings and bathtubs, minibars and TVs; some rooms have tiny 'smoking' balconies. Wi-Fi throughout. Breakfast served on the upstairs veranda.

E Pon's Hotel and Restaurant, T031-214037. The large, spotless rooms are very good value, with hot showers, mosquito nets and comfortable beds. For 50,000 kip more you get a/c. Mr Pon, who speaks French and English, is perhaps the most helpful of all accommodation proprietors on the island and can offer an endless supply of

tourist information and travel arrangements. Motorbike and bike rental and he can also arrange trips to the Cambodian border, to Don Deth and Don Khon and back to Pakse. In fact, Mr Pon should be your first point of contact for any needs. Recommended. The restaurant is the most popular on the island.

E-F Souksan Hotel, northern end of town near Wat Chom Thong, T031-212071. The reception is in a homely building at the front, while the main accommodation area is in a block further back. Well-designed a/c rooms with en suite bathrooms and hot water set around a concrete garden. In a separate building, with bizarre river landscape paintings, the rooms are nicely decorated and comfortable with desk, cane chairs, tiled floorboards and hot water. Fan rooms are cheaper and represent good value. They also run one of the most up-market guesthouses on Don Deth. Friendly management.

F Villa Khang Kong, set back from the main road, near the ferry point, T031-213539. Fantastic traditional Lao wooden building spruced up with some colourful paint with a great veranda and fab communal lounging area. Spacious clean rooms, with or without a/c. No river views.

Don Deth *p446, map p445*

Many people tend to make their choice of accommodation based on word-of-mouth recommendations from other travellers. Accommodation normally consists of spartan, threadbare bungalows with bed, mosquito net, hammock and shared squat toilets (unless otherwise stated). Always opt for a bungalow with a window, as the huts can get very hot. The wooden bungalows don't provide as much ventilation as the rattan equivalents but tend to attract fewer insects. Also note that tin-roofed huts will heat up quicker than thatch-roofed ones.

The accommodation runs across the both sides of the island, known as the **Sunset Side** and the **Sunrise Side**. As a general rule, if you want peace and quiet, head for the bungalows towards the mid-point along each coast; ask the boat drivers to drop you off directly at the bungalows as it can be a difficult hike with bags.

Sunset side

D-E Little Eden, Hua Det, T020-7773 9045, www.littleedenguesthouse-dondet.com. Very close to the island tip and a small hike from the main drop-off dock, this place offers the best view of the stunning sunsets. Miss Noy and her husband Mathieu have built the best concrete bungalows on the island: 5 smart and spacious rooms with fan and a/c, mosquito net, hot water and even a bookcase in the rooms. The restaurant serving top-notch Asian and European dishes (and Belgian fries) is in a prime position. Mathieu is very helpful with information.
G Mr B's Sunset View Bungalow, near the northern tip, T020-5418 1171. The bungalows and grounds themselves are a bit lacklustre. However, the river views and the helpful staff make this a good option. The best options are the well-located 4 riverside rooms. Of the others the rooms without shower are nicer and bigger than those with shower.

Sunrise side

F-G Deng Guesthouse, next to Mr Oudomsouk's. Wooden bungalows on stilts. Very popular with those who want to laze in a hammock overlooking the water.
G Mr Phao's Riverview, on the riverfront, T020-5656 9651. Brand spanking new 7 wooden bungalows with lovely carved wooden furniture; 2 have inside shower. Mr Phao is one of the friendliest folk on the island and super helpful. He has a new toilet block with Western loo and squat options. He will take guests across to opposite Aan island where there is a wat (10,000 kip) and will make an ATM run for 120,000 kip return, see Banks, page 459.
G Mr Tho's, T020-5656 7502. Wooden stilt bungalows, good hammocks and views of Don Khone. The staff are friendly.

Rooms have been given unusual names, such as 'sticky rice bungalow' and 'bamboo bungalow'. Restaurant attached.
G Santiphab Guesthouse, far end of the island next to the bridge, T020-5461 4231, www.santiphab-don-det.com. 7 basic rattan bungalows right beside the bridge, most have the quintessential hammock. Idyllic setting, flanked by the Mekong on one side and rice paddies on the other. Good for those who want seclusion but also quick access to Don Khone. Very cheap restaurant serves tasty fare with buckets of atmosphere. Very little English spoken. A friendly, timeless place.

Don Khone p446, map p445

Although Don Deth attracts the vast majority of tourists, Don Khone has a much friendlier atmosphere.
B Auberge Sala Don Khone, T030-525 6390, www.salalao.com. A former French hospital built in 1927, this is one of the nicest places to stay on the island with 3 rooms, original tiles and 4 poster beds. In addition, traditional Luang Prabang-style houses have been built in the grounds, with 8 twin rooms, all with en suite hot shower and toilet. 2 rooms have unusual paddy-field views. Breakfast is included. The captured gibbon in a cage in the front garden is a disgrace.
B Salaphae, T030-525 6390, www.salalao.com. This is the most unusual accommodation in the whole Siphandon area. 3 rafts (and 6 rooms) are managed by ex-lawyer, Luesak. Rooms have been decorated simply, with all the minor touches that can make accommodation outstanding. Hot water bathrooms. A wonderful deck, with seating overlooks the stunning river scenery.
D-E Pan's Guesthouse, T030-534 6939. A relative newcomer to Don Khone, these wooden bungalows are exceptionally good value for money. The 6 riverside bungalows with hot water, fan and comfy mattresses are simple but comfortable and ultra clean. The owner is one of the most helpful hosts

in Siphandon. Highly recommended for those on a limited budget. New rooms are under construction. Breakfast included.

G Boun Guesthouse, next door to Auberge Sala Don Khone, T020-2271 0163. Mr Boun has built a couple of cream-painted wooden bungalows, with en suite bathrooms but a private concrete block in the garden obscures the view from some of his wooden rooms.

🍴 Eating

Pakse *p435, map 436*

There are a couple of fantastic *sindat* (barbeque) places near the Da Heung market that are extremely popular with the locals.

If the weather is fine, the **Pakse Hotel** has a fantastic rooftop restaurant offering a range of Lao dishes plus pretty good pizza, totally delicious chicken curry soup and some delectable mojitos from 1600. It has an excellent selection of coffees.

🍴 Delta Coffee, Route 13, opposite the Champasak Palace Hotel, T020-5534 5895. This place is a real find for those craving some Western comfort food. The extensive menu is varied and offers everything from pizza and lasagne to Thai noodles. The coffee is brilliant and the staff are very friendly.

🍴 Jasmine Restaurant, No 13 Rd, T031-251002. This small place has outdoor seating and is a firm favourite with travellers. Offering the standard Indian fare and a few Malaysian dishes, it's reasonable value.

🍴 Nazim's Restaurant, in a new location, T031-252912. Serving a very similar selection of Indian/Malaysian dishes, although the service is a little slower.

🍴 Xuan Mai, near Pakse Hotel, T031-213245. Vietnamese restaurant with outdoor kitchen and eating area. Good shakes and fresh spring rolls. Can be a bit hit and miss.

Champasak *p436*

Most restaurants are located in the guesthouses; all are cheap (🍴).

🍴 Anouxa Guesthouse, see Sleeping. Has a small but delectable menu and lovely restaurant set over the river; opt for a fish dish. They also have a selection of wines.

🍴 Inthira Champakone Hotel, see Sleeping. The Inthira does Western burgers and pizzas and Asian dishes too in handsome surrounds. The iced coffee is fabulous.

🍴 Vong Paseud Guesthouse, see Sleeping. Has a cheap and extensive menu ranging from backpacker favourites like pancakes through to *tom yum* soup.

Xe Pian National Protected Area *p439*

Eating in Ban Kiet Ngong is very basic and you will have to rely on the local food. *Feu* and noodle soup can be made on the spot.

🍴 The Kingfisher Ecolodge, see Sleeping. A fantastic restaurant serving a range of Western and Lao dishes. Also stocks wine.

Paksong and around *p440*

🍴 Borravan Plateau, Route 23 about 1 km from the market towards Tha Teng. Standard selection of Lao dishes in an indoor setting, safe from the weather. Unfortunately there is no menu and no English spoken – so opt for something easy like *feu* or *laap*. The owner is very friendly.

Tad Lo and around *p441*

🍴 Tad Lo Lodge, see Sleeping. A variety of Thai, Lao and Western dishes on offer.

🍴 Tim Guesthouse & Restaurant, see Sleeping. A popular restaurant serving good hearty breakfasts and generic Western dishes.

Don Khong *p442*

The majority of restaurants only serve fish and chicken. In the low season most restaurants will only be able to fulfil about half of the menu options. Special dishes such as a roast or *hor mok* will also need to be ordered at least a few hours, if not a day, in advance to ensure the proprietors have the required produce in stock. Although many other towns and areas also make such a claim, Don Khong is renowned for the quality of its *lao-lao* (rice liquor). Local fish with coconut milk cooked in banana leaves, *mok pa*, is truly a divine local speciality and makes a trip to the islands worthwhile in itself.

Ψ-Ψ Souksan Chinese Restaurant. Attractive place with a stunning, unobscured view of the river. Funnily enough there is an absence of Chinese food but there are other more generic Asian options including good local fish, tasty honeyed chicken and basil pork with chilli.

Ψ Pon's Hotel and Restaurant, see Sleeping. Good atmosphere and excellent food, try the fish soup. Also the *mok pa* here is excellent, order 2 hrs in advance. Very popular.

Don Deth *p446, map p445*

Most people choose to eat at their guest-houses; they all have pretty much the same menu.

Ψ-Ψ Lamphone, see Sleeping. The resident Australian baker cooks up a mean focaccia, and chocolate and banana donuts and other delicious freshly baked goodies including carrot cake and lemon sponge. Also burgers in freshly baked buns and other dishes bringing variety to the island's offerings.

Ψ-Ψ Little Eden, see Sleeping. A large menu with some good Western dishes: grilled chicken breast and creamy pepper sauce, salads, sandwiches and soup and lots of catfish dishes; for example, grilled catfish in a white wine sauce. It's a change from the rest of the places on the island.

Ψ-Ψ Mr B's Sunset View Bungalow, near the northern tip. Italian bruschetta, rice pudding and a selection of burgers including chicken and pumpkin. Good cocktails.

Ψ The Pool Bar and Restaurant, near the main port. Has a pool table and fantastic Indian and Malay food. Good service. Good book exchange.

Don Khone *p446, map p445*

Ψ Auberge Sala Don Khone, see Sleeping. There's a beautiful view from the restaurant and some fine options on the menu, such

as tuna and orange salad or steak salad. Unfortunately, the service has deteriorated significantly and is too slow. Lunch menu is sandwich-based and not all ingredients may be available.

Ψ Anny's, village centre. A new addition to the eating scene, this popular place is offering dishes on smart plates. The fried garlic fish is recommended.

Ψ Pan's Restaurant, see Sleeping. Across from the guesthouse, this is a fantastic, cheap option serving up brilliant home-made meals. The fish here is outstanding.

⊛ Festivals and events

Wat Phou *p437*

Feb (movable) **Wat Phou Festival** lasts for 3 days around the full moon of the 3rd lunar month. Pilgrims come from far and wide to leave offerings at the temple. In the evening there are competitions – football, boat racing, bullfighting and cockfighting, Thai boxing, singing contests and the like.

Don Khong *p442*

Dec A 5-day **Boat Racing** festival on the river opposite Muang Khong. It coincides with National Day on 2 Dec and is accompanied by a great deal of celebration, eating and drinking.

O Shopping

Don Deth *p446, map p445*

There isn't much to buy here. A small grocery store just down from the port has a few essential items and snacks but is not well stocked. If you're in desperate need of any items, make a quick trip to Ban Nakasang and pick up things from the market there. Most guesthouses go to Ban Nakasang on an almost daily basis and will usually buy things for you if you pay them 5000 kip or so.

⚙ Activities and tours

Pakse *p435, map p436*

Most of the hotels in town arrange day tours to Wat Phou and Tad Lo; of these the best is the **Pakse Hotel**. There are a number of tour agencies in town.

Green Discovery, on the main road, T031-252908, www.greendiscoverylaos.com. Offers a range of adventure tours and eco-tourism treks around Champasak Province including Ban Kiet Ngong, rafting, kayaking and cycling trips. Highly recommended.

Sabaidy 2, see Sleeping, T031-212992. Mr Vong and crew offer a wide range of tours around a variety of top-notch provincial sites, very good value and recommended for visitors who are only around for 1-2 days. The 1-day Bolaven tour costs US$24 per person and is great fun. Mr Vong contributes to a school project charity in the province: www.kokphungtai-primaryschool-fund.com.

Xplore Asia, opposite Jasmine Restaurant, Rd 13, T031-212893, www.xplore-laos.com. Offers a variety of tours and useful tour services (including a minivan service to Siphandon). Open-tour trip to Bolaven with stops at Tad Fane, Tad Yuang, Tad Lo, Lao Ngam, 140,000 kip.

Xe Pian National Protected Area *p439*

There are several 2- to 3-day trekking/ homestay trips offered in the area. These include elephant treks across the **Xe Pian** forests, wetlands and rocky outcrops; treks from Kiet Ngong Village to the top of **Phu Asa** (this one takes about 2 hrs; the elephant baskets can carry 2 people); and birdwatching trips. There is a 2-day canoe/ trekking/homestay trip called the **Ban Ta Ong Trail** with guides trained in wildlife and the medicinal uses of plants (from US$95 per person; min 2 people). A challenging 3-day camping Kiet Ngong-Ta Ong Trail is a walking/elephant back/ canoeing trip in Xe Pian from US$280 per person. These tours are designed to ensure

that local communities reap the rewards of tourism in a sustainable fashion and are highly recommended. The best time for birdwatching is between Dec and Feb.

The **Kingfisher Ecolodge** (see Sleeping), T030-534 5016, can arrange for you to train to be a bona fide elephant rider with a traditional *mahout* (elephant keeper).

Tour operators in Pakse can also organize trips to the area. Contact the **Provincial Tourism Office** in Pakse for complete information, T031-676 4144, www.xepian. org. It can also offer a 1-day elephant safari from US$100 per person, for 2 people.

Bolaven Plateau *p454*

To organize kayaking and rafting trips to the Bolaven Plateau contact **Green Discovery** in Pakse, see above.

Tad Lo and around *p441*
Elephant treks

This is an excellent way to see the area as there are few roads on the plateau and elephants can go where jeeps cannot. The Tad Lo lodge organizes treks at 0800, 1000, 1300 and 1500, 85,000 kip per person (2 people per elephant).

Don Khong *p442*

All the guesthouses run tours to Don Deth and Don Khone taking in the Phaphaeng Falls and dolphin watching. Mr Pon's charges 150,000 kip per person for a full-day trip. The national tourist authority is due to open an office in Don Khong and plan to run guided treks to the interior of the island.

Don Deth and Don Khone *p446, map p445*

Almost every guesthouse on the island can arrange tours, transport and tickets. All tour operators offer trips to Khong Phapheng, 60,000-70,000 kip each, minimum 4 people. From Don Khone, it is possible to hire a boat for the day, to visit the islands including one where the rice pots are made. Ask at **Mr Pan's**; 2-3 hrs, 150,000 kip for 4 people.

Dolphin watching

From **Don Khone**, it is possible to hire a boat from Kong Ngay, 90,000 kip, maximum 3 people to a boat Further south, at Ban Hang Khon, it's 60,000 kip per boat, maximum 3 people. Tours from Don Deth to the dolphins and Phapheng Falls cost 80,000 kip per person, minimum 6 people. **X-plore Asia** runs tours to the Phapheng tours and dolphin watching for 180,000 per person, minimum 2 people. Costs reduce the larger the group of people. Note that if the dolphins are hanging out across the border in Cambodia, you will need to pay an extra US$1 per person to criss-cross the waters. (There are now restaurants at Hang Khon and Kong Ngay).

Fishing and kayaking

Most tour operators would be able to arrange a day out fishing if you asked. **Happy Island Adventure Tour**, T020-2267 7698, happytour_bs@hotmail.com runs fishing trips for 120,000 per person, minimum 5 people. Kayaking is also possible including trips to the falls and dolphins, 200,000 kip per person, minimum 3 people.

For boat trips further afield, see Transport, page xxx.

⊖ Transport

Pakse *p435, map p436*
Air
To **Vientiane**, **Luang Prabang**, **Siem Reap** and **Bangkok**. Lao Airlines has offices at the airport and by the river in town, T031-212140. **Bangkok Airways** also runs flights direct to/from **Bangkok** and to **Siem Reap**.

Boat
A boat to **Champasak** leaves at 0830 daily, 80,000 kip, 2 hrs. If you have enough people and money it is possible to charter a boat to **Don Khong** or **Champasak**, contact **Mr Boun My**, T020-5563 1008. A charter to Champasak, US$70; to the **4000 Islands**, US$210.

The **Luang Say** company and **Mekong Islands Tours** run cruises from Pakse to Wat Phou and down to the 4000 Islands. The **Vat Phou** (T031-251446, www.vatphou.com) offers 3-day cruises in 12 cabins from €419. The **Mekong Islands** has 11 cabins (T031-410155, www.mekongislands.com). Its 4-night cruise costs from €620.

Bus
You can charter a tuk-tuk to the airport, northern bus station or southern bus station for about 15,000 kip. To get to the VIP bus station, 2 km from the town centre, at *talaat lak song*, costs about 10,000 kip.

Northern terminal 7 km north of town on Route 13. Hourly departures daily 0730-1630 to **Savannakhet**, 250 km, 5 hrs, 40,000 kip; to **Thakhek**, 7-8 hrs, 55,000 kip; to **Vientiane**, 16-18 hrs, 100,000 kip. Local buses can be painfully slow due to the number of stops they make. For those heading to Vientiane it makes more sense to pay a couple of extra dollars and get on the much quicker and more comfortable VIP bus at the VIP station.

Southern terminal 8 km south of town of Route 13. There are regular connections with **Champasak** from 1030-1400, 20,000 kip including the ferry fare; stay on the bus if you are travelling to **Wat Phou** (see page 437). Ask for Ban Lak Sarm Sip (translates as 'village 30 km'), here there is a signpost and you turn right and travel 4 km towards Ban Muang (5 km). In the village there are people selling tickets for the ferry. Local buses coming through from Vientiane provide the main means of transport to other destinations down south, so can be slightly off kilter. *Songthaews* to the **Bolaven Plateau**; **Paksong**, 0930, 1000, 1230, 20,000 kip; **Tad Fan**, 5 morning departures, 1 hr, 20,000 kip. A *songthaew* leaves for **Ban Kiet Ngong** 1200, 2 hrs, 25,000 kip.

Buses/*songthaews* leave for **Siphandon** (Muang Khong) at 0830, 1030, 1130, 1300 and 1430 3-4 hrs, 30,000 kip; for **Ban Nakasang** (the closest port to Don Deth/

Don Khone) several departures at 0700, 0800, 0900, 1130, 1200, 1430 and 1400, 30,000 kip, 3-4 hrs. Several of the buses to Ban Nakasang also stop at **Ban Hat Xai Khoune** (the stop-off for Don Khong). Make sure that you let the bus/*songthaew* driver know that you are going to Ban Nakasang or Ban Hat Xai Khoune rather than saying the name of the islands.

A more comfortable alternative to Siphandon is to take the minivan service to **Don Deth/Don Khong** offered by Pakse operators, 2-2½ hrs, 60,000 kip. This is highly recommended as, once you have paid all the fees involved with local transport, it costs about the same. It is also a shorter trip.

Kiang Kai, VIP and international bus terminal Near the football stadium and Talaat Lak Song, T031-212228, just off Route 13. VIP buses to **Ubon** (Thailand) leave at 0830 and 1530, 55,000 kip, 3 hrs; VIP seat buses leave for **Vientiane** at 2000 arriving at 0600 (stopping in **Thakhek** en route), 150,000 kip. A VIP sleeping bus with comfy beds, duvet, cake and films leaves at 0830 arriving in Vientiane at 0600 (stopping en route to Thakhek), 150,000 kip. The beds are double, so unless you book 2 spaces you might end up sleeping next to a stranger. If you are tall ask for a bed towards the back of the bus. Make sure you secure your belongings on any of the overnight buses, as some passengers have sticky fingers.

Buses to Vietnam Buses leave for Vietnam via the Bo Y border. To **Danang**, 1900, 18 hrs, 200,000 kip; to **Hué**, 1830, 15.5 hrs, 190,000 kip; to **Dong Ha**, 1800, 14hrs, 150,000 kip; to **Lao Bao**, 1700, 11 hrs, 120,000 kip.

Buses to Cambodia Leave from the adjacent Seangchaolearn terminal. Sorya buses (www.ppsoryatransport. com) leave Pakse for **Stung Treng** at 0730, US$15, 4.5hrs; to **Kratie**, US$15, 6.5 hrs, to **Kampong Cham**, 0730, US$15, 9.5 hrs; to **Phnom Penh** at 0730, US$30, 13.5 hrs. Warning: that it is not possible to get to

Siem Reap in 1 day from southern Laos. You will need to stay the night in Kampong Cham. Agents that tell you it's possible appear to be operating a scam in southern Laos where they charge travellers extra to transfer onto a minibus at Kampong Cham to get to the traveller to Siem Reap well into the night. **Sorya** is a bit more expensive than most operators, but reliable and recommended.

Motorbike/bicycle
The **Lankham Hotel**, near the Xplore Asia office, rents out bicycles (US$1 per day) standard small bikes (US$8 per day) and larger dirt bikes (US$20 per day). Guesthouses and travel agencies are starting to withdraw motorbike hire because of the responsibility. Tourists who have never hired motorbikes before and the death of a US citizen in Sekong in November 2009 in a motorbike accident are too much to bear. The **Sang Aroun** rents bicycles for 30,000 kip.

Private transport
If you miss public transport, a private *songthaew* from Pakse to Champasak (with ferry and tuk-tuk included) will cost you 300,000 kip. A half day Pakse City tour costs 150,000 kip, full-day 250,000 kip. Ask at **Pakse Hotel** for reliable drivers.

Tuk-tuk/saamlor
A tuk-tuk to the northern bus station should cost 30,000 kip. Shared tuk-tuks to local villages leave from the Daoheung market and from the stop on No 11 Rd near the jetty. Tuk-tuks can also be chartered by the hour.

Champasak p436
Bus/songthaew
A shared local *songthaew* to **Ban Thong Kop**, the village opposite Wat Phou costs around 10,000 kip; direct to **Wat Phou** is 60-80,000 kip return (chartered).To **Pakse** direct at 0630, 0730 and 0800, 15,000 kip 2 hrs (with wait for ferry). A private chartered

Border essentials: Voen Kham-Don Kralor (Cambodia)

It's easy to get to Cambodia from the islands of Siphandon, although rules and regulations change regularly so it is better to check in advance. Cambodian visas are available on the border and cost US$20 for 30 days. You'll need two passport photographs; for a hefty fee, the Cambodian officials are happy to provide you with some. Lao visas are now available at the border from 2010. The border is officially open daily 0800-1600; however, border officials will process outside of these times for a overtime fee so expect to pay anywhere between US$3 and US$5 on the Cambodian side and a little less on the Lao side. On both sides of the border, officials will charge US$2-3 to stamp your passport.

Most tourism operators can arrange buses from Don Khong, Don Deth and Done Khone to the border and beyond. You will need to change vehicles on the Cambodian side on most transport although Sorya is the only company that passes right through. Transport is available to Stung Treng, Phnom Penh and Kampong Cham. See the warning under Pakse, page 456 for through transport to Siem Reap from Laos. Mr Pon can also organize transport for visitors from the Cambodian side back to Don Khong.

van to **Pakse** costs 500,000 kip; to **Paksong**, 700,000 kip, to **Ban Kiet Ngong**, 400,000 kip.

A tourist minibus leaves from the tourist information centre daily at 0800 for **Siphandon**, 70,000 kip. Most of the guesthouses can organize tickets.

Boat

A tuk-tuk from the ferry port to Champasak town is 5000 kip. The return boat journey to **Ban Muang** depends on passengers but it usually returns at 1430, 70,000 kip. A tuk-tuk from Ban Muang on the other side of the river to Ban Lak Sarm Sip on the main road is 10,000 kip.

A ferry to **Don Daeng** island costs 50,000 kip and can be arranged through the Champasak tourist office. The boat departs from behind the tourist office.

Paksong and around *p440*
Regular connections to **Pakse**, 0830-1530, 1½ hrs, 20,000 kip.

Tad Lo *p441*
There are buses from Ban Houei Set (1.8 km north of Tad Lo) to **Pakse**, hourly 0730-1130 then 1300 and 1400, 20,000 kip. You may be able to catch the daily service to **Vientiane**

on its way north, daily 1600 but you will need to book.

Don Khong *p442*
Boat

See also Ins and outs, page 442. **Pon's Hotel** (reliable and recommended) can arrange boats to **Don Deth** or **Don Khone**, 30,000 kip, 1.5 hrs. Other guesthouses also offer this price (Don Khong guesthouse) while **Villa Muang Khong** and **Senesothxeune** are a bit more expensive There are also several boatmen on the riverfront who are more than happy to take people for the right price. Fares tend to fluctuate according to international fuel prices but the going rate at the time of publication was 150,000 kip for up to 10 people, 1 way. Most boats leave at 0830. Private boat charter to Pakse, US$150.

Bus/songthaew
Songthaew and buses head to **Pakse** at 0630, 0700, 0800, 0830, 3-4 hrs, from in front of What Kan Khong, 30,000 kip. Or cross to Ban Hat Xai Khoune and try for transport south.

The minibus service back to Pakse can be organized by Mr Pon, it costs 50,000 kip and includes ferry and drop off directly at your hotel in Pakse (2 hrs). Leaves at 1130; drop off at Ban Muang for Champasak possible, 50,000 kip. Xplore-Asia also passes the Don Khong turn-off at 1230 for the return journey, 50,000 kip.

Guesthouses also arrange transport to the Cambodian border and beyond (to **Siem Reap**, US$23; to **Phnom Penh**, US$18, **Kratie**, US$12, **Stung Treng**, US$8; to the **border** US$5. Private transport to anywhere can also be arranged eg transfer to **Pakse Airport**, US$80; to **Kingfisher Ecolodge**, US$60.

Motorbike & bicycle
Many of the gueshouses offer motorbikes (100,000 kip a day at Senesothxeune; 80,000 kip with Mr Pon) and bikes (10,000-20,000 kip).

Don Deth, Don Khone and around
p446, map p445
Ban Nakasang
To **Don Deth** and **Don Khone**, 15-20 mins, 20,000 kip per person. To **Don Khong**, 2 hrs, 180,000 per boat. Between Don Khone and Don Deth, 30,000 kip.

Bus/songthaew
Decent buses depart from Ban Nakasang's market, hourly from 0600-1000 daily, northbound for **Pakse**, 40,000 kip; some continue onwards to **Vientiane**; get off at **Ban Hat Xai Khoune** for the crossing to **Don Khong**. Xplore-Asia tourist buses go to Pakse at 1100, 50,000 kip including ferry crossing. The same minivan will stop at **Ban Muang** for **Champasak**, 50,000 kip. To get to **Don Kralor** (on the Cambodian border) most guesthouses can organize the trip on a minivan. (There is no public transport now; a motorbike taxi costs 40,000 kip). Cambodian visas are available on the border and Lao visas are now available. To **Don Kralor**, the largest town on the other side of th Cambodian border, US$4, 2 hrs. Tickets can also be bought further to **Stung**

Treng, US$6, **Kratie**, US$11, **Kampong Cham**, US$12 or **Phnom Penh**, US$13. The Siem Reap bus requires an overnight stop in Kampong Cham, US$18. Note that the **Paramount** company requires a change of bus in Cambodia but the **Sorya** company goes right through to the further destinations. But see warning under Transport, Pakse page 456. For the Cambodia border; see page 457).

X-plore Asia and other agencies can also arrange bus tickets to further afield: **Attapeu**, 120,000 kip, **Ubon Ratchathani**, 110,000 kip, **Bangkok**, 250,000 kip and **Vientiane**, 220,000 kip.

Don Deth and Don Khone
To **Ban Nakasang**, 20,000 kip per person. The first boat is the market boat at 0630; before that you will need to pay 40,000 kip

There are 2 ways to get to **Don Khong**, from Ban Nakasang, either by boat, 2 hrs,180,000 kip per boat (bargain hard), or by bus (see above); motorbike taxis also make the trip for US$3. Although it's slower and more expensive, the boat trip is one of the loveliest in Laos. Boats between Don Khong and Don Deth cost 30,000 kip.

❶ Directory

Pakse *p435, map p436*
Banks BCEL Bank, No 11 Rd (beside the river), changes US$ and most currencies, and offers a better commission rate on cash exchange than other banks, also Visa/MasterCard cash advances at 3% commission, Mon-Fri 0830-1530, they have 2 ATMs; Lao Development Bank, No 13 Rd, T031-212168, cash and TCs exchanged. **Embassies and consulates** Vietnam, No 24 Rd, T031-212827, Mon-Fri 0830-1330, 1400-1630, visas for Vietnam cost US$45 and take 4 days to process, so you are better off organizing your Vietnamese visa in Vientiane. **Internet** Expect to pay around

200 kip per min but discounts kick in usually after 1 hr: **SK internet**, No 13 Rd.

Medical services There is a huge hospital between No 1 Rd and No 46 Rd, T031-212018, but neither their English skills nor medical service will suffice for complex cases; in case of emergencies go across to Ubon in Thailand; there is a pretty good pharmacy at the hospital that stocks most medications. A new international clinic is under construction. **Police** T031-212641.

Post office No 8 Rd, overseas telephone calls can also be made from here.

Telephone Telecommunications office for fax and overseas calls on No 1 Rd, near No 13 Rd; all internet cafés have Skype.

Champasak *p436*

Banks Lao Development Bank, changes cash only Mon-Fri. **Internet** There are 3 internet places including the school and Inthira Hotel.

Don Khong *p442*
Muang Khong

Banks There is a basic Lao Agriculture Promotion bank in town, hours are erratic and it accepts only US$ or Thai.

Internet Nearly all the accommodation offer internet at between 500-1000 kip per minute. **Senesothxeune** also offers Wi-Fi (US$5 a day); **Mr Pon's Arena Hotel** also has Wi-Fi.

Don Deth, Don Khone and around *p446, map p445*

Banks There are no banks on the islands; some guesthouses will change money. Mr Phao of **Phao's Riverview** on Don Deth will take you by boat to Ban Khinak, north of Ban Nakasang where there is a Visa and MasterCard ATM for 120,000 kip return.

Internet There are several internet cafés on Don Deth and Don Khone; minimum 400 kip per min; calls can also be made, minimum 10 mins. **Telephone** The best way to make a call is via the net, although most guesthouses will let you make calls from their mobiles, which can be incredibly expensive, up to US$4 per min.

Background

Scholars of Lao history, before they even begin, need to decide whether they are writing a history of Laos; a history of the Lao ethnic group; or histories of the various kingdoms and principalities that have, through time, been encompassed by the present boundaries of the Lao People's Democratic Republic. Historians have tended to confront this problem in different ways without, often, acknowledging on what basis their 'history' is built. It is common to see 1365, the date of the foundation of the kingdom of Lane Xang, as marking the beginning of Lao history. But, as Martin Stuart-Fox points out, prior to Lane Xang, the principality of Muang Swa, occupying the same geographical space, was headed by a Lao. The following account provides a brief overview of the histories of those peoples who have occupied what is now the territory of the Lao PDR.

Archaeological and historical evidence indicates that most Lao originally migrated south from China. This was followed by an influx of ideas and culture from the Indian subcontinent via Myanmar (Burma), Thailand and Cambodia – something which is reflected in the state religion, Theravada Buddhism.

Being surrounded by large, powerful neighbours, Laos has been repeatedly invaded over the centuries by the Thais (or Siamese) and the Vietnamese – who both thought of Laos as their buffer zone and backyard. They too have both left their mark on Lao culture. In recent history, Laos has been influenced by the French during the colonial era, the Japanese during the Second World War, the Americans during the Indochinese wars and, between 1975 and the early 1990s, by Marxism-Leninism.

It is also worth noting, in introduction, that historians and regimes have axes to grind. The French were anxious to justify their annexation of Laos and so used dubious Vietnamese documents to provide a thin legal gloss to their actions. Western historians, lumbered with the baggage of Western historiography, ignored indigenous histories. And the Lao People's Revolutionary Party uses history for its own ends too. The official three volume *History of Laos* is currently being written by Party-approved history hacks. The third volume (chronologically speaking) was published in 1989 and, working back in time, the first and second thereafter. As Martin Stuart-Fox remarks in his *A History of Laos*, "the Communist regime is as anxious as was the previous Royal Lao government [pre-1975] to establish that Laos has a long and glorious past and that a continuity exists between the past and the present Lao state". In other words, Laos has not one history, but many.

First kingdom of Laos

Myth, archaeology and history all point to a number of early feudal Lao kingdoms in what is now South China and North Vietnam. External pressures from the Mongols under Kublai Khan and the Han Chinese forced the Tai tribes to migrate south into what had been part of the Khmer Empire. The mountains to the north and east served as a cultural barrier to Vietnam and China, leaving the Lao exposed to influences from India and the West. There are no documentary records of early Lao history (the first date in the Lao chronicles to which historians attach any real veracity is 1271), although it seems probable that parts of present-day Laos were annexed by Lannathai (Chiang Mai) in the 11th century and by the **Khmer Empire** during the 12th century. But neither of these states held sway over the entire area of Laos. Xieng Khouang, for example, was probably never under Khmer domination. This was followed by strong Siamese influence over the cities of Luang Prabang and Vientiane under the Siamese Sukhothai Dynasty. Laos (the country) in effect did not exist, although the Laos (the people) certainly did.

The downfall of the kingdom of Sukhothai in 1345 and its submission to the new Siamese Dynasty at Ayutthaya (founded in 1349) was the catalyst for the foundation of what is commonly regarded as the first truly independent Lao Kingdom – although there were smaller semi-independent Lao *muang* (city states) existing prior to that date.

Fa Ngum and Lane Xang

The kingdom of Lane Xang (Lan Chang) emerged in 1353 under Fa Ngum, a Lao prince who had grown up in the Khmer court of Angkor. There is more written about Fa Ngum than about the following two centuries of Lao history. It is also safe to say that his life is more fiction than fact. Fa Ngum was reputedly born with 33 teeth and was banished to Angkor after his father, Prince Yakfah, was convicted of having an incestuous affair with a wife of King Suvarna Kamphong. In 1353 Fa Ngum led an army to Luang Prabang and confronted his grandfather, King Suvarna Kamphong. Unable to defeat his grandson on the battlefield, the aged king is said to have hanged himself and Fa Ngum was invited to take the throne. Three years later, in 1356, Fa Ngum marched on Vientiane – which he took with ease – and then on Vienkam, which proved more of a challenge. He is credited with piecing together Lang Xang – the Land of a Million Elephants – the golden age to which all histories of Laos refer to justify the existence (and greatness) of Laos.

In some accounts Lang Xang is portrayed as stretching from China to Cambodia and from the Khorat Plateau in present-day Northeast Thailand to the Annamite mountains in the east. But it would be entirely wrong to envisage the kingdom controlling all these regions. Lane Xang probably only had total control over a comparatively small area of present-day Laos and parts of Northeast Thailand; the bulk of this grand empire would have been contested with other surrounding kingdoms. In addition, the smaller *muang* and principalities would themselves have played competing powers off, one against another, in an attempt to maximize their own autonomy. It is this 'messiness' that led scholars of Southeast Asian history to suggest that territories as such did not exist, but rather zones of variable control. The historian OW Wolters coined the term *mandala* for "a particular and often unstable political situation in a vaguely defined geographical area without fixed boundaries and where smaller centres tended to look in all directions for security. *Mandalas* would expand and contract in concertina-like fashion. Each one contained several tributary rulers, some of whom would repudiate their vassal status when the opportunity arose and try to build up their own network of vassals".

Legend relates that Fa Ngum was a descendant of Khoum Borom, "a king who came out of the sky from South China". He is said to have succeeded to the throne of Nanchao in 729, aged 31, and died 20 years later, although this historical record is, as they say, exceedingly thin. Khoum Borom is credited with giving birth to the Lao people by slicing open a gourd in Muong Taeng (Dien Bien Phu, Vietnam) and his seven sons established the great Tai kingdoms. He returned to his country with a detachment of Khmer soldiers and united several scattered Lao fiefdoms. In those days, conquered lands were usually razed and the people taken as slaves to build up the population of the conquering group. (This largely explains why today there are far more Lao in northeastern Thailand than in Laos – they were forcibly settled there after King Anou was defeated by King Rama III of Siam in 1827 – see page 464). The kings of Lane Xang were less philistine, demanding

Kings of Lane Xang

Fa Ngum	1353-1373	Pothisarath	1520-1548
Samsenthai	1373-1416	Setthathirat	1548-1571
Lan Kamdaeng	1417-1428	Saensurin	1572-1574
Phommathat	1428-1429	Mahaupahat (under Burmese control)	
Mun Sai	1429-1430		1574-1580
Fa Khai	1430-1433	Saensurin	1580-1582
Khong Kham	1433-1434	Nakhon Noi (under Burmese control)	
Yukhon	1434-1435		1582-1583
Kham Keut	1435-1441	Interregnum	1583-1591
Chaiyachakkapat-Phaenphaeo		Nokeo Koumone	1591-1596
(aka Sao Tiakaphat)	1441-1478	Thammikarath	1596-1622
Suvarna Banlang		Upanyuvarat	1622-1623
(aka Theng Kham)	1478-1485	Pothisarat	1623-1627
Lahsaenthai Puvanart	1485-1495	Mon Keo	1627
Sompou	1497-1500	Unstable period	1627-1637
Visunarat	1500-1520	Sulinya Vongsa	1637-1694

only subordination and allegiance as one part of a larger *mandala*.

Luang Prabang became the capital of the kingdom of Lane Xang. The unruly highland tribes of the northeast did not come under the kingdom's control at that time. Fa Ngum made Theravada Buddhism the official religion. He married the Cambodian king's daughter, Princess Keo Kaengkanya, and was given the Pra Bang (a golden statue, the most revered religious symbol of Laos), by the Khmer court.

It is common to read of Lane Xang as the first kingdom of Laos; as encompassing the territory of present-day Laos; and as marking the introduction of Theravada Buddhism to the country. On all counts this portrait is, if not false, then deeply flawed. As noted above, there were Lao states that predated Lane Xang; Lane Xang never controlled Laos as it currently exists; and Buddhism had made an impact on the Lao people before 1365. Fa Ngum did not create a kingdom; rather he brought together various pre-existing *muang* (city states) into a powerful *mandala*. As Martin Stuart-Fox writes, "From this derives [Fa Ngum's] historical claim to hero status as the founder of the Lao Kingdom." But, as Stuart-Fox goes on to explain, there was no central authority and rulers of individual *muang* were permitted considerable autonomy.

After Fa Ngum's wife died in 1368, he became so debauched, it is said, that he was deposed in favour of his son, Samsenthai (1373-1416), who was barely 18 when he acceded the throne. He was named after the 1376 census, which concluded that he ruled over 300,000 Tais living in Laos; *samsen* means, literally, 300,000. He set up a new administrative system based on the existing *muang*, nominating governors to each that lasted until it was abolished by the Communist government in 1975. Samsenthai's death was followed by a period of unrest. Under King Chaiyachakkapat-Phaenphaeo (1441-1478), the kingdom came under increasing threat from the Vietnamese. How the Vietnamese came to be peeved with the Lao is another story which smacks of fable more than fact. King Chaiyachakkapat's eldest son, the Prince of Chienglaw, secured a holy white elephant. The emperor of Vietnam, learning of this momentous discovery, asked to be sent some of the beast's hairs. Disliking the Vietnamese, the Prince dispatched a box of its excrement instead, whereupon the Emperor formed an army of an improbably large 550,000 men. The Prince's army numbered 200,000 and 2000 elephants. The massive Vietnamese army finally prevailed and entered and sacked Luang Prabang. But shortly thereafter they were driven out by Chaiyachakkapat-Phaenphaeo's son, King Suvarna Banlang (1478-1485). Peace was only fully restored under King Visunarat (1500-1520).

Increasing prominence and Burmese incursions

Under King Pothisarath (1520-1548) Vientiane became prominent as a trading and religious centre. He married a Lanna (Chiang Mai) princess, Queen Yotkamtip, and when the Siamese King Ketklao was put to death in 1545, Pothisarath's son claimed the throne at Lanna. He returned to Lane Xang when his father died in 1548. Asserting his right as successor to the throne, he was crowned Setthathirat in 1548 and ruled until 1571 – the last of the great kings of Lane Xang.

At the same time, the Burmese were expanding East and in 1556 Lanna fell into their hands. Setthathirat gave up his claim to that throne, to a Siamese prince, who ruled under Burmese authority. (He also took the **Phra Kaeo** – Thailand's famous 'Emerald' Buddha and its most sacred and revered image – with him to Luang Prabang and then to Vientiane. The Phra Kaeo stayed in Vientiane until 1778 when the Thai general Phya Chakri 'repatriated' it to Thailand.) In 1563 Setthathirat pronounced Vieng Chan (Vientiane) the principal capital of Lane Xang. Seven years later, the Burmese King Bayinnaung launched an unsuccessful attack on Vieng Chan itself.

Setthathirat is revered as one of the great Lao kings, having protected the country from foreign domination. He built Wat Phra Kaeo (see page 361) in Vientiane, in which he placed the famous Emerald Buddha brought from Lanna. Setthathirat mysteriously disappeared during a campaign in the southern province of Attapeu in 1574, which threw the kingdom into crisis. Vientiane fell to invading Burmese the following year and remained under Burmese control for seven years. Finally the anarchic kingdoms of Luang Prabang and Vientiane were reunified under Nokeo Koumane (1591-96) and Thammikarath (1596-1622).

Disputed territory

From the time of the formation of the kingdom of Lane Xang to the arrival of the French, the history of Laos was dominated by the struggle to retain the lands it had conquered. Following King Setthathirat's death, a series of kings came to the throne in quick succession. King Souligna Vongsa, crowned in 1633, brought long awaited peace to Laos. The 61 years he was on the throne are regarded as Lane Xang's golden age. Under him, the kingdom's influence spread to Yunnan in South China, the Burmese Shan States, Issan in Northeast Thailand and areas of Vietnam and Cambodia.

Souligna Vongsa was even on friendly terms with the Vietnamese: he married Emperor Le Thanh Ton's daughter and he and the Emperor agreed the borders between the two countries. The frontier was settled in a deterministic – but nonetheless amicable – fashion: those living in houses built on stilts with verandas were considered Lao subjects and those living in houses without piles and verandas owed allegiance to Vietnam.

During his reign foreigners first visited the country, but other than a handful of adventurers, Laos remained on the outer periphery of European concerns and influence.

The three kingdoms

After Souligna Vongsa died in 1694, leaving no heir, dynastic quarrels and feudal rivalries once again erupted, undermining the kingdom's cohesion. In 1700 Lane Xang split into three: Luang Prabang under Souligna's grandson, Vientiane under Souligna's nephew and the new kingdom of Champasak was founded in the south 'panhandle'. This weakened the country and allowed the Siamese and Vietnamese to encroach. Muang, which previously owed clear allegiance to Lane Xang, began to look towards Vietnam or Siam. Isan muang in present day Northeast Thailand, for example, paid tribute to Bangkok; while Xieng Khouang did the same to Hanoi and, later, to Hué. The three main kingdoms that emerged with the disintegration of Lane Xang leant in different directions: Luang Prabang had close links with China, Vientiane with Vietnam's Hanoi/Hué and Champassak with Siam.

By the mid-1760s Burmese influence once again held sway in Vientiane and Luang Prabang and before the turn of the decade, they sacked Ayutthaya, the capital of Siam. Somehow the Siamese managed to pull themselves together and only two years later in 1778 successfully rampaged through Vientiane. The two sacred Buddhas, the Phra Bang and the Phra Kaeo (Emerald Buddha), were taken as booty back to Bangkok. The Emerald Buddha was never returned and now sits in Bangkok's Wat Phra Kaeo.

King Anou (an abbreviation of Anurutha), was placed on the Vientiane throne by the Siamese. With the death of King Rama II of Siam, King Anou saw his chance of rebellion, asked Vietnam for assistance, formed an army and marched on Bangkok in 1827. In mounting this brave – some would say foolhardy – assault, Anou was apparently trying to emulate the great Fa Ngum. Unfortunately, he got no further than the Northeast Thai town of Korat where his forces suffered a defeat and were driven back. Nonetheless, Anou's rebellion is considered one of the most daring and ruthless rebellions in Siamese history and he was lauded as a war hero back home.

King Anou's brief stab at regional power was to result in catastrophe for Laos – and tragedy for King Anou. The first US arms shipment to Siam allowed the Siamese to sack Vientiane, a task to which they had grown accustomed over the years. (This marks America's first intervention in Southeast Asia.) Lao artisans were frogmarched to Bangkok and many of the inhabitants were resettled in Northeast Siam. Rama III had Chao Anou locked in a cage where he was taunted and abused by the population of Bangkok. He died soon afterwards, at the age of 62. One of his supporters is said to have taken pity on the king and brought him poison, other explanations simply say that he wished himself dead or that he choked. Whatever the cause, the disconsolate Anou, before he died, put a curse on Siam's monarchy, promising that the next time a Thai king set foot on Lao soil, he would die. To this day no Thai king has crossed the Mekong River. When the agreement for the supply of hydroelectric power was signed with Thailand in the 1970s, the Thai king opened the Nam Ngum Dam from a sandbank in the middle of the Mekong.

Disintegration of the kingdom

Over the next 50 years, Anou's kingdom was destroyed. By the time the French arrived in the late 19th century, the virtually unoccupied city was subsumed into the Siamese sphere of influence. Luang Prabang also became a Siamese vassal state, while Xieng Khouang province was invaded by Chinese rebels – to the chagrin of the Vietnamese, who had always considered the Hmong mountain kingdom (they called it Tran Ninh), to be their exclusive source of slaves. The Chinese had designs on Luang Prabang too and in order to quash their expansionist instincts, Bangkok dispatched an army there in 1885 to pacify the region and ensure the north remained firmly within the Siamese sphere of influence. This period was one of confusion and rapidly shifting allegiances.

The history of Laos during this period becomes, essentially, the history of only a small part of the current territory of the country: namely, the history of Luang Prabang. And because Luang Prabang was a suzerain state of Bangkok, the history of that kingdom is, in turn, sometimes relegated to a mere footnote in the history of Siam.

The French and independence

Following King Anou's death, Laos became the centre of Southeast Asian rivalry between Britain, expanding east from Burma, and France, pushing west through Vietnam. In 1868, following the French annexation of South Vietnam and the formation of a protectorate in Cambodia, an expedition set out to explore the Mekong trade route to China. Once central and north Vietnam had come under the influence of the Quai d'Orsay in Paris, the French became increasingly curious about Vietnamese claims to chunks of Laos. Unlike the Siamese, the French – like the British – were concerned with demarcating borders and establishing explicit areas of sovereignty. This seemed extraordinary to most Southeast Asians at the time, who could not see the point of mapping space when land was so abundant. However, it did not take long for the Siamese king to realize the importance of maintaining his claim to Siamese territories if the French in the east and the British in the south (Malaya) and west (Burma) were not to squeeze Siam to nothing.

However, King Chulalongkorn was not in a position to confront the French militarily and instead he had to play a clever diplomatic game if his kingdom was to survive. The French, for their part, were anxious to continue to press westwards from Vietnam into the Lao lands over which Siam held suzerainty. Martin Stuart-Fox argues that there were four main reasons underlying France's desire to expand West: the lingering hope that the Mekong might still offer a 'back door' into China; the consolidation of Vietnam against attack; the 'rounding out' of their Indochina possessions; and a means of further pressuring Bangkok. In 1886, the French received reluctant Siamese permission to post a vice consul to Luang Prabang and a year later he persuaded the Thais to leave. However, even greater humiliation was to come in 1893 when the French, through crude gunboat diplomacy – the so-called Paknam incident – forced King Chulalongkorn to give up all claim to Laos on the flimsiest of historical pretexts. Despite attempts by Prince Devawongse to manufacture a compromise, the French forced Siam to cede Laos to France and, what's more, to pay compensation. It is said that after this humiliation, King Chulalongkorn retired from public life, broken in spirit and health. So the French colonial era in Laos began.

What is notable about this spat between France and Siam is that Laos – the country over which they were fighting – scarcely figures. As was to happen again in Laos' history, the country was caught between two competing powers who used Laos as a stage on which to fight a wider and to them, more important, conflict.

Union of Indochina

In 1893 France occupied the left bank of the Mekong and forced Thailand to recognize the river as the boundary. The French Union of Indochina denied Laos the area that is now Isan, northeast Thailand, and this was the start of 50 years of colonial rule. Laos became a protectorate with a *résident-superieur* in Vientiane and a vice-consul in Luang Prabang. However, Laos could hardly be construed as a 'country' during the colonial period. "Laos existed again", writes Martin Stuart-Fox, "but not yet as a political entity in its own right, for no independent centre of Lao political power existed. Laos was but a territorial entity within French Indochina." The French were not interested in establishing an identifiable Lao state; they saw Laos as a part and a subservient part at that, of Vietnam, serving as a resource-rich appendage. Though they had grand plans for the development of Laos, these were only expressed airily and none of them came to anything. "The French were never sure what to do with Laos", Stuart-Fox writes. Unlike Cambodia to the south, the French did not perceive Laos to have any historical unity or coherence and therefore it could be hacked about and developed or otherwise, according to their whim.

In 1904 the Franco-British convention delimited respective zones of influence. Only a few hundred French civil servants were ever in Vientiane at any one time and their attitude to colonial administration – described as 'benign neglect' – was as relaxed as the people they governed. To the displeasure of the Lao, France brought in Vietnamese to run the civil service (in the way the British used Indian bureaucrats in Burma). But for the most part, the French colonial period was a 50-year siesta for Laos. The king was allowed to stay in Luang Prabang, but had little say in administration. Trade and commerce was left to the omni-present Chinese and the Vietnamese. A small, French-educated Lao élite did grow up and by the 1940s they had become the core of a typically laid-back Lao nationalist movement.

Japanese coup

Towards the end of the Second World War, Japan ousted the French administration in Laos in a coup in March 1945. The eventual surrender of the Japanese in August that year gave impetus to the Lao independence movement. Prince Phetsarath, hereditary viceroy and premier of the Luang Prabang Kingdom, took over the leadership of the Lao Issara, the Free Laos Movement (originally a resistance movement against the Japanese). They prevented the French from seizing power again and declared Lao independence on 1 September 1945. Two weeks later, the north and south provinces were reunified and in October, Phetsarath formed a Lao Issara government headed by Prince Phaya Khammao.

France refused to recognize the new state and crushed the Lao resistance. King Sisavang Vong, unimpressed by Prince Phetsarath's move, sided with the French, who had their colony handed back by British forces. He was crowned the constitutional monarch of the new protectorate in 1946. The rebel government took refuge in Bangkok. Historians believe the Issara movement was aided in their resistance to the French by the Viet Minh – Hanoi's Communists.

Independence

In response to nationalist pressures, France was obliged to grant Laos ever greater self government and, eventually, formal independence within the framework of the newly reconstructed French Union in July 1949. Meanwhile, in Bangkok, the Issara movement had formed a government-in-exile, headed by Phetsarath and his half-brothers: Prince Souvanna Phouma (see box, page 468) and Prince Souphanouvong. Both were refined, French-educated men. The Issara's military wing was led by Souphanouvong who, even at that stage, was known for his Communist sympathies. This was due to a temporary alliance between the Issara and the Viet Minh, who had the common cause of ridding their respective countries of the French. Within just a few months the so-called Red Prince had been ousted by his half-brothers and joined the Viet Minh where he is said to have been the moving force behind the declaration of the Democratic Republic of Laos by the newly-formed Lao National Assembly. The Lao People's Democratic Republic emerged – albeit in name only – somewhere inside Vietnam, in August 1949. Soon afterwards, the Pathet Lao (the Lao Nation) was born. The Issara movement quickly folded and Souvanna Phouma went back to Vientiane and joined the newly formed Royal Lao Government.

By 1953, Prince Souphanouvong had managed to move his Pathet Lao headquarters inside Laos and with the French losing their grip on the north provinces, the weary colonizers granted the country full independence. France signed a treaty of friendship and association with the new royalist government and made the country a French protectorate.

The rise of Communism

French defeat
While all this was going on, King Sisavang Vong sat tight in Luang Prabang instead of moving to Vientiane. But within a few months of independence, the ancient royal capital was under threat from the Communist Viet Minh and Pathet Lao. Honouring the terms of the new treaty, French commander General Henri Navarre determined in late 1953 to take the pressure off Luang Prabang by confronting the Viet Minh who controlled the strategic approach to the city at Dien Bien Phu. The French suffered a stunning defeat that presaged their withdrawal from Indochina. The subsequent occupation of two north Lao provinces by the Vietnam-backed Pathet Lao forces, meant the kingdom's days as a Western buffer state were numbered. The Vietnamese, not unlike their previous neighbours, did not respect Laos as a state, but as a extension of their own territory to be utilized for their own strategic purposes during the ensuing war.

With the **Geneva Accord** in July 1954, following the fall of Dien Bien Phu in May, Ho Chi Minh's government gained control of all territory north of the 17th parallel in neighbouring Vietnam. The Accord guaranteed Laos' freedom and neutrality, but with the Communists on the threshold, the US was not prepared to be a passive spectator: the demise of the French sparked an increasing US involvement. In an operation that was to mirror the much more famous war with Vietnam to the East, Washington soon found itself supplying and paying the salaries of 50,000 royalist troops and their corrupt officers. Clandestine military assistance grew, undercover special forces were mobilized and the CIA began meddling in Lao politics. In 1960 a consignment of weapons was dispatched by the CIA to a major in the Royal Lao Army called Vang Pao – or VP, as he became known – who was destined to become the leader of the Hmong.

US involvement: the domino effect
Laos had become the dreaded first domino, which, using the scheme of US President Dwight D Eisenhower's famous analogy, would trigger the rapid spread of Communism if ever it fell. The time-trapped little kingdom became the focus of superpower brinkmanship. At a press conference in March 1961, President Kennedy is said to have been too abashed to announce to the American people that US forces might soon become embroiled in conflict in a far-away flashpoint that went by the inglorious name of 'Louse'. For three decades Americans have unwittingly mispronounced the country's name as Kennedy decided, euphemistically, to label it 'Lay-os' throughout his national television broadcast.

Coalitions, coups and counter-coups
The US-backed Royal Lao Government of independent Laos – even though it was headed by the neutralist, Prince Souvanna Phouma – ruled over a divided country from 1951 to 1954. The US played havoc with Laos' domestic politics, running anti-Communist campaigns,

Prince Souvanna Phouma

Prince Souvanna Phouma was Laos' greatest statesman. He was prime minister on no less than eight occasions for a total of 20 years between 1951 and 1975. He dominated mainstream politics from independence until the victory of the Pathet Lao in 1975. But he was never able to preserve the integrity of Laos in the face of much stronger external forces. "Souvanna stands as a tragic figure in modern Lao history," Martin Stuart-Fox writes, a "stubborn symbol of an alternative, neutral, 'middle way'."

In 1950 Souvanna became a co-founder of the Progressive Party and in the elections of 1951 he headed his first government, which negotiated and secured full independence from France.

Souvanna made two key errors of judgement during these early years. First, he ignored the need for nation building in Laos. Second, he underestimated the threat that the Communists posed to the country. With regard to the first of these misjudgements, he seemed to believe – and it is perhaps no accident that he trained as an engineer and architect – that Laos just needed to be administered efficiently to become a modern state. He appeared either to reject or ignore the idea that the government first had to try and inculcate a sense of Lao nationhood.

backing the royalist army and lending support to political figures on the right (even if they lacked experience or political qualifications). The Communist Pathet Lao, headed by Prince Souphanouvong and overseen and sponsored by North Vietnam's Lao Dong party since 1949, emerged as the only strong opposition. By the mid-1950s, Kaysone Phomvihane, later prime minister of the Lao PDR, began to make a name for himself in the Indochinese Communist Party. Indeed the close association between Laos and Vietnam went deeper than just ideology. Kaysone's father was Vietnamese, while Prince Souphanouvong and Nouhak Phounsavanh both married Vietnamese women.

Government of National Union

Elections were held in Vientiane in July 1955 but were boycotted by the Pathet Lao. Souvanna Phouma became prime minister in March 1956. He aimed to try to negotiate the integration of his half-brother's Pathet Lao provinces into a unified administration and coax the Communists into a coalition government. In 1957 the disputed provinces were returned to royal government control under the first coalition government. This coalition government, much to US discontent, contained two Pathet Lao ministers including Souphanouvong and Phoumi Vongvichit. This was one of Souvanna Phouma's achievements in trying to combine the two sides to ensure neutrality, although it was only short-lived. In May 1958 elections were held. This time the Communists' Lao Patriotic Front (Neo Lao Hak Xat) clinched 13 of the 21 seats in the Government of National Union. The Red Prince, Souphanouvong and one of his aides were included in the cabinet and former Pathet Lao members were elected deputies of the National Assembly.

Almost immediately problems that had been beneath the surface emerged to plague the government. The rightists and their US supporters were shaken by the result and the much-vaunted coalition lasted just two months. Driven by Cold War prerogatives, the US could not abide by any government that contained Communist members and withdrew their aid, which the country had become much dependent upon. Between

The second misjudgement was his long-held belief that the Pathet Lao was a nationalist and not a Communist organization. He let the Pathet Lao grow in strength and this, in turn, brought the US into Lao affairs.

By the time the US began to intervene in the late 1950s, the country already seemed to be heading for catastrophe. But in his struggle to maintain some semblance of independence for his tiny country, he ignored the degree to which Laos was being sucked into the quagmire of Indochina. As Martin Stuart-Fox writes: "He [Souvanna] knew he was being used, and that he had no power to protect his country from the war that increasingly engulfed it. But he was too proud meekly to submit to US demands – even as Laos was subjected to the heaviest bombing in the history of warfare. At least a form of independence had to be maintained."

When the Pathet Lao entered Vientiane in victory in 1975, Souvanna did not flee into exile. He remained to help in the transfer of power. The Pathet Lao, of course, gave him a title and then largely ignored him as they pursued their Communist manifesto.

From Martin Stuart-Fox's *Buddhist Kingdom, Marxist State: the Making of Modern Laos* (White Lotus, 1996).

1955 and 1958 the US had given four times more aid to Laos than the French had done in the prior eight years and it had become the backbone of the Lao economy. If Laos was not so dependent on this aid, it is quite plausible that the coalition government may have survived. The National Union fell apart in July 1958 and Souvanna Phouma was forced out of power. Pathet Lao leaders were jailed and the rightwing Phoui Sananikone came to power. With anti-Communists in control, Pathet Lao forces withdrew to the Plain of Jars in Xieng Khouang province. A three-way civil war ensued, between the rightists (backed by the US), the Communists (backed by North Vietnam) and the neutralists (led by Souvanna Phouma, who wanted to maintain independence).

Civil war

CIA-backed strongman General Phoumi Nosavan thought Phoui's politics rather tame and with a nod from Washington he stepped into the breach in January 1959, eventually overthrowing Phoui in a coup in December and placing Prince Boun Oum in power. Pathet Lao leaders were imprisoned without trial.

Within a year, the rightist regime was overthrown by a neutralist *coup d'état* led by General Kong Lae and Prince Souvanna Phouma was recalled from exile in Cambodia to become prime minister of the first National Union. Souvanna Phouma incurred American wrath by inviting a Soviet ambassador to Vientiane in October. With US support, Nosavan staged yet another armed rebellion in December and sparked a new civil war. In the 1960 general elections, provincial authorities were threatened with military action if they did not support the rightwing groups and were rigged to ensure no Pathet Lao cadres could obtain a seat in office. By this stage, the Pathet Lao had consolidated considerable forces in the region surrounding the Plain of Jars and, with support from the Vietnamese, had been able to expand their territorial control in the north. This represented a major crisis to the incoming Kennedy administration that Stuart Martin-Fox describes as "second only to Cuba".

Zurich talks and the Geneva Accord

The new prime minister, the old one and his Marxist half-brother finally sat down to talks in Zurich in June 1961, but any hope of an agreement was overshadowed by escalating tensions between the superpowers. In 1962, an international agreement on Laos was hammered out in Geneva by 14 participating nations and accords were signed, once again guaranteeing Lao neutrality. By implication, the accords denied the Viet Minh access to the **Ho Chi Minh Trail**. But aware of the reality of constant North Vietnamese infiltration through Laos into South Vietnam, the head of the American mission concluded that the agreement was "a good bad deal".

Another coalition government of National Union was formed under the determined neutralist Prince Souvanna Phouma (as prime minister), with Prince Souphanouvong for the Pathet Lao and Prince Boun Oum representing the right. A number of political assassinations derailed the process of reconciliation. Moreover, antagonisms between the left and the right, both backed financially by their respective allies, made it impossible for the unfunded neutralists to balance the two sides into any form of neutrality. It was no surprise when the coalition government collapsed within a few months and fighting resumed. This time the international community just shrugged and watched Laos sink back into civil war. Unbeknown to the outside world, the conflict was rapidly degenerating into a war between the CIA and North Vietnamese jungle guerrillas.

Secret war

The war that wasn't

In the aftermath of the Geneva agreement, the North Vietnamese, rather than reducing their forces in Laos, continued to increase their manpower on the ground. With the Viet Minh denying the existence of the Ho Chi Minh Trail, while at the same time enlarging it, Kennedy dispatched an undercover force of CIA men, green berets and US-trained Thai mercenaries to command 9000 Lao soldiers. By 1963, these American forces had grown to 30,000 men. Historian Roger Warner believes that by 1965 "word spread among a select circle of congressmen and senators about this exotic program run by Lone Star rednecks and Asian hillbillies that was better and cheaper than anything the Pentagon was doing in South Vietnam." To the north, the US also supplied Vang Pao's force of Hmong guerrillas, dubbed 'Mobile Strike Forces'. With the cooperation of Prince Souvanna Phouma, the CIA's commercial airline, Air America, ferried men and equipment into Laos from Thailand (and opium out, it is believed). Caught between Cold War antagonisms it was impossible to maintain a modicum of neutrality as even the most staunch neutralist, Souvanna Phouma, began to become entangled. As Robbins argues, by the early 1960s, Sovanna Phouma – trying to reinforce the middle way – had given permission "for every clandestine manoeuvre the United States made to match the North Vietnamese. In turn Souvanna demanded that his complicity in such arrangements be kept secret, lest his position in the country become untenable." Owing to the clandestine nature of the military intervention in Laos, the rest of the world – believing that the Geneva settlement had solved the foreign interventionist problem – was oblivious as to what was happening on the ground. Right up until 1970, Washington never admitted to any activity in Laos beyond 'armed reconnaissance' flights over northern provinces.

Meanwhile the North Vietnamese were fulfilling their two major strategic priorities in the country: continued use of the Ho Chi Minh trail (by this stage the majority of North Vietnamese munitions and personnel for the Viet Cong was being shuffled along the trail) and ensuring that the Plain of Jars did not fall under the control of the right, where the US could launch attacks on North Vietnam. This latter goal amounted to supporting the Pathet Lao in their aim to hold on to as much territory as possible in the north. The Pathet Lao, in turn, were dependent on the North Vietnamese for supplies – both material and manpower. With both the US bankrolling the Royalist right and the Vietnamese puppeteering the Pathet Lao, within the country any pretence of maintaining a balance in the face of Cold War hostilities was shattered for neutralists like Souvanna Phouma.

Souvanna Phouma appropriately referred to it as 'the forgotten war' and it is often termed now the 'non-attributable war'. The willingness on the part of the Americans to dump millions of tonnes of ordnance on a country which was ostensibly neutral may have been made easier by the fact that some people in the administration did not believe Laos to be a country at all. Bernard Fall wrote that Laos at the time was "neither a geographical nor an ethnic or social entity, but merely a political convenience", while a Rand Corporation report written in 1970 described Laos as "hardly a country except in the legal sense". More colourfully, Secretary of State Dean Rusk described it as a "wart on the hog of Vietnam". Perhaps those in Washington could feel a touch better about bombing the hell out of a country which, in their view, occupied a sort of political never never land – or which they could liken to an unfortunate skin complaint.

Not everyone agrees with this view that Laos never existed until the French wished it into existence. Scholar of Laos Arthur Dommen, for example, traces a true and coherent Lao identity back to Fa Ngum and his creation of the kingdom of Lane Xang in 1353, writing that it was "a state in the true sense of the term, delineated by borders clearly defined and consecrated by treaty" for 350 years. He goes on:

"Lao historians see a positive proof of the existence of a distinct Lao race (*sua sat Lao*), a Lao nation (*sat Lao*), a Lao country (*muong Lao*) and a Lao state (*pathet Lao*). In view of these facts, we may safely reject the notion, fashionable among apologists for a colonial enterprise of a later day, that Laos was a creation of French colonial policy and administration".

American bombing of the North Vietnamese Army's supply lines through Laos to South Vietnam along the Ho Chi Minh Trail in East Laos started in 1964 and fuelled the conflict between the Royalist Vientiane government and the Pathet Lao. The neutralists had been forced into alliance with the Royalists to avoid defeat in Xieng Kouang province. US bombers crossed Laos on bombing runs to Hanoi from air bases in Thailand and gradually the war in Laos escalated.

America's side of the secret war was conducted from a one-room shack at the US base in Udon Thani, 'across the fence' in Thailand. This was the CIA's Air America operations room and in the same compound was stationed the 4802 Joint Liaison Detachment – or the CIA logistics office. In Vientiane, US pilots supporting Hmong General Vang Pao's rag-tag army, were given a new identity as rangers for the US Agency for International Development; they reported directly to the air attaché at the US embassy. In his book *The Ravens* (1987), Christopher Robbins writes that they "were military men, but flew into battle in civilian clothes – denim cut-offs, T-shirts, cowboy hats and dark glasses. Their job was to fly as the winged artillery of some fearsome warlord, who led an army of stone age mercenaries in the pay of the CIA and they operated out of a secret city hidden in the mountains of a jungle kingdom."

The most notorious of the CIA's unsavoury operatives was Anthony Posepny – known as Tony Poe, on whom the character of Kurtz, the crazy colonel played by Marlon Brando in the film *Apocalypse Now*, was based. Originally, Poe had worked as Vang Pao's case officer; he then moved to North Laos and operated for years, on his own, in Burmese and Chinese border territories, offering his tribal recruits one US dollar for each set of Communist ears they brought back. Many of the spies and pilots of this secret war have re-emerged in recent years in covert and illegal arms-smuggling rackets to Libya, Iran and the Nicaraguan Contras.

By contrast, the Royalist forces were reluctant warriors: despite the fact that civil war was a deeply ingrained tradition in Laos, the Lao themselves would go to great lengths to avoid fighting each other. One foreign journalist, reporting from Luang Prabang in the latter stages of the war, related how Royalist and Pathet Lao troops, encamped on opposite banks of the Nam Ou, agreed an informal ceasefire over Pi Mai (Lao New Year), to jointly celebrate the king's annual visit to the sacred Pak Ou Caves (see page 391). Most Lao did not want to fight. Correspondents who covered the war noted that without the constant goading of their respective US and North Vietnamese masters, many Lao soldiers would have happily gone home. Prior to the war, one military strategist described the Lao forces as one of the worst armies ever seen, adding that they made the (poorly regarded) "South Vietnamese Army look like Storm Troopers". "The troops lack the basic will to fight. They do not take initiative. A typical characteristic of the Laotian Army is to leave an escape route. US technicians attached to the various training institutions have not been able to overcome Lao apathy". (Ratnam, P, *Laos and the Superpowers*, 1980).

Air Force planes were often used to carry passengers for money – or to smuggle opium out of the **Golden Triangle**. In the field, soldiers of the Royal Lao Army regularly fled when faced with a frontal assault by the Vietnam People's Army (NVA). The officer corps was uncommitted, lazy and corrupt; many ran opium-smuggling rackets and saw the war as a ticket to get rich quick. In the south, the Americans considered Royal Lao Air Force pilots unreliable because they were loath to bomb their own people and cultural heritage.

The air war

The clandestine bombing of the Ho Chi Minh Trail caused many civilian casualties and displaced much of the population in Laos' eastern provinces. By 1973, when the bombing stopped, the US had dropped over two million tonnes of bombs on Laos – equivalent to 700 kg of explosives for every man, woman and child in the country. It is reported that up to 70% of all B-52 strikes in Indochina were targeted at Laos. To pulverize the country to this degree 580,994 bombing sorties were flown. The bombing intensified during the Nixon administration: up to 1969 less than 500,000 tonnes of bombs had been dropped on Laos; from then on nearly that amount was dropped each year. In the 1960s and early 1970s, more bombs rained on Laos than were dropped during the Second World War – the equivalent of a plane load of bombs every eight minutes around the clock for nine years. This campaign cost American taxpayers more than US$2 million a day but the cost to Laos was incalculable. The activist Fred Branfman, quoted by Roger Warner in *Shooting at the Moon*, wrote: "Nine years of bombing, two million tons of bombs, whole rural societies wiped off the map, hundreds of thousands of peasants treated like herds of animals in a Clockwork Orange fantasy of an aerial African Hunting safari."

The war was not restricted to bombing missions – once potential Pathet Lao strong-holds had been identified, fighters, using rockets, were sent to attempt to destroy them. Such was the intensity of the bombing campaign that villagers in Pathet Lao-controlled areas are said to have turned to planting and harvesting their rice at night. Few of those living in Xieng Khouang province, the Bolaven Plateau or along the Ho Chi Minh Trail had any idea of who was bombing them or why. The consequences were often tragic, as in the case of Tham Piu Cave (see page 420).

After the war, the collection and sale of war debris turned into a valuable scrap metal industry for tribes' people in Xieng Khouang province and along the Ho Chi Minh Trail. Bomb casings, aircraft fuel tanks and other bits and pieces that were not sold to Thailand have been put to every possible use in rural Laos. They are used as cattle troughs, fence posts, flower pots, stilts for houses, water carriers, temple bells, knives and ploughs.

But the bombing campaign has also left a more deadly legacy of unexploded bombs and anti-personnel mines. Today, over 30 years after the air war, over 500,000 tonnes of deadly **unexploded ordnance** (UXO) is believed to still be scattered throughout nine of Laos' 13 provinces. Most casualties are caused by cluster bombs, or 'bombis' as they have become known. Cluster bombs are carried in large canisters called Cluster Bomb Units (CBUs), which open in mid-air, releasing around 670 tennis ball-sized bomblets. Upon detonation, the bombie propels around 200,000 pieces of shrapnel over an area the size of several football fields. This UXO contamination inhibits long-term development, especially in Xieng Khouang Province, turning Laos' fertile fields, which are critical for agricultural production, into killing zones.

The land war

Within Laos, the war largely focused on the strategic Plain of Jars in Xieng Khouang province and was co-ordinated from the town of Long Tien (the secret city), tucked into the limestone hills to the southwest of the plain. Known as the most secret spot on earth, it was not marked on maps and was populated by the CIA, the Ravens (the air controllers who flew spotter planes and called in air strikes) and the Hmong.

The Pathet Lao were headquartered in caves in Xam Neua province, to the north of the plain. Their base was equipped with a hotel cave (for visiting dignitaries), a hospital cave, embassy caves and even a theatre cave.

The Plain of Jars (colloquially known as the PDJ, after the French Plaine de Jarres), was the scene of some of the heaviest fighting and changed hands countless times, the Royalist and Hmong forces occupying it during the wet season, the Pathet Lao in the dry. During this period in the conflict the town of Long Tien, known as one of the country's 'alternate' bases to keep nosy journalists away (the word 'alternate' was meant to indicate that it was unimportant), grew to such an extent that it became Laos' second city. James Parker in his book *Codename Mule* claims that the air base was so busy that at its peak it was handling more daily flights than Chicago's O'Hare airport. Others claim that it was the busiest airport in the world. There was also fighting around Luang Prabang and the Bolaven Plateau to the south.

The end of the war

Although the origins of the war in Laos were distinct from those that fuelled the conflict in Vietnam, the two wars had effectively merged by the early 1970s and it became inevitable that the fate of the Americans to the east would determine the outcome of the secret war on the other side of the Annamite Range. By 1970 it was no longer possible for the US administration to shroud the war in secrecy: a flood of refugees had arrived in Vientiane in an effort to escape the conflict.

During the dying days of the US-backed regime in Vientiane, CIA agents and Ravens lived in quarters south of the capital, known as KM-6 – because it was 6 km from town.

Another compound in downtown Vientiane was known as 'Silver City' and reputedly also sometimes housed CIA agents. On the departure of the Americans and the arrival of the new regime in 1975, the Communists' secret police made Silver City their new home. Today, Lao people still call military intelligence officers 'Silvers' – and from time to time during the early 1990s, as Laos was opening up to tourism, Silvers were assigned as tour guides.

A ceasefire was agreed in February 1973, a month after Washington and Hanoi struck a similar deal in Paris. Power was transferred in April 1974 to yet another coalition government set up in Vientiane under the premiership of the ever-ready Souvanna Phouma. The neutralist prince once again had a Communist deputy and foreign affairs minister. The Red Prince, Souphanouvong, headed the Joint National Political Council. Foreign troops were given two months to leave the country. The North Vietnamese were allowed to remain along the Ho Chi Minh Trail, for although US forces had withdrawn from South Vietnam, the war there was not over.

The Communists' final victories over Saigon (and Phnom Penh) in April 1975 were a catalyst for the Pathet Lao who advanced on the capital. Grant Evans in a *Short History of Laos* says that the most intriguing element of the Communist takeover of Laos was the slow pace in which it was executed. It is widely hailed as the 'bloodless' takeover. Due to the country's mixed loyalties the Pathet Lao government undertook a gradual process of eroding away existing loyalties to the Royalist government. As the end drew near and the Pathet Lao began to advance out of the mountains and towards the more populated areas of the Mekong valley – the heartland of the Royalist government – province after province fell with scarcely a shot being fired. The mere arrival of a small contingent of Pathet Lao soldiers was sufficient to secure victory – even though these soldiers arrived at Wattay Airport on Chinese transport planes to be greeted by representatives of the Royal Lao government. It is possible that they were not even armed.

Administration of Vientiane by the People's Revolutionary Committee was secured on 18 August. The atmosphere was very different from that which accompanied the Communist's occupation of Saigon in Vietnam the same year. In Vientiane peaceful crowds of several hundred thousand turned out to hear speeches by Pathet Lao cadres. The King remained unharmed in his palace and while a coffin representing 'dead American imperialism' was ceremonially burned this was done in a 'carnival' atmosphere. Vientiane was declared 'officially liberated' on 23 August 1975. The coalition government was dismissed and Souvanna Phouma resigned for the last time. All communications with the outside world were cut.

While August 1975 represents a watershed in the history of Laos, scholars are left with something of a problem: explaining why the Pathet Lao prevailed. According to Martin Stuart-Fox, the Lao revolutionary movement "had not mobilized an exploited peasantry with promises of land reform, for most of the country was underpopulated and peasant families generally owned sufficient land for their subsistence needs. The appeal of the Pathet Lao to their lowland Lao compatriots was in terms of nationalism and independence and the preservation of Lao culture from the corrosive American influence; but no urban uprising occurred until the very last minute when effective government had virtually ceased to exist … The small Lao intelligentsia, though critical of the Royal Lao government, did not desert it entirely and their recruitment to the Pathet Lao was minimal. Neither the monarchy, still less Buddhism, lost legitimacy." He concludes that it was external factors, and in particular the intervention of outside powers, which led to the victory of the Pathet Lao. Without the Vietnamese and Americans, the Pathet Lao would not have won. For the great mass of Laos' population before 1975, Communism meant nothing. This was not a mass uprising but a victory secured by a small ideologically committed elite and forged in the furnace of the war in Indochina.

As the Pathet Lao seized power, rightist ministers, ranking civil servants, doctors, much of the intelligentsia and around 30,000 Hmong escaped into Thailand, fearing they would face persecution from the Pathet Lao. Although the initial exodus was large, the majority of refugees fled in the next few years up until 1980 as the Lao government introduced new reforms aimed at wiping out decadence and reforming the economic system.

The refugee camps
By the late 1980s, a total of 340,000 people – 10% of the population and mostly middle class – had fled the country. At least half of the refugees were Hmong, the US's key allies during the war, who feared reprisals and persecution. From 1988, refugees who had made it across the border began to head back across the Mekong from camps in Thailand and to asylum in the US and France. More than 2000 refugees were also repatriated from Yunnan Province in China. For those prepared to return from exile overseas, the government offered to give them back confiscated property so long as they stayed for at least six months and become Lao citizens once again.

Nonetheless, many lived for years in squalid refugee camps, although the better connected and those with skills to sell secured US, Australian and French passports. For Laos, a large proportion of its human capital drained westwards, creating a vacuum of skilled personnel that would hamper – and still does – efforts at reconstruction and development. But while many people fled across the Mekong, a significant number who had aligned themselves with the Royalists decided to stay and help build a new Laos.

Laos under communism

The People's Democratic Republic of Laos was proclaimed in December 1975 with Prince Souphanouvong as president and Kaysone Phomvihane as secretary-general of the Lao People's Revolutionary Party (a post he had held since its formation in 1955). The king's abdication was accepted and the ancient Lao monarchy was abolished, together with King Samsenthai's 600-year-old system of village autonomy. But instead of executing their vanquished foes, the LPRP installed Souvanna and the ex-king, Savang Vatthana, as 'special advisers' to the politburo. On Souvanna's death in 1984, he was accorded a full state funeral. The king did not fare so well: he later died ignominiously while in detention after his alleged involvement in a counter-revolutionary plot (see below).

Surprisingly, the first actions of the new revolutionary government was not to build a new revolutionary economy and society, but to stamp out unsavoury behaviour. Dress and hairstyles, dancing and singing, even the food that was served at family celebrations, was all subject to rigorous official scrutiny by so-called 'Investigation Cadres'. If the person(s) concerned were found not to match up to the Party's scrupulous standards of good taste they were bundled off to re-education camps.

Relations with Thailand, which in the immediate wake of the revolution remained cordial, deteriorated in late 1976. A military coup in Bangkok led to rumours that the Thai military, backed by the CIA, was supporting Hmong and other right-wing Lao rebels. The regime feared that Thailand would be used as a spring-board for a royalist coup attempt by exiled reactionaries. This prompted the arrest of King Savang Vatthana, together with his family and Crown Prince Vongsavang, who were all dispatched to a Seminar re-education camp in Sam Neua province. They were never heard of again. In December 1989 Kaysone Phomvihane admitted in Paris, for the first time, that the king had died of malaria in 1984 and that the queen had also died "of natural causes" – no mention was made of Vongsavang. The Lao people have still to be officially informed of his demise.

Re-education camps

Between 30,000 and 40,000 reactionaries who had been unable to flee the country were interned in remote, disease-ridden camps for 're-education'. These camps, referred to as *Samanaya*, took their name from the Western word, seminar. The reluctant scholars were forced into slave labour in squalid jungle conditions and subjected to incessant political propaganda for anything from a few months up to 15 years. Historian Grant Evans suggests that many internees were duped into believing that the government wanted complete reconciliation and so went away for re-education willingly. Evans says the purpose of the camps was to "break the will of members of the old regime and instil in them fear of the new regime." Old men, released back into society after more than 15 years of re-education were cowed and subdued, although some were prepared to talk in paranoid whispers about their grim experiences in Xam Neua.

By 1978, the re-education policy was starting to wind down, although, in 1986, Amnesty International released a report on the forgotten inhabitants of the re-education camps, claiming that 6000-7000 were still being held. By that time incarceration behind barbed wire had ended and the internees were 'arbitrarily restricted' rather than imprisoned. They were assigned to road construction teams and other public works projects. Nonetheless, conditions for these victims of the war in Indochina suffered from malnutrition, disease and many died prematurely in captivity. It is unclear how many died, but at least 15,000 have been freed. Officials of the old regime, ex-government ministers and former Royalist air force and army officers, together with thousands of others unlucky enough to have been on the wrong side, were released from the camps, largely during the mid to late 1980s. Most of the surviving political prisoners have now been re-integrated into society. Some work in the tourism industry and one, a former colonel in the Royal Lao Army, jointly owns the Asian Pavilion Hotel (formerly the Vieng Vilai) on Samsenthai Road in downtown Vientiane. After years of being force-fed Communist propaganda he now enjoys full government support as an ardent capitalist entrepreneur.

The Lao are a gentle people and it is hard not to leave the country without that view being reinforced. Even the Lao People's Revolutionary Party seems quaintly inept and it is hard to equate it with its more brutal sister parties in Vietnam, Cambodia, China or the former Soviet Union. Yet five students who meekly called for greater political freedom in 1999 were whisked off by police and have not been heard of since.

Reflecting on 10 years of 'reconstruction'

It is worth ending this short account of the country's history by noting the brevity of Laos' experiment with full-blown Communism. Just 10 years after the Pathet Lao took control of Vientiane, the leadership were on the brink of far-reaching economic reforms. By the mid-1980s it was widely acknowledged that Marxism-Leninism had failed the country and its people. The population were still dreadfully poor; the ideology of Communism had failed to entice more than a handful into serious and enthusiastic support for the party and its ways; and graft and nepotism were on the rise.

Nam Theun II and the lure of hydro-gold

One of Laos' greatest economic resources is hydropower, leading to it being dubbed the 'battery' or 'Kuwait' of Southeast Asia with only 1% of the country's hydropower potential of some 18,000 MW so far exploited and myriad schemes being discussed. By far the largest of these is Nam Theun II, which became operational in 2010. The huge dam is expected to generate up to US$150 million revenue a year for Laos or approximately US$2 billion over a 25-year period.

Funded by the World Bank, Nam Theun II was delayed by the discoveries of rare bats and birds. The World Bank, all too conscious that its environmental credentials have been tarnished by dam developments in India and elsewhere, went out of its way to ensure that all the required studies were undertaken.

But Nam Theun II dam is not quite the open-and-shut case it might appear, with the international environmental lobby on the side of local people and animals and the dastardly World Bank supporting businessmen and the interests of international capital. When local people were asked their views of the dam, many apparently welcomed it. Even some environmentalists argued that having the dam might be preferable to having the forests logged (for without the money to be gained from selling electricity to Thailand, one of the few alternatives is selling wood).

With the dam in its early operational stage, the results are yet to be fully determined. The majority of villagers seem happy with relocation efforts, while conservationists argue that the environmental damage is yet to be properly evaluated. Plans are underway to further exploit the potential of the Mekong and its tributaries, with over 60 projects slated for development over the next decade.

Modern Laos

Politics

President Kaysone Phomvihane died in November 1992, aged 71. (His right-hand man, Prince Souphanouvong died just over two years later, on 9 January 1995.) As one obituary put it, Kaysone was older than he seemed, both historically and ideologically. He had been chairman of the LPRP since the mid-1950s and had been a protégé and comrade of Ho Chi Minh, who led the Vietnamese struggle for independence from the French. After leading the Lao Resistance Government – or Pathet Lao – from caves in Xam Neua province in the north, Kaysone assumed the premiership on the abolition of the monarchy in 1975. But under his leadership – and following the example of his mentors in Hanoi – Kaysone became the driving force behind the market-orientated reforms. The year before he died, he gave up the post of prime minister for that of president.

His death didn't change much, as other members of the old guard stepped into the breach. Nouhak Phounsavanh – a 78-year-old former truck driver and hardline Communist – succeeded him as president. Nouhak didn't last long in the position and in February 1998 he was replaced by 75-year-old General Khamtai Siphandon – the outgoing prime minister and head of the LPRP. Khamtai represents the last of the revolutionary Pathet Lao leaders who fought the Royalists and the Americans. In April 2006, Siphandon, the last of the old guard from the caves in Vieng Xai, was replaced as president by Choummaly Sayasone.

Recent years

With the introduction of the New Economic Mechanism in 1986 there were hopes, in some quarters at least, that economic liberalization would be matched by political *glasnost*. So far, however, the monolithic Party shows few signs of equating capitalism with democracy. While the Lao brand of Communism has always been seen as relatively tame, it remains a far cry from political pluralism.

In 2010, the politburo still largely controlled the country and, for now, sweeping changes are unlikely. Most of the country's leaders are well into their 60s and were educated in Communist countries like Russia and Vietnam. However, the younger Lao (particularly those who have studied in Japan, Australia, the UK or the US) are starting to embrace new political and economic ideas. The government takes inspiration from Vietnam's success and is more likely to follow its neighbour's lead than adopt any Western model of government.

As Laos moved towards the end of the first decade of the 21st century progress was being maintained. The troublesome Hmong, whose US-based leadership's attempts to undermine the Laos government's authority came to nothing. The nation's first railway line opened in early 2009 and huge Chinese investment poured into the country. With the ASEAN Free Trade Agreement set to open up trade throughout the region in 2010 (Laos will be subject to this in 2015), the inauguration of the Nam Theun II dam (see box, page 477) and Laos still working on joining the World Trade Organisation, the challenges facing Laos are some of the greatest in its history.

In 2010 the country opened its own stock market in Vientiane in conjunction with Korea Exchange to invigorate the economy in the downturn and prime minster Bouasone Bouphavanh told the World Economic Forum on East Asia in June 2010 that Laos is aiming for 'no less than' eight percent annual economic growth until 2015. It also wants to elevate its status out of that of underdevelopment by 2020, Bouphavanh told the conference.

People

Laos has a population of 6.8 million people, with an estimated annual growth rate of 2.3%, one of the highest in Southeast Asia. Savannakhet has the largest population among provinces, with around 721,500 people. Vientiane is second with around 695,473 people, while Champasak province is in third place, with 603,880 people.

Ethnic groups

Laos is less a nation state than a collection of different tribes and languages. Its enormous ethnic diversity has long been an impediment to national integration. In total there are more than 60 ethnic groups, which are often described as living in isolated, self-sufficient communities. Although communication and intercourse may have been difficult – and remains so – there has always been communication, trade and inter-marriage between the different Lao 'worlds' and today, with even greater interaction, the walls between them are becoming more permeable still.

Laos' ethnically diverse population is usually – and rather simplistically – divided by ecological zone into three groups: the wet rice cultivating, Buddhist Lao Loum of the lowlands, who are politically and numerically dominant, constituting just under half of the total population; the Lao Theung who occupy the mountain slopes and make up about a third of the population; and the Lao Soung, or upland Lao, who live in the high mountains and practise shifting cultivation and who represent less than a fifth of Laos' total population.

Lao, Laos and Laotians

Most Lao are not Laotians. And not all Laotians are Lao. Lao tends to be used to describe people of Lao stock. There are, in fact, several times more Lao in neighbouring northeastern Thailand (Issan) – roughly 20 million – than there are in Laos, with a total population of some five million of whom perhaps a little over a half are ethnic Lao. At the same time not all Laotians – people who are nationals of Laos – are ethnic Lao. There are also significant minority populations including Chinese, Vietnamese, the Mon-Khmer Lao Theung and the many tribal groups that comprise the Lao Soung. After a few too many lau-lao it is easy to get confused.

Overall, in Laos the ethnic majority, Lao Loum, are in the minority. The terms were brought into general usage by the Pathet Lao who wished to emphasize that all of Laos' inhabitants were 'Lao' and to avoid the more derogatory terms that had been used in the past – such as the Thai word *kha*, (slave), to describe the Mon-Khmer Lao Theung like the Khmu and Lamet. Stereotypical representations of each category are depicted on the 1000 kip note.

Although the words have a geographical connotation, they should be viewed more as contrasting pairs of terms: *loum* and *theung* mean 'below' and 'above' (rather than hillsides and lowland), while *soung* is paired with *tam*, meaning 'high' and 'low'. These two pairs of oppositions were then brought together by the Pathet Lao into one three-fold division. Thus, the Lao Theung in one area may, in practice, occupy a higher location than Lao Soung in another area. In addition, economic change, greater interaction between the groups and the settlement of lowland peoples in hill areas means that it is possible to find Lao Loum villages in upland areas, where the inhabitants practise swidden, not wet rice, agriculture. So, although it is broadly possible to characterize the mountain slopes as inhabited by shifting cultivating Lao Theung of Mon-Khmer descent, in practice the neat delimitation of people into discrete spatial units breaks down and as the years go by is becoming increasingly untenable.

Lao Loum

It has been noted that the Lao who have reaped the rewards of reform are the Lao Loum of T'ai stock – not the Lao Theung who are of Mon-Khmer descent or the ethnic Lao Soung, such as the Hmong but also Akha and Lahu. Ing-Britt Trankell, in her book *On the Road in Laos: an Anthropological Study of Road Construction and Rural Communities* (1993), writes that the Lao Loum's "sense of [cultural and moral] superiority is often manifested in both a patronizing and contemptuous attitude toward the Lao Theung and Lao Sung, who are thought of as backward and less susceptible to socio-economic development because they are still governed by their archaic cultural traditions". This attitude is still prevalent today, where Lao Loum sneer at the cultural practices of other ethnic groups, such as the Akha, as being unmodern. As a result many of these groups are ashamed to wear their traditional clothes around as it has a stigma attached to it.

During the sixth and seventh centuries the Lao Loum arrived from the southern provinces of China. They occupied the valleys along the Mekong and its tributaries and drove the Lao Theung to more mountainous areas. The Lao Loum, who are ethnically almost indistinguishable from the Thais of the Isan region (the Northeast of Thailand), came under the influence of the Khmer and Indonesian cultures and sometime before the emergence of Lane Xang in the 14th century embraced Theravada Buddhism.

Population by ethnic group

Group	Official category	% of total population
Tai	Lao Loum	55
Mon-Khmer	Lao Theung	35
Tibeto-Burman	Lao Soung	10

The majority of Lao are Buddhist but retain many of their animist beliefs. Remote Lao Loum communities still usually have a *mor du* (a doctor who 'sees') or medium. The medium's job description is demanding: he must concoct love potions, heal the sick, devise and design protective charms and read the future.

Today, the Lao Loum are the principal ethnic group, accounting for nearly half the population, and Lao is their mother tongue. As the lowland Lao, they occupy the ricelands of the Mekong and its main tributary valleys. Their houses are traditionally made of wood and are built on stilts with thatched roofs – although tin roofs and Thai concrete houses are much more popular these days. The extended family is usually spread throughout several houses in one compound.

There are also several tribal sub-groups of this main Thai-Lao group; they are conveniently colour-coded and readily identifiable by their sartorial traits. There are, for example, the Red Tai, the White Tai and the Black Tai – who live in the upland valley areas in Xieng Khouang and Hua Phan provinces. That they live in the hills suggests they are Lao Theung, but ethnically and culturally they are closer to the Lao Loum.

Lao Theung

The Lao Theung, consisting of 45 different sub-groups, are the descendants of the oldest inhabitants of the country and are of Mon-Khmer descent. They are sometimes called *Kha* (slave), as they were used as labourers by the Thai and Lao kings and are still poorer than the Lao Loum. Traditionally, the Lao Theung were semi-nomadic and they still live mainly on the mountain slopes of the interior, along the whole length of the Annamite Chain from South China. There are concentrations of Akha, Alak and Ta-Oy on the Bolaven Plateau in the south (see page 480) and Khmu in the north.

The Lao Theung's reliance on slash-and-burn, or shifting, agriculture is slowly being phased out. Traditionally, they would burn a small area of forest, cultivate it for a few years and then, when the soil was exhausted, abandon the land until the vegetation had regenerated to replenish the soil. Some groups merely shifted fields in a 10-15 year rotation; others not only shifted fields but also their villages, relocating in a fresh area of forest when the land had become depleted of nutrients. To obtain salt, metal implements and other goods which could not be made or found in the hills, the tribal peoples would trade forest products such as resins and animal skins with the settled lowland Lao. Some groups, mainly those living closer to towns, have converted to Buddhism but many are still animist.

The social and religious beliefs of the Lao Theung and their general outlook on health and happiness are governed by their belief in spirits. The shaman is a key personality in any village. The Alak, from the Bolaven Plateau (see page 480) test the prospects of a marriage by killing a chicken: the manner in which it bleeds will determine whether the marriage will be propitious. Buffalo sacrifices are also common in Lao Theung villages and it is not unusual for a community to slaughter all its livestock to appease the spirits.

Viet Minh guerrillas and American B-52s made life difficult for many of the Lao Theung tribes living in East Laos, who were forced to move away from the Ho Chi Minh Trail. By leaving their birth places the Lao Theung left their protecting spirits, forcing them to find new and unfamiliar ones.

Lao Soung

The Lao Soung began migrating to Laos from South China, Tibet and Burma, in the early 18th century, settling high in the mountains (some up to 2500 m). The Hmong(formerly known as the Meo) and Yao (also called the Mien) are the principal Lao Soung groups.

Yao (or Mien)

The Yao mainly live around Nam Tha – deep inside the Golden Triangle, near the borders with Thailand, Myanmar (Burma) and China. They are best known as craftspeople – the men make knives, crossbows, rifles and high-quality, elaborately designed silver jewellery, which is worn by the women. Silver is a symbol of wealth among the Yao and Hmong.

The Mien or Yao are unique among the hilltribes in that they have a tradition of writing based on Chinese characters. Mien legend has it that they came from 'across the sea' during the 14th century, although it is generally thought that their roots are in South China where they originated about 2000 years ago.

The Mien village is not enclosed and is usually found on sloping ground. The houses are large, wooden and need to accommodate an extended family of sometimes 20 or more. They are built on the ground, not on stilts and have one large living area and four or more bedrooms. As with other tribes, the construction of the house must be undertaken carefully. The house needs to be orientated appropriately, so that the spirits are not disturbed and the ancestral altar installed on an auspicious day.

The Mien combine two religious beliefs: on the one hand they recognize and pay their dues to spirits and ancestors (informing them of family developments); and on the other, they follow Taoism as it was practised in China in the 13th and 14th centuries. The Taoist rituals are expensive and the Mien appear to spend a great deal of their lives struggling to save enough money to afford the various life cycle ceremonies, such as weddings and death ceremonies. The Mien economy is based upon the shifting cultivation of dry rice, maize and small quantities of opium poppy.

Material culture The Mien women dress distinctively, with black turbans and red-ruffed tunics, making them easy to distinguish from the other hilltribes. All their clothes are made of black or indigo-dyed homespun cotton, which is then embroidered using distinctive cross-stitching. Their trousers are the most elaborate garments. Unusually, they sew from the back of the cloth and cannot see the pattern they are making. The children wear embroidered caps with red pompoms on the top and by the ears. The men's dress is a simple indigo-dyed jacket and trousers, with little embroidery. They have been dubbed "the most elegantly dressed but worst-housed people in the world".

Akha (or Kaw)

The Akha, also called as the Ikho, Kho or Kha, have their origins in Yunnan, southern China, and from there spread into Burma (where there are nearly 200,000) and Laos and rather later into Thailand. There are three different Akha groups in northern Laos: the Akha Pouli, the Akha Pen and the Akha Jijaw. Around Muang Sing (see page 404) they constitute 22% of the population. They traditionally speak a Tibeto-Burmese language, which is believed to be represented in nine different written forms.

The Akha are shifting cultivators, growing primarily dry rice on mountainsides but also a wide variety of vegetables. The cultivation of rice is bound up with myths and rituals: the rice plant is regarded as a sentient being and the selection of the swidden, its clearance, the planting of the rice seed, the care of the growing plants and finally the harvest of the rice, must all be done according to the Akha Way. Any offence to the rice soul must be rectified by ceremonies. The Akha have no word for religion but believe in the 'Akha Way'. They are able to recite the names of all their male ancestors (60 names or more) and they keep an ancestral altar in their homes, at which food is offered up at important festivals and after the rice harvest. The two most important Akha festivals are the four-day Swinging Ceremony, celebrated during August, and New Year, when festivities also extend over four days. When someone dies they are wrapped in cloth, poor people in a white cloth, and rich people in a black cloth. They are kept in a wooden coffin, with a lid similar to a xylophone, for up to a month. A usual ritual *baci* will follow.

Akha villages are identified by their gates, a village swing and high-roofed houses on posts. At the upper and lower ends of the village are gates which are renewed every year. Visitors should walk through them in order to rid themselves of the spirit of the jungle. The gates are sacred and must not be defiled. Visitors must not touch the gates and should avoid going through them if they do not intend to enter a house in the village. A pair of wooden male and female carved figures are placed inside the entrance to signify that this is the realm of human beings. The female and male parts of the house are divided and two doorways enter the house, one which is entered through and the other which serves as the exit.

The Akha are relatively sexually liberal. Each village usually has a small courting house, where young men and women can rendezvous privately. Women will generally have a number of partners before settling into marriage and pregnancy prior to marriage is not deemed as being shameful but rather as a sign of fecundity. Sexual abstinence is often used as punishment for those who commit offences. Marriage is monogamous; however, the rich and powerful are entitled to additional wives if their first wives can't conceive. Women adopt the husband's lineage upon marriage and usually move into or close to her partner's family home. Divorce exists but is not common, due to the financial pressures of raising children. A midwife generally delivers babies and men are not allowed in the house when the woman is in labour. Historically, twins born in villages were regarded as a very bad omen and were killed but this practice has now been outlawed and the children are put up for adoption.

Today the Akha are finding it increasingly difficult to follow the 'Akha Way'. Their complex rituals set them apart from both the lowland Lao and from the other hilltribes. The conflicts and pressures which the Akha currently face and their inability to reconcile the old with the new is claimed by some to explain why the incidence of opium addiction among the Akha is so high.

Material culture Akha clothing is made of homespun blue-black cloth (dyed from indigo), which is appliquéd for decoration. The basic clothing of an Akha woman is a head-dress, a jacket, a short skirt worn on the hips, with a sash and leggings worn from the ankle to below the knee, though many are starting to wear more mainstream clothing, as they are self-conscious of their traditional dress. They wear their jewellery as an integral part of their clothing, mostly sewn to their head dresses. This is the most characteristic item of Akha clothing and is adorned with jewellery and coins. The coins are made of pure silver and are used as currency (the small coins are worth about 15,000 kip and the large are worth about 50,000 kip). Girls wear similar clothing to the women, except that they sport caps rather than the elaborate head-dress of the mature women. The change from girl's clothes to women's clothes occurs through four stages during adolescence. Unmarried girls can be identified by the small gourds tied to their waist and head-dress. Men's clothing is much less elaborate. They wear loose-fitting Chinese-style black pants and a black jacket which may be embroidered. Both men and women use cloth shoulder bags.

Hmong

Origins The Hmong are probably the best-known tribe in Laos. In the 19th century, Chinese opium farmers drove many thousands of Hmong off their poppy fields and forced them south into the mountains of Laos. The Hmong did not have a written language before contact with Europeans and Americans and their heritage is mainly preserved through oral tradition. Hmong mythology relates how they flew in from South China on magic carpets. Village storytellers also like to propagate the notion that the Hmong are in fact werewolves, who happily devour the livers of their victims. This warrior tribe now mainly inhabits the mountain areas of Luang Prabang, Xieng Khouang and Xam Neua provinces where they practise shifting cultivation.

Economy and society Until a few years ago, other Lao and the rest of the world knew the Hmong as the Meo. Unbeknown to anyone except the Hmong, 'Meo' was a Chinese insult meaning 'barbarian' – conferred on them several millennia ago by Chinese who developed an intense disliking for the tribe. Returning from university in France in the mid-1970s, the Hmong's first highly qualified academic decided it was time to educate the world. Due to his prompting, the tribe was rechristened Hmong, their word for 'mankind'. This change in nomenclature has not stopped the Hmong from continuing to refer to the Chinese as 'sons of dogs'. Nor has it stopped the Lao Loum from regarding the Hmong as their cultural inferiors. But, again, the feelings are reciprocated: the Hmong have an inherent mistrust of the lowland Lao – exacerbated by years of war – and Lao Loum guides reluctantly enter Hmong villages.

The Hmong value their independence and tend to live at high altitudes, away from other tribes. This independence in addition to their former association with poppy cultivation and their siding with the US during the war has meant that of all the hilltribes, it is the Hmong who have been most severely persecuted. They have, in recent history, been perceived as a threat to the security of the state; a group that needs to be controlled and carefully watched.

Hmong villages tend not to be fenced, while their houses are built of wood or bamboo at ground level. Each house has a main living area and two or three sleeping rooms. The extended family is headed by the oldest male; he settles family disputes and has supreme authority over family affairs. The Hmong too are spirit worshippers and believe in household spirits. Every house has an altar, where protection for the household is sought.

As animists, the Hmong believe everything from mountains and opium poppies to cluster bombs, has a spirit – or *phi* – some bad, some good. Shamans – or witchdoctors – play a central role in village life and decision making. The *phi* need to be placated incessantly to ward off sickness and catastrophe. It is the shaman's job to exorcise the bad *phi* from his patients. Until modern medicine arrived in Laos along with the Americans, opium was the Hmong's only palliative drug. Due to their lack of resistance to pharmaceuticals, the Hmong responded miraculously to the smallest doses of penicillin. Even plasters were revered as they were thought to contain magical powers which drew out bad *phi*.

Material culture The Hmong are the only tribe in Laos who make batik; indigo-dyed batik makes up the main panel of their skirts, with appliqué and embroidery added to it. The women traditionally wore black leggings from their knees to their ankles, black jackets (with embroidery) and a black panel or 'apron', held in place with a cummerbund. Even the youngest children wore clothes of intricate design with exquisite needlework. Traditionally the cloth would have been woven by hand on a foot-treddle/back-strap loom; today it is increasingly purchased from markets and often made of synthetic fabrics. Most Hmong today tend to wear Western-style clothes except for on auspicious occasions, such as Hmong New Year.

The White Hmong tend to wear less elaborate clothing from day to day, saving it for special occasions only. Hmong men wear loose-fitting black trousers, black jackets (sometimes embroidered) and coloured or embroidered sashes.

The Hmong particularly value silver jewellery; it signifies wealth and a good life. Men, women and children wear silver – tiers of neck rings, heavy silver chains with lock-shaped pendants, earrings and pointed rings on every finger. Through their life the Hmong will collect these heavy bands and lock them together with a spirit lock, which holds in their 32 souls. All the family jewellery is brought out at New Year and is an impressive sight, symbolizing the wealth of the family.

Hmong fighters in the 20th century In the dying days of the French colonial administration, thousands of Hmong were recruited to help fight the Vietnamese Communists. Vang Pao – known as VP – who would later command 30,000 Hmong mercenaries in the US-backed war against the Pathet Lao, was first picked out by a French colonel in charge of these *maquisards* (native movements). Later, the Hmong were recruited and paid by the CIA to fight the Pathet Lao. Under General VP, remote mountain villagers with no education were trained to fly T-28 fighter-bombers. It is said that when these US aircraft first started landing in remote villages, locals would carefully examine the undercarriage to see what sex they were.

At its peak, VP's army consisted of 250,000 fighters, the majority of whom were Hmong. Around 30,000 Hmong lost their life in the war, over a tenth of the Hmong population at the time. Even after the Pathet Lao's 'liberation' of Vientiane in 1975, Hmong refugees, encamped in hills to the south of the Plain of Jars, were attacked and flushed out by Vietnamese troops. The Hmong claimed that chemical weapons were being used against them, most notably 'yellow rain' (the biological agent, trichothecane mycotoxins), although biologists at Yale University suggested the substance was, in fact, faeces from swarms of over-flying bees.

When the war ended in 1975 there was a mass exodus of Hmong from Laos. Hmong refugees poured into Thailand, the exodus reaching a peak in 1979 when 3000 a month were fleeing across the Mekong. Many ended up in Thai refugee camps, where they lived in terrible conditions, for many years, sometimes decades. A temporary refugee camp called Ban Vinai was established by the Thai government in June 1975 solely to accommodate the Hmong. These camps are now part of history but one of the best accounts of this period can be read in Lynellyn D Long's *Ban Vinai: the Refugee Camp*. As a Jesuit priest who worked at the camp explained to the author: "Before, they [the refugees] had a life revolving around the seasons ... Here they cannot really work ... Here people make only dreams."

Thousands of Hmong also ended up in the US and France, fresh from the mountains of Laos: unsurprisingly they did not adapt easily. Various stress disorders were thought to have triggered heart attacks in many healthy young Hmong – a condition referred to as Sudden Unexplained Nocturnal Death Syndrome. In *The Ravens*, Robbins comments that "in a simpler age, it would have been said that the Hmong are dying of a broken heart". Today more than 100,000 Hmong live in the US – mostly on the west coast and in Minnesota – where they regularly lobby politicians. They are a very powerful pressure group but they are increasingly out of touch with the situation in Laos. Where the US-based Hmong remain important, however, is in the money they remit to their relatives in Laos.

Hmong insurgency A small group of Hmong, led by Vang Pao in the US, remained in Laos and continued to fight the Lao government through the 1980s and 1990s. There are probably still a small number of disaffected Hmong who cling to the cause but they have lost what credibility they may have had and, for the most part rely on leftover ammunition and guerilla tactics. The rebels' biggest public relations disaster came in 1989 when they shot dead several Buddhist monks while attacking a government convoy on the road to Luang Prabang.

Hmong insurgents have been staging reasonably regular attacks for years. A spate of bombings in Vientiane in 2000 was probably linked to the Hmong resistance and in 2004-2005 at least 15 civilians were killed by Hmong insurgents in the north of the country. The Hmong claim to be fighting for democracy and freedom but most are living in terrible conditions and starving, so robbery seems a more likely motivation behind their attacks.

The Lao government tends publicly to sidestep the issue, saying there is no official policy towards the Hmong. However, the eradication of opium and related resettlement programme has had a negative impact on the Hmong and there is undisputable evidence of human rights violations against the Hmong by the Lao government. In 2004, video footage was smuggled out of Laos showing the carnage of a military attack on a Hmong rebel group that had taken place in May 2004; the victims were children. On the other hand, the Lao government has appointed Hmong as governors of Phonsavanh, Xam Neua and Sayaboury provinces.

The donor community and international organizations continue keenly to watch the Lao government's response to the Hmong. Unfortunately, international pressure can destabilize important domestic policies. In 2005 it was reported that the government had requested groups involved in poverty alleviation in some provinces to prioritize the Hmong above all other ethnic groups when provincial budgets are allocated, regardless of their relative need.

Between 2004 and 2006 several groups of hundreds of Hmong insurgents surrendered. In December 2006 alone more than 400 members of the Hmong ethnic insurgents and their families came out of the jungle and surrendered to the authorities.

In 2007 American officials in the US arrested Vang Pao, the 77-year-old former CIA-backed general of the Royal Army in Laos, on a conspiracy to stage a coup in Vientiane. The criminal complaint said Vang Pao and the other Hmong defendants formed a committee "to evaluate the feasibility of conducting a military expedition or enterprise to engage in the overthrow of the existing government of Laos by violent means, including murder, assaults on both military and civilian officials of Laos and destruction of buildings and property." This included charges of inspecting shipments of military equipment that were to be purchased and shipped to Thailand. That equipment included machine guns, ammunition, rocket-propelled grenade launchers, anti-tank rockets, stinger missiles, mines and C-4 explosives.

In 2009, the US dropped the charges against Vang Pao. He made plans to return to Laos but the government communicated that he would be executed if he set foot on Laos soil. In late 2009 more than 4000 Hmong refugees living in Thailand were forcibly repatriated to Laos.

Other communities

The largest non-Lao groups in Laos are the Chinese and Vietnamese communities in the main cities. Many of the Vietnamese were brought in by the French to run the country and stayed. In more recent years, Vietnam also tried to colonize parts of Laos. The Chinese have been migrating to Laos for centuries and are usually traders, restaurateurs and shop owners. Chinese immigration has increased greatly in recent years. With the relaxation in Communist policies in recent years, there has been a large influx of Thais; most are involved in business. In Vientiane there is also a small community of Indians running restaurants, jewellery and tailors' shops. The majority of the Europeans in Laos are NGO, embassy or mining company staff.

Language

The official language is Lao, the language of the ethnic majority. Lao is basically a monosyllabic, tonal language. It contains many polysyllabic words borrowed from Pali and Sanskrit (ancient Indian dialects) as well as words borrowed from Khmer. It has six tones, 33 consonants and 28 vowels. Lao is also spoken in Northeast Thailand and North Cambodia, which was originally part of the kingdom of Lane Xang. Lao and Thai, particularly the Northeast dialect, are mutually intelligible. Differences have mainly developed since French colonial days when Laos was insulated from developments of the Thai language. French is still spoken in towns – particularly by the older generation – and is often used in government but English is being increasingly used. Significant numbers of Lao have been to universities and colleges in the former Soviet Union and Eastern Europe, so Eastern European languages and Russian are also spoken, but not widely.

Many of the tribal groups have no system of writing and the Lao script is similar to Thai, to which it is closely related. One of the kings of the Sukhothai Dynasty, Ramkhamhaeng, devised the Thai alphabet in 1283 and introduced the Thai system of writing. Lao script is modelled on the early Thai script and is written from left to right with no spacing between the words.

Like many other newly independent countries, the leadership in the Lao PDR have attempted to make Lao the national language, in fact as well as in rhetoric. An oft-quoted phrase is 'Language reveals one's nationhood, manners reveals one's lineage'. Because Lao is so similar to Thai, there has also been a conscious attempt to maintain a sense of difference between the two countries' languages. Otherwise, some people believe, there exists the danger that Laos might simply become culturally absorbed within Greater Thailand. As scholars have pointed out, the cultural flows have essentially been one way: most people in Laos can understand Standard Thai, but few Thais (except in the Northeastern region) can understand Lao. Linguistically, Lao and Thai are both dialects of the same root language, but neither is the dialect of the other. (Many Thais view Lao as a linguistic offshoot of Thai and hence subordinate to Thai. Understandably, people in Laos take offence at this intimation.)

Because of this delicate intersection of nationality, identity and language, there has been a studied attempt to establish language principles for Lao that clearly separates it from Thai. To begin with it was necessary to establish an accepted, national version of spoken Lao (there are significant differences between areas). In other words, to produce Standard Lao which could be taught in schools, promoted in the media, and used in government. This effort at language engineering can be dated from the 1930s, and saw further refinements in the 1940s, 1950s, 1970s and 1990s. (Note that these attempts to develop Standard Lao bridge the colonial, royalist and communist periods.) While this has been successful to the extent that Lao remains noticeably and significantly different from Thai, the major influence on the Lao language today remains that of Thai. ▶▶ *See also Language, page 487; and Useful words and phrases, page 498.*

Religion

Theravada Buddhism

Theravada Buddhism, from the Pali word *thera* (elders), means the 'way of the elders' and is distinct from the dominant Buddhism practised in India, Mahayana Buddhism or the 'Greater Vehicle'. The sacred language of Theravada Buddhism is Pali rather than Sanskrit, Bodhisattvas (future Buddhas) are not given much attention and emphasis is placed upon a precise and 'fundamental' interpretation of the Buddha's teachings, as they were originally recorded. By the 15th century, Theravada Buddhism was the dominant religion in Laos – as it was in neighbouring Siam (Thailand), Myanmar and Cambodia. Buddhism shares the belief, in common with Hinduism, in rebirth. A person goes through countless lives and the experience of one life is conditioned by the acts in a previous one. This is the Law of Karma (act or deed, from Pali *kamma*), the law of cause and effect. But, it is not, as commonly thought in the West, equivalent to fate.

For most people, nirvana is a distant goal and they merely aim to accumulate merit by living good lives and performing good deeds such as giving alms to monks. In this way the layman embarks on the path to heaven. It is also common for a layman to become ordained, at some point in his life (usually as a young man), for a three month period during the Buddhist Rains Retreat.

Monks should endeavour to lead stringently ascetic lives. They must refrain from murder, theft, sexual intercourse, untruths, eating after noon, alcohol, entertainment, ornament, comfortable beds and wealth. They are allowed to own only a begging bowl, three pieces of clothing, a razor, needle, belt and water filter. They can only eat food that they have received through begging. Anyone who is male, over 20 and not a criminal can become a monk.

The 'Way of the Elders', is believed to be closest to Buddhist as it originally developed in India. It is often referred to by the term 'Hinayana' (Lesser Vehicle), a disparaging name foisted onto Theravadans by Mahayanists. This form of Buddhism is the dominant contemporary religion in the mainland Southeast Asian countries of Laos, Thailand, Cambodia and Myanmar (Burma).

In Theravadan Buddhism, the historic Buddha, Sakyamuni, is revered above all else and most images of the Buddha are of Sakyamuni. Importantly and unlike Mahayana Buddhism, the Buddha image is only meant to serve as a meditation aid; it does not embody supernatural powers and is not supposed to be worshipped. However, the popular need for objects of veneration has meant that most images are worshipped. Pilgrims bring flowers and incense and prostrate themselves in front of the image. This is a Mahayanist influence which has been embraced by Theravadans.

Buddhism in Laos

The Lao often maintain that the Vientiane area converted to Buddhism at the time of the Moghul emperor Asoka. This seems suspiciously early and is probably untrue. The original stupa at That Luang, so it is claimed, was built to encase a piece of the Buddha's breastbone provided by Asoka. Buddhism was undoubtedly practised before Fa Ngum united Lane Xang and created a Buddhist Kingdom in the mid-14th century. He was known as the Great Protector of the Faith and brought the Phra Bang, the famous golden statue – the symbol of Buddhism in Laos – from Angkor in Cambodia to Laos.

Buddhism was gradually accepted among the lowland Lao but many of the highland tribes remain animist. Even where Buddhism has been practised for centuries, it is usually interwoven with the superstitions and rituals of animist beliefs. Appeasing the spirits and gaining merit are both integral features of life. Most highlanders are animists and the worship of *phi* or spirits has remained central to village life throughout the revolutionary years, despite the fact that it was officially banned by the government. Similarly, the *baci* ceremony – when strings representing guardian spirits are tied around the wrists of guests – is still practised in Laos.

In the late 1500s, King Setthathirat promoted Buddhism and built many monasteries or wats. Buddhism was first taught in schools in the 17th century and prospered until the Thai and Ho invasions of the 18th and 19th centuries when many of the wats were destroyed. With the introduction of socialism in 1975, Buddhism was banned from primary schools and people prohibited from giving alms to monks. With the increasing religious tolerance of the regime it is now undergoing a revival and many of the wats are being rebuilt and redecorated. All members of the priesthood are placed under the authority of a superior – the *Phra Sangharaja* – whose seat was traditionally in the capital of the kingdom.

In line with Buddhist tradition, materialism and the accumulation of personal wealth is generally frowned on in Laos. Poverty is admired as a form of spirituality. This belief proved rather convenient for the Communist regime, when it was taken to extremes. Today, in the new capitalist climate, the traditional attributes of spirituality sit uncomfortably with Laos' increasingly bourgeois aspirations.

Buddhism, as it is practised in Laos, is not the 'other-worldly' religion of Western conception. Ultimate salvation – enlightenment, or *nirvana* – is a distant goal for most people. Lao Buddhists pursue the Law of Karma, the reduction of suffering. Meritorious acts are undertaken and demeritorious ones avoided so that life and more particularly future life, might be improved. Karma is often thought of in the West as fate. It is not. It is true that previous karma determines a person's position in society, but there is still room for individual action – and a person is ultimately responsible for that action. It is the law of cause and effect.

It is important to draw a distinction between 'academic' Buddhism, as it tends to be understood in the West and 'popular' Buddhism, as it is practised in Laos. In Laos, Buddhism is a syncretic religion: it incorporates elements of Brahmanism, animism and ancestor worship. Amulets are worn to protect against harm and are often sold in temple compounds. In the countryside, farmers have what they consider to be a healthy regard for the spirits (*phi*) and demons that inhabit the rivers, trees and forests. Astrologers are widely consulted by urban and rural dwellers alike. It is these aspects of Lao Buddhism which help to provide worldly assurance and they are perceived to be complementary, not in contradiction, with Buddhist teachings.

Most Lao villages will contain a temple, monastery or wat (the word does not translate accurately). The wat represents the mental heart of each community and most young men at some point in their lives will become ordained as monks. Previously this period represented the only opportunity for a young man to gain an education and to learn how to read. An equally important reason for a man to become ordained is so that he can accumulate merit for his family, particularly for his mother, who as a woman cannot become ordained.

As in Thailand, Laos has adopted the Indian epic the *Ramayana*, which has been the inspiration for much Lao art and sculpture. Complete manuscripts of the Lao *Ramayana* – known as the *Phra Lak Phra Lam* – used to be kept at Wat Phra Kaeo and Wat Sisaket.

Buddhism under Communism

Buddhism's relationship with Communism has been complex and usually ambivalent. As the Pathet Lao began their revolutionary mission they saw in the country's monks a useful means by which to spread their message. Many monks, though they may themselves have renounced material possessions and all desires, were conscious of the inequalities in society and the impoverished conditions in which many people lived their lives. Indeed most of them came from poor rural backgrounds. In addition many monks saw themselves as the guardians of Lao culture and as the US became more closely involved in the country so they increasingly felt that it was their job to protect the people against the spread of an alien culture and mores. Therefore, right from the start, monks had a natural sympathy with the ideals of the Pathet Lao. Indeed, significant numbers renounced their vows and joined the revolution. Others stayed on in their monasteries, but used their positions and the teachings of the Buddha to further the revolutionary cause. The Pathet Lao, for their part, saw the monks as a legitimizing force which would assist in their revolutionary efforts. Monks were often the most respected individuals in society and if the Pathet Lao could somehow piggy-back on this respect then they too, it was reasoned, would gain in credibility and respect. The Rightist government also tried to do the same, but with notably less success.

With the victory of the Pathet Lao in 1975, their view of the *sangha* (monkhood) changed. No longer were monks a useful vehicle in building revolution; overnight they became a potential threat. Monks were forced to attend re-education seminars where they were instructed that they could no longer teach about merit or *karma*, two central pillars of Buddhism. Their sermons were taped by Pathet Lao cadres to be scrutinized for subversive propaganda and a stream of disillusioned monks began to flee to Thailand. So the *sangha* was emasculated as an independent force. Monks were forced to follow the directives of the Lao People's Revolutionary Party and the *sangha* came under strict Party control. Monasteries were expected to become mini-cooperatives so that they did not have to depend on the laity for alms and they were paid a small salary by the state for undertaking teaching and health work. In short, the LPDR seemed intent on undermining the *sangha* as an independent force in Lao society, making it dependent on the state for its survival and largely irrelevant to wider society. The success of the Pathet Lao's policy of marginalization can be seen in the number of monks in the country. In 1975 there were 20,000 monks. By 1979 this had shrunk to just 1700.

However, before the *sangha* could sink into obscurity and irrelevance, the government eased its policy in 1979 and began to allow monks and the *sangha* greater latitude. In addition and perhaps more importantly, the leadership embraced certain aspects of Lao culture, one of which was Theravada Buddhism. The memorial to the revolutionary struggle in Vientiane, for example, was designed as a Buddhist *that* (stupa) and government ministers enthusiastically join in the celebration of Buddhist festivals.

Animism

While the majority of the population (about 60-65%) follow Theravada Buddhism, Animism is practised by about 30% of the population. The term Animism derives from the Latin word 'anima', meaning mind or soul. At a very basic level, Animism refers to a belief in spirits. Animism is particularly common among Lao Theung and Lao Soung groups minority groups but elements of Animism have also infiltrated or been grafted onto Buddhism and Lao culture at a broader level. Most people believe in *phi*, spirits, which are seen as fundamental to their relationship with nature and the community. The word *phi* has even been adopted into Lao language to mean ghost, while *phi-baa* means crazy. Many Lao people believe that spiritual forces need to be placated, usually through a *baci* ceremony, as they can cause illness, disease or bad luck. Inexplicable events – including strange behaviour by foreign visitors – are often attributed to 'ghosts'. Buddhist monks are often called upon to exorcize bad spirits and most wats have a small spirit house built on the monastic grounds. Animists generally suffer little discrimination from the government; however, some practises are discouraged for health and security reasons.

Christianity in post-1975 Laos

The smallest religious group represented in Laos are Christians, including Roman Catholics, who account for around 2% of the population. There are around 30,000 to 40,000 Catholics in the country, many of whom are ethnic Vietnamese, concentrated in major urban centres along the Mekong River.

Following the revolution, many churches in provincial towns were turned into community centres and meeting halls. Vientiane's Evangelical Church has held a Sunday service ever since 1979 but it is only in recent years that Christians have felt free to worship openly and even this 'freedom' comes with qualifications. In 1989 the first consultation between the country's Christian leaders (Protestant and Roman Catholic) was authorized by the government; it was the first such meeting since 'liberation' and was also attended by government representatives and two Hmong leaders of the Buddhist Federation.

It's illegal for foreigners to proselytize in Laos; persons found guilty can be subject to arrest and deportation for 'creating social divisions'. Foreign missionaries were ejected from Laos in 1975 and, today, foreign NGOs affiliated with religious organizations are only allowed to work in the country on the condition that they don't try to spread their religion. Not many Buddhists have converted to Christianity but it seems to be growing among the animist hilltribes. The US Bible Society has recently published a modern translation of the Bible into Lao but tribal-language editions do not yet exist. The shortage of bibles and other literature has prompted Christian leaders to offer unsolicited gifts to the department of religious affairs to ease restrictions on the import of hymn books and bibles from Thailand.

While there is more freedom to worship today than during the pre-reform period, there is still a sense in the leadership that Christians are a political threat. In 1998 the authorities arrested 44 Christians, among them three Americans, for conducting unauthorized church services in people's private homes. The Americans were expelled but the Laotians were thrown in prison. This sort of knee-jerk reaction usually ends up being counter-productive. The US Congress responded to what they saw as religious persecution by blocking an economic agreement that was likely to significantly boost textile exports to the US. The fact that the leadership in Laos is hypersensitive to such issues was reinforced in November 1999 when six Christian leaders were reportedly arrested and imprisoned for planning a pro-democracy rally along with around 100 other activists.

Geography

Laos stretches about 1000 km from north to south, while distances from east to west range from 140 to 500 km. The country covers 236,800 sq km – less than half the size of France and just a third of the size of Texas. Only 24% of the population lives in towns. The country has the lowest population density in Asia, with 22 people per sq km.

Rugged mountains cover more than three-quarters of the country and with few all-weather roads (there are just 4000 km of sealed roads in the entire country), rivers remain important communication routes. Historically, the Mekong River has been the country's economic artery. On its banks nestle Laos' most important cities: in the north the small, colourful former royal capital of Luang Prabang, further south the administrative and political capital of Vientiane and farther south still the regional centres of Thakhek, Savannakhet and Pakse.

Laos is dominated by the Mekong River and the Annamite chain of mountains which both run southeast towards the East Sea (South China Sea). Flowing along the borders of Laos are 1865 km of the 4000km-long Mekong River. The lowlands of the Mekong valley form the principal agricultural areas, especially around Vientiane and Savannakhet and these are home to the lowland Lao – sometimes argued to be the 'true' Lao. The Mekong has three main tributaries: the Nam Ou and Nam Tha from the north and the Nam Ngum, which flows into Vientiane province.

Much of the northern half of Laos is 1500 m or more above sea level and its karst limestone outcrops are deeply dissected by steep-sided river valleys. Further south, the Annamite chain has an average height of 1200 m. Heavily forested, rugged mountains form a natural barrier between Laos and Vietnam. Most of the country is a mixture of mountains and high plateau. There are four main plateau: the Xieng Khouang plateau, better known as the Plain of Jars, in the north, the Nakai and the limestone Khammuoane plateau in the centre and the 10,000 sq km Bolaven Plateau to the south. The highest peak is the 2800 m Bia Mountain, which rises above the Xieng Khouang plateau to the northeast.

Climate

The rainy season is from May through to September-October; the tropical lowlands receive an annual average rainfall of 1250 mm a year. Temperatures during these months are between 30 and 40°C. In mountainous Xieng Khoung Province, it is cooler and temperatures can drop to freezing point in December and January. The first half of the dry season, from November to April, is cool, with temperatures between 10 and 20°C. This gives way to a hot, dry season from March to June when temperatures soar and are often in excess of 35°C. Average rainfall in Vientiane is 1700 mm, although in North Laos and the highlands it is much wetter, with more than 3000 mm each year.

Vegetation

Much of Laos is forested. The vegetation is rich and diverse: a mix of tropical and subtropical species. Grassy savannah predominates on plateau areas such as the Plain of Jars. In the forests, some hardwoods tower to over 30 m, while tropical palms and mango are found in the lowlands and large stands of pine in the remote northern hills.

Rural people rely heavily on the Mekong River and its watershed for everything from transport to rice production and fishing. It is estimated that 80% of the country is located near the Mekong, its tributaries or in the watershed. Over half of all vital protein consumed in rural areas comes from fish, frogs and other river creatures. Agriculture is of utmost importance to Lao people, with about 80% of the population engaged in subsistence farming.

In the mid-20th century over 70% of the country was covered with forest. Today, this number has been reduced to around 40% and of this only 17% remains old growth tropical forest. The rattan, cardamom, mushrooms, orchids and wild meat gathered from these forests are essential to rural livelihoods and in many cases generate over half of the income of a rural family. The Lao government has established 20 National Protected Areas or NPAs (formerly known as National Biodiversity Conservation Areas, NBCAs), plus two corridor areas, covering 14.3% of the country. Although this is a step forward, illegal hunting and logging is still rife in most areas.

Logging provides Laos with a large proportion of its export earnings. Officially, around 450,000 cu m of forest are felled each year for commercial purposes but this is probably an underestimate owing to the activities of illegal loggers, many of whom are Chinese, Vietnamese and Thai. A ban on the export of logs in 1988 caused official timber export earnings to slump 30% but environmentalists claim that the ban has had little impact on the number of logs being exported. Another ban was imposed in late 1991. In addition, shifting cultivators clear an estimated 100,000 ha of forest a year. The government sees shifting cultivators (most of whom are from one of Laos' ethnic minorities) as the primary cause of forest loss and the current five-year development plan has reiterated the government's commitment to 'totally eradicating' shifting cultivation. But if the situation is similar to neighbouring countries like Thailand and Vietnam then this will do little to preserve the forest because the primary culprits are commercial logging concerns. Government reforestation programmes far from compensate for the destruction. In October 1989 the Council of Ministers issued a decree on the preservation of forests of which the people appear to be blissfully unaware. There was a half-hearted propaganda campaign to 'teach every Lao citizen to love nature and develop a sense of responsibility for the preservation of forests'.

Wildlife

Mammals include everything from wildcats, leopards and tigers to bears, wild cattle and small barking deer. Laos is also home to the large Asian elk, rhinoceros, elephants, monkeys, gibbons and ubiquitous rabbits and squirrels. Ornithological life encompasses pheasants, partridges, many songbirds, ducks and some hawks and eagles – although in rural areas many birds (and other animals) have been killed for food. There is an abundant reptilian population, including cobras, kraits, crocodiles and lizards. The lower reaches of the Mekong River, marking the border between Cambodia and Laos, is the last place in Indochina where the rare Irrawaddy dolphin is to be found. However, dynamite fishing has decimated the population and today there are probably under 20 left. Another rare denizen of the Mekong, but one that stands a greater chance of survival, is the pa buk catfish (*Pangasianodon gigas*) which weighs up to 340 kg. This riverbed-dwelling fish was first described by Western science only in 1930, although Lao fishermen and their Thai counterparts had been catching it for many years – as James McCarthy notes in the account of his travels through Siam and Laos published in 1900.

Historically, the fish is a delicacy– its roe was paid as tribute to China in the late 19th century. Due to overfishing, by the 1980s the numbers of pa buk had become severely depleted. However, a breeding programme is having some success and young pa buk fingerlings are now being released into the Mekong.

There is an enormous problem of smuggling rare animals out of Laos, mainly to South Korea and China. In 1978, the gall bladder of a black bear from Laos was auctioned in Seoul for US$55,000. Teeth and bones of wild cats from Laos are in demand for Chinese medicine. The English-language daily, *Khao San Pathet Lao*, published a report estimating that in 1992 more than 10 tonnes of protected wild animals had been slaughtered for export in the northeastern province of Houa Phanh.

Laos' wildlife has taken a caning due to poachers peddling animals across the country's borders. In 2001 the authors of 'Wildlife Trade in Laos: the End of the Game' suspected that wildlife trade was the largest source of income in Lao villages after fishing and was worth a conservative estimate of US$35 million per year. A damning report in the Guardian shows there is little hope: www.guardian.co.uk/environment/2010/feb/21/illegal-wildlife-trade.

In 2004, the Lao government joined CITES, the world's foremost conservation treaty regulating the international trade in endangered species. Regardless, Laos is still home to a diverse range of wildlife will some 800 bird and 100 mammal species. New species are popping up on an almost annual basis.

The degree to which Laos' flora and fauna are under-researched was illustrated in August 1999 when it was announced that a previously unknown species of striped rabbit had been discovered quietly nibbling the grass in the mountains dividing Laos from Vietnam. This area of Indochina has proved a veritable cornucopia of unknown animals. During the 1990s scientists have discovered one antelope, several species of deer, an ox and even a remnant herd of Javan rhinoceros, a species which was previously thought to be confined to a small corner of West Java.

Birds

Laos is nowhere near as popular a destination for birdwatchers as neighbouring Vietnam and Cambodia but there has been a flurry of interest in the birding community since the discovery of a bizarre-looking bald-headed bird in 2009. The bare-faced bulbul, first found by a team of scientists from the Wildlife Conservation Society and the University of Melbourne, is the first new species of Asian bulbul to be discovered in more than 100 years. It inhabits a remote area of rugged limestone karsts in Kammouane Province, 250 km south of Vientiane. Two other scarce inhabitants of limestone karst forest in the region, the sooty babbler and red-collared woodpecker can also be found here. See www.vietnambirding.com for further information.

Books

Art and culture

Dakin, Brett (2003) *Another Quiet American*, Asia Books. Dakin's experiences of working in Laos, with some interesting cultural insights.

Evans, Grant (1999) *Laos: Culture and Society*, Chiang Mai, Thailand: Silkworm Books. Edited volume written by assorted scholars of Laos. Highly informed; for those who really want to know about the country.

Fay, Kim (2005) *To Asia with Love: A Connoisseur's Guide to Cambodia, Laos, Thailand Vietnam*, Global Directions Inc/Things Asian Press. Great anthology of ideas, inspirations and experiences of Southeast Asia from the people who live there.

Phia Sing (1995) *Traditional Recipes of Laos*, Totnes, Devon, UK: Prospect Books. The best Lao cookbook available.

The recipes were collected by the chief chef at the Royal Palace in Luang Prabang, Phia Sing, in the 1960s. They have been translated into English and made West-friendly by replacing some of the more esoteric ingredients.

Economics, politics and development

Dommen, Arthur J (1985) *Laos: Keystone of Indochina*, Boulder: Westview Press. Out of date but a reasonable overview.

Evans, Grant (1990) *Lao Peasants under Socialism*, New Haven: Yale University Press. The definitive account of farmers in modern Laos. A new edition published by Silkworm Books in Chiang Mai (Thailand) takes into account economic changes brought about by the New Economic Mechanism.

Stuart-Fox, Martin (1982) *Contemporary Laos*, St Lucia: Queensland University Press. A useful overview of Laos up to 1980.

Stuart-Fox, Martin (1986) *Laos – Politics, Economics and Society*, London: Francis Pinter. Out of date but a good single volume summary of the country providing historical and cultural background.

Stuart-Fox, Martin (1996) *Buddhist Kingdom, Marxist State: the Making of Modern Laos*, Bangkok: White Lotus. A collection of Stuart-Fox's various papers published over the years and brought up to date. Especially good on recent history.

Zasloff, J J and Unger, L (1991) (eds) *Laos: Beyond the Revolution*, Macmillan, Basingstoke. Edited volume with a mixed collection of papers; economics/politics chapters are already rather dated.

History

Kremmer, Christopher, *Bamboo Palace*, HarperCollins Australia. Traces Kremmer's attempts to unravel the mystery surrounding the Lao royal family.

Stuart-Fox, Martin and Kooyman, Mary (1992), *Historical Dictionary of Laos*, New York: the Scarecrow Press. Takes a dictionary approach to Laos' history which is fine if you are looking up a fact, but doesn't really lend itself to telling a narrative.

Stuart-Fox, Martin (1997), *A History of Laos*, CUP: Cambridge. Concentrates on the modern period.

McCoy, Alfred W (1991) *The Politics of Heroin: CIA Complicity in the Global Drugs Trade*, Lawrence Hill/Chicago Review Press. Originally published at the beginning of the 1970s; the classic study of the politics of drugs in mainland Southeast Asia.

Parker, James (1995) *Codename Mule: Fighting the Secret War in Laos for the CIA*, Annapolis, Maryland: Naval Institute Press. Personal story of Americans fighting in Laos. Much of it deals with fighting on the Plain of Jars.

Pyle and Faas (2003) *Lost Over Laos*, De Capo Press. The story of 4 photographers who died in Laos in 1971 and the search, years later, to recover the crash site.

Ratnam, P (1980) *Laos and the Superpowers*, Tulsi Publishing, India.

Robbins, Christopher (1979) *Air America: the Story of the CIS's Secret Airlines*, New York: Putnam Books. The earlier of Robbins' 2 books on the secret war. Made into a film of the same name with Mel Gibson in the starring role.

Robbins, Christopher (1989) *The Ravens: Pilots of the Secret War of Laos*, New York: Bantam Press. The best known of all the books on America's secret war in Laos. The story it tells seems almost too incredible to be true.

Warner, Roger (1995) *Back Fire: the CIA's Secret War in Laos and its Link to the War in Vietnam*, New York: Simon and Schuster. The best of the more recent books recounting the experiences of US servicemen in Laos. Excellent, engaging read. Also published as *Shooting at the Moon*.

Language

Higbie, James, *Lao-English/English-Lao Dictionary and Phrasebook*, Hippocrene Books, Inc.

Marcus, Russell (1983) *Lao-English/ English- Lao Dictionary*, Charles E Tuttle Co, USA. Perhaps the best dictionary available;

US$16.95 from www.worldlanguage.com.

Phone Bouaravong, *Learning Lao for Everyone*. Locally produced, with tapes.

Werner, Klaus *Learning and Speaking Lao*. Useful and cheaper than Marcus.

Travel and geography

De Carne, Louis (1872) *Travels in Indochina and the Chinese Empire*, London: Chapman Hall. Recounts De Carne's experiences in Laos in 1872, some years before the country was colonized by the French.

Du Pont De Bie, Natacha (2004) *Ant Egg Soup: The Adventures of a Food Tourist in Laos*, Sceptre. A wonderful portrait of Lao culture and food through the eyes of a food tourist.

Garstin, Crosbie (1928), *The Voyage from London to Indochina*, Heinemann. Hilarious, irreverent journey through Indochina.

Hoskins, John (1991), *The Mekong*, Bangkok: Post Publishing. A large format coffee table book with good photographs and a modest text. Widely available in Bangkok.

Lewis, Norman (1951), *A Dragon Apparent: Travels in Cambodia, Laos and Vietnam*. One of the finest travel books; reprinted by Eland Books but also available second-hand from many bookshops.

Maugham, Somerset (1930) *The Gentlemen in the Parlour: a Record of a Journey from Rangoon to Haiphong*, Heinemann: London. An account of Maugham's journey through Southeast Asia, in classic limpid prose.

McCarthy, James (1994) *Surveying and Exploring in Siam with Descriptions of Laos Dependencies and of Battles against the Chinese Haws*, White Lotus: Bangkok. First published in 1900. An interesting account by Englishman James McCarthy, who was employed by the government of Siam as a surveyor and adviser.

Mouhot, Henri (1986) *Travels in Indochina*, Bangkok: White Lotus. An account of Laos by France's most famous explorer of Southeast Asia. He tried to discover a 'back door' into China by travelling up the Mekong, but died of Malaria in Luang Prabang in 1860. The book has been republished by White Lotus and is easily available in Bangkok; there is also a more expensive reprint available from OUP (Kuala Lumpur).

Murphy, Dervla (1999) *One Foot in Laos*, John Murphy Publisher. An interesting, off-the-beaten-track travelogue of adventures and mishaps through Laos.

Stewart, Lucretia (1998), *Tiger Balm: Travels in Laos, Cambodia and Vietnam*, London: Chatto and Windus

Contents

Footnotes

Useful words and phrases

Greetings
Hello/goodbye
xin chào (Vietnam)
joom ree-up soo-a/lee-a hai (Cambodia)
suh-bye-dee/lah-gohn (Laos)

what is your name?
ông/bà tên là gì? (Vietam)
Neak ch'muah ei? (Cambodia)
Chow seu yang? (Laos)

my name is …
Tôi tên là … (Vietnam)
k'nyom tch much … (Cambodia)
koi seu … (Laos)

Getting around
where is the …?
O dâu …? (Vietnam)
noev eah nah …? (Cambodia)
Sa ta ni lot …? (Laos)

is it far?
Có xa không? (Vietnam)
Ch'ngai dtay? (Cambodia)
Kai baw? (Laos)

turn left/right
queo rë trái/queo rë phai (Vietnam)
bot dtoh kahng ch'wayng s'dum (Cambodia)
leo sai/leo qua (Laos)

go straight on
di thang (Vietnam)
ondtoh dtrong (Cambodia)
pai leuy (Laos)

Time
today
hôm nay (Vietnam)
t'ngai ni(h) (Cambodia)
Muh-nee (Laos)

tomorrow
ngày mai (Vietnam)
Sa-aik (Cambodia)
Muh-ouhn (Laos)

Monday
thu hai (Vietnam)
t'ngai jan (Cambodia)
Van Chanh (Laos)

Tuesday
thu ba (Vietnam)
t'ngai ong-gee-a (Cambodia)
Van Ang Khan (Laos)

Wednesday
thu tu (Vietnam)
t'ngai bpoot (Cambodia)
Van Pud (Laos)

Thursday
thu nam (Vietnam)
t'ngai bpra-hoa-a (Cambodia)
Van Pa Had (Laos)

Friday
thu sáu (Vietnam)
t'ngai sok (Cambodia)
Van Sook (Laos)

Saturday
thu bay (Vietnam)
t'ngai sao (Cambodia)
Van Sao (Laos)

Sunday
chu nhât (Vietnam)
t'ngai aa-dteut (Cambodia)
Van Arthid (Laos)

Numbers
1
môt (Vietnam)
moo-ay (Cambodia)
nung (Laos)

2
hai (Vietnam)
bpee (Cambodia)
song (Laos)

3
ba (Vietnam)
bay (Cambodia)
sahm (Laos)

4
bon (Vietnam)
boo-un (Cambodia)
see (Laos)

5
nam (Vietnam)
bprum (Cambodia)
hah (Laos)

6
sáu (Vietnam)
bprum moo-ay (Cambodia)
hoke (Laos)

7
bay (Vietnam)
bprum bpee (Cambodia)
chet (Laos)

8
tám (Vietnam)
bprum bay (Cambodia)
pet (Laos)

9
chin (Vietnam)
bprum boo-un (Cambodia)
cow (Laos)

10
muoi/môt chuc (Vietnam)
dop (Cambodia)
sip (Laos)

11
muoi môt (Vietnam)
dop moo-ay (Cambodia)
sip-et (Laos)

12
muoi hai (Vietnam)
dop bpee (Cambodia)
sip-song (Laos)

1000
môt ngàn (Vietnam)
moo-ay bpohn (Cambodia)
phan (Laos)

10,000
muoi ngàn (Vietnam)
moo-ay meun (Cambodia)
sip-phan (Laos)

100,000
môt tram nghìn (Vietnam)
moo-ay sain (Cambodia)
muun (Laos)

Further reading

See also Books sections at the end of each country's Background section.

White Lotus, www.whitelotuspress.com, is a Bangkok-based publisher specializing in English language books (with many reprints of old books) on the region.

Dingwall, Alastair (1994) *Traveller's Literary Companion to Southeast Asia.* (In Print: Brighton, 1994.) Extracts from books by Western and regional writers on Southeast Asia. A good overview of what is available.

Dumarçay, Jacques *The Palaces of South-East Asia: architecture and customs.* (Singapore: OUP, 1991.) A broad summary of the palace art and architecture in both.

Fenton, James *All the Wrong Places: adrift in the politics of Asia.* (London: Penguin, 1988.) British journalist James Fenton skilfully and entertainingly recounts his experiences.

Fraser-Lu, Sylvia *Handwoven Textiles of South-East Asia.* (OUP: Singapore 1988.) Large well-illustrated book.

Higham, Charles *The Archaeology of Mainland Southeast Asia from 10,000 BC to the Fall of Angkor.* (Cambridge: Cambridge University Press, 1989.) Best summary of changing views of the archaeology of the mainland.

King, Ben F and Dickinson, EC *A Field Guide to the Birds of South-East Asia.* (London: Collins, 1975.) Best regional guide to the birds of the region.

Osborne, Milton *Southeast Asia: an introductory history.* (Sydney: Allen & Unwin, 1979.) Good introductory history, clearly written, published in a portable paperback edition.

Rawson, Philip *The Art of Southeast Asia.* (London: Thames & Hudson, 1967.) Portable general art history of Cambodia, Vietnam, Thailand, Laos, Burma, Java and Bali; by necessity, rather superficial.

Reid, Anthony *Southeast Asia in the Age of Commerce 1450-1680: the lands below the winds.* (New Haven: Yale University Press, 1988.) Perhaps the best history of everyday life in Southeast Asia, looking at such themes as physical well-being, material culture and social organization.

Reid, Anthony *Southeast Asia in the age of commerce 1450-1680: expansion and crisis.* (Yale University Press: New Haven. Volume 2, 1993.)

Rigg, Jonathan *Southeast Asia: the Human Landscape of Modernization and Development.* (London: Routledge, 1997.) Focuses on how people have responded to the challenges and tensions of modernization.

SarDesai, DR *Southeast Asia: Past and Present.* (Macmillan: London, 1989.) Skilful but at times frustratingly thin history of the region from the first century to the withdrawal of US forces from Vietnam.

Sesser, Stan *The Lands of Charm and Cruelty: travels in Southeast Asia.* (Basingstoke: Picador, 1993.) A series of collected narratives first published in the *New Yorker* including essays on Singapore, Laos, Cambodia, Burma and Borneo. Finely observed and thoughtful, the book is an excellent travel companion.

Steinberg, DJ et al *In Search of Southeast Asia: a modern history.* (Honolulu: University of Hawaii Press, 1987.) The best standard history of the region; it skilfully examines and assesses general processes of change and their impacts from the arrival of the Europeans in the region.

Tarling, Nicholas *Cambridge History of Southeast Asia.* (Cambridge: Cambridge University Press, 1992.) Two-volume edited study, long and expensive with contributions from most of the leading historians of the region. A thematic and regional approach is taken, not a country one, although the history is fairly conventional.

Waterson, Roxana *The Living House: An Anthropology of Architecture in South-East Asia* (OUP: Singapore, 1990). An academic but extensively illustrated book on the region's architecture and how it links with lives and livelihoods. Fascinating material.

Index → Entries in bold refer to maps.

Advertisers' index

Credits

Footprint credits
Project Editor: Jo Williams
Layout and production: Kelly Pipes,
Angus Dawson
Colour section: Pepi Bluck
Maps: Kevin Feeney
Proofreader: Ria Gane

Managing Director: Andy Riddle
Commercial Director: Patrick Dawson
Publisher: Alan Murphy
Publishing Managers: Jo Williams,
Felicity Laughton, Jen Haddington
Series design: Mytton Williams
Marketing and PR: Liz Harper
Sales: Diane McEntee
Advertising: Renu Sibal
Finance and administration: Elizabeth Taylor

Photography credits
Front cover: David Noton Photography/
Alamy
Back cover: René Mattes/hemis.fr

Printed in India by Nutech Print Services, Delhi.

Every effort has been made to ensure that the
facts in this guidebook are accurate. However,
travellers should still obtain advice from
consulates, airlines, etc about travel and visa
requirements before travelling. The authors and
publishers cannot accept responsibility for any
loss, injury or inconvenience however caused.

Publishing information
Footprint Vietnam, Cambodia & Laos
3rd edition
© Footprint Handbooks Ltd
October 2010

ISBN: 978 1 907263 16 3
CIP DATA: A catalogue record for this book is
available from the British Library

® Footprint Handbooks and the Footprint
mark are a registered trademark of Footprint
Handbooks Ltd

Published by Footprint
6 Riverside Court
Lower Bristol Road
Bath BA2 3DZ, UK
T +44 (0)1225 469141
F +44 (0)1225 469461
footprinttravelguides.com

Distributed in the USA by Globe Pequot
Press, Guilford, Connecticut

Colour section photography credits
Page 1: Michel Gotin/hemis.fr. Page 2: Keith Levit Photography/Photolibrary. Page 6:
Ludovic Maisant/hemis.fr, Bruno Morandi/hemis.fr, Vito Arcomano/Alamy, Jean Kugler/
Photolibrary. Page 7: Romain Cintract/hemis.fr, Peter Schickert/Alamy. Page 8: Bruno
Morandi/hemis.fr. Page 9: Chris Caldicott/Axiom, Peter Weld/Robert Harding World
Imagery, Jean Du Boisberranger/hemis.fr, Chris Caldicott/Axiom, Andrew McConnell/
Robert Harding World Imagery. Page 10: Per-Andre Hoffmann/Photolibrary, Travis Rowan/
Alamy, Claire Boobbyer. Page 11: Christophe Boisvieux/hemis.fr, Stéphane Frances/hemis.
fr. Page 12: Bertrand Gardel/hemis.fr

Acknowledgements

Claire Boobyer would like to thank the following people for their help in updating Laos. She would not have got anywhere without the considerable help of Jason Rolan, country manager at Buffalo Tours. Sincere thanks also to Steven Schipani, senior tourism advisor at LNTA, Oudomxay Thongsavath at Savannakhet Eco-Guide Unit, Friederike Heeschen at NGO ded in Vientiane and the exceptionally helpful Sibylle Creutz working in Xieng Khouang province.

Her thanks also to the following: Gabriel Kuperman in Luang Prabang, Stefan and Magdalena from Germany, Lee Sheridan in Vientiane, Siegfried Moser working in Udomxai, Mr Vong and Jerome and Noy in Pakse, Kristen Focken at LNTA, Richard Craik at Vietnam Birding, Nathalie Pouliot in Luang Prabang, Bangkok Airways, and Klaus Schwettman at Green Discovery Laos.

Thanks also due to Jock O'Tailan for the previous sterling work on Laos in the last few editions of the guide.

For Vietnam, many thanks to writer Adam Bray (www.muine beach.net, www.fisheggtree.com), who updated the Central Highlands chapter, Mui Ne and Phan Thiet, and to writer Helen Clark who helped update much of the Hanoi chapter.
This edition would not have been possible without the help of Do Thu Trang at Buffalo Tours, Gabriel Kuperman (www.gabriel shaya.com), Nguyen Anh Tuan, Quyen Do, Christine Andrews in Hanoi, An at Hidden Hanoi, Phil Harman of SNV, Vasu Thirasak in Bangkok, Kiwi Natasha Buckley, Magdalena Buhl and Stefan from Germany, and Anne Courtney Cruickshanks.

Thanks also to editor Jo Williams at Footprint who juggled whole reams of Indochina text and sorted it out.

Andrew Spooner would like to thank Len Austin, Jo Owen, Jo Williams and Alan Murphy at Footprint, Chris Coles, Thomas Holdo Hansen, Kristin Holdo Hansen, Nanthida Rakwong, Alex Aziz, Hak Try and all the drivers, guesthouse and hotel staff, etc who had to endure him during his work in Cambodia.

Journey through lost kingdoms and discover the hidden history of Asia to let Asian Trails be your guide!

CAMBODIA

Asian Trails Ltd. (Phnom Penh Office)

No. 22, Street 294, Sangkat Boeng Keng Kong I

Khan Chamkarmorn, P.O. Box 621, Phnom Penh, Cambodia

Tel: (855 23) 216 555 Fax: (855 23) 216 591

E-mail: res@asiantrails.com.kh

CHINA

Asian Trails China

Rm. 1001, Scitech Tower, No. 22 Jianguomenwai Avenue

Beijing 100004, P.R. China

Tel: (86 10) 6515 9259 & 9279 & 9260 Fax: (86 10) 6515 9293

E-mail: kris.vangoethem@asiantrailschina.com

INDONESIA

P.T. Asian Trails Indonesia

Jl. By Pass Ngurah Rai No. 260 Sanur

Denpasar 80228, Bali, Indonesia

Tel: (62 361) 285 771 Fax: (62 361) 281 515

E-mail: info@asiantrailsbali.com

LAO P.D.R.

Asian Trails Laos (AT Lao Co., Ltd.)

P.O. Box 5422, Unit 10, Ban Khounta Thong

Sikhottabong District, Vientiane, Lao P.D.R.

Tel: (856 21) 263 936 Fax: (856 21) 262 956

E-mail: vte@asiantrails.laopdr.com

MALAYSIA

Asian Trails (M) Sdn. Bhd.

11-2-B Jalan Manau off Jalan Kg. Attap 50460

Kuala Lumpur, Malaysia

Tel: (60 3) 2274 9488 Fax: (60 3) 2274 9588

E-mail: res@asiantrails.com.my

MYANMAR

Asian Trails Tour Ltd.

73 Pyay Road, Dagon Township, Yangon, Myanmar

Tel: (95 1) 211 212, 223 262 Fax: (95 1) 211 670

E-mail: res@asiantrails.com.mm

THAILAND

Asian Trails Ltd.

9th Floor, SG Tower, 161/1 Soi Mahadlek Luang 3, Rajdamri Road

Lumpini, Pathumwan, Bangkok 10330

Tel: (66 2) 626 2000 Fax: (66 2) 651 8111

E-mail: res@asiantrails.org

VIETNAM

Asian Trails Co., Ltd.

5th Floor, 21 Nguyen Trung Ngan Street, District 1

Ho Chi Minh City, Vietnam

Tel: (84 8) 3 910 2871 Fax: (84 8) 3 910 2874

E-mail: vietnam@asiantrails.com.vn

CONTACT

Contact us for our brochure or log into

www.asiantrails.info   www.asiantrails.net   www.asiantrails.com   www.asiantrails.travel